*The*
*Power*
*of*
*Kings*

# THE

# *POWER*

## OF

# *KINGS*

*Monarchy and Religion in Europe*

*1589–1715*

PAUL KLÉBER MONOD

*Yale University Press    New Haven and London*

Designed by James J. Johnson and Set in Fournier Roman type
by Keystone Typesetting, Inc., Orwigsburg, Pennsylvania
Printed in the United States of America by Edwards Brothers, Inc.,
Ann Arbor, Michigan.

*Library of Congress Cataloging-in-Publication Data*

Monod, Paul Kléber.
    The power of kings : monarchy and religion in Europe, 1589–1715 /
Paul Kléber Monod.
        p.      cm.
    Includes bibliographical references and index.
    ISBN 0-300-07810-2 (cloth : alk. paper)
    ISBN 0-300-09066-8 (pbk. : alk. paper)

    1. Kings and rulers—Religious aspects—Christianity—History.
2. Europe—Politics and government—1517–1648.    3. Europe—Politics
and government—1648–1715.    4. Europe—Kings and rulers—History.
I. Title.
BR115.K55M66    1999
321'.6'0940903—dc21                                          99-17815

A catalogue record for this book is available from the British Library.

2    4    6    8    10    9    7    5    3

*For Jan and Evan*

# Contents

# Acknowledgments

THE IDEA FOR THIS BOOK began to germinate a decade ago, as a result of conversations with my former dissertation advisor, the sagacious Linda Colley, and her husband, David Cannadine. At first the project was even more ambitious in scope, but after a few years of trying vainly to grasp the essentials of West African religion, Shinto rituals, and Mughal politics, I decided to restrict it to Europe. The inclusion of Russia and Poland was a difficult decision, because I do not know their languages, but I decided that to cut them out would be arbitrary.

This has not been an easy book to write. My previous work dealt with England after 1689, and I was unfamiliar with the historiography of other nations or earlier periods. At times, I have felt like Casaubon in George Eliot's *Middlemarch*, obsessed with a massive endeavour that must ultimately prove futile. Luckily, my wife, Jan Albers, has been unflagging in her encouragement and optimism. Whatever merit this book may have is due to her intellectual companionship and constant love. My second debt is to a six-year-old, our son, Evan, whose endless energy and precocious humour have revealed to me how far scholarship is from the greatest joys of life. Born very prematurely, he has overcome much more than I have in the past few years, and has done it with a better grace. Third, I thank Joan Monod for her absolute confidence that my writing must be going well, simply because I am her son.

A number of other people in the United States and Europe have helped this project in direct or indirect ways, and deserve heartfelt thanks. They include Susan Amussen, José Andrés-Gallego, Alfonso Bullón de Mendoza, J. C. D. Clark, Eveline Cruickshanks, Howard Erskine-Hill, Xavier Gil Pujol, William Lamont, Isabel de Madariaga, Jeffrey Merrick, René Pillorget, J. G. A. Pocock, Conrad Russell, Elizabeth Russell, and Daniel Szechi. Closer to home, I have often relied on the counsels of friends, among them Richard Arthur, Cates Baldridge, Darién Davis, Diana Henderson, Karin Hanta, Steve Jensen, Marjorie Lamberti, David Macey, David Napier, Victor Nuovo, Ellen Oxfeld, José Alberto Portugal, Cassandra Potts, and Sharon Rybak. I am very grateful to the reader for Yale University Press, who suggested many important changes to the original draft, and to my editor at the Press, Otto Bohlmann. Middlebury College has generously supported my work through funding numerous research trips and granting me two leaves. The Leverhulme Trust and the University of Sussex provided me with a much-appreciated visiting fellowship in 1990 and 1991. The Universidad Complutense of Madrid sponsored a summer session at which portions of the last chapter were presented in 1994.

The research for this book was begun at the University of Sussex and the Institute for Historical Research in London, but most of it was done at Middlebury College, the University of Vermont, Yale University, and McGill University. The assistance of library staffs at these institutions has been vital. I would particularly like to thank the indefatigable Interlibrary Loan staff at Middlebury for their unstinting assistance.

A few points about the text should be mentioned. The names of rulers have been given in the forms I found most commonly used in English sources. Dates have not been standardized to remove the differences between the Gregorian and Julian calendars, but the year is taken to begin on the first day of January. Unless otherwise noted, translations are my own. Unlike Casaubon, I have learned not to aspire to a perfection that leads only to doubt and silence. My readers will have to decide for themselves how wise this choice has been.

# CHAPTER ONE

# Introduction

Let us keep in mind, that King Saul had been chosen and anointed.
—ST. TERESA OF AVILA to Philip II, 1569

UCKED INTO A CORNER of that massive Spanish royal fantasy, the monastery-palace of San Lorenzo de El Escorial, are the tranquil spaces known as the chapter rooms. Their plain walls are adorned with religious paintings chosen by the great court artist Diego Velázquez. Visitors are often drawn to one small, crowded canvas, a puzzling allegory painted in 1579 by El Greco. Kneeling at the bottom of the picture, dressed in black, is King Philip II of Spain, who built the Escorial. He prays serenely at the center of a visionary vortex. Behind him open the jaws of hell, where the damned writhe in agony; beyond him lies purgatory; above him floats a chorus of angels, adoring the holy name of Jesus. The light from the divine symbol shines directly upon the king, who reflects it towards the viewer. It also illuminates a rock in the lower left, which bears the artist's name. The rock represents El Greco's Christian self, humble yet indivisible. The implied link between the painter's name and the holy name indicates a hope of personal salvation, which is also extended to us, through the king. By placing our gaze in line with his, we can rise above the twisting, confused bodies of men and angels and witness the perfect sign of God. Our own salvation seems to depend upon acceptance of the monarch's role as intermediary between us and Christ.[1]

Why should the king enjoy this significance? Because for El Greco, as

1. Domenikos Theotokopoulos, called El Greco, *Allegory of the Holy League* (ca. 1579), painting. Monastery-Palace of El Escorial.

Photo: Patrimonio nacional, Madrid.

for most European Christians of his time, monarchy was not just a system of worldly dominance; it was a reflection of God, and an ideal mirror of human identity. It was a link between the sacred and the self. In turn, the mediation of the royal person had become essential to Christian conceptions of political authority. This book is about how such mediation worked and how over time its terms were altered. It is, therefore, a book about kings; but it is concerned less with their deeds, their characters, or their administrations than with their intellectual, spiritual, and even mystical powers over the minds and hearts of their subjects—the powers that are summed up in El Greco's kneeling figure of Philip II.

Between the sixteenth and the eighteenth centuries these mediating powers changed in fundamental ways, so that by 1715 El Greco's intensely personal vision of Christian kingship would have seemed quite outdated. There had been a marked decline in the effectiveness of political explanations that rested on the assumption of sacredness or divine grace. What had supplanted them was not secularism but a religiously based obedience to an abstract, unitary human authority, combined with a deepened sense of individual moral responsibility—in short, sovereignty plus self-discipline. These were the foundations of what will be called the rational state, whose visible sign was the king. It was a momentous change, the beginning of what the German sociologist Max Weber dubbed a "de-enchantment of the world." We still live in its shadow.

There are many excellent books that deal with the formation of the state in early modern Europe.[2] Some have already brilliantly surveyed the political thought of the period, including the idea of kingship.[3] The approach adopted in this book is different from them in three ways. First, greater emphasis is placed here on the overarching cultural importance of religious beliefs. It would not have surprised El Greco to be told that religion provided the bonding element in his social, intellectual, and political atmosphere. It was the glue that held together what sociologists have called *habitus*, the embodiment of social learning in human relations.[4] Historians of the state, however, have usually shown more interest in non-religious influences on human behaviour and in what they have regarded as secular aspects of political thought. They have looked upon the rational state as the product of class conflict, militarism, fiscal reform, and hierarchical organization. In this book, by contrast, state development is interpreted through the prism of religious faith, at whose centre lies a vision (or illusion) of the sacred.

The second distinctive feature of this approach is that it connects the emergence of state ideologies with the redefinition of a moral persona that will be called the self. The self was the humble rock in El Greco's painting, an idealized yet specific identity that was assumed to lie beneath the diverse features of worldly personhood. A particular awareness of the self was woven into the fabric of Christian teachings. Early modern religious movements, as we shall see, sought to reform or purify the self by espousing a simplified, internalized piety. Out of this reformed Christian self emerged the idea of a new kind of political subject, one who had enough self-regulated discipline to become a tacit participant in the state. The responsible subject was imagined as an adult male of independent judgment, who had surrendered part of his self-determination to a worldly monarchy that claimed to reflect his own inner values. In practice, such a pact may seldom have been consciously entered into, and it was almost never smoothly attained, but the myth of its existence was vital to the preservation of state authority.

The third aspect of this book that differs from previous accounts is that it blends the intellectual discourse of the time with the images and rituals of rulership. Its sources are not just political writings but also accounts of public ceremonies, court etiquette, paintings, prints, and commemorative verse. This sort of historical evidence has been used before to good effect and has enlivened many recent cultural studies.[5] It has sustained anthropological theories about kingship, such as those of the eccentric A. M. Hocart, who argued that all the structures of royal government had ritual origins, or of Clifford Geertz, who described the monarch as the "exemplary centre" of a symbolic system.[6] This book, however, examines the representations of royalty neither as emblems of a stable authority nor as examples of an accepted iconographic tradition but as the shifting strategies of political persuasion. Although rituals or icons might claim to express universal, settled meanings, in fact they changed form and significance depending on circumstances and the audiences they were meant to address. They became aspects of an emerging language of politics, one that linked subjects to rulers in a continuing dialogue about dominance and obedience.

As an analysis of representations, this book can be considered an essay in cultural history. The term deserves some clarification. Cultural history assumes that human behaviour can be interpreted through language (including graphic and behavioral expressions), or, more precisely, through the linguistic signifiers by which we try to communicate. The purpose of cultural history is to analyse these signifiers so as to find out how they indicate social, intellectual, or ideological motivations, distinctions of value, and power relations.[7] The task is far from easy. Language is a notoriously ambiguous instrument that may point in different directions at the same time. Signifiers may conflict and compete with one another. In addition, not every linguistic example can be read as representative of the whole culture that produces it; it may belong to a subculture or be unique to some quirkily individual viewpoint. An approach that sees every cultural expression as the outcome of uniform processes of construction would be crudely reductionist. It could not account for the diversity of thought that may be found in even the most apparently homogeneous societies.

Cultural historians, therefore, have to be discriminating in their use of evidence and cautious in amassing, assorting, and explaining it. Even taken together, a given collection of signifiers may not comprise a definable cultural pattern. Moreover, in trying to determine the historical coherence of any set of linguistic expressions, we cannot simply dissect them, as if they clearly displayed within themselves all the elements of their making. We have to bring to the task some previous understanding of the structures of life—social hierarchy, economic activity, political organization—that prevailed at the time of their creation. Perhaps we should not separately distinguish such structures as "background" or "context," because they are integrated into culture, visibly or invisibly, and have to be expressed through language. Yet there is no satisfactory way to describe them except as contextual. They have a constant, practical impact on everyday existence that cannot be grasped if we study them only as cultural representations. To examine life in the past as if it consisted of a set of interlocking images, a unified foreground with no background, will not tell us much about how it was experienced by the men and women who lived it.

Languages are not constructed for the benefit of students of culture. They are made by living people, motivated by emotions and desires with which we can partially identify, because we are human; so it is misleading to interpret cultural history as if it were an endless, self-referential series of signifiers, always conveniently distanced from our own critical minds. Language is designed, however arbitrarily, to refer to something beyond itself—to what used to be called "the real world." We may not ourselves be able to conceive of anything that lies outside language; we may not be willing to commit ourselves to the immanence of some "reality" beyond it. Still, we should recognize that others have been able and willing to do so, that their ways of thinking and communicating were based on this assumption.

With such caveats in mind, this book is an attempt at cultural history. It is also a political history, which is to say that it pays attention to the course of political events. Events are not wholly predictable. They can disrupt a socio-economic structure or upset the certainty of a cultural system. Because rituals are also events, they do not always work as they are supposed to, and they can be altered. To ignore events is to downplay the role of inconsistency in history, and unduly to regularize change.

The next chapter of the book begins with an event: the assassination of King Henry III of France in 1589. In itself, the killing of a king was a momentous political occurrence; but it was also an unmistakable sign of the waning of sacral monarchy throughout Europe, the outcome of seven decades of religious reformation. The last chapter ends in 1715, with the death of Louis XIV. By that point, the transformation of kingship and the self had been firmly set in motion, not just in France but also in Britain, Scandinavia, Russia, and, to a lesser extent, the Habsburg monarchies. The events of 1715, therefore, are notable not so much for the temporary disruptions they may have caused as for their consolidation of long-term structural changes.

Each of the following chapters concentrates on a chronological stage in the developing relationship of kings with Christian selves. Chapter 2 deals with the crisis of Renaissance monarchy, a rulership centred on the sacredness of the royal body, which was challenged by reformed religion. Chapter 3 shows how Renaissance monarchy gave way to the theatre of baroque kingship, which tried to assert control over a broad, confession-alized audience. As chapter 4 relates, however, many of the devout re-mained dissatisfied with a politics guided by "reason of state," and they supported the rebellions of the mid-seventeenth century. The outcome of this crisis, described in chapter 5, was not the collapse of kingship but a renewed attempt to fashion the godly self into a loyal subject through an implicit pact with the ruler. The concluding chapter argues that by 1715 monarchy had appropriated many of the elements of religious identity and had begun to reshape them to conform to an abstract collectivity: the rational state.

Although these stages of development varied considerably among different countries, they followed fairly consistent patterns throughout Europe. The reasons for that consistency are not hard to find. First, the motor of change in kingship and the self was religious reform—whether Protestant, Catholic, or after 1600 Orthodox—which tended to have similar social and cultural effects wherever it emerged. Second, by the late 1500s the impact of printing, improvements in transport and communications systems, the formalization of diplomacy, and a preoccupation with rapidly changing military technology had made ruling elites throughout the continent more keenly aware of what was happening elsewhere. These changes also brought new segments of the population, especially the lesser nobility and the middling classes, towards political consciousness. Third, the Renaissance idea of glory had generated a frenetic competition among kings, drawing them towards standard choices and responses in dealing with the problems of their realms.

I use "king" or "monarch" to refer to the ruler or head of a polity, who holds that position for life, and whose authority adheres at least in part to the person rather than the office. Although their powers may be limited, kings are not fully subjected to other earthly rulers. At times I employ the term *king* for members of a collective category including kings and ruling queens, emperors, and tsars. Such usage is not intended to minimize the significance of constitutional or gender differences. Rather, it reflects the tendency of early modern political writers to lump various types of rulers together as "kings" and to interpret "kingship" as a fundamentally masculine quality. "Queenship" was exceptional, and each case has to be examined separately.

The book does not provide a key to all royal mythologies. It will not seek to argue, like J. G. A. Frazer, that the king was essentially a god of vegetation or, like A. M. Hocart, that he always represented the sun.[8] Of course, at times he was both these things. Perhaps the most common explanation of kingship has related it to fatherhood. In a version of this argument, Sigmund Freud suggested that kingship developed out of a universal struggle between fathers and sons to achieve sexual dominance over women. According to Freud, rebellious sons in "primitive" societies, having overthrown the authority of their sire, created sacred totems representing the father in order to relieve their emotional ambivalence towards him. The father, however, eventually had a psychological revenge in the emergence of kingship and incest taboos, which imposed a harsh authority on his guilt-ridden heirs.[9] Freud's theory is hard to swallow without considerable reservation, not least because the meaning of patriarchy varied among societies. Nevertheless, his theme of emotional ambivalence towards a patriarchal ruler will recur in later chapters.

The book also does not seek to construct a comprehensive political model to explain the development of European government. Nothing has been more misleading for historians than the assumption that the early modern state converged upon a single dominant type—which usually turns out to be the so-called absolutism of the French Bourbons. Absolutism was not the necessary goal of monarchs. Most of them already thought of themselves as "absolute" in some sense, because they were responsible directly to God rather than to their subjects. Although all kings tried to expand their authority wherever they could, there was no fixed pattern of absolutist governance that was imitated throughout Europe.[10]

I use the term *religion* to mean a system of belief in a god or gods, which unites specific behavioral constraints with the possibility of personal revelation or salvation. Religion encompasses informal cults and organized devotions, private prayer and public rituals, theological dogma and occult speculation, the formulation of moral values and the imposition of social norms. Does it also include magic? The line that divides religion from magic is certainly blurred. Magic is not necessarily more "primitive" than religion, although Frazer tried to prove that it was. The historian Keith Thomas has contrasted the "multi-dimensional character" of religion with the single-minded, worldly efficacy of magic, but he admits that the two are not always clearly distinguishable. This is particularly true when dealing with a quasi-magical category like sacred kingship. In many cases, what was condemned as magic consisted of religious practices that had simply become unacceptable to the arbiters of formal doctrine.[11]

The field of investigation in this book is the Europe of Christian rulers and subjects, which lay outside the Ottoman Empire. I make no attempt to deal with Muslim-dominated societies, with Islamic and Jewish political ideas, and with events of importance chiefly to non-Christian minorities. Nor do I say much about the papacy. As the universal spiritual governor of the church, the pope was something more than a king; as a ruler lacking temporal authority, except within the oligarchical regime known as the Papal States, he was something less. The papacy is considered mainly in its role as an obstacle to monarchical power.

The argument of the book rests on three other concepts: the state, the sacred, and the self. How have they been conceived of by previous scholars, and how may they be related to one another?

## Sacred State, Sacred Self

The state and the sacred seem to be opposites. The state, a human and profane institution, bears an aura of secular rather than divine power. Its inner workings are determined by reason, not by revelation or grace. The meaning of the state is supposed to be discernible to the rational mind, while the ultimate meaning of the sacred is hidden or secret. The state suggests structure, governance, and control; the sacred implies freedom from human structure, a release from worldly disciplines. The domain of the state is within the limits of human culture; the domain of the sacred is the unbounded sphere of the divine. Yet the two may not really be so far apart. As we shall see, they have been linked as idealized constructions that gave order and unity to the self.

### THE STATE

The state is more than a set of governing structures or functions. It is also an ideal of governance. In monarchical states, kings have been seen as the human representatives of that ideal. The philosopher G. W. F. Hegel, in a famous formulation, described the monarch as "the personality of the whole . . . the ultimate self in which the will of the state is concentrated."[12] Hegel assumed a total subordination of the self to a godlike ruler, in whom every particular will was included. Some version of this idealized relationship may have been at the heart of all monarchical states.

At the beginning of the twentieth century the social theorist Max Weber envisioned three ideal types of state authority, or what he called legitimate domination. The first was rational authority, which produced impersonal rules of discipline to which everyone was subject. It typified modern European governments, according to Weber. The second type of legitimate domination was traditional authority, in which "obedience is owed not to enacted rules but to the person who occupies a position of authority by tradition." Kingship was in Weber's view more suited to traditional than to rational authority. He suggested that all states were bound to evolve out of one, towards the other.[13] Weber's third category of domination, however, was more elusive and problematic. He defined "charismatic" authority as "a certain quality of an individual personality by virtue of which he is considered extraordinary and treated as endowed with supernatural, superhuman, or at least specifically exceptional powers or qualities. These are such as are not accessible to the ordinary person, but are regarded as of divine origin or as exemplary, and on the basis of them the individual is treated as a 'leader.'"[14] At its inception, according to Weber, charismatic authority was revolutionary and irrational, but eventually it became stable and routine. In other words, charisma began as divine grace and ended as human discipline. Thus, it might connect the sacred with the state, the divinity of the sanctified person with the establishment of rational authority. It also hinted at an irrational foundation for the state, one that could be papered over by laws or stabilizing rituals but could never entirely be effaced.[15]

Weber's categories have been applied to European and global history by scholars who have tended to emphasize the progressive divergence of rational from irrational authority, without paying much attention to the possible connections between the two.[16] The same distinction underlay the quasi-Weberian concept of the *Machtstaat*, or "power-state," developed by the German historian Otto Hintze. In the Machtstaat, the rational state took on a militarized, anti-democratic air. Hintze asserted that "the form and spirit of the state's organization" was determined "primarily by the necessities of defense and offense, that is, by the organization of the army and of warfare." The late seventeenth century witnessed the apogee of the "absolutist military state" and the emergence of the "tutelary police state," which placed the whole of society at its service. While he recognized the importance of religion to the Machtstaat, Hintze saw it mainly as a means of justifying a purely secular "reason of state."[17]

Weber's terminology can serve many different agendas, and it has to be employed with caution. Weber has been justly criticised for equating rationalism with a uniquely European standard of modernity. By contrast, the argument of this book interprets rationalism in an historically conditioned rather than an absolute sense. Rationalism describes thought and behaviour that are consistent with generally accepted contemporary principles of reason. It was a feature of seventeenth-century western philosophy, but it can also be observed in religious thought, both European and non-European, a point Weber himself recognized.[18] The rational state was not antithetical to traditional or charismatic dominance, and it did not inevitably culminate in either popular democracy or the Machtstaat.

As an alternative to Weber, we may point to theories that have derived the significance of the state from more fundamental structures of society or culture: in particular, those of Marx, Engels, Elias, and Foucault. Karl Marx saw the state as a manifestation of class relations. An essentially bourgeois formation, the state had "organs wrought after the plan of a systematic and hierarchic division of labour." Marx asserted that "all struggles within the State . . . are merely the illusory forms in which the real struggles of the different classes are fought out among one another." The state, in other words, disguised the real nature of class conflict. Marx was not much interested in the theatrical methods used to prop up the state, and he dismissed the rituals of kingship as "medieval rubbish." Still, he described the state as if it were a vital entity (with "organs"), and when he mentioned kings directly, he implied that they were to some extent self-serving agents, capable of guiding class struggles in a particular direction.[19]

In fact, it was difficult for Marx to work back from the illusory power of the state to its "real" origins, to strip ideal authority down to a convincingly materialist basis. It has remained difficult for Marxist historians ever since. The problem is imaginatively addressed, although not solved, in Perry Anderson's wide-ranging Marxist examination of the absolutist state. Anderson argues that absolutism "fundamentally represented an apparatus for the protection of aristocratic property and privileges, yet at the same time . . . could *simultaneously* ensure the basic interests of the nascent mercantile and manufacturing classes."[20] Somewhat obscurely, he describes this situation as a socio-economic "over-determination," rather than a deliberate balancing act. As in Marx's own writings, it is not always obvious in Anderson's critique who or what was represented by kings. On the other hand, can we simply deny the importance of social conflict in state development?

Marx's colleague Friedrich Engels offered a solution to the problem of finding a materialist basis for state power that made some concessions to idealism. He proposed that the earliest human society was structured according to common ownership and elected government. This happy world was transformed by the introduction of property rights, which led to patriarchy and the creation of kingship. The monarchical state protected the owners of property, who were the male heads of families, from the wrath of the whole clan. But the state was not merely their tool. According to Engels, it was "a power seemingly standing above society," a "moderating" influence in class conflict—in other words, an ideal authority that bears some resemblance both to Weber's traditional dominance and to the sacred patriarchal totem described by Freud.[21]

For the sociologist Norbert Elias, as for Marx and Engels, government was built on social relations rather than Weber's ideal forms; but his writings were more rooted in historical research. Elias perceived the state as a testing ground for social constructions. He was particularly interested in the development of modern forms of "civilizing" behaviour, from guarding one's temper to blowing one's nose. He argued that changing rules of conduct marked shifts in social as well as personal discipline. The honour codes of knightly violence had given way to bourgeois standards of civility or self-control. Through etiquette and ceremony, Elias maintained, the early modern "court society" reproduced and validated a *habitus*, a comprehensive structure of dominance over others. At its centre was the absolute monarch, the arbiter of status distinctions among the nobility of the kingdom.[22]

Elias was a provocative thinker, but he was imprecise about the origins of specific behavioral patterns. He saw the state, and the civility that suffused it, as reiterations of underlying realities of power. While there is a refreshing simplicity in such an approach, it begs the question of how such power was formed. Was it an ideal conception, or a manifestation of physical force? Was it precisely mirrored in prevailing behavioral patterns, or did other cultural values come into play? Elias gave no consideration at all to the importance of religious beliefs, which had an undeniable impact on the definition of power. While his analytical framework is compelling—it will surface again in later chapters—it has serious limitations.

Like Elias, the French philosopher Michel Foucault emphasized holistic networks of significance built around the central importance of personal discipline. Foucault envisaged power as equivalent to the imposition of order on the world by language systems. A particular disposition of power is built into language, and through language into perceptions of the body and the self. The state is nothing more than the political expression of this power, part of an all-encompassing system of discipline, or "epistemic field," with its own laws and logic.[23] Foucault's "archaeology of knowledge," however, was based on formal philosophic and didactic sources, which he accepted as normative. He was not much interested in the varieties of actual experience. For him, all forms of power were equally rigid and inclusive, which made it very difficult to account for cultural change. During most of his career, Foucault refused to allow for the possibility that cultures alter because they are not monolithic entities. Only towards the end of his life did he become interested in the "genealogical fragments" of "suppressed knowledge" that could produce diversity. Pushing the point further, we might propose that the "archaeology of knowledge" is full of such fragments, whose anomalies and contradictions raise the possibility of change.

In the works of Foucault, as in those of Elias, the state virtually disappears, because its controlling apparatus becomes indistinguishable from the nexus of social relations or the field of cultural power that informs it. If we accept that the state's importance in history cannot fully be comprehended unless we consider it as a partially separate entity, with its own rules, mechanisms, and interests, then we are again pulled back towards Weber's ideal types. It would seem that if we do not imagine the state as an idealized category it loses most of its analytical purpose.

## THE SACRED

Can the same be said of the sacred? Modern theories of the sacred that are not primarily theological look back to the work of the sociologist Emil

Durkheim. Instead of treating religious life as a distorted, and necessarily falsified, reflection of social or material life, Durkheim argued that it was a "collective ideal" that raised ordinary existence to what was imagined to be a higher reality. He defined the sacred as "something added to and above the real," in other words, the ultimate collective idealization.[24] The parallel between Durkheim's view of the sacred and Weber's concept of the state appears obvious. Both are ideal types; both are products of group consciousness; both give coherence and direction to individuals within a social collectivity.

Durkheim did not examine the ways by which the sacred can suddenly reintroduce itself back into ordinary social life, with transforming effect. This was a central aspect of the writings of the controversial Romanian scholar Mircea Eliade. His work can best be approached not as a credulous alternative to Durkheim's thesis but as an extension of it. Eliade proposed the term *hierophany* to describe "the *act of manifestation* of the sacred," by which the individual comes into contact with an organic, cosmic space and a perception of time as "a sort of eternal mythic present."[25] We do not have to subscribe to the existence of divine forces in order to appreciate that this is how many people claim to have known the sacred—not only as a collective idealization but also as a personal experience of universal order.

In his category of charismatic domination, Weber suggested how this view of the sacred can be connected with the state. Through charisma (or grace, in Christian terms), an element of the sacred manifests itself, suddenly and evocatively, as the point of origin of the state, a kind of political hierophany. Weber thought that charisma had to attach itself to a single leader or prophet, but there is no reason why it could not express itself through a collective ideal—the myth of belonging to a people chosen by God, for example. Charisma might then be transferred from generation to generation as part of a common identity.

Eliade's concept of the sacred includes violent states of spiritual exaltation. René Girard has even more closely associated the sacred with violence—specifically, the sacrificial violence that is seen as necessary to repair social order during a period of crisis. Girard suggests that all forms of religion and ideology have their origins in an act of expiatory violence, by which the threat of chaos is symbolically overcome. He may carry this argument too far—after all, it is possible to imagine certain experiences of the sacred (prayer, for example, or contemplation, or the reading of Scripture) that are not in any direct way linked to rituals of blood sacrifice. Still, as Girard insists, sacrality tends to protect against the dangers of the world by invoking a different, perhaps equally dangerous, irrationality, to which the person of the believer is subjected.[26]

The sacred, in other words, pursues the rational end of control or stability by irrational means. This contradiction has alarmed some scholars, who see in the sacred little more than violent emotionalism. For them, ethical participation in the state offers a promise of spiritual stability without the dangers of "possession by the Sacred."[27] Thus, the philosopher Jacques Derrida—somewhat surprisingly, considering the deconstructive tone of his earlier works—has written that "religion exists once the secret of the sacred, orgiastic, or demonic mystery has been, if not destroyed, at least integrated, and finally subjected to the sphere of responsibility."[28] That sphere of responsibility might be coterminous with the rational state.

Could such an integration remove the remnant of "demonic mystery" that continually resurfaces within religion? Julia Kristeva has suggested that it could not. In her study of what she calls "abjection," she connects "the abject" with all those aspects of the body (death, childbearing, even incest) that are culturally associated with disgust, horror, or impurity, particularly female impurity. The abject, for Kristeva, is the source of a "psychic" disorder that has to be expunged by the expiatory violence described by Girard. Ritual purification, however, is never successful; the trace of abjection always remains. Kristeva therefore imagines the sacred as "two-faced," with one side characterized by formal rituals, while the other remains "an understudy, still more secret and invisible, unrepresentable, turned towards those uncertain spaces of an unstable identity."[29] Although it is opaque and laden with unsupported assumptions, Kristeva's argument presents an obstacle to those who prefer a purely ethical approach to religion. Full human responsibility could emerge only if the abject, and with it the instability of the body itself, were somehow subjugated.

The notion of the abject echoes some long-standing Christian beliefs about the body, connected with physical penitence or mystical divisions of the self.[30] It might also be applied to another quintessentially medieval construct, the royal body. The figure of the sacred king seems to carry within it a two-faced identity. Alongside the dominant presence of the divine, a disturbing taint of human impurity or abjection can always be detected. For Christians, however, this bifurcated identity reflected an underlying order, designed by God, in which even impurity or abjection had a sacred purpose. Through his debased flesh and exalted person, the monarch represented both the earthly wretchedness of the self and its potential glorification in heaven. To make a human being into such a powerful symbol of divine order is an astonishing claim, and for most of us today an utterly unbelievable one. Sacred kingship, therefore, is the most obvious and hollow of cultural constructions; but it is also one of the most historically important. It is much easier to embrace its charisma blindly, or reject it impatiently, than to understand it.

## The Person and the Self

If we wish to understand sacred monarchy as a symbol of individual destiny, we have to decide what is meant by the person and the self. Surprisingly, historians have had little to say about either term until very recently.[31] "The concept of the person," however, has been the subject of debate among anthropologists since Marcel Mauss first proposed it as "a category of the human mind" in 1938. Mauss also employed the term *the self* (*le soi*) in a specific historical fashion, although some scholars have used it more or less interchangeably with "the person," and others have seen it as a basic psychological formation.

Mauss did not deny that all societies accept some sense of individual identity, but he argued that personhood had evolved over time, primarily in Europe. The "primitive" person, said Mauss, was defined by a carefully prescribed role within the family or clan, not by individual autonomy. The Romans were the first to envisage personhood as a form of public representation, whereby an individual was characterized by a *persona*, or mask. The concept of a real or inner moral persona was developed by the Stoics and given a unified direction by Christianity. "Our own notion of the human person," according to Mauss, "is still basically the Christian one." In the seventeenth and eighteenth centuries "the category of self" became the primary focus of consciousness, through the influence not only of rationalist philosophers like Descartes and Spinoza but also of sectarian religious movements, from Puritans to Pietists. The Enlightenment ensured the final triumph of the self in the western world.[32] This is a simplified and blatantly "progressive" chronology, but it has yet to be replaced with a more convincing one.

Mauss set the tone for later discussions in two major ways. First, he assumed that personhood was not a fixed or unchanging feature of human identity. Most subsequent scholarship has followed his lead, and both the person and the self have gradually become more and more unfixed. Some have argued, as Mauss did not, that they lack any inner coherence or core. This could be inferred from the work of the sociologist Erving Goffman, who suggested that the self was structured by the theatrical techniques of its outward presentation. Nothing essential seems to lie behind the masks used in these performances. Goffman, however, did not explore the moral or cultural values that underlie everyday transactions.[33] They may give more unity and coherence to the theatre of the self than he assumed.

Second, Mauss stressed the contrast between western individualism and the "holism," or subordination of the person to the whole, that appeared to dominate other societies. Recent anthropological theory has tended to underline the distinction between individualist conceptions of the person, based on privacy, and holistic ones, "where the person receives no abstract, context-independent recognition." Some scholars have objected, however, that the western concept of the person is far from autonomous and, conversely, that a consciousness of one's own individuality is found in all cultures.[34] Indeed, from the perspective of European history, it is difficult to justify a severe dichotomy between individualism and holism, which seem always to have complemented one another.

Mauss was less influential in trying to separate the outward-looking person from the inward-looking self. Later anthropological scholarship has tended to confute the two. Psychologists, however, have maintained a distinction similar to that made by Mauss. They have developed their own concept of the self as the clearing house of human consciousness, at once more primal and more mysterious than the fully socialized person. For Freud, the self was formed through an internal process of control whereby desires and urges were subjected to a repressive "superego." In an overwrought Freudian analysis, Jacques Lacan envisaged the creation of the self as a violent psychological disruption. An externally based perception of coherent ego is imposed on the fragmented consciousness of infants.

Figures of authority (the father, the phallus, language, presumably the king) manifest the brutal integration of the self. Lacan's dramatic theory has had a considerable impact on scholars who have sought to depict the self as divided or as lacking essential coherence.[35]

Psychoanalytical models of the self are vexing for historians, because they make it difficult to distinguish inevitable stages from those that are conditioned by changing circumstances. If everybody's consciousness goes through roughly the same processes, as Freud and Lacan imply, then historical context becomes irrelevant. On the other hand, we may wonder whether there is something more to the self than social or linguistic interactions. In spite of its many shortcomings, psychoanalysis attempts to explain internalized emotional structures that may be buried within cultural formulations. It is therefore not without historical value, although it has to be used with care.

The treatment of the self adopted in this book will not satisfy everyone, but it will serve the purposes of an argument about early modern European politics and religion. Person and self will be understood as overlapping but somewhat different categories. Person will refer to social identity in its broadest sense, the Freudian superego, from official roles and economic interactions to conventional relations among family members; the self, to a more inwardly focused emotional and moral identity, similar in some respects to what Freud called the "ego." Both were multi-faceted, with sides to them that were holistic, others that were individualistic. The person was seen as dependent on the self and governed by it, at least in an ideally balanced consciousness. Identity, therefore, was not fully integrated, but neither was it based on a stark duality. The self aspired to be a coherent whole, especially in relation to God, although its connections with others might be fraught with division or instability. It was assumed that the self had an essential core, and that its expressions were authentic. Whether or not such assumptions reflected some inherent reality, common to all human beings, is a question historians cannot answer satisfactorily. Certainly we can find different configurations of the self in other societies or time periods.

The person was rooted in the world, while the focus of the self was on universal and unworldly things, above all the sacred. The sacred monarch was meant to belong to the realm of the self. Although he headed the social order, he did not symbolize the heterogeneous strands of the person. Rather, he was the symbol of a higher spiritual order found in self-identity. For Christians, therefore, the analogy between the self and sacred monarchy was always obvious: the first united and gave direction to the soul and body just as the second unified and led the polity.

## THE CHRISTIAN SELF

These points about the person and the self need further historical illustration. Personhood or social identity was important in early modern Europe, not as the basis of individual autonomy but as an indicator of family, rank, gender, honour, economic status, marital condition, nationality, geographical origins, personal beauty. All could be summed up in a name. For anyone who aspired to a modicum of social respectability, one's name—often made more specific through a patronymic or honorific through a title—was not separable from one's background, one's rank, or what one owned. Only criminals, vagabonds, and beggars used nicknames and aliases to disguise themselves. A lot of people shared the same name in early modern societies, yet it was a terrible crime to impersonate another by taking his or her name, as was shown by the strange story of Arnauld du Tilh, a French peasant executed in 1560 for pretending to be someone named Martin Guerre.[36]

The vesting of worldly reputation in a name was as old as Odysseus. In Christian Europe, however, there was a further and more spiritual reason for guarding one's name. For Christians, self-identity was a fundamental religious precept. The Christian self consisted of a particular immortal soul lodged in a particular mortal body. "The soul is in its body somewhat as God in the world. Everywhere, and everywhere entire," wrote William of St. Thierry in the twelfth century.[37] Together, soul and body comprised a specific human being, whose individuality was essential to salvation. In the afterlife one was rewarded for personal acts of faith, punished for personal sins. This eternal destiny applied to the body as well as the soul. St. Augustine had maintained that the physical form, separated from the soul at death, would be resurrected pure and intact at the end of time, so that the whole individual would be reunited in glory. "The bodies of the righteous, after resurrection . . . will be endowed with the gift of assured and

inviolable immortality," he confidently asserted.[38] St. Thomas Aquinas reiterated the point several centuries later. The soul was not anonymous, collective, or migrant, according to Aquinas; it was "an individuated form,"
lodged in the body. It had a single, permanent character, which would be
rewarded or punished in the afterlife.[39] The doctrine is illustrated in the last
cantos of Dante's *Paradiso*, where the souls of the blessed retain their
individual traits, their bodies as well as their names, even in the rapture of
direct contemplation of God.

Eastern Christianity used a different vocabulary, which placed more
emphasis on direct spiritual communion with God. Yet basic assumptions
about the coherence of the self in Orthodox lands were not dissimilar to
those of the west. According to the seventh-century writer Maximus Confessor, whose influence made him a sort of Greek Augustine, salvation
meant that both soul and body would be "deified" through "partaking" in
God, so that the reunited self would actually become a god, while retaining
its individuality. Later, Byzantine theologians like Michael Psellus wrote of
soul and body as "contemporaneous," meaning that one could not exist
without the other.[40]

In principle, Christian identity was not supposed to have anything to
do with personhood or the ethnic, social, and gender distinctions of earthly
existence. As St. Paul put it, "There is neither Jew nor Greek, there is
neither bond nor free, there is neither male nor female: for you are all one
in Christ Jesus" (Galatians 3:28). The self should depend wholly on God.
"His gifts are good and the sum of them all is my own self," St. Augustine
observed in his *Confessions*.[41] Yet person and self shared the same name, the
same body. To assert that they were entirely separate, that spiritual identity
wholly superseded worldly identity, was to repeat the dualist heresy of
Gnosticism. Christians instead upheld the moral unity of both person and
self, of outward and inward identity. The doctrine of individual unity,
however, brought together two moral opposites: on the one hand, a corrupt, worldly identity, invested in the material body, or "the flesh," and
expressed through the social roles of personhood; on the other, an eternal
spiritual identity that was associated with physical as well as mental purification. Thus, the integration of the Christian self with the person represented a major moral compromise.

It was a compromise crucial to the expansion and security of the Church, because a wholesale rejection of personhood was not an option widely acceptable to those who held status and privilege. From the beginning, they were not willing to sacrifice their worldly identities for the sake of salvation. Eventually, as Jacques le Goff has argued, the western Church even extended the socio-economic distinctions of personal identity into the afterlife by the invention of purgatory, which allowed the living to help the dead up to heaven through financial contributions.[42] Thus, in both life and death the integration of the religious self with the social person was preserved. This may not always have been easy for the poor to swallow. The popular Cathar heresy denied the compromise between self and person, preaching an absolute separation between the reality of the spirit and the evil illusion of the physical world.[43] Cathar dualism, however, was eventually defeated in both western and eastern Europe, rooted out by Catholic doctrines that preached moral dominance over the whole individual.

The poor were not the only ones who may have felt marginalized by the close integration of Christian identity. Women of the middle and upper ranks might also be penalized by it, because their social or worldly persons were held to be subordinate to those of men. Against this, they might appeal to the basic equality of all Christian selves, as maintained by St. Paul and St. Augustine. The doctrine of equal participation in Christ, however, flew in the face of strong gender prejudices. The belief, inherited from classical science, that females were defined more by nature than by reason, more by their reproductive functions than by their judgment, fostered the perception that they were morally lesser beings. They were often associated with impurity—physical, sexual, and religious. A deep misogyny among the male clergy, especially monks, led to much fuming against women as incapable of becoming full Christians. Godly women, however, kept up a lively opposition to this view, and it never became a full-blown dogma of the Church.[44]

At the same time, female mystics turned against worldly personhood and immersed themselves in the ideal of the Christian self. Their piety was marked by a strong emphasis on abjection leading to exaltation, both spiritual and physical. Margery Kempe, for example, described herself as "a creature set in great pomp and pride of the world, who later was drawn to the Lord by great poverty, sickness, shame, and great reproofs." Her sense of unworthiness did not prevent her from speaking to and touching Christ.[45]

For men as well as women, the features of the Christian self were never free from tension, but they endured with remarkably little change through the Middle Ages. They were shaken up after 1400, however, by Renaissance humanism and its revival of classical learning. Humanism has been seen as fostering a competing, secular ideal of the self. Jacob Burckhardt, for example, wrote of "the growth of individual character" in Renaissance Italy as a liberation of innate human qualities, above all the desire for fame, that had little to do with Augustinian theology. As if to defend such a view, Pico della Mirandola envisaged God telling Adam, "Thou, constrained by no limits, in accordance with thy own free will, . . . shalt ordain for thyself the limits of thy nature."[46] The apogee of Renaissance individualism can be found in the essays of the French humanist Michel de Montaigne, which contain a remarkable series of explorations of the natural self in all its diversity. "As for me," Montaigne wrote, "I turn my gaze inward, I fix it there and keep it busy."[47] He was not much interested in Augustine, and he happily transposed aspects of the outer person onto those of the inner self.

Unlike Burckhardt, scholars of the Renaissance no longer see "individual character" as innately human or necessarily liberating. Stephen Greenblatt has suggested that educated men of the period engaged in what he calls "self-fashioning" in order to ease the anxiety generated by classical knowledge. Self-fashioning involved "submission to an absolute power or authority situated at least partially outside the self," and it was "achieved in relation to something perceived as alien, strange or hostile."[48] For Montaigne, the "outside power" was ancient Rome. For others, it was an earthly monarch, and the "alien" element was the lower classes or women, whose lack of education and perceived incivility made them objects of increased scrutiny and control.[49] Greenblatt's concept of self-fashioning is far removed from the "self-liberation" found in Burckhardt, although it still suggests that the Renaissance individual enjoyed considerable autonomy in shaping his (or, more rarely, her) identity.

This may overstate the case. Humanism disturbed, but it did not replace, the older theology of self. Recent historians of the Renaissance self have stressed that the renewal of interest in ancient pagan standards of virtue took place in an environment that remained essentially Christian. Divine approval or grace, for example, remained essential to any final estimation of human worthiness. Montaigne admitted that man "cannot raise himself above himself and humanity. . . . He will rise, if God by exception lends him a hand."[50] Even so bloated a personality as the artist Benvenuto Cellini looked to grace, and to the Christian self, at a critical moment in his *Autobiography*, that blustering masterpiece of Renaissance bragadoccio. Suffering wrongful imprisonment in a windowless cell, Cellini prays for divine guidance. He is rewarded with a vision of Christ and the Virgin. He cries out: "God in His greatness has made me worthy to set eyes on His glory. . . . So this proves my freedom, and my happiness, and my favour with God."[51] Ultimately, Cellini's self-worth depended on the deity and an internal spiritual assurance, not on the approval of other men.

The point was made more emphatically by religious writers of the time. "Thou wilt never be interior or devout unless thou pass over in silence other men's affairs, and look especially to thyself," advised the Augustinian monk Thomas à Kempis around 1450. "If thou attend wholly to thyself and to God," he added, "what thou seest abroad will affect thee but little."[52] The seventeenth-century English poet and divine John Donne echoed this Augustinian theme in his "Holy Sonnets," which were addressed to God: "I am thy sonne, made with thy selfe to shine, / Thy servant, whose paines thou hast still repaid, / Thy sheepe, thine Image, and, till I betray'd / My selfe, a temple of thy Spirit divine."[53] Line by line, Donne's classical egoism grudgingly surrenders to a reliance on the grace of God.

The "temple of thy Spirit divine" might take a political form as well. From Augustine to Donne it was imagined that the perfect Christian polity would reflect the ordering of the self. Sacred authority would be merged with the power of the "temporal sword," mirroring the unification of the self and the person. Just as obedience to divine government would establish spiritual harmony within the soul and the body, so too obedience to human government would maintain worldly control over "the flesh." The charisma of the monarch, representing that of the deity, would infuse the polity in much the same way as divine grace infused the self. In the powers of a godly king, therefore, Christian subjects would behold a collective and earthbound but still recognizeable image of their own powers over themselves.

Of course, no perfect Christian polity ever existed. Throughout early modern Europe subjects lived under spiritually imperfect governments, beset by a host of pressing realities: demographic, economic, social, fiscal, and constitutional. These factors conditioned the elements of social personhood, and they impinged upon the idealized definition of the self. They also affected the hoped-for sense of identification between kings and subjects. Let us consider some of these realities, the historical structures that framed Christian rulership in the sixteenth and seventeenth centuries.

## Cabbages and Kings

In 1589, kings ruled almost everywhere. Only one European state was recognized by its neighbours as an independent republic: Venice. The Swiss Confederation was still nominally part of the Holy Roman Empire; San Marino was claimed by the pope; Genoa was a Spanish satellite; and the rebel provinces of the Netherlands had not yet defeated the claims of their erstwhile overlord, Philip II. All of the other territories in Europe were subject in law and in fact to a single ruler—a king, an emperor, a tsar.[54]

The states of early modern Europe have been described by the historian J. H. Elliott as "composite monarchies," loose unions of semi-autonomous territories. Some were "multiple kingdoms," a term coined by Conrad Russell to describe the combination of more than one monarchy in a single person.[55] England had swallowed up Wales, subjugated Ireland by 1601, and united its Crown with that of Scotland in 1603; but each kingdom kept its own parliament and laws. France was made up of a number of large provinces with powerful local administrations as well as a multiplicity of legal and fiscal customs. Royal edicts had to be registered in the Parlement of Paris, the supreme law court, but by the end of the sixteenth century there were seven other provincial parlements guarding local legal traditions. An extreme example of disunity, Spain consisted of the separate kingdoms of Castile, Aragon, Navarre, Portugal, and the three Basque provinces. All these realms had their own Cortes, or Estates, including one each in the Aragonese provinces of Aragon, Valencia, and Catalonia. Within the Holy Roman Empire were over one thousand territorial entities, many of which had their own Estates, or *Stände*. The king of Denmark ruled both Norway, which had its own language, laws, and Estates, and the virtually self-governing territory of Iceland. Finland was a duchy within Sweden, with a partially independent administration. Poland was united with Lithuania, which kept its own laws; the Polish provinces, moreover, had local assemblies, or *sejmiki,* with extensive powers.

A seeming exception to this composite confusion was Russia, where the Grand Prince of Moscow had simply eliminated most of the local institutions in areas annexed to his territory; but he too had to rely on gentry administrators whose first loyalty was to their own communities.

All European monarchies contained representative assemblies, or Estates, whose prerogatives differed widely. In Russia the *zemsky sobor,* or assembly of the land, met in the succession crises of 1589 and 1613, but it had no fixed role in determining policy. In the French *pays d'élection* the Estates General did not have to be consulted in order to alter or create taxes. In the rest of Europe, however, it was almost impossible to create a direct tax, especially one on land, without the consent of a representative assembly. The Estates usually consisted of two or three houses representing the main "orders" of the kingdom, such as the clergy, the nobility, and the town burgesses, but there was a lot of national and even provincial variation. The Polish *Sejm* had two chambers, one for royal and church officials, the other for the lesser nobility; representatives of the towns were summoned only for the election of a king. The Castilian Cortes, on the other hand, consisted entirely of burgesses; the fractious nobles and clergy had been excluded from attending by the Crown. The Swedish *Riksdag* contained a fourth house for the free peasantry, a unique feature. In the English Parliament, bishops sat in the House of Lords, and the lower House of Commons was dominated by gentry rather than by townsmen. The *Reichstag* of the Holy Roman Empire included a separate house for the seven Imperial Electors, another for the eighty lay and ecclesiastical Imperial princes, and a third for the sixty-five or so Free Towns.

Within composite monarchies one might owe allegiance to a number of masters—a local landlord, a great provincial magnate, a territorial prince, a king, an emperor. Regional affiliations almost always proved stronger than ties to the Crown, particularly in border areas, as Peter Sahlins has shown in his study of the shifting Franco-Spanish boundary in the Pyrenees.[56] The ruler himself might be a composite person, like the king of Spain, who governed each of his kingdoms through different titles and in Barcelona was officially considered merely a count. In spite of these factors, Europe's monarchs saw themselves, without exception, as representatives of God. None of them, not even the elective kings of Poland, regarded the regal office as dependent upon the approval of the people. This gave them an appearance of formidable power. In practice, however, the exercise of royal government was constrained by local or provincial customs, laws, and institutions.

The political situation was aggravated by the fact that Europe's monarchs ruled over more subjects than ever before. From a low point of about fifty-five million in 1450, Europe's population had expanded to about eighty million in 1550 and perhaps one hundred million in 1600. This growth in numbers reflected relatively good economic conditions. By the late sixteenth century, however, overpopulation was bringing that moderate prosperity to an end. Rising demand spurred inflation, and the real purchasing power of wages declined almost everywhere. The period from 1600 to 1650 saw severe economic hardship in many parts of Europe, aggravated by war. Only after the mid-seventeenth century did prices stabilize and wages improve, so that living conditions by 1715 were in most places better than they had been for some time. By then there were perhaps 118 million people living between the Urals and the Atlantic.

These demographic and economic fluctuations put enormous strains on underproductive systems of agriculture and manufacturing. The common response from landowners and merchants was to intensify existing methods rather than to adopt new ones. In eastern Europe this meant a steady augmentation in the labour services owed by a peasant to his lord, and the imposition of what has been called a new serfdom. In western Europe, where the peasantry was free of most direct service obligations, the economic crisis often led to higher rents, subdivision of small-holdings, and increasing landlessness. The domestic production of textiles expanded as an alternative to low agricultural wages. For an unskilled labourer, it was not a happy time to be alive.

Whether or not the economic downturn undermined the old aristocracies and prepared the way for the rise of new elites is a controversial question. What can be suggested with some certainty is that shifting fortunes, greater social mobility, and the disruption of clientage systems sapped confidence in the continuity of existing social structures. The perception of change was widespread, even in countries where its practical effects were limited. The great nobles were usually most threatened by change; lesser nobles and members of the middle classes were often most able to exploit it. The fears and expectations of artisans and labourers were sometimes raised to a fever pitch, making them susceptible to religious or political movements that promised a measure of social justice.

Apprehensions about social instability also encouraged the spread of campaigns against public vice, including popular customs that were viewed as immoral or superstitious—carnivals, spring dances, harvest festivals. Leading clerics and members of governing elites had long wanted to clean up the obnoxious behaviour of the lower orders. The climate of uncertainty in the sixteenth and seventeenth centuries intensified their efforts.[57] The effectiveness of the assault on popular culture, however, remains debatable. Numerous practices that were abhorrent to moralists survived until the eighteenth century and beyond. Vices like drinking or swearing were often transferred from public to private milieus, but they did not disappear. Self-discipline was never as widespread or as internalized as the reformers sought to make it.

The atmosphere of economic, social, and moral crisis was not created by kings, but they were often blamed for it. They were viewed as responsible for the welfare and prosperity of their people, although they were almost wholly ignorant of how to bring them about. When lobbied by self-interested groups of merchants, they might grant trade monopolies to companies or individuals, issue regulations for manufacturing, or forbid certain imports; but these measures were designed to reward loyalty or to raise the Crown's revenues, not to effect economic reform. A change in the value of currency or a declaration of bankruptcy by a ruler had wider-ranging, and almost always negative, implications. Here again, however, kings acted to shore up their own income or to dispose of their debts, rather than to promote a coherent economic policy.

They were driven to such shifts because no European kingdom was financially secure. In most places, nobles and clergy were free from taxes, and many towns had obtained similar exemptions. The fiscal burden fell most heavily on peasants. To make matters worse, tax collection was often in private hands, and at every level contractors or officials would take a cut for themselves, which meant less for the royal treasury. These structural problems were compounded by worsening economic conditions, which cut away at royal revenues every year. The costs of hiring mercenaries and of updating military technology led to hefty increases in expenditure. On top of all this was added the costly magnificence of Renaissance courts.

Few kings could rely on a steady income to meet such demands. The French *taille*, a permanent annual land tax, was highly exceptional; elsewhere, rulers mainly depended on customs duties like tonnage and poundage in England or sales taxes like the Spanish *alcabala*. These regular revenues might be augmented by special subsidies, but such impositions were unpopular and were often resisted. The sale of public offices brought in a lot of money for the French kings, a strategy imitated by James I of England, who sold off scores of aristocratic titles. The king of Spain did a brisk traffic in the mayoralities of Castilian towns. In most countries, however, venality or the sale of offices was restricted to minor positions, and even in France there was a limit on the number of new municipal judgeships, court clerkships, or forestry positions that could be created. Beyond these expedients, monarchs had to borrow, either from private financiers, such as the syndicates of *partisans* who leased the tax farms in France, or through public funds like the French *rentes* or Spanish *juros*, which were heritable annuities. Kings often failed to pay their debts; Philip II of Spain declared bankruptcy three times, with devastating consequences for his Genoese bankers.

As for civil administration, the responsibilities of European monarchs were relatively well defined in just two major areas: justice and warfare. Both were seen as essential to the good order of the kingdom. Although rulers no longer exercised many judicial functions, the justice administered by their courts was a measure of their own fairness, in the same way that their success in war was an indication of their own valour. Besides, justice was a form of personal dominance, reflecting the subordination of those who sought it to those who meted it out. Similarly, the pursuit of war depended on the ability to command military service. For these reasons, European monarchs continually strove to make themselves the sole sources of justice and the only leaders in times of war.

They also tried to establish control over the Christian churches, which were major sources of wealth and patronage. The churches levied tithes, owned vast tracts of land, bought and sold serfs, and ran big legal and fiscal bureaucracies. They enjoyed an unmatched cultural influence. Although it is hard to measure the extent of ignorance or of indifference to religion, most Europeans were guided through birth, marriage, and death by the ministrations of clerics. Sundays and saint's days regulated the cycles of the week and year. Pastors and priests marked out the hard path to salvation and the slippery slope to hell. Cathedrals dominated the politics and social life of many major towns. The parish church was the centre of community and the repository of its most treasured objects: icons, bells, relics, paintings, statuary. Clerics preached in praise of the king's justice, blessed his armies, bestowed sacredness upon him. It is hardly surprising, therefore, that every monarchy aspired to bring the church under its sway.[58]

Royal efforts to dominate justice, warfare, and the church produced sporadic attempts to centralize administrative authority. It should be pointed out that there was nothing particularly "modern" or European about centralization. The Mughal emperors of India and the Manchus in China pursued it, as had Charlemagne. The European rulers of the sixteenth and seventeenth centuries did not have very different methods. To counter the influence of the nobility over local justice, they set up new central courts, fiscal courts, and courts of appeal that were under royal control—the *Reichshofrat* in the Holy Roman Empire, Star Chamber in England, the *audiencias* in Spain, the *chambres des comptes* and *cours des aides* in France. To overcome the particularism of provincial governors and elites, they appointed new judicial, fiscal, or military officials who were directly responsible to the Crown—*corregidores* in Spain, *élus*, *commissaires*, and later *intendants* in France, *voivodes* or "commanders" in Russia. To ensure that they would always have military forces at their disposal, kings turned from feudal levies to the hiring of mercenaries, dealing a final death blow to the already decrepit feudal system. To facilitate the flow of administrative business, they established secretaries of state, fiscal chancelleries, and councils to deal with specific concerns.

All of this was done in piecemeal fashion; none of it followed an overall plan. The only general scheme to transform government in the sixteenth century, Ivan the Terrible's secretive and ruthless *oprichnina*, ended in total failure.

As for the churches, kings imposed control from the top down, by claiming rights over appointments to high ecclesiastical offices. In Protestant nations and Orthodox Russia there was no effective check on royal appointment except the disapproval of leading clerics. In France, Spain, and the Habsburg lands the monarch appointed bishops, ostensibly with the approval of the pope. The Polish king did not directly appoint but did confirm bishops and abbots of the Uniate and the Orthodox as well as the Catholic faiths. Monarchs also tried to tap into the wealth of the church, whether through clerical tax contributions like the Spanish *cru\i{}ada*, the remission to the French Crown of benefices from empty bishoprics, or the direct confiscation of monastic property in Protestant kingdoms.

In general, kings would have preferred to pursue such initiatives without the interference of Estates. No ruler, however, was able to dispense with Estates entirely; the king of France himself had to consult them in the *pays d'état* where the taille was not permanent. They represented powerful interests and could provide a sense of national purpose, which might be turned in favour of the monarchy. In the 1530s Henry VIII had used Parliament to promote the Reformation in England; in the 1590s Charles IX allied with the Riksdag to legitimize his seizure of power in Sweden. The Austrian Estates eagerly supported the military efforts of the Habsburgs against the Turks. The Castilian Cortes was able to exert an important influence over royal fiscal policy until the 1630s. Even the French Estates General were summoned by Louis XIII in 1614 to promote national reconciliation.

If the Estates or other interests opposed his plans, the king might have to command obedience, or plead for public support. But he did not possess many effective means by which to spread his messages. Royal proclamations might be read or understood by very few people. State rituals were mostly attended by the nobles and clerics of the king's court. A coronation, royal entry, or great festival might bring the ruler face to face with large numbers of his subjects, but these were rare occasions. Most of the common people, in short, had little direct contact with monarchy, although it touched them obliquely through justice, war, taxes, coinage, and the images they encountered in storytelling or popular literature. Perhaps the only sure way to disseminate a message of obedience was through the churches, which had branches in every parish. Religious propaganda, however, was dependent on the adherence of local elites and the acquiescence of ordinary believers. No church was capable of carrying out a program of forced political indoctrination. The king's name might be read at prayers every Sunday, but would that guarantee submission to him?

The call to obedience was not, of course, a pointless exhortation, because almost everyone in Christian Europe believed it was the necessary adhesive for any society. Subjects were supposed to obey kings, just as peasants or serfs were supposed to obey the nobles who held sway over them. Apprentices or servants were obliged by law to bend their will to that of their masters. Wives swore obedience to their husbands in their marriage vows, and parents were given command over their children by nature itself. Everyone was expected to submit without protest to the sovereign will of God, expressed through his church. Hardly anyone, aside from a few ecstatic religious visionaries, openly criticized this seemingly unbreakable chain of hierarchical deference. In practice, however, there were plenty of weak or even severed links. One does not have to look far in any early modern society to find anti-clerical sceptics, recalcitrant children, wayward wives, riotous apprentices, rebellious peasants, or obstinate subjects. Few of them would have described themselves as disobedient. Rather, they saw their disruptive actions as justified by some higher power—usually God. This was why authority in early modern Europe was not a fixed assumption; it was a constant process of negotiation between rulers and ruled, with divine providence as the ultimate mediator. In the century after 1589, as we shall see, that process heated up, and it brought the kingdoms of Europe to the verge of a transformation of the state and the self.

2. *Truthful New Report of How Henry the Third, King of France, Has Been Stabbed by a Dominican Monk* (1589), German colored print.

Photo: Bibliothèque nationale de France, Paris.

# CHAPTER TWO

# The Sickness of the Royal Body, 1589–1610

To conquering Monarchs the red surcoat of arms
Justly belongs. That victorious King
Is justly dressed by these mocking men at arms
In a mantle which marks him as both Prince and glorious.

—JEAN DE LA CEPPÈDE,
*Les théorèmes sur le sacré mystère de nostre redemption*,
Sonnet 63 (1613)

T 8 A.M. ON 1 AUGUST 1589, in a mansion at St. Cloud near Paris, a passionate young Dominican monk named Jacques Clément stabbed King Henry III of France in the abdomen. The dagger appeared suddenly from the assassin's sleeve, and it made a single fatal blow. "Ah! My God! This wretch has wounded me!" cried King Henry, who was still wearing his dressing gown. Recovering quickly from the shock, he angrily drew the knife from his own body and struck his astonished assassin with it in the face. The hapless murderer was then cut to pieces by the king's retainers and thrown out of a window. His corpse was later recovered, pulled apart by four horses, and burned. The ashes were scattered in a river. Clément was dismembered and annihilated because he had countenanced the destruction of the body politic. As for King Henry's natural body, it lingered in agony for almost a day before dying.[1]

The crime of Jacques Clément was inspired by the Catholic League, a rebellious religious movement that controlled Paris and much of the kingdom. Some supporters of the League openly denied that kings were sacred. They despised Henry III, whom they accused of turning against the true faith by accepting as his heir a Protestant heretic, Henry of Navarre. The body of the Valois king possessed no special dignity in their eyes; it was mortal and corrupt, and it threatened to pull the whole kingdom into impurity. Accordingly, the murder had conformed to a typology of ritual purification. Following the biblical example of Ehud, the Israelite "deliverer" who stabbed the idolatrous King Eglon in the belly (Judges 3:12–26), Jacques Clément had pointed his blade at the abdomen, the centre of base desire. The righteous Dominican saw his knife sink into the degraded human flesh of a tyrant, not into a holy object.

"Oh execrable parricide! That a monk could have been so unhappy and wicked as to assassinate his King! The most Catholic King, I say, who ever was, among all the Catholics!"[2] This was the horrified reaction of the lawyer, historian, and poet Etienne Pasquier to the murder of Henry III. As attorney-general of the cour des comptes, Pasquier was a partisan of the king. Yet even he had been troubled by dark visions of the decay of the royal body. Pasquier recorded his fears in the form of a medical diagnosis: "Just as in a human body which is disposed to sickness, we accumulate bad humours, little by little, which are recalled to us suddenly, when we think we are less ill, thus has the King been stricken . . . so many malignant humours [were] built up in the body of our Republic, which gave us nothing, other than the great outburst of scandal, which we have seen in Paris. It was a pus; it was a slime which flowed in us, which the supernatural doctor wanted to let out, when none of us was thinking of it."[3] Pasquier was further troubled by physical signs of weakness in King Henry, which might betoken a loss of legitimacy: "What made me fear the most, was, that to conserve his health, he wore his head shaved, by the advice of his Doctors, using a false wig; & I would say, that long hair, under the first dynasty of our Kings, was the most signal indication of their Royalty."[4]

We may be amused by Pasquier's concern with bad humours or long hair, a symbol of masculine sexual potency; but he was not hidebound or credulous. On the contrary, he was a Renaissance humanist, learned in classical scholarship. His use of medical and historical analogies suited a humanist belief in man as the measure of all things. He exalted the king's body as the symbol of a collective body, "the Republic." He perceived the condition of the royal body as sympathetically tied to the welfare of the whole people, so that the king's lack of physical health was mirrored in the deterioration of the Republic. A misguided ruler would allow sickness to fester, in himself as in the polity. Nevertheless, Pasquier could not countenance an outright desecration of the royal person, which was an attack on the representative of natural and divine order. The monk Clément's deed was for him the worst offence against both nature and God, a parricide.

The crime of Jacques Clément marked the height of a crisis in the Renaissance conception of sacred monarchy, which had been challenged by a revived preoccupation with the religious purity of the Christian self. The result was a loss of public confidence in the mystical powers of kingship. Pasquier's anxious letters are evidence of this. So too was the highly irregular treatment of Henry III's corpse. Normally, the king's body would have received elaborate attention, because it did not cease to incorporate the spiritual presence of royalty. The continuity of power would have been represented in a wax effigy of the late king on the royal coffin. The effigy was treated like a living being—it wore the deceased king's clothes, carried his royal insignia, and was even fed meals twice a day. The king's successor would not appear in public until the effigy had been removed and the body interred at the abbey of St. Denis. Only then was the authority of the new king brought to life.[5]

In 1589, however, the ceremonies were altered. Because the Catholic League held St. Denis, the king's body could not be buried there. Instead, his successor staged a brief mourning ceremony in the chamber where his predecessor had died. Quickly embalmed, the late king's corpse was laid in a lead coffin. The heart, the centre of the king's love for God, was interred at St. Cloud; the rest of him was carried to an abbey at Compiègne, where it was placed under a wooden canopy festooned with candles. Not until 1610 was the body of Henry III removed to St. Denis.

The assassination of King Henry had taken the court by surprise, at a moment when a full royal funeral was impossible. Nevertheless, the departure from the usual ceremonies—the lack of an effigy, the appearance of Henry IV at the makeshift rites, the obscure resting place and separate burial of the heart—went beyond necessity. These anomalies were the first faltering steps in an almost desperate reformulation of the powers of the royal body. From now on, the king's majesty must be a fixed legal quality, not a personal charisma that might be squandered by error or sin. From now on, the king must never die. Through this slogan, Henry IV tried to staunch the wound made by Jacques Clément's knife.

By 1589 the sacred royal body was sick not just in France but throughout Europe. It was under severe assault from religious reformers, both Protestant and Catholic, who called for a stripping away of its mystical trappings and a return to a godly or purified governance more compatible with the piety of the Christian self. Confessional reform was sapping the strength of Renaissance monarchy from Stockholm to Madrid. It helped to foment civil wars, rebellions, and insurrections throughout the 1590s.[6] The response from royal apologists, most of them steeped in humanism, was a series of attempts to patch up the differences between kingly power and religious belief. In France their efforts converged on the idea of sovereignty, which would give legal substance to sacral kingship. To understand the processes that led to such a change, however, we have to go back to the origins of the sacred royal body and trace the pathology of the ailments that by 1589 had filled it with such malignant humours.

## Body Politics

The body is now a fashionable subject among historians. They have approached it as a cultural construction, observing it through rules and prescriptions that have been aimed at disciplining it. "There is no law that is not inscribed on bodies," Michel de Certeau pronounced. Of course, the body encompasses a variety of physical realities as well, which no law can fully take into account. "Bodies are not merely the creations of discourse," as Lyndal Roper has cautioned; they also live and move, and do not always behave as the makers of discourse intend.[7]

The sacred royal body was a creation of discourse, but it was far from being a secure legal concept. It was a quasi-theological notion, bound up with the ideal Christian self, and was thereby distinguished, at least to some extent, from the worldly or natural body that was the concern of physicians. Although Etienne Pasquier described the ailments of the royal body in the medical language of heats and humours, he did not mean to suggest that it could be cured through natural science or medicine. It suffered from a spiritual disorder that had to be examined through moral and religious precepts. For Pasquier, the health of the king's sacred body was ultimately determined by the "supernatural doctor," God.[8]

How did the notion of the sacred royal body originate? As we saw in the previous chapter, Christianity promoted a highly ambivalent view of human bodies as on the one hand irredeemably corrupt and on the other potentially sacred. The Christian formulation of kingship could not escape being affected by such attitudes. The body of the king, like that of his subjects, was both a reflection of the divine and a repository of human weakness or abjection. Over time, however, monarchs began to assert a personal sacredness that had once been reserved for priests and saints. Clerics tried to keep such claims under control by placing royal sanctity not in a natural form but in an idealized, collective *corpus mysticum*, or mystical body.

The beginnings of this long process of abstraction lie in the Book of Genesis, where God created man (and perhaps woman) "in his own image" and then cast his creations out of Paradise, branding them with original sin. The Christian body was therefore a reflection of God, the repository of the soul and the moral will; but it also included the flesh, a corrupting and evil influence. The early Christians, as Peter Brown has shown, often expressed a contempt for the unredeemed flesh as the source of worldly vice, especially sexual desire. They rejected the normative social ethics of their pagan neighbours, for whom the desires of the body were beneficial within a proper domain of moderation. Instead, Christians thought the body could be purified only through self-denial and punishment. St. Paul exhorted his readers to spurn the flesh and make their bodies holy: "Know ye not that your bodies are the members of Christ? . . . Know ye not that your body is the temple of the Holy Ghost which is in you, which ye have of God, and ye are not your own?" (I Corinthians 6:15, 19). Marriage was acceptable only for those who were too weak to keep themselves from fornication. Following Paul, many Christians rejected family life, choosing instead a rigorous chastity, often accompanied by self-mortification. Their goal was to purify their physical forms by imitating the sanctity of Jesus himself. For female devotees in particular, this could offer liberation from society's patriarchal bonds.[9]

Christian asceticism, however, was attractive to only a few, and it increasingly conflicted with the social aims of an expanding church. St.

Augustine spelled out a compromise whereby normative family ethics could be reconciled with Christian doctrine. He noted that "God created man with the added power of propagation, so that he could beget other human beings"; and he marvelled that "even in the body . . . what evidence we find of the goodness of God, of the providence of the mighty Creator!"[10] Eventually, the western church was able to impose an Augustinian solution: marriage and family for the multitude, chastity and personal holiness for the clergy. The ordinary believer's body was subjected to a social morality based on rational ethics. As William of St. Thierry put it in the 1100s, "Nature prepares and adapts the instrument of the body to the use of reason in everything."[11] This was a far cry from ascetic torments, or St. Paul's contempt for the flesh.

Asceticism persisted, but the medieval church worked to prevent it from becoming a radical force by emphasizing common membership in a society of believers. The ascetic body was absorbed into the body of the church and was required to heed its collective authority, which was derived from Christ. St. Paul himself had taught that the church must be a single body, which he identified with that of Christ. "For as the body is one," he wrote, "and hath many members, and all the members of that one body, being many, are one body: so also is Christ. . . . Now ye are the body of Christ" (I Corinthians 7:12, 27). Augustine noted "that sometimes the head and the body, that is, Christ and the Church, are indicated to us as one person." The unifying image of Christ's body was constantly reiterated by ecclesiastical writers of the Middle Ages, who depicted the clergy as its soul, the laity as its physical parts.[12] Only priests and members of religious orders could claim a personal resemblance to Christ, because only their male bodies were ordained by the church and made holy. Yet the body of any believer might be sanctified at the end of time.

The medieval Church was not the body of Christ in a strictly material sense; the relationship was understood as mystical. Christ, in other words, had two bodies: a human one and a "spiritual collegiate" one, a corpus mysticum, or mystical body, which was the Church. The first, although divine, was finite, historical, and male. The second was universal, perpetual, and perhaps female—ecclesia was usually represented as a woman.[13] The two bodies of Christ resembled the idea of his two natures: his divine and human elements. In fact, as Ernst Kantorowicz pointed out, the term *corpus mysticum* was first applied to the real presence of Christ in the Eucharist; but after 1150 it was increasingly used to describe the Church.[14] In both cases, it was a way of imbuing a physical entity with the sanctity of Christ's body. The idea of a corpus mysticum, however, also served to legitimate clerical dominance, because it distanced the lay Christian from personal holiness. Although regarded as part of a mystical body, the ordinary believer was not encouraged to imitate the actual body of Christ.

The corpus mysticum was soon given a secular application, as an answer to royal pretensions. From the conversion of Constantine onwards, the church had provided justification and sanction for temporal rulers. Divine approval set kings apart from lesser lords. They were said to govern "by the grace of God," a formula which meant that they had been specially chosen to act as secular agents of the deity.[15] Ecclesiastical sanction took concrete form as a consecration or anointment with holy oil performed by bishops at the royal coronation ceremony. The model for this was Charlemagne, crowned and anointed in 800 as the first Holy Roman Emperor. From the first, royal apologists asserted that consecration transformed the king into a quasi-sacred personage, a living imitator of Christ himself.[16] Through the ritual application of holy oil, it was claimed, the king's body became holy, like that of a priest. Of course, few kings were chaste—most were far from it—and their bodies were purified simply by anointment, not by any personal efforts. The ascetic ideal of the holy body had thus been doubly twisted, by both ecclesiastical and secular rulers, into what St. Paul might have considered a grotesque parody reminiscent of the divinity of Roman emperors.

Royal sanctity was permissible to the church so long as the king remained merely part of its body; but soon the Holy Roman Emperor began to claim that his sacred authority was derived directly from God, not from the pope. Had not St. Paul written that "there is no power but of God: the powers that be are ordained of God" (Romans 13:1)?[17] The pope shot back at the emperor with reassertions of his own authority over an ecclesiastical corpus mysticum that took pre-eminence over all other corporate bodies. Before long, however, the kings of France, the emperor's main competitors for the mantle of Charlemagne, began to advance their own pretensions to the direct sanction of God. The French example was soon followed by England, whose Angevin rulers were eager to outpace their Capetian rivals in sacredness.[18]

In 1159 the English cleric John of Salisbury proposed a compromise between clerical and royal authority. John compared the polity to "a sort of body which is animated by the grant of divine reward . . . and ruled by a sort of rational management." While the soul of the polity was "those who direct the practice of religion," its head was the prince, "subject only to God and to those who act in His place on earth [that is, priests]." John claimed to have derived the body metaphor from a lost treatise by Plutarch (which he may have invented), but it was clearly a version of the mystical body of Christ.[19] The *corpus ecclesiae mysticum*, the mystical body of the church, was now matched by the *corpus reipublicae mysticum*—the mystical body of the republic, with the king as its head.

In the corpus reipublicae mysticum can dimly be observed the origins of the rational state. It was a collective idealization of governance, an abstract yet organic concept that included everyone, and mirrored the order of the self. As a political compromise, however, it was shaky from the first, because it subordinated the ruler to the church and to the corporate polity of which he was the head. Ambitious monarchs could not settle for this; so they bolstered it with further inventions that would give them more Christ-like authority. Was the king not a sacred being, consecrated by God? Why, then, should he not be able to perform miracles, as Christ and the saints had done? Already in the early eleventh century the Capetian kings of France had begun to claim the ability to cure scrofula, a tubercular inflammation of the lymph nodes, by laying on their hands. The Royal Touch, as it was called, soon spread to England.[20] Ostensibly, the miraculous power of touching arose from the anointing ceremony, and it was attributed to God's grace; but it bestowed on monarchs a divine aura that adhered to the royal body itself. It must have seemed to many that the king, like Christ, encompassed a mystical body in his own.

There remained an unfortunate flaw in such high-flown royalist formulations. Unlike Christ, kings retained the embarrassingly mortal trait of dying. How was it possible for an everlasting authority to be attached to a deceased head or be incarnated in a cadaver? Perhaps the mystical political body might have a mystical head or ruling part—the crown, as it was sometimes called—which did not die. The crown might then be contained within the king, as an invisible element known as his *dignitas*. While the physical body of the ruler could expire, the dignitas was immortal, so that at least part of him never died. This was the imaginative solution arrived at by 1500 in France and England.[21]

The sacred king and his undying dignitas may seem far removed from the ascetic Christian body envisioned by St. Paul, but one was actually a political distortion of the other. The western church had sought to tame the asceticism of the Christian self by harnessing it within the normative rules of a unified corpus mysticum. Medieval kings tried to break free from those rules by reviving the destabilizing concept of personal sacredness, detaching it from priestly chastity and making it the foundation of their human dominance. Over time, however, their quasi-divinity became invested less in their natural bodies than in an imaginary corpus mysticum of the polity that was somehow attached to their persons. Thus, the sacredness of kings was made less threatening to the church, although its more alarming aspects were never entirely forgotten.

The Christian version of sacred monarchy, unlike divine rulership in the ancient world, did not involve making the king into an actual god; he was always essentially human. The sense of "the abject," of human weakness underlying the sacred, was therefore never expunged from western European monarchy. On the other hand, there was no danger that Christian kingship might become a symbolic religious office, disengaged from everyday governance, as happened in Japan or parts of Africa. The body of the Christian king had not been bestowed with divinity by communal religious traditions; it had seized its sacrality from the community of the church, as a justification for temporal dominance. Its holiness was active, not passive.

The sacral model tended to absorb other theories of authority—for example, patriarchy. The king was often seen as a father figure who ruled like the head of a family. Philip Augustus of France was referred to as a "king-father" who had "paternal" affection for his subjects. Of course, patriarchal kingship had biblical origins, because God was also referred to as a father; and it had sanction from St. Paul, who had exhorted obedience to fathers (Ephesians 5–6). It could therefore become a feature of sacrality.[22] Theories of natural authority, based on the revival of Aristotle, proved more difficult to integrate with quasi-divine kingship. Aristotelianism helped to shape the concept of *dominium politicum et regale* (political and regal lordship), which for some theorists, like Thomas Aquinas or the English jurist Sir John Fortescue, was held by the consent of the people and was strictly limited by law and convention. Within such a framework, however, the king remained the head of a mystical body politic, and his power still reflected that of the Christian deity. Fortescue even saw kings as ruling like God, in harmony with his saints.[23] However strong the intellectual pull of Aristotle, the image of monarchy throughout medieval Europe remained fundamentally Christian and sacred.

## Bodies Politic

In practice, of course, not all European monarchs could aspire to the same degree of quasi-divinity. Only in England and France was the full panoply of sacred monarchy unfurled, from consecration to the royal touch to the immortality of the royal *dignitas*. For the monarchs of Sweden and Denmark, on the other hand, sacrality was more tenuous. Although both were anointed at their coronations, neither could lay much claim to divine right. In Sweden the Crown became hereditary only in 1534, and the line of inheritance was uncertain until the end of the sixteenth century. In Denmark the accession of a new ruler had to be approved by the royal council. In neither kingdom was the political theology of the royal body fully developed.

The sacrality of elective monarchs, like the Holy Roman Emperor and the king of Poland, was even more questionable. The emperor was chosen by seven Electors, to whom he swore an oath known as the *Wahlkapitulation*. He bore no inherent divinity, although his subsequent crowning and consecration gave him a measure of heavenly sanction.[24] Similarly, the Polish king was elected in an often riotous Diet of ten thousand to fifteen thousand nobles, who bound him to tight restrictions, known as the *Pacta Conventa*. The choice of ruler, however, was thought to be inspired from above. The Polish king was duly crowned and anointed, and his publicity would continue to stress his divine selection. Despite such rhetoric, the king of Poland remained in practice a "lifelong manager," a mere mortal politically beholden to the great magnates who had picked him.[25]

In Spain a powerful but relatively new monarchy enjoyed few of the conventional attributes of sacred rulership. This may have stemmed partly from the influence of Islam; for a Muslim ruler to claim personal divinity would have been a terrible blasphemy. The customs associated with Castilian kingship, like the raising of banners at an accession to the throne and the practice of allowing no one else to ride the king's horse, had Islamic origins. After the coronation ceremony had died out in the fourteenth century, Castilian kings were neither consecrated nor crowned, and they possessed no regalia—no sceptre, no throne, no crown. In Aragon the authority of the Habsburg monarchs was seen as dependent on their defence of the privileges of the realm, to which they committed themselves in jurisdictional oaths sworn before the chief *justiciar* and the Cortes. Although the famous Oath of the Aragonese, beginning "We, who are worth as much as you" (that is, the king) and ending with a strident "and if not, not," was a sixteenth-century fabrication, it showed how far some of the educated elite were willing to go in justifying constitutional limits on monarchy.[26]

Nevertheless, the loftier elements of western Christian kingship were certainly not alien to Spain, and its monarchs were not ordinary human beings. References to the corpus reipublicae mysticum have been noted in Castilian political writings of the 1400s, and they did not wholly disappear in the following century.[27] The king of Spain ruled "by the grace of God," and he saw himself as the Lord's champion in the defence of Catholic orthodoxy. J. H. Elliott has pointed to "the recurring identification of king and altar" as one of the main props of Spanish monarchy.[28] The boundary between royal humanity and sacrality was vague, and it was frequently crossed by court writers. As Lope de Vega put it, "That princes are human, nobody can doubt, / But poetry must make their divinity shine."[29]

Christian rulership did not follow the same pattern in the east as in the west, in part because the ascetic ideal of the self was never fully tamed there by the authority of an Augustine. Byzantine theologians like the fourteenth-century monk Gregory Palamas continued to uphold asceticism, leading to mystic union with God, as the highest form of religious experience. These teachings were spread in fifteenth-century Russia by St. Nilus Sorski and his followers. Self-purification, however, applied only to celibate monks, not to the married parish clergy or to women. A countervailing Russian religious tendency of the same period, represented by St. Joseph of Volok, emphasized physical self-control, social discipline, and obedience to earthly rulers. But it never succeeded in displacing the ascetic ideal, and eastern Christian rulers absorbed in their persons a highly exclusive and wholeheartedly ascetic understanding of holiness, rather than the Augustinian view of it.[30]

As a result, the sacred body of the Orthodox monarch was relatively untrammelled by concerns about its basic humanity. The Byzantine emperors had seen themselves as "the living law," subject to no restraints, and had treated the church as if it were part of their inheritance. The divine element in the Byzantine imperial body was to be found in its animate or physical nature, not in a mystical dignitas—which explains why bodily handicaps, especially blindness, disqualified candidates from the throne.[31] Aspects of Byzantine monarchy migrated north to Muscovy, where after 1547, princes were crowned with regalia that had purportedly belonged to the eastern emperors. They also imitated the physical sanctification of the Byzantines, which led to rulers becoming saints. By the eighteenth century, of the eight hundred saints recognized by the Russian Orthodox Church, more than one hundred were princes or princesses, many of them martyrs for the faith.

Princely sainthood carried an implication of physical exaltation—the ruler's divinity, in other words, was rooted in his natural as well as his spiritual body. "In Russia," as the historian Michael Cherniavsky noted, "the tension was between the divine nature of princely power and the saintly nature of the prince as a man . . . the two aspects, princely and human, were equally deified."[32] The realm was not a corpus mysticum attached to the natural body of the ruler. On the contrary, it was described simply as the personal property of the prince, just as government was an extension of the administration of his own lands.[33]

The contrast with western Europe is easy to discern—but it is also easily exaggerated. Russia was not entirely dissimilar to other Christian nations, where sacrality was intermixed with human virtue and dominium was akin to ownership. Nor did the grandiose titles claimed by its rulers set Muscovy apart from the kings and emperors of western Europe. The name *tsar,* or *Caesar,* taken by the Grand Prince of Moscow after 1547, would have been coveted by any of the kings of Renaissance Europe. It was not an exclusive designation of Russian imperial authority and was used to denote any great ruler. The tsar was also called *gosudar' i samoderzhets,* which is often translated as "autocrat," but according to Marc Szeftel may be more properly rendered as "lord and sovereign." It too would not have been an unfamiliar term in the west.[34]

The Russian prince was no despot; like other Christian rulers, he was subject to God and to the ordinances of the church. To be sure, some tsars treated the leaders of the church with contempt—Ivan IV, known as "the Terrible," had ordered the metropolitan, or chief cleric, of Moscow to be strangled to death for criticizing him in 1568. No tsar, however, could afford to dispense with the sanction offered by religion, bestowed in rituals like the annual Epiphany ceremony, when the metropolitan blessed the tsar and his court with "holy" water drawn from the frozen Moscow River.[35] Eager for such legitimation, the regent Boris Godunov arranged in 1589 for the metropolitan to be raised to the higher status of patriarch, a move that gave Boris much-needed clerical support when he eventually usurped the throne. Russians in the troubled late sixteenth century continued to look to religious leaders for the political guidance that an unstable monarchy could not provide. The corpus mysticum of the Russian people did exist, therefore, but it was in the care of the church.[36]

What firmly set western European government apart from eastern—at least until after 1650—was not theological assumptions so much as the influence of classical learning. This became particularly marked during the Renaissance, which raised the medieval exaltation of kingship to new levels. The humanism of the Renaissance elaborated upon pre-existing themes of bodily sacrality, developing them in ways that could seem religiously suspect. By placing new emphasis on ancient models of virtue, humanist scholars stirred kings to worldly achievement in everything from art patronage to military science. The quasi-divinity of the royal body could now manifest itself through a variety of secular endeavours, and its excellence could be compared directly to that of pagan rulers like Alexander the Great and the emperors of Rome. Humanism also created models of courtly behaviour, and it animated court circles through the spread of Italian culture, etiquette, and ceremonies. To critics, however, the courtier might seem to be an artificial creature whose conduct depended on externalized codes of conduct rather than internal moral standards. Worse still, the sacred centre of the Renaissance court appeared to be the royal body itself, rather than the God whom it imperfectly represented.[37]

Some humanist intellectuals longed for a universal ruler who would provide an unchanging, irreducible source of worldly harmony—a paradise on earth. Although early formulations of this idea, as in Dante's *De monarchia*, were scrupulously orthodox, by the seventeenth century the dream of universal monarchy was producing utopian visions like the friar Tommaso Campanella's famous "City of the Sun," a communalist state based on natural religion and ruled by a "Prince Prelate." Campanella's work ends with a prediction of "a great new monarchy, reformation of laws and of arts, new prophets, and a general renewal."[38] Such cosmic fantasies proliferated in war-torn Italy, giving a considerable cultural boost to the already heightened pretensions of kings. At the same time, Renaissance Neoplatonism opened up to scholars—and to would-be universal monarchs—the natural secrets of science and magic by pursuing the hidden wisdom of ancient symbols. By the late sixteenth century, Neoplatonism pervaded the imagery of western European monarchy, especially in festivals and rituals that mimicked the antique.[39]

Thus, the Renaissance king became a classical god, a supernatural hero, or the subject of elaborate allegories with layers of disguised meaning. Garbed in such elaborate costumes, glowing even brighter to the educated few, the dazzling body of the king was further removed from the controlling shadow of the pope. But the monarch was also further separated from the mass of his subjects and brought closer to the borders of Christianity. The cosmic mysteries of Neoplatonic kingship were a far cry from the pious teachings of late medieval reformers like Thomas à Kempis, who exhorted: "Let not the beautiful and subtle sayings of men affect thee; for the kingdom of God consisteth not in speech, but in virtue."[40] How could the virtuous Christian self recognize its own divinely appointed order in the "subtle sayings" and Neoplatonic rituals of Renaissance monarchy? How could the pagan splendours of humanist courts be reconciled with the austere injunctions of Scripture?

Martin Luther did not set out to answer those questions. The Protestant reformer did not wish to make kings tremble; on the contrary, like St. Paul, he sought to preserve the powers that were, as bulwarks against wickedness. Yet the primacy of faith, a tenet that he bellowed out so fiercely, stirred up the old struggle between religion and monarchy. Like a whirl-wind, reformed teachings blew strong against the magnificent stage props of Renaissance rulership and rudely shook the sacred body of the king.

## Reforming the Body

The religious movements of the sixteenth century threatened the Renaissance conception of the royal body, because they redefined the potential sacredness of the human body and reconfigured the spiritual balance of the Christian self. Protestantism rejected the idea of two paths to holiness—chastity for clerics, social conformity for the laity. Instead, it espoused a single ideal of the wholly integrated Christian. Salvation was attained by the workings of divine grace in both the person and the self. Ordinary social life was affected as much as the "inner man." Because Protestantism rejected physical holiness, moreover, it could easily clash with a kingship that made the body of the ruler sacred.

For Martin Luther, asceticism belonged to the realm of works, not faith. In consequence, St. Paul's call to sexual abstinence was reversed: virginity was denigrated and marriage exalted. Luther wrote that "neither Christ nor the Apostles sought to make chastity a matter of obligation."[41] This rejection of bodily purity and emphasis on the workings of grace in ordinary life was bound to have an impact on the corpus mysticum of the polity. For a start, the king's body was perceived as no more divine than anybody else's. When Luther wrote about secular government, he gave it no sacred attributes at all. On the contrary, authority consisted of mere force, a "temporal sword" that had to be used to maintain the church and keep the unvirtuous under control. Christians, he admitted, "are subject neither to law nor sword, and have need of neither"; but government remained necessary because most people were not true Christians.[42] Deeply conservative, Luther nonetheless opened the way towards a radical de-mystification of human authority.

The path he laid out was followed by later Lutheran political writers like Henning Arnisaeus, professor of medicine at Helmstadt University, whose comprehensive *Doctrina politica* appeared in 1609. A disciple of Aristotle as well as of Luther, Arnisaeus maintained that monarchy was the best type of government, not because it was divinely instituted but because it was an extension of the organization of the family, the basic unit of society. He called for the monarch to uphold a single state church and to defend true religion; but he also argued in favour of "mixed republics," in which rulers and assemblies shared power. Although he was a medical practitioner, he showed no interest in the attributes of the royal body. Like all the Lutheran political theorists of his time, Arnisaeus upheld the temporal authority of kings, but he did not bestow any quasi-divine characteristics on them.[43]

The two Lutheran monarchies of Denmark and Sweden were strongly affected by such teachings. In neither kingdom had monarchy ever enjoyed much physical sanctity. In both, the Reformation strengthened the ruler as the protector of religion but did not enhance the sacredness of his body. At the coronation of Denmark's Christian IV in 1596, the bishop of Zealand exuberantly praised the monarch as "a reflection of God on earth," but he made it clear that the new king was an "agent" of heaven, expected to defend the community of the faithful against Satan's wiles, rather than an avatar of Christ. It was the leading nobles, moreover, not the bishop, who claimed the right to give him his crown.[44] As for the Swedish monarchy, the political struggles of the Reformation period virtually wiped out any claims it may have had to sacrality. In 1599 the Lutheran Duke Charles of Östermanland usurped the throne from his Roman Catholic nephew, Sigismund of Poland. Utterly lacking in sacral pretensions, Charles would at first only accept the position of regent. He was not crowned until 1607, and he waited another four years to perform the constitutional requirement of making a ceremonial progress around his kingdom. Acting like Luther's "temporal sword," Charles put to death many leading nobles for backing his Catholic rival. Although his publicists proclaimed that he was divinely chosen, they also asserted that Sweden was a "mixed monarchy" and freely placed royal authority on a par with that of the Riksdag. It was not clear that anyone, including the king himself, regarded the body of Charles IX as sacred.[45]

Compared to the Lutheran, the Calvinist approach to the royal body was less straightforward, in part because it stayed closer to the teachings of Augustine. Jean Calvin struck a more worried note than Luther on matters pertaining to the body, both physical and politic. He did not trust the flesh as much as the German reformer did. In *The Institutes of the Christian*

*Religion,* published in 1536, Calvin dwelled on the corruption of human nature, posing the rhetorical query, "Is the flesh so perverse that it is wholly disposed to bear a grudge against God?" Yet he was firmly opposed to asceticism and had no hesitation in condemning clerical celibacy: "It was an astonishing shamelessness . . . to peddle this ornament of chastity as something necessary."[46] Instead, Calvin constantly praised the married household as the foundation of godly Christian governance, a "mirror to set the example to those who show themselves rather indocile," the basis of "a good discipline for repressing vices and occasions of scandal."[47]

This household governance was not merely human. How could it be, when it had to control the unruly flesh? Calvin bestowed a divine authority on the heads of families, as well as on political leaders. He compared magistrates to "gods," a curiously pagan concept derived from the Old Testament: "Since those who serve as magistrates are called 'gods' . . . let no one think that their being so-called is of slight importance. For it signifies that they have a mandate from God, have been invested with divine authority, and are wholly God's representatives, in a manner, acting as his vicegerents. This is no subtlety of mine, but Christ's explanation."[48] Although he was not arguing for personal sacrality, Calvin clearly wanted Christians to accept the power of rulers as more than worldly. Kings should be obeyed in all things, because "when once the Lord advances any man to kingly rank, he attests to us his determination that he would have him reign."[49] Admittedly, Calvin was uneasy about some of these assertions, which seemed to contradict his oft-repeated aversion to "the wilfulness of kings." Indeed, it is hard to comprehend how a mere human being, a piece of corrupted flesh, could represent a God as omnipotent as Calvin's.

In the face of oppression by secular rulers, the followers of Calvin often tended to ignore his advice about obedience and gave the special authority mentioned in the *Institutes* to magistrates other than the king.[50] Some French Calvinists came to regard monarchy as a contractual and elective institution. The famous *Vindiciae contra tyrannos* of 1579, written jointly by Hubert Languet and Philippe Duplessis-Mornay, began with the argument that kings are not substitutes for God but are his servants. It followed that "no one is born a king, and no one is a king by nature . . . [they] became kings only when they have received the office, together with the sceptre and crown, from those who represent the people's majesty."[51]

Monarchy, according to the *Vindiciae,* was founded on two covenants, "the first, between God, the king, and the people, that they will be God's people; the second, between the king and the people that if he is a proper ruler, he will be obeyed accordingly."[52] There was no separate covenant between the ruler and God. Here was the basis for an utterly desacralized kingship.

Similar views were echoed by Calvinist writers in the rebellious Netherlands and by the Scots Calvinist George Buchanan, who went further than the authors of the *Vindiciae* in giving the power of resistance to the whole people rather than just the magistrates.[53] The most influential Calvinist political writer of the early seventeenth century, however, was Johannes Althusius of Herborn College in north Germany. Like Languet and Duplessis-Mornay, Althusius envisioned a "mixed monarchy" in which the elected representatives of the people, called "ephors," chose the "supreme magistrate." Opposing himself directly to royal dominance, Althusius argued that the king could rule over the ephors while remaining accountable to them — "the king is over and the king is subjected. . . . For he who is greater or equal to another can be subjected to the jurisdiction of another."[54] Althusius accepted that "supreme magistrates bear and represent the person of the entire realm, of all subjects hereof, and of God from whom all power derives," but they held this status only because they were beacons of godliness. He accordingly granted them "inspection, defence, care and direction of ecclesiastical matters," as part of their covenant with God.[55]

Staunchly Protestant monarchs could easily find themselves at odds with radical Calvinist political thought, as happened in Scotland. The regents who deposed Mary, Queen of Scots in 1567 actually appointed George Buchanan as tutor to her son, James VI. The boy came to hate his instructor's political principles, which would have made him a mere cipher.[56] James was equally disgusted by those Calvinist radicals who called for presbyterianism, or church government by lay elders, within the Scottish kirk. His dislike of them was confirmed by a famous confrontation of 1596 with the Presbyterian leader, Andrew Melville. After calling him "God's sillie vassale" to his face, Melville informed James that "there is two Kings and two Kingdoms in Scotland. There is Christ Jesus the King, and his kingdom the Kirk; whose subject King James the Sixth is, and of

whose kingdom not a King, nor a lord, nor a head, but a member!"[57]
Melville meant that there should in fact be one kingdom—a political as well
as religious body, with the real Christ at its head. The idea that Jesus was
the true king of this world was even more explosive than Buchanan's
populism, because the subjects of such a divine ruler might all be regarded
as equal. No wonder that James was moved to write a treatise rejecting it in
the strongest terms! Yet the king retained doubts in his own mind about his
personal divinity, as we shall see.

Given the ideological dangers of Protestantism, did sacral monarchs
find greater solace in Catholicism? On the contrary. The reforming direction taken by the old religion after 1540 was even less agreeable to divine
kingship. If Protestantism pointed towards demystifying the royal body,
Counter Reformation Catholicism often did so much more boldly, by
reasserting the purificatory ideal of the ascetic self. Spearheaded by the
new Catholic preaching orders, the Counter Reformation spread a message
of contempt for the world and the flesh, of redemption through denial and
mortification. Family life was frequently criticized rather than praised and
was subjected to the strict regulation of the clergy.[58] Lay Catholics of the
middle and upper classes took up the call to purify not only their own
bodies but the church and society as well. As Louis Chatellier has put it,
they sought "the realization of the Christian state" through moral control
of the mechanisms of governance.[59] The communal work of faith was to be
carried out by the whole body of the church, led by the pope and clergy.
Secular rulers could only serve as auxiliaries in the great process of spiritual renovation.

Hand in hand with reformed Catholic piety came a renewed scrutiny
of kingship, carried out mostly by Spanish Jesuits. They argued that kings
were responsible to the church, to the pope, perhaps even to the people.
Father Pedro de Rivadeneira warned the Christian prince "not to puff
himself up with the authority or with the power and sovereignty of the
king . . . [kings are] no more than a little dust and ashes."[60] The king should
act as the obedient instrument of God and the church: "No king is absolute
or independent or proprietary, but is a lieutenant and minister of God. . . .
[Princes] are guardians of the law of God, but not interpreters; ministers of
the Church, but not judges. . . . If sometimes, as men, they will fall into
some grave crime, they should recognize it and humiliate themselves, and

subject themselves to the ecclesiastical canons and the censure and correction of the Church."[61]

Harsher words would follow from other Spanish Jesuits. Father Juan de Mariana went so far as to justify assassination as a legitimate means of removing a tyrant, for "if every hope is gone, if the public safety and the sanctity of religion are put in danger, who will be so unintelligent as not to admit that it is permissible to take arms and kill the tyrant, justly and according to the statutes?"[62] The formidable Father Francisco Suárez asserted that "the power of political dominion or rule over men has not been granted, directly by God, to any particular human individual." Government was created by "the multitude of mankind . . . they form a single mystical body which, morally speaking, may be termed essentially a unity; and that body accordingly needs a single head."[63] The corpus mysticum, in other words, resided in the people, not the ruler. Suárez hastened to add that subjects were bound by God to obey their rulers, but he also argued that they had a right to defend themselves through a just war against a tyrant.[64]

The Jesuits were not enemies of monarchy; in Poland, for example, they upheld it strongly against the power of the nobles. The Jesuit court chaplain Piotr Skarga alarmed the Polish Sejm with his fierce sermons in defence of royal authority in 1597. Yet Skarga also praised the "golden freedom" of Poland's limited monarchy, which included the right of resistance to tyrants, and he associated "absolute dominion" with the Turks, Tartars, and Muscovites. He praised Polish kingship chiefly as a means of enforcing religious unity.[65] Like other members of his order, Skarga was no admirer of sacred rulership. His employer, Sigismund III, was imbued with the same attitudes and saw himself first and foremost as a servant of the church. This was epitomized in the pious inscription on a medal struck in honour of the royal founding of a Jesuit church in Cracow: "God has given the realm to the king. The king has erected a sanctuary to God. Thus God honours the king in heaven. Thus the king adores God on earth."[66]

The writings of the Jesuits inspired widespread Catholic attacks on the sacral pretensions of kings. In a pamphlet of 1583, for example, the priest William Allen scathingly condemned the usurpation of spiritual authority by the English Crown: "As though there were no difference between a king and a priest. As though there were no distinction between Christ's Body Mystical and a body politic or human commonwealth. As though Christ had given His said Body, Spouse and spiritual Commonwealth to be governed either unto kings or emperors."[67] While it proceeded from different premises, this was just as radical an attack on established forms of monarchy as the *Vindiciae contra tyrannos*. Christian kings were no more divine than any other creature, and they did not exercise a priestly role. James I was so alarmed by such views that he wrote three major works refuting them between 1607 and 1615. He unleashed far more invective against the Jesuits than he did against radical Protestants.[68]

Protestant and Catholic reformers had much in common. Luther was as keen as Suárez to separate what was holy from what was not, and to set the spiritual freedom of the Christian self above worldly governance. Sacred monarchs, therefore, could find little consolation in reformed religion, of whatever variety. They might, however, discover in it a different justification for their earthly powers, if only they were willing to make themselves into what Luther called a "temporal sword" or what Rivadeneira dubbed "a minister of God"—in other words, to become representatives of the reformed Christian self. German historians have called this approach confessionalization.[69] First adopted by princes in the territorial states of the Holy Roman Empire, it was based on political alliances between godly reformers and secular rulers. The reformers emphasized the moral necessity of submission to earthly authority, while princes enforced doctrinal unity and moral discipline. Subjects were exhorted to obedience by the new imperatives of salvation. Thus, the power of the prince was yoked to the confessional transformation of public and private life.

Unlike territorial princes, however, most anointed kings continued to fear confessionalization, because it limited their sacral claims and was associated with the dangers of godly zeal. Besides, monarchs wanted to preserve doctrinal peace in their diverse dominions, not to impose further changes. They were reluctant to commit themselves to a role as instruments in the struggle to spread reform, which might subordinate them to clerical bodies or require them to satisfy a broader audience. In the short term their fears were partly justified, because confessional upheavals cleared the way for a loss of royal sacrality and the growth of an engaged political public. In the longer term, however, confessionalization would become the chief pillar of baroque monarchy and would prepare the way for the emergence of the rational state.[70]

This lay in the future. In the late 1500s confessional reform was still unwelcome to sacred monarchs, even to those who, like Henry III, wanted to be perceived as devout. Indeed, religious change engendered a crisis in Renaissance monarchy. It brought confusion to the great ruling houses of western Europe: to both branches of the Habsburgs, to the first Stuart monarch of England, to the last Valois king of France and his Bourbon successor. Throughout Europe the renewed piety of the Christian self deftly subverted the cosmic designs of Renaissance kingship and placed a cloud over the shining divinity of the royal body.

## Vertumnus in Autumn: The Habsburgs

### THE ROYAL HIEROGLYPH

The Habsburgs were not just the ruling house of Spain and the Holy Roman Empire; they were an international governing consortium with their own mythology and a strong sense of destiny. They believed that their family possessed a God-given mission to protect the church, as evidenced by an accumulation of legends. According to the original Habsburg myth, dating from around 1340, Rudolf I, the south German founder of the dynasty, was riding with his followers when he met a priest carrying the viaticum, the Communion Host administered to the dying. Rudolf dismounted at once and gave his horse to the priest, "out of reverence for the love of God."[71] By the sixteenth century the story was interpreted to reveal a promise of world empire given to the Habsburgs. Just as they were protectors of the Eucharist, which is Christ's body, so too would they be given temporal custody of his other body, the universal Church.

Inspired by such tales, the Habsburgs nurtured vast ambitions, which the culture of Renaissance monarchy raised to ever more dizzying heights. None grasped higher than Charles I and V, who tirelessly pursued the universalist aims of his family. He was depicted as the descendant of Aeneas, heir to the Roman Empire, the secular counterpart to the church. His lifelong dream was to lead a crusade against the Turks and bring the

Ottoman domains back into the Christian fold. As Holy Roman Emperor and king of Spain, with all its American dominions, it must have seemed for a time that Charles really was emperor of the world. He did not hesitate to proclaim the title through his personal device—two columns representing the Pillars of Hercules, gateway to the oceans and link between continents.[72] His dreams, however, were never realized. Defeated and exhausted by the rise of Protestantism, he abdicated in 1555. The religious split in the Empire was recognized by the Peace of Augsburg, which allowed territorial rulers to determine whether the faith of their subjects would be Catholic or Lutheran. By 1600 most of the inhabitants of the *Erblande*, or Habsburg hereditary lands—Austria, Bohemia, and parts of Hungary— were Protestants of one sort or another.[73]

Charles V's Imperial successors began to lose confidence in the efficacy of the old Habsburg ideology, and they tried to prop it up with new cultural supports. Rudolf II commissioned in 1589 what is perhaps the strangest royal portrait of the early modern age: Giuseppe Arcimboldo's representation of the emperor in the guise of the Roman god Vertumnus. In this bizarre painting, the face and body of the Habsburg emperor consist of a wild medley of fruits and vegetables—corn for his hair, a pear for his nose, apples for his cheeks, cucumber and garlic and onions and marrow delineating his imperial chest. What sort of royal power displays itself as a pile of agricultural produce?

As the art historian Thomas DaCosta Kaufmann has pointed out, the painting was not an elaborate joke. Arcimboldo had already painted two series of fantastic heads showing the seasons and the elements. They were intended as political allegories, representing the imperial claim to domination of the entire world. All parts of nature were "servants" of the emperor. In the Vertumnus painting, however, it is the emperor himself who embodies nature, as a deity of the seasons and elements. His vigour generates an eternal fruitfulness that is meant to remind us of the Golden Age of Rome.[74]

Still, the painting remains very odd. It is certainly not a familiar type of royal allegory; indeed, for a long time it was thought to be a portrait of the emperor's gardener. The hidden face of Rudolf can be seen only by those who have special knowledge—by "adepts," to use contemporary terminology. The portrait suggests magical implications, for how could a human

3. Giuseppe Arcimboldo, *Rudolf II as Vertumnus* (1589), painting.
Photo: Skoklosters slott, Stockholm.

form be metamorphosed into such a grotesque shape other than by necro-
mancy? Certainly not through conventional religion, for this is not a very
Christian work. The Christian God is fixed and unchanging; the pagan
Vertumnus is a god of mutability. Moreover, Vertumnus-Rudolf seems to
owe his natural and eternal dominance to nothing but himself. A poem by

Gregorio Comanini, probably written to accompany the portrait, describes Vertumnus as "the bold, the skilful / Rival of mighty Jove."[75] Should we equate Jove with Jehovah and see this work as an impious assertion of Rudolf's divine majesty?

Rudolf II has been seen as mad; he was certainly eccentric. At his magnificent court at the Hradschin Castle in Prague he gathered together an extraordinary collection of paintings (many of them erotic), manuscripts, jewels, clocks, scientific instruments, natural artefacts—everything from classical statues to mechanical toys and the horn of a unicorn. His aim was to create a "museum of the world," a microcosm of the universe that would put all of human knowledge at his disposal.[76] What was the ultimate significance of this marvellous jumble sale of bits and pieces? To a reformed Christian mind, a "universal museum" would reflect God's creation, its underlying plan unknowable to humankind. Rudolf, however, longed to know it all, and he employed an army of astrologers, alchemists, seers, and magicians to work it out. Rudolf's intellectual circle sought to explain the world in natural ways that were not always entirely consonant with Christian revelation.[77] They had a Neoplatonic fascination with magical symbols and signs. They were enraptured by hieroglyphics, the picture writing of the ancient Egyptians, which they saw as a sacred language capturing the exact meaning of things. The poet Comanini compared Arcimboldo to "a learned Egyptian" who had "veiled / Your [Rudolf's] divine countenance with beauteous fruits."[78]

R. J. W. Evans has emphasized that the Rudolfine fascination with magic was a serious attempt to reconstruct certainty in a world of religious division and doubt. Similar preoccupations were shared by many of Rudolf's contemporaries, among them the Lutheran cobbler and mystic of Upper Lusatia, Jakob Boehme, who turned to the occult science of Paracelsus in hope of finding *pansophia*, a universal synthesis of beliefs. Like Boehme, Rudolf was suspected of heterodoxy. His religious views were apparently eclectic, although he remained a practising Catholic.[79] At the same time, his desire to understand nature was not just philosophical; it indicated a search for a political synthesis as well, one ultimately centred on himself. Like Montaigne, Rudolf made the exploration of self his main concern. Perhaps he hoped that, through the magical powers vested in his royal being, he could bring his fragmented empire together like the varied fruits that comprised the body of Vertumnus. His aims were those of Renaissance Neoplatonism, but he adapted them to his own fantastic megalomania.

Rudolf's court was shaped to his own cultural interests rather than to the aspirations of the religious groups over which he ruled. It was therefore ineffective as an integrating force within the Empire.[80] In general, Rudolf turned his back on confessional politics. He ignored those Protestants who, finding themselves outnumbered in the Diet and the *Reichskammergericht*, looked to the emperor as a potential ally. In vain they urged him to assert his independence of the pope and become the "temporal sword" of a church reunited under his authority. The Calvinist jurist Melchior Goldast edited three gigantic volumes of Latin texts between 1611 and 1614 in an effort to prove that papal power was subordinate to that of the emperor. He boldly declared, in the words of Constantine the Great, "*Imperator est Pontifex Maximus*"—the emperor is the supreme bishop.[81] Like Althusius, Goldast sought to elevate monarchical power over religious life, while simultaneously subjecting it to the approval of the godly community.

Rudolf II would not have approved of such views. To have espoused the aims of Protestant jurists would have violated both the Habsburg religious heritage and the emperor's self-image as a harmonizing presence who stood above confessional interests. By the same token, Rudolf never took the lead in campaigns for Catholic conformity. While the mayor of Vienna published stringent decrees against walking, riding, or driving on Sundays "to hear the sectarian, seductive preachers" at places outside the town, the emperor did not lend his political weight to such campaigns. He left to lesser authorities the business of protecting public morality, which they did through the gloomy ordinances that proliferated in the 1590s, condemning "singing, whistling, dancing, masques, promenading in the streets and other merry-making."[82]

Rudolf's stratagems were more cosmic, but they came to nothing; he was unable to unite the Empire either spiritually or temporally. Rudolf was seen as weak and possibly deranged by his family, who rallied behind his brother Matthias in the bitter feud known as the *Bruderzwist in Habsburg*. Matthias cunningly played religious politics, allying himself with the Inner Austrian Estates, whose Protestant leader, Georg Erasmus Tschernembl, was an admirer of the dreaded Althusius. Matthias seized the Bohemian

Crown, and Rudolf became an isolated recluse in the Hradschin. Finally, in January 1612, the mutable Vertumnus met immutable death at Prague, and his magical court suddenly vanished.[83]

## THE NEGLIGENT ONE

It would seem at first unlikely that Rudolf II's predicament was shared by "the prudent king" Philip II, his cousin (and, through frequent Habsburg intermarriages, his uncle and brother-in-law). After all, the Protestant Reformation had never taken hold in Spain, and Philip was renowned as the first monarch in Europe to accept the work of the Council of Trent. He has often been depicted as a crusader against heresy. He promoted religious unity, however, as an aspect of his family's leadership within Catholicism—not to strengthen the pope, with whom he often quarrelled —and he usually did not press it further than the constitutions of his kingdoms would allow.[84] Although Philip was initially zealous for reform, a word he used freely in his correspondence, his efforts to implement it gradually diminished as obstacles appeared, often through local resistance to standardized practices. The provincial councils of the clergy, which were called frequently in the 1560s to issue reform decrees, had ceased to meet almost everywhere in Spain by the 1590s.[85]

Philip II was more a Renaissance monarch than a minister of God. He saw himself as a universal ruler, whose person was close to sacred. The features of his kingship were enshrined in the spectacular monastery-palace of El Escorial. The monk José de Sigüenza pointed out that, by dedicating the mountain retreat to St. Lawrence, Philip was comparing himself to Constantine, the typological universal Christian emperor, who built the martyr's first church soon after his conversion. The massive complex at El Escorial was supposedly designed by its principal architect, Juan de Herrera, to resemble both Solomon's Temple and the heavenly Jerusalem. Sigüenza had doubts about such mystical comparisons, but he admitted that many people believed them.[86] Why should they not have, if they knew that in the Holy of Holies at El Escorial's centre the body of Christ was housed alongside that of the king? This symbiotic relationship can still be glimpsed dramatically in the royal apartment, where a small window next to the bed looks directly at the Eucharist, displayed on the high altar of the Basilica. The sacred dimensions of Philip's kingship were further reinforced by his exemplary death in the monastery-palace and his interment directly below the altar.[87]

El Escorial may also reveal the influence of Neoplatonism and other hermetic philosophies on Philip's court. Juan de Herrera was apparently fascinated with "divine proportions," and he tried to make the palace a microcosm of the universe. Occult symbols and quasi-magical references saturate the painted walls and ceilings of the Royal Library, and they can even be spotted in the decorations of the basilica. The pious Brother Sigüenza was embarrassed by all this and felt obliged to chastise those "ignorant or hypocritical people" who complained about the mixture of sacred and profane motifs in the library. He argued somewhat weakly that there, "as at the Royal table, all tastes have to find what suits them."[88] Philip may have found much to suit him in Herrera's hermeticism, as he reportedly shared an interest in magic. It was even said that the king liked to dress in black because he connected the colour with the occult power of the planet Saturn.[89]

In keeping with the humanist patterns of Renaissance monarchy, Philip's court was never a seedbed for confessional discipline. There, as elsewhere, codes of honour remained more important than reformed Catholic morality in shaping upper-class social behaviour. "A good reputation saves us from many sins," quipped a contemporary aristocratic writer. Philip did little to curb the preoccupation with honour and reputation, or to turn it in the direction of internal self-control.[90] His court made no noticeable contribution to the "civilizing process" so deftly outlined by Norbert Elias.

As is well known, Philip's regime was more personal than bureaucratic. Its success depended on the king's own energy, and it began to falter as his powers declined. The grim events of 1588 to 1598—the fiasco of the great Armada, the sack of Cadiz, and above all the continuance of the Dutch rebellion—took place against a background of harvest failures and spiralling royal debt. Central government seemed to be disintegrating, and banditry was everywhere observed to be increasing.[91] Sickness in the kingdom was blamed on the debility of the king, as it was throughout Europe; but the clergy of Spain were far more open than most in their criticism of a monarch whom many perceived as no more than human. As early as 1583 a reforming preacher in Barcelona conjured up the dire prospect of "the king don Felipe, an old and sick man; the kingdom poor and worn out, for many a year nothing has gone right; the land full of thieves, murderers, idlers, the sick and the wretched; everything in ruins."[92]

Around the same time, as the historian Richard Kagan has recounted, a young middle-class woman of Madrid named Lucrecia de León began to have prophetic dreams. She saw the courtiers of Philip II engaged in diabolic dances; she witnessed the king dead and lying in mud; she imagined that she crept into his bedroom and stole his sword, or that a dream guide decapitated him with a saw. Lucrecia regarded the king as a father, and her fantasies of his symbolic castration violated all the patriarchal taboos that Freud would later reconstruct. Yet she had no deep qualms or emotional ambivalence about such unnatural thoughts, and she did not see herself as a rebel. Rather, it was the king himself who had undermined the monarchy, through his own weakness and decrepitude. In one Daliesque vision, Lucrecia saw Philip sitting asleep in a chair, holding a placard inscribed "The Negligent One," while insects crawled in and out of his mouth! The building of the Escorial had not helped him, she declared, because it was "not pleasing to God."[93]

In Lucrecia's dreams the Renaissance monarch and his court were debased and debunked by a reluctant Judith whose solution to the nation's ills was personal religious purification, for both subject and ruler. Such attitudes had become alarmingly widespread among the nobility of Spain. In 1591 they motivated a sudden rash of provincial disorders. Seditious posters appeared in pious Avila, prompting a vicious crackdown against several leading families. Town officials in Valencia made angry demonstrations against the Inquisition. Finally, the city of Zaragoza, capital of Aragon, rose up in revolt over the sordid affair of the king's former secretary, Antonio Pérez. The king had imprisoned him for a political murder; but in 1590 Pérez escaped to Zaragoza, where he put himself under the protection of Aragon's unique legal system. There he began to publicize allegations about the king's complicity in the crime of which he was accused. A frustrated Philip tried to prosecute him in the court of the Inquisition, a royal institution widely disliked in Aragon. The trial caused a riotous uprising that led to Pérez's rescue and the death of the king's viceroy. In the end, Philip brought an army to Aragon, the revolt collapsed, and Pérez fled to France.[94]

The rebellion had deep religious undertones. One of its causes was resentment—flaring up into gang warfare—between Aragonese Christians and *Moriscos*, or Muslims, whose very existence in a Catholic kingdom was a reproach to the monarch. In addition, the revelations of Antonio Pérez, like Lucrecia's dreams, were profound insults to the moral foundations of Philip's authority. Although the secretary himself was a courtier and humanist rather than a reformed Christian, several of his supporters in Madrid joined Lucrecia's circle of aristocratic admirers. They also sponsored a second popular religious prophet of the time, who forecast "the imminent destruction of Spain." No wonder Philip's English enemies hoped that the Aragonese uprising was "a secret iudgement of the Lorde to cause . . . so great a floud that may drowne all Spaine for their sinnes."[95] The thought was shared with apprehension by many in Spain itself.

Throughout Philip II's kingdoms, a court-based Renaissance monarchy with universalist and sacral pretensions was in ideological jeopardy by the end of the sixteenth century, under pressure from groups bent on political renewal through religious reform. After the death of the king in 1598, it was left to his son and successor, Philip III, to complete the moral degradation of the monarchy, through making a peace with the English and a truce with the Dutch. Protestant merchants were even allowed to trade unmolested in Spanish ports—a small but ominous step towards toleration. As one Dutch peace negotiator aptly noted, Philip's commissioners "came here [the Hague] at the cost of the reputation of their king and princes."[96] On the same day that the truce was signed, Philip III took the cruel step of expelling the Moriscos from Spain. Three hundred thousand people went into exile, salvaging at least part of the Spanish monarchy's reputation for confessional purity. Whether or not the renewed effort at reform succeeded in creating a godly kingdom is an issue we shall address in the next chapter.

## Two Bodies: Elizabeth to James

The Habsburgs ruled over universal empires; the Tudors, by contrast, governed a mere nation. Like other Renaissance monarchs, however, the Tudors defined "the nation" in terms of *imperium*, or undivided rulership, not common identity. England was an extension of the Crown; it was, in

Shakespeare's words, "This royal seat of kings, this sceptr'd isle." Parliament announced at the onset of the Reformation that "this realm of England is an empire," whose king possessed "a body politic, compact of all sorts and degrees of people" and containing "that part . . . called the spirituality, now being usually called the English Church."[97] In short, people and church were both part of the sacred royal body. Let us consider the tenuous survival of that unorthodox Renaissance idea, and its disintegration from the 1590s onwards.

The perfect unity of church and state did not long survive the death of Henry VIII. When Elizabeth I succeeded to the throne in 1558, the bishops of the Church of England showed deep reservations about conferring on a female ruler the kind of religious powers her father had enjoyed. The archbishop of York was rude enough to state that a woman could not be head of the church.[98] The queen ended up accepting from Parliament the title of governor rather than head, a big concession, because it meant that her dominance over the church's mystical body was political rather than personal.

Elizabeth agreed to this lesser status because she was more interested in securing power than in extending it. Always cautious in confessional matters, she was no champion of radical Protestantism, and her court was lacking in exemplary piety.[99] Yet she did not reject the adulation showered on her by the hotter Protestants. Early in her reign they had hailed her as "the English Deborah," whose original appears in Scripture as "a prophetess" and a judge in Israel (Judges 4:4–5). Judges were closer to the godly ideal of magistracy than sacred monarchs. In the 1560s, however, the Protestant Deborah was overwhelmed by the advent of so-called two-bodies legalism and by the astonishing "cult of Elizabeth."[100] They marked the culmination of Renaissance monarchy in Tudor England.

The legal concept of the "king's two bodies" was invented by jurists, who delineated it in a series of high-court decisions. Perhaps the most succinct statement of the doctrine was made by Crown lawyers in 1561: "The King has in him two Bodies, *viz.*, a Body natural, and a Body politic. His Body natural . . . is a Body mortal, subject to all Infirmities that come by Nature or Accident. . . . But his Body politic is a Body that cannot be seen or handled, consisting of Policy and Government, and constituted for the Direction of the People, and the Management of the public weal, and this Body is utterly void of Infancy, and old Age, and other natural Defects and Imbecilities, which the Body natural is subject to."[101] This implied that, while she had in her own words "the body of a weak and feeble woman," Elizabeth nevertheless possessed a political body that knew no physical handicaps, including death.

The doctrine was clearly intended to strengthen the mystical powers of monarchy, by legally defining its sacred part. The historian F. W. Maitland, however, considered it "abortive" and found that it "stubbornly refuses to do any real work in the case of jurisprudence."[102] It assumed not simply the resemblance of the ruler to God but the existence of a divine presence fully formed within the corporeal body of the ruler, a miracle of incarnation that rivalled Christ's own double nature. Such a mystification was very hard to maintain in legal practice or to reconcile with reformed theology. Not surprisingly, the clergy do not seem to have been enamoured of it. The sacredness of the queen's body did not prevent the high-minded Archbishop Grindal from reminding her that she was a mortal creature, or telling her that "in God's matters all princes ought to bow their sceptres to the Son of God."[103] It is noteworthy that none of the statements defining the "two bodies" was penned by a clergyman.

Similarly, it was courtiers, not clerics, who gave shape to the amazing "cult of Elizabeth." In a remarkable series of festivals, pageants, and tournaments, members of the court acted out their passionate attachment to a virgin goddess—Diana, Cynthia, Astraea—who commanded both allegiance and love but remained eternally chaste.[104] These Neoplatonic spectacles were mostly designed for Elizabeth's inner circle, not for popular audiences. They typified a court-based culture that sought to separate itself from both vulgar amusements and the rigours of the new religion. A product of Renaissance courtly values, the cult of Elizabeth was more concerned with knightly honour than with personal discipline or self-control.[105]

The image of the "Virgin Queen" was potentially divisive, because it was modelled on the Virgin Mary, never a favourite with godly Protestants. Compare Calvin's views on chastity with the praises lavished on Elizabeth by the poet Edmund Spenser: "It falles me here to write of Chastity, / That fairest vertue, farre aboue the rest; / For which what needs me fetch from *Faery* / Forreine ensamples, it to haue exprest? / Sith it is shrined in my Soueraines brest."[106] The second part of Spenser's *Faerie Queene* contained a panegyric to "that sacred Saint my souveraigne Queene." This seems far removed from the rigours of Calvinist election, and the poet's profane love for the queen verges on idolatry. To be sure, Spenser tempered the crypto-Catholic implications of his "Book of Chastity" through multiple portrayals of Elizabeth. She appears in the poem not only as the virginal moon goddess Belphoebe but also as the heroic Britomart, who personifies the Protestant ideal of a godly, crusading, and married monarch. Significantly, Spenser did not try to reconcile these royal images in a single figure.[107]

The real Elizabeth was similarly obliged to adopt a multiplicity of personae in order to please a divided political establishment. Her admirers praised this as an aspect of her godlike powers, but it chiefly reflected her need for legitimation as a female ruler. Elizabeth was able to make her "changeable" femininity into a political asset without offending against the accepted rules of gender.[108] Nevertheless, the crypto-Catholic imagery of her monarchy may have irritated godly clerics and magistrates, advocates of the integrated Christian self, who were bent on a hotter reformation that would eliminate all trace of popish superstitions. If they did not criticize her openly, it was because they never forgot that the queen was at least a Protestant, while her presumed heir, until 1587, was a Catholic.[109]

Even the godly, of course, were drawn into the tremendous enthusiasm that accompanied the war against Spain, which became a Protestant crusade. Elated by the initial victory over the Armada in 1588, Elizabeth's subjects gloried in annual commemorations of the event. England might now truly be seen as the second Israel, "defended by God, and governed by so virtuous a princess as God hath chosen after his own heart."[110] Elizabeth's great domestic propaganda victory, however, was short-lived. The queen's magic soon began to wear thin, as it had to cope with rebellion in Ireland, religious disputes, mounting financial commitments, and a dearth of foodstuffs.[111] Meanwhile, the royal cult had not become any more attractive to clerics. When Richard Hooker wrote his magisterial *Laws of Ecclesiasticall Politie* in the 1590s, he never mentioned the "two bodies." Instead, he argued for the origins of government in natural law, which gave legislative power to "entire societies." The ruler was separate from and subordinate to the body politic: "Original influence of power from the body into the king, is cause of the king's dependency in power upon the body." The similarity to Suárez is striking, although Hooker defended the Royal Supremacy, which made the English monarch the "only supreme power in ecclesiastical affairs or causes."[112]

The suggestion that the queen was not a divine being was made more crudely through the attempted coup by the earl of Essex in 1601. While ostensibly directed at her chief advisor, Robert Cecil, rather than at Elizabeth herself, Essex's revolt nonetheless gave shocking proof that the moon goddess could not trust her supposedly ardent male devotees. Motivated by the warrior ideals of masculine aristocratic honour, Essex had chafed at the female "weakness" of the queen—just as his friend and advisor, the exiled Antonio Pérez, had condemned the feebleness of Philip II. Before the rising, Essex's "swordsmen" had arranged a performance of Shakespeare's *Richard II*, including the suppressed deposition scene, in which the effeminate ruler "unkings" himself. Did they mean to imply that Elizabeth should likewise surrender the Crown—"With mine own tongue deny my sacred state"?[113] Of course, she did not do so; and it was Essex rather than the despised Cecil who ended up on the block.

The factionalism that the royal cult had controlled for decades was now tearing at Astraea's mask. She fought back by becoming a Protestant Deborah again. In her "Golden Speech" to the 1601 Parliament, she described herself as "[God's] instrument to preserve you from every peril, dishonour, shame, tyranny and oppression." By the time she died in 1603, however, complaints about Elizabeth's rule, and her sex, were spreading. "Wee worship no saintes, but wee prayd to ladyes, in the Q[ueenes] tyme," snipped one disgruntled law student shortly after her death, adding that "this superstition shall be abolished, we hope in our kinges raigne."[114] The Protestant memory of Elizabeth as "God's instrument" was still fondly held—it appeared, for example, in the posthumous print by Crispin van de Passe that shows her in full regalia next to a sword of justice and a Bible. The godly hoped that the more pagan aspects of the royal cult would be interred with her bones.

---

4. Crispin van de Passe the elder, after Isaac Oliver, *Elizabeth I Memorial Portrait* (1603), engraving.

Photo: The Huntington Library, San Marino, California.

POSVI DEVM ADIVTOREM MEVM

Aeterna amo
MIserICorDIæ.

NONI SOLI QVI MAI PENSE

SEMPER EADEM

Nata Grœnwiciæ
anno Christi
MDXXXIII.
6. Id. Sept.

DEI · IVSTITIA

VERBVM

**ELISABET D.G. ANGLIAE, FRANCIAE, HIBERNIAE, ET VERGINIAE REGINA,**
**FIDEI CHRISTIANAE PROPVGNATRIX ACERRIMA. NVNC IN DNO REQVIESCENS**

Virginis os habitumque geris, diuina virago;          Vas tu Semiramiden Babylon super æthera tollat,          Isaac Oliuier
Sed supra sexum dotes animumque virilem;              Efferat et Didona suam Sidonia tellus,                           effigiebat.
Quod sæpe allatum docuit rerum exitus ingens;        Gens Es Ebræn Iudæa, Camillam Volscæ propago,       Crispin van de Passe
Vnde tibi et Regni populi debere fatentur;             Aut Constantini matrem Byzantion ingens,                  incidebat.
Christiadumque cohors, astio rumpantur ut hostes,    Atque alias aliæ gentes: tete Anglia forcis               procurantur Ioanne
Queram Deus tua ratios nil morte lucrata est.          Vt quondam fructus esse sic nunc clarescat alumna.   Woldendo

P.B.M.Q. Inden.

The new king, James VI of Scotland and James I of England, was an intellectual who aspired to make the royal body more acceptable to Protestants. His views on kingship were expressed in *The Trew Law of Free Monarchies* (1598) and the *Basilikon Doron* (1599), which provided advice on ruling to his heir.[115] Calvin himself would probably have found nothing objectionable in either of these treatises. James's approach was based on a sound knowledge of Scripture and was devoid not only of mystical doctrines but also of extravagant pagan allusions. The king was not compared to Christ, endowed with miraculous qualities, or dressed up as an Olympian deity. In the *Trew Law,* James echoed Calvin in remarking that "Kings are called Gods by the propheticall King *David,* because they sit vpon GOD his Throne in the earth." He further maintained that "by the Law of nature the King becomes a naturall Father to all his Lieges."[116] In the *Basilikon doron* James firmly upheld the pure doctrine of salvation by faith, "the nourisher and quickner of Religion . . . *the free gift of God.*" He recommended frequent reading of the Bible, condemned "that sickenesse of superstition," and praised the institution of marriage. As a striking reminder that monarchs were only human, James exhorted his son to "speake with all reuerence" when praying to God, "for if a subiect will not speake but reuerently to a King, much less should any flesh presume to talke with God as with his companion." No wonder that this little work was very popular in Protestant England, where some sixteen thousand copies of it were printed in the year of James's accession.[117]

King James's writings on monarchy spoke directly to the reformed Protestant self. Yet they did not lead to an overhaul of the practices of English sacral kingship. For example, although James regarded the royal touch to cure scrofula as a popish practice, he continued to administer it on the advice of his courtiers. He insisted publicly that it was not a miracle, only a kind of prayer for healing; but many people continued to think of it as a claim to personal divinity.[118] James even resorted to the two-bodies theory in order to salvage a favourite project, his scheme for uniting England and Scotland. To make a case for union in the courts, the Crown lawyers argued in Calvin's Case of 1608 that no legal distinction could be made between the two kingdoms, since both swore allegiance to the same "body natural" of the monarch.[119] James's interest in the two-bodies doctrine seems to have been momentary, as he never referred to it in his own writings or speeches. Calvin's Case, however, reveals that he did not leave all the mystifications of Tudor monarchy buried in Queen Elizabeth's tomb.

James's godly English subjects had expected reform at court, so that the "humour of luxuriousness" would be replaced by "our ancient native modesty."[120] Such hopes were soon dashed. Infested (at least in English eyes) by ambitious Scots, the Stuart court became notorious for political corruption.[121] Court culture, moreover, was not purged of impious or semi-pagan overtones. The masques of Ben Jonson and Inigo Jones kept alive the Neoplatonic spectacles of Elizabeth's reign, in which the presence of the king or queen restored harmony to a distempered world. Admittedly, King James was not much interested in masques; he preferred to see himself as David or Solomon rather than as Neptune or Pan. Jonson's masques were mostly written for James's crypto-Catholic queen, Anne of Denmark, or for their sons, Princes Henry and Charles. Yet James did nothing to make these lavish entertainments more godly, or less costly.[122] To the further disappointment of those puritans who had longed for a Protestant Caesar to lead them with manly vigour against Catholics at home and abroad, James turned out to be tolerant and unwarlike. One country gentleman, perhaps unfairly, called him "the most cowardly man that ever I knew."[123]

James I did not fail in everything, as historians once liked to argue. By 1610 the royal body was partially demystified and centred in one male persona, not in the many pagan goddesses of the Elizabethan cult. His homosexual longings notwithstanding, James exalted the family and marriage. All of these Protestant attributes would endure beyond the attempted revival of Renaissance kingship by Charles I after 1625. James was no reformer, however, and he disappointed hopes of a godly kingship. As a result, the crisis atmosphere of the 1590s never fully dissipated during his reign.

## The Sovereign Body: Valois to Bourbon

James I's confessionalism differed markedly from the approach of France's Henry IV, who was more concerned with defining the sovereignty inherent in the royal body than with accommodating himself to the demands of reformed religion. Henry was responding to a radical Catholic threat that would have shorn him of his divine attributes and made the kingdom into a utopia for the Christian self. The sovereign royal body that emerged in opposition to such millenarian visions was a more potent legal fiction than the English two-bodies doctrine, but its cultural roots were weak, because it was so heavily dependent on humanist concepts of natural dominance rather than on confessional doctrines.

During the 1560s and 1570s reforming French Catholics took the business of purification into their own hands, in a tumultuous reassertion of the ascetic foundations of their faith. Scenes of public expiation and self-denial were accompanied by the horrible mass killings of Huguenots. The historians Natalie Davis and Denis Crouzet have argued that these massacres were not frenzied or indiscriminate acts; they were governed by an adherence to confessional "rites of violence" that made them legitimate in the minds of their perpetrators. The crowds saw themselves as possessed by the spirit of God in purifying the community, which they identified with the sacred body of Christ and with the church.[124]

This was a doctrine as dangerous for the kings of France as it was for their Huguenot subjects. The last Valois were quintessential Renaissance rulers. Their court surpassed Queen Elizabeth's in its sumptuous Neoplatonic entertainments. Ballets and other Italianate festivals portrayed, through emblems, rituals, and gorgeous costumes, the sacral mysteries of a many-faced kingship. The court was a forum for aristocratic display, not for self-discipline. It was peripatetic, reflecting the fragmented focal points of a state that depended on personal contacts.[125] Less consistent in policy than in pursuing clientage, the royal attitude towards Protestantism wavered between tacit toleration and fierce prosecution. At times, the king placed himself in the vanguard of the holy war of Catholic purification; but he did so reluctantly, because it made his personal sacrality contingent on carrying out the divinely appointed communal mission of violence.[126]

In 1584 King Henry III's lineal successor became his cousin and brother-in-law, Henry of Bourbon, King of Navarre, a convinced Huguenot who was unacceptable to the Catholic party. The result was a revival of religious militancy, centred on a national association, the Catholic League. Although it was led by the aristocratic Guise family, the League's strength was based on popular preachers and the urban middle classes. At first the king tried to ally himself with them by making public affirmations of piety and marching in penitential processions. None of this convinced his critics. As Montaigne insinuated, Henry tended "to injure his reputation for religion by making a display of religion beyond all example of men of his sort."[127] In December 1587 the diarist Pierre de L'Estoile, chief clerk to the Parlement of Paris, noted sardonically that the doctors of the Sorbonne, "who dispose of sceptres and crowns . . . [had] made a secret decision (though not so secret that everyone didn't hear of it, and the King among the first) that one could remove the power of government from the hands of incapable princes."[128] Four months later, on the "Day of the Barricades," the League rose in rebellion against the king, who fled from Paris.

For the next six years the League ruled the capital, as well as most of the major cities of France.[129] Its control was upheld by sermons, public ceremonies, and especially penitential processions that emphasized the necessity of purification, both personal and political. During these processions, heavily armed "flagellants" wearing hooded gowns marched through the streets to the accompaniment of martial music. Such tumultuous scenes, combining expiation with defiance, played out the theories of René Girard: through ritual violence, whether self-inflicted or meted out to scapegoats, the sins of the nation were erased and sacred order was restored. The League was not, after all, just a political movement; as Denis Crouzet has argued, its supporters dreamed of an earthly Jerusalem and of the millennium, which were symbolically realized through collective rites that submerged worldly personhood in a spiritual community.[130] The League also resurrected the ascetic ideal of the human body, with all its radical social and gender implications. At Mardi Gras in 1589, for example, a scandalized Pierre de L'Estoile noted that men and women, boys and girls, marched through the streets of Paris "naked or in shirts, with bare feet, carrying lighted candles, and singing devoutly."[131] In the new age of the purified Christian self, "abjection" had become the basis of political participation.

While they purged their own bodies and the urban body politic, the Leaguers denied any special sanctity to the body of the monarch. This was a great affront to Henry III. Convinced of his own sacrality, Henry frequently used the royal touch and even communicated in two kinds, like a priest.[132] De L'Estoile, who remained a *politique,* or supporter of the king, was horrified to hear contemptuous references to "Henri de Valois," and he recorded that "the preachers called the King dog, tiger, heretic, tyrant . . . and wouldn't allow him to be spoken of otherwise." The assiduous *audiencier* collected no fewer than three hundred libels against Henry that were peddled in the streets of Paris.[133] Like Calvinist radicals, the Leaguers asserted that the ruler was responsible to the body of the people, particularly to the Estates General, which met at Blois in October 1588. When King Henry had the duke of Guise murdered in December, the Sorbonne announced that all subjects were absolved from obedience to him. The propaganda of the League now claimed the right to assassinate a tyrant. The doctrine of tyrannicide was finally put into practice by Jacques Clément in August 1589.

Locked into an all-out struggle against the new king, Henry IV, the ascetic fervour of the Leaguers grew even more radical. One of the most extreme examples of Leaguer anti-royalism was the 1593 *Dialogue d'entre le maheustre et le manant,* which translates very roughly as "dialogue between a crotch-stuffing courtier and an honest citizen." When challenged to identify himself, the good citizen says he is simply "a Catholic." In other words, he has no identity beyond that of the Christian self. He then takes pains to correct the misguided views of the court creature on monarchy: "You suppose that one is born King, or by birth and nature has a right to the throne, which among men is false, and is only true in the person of Jesus Christ who would have been King of the Jews, having right to the kingdom by birth and the real title and property to it, but of which he never took possession . . . and among men the right to the kingdom passes to a man by the force of law imposed by the people and agreed to by God if it is acceptable to the people."[134] Only Jesus is born pure; only Jesus is born king. No human has a right by birth to ascend the throne, and heretics have no right to it at all. The people, through their laws, will decide who should reign. This reflects a kind of Christian egalitarianism: because all human bodies are corrupt, none can claim to represent in itself the body of Christ. Some League writers abandoned all plans for changing earthly governance and placed their hopes in the Second Coming of Christ. As one pamphleteer put it in 1587, "Jesus Christ will reign. Jesus Christ will be King of France."[135]

Other than Jesus, the Catholic League had no viable candidate for the

throne. In spite of such a fundamental weakness, it cost the hated Huguenot successor five years of fighting and conversion to Catholicism before
Paris finally surrendered to him.[136] The long resistance of the League had
fatally wounded the Renaissance fictions of Valois monarchy. The Bourbon dynasty looked instead towards the redefinitions of royal power offered in the works of lawyers and jurists, the class of educated officials to
which Montaigne, Pasquier, and Pierre de L'Estoile belonged. Steeped in
humanism, they had little desire to exchange classical models of kingship
for the earthly paradise promised by the Leaguers. Under Henry IV, legal
officials increasingly came to accept that the king held an unbreakable
supreme power, known as sovereignty. The idea had been circulating for
some time as a means of enhancing the French king's position in relation to
the pope. Montaigne, however, had used the language of sovereignty to
describe his command over himself: "I who am king of the matter I treat,
and who owe an accounting for it to no one."[137] Sovereignty was part of the
rhetoric of humanist selfhood. Its clearest political expression was found in
the celebrated *Six Books of the Commonwealth* by the lawyer Jean Bodin,
which appeared in 1576.

Bodin was a contradictory figure, a man of reputedly Protestant leanings who had collaborated openly with the League.[138] His writings on
monarchy, however, showed little sympathy with the League's principles.
On the other hand, he was not much interested in the Neoplatonic myths of
monarchy either. His chief concern was with sovereignty, "the absolute
and perpetual power of a commonwealth."[139] He allowed that it might be
conferred originally by the people, who could not then place any subsequent restrictions on the ruler. Bodin saw sovereignty as the sole source of
law. It was indivisible; no part of it could be granted to other institutions.
Its locus was the physical body of the king, not a mystical persona.

Bodin's brand of sovereignty was derived from the patriarchal power
exerted by fathers over their wives and children. He argued that "as a
familie well and wisely ordered, is the true image of a Citie, and the
domesticall government, in sort like unto the soveraigntie in a Commonweale: so also is the manner of the government of an house or familie, the
true modell for the government of a Commonweale."[140] In a sense, Bodin
exchanged the mystical image of the king for that of a father figure, who
derived his authority from a social institution, the family. The natural body

of the *paterfamilias* had replaced the spiritual body of Christ. Bodin's patriarchalism may have been influenced by Protestant ideas, but he went much further than writers who saw patriarchy as one of several justifications of monarchy, as James I did, or who simply noted the resemblances between rule by fathers and by kings, like Luther or Arnisaeus.

Bodin, however, did not base his argument on purely secular reason. He saw the family as divinely ordained, as did Calvin, and he imbued patriarchy with a religious aura, describing fathers as "the true Image of the great and Almightie God the Father of all things."[141] His concept of sovereignty, moreover, bore supernatural attributes, which gave a godlike quality to an abstract principle. Like Christian divinity, sovereignty was perfect, unified, absolute. Residing in a human body, it was nonetheless perpetual, or, as the first English translation of the *Six Books* put it, "the king doth never die."[142] The sovereign authority inherent in the king's mortal coil passed immediately upon his demise to his successor. Bodin nowhere wrote of "two bodies" or of a transcendent dignitas separate from the king's human form. In effect, he eliminated the duality between the physical being of the ruler and the immortal body politic. Both were completely united through the possession of sovereignty, which raised the innate powers of the king's body to the highest level imaginable. Instead of making the ruler into a demigod, sovereignty made him the incarnation of a quasi-divine juridical principle. Through this spiritual legalism, a strange mingling of faith and law, Bodin gave new strength to the humanist conception of monarchy by combining it with the strict integration of the reformed Christian self.

The notion of perpetual sovereignty was soon adopted by the French legal establishment, although with modifications. Lawyers saw themselves as guardians of the fundamental law, which for some was a power higher than the king himself. In addition, the high courts, or parlements, possessed the right to register royal edicts, and their members did not always defer gracefully to the authority of the monarch.[143] The Catholic League, however, had bullied the Parlement of Paris, so the lawyers of the capital were happy to see Henry IV enter the city in 1594. The king was greeted with a fulsome address in the *Grand'-Chambre* of the parlement, delivered by the leading jurist Antoine Loisel. "TOUCH NOT THE KING OR THE FUNDA-MENTAL LAW OF THE KINGDOM," he exhorted his compatriots, a traditional formula that gave precedence to neither king nor law. But he added almost immediately that when French kings die, "there is reborn from them whole another of similar material and quality as the deceased," like the mythical phoenix.[144] In other words, the authority of monarchy was perpetual, as Bodin had asserted.

Some years later, Loisel included "the king never dies," which he ascribed to Bodin, in a collection of legal maxims.[145] By then, the full-blown conception of sovereignty had attained legal acceptance. It was incorporated in 1608 into an enormously influential treatise on seigneurial ownership by the jurist Charles Loyseau. "The state and sovereignty . . . are synonymous," Loyseau opined. The king was the ultimate proprietor of public power, which gave definition to the state; but he could not thereby claim to possess the lands and goods of his subjects. Loyseau saw "fundamental law" as compatible with sovereignty.[146] In general, the lawyers tried to place sovereign authority within the framework of the traditional constitution. Bodin had implied as much himself when he acknowledged that "as for laws which concern the state of the kingdom and its basic form, since these are annexed and united to the crown like the Salic law, the prince cannot detract from them."[147]

Henry IV probably never read Bodin, but he did grasp the implications of sovereignty, which became the core of his royal self-fashioning. When he failed to give his predecessor a state burial, Henry rejected the "ceremonial interregnum" between the death of an old king and the public appearance of the new, implying that the king never died.[148] His coronation was held at Chartres rather than in the League-held town of Rheims, as if to show that it was the king himself who made the ritual, not vice versa. In an unusual addition to the ceremony, Henry was given a ring as a symbol of his "marriage" to the nation. He thus declared his patriarchal lordship over the territory of France. It was carefully noted, moreover, that the popular acclamation at his coronation did not mean he owed his power to the people: he ruled by hereditary right alone, infused in his blood by God.[149]

Henry was keenly concerned with creating a public image focused less on Neoplatonic symbolism than on displays of personal charisma, manliness, and warlike virtue. He touched huge numbers of scrofulitics. His physician even wrote a learned book claiming that the royal touch was a miraculous power given direct to the king by God. The contrast between

5. Thomas de Leu, *The Sacred Gallic Hercules* (c. 1595), engraving.
Photo: Bibliothèque nationale de France, Paris.

Henry and his Protestant contemporary James I could not be more striking.[150] The lavish court festivals of the Valois, which promoted a mystical,
mutable, and somewhat androgynous kingship, were not replicated at the
"rustic" court of the manly Gascon king. Instead, entertainments like the
ballet became more private, while public rituals concentrated on shows of
majesty, like the triumphal *entrées* into important towns.[151] Henry's warrior
image was disseminated in an unprecedented number of prints and portraits of the king as a Caesar, an Alexander, a Charlemagne—all founders

of empires based on the sword. He was the *Grand Capitaine*, a gallant Renaissance knight battling the enemies of France, although clergymen hastened to add that he was a holy warrior, chosen by God. He was lauded as a Gallic Hercules, an invincible hero who had overcome the many-headed hydra of popular rebellion.[152] The comparison with the unconquerable Greek muscle-man suggested that sovereignty was to some extent based on sheer force, that Bourbon authority was due as much to rightful conquest as to dynastic succession.

Henry's publicity was marked by themes of virile energy and constant motion that could be interpreted as signs of an underlying instability. Sovereignty, in fact, was a culturally insecure concept. It required an internal surrender of the Christian self to a human authority, which most were not prepared to make. Meanwhile, the devout desire for purification of the polity had been neither destroyed nor displaced; it was simply waiting for its next opportunity. It might have been given one by a contradiction that lay at the heart of Bourbon sovereignty: the Edict of Nantes. Eschewing a policy of Catholic confessionalization, Henry granted to Huguenots not only toleration but even the right to hold fortified towns with their own troops. He thus partly violated his own indivisible authority. The edict rankled the devout and would bother a later Bourbon king as an unbearable breach of sovereign power, which it clearly was. Henry did not care; he needed the Huguenots as allies and showed little concern about the limits the edict set on future rulers. By 1610 his suppleness seemed to have worked. The pacification of France was complete, and even the king's public image was changing from warrior to peace giver.[153] Then, suddenly, Henry too was stabbed to death, by the hand of another Catholic assassin, the insane monk François Ravaillac.

Henry's murder glaringly revealed the continuing fragility of French monarchy. All at once government returned to a state of crisis, from which it had to be rescued by improvised rituals of sovereignty. Within hours of the assassination, Henry's eight-year-old successor, Louis XIII, held a *lit de justice* in the Parlement of Paris—an assembly of princes, nobles, bishops, Crown officers, and lawyers before whom the king could declare his will. By appearing in public prior to the burial of his father, the soft-spoken Louis (or rather his mother, Queen Marie de Médicis) signalled that the ceremonial interregnum of the royal funeral, which had lapsed in 1589, was now meaningless. Louis appeared as "the living image" of the dead monarch, a role previously played by the funeral effigy. Nobody could doubt that sovereignty was perpetual, that the king never died.[154] Some observers were shocked by the innovation; the Protestant duc de Sully, for instance, was ordered to attend but "felt an extreme repugnance for what was required of me."[155]

The coronation of the young king five months later was designed as a mere recognition of the royal power he already fully held. As in 1594, the ceremony highlighted the innate and perpetual sovereignty of French kings. Louis made his formal entrance into Rheims surrounded by images of the phoenix and the rising sun—for undying kingship knows no setting sun.[156] The following day, in a ritual loosely based on medieval precedents, the king was wakened from sleep on the morning of the ceremony by a group of peers, who stood at his chamber door and asked for him three times. Twice they requested "Louis XIII, son of Henry the Great," and were refused. Then they asked for "Louis XIII, whom God has given us for King," and the king appeared. Louis was no longer the son of his earthly father; he had been awakened to a new, divinely appointed identity which ran in his blood, and which he had possessed even in his sleep. The coronation ring ceremony was replayed, and it was now openly interpreted by jurists as a fulfilment of the "betrothal" already made at Louis's inaugural lit de justice.[157]

The concept of sovereignty was made integral to French monarchy by the assassinations of 1589 and 1610. As recurring crises were to show, however, it bestowed merely the appearance rather than the reality of absolute power. It did not alter the cumbersome structure of French government; instead, it fostered a myth of unified authority that did not always correspond to administrative practice.[158] Moreover, it was a Renaissance survival, emphasizing masculine and heroic virtues. These were not the values of Catholic selfhood, which set the purified body and the devout soul above the pride of the warrior.

Was the concept of sovereignty unique to France? Although Bodin was read throughout Europe, his ideas were absorbed in conflicting ways. He was heartily detested in Spain, where Ribadeneira condemned him as "neither schooled in theology nor practised in piety." In the Netherlands he was cited in defence not of a king but of the sovereignty of the Estates General.[159] German Protestant scholars diligently mined Bodin's writings; between 1592 and 1626, sixteen treatises were published at imperial and Swiss universities on the subject of sovereignty. The jurists of the *Reich*, however, tended to argue that while supreme authority ought in theory to be indivisible, in practice it might be partitioned. Arnisaeus, for example, accepted Bodin's definition of sovereignty but thought it could be vested in diverse elements of the imperial constitution, so long as they acted in unison. Some German jurists envisioned a *maiestas duplex*, a double majesty, consisting of an instrumental part, held by the Diet, the territorial princes, and the Estates, and a personal or symbolic part, enjoyed by the emperor alone.[160]

Bodin's warmest foreign reception was in England. By 1603 the idea that the king never dies had spread across the Channel. "Noe vacancy, noe interregnum, noe interruption of government, as in Rome an[d] other places," one preacher remarked shortly after Elizabeth's death.[161] The image of the phoenix rising again from its own funeral pyre appeared frequently in the congratulatory verses welcoming King James to England. A translation of the *Six Books of the Commonwealth* was published in 1606, and the work won admirers at the English court. Still, as a clerical observer noted, sovereignty remained *Vox Gallica*, a French term.[162] Undivided sovereignty was an unattractive innovation to most of the English governing class, because it implied a weak Parliament, an overweening court, and, worst of all, political unity with Scotland. James I was not able to bind together his kingdoms; by contrast, Henry IV was not allowed to separate his. The Parlement of Paris flatly rejected Henry's desire to rule Navarre as a distinct territory, insisting that his domains were indivisible.[163] Not even the king could violate the unity of his own power.

England and France, however, were similar in other ways. In both kingdoms—but not yet in Spain or the Holy Roman Empire—the challenge of reformed religion had by 1610 brought about a tempering of the multivalent sacrality of Renaissance monarchy and a partial reshaping of the royal body. Some of the quasi-pagan, magical aspects of kingship had been discarded. These changes were still to be consolidated, and they had not had much direct impact on subjects. The potentially explosive moralizing and ascetic tendencies of the reformed Christian self had not been defused. Instead, they began to channel themselves into the development of a political public, and a public politics: in other words, a new kind of audience for the theatre of kingship. Over the next three decades, kings would begin to address this audience and to learn how the image of godly rulership might be used to assert their authority over every household, over every soul, over every human body.

# CHAPTER THREE

# The Theatre of Royal Virtue, 1610–1637

This wicked man prospereth. That Tyrant liueth. Let be awhiles. Remember it is but the first Act, and consider aforehande in thy mind, that sobs and sorrowes will ensue vppon their sollace. . . . For that Poet of ours is singular cunning in his art, and will not lightly transgresse the lawes of his Tragedie.

—JUSTUS LIPSIUS, *Two Bookes of Constancie*, trans. Sir John Stradling (1584)

N JUNE 1619 Ferdinand of Bohemia, king of the Romans and soon to be Holy Roman Emperor, found himself besieged in the city of Vienna. Outside its walls camped the Protestant army of the rebellious Estates of Bohemia; inside, the angry leaders of the Estates of Lower Austria, spurred on by the fiery Georg Erasmus Tschernembl, were trying to force Ferdinand to issue a decree of toleration for Protestants.[1] Cornered but not defeated, he knelt in prayer before a crucifix in his private chapel in the Hofburg Palace. Suddenly, amazingly, Christ seemed to speak to him from the cross with words of hope: *"Ferdinande, non te deseram!"* — "Ferdinand, I will not desert you!" Here at last was irrevocable proof of the divine assistance always granted to the pious Habsburgs. And the Lord did not desert his servant Ferdinand, for within a week the Bohemians had withdrawn from the gates of Vienna, while the leaders of the Austrian Estates ended up in exile at Prague. Admittedly, it was the intervention of a Bavarian army, not of Christ himself, that caused the Bohemians to retreat. Admittedly, too, the miracle of the talking crucifix was not publicly mentioned until long after, and Ferdinand's own Jesuit confessor would neither confirm nor deny that it had taken place. Nonetheless, in later years the great event was publicly commemorated at Vienna with elaborate pomp and ecclesiastical ritual.[2]

6. *Emperor Ferdinand II as Christ on the Mount of Olives* (1622–23),
engraved broadsheet.

Photo: Kunstsammlungen der Veste, Coburg.

Christ's words to Ferdinand constituted a theatrical reaffirmation of
the Habsburg family myth and dramatically rescued a kingship threatened
by godly rebellion. The event paralleled the miracle of Constantine the
Great, the first Christian emperor, to whom a heavenly cross had appeared
as a sign of victory. The connection between the two devout rulers had
already been noticed by the Jesuits, who had staged a play on Constantine's
victory to celebrate Ferdinand's coronation at Prague in 1617.[3] Not surprisingly, Constantine's triumph became a favourite theme of the Viennese
theatre in the following decades. It was re-enacted on the Jesuit stage for
Ferdinand III in 1627, and for Leopold I in 1659. The introduction to the
last of these plays states that "the beginning of rulership is the propagation
of godly spirituality."[4] The stage itself had become an important medium
for political as well as spiritual propagation. The process of confessionalization was taking shape as a kind of royal theatre, designed to transform
willing listeners into more obedient subjects.

The theatre of royal virtue was born out of a crisis over what the royal
body represented. By 1600, as we have seen, medieval and Renaissance

assumptions about the monarch's physical sacrality were widely challenged. The king's body no longer provided an uncontested representation of order in the polity and the self. For many reformed Christians, the king was divinely sanctioned only insofar as he accepted his human unworthiness and promoted the designs of heaven. To ensure continuing allegiance, the ruler would have to align himself with devout aspirations by submitting both his own body and the mystical body of the polity to reformed discipline. He might thereby gain new powers of personal control over all of his subjects. On the other hand, he might find himself under the sway of a godly faction and opposed by the humanist lawyers and venal office-bearers who were indispensable to centralized administration. In any case, the king would have to take dangerous steps, shedding part of the Renaissance mantle of glory, transforming himself from a sacred object into a political actor, inuring himself to the limelight of constant publicity. He would have to recognize that his subjects comprised a public that was not simply subsumed in his own body. In short, he would have to embrace the techniques of the theatre.

This amounted to a significant change. Before the age of religious reform, European monarchs had played out the hieratic gestures of rulership before tiny audiences of courtiers. Their sacred bodies were seldom seen and were never meant to be comprehended by their subjects. Their relative freedom from public scrutiny allowed them easily to mix ritual offices with their own pleasures. No clear boundary separated their public and private lives. By the early seventeenth century, however, kings were expected to uphold in their persons the constant religious and moral principles that bound together the Christian community. The most conniving politicians concurred with this expectation. "The good conduct of a moral prince," Cardinal Richelieu advised Louis XIII, "banishes more vice from his realms than all the orders he can give."[5] It was no longer enough for monarchs to claim that they incorporated holiness; they had to imitate it in their lives and behaviour and display it to their subjects. In doing so, they broadened the use of older methods—court rituals, processions, proclamations—and made them into what Michèle Fogel has called "ceremonies of information," public enunciations of the theme of authority.[6] Royal publicists also resorted to a fledgling popular press that turned out piles of broadsheets, pamphlets, and gazettes concerned with the lives of rulers. Through group readings, rumour, and gossip, even the illiterate had some access to this material.

In consequence, royal performances became more open, ruling mythologies less impenetrable. It became difficult for kings to have any life at all beyond the glare of publicity. Any vices now had to be kept behind the scenes, creating a more restrictive definition of royal privacy.

In rituals, ceremonies, paintings, and literature, monarchs began to adopt the techniques of the burgeoning public theatre—the theatre of Shakespeare and Jonson, Gryphius and Corneille, Lope de Vega and Calderón. The theatre spoke to a broad and respectable audience. It had evolved its own rhetoric, its own narrative style, its own rationality, which enabled it to impart didactic messages to its viewers. Cervantes wrote that "the principal purpose for which well-ordered states allow public plays to be acted is to give the common people a respectable entertainment, and to divert the ill-humours which idleness at times engenders."[7] It was specifically to control confessional "ill-humours" that kings were encouraged to become actors. They began to present themselves as coherent personalities, who played out their parts according to conventional moral archetypes. They constructed naturalistic characters with whom everyone could in some measure identify: pious heroes in trial or triumph. The plots in which they embroiled themselves might involve miracles but were relatively free of recourse to magical interventions or occult meanings. Instead, they were imbued with messages of confessional unity and moral discipline. Throughout the whole performance, the royal actors appeared to keep their eyes fixed on heaven and to look for support only to God. In return, they were covered by the public with the aura of divine approbation.

The theatre of royal virtue was a move away from what Weber called traditional authority and was an essential preliminary to the construction of the rational state. It entailed a change in the concept of political representation, because the significance of the royal body was no longer centred on its sacred status. Kingly charisma became dependent upon the norms and values of an audience composed of provincial nobles, merchants, even urban shopkeepers and artisans. Both sides in this theatrical exchange had powers; neither could take the other for granted. Confessional politics therefore took on some of the features of the "public sphere" that Jürgen

Habermas has associated with a later age of bourgeois culture: a commitment to the clear formulation of discourse, a hitherto unknown level of openness, a need to establish rational justifications.[8] The confessional audience of the seventeenth century was not solely or even predominantly bourgeois, of course, but many of its values would be bequeathed as a cultural inheritance to the middle classes of subsequent periods. The public sphere, in short, had religious and political as well as socio-economic origins. It provided an indispensable basis for the further rationalization of monarchical government.

Contemporary literature did not mention a public sphere, but it did contain many references to the *Theatrum Mundi*, or theatre of the world. The term appeared everywhere, from the plays of Shakespeare and Calderón to the pamphlets of the German Rosicrucians. By the mid-1600s, for example, a chronicle of literary publications and political events entitled *Theatrum Europaeum* was regularly published at Frankfurt.[9] The Spanish historian José Antonio Maravall linked this widespread theatre of the world motif with what he called the "mass culture" of the baroque age. More controlled than traditional popular beliefs and practices, mass culture combined a broad level of participation with heavy doses of indoctrination.[10] Because he saw mass culture as created from the top down, to prop up a precarious social hierarchy, Maravall may have undervalued the considerable importance of cultural exchange between governing elites and a widened audience; but he accurately perceived the significance of the theatre of the world as a tool of social change and a means of identification with the state.

Yet to describe politics, especially religious politics, as a kind of theatre was a problematic comparison for the godly. Play-acting had negative associations with artifice or deception. It seemed to compromise the authenticity of the Christian self. It was active rather than introspective, worldly rather than spiritual—faults that some among the devout would fiercely denounce. The extravagances of baroque culture might therefore be greeted with suspicion. In a political sense, moreover, theatricality might be associated with what was called "reason of state"—that is, doing bad deeds for good ends. For many pious observers, reason of state was Machiavellian, profoundly un-Christian, and to be avoided.[11] If the theatre of politics was to be acceptable to the devout, it had to restrict itself to what

was truthful and without ambiguity; in other words, to the simple ve-
racities of revealed religion. The carefully controlled words and gestures
of the Jesuit stage tried to meet this demand. Jesuit theatre was supposed
to provide not a furtive, illusory, or ironic entertainment but a direct sen-
sory experience of the sacred, a "hierophany." In its simple, emotionally
charged presentation of divine verities, it resembled the Mass itself.[12] To
some extent, however, pretence and artifice were mixed up in all theatre,
and in all politics. In time, as we shall see, many of the godly became
heartily disillusioned by both.

To make things worse, royal actors kept slipping into an older rhetoric
of humanism that emphasized natural order or classical virtue rather than
godly reform. Most royal performances, therefore, received lukewarm
reviews from the devout. But every king hoped that, if the play were
successful, if the arts of dissimulation and rhetoric were not seen to be
abused, he might reconcile all the disharmonies in the script and mould his
listeners into willing servants of the state. Let us look at how this authoritarian vision sustained the dialogue of politics in the baroque age, preparing the way for a broader level of identification with, and acquiescence in,
the workings of government. The godly public always wanted to see true
religion triumph over reason of state. When this did not happen, as the next
chapter will show, an angry audience might actually mount the stage.

## Ferdinand on the Mount of Olives

To understand the theatrical politics of the early seventeenth century, we
have to consider the emperor Ferdinand II carefully. He is a figure little
known today outside Austrian historiography, but in his own times he cast
a large shadow on the theatre of the world. What made him the pre-
eminent example of a confessionalized monarch? The answers lie in his
public image, specifically his Christian Neostoicism, his cultivation of the
role of "evangelical house-father," his constitutional propriety, and his
avoidance of the wicked paths of reason of state. Together, these factors
combined to form an effective, unified moral persona, whose exemplary
actions would have a profound impact on the confessional identities of
his subjects.

In formulating his public image, Ferdinand drew direct inspiration from the writings of the Neostoic philosopher Justus Lipsius. Like his fellow Netherlander Erasmus, Lipsius merged classical precepts with the discipline of the Christian self; but he lived in an age of humanist disillusionment and had to come to terms with the consequences of confessional strife. In his *Six Books of Politics* of 1589, Lipsius set down what he saw as universal principles of virtue, derived from Tacitus and the Roman Stoics, particularly Seneca. Prudence, constancy, fortitude, and severity were Lipsius's watchwords. What they amounted to was perfect self-control, in both public and private life. The prince had to maintain in his conduct the highest moral values and set an unimpeachable example to his subjects.[13] Lipsius acknowledged that some measure of deceit was necessary in governance—"I always mean but a small deale, and to a good end." The prince sometimes had to be *"as craftie as a Foxe"* in his dealings. Still, he had to remember that majesty was based on the appearance of personal probity.[14]

Lipsius was the most influential acting coach in the theatre of royal virtue. He was interested less in analyzing power than in providing instructions for its effective projection. He took classical principles of active political engagement, principles beloved by humanists, and made them safe for emulation by Christian monarchs. Underlying his high-minded maxims, however, was an understanding of government as a human art rather than a manifestation of divine order. The aim of Neostoic politics was to present an outward impression of perfect harmony and discipline, not to purify the self or create a moral utopia. Its purpose was to smooth over conflict, particularly confessional strife, rather than find ultimate solutions to ethical questions.

Having taught at both the Calvinist bastion of Leiden and at the Catholic University of Louvain, Lipsius had experience of both sides of the religious divide. He may have preserved secret connections with heterodox groups, but in his published works he stipulated that religious unity must be preserved within the state at all costs. While he allowed that private opinions on religion might sometimes be tolerated, visible heresy was to be stamped out: "Here is no place for clemencie, burne, sawe asunder, for it is better that one member be cast away, then that the whole body runne to ruyne."[15] The arts of Neostoic politics, therefore, lent themselves to a sometimes brutal confessional control; but they did not reach very deeply into the inner recesses of the Christian self.

As the late Gerhard Oestreich demonstrated, Lipsian Neostoicism attracted reforming rulers like Ferdinand II, who sought to extend a rigorous external discipline over their subjects.[16] Within the Empire, moreover, Lipsius was read in the context of his devotion to the Habsburg dynastic mission. During the last years of his life the ageing professor enjoyed a special relationship with Philip II, who made him a royal historiographer. Lipsius praised the Habsburgs as ideal Christian monarchs; he even glorified the myth of Rudolf I and the viaticum. Ferdinand II's devotion to Lipsius was so well known as to fuel a rumour that the emperor himself had written a Neostoic tract on princely virtue, *Princeps in compendio*, published in 1632.[17]

Ferdinand used the Neostoic art of politics to project the image of a Christian patriarch, or what contemporary Jesuit plays called "the evangelical house-father."[18] The emperor's renowned personal piety bolstered his claim to be father or leader of the spiritual family of his Catholic subjects. He attended two private masses each day, as well as public masses and vespers on Sundays and feast days. He was frequently seen venerating the Eucharist. He marched yearly at the head of the Corpus Christi procession, the central public ritual of Catholic unity, in which the assembled social orders carried the body of Christ. Thus, Ferdinand made himself first among believers. On the Jesuit stage, he was portrayed as the biblical patriarch Joseph. He chose as his personal protector and consort the Virgin Mary. By naming her honorary "Generalissima" of his armies, he tied military success to the triumph of motherhood and purity. His publicity also made frequent comparisons between the holy family and the Habsburg clan.[19] Imperial patriarchy, it should be noted, was built on Catholic, not Lutheran, assumptions. It envisioned the family as serving spiritual rather than social ends, and it elevated fatherhood not as the foundation of human authority but as a prop of the universal Church.

Thus, the evangelical house-father was first and foremost an imitator of Christ. At times, this meant that he could be imagined as a sacrificial scapegoat, fulfilling the role described by René Girard. Symbolic violence against his body would indicate to his people the path back to sacred order. A popular woodcut of 1622, for example, showed Ferdinand in the guise of Jesus praying on the Mount of Olives, surrounded by the sleeping Electors. While the devil leads on the forces of rebellion, an angel hands to the emperor the accoutrements of royalty, along with a victor's laurel wreath.[20] The print implies a correspondence between Christ and Ferdinand, although not an equivalence in their natures—the emperor remains a human reflection of the sacred. The representation of sacrificial royal devotion to the faith was nonetheless moving, and it became a common theme in Imperial mass culture. Jesuit plays restated it through frequent depiction of Hermenegildus, the Ostrogothic prince who was martyred for opposing the Arian heresy. The martyr image of Habsburg rulership reached a sort of grim apotheosis on the high altar of the church at Wasserburg-am-Inn, where the emperor Ferdinand III was depicted as a suffering St. Sebastian.[21] This was in part an admission of Imperial humanity or abjection; but it also promised a crown of glory to a ruler whose faith would stand firm against the arrows of heresy.

The emperor exploited his role as martyr and evangelical house-father in order to extend throughout Austria and Bohemia a programme of confessional discipline. This programme entailed not only religious reconversion but also changes in marriage and funeral customs, the suppression of festivals and popular holidays, the creation of charity schools and catechism classes, the founding of Jesuit academies for upper-class boys, and the renewed obligation of confession. From 1633 onwards the emperor issued a series of ordinances dealing with "virtuous conduct," calling for the use of informers to check on Sunday observances and for police measures to enforce Easter Communion. Habsburg "family discipline" also encompassed an attack on the popular magic of the peasantry. Quasi-pagan practices and superstitions were suppressed and replaced by belief in the miracles wrought by saints. Towards the end of the Thirty Years' War, prosecutions of witchcraft began to proliferate in Austria, Bohemia, and Hungary; they did not cease until the eighteenth century. The victims were often village "wise women," who offered cures and advice that infringed on the prerogatives of the church's male hierarchy.[22] Through such methods the rod of godly rulership was felt in every village of the Erblande.

It would be absurd, however, to depict Ferdinand's patriarchal reformism as purely coercive, just as it would be to assume that peasants were forced to believe whatever they were shown on the Jesuit stage. Confessional discipline did not simply entail a repression or "acculturation" of the common people.[23] The dramatic successes of reform depended largely on persuasion and the recruitment of allies among the middle and lower classes. In a study of property relations in Upper Austria, Hermann Rebel has examined the effects of the Habsburg policy of *Bauernschutz*, or peasant protection. Little by little the state took charge of property relations, changing obligations to landlords, like the hated labour duty called *Robot*, into money payments. The legalization of ownership favoured house-holders over the unhoused, masters over servants, fathers over recalcitrant children. Rebel notes that the great Austrian peasant uprising of 1626 was the last to be led by substantial peasant farmers; thereafter, it was only the "dispossessed"—the landless and the indigent—who took part in revolts.[24] Increasingly, the Habsburg monarchy could rely on the heads of village households, little house-fathers for whom the road to religious conversion was now made smooth.

At a higher social level, the Imperial house-father won the support of the great magnate families of Austria and Bohemia—the Liechtensteins, Lobkovices, Dietrichsteins, Pálffys, and so forth—as well as ambitious petty gentry, like the Hungarian Esterhazys, and upwardly mobile bur-ghers, such as Hans Ulrich von Eggenberg, director of the Imperial Privy Council. They were rewarded with offices and positions, so that gradually the Habsburg court began to revive as the nerve centre of Imperial author-ity.[25] Those who sided with Ferdinand's vision of patriarchal political order were obliged to embrace Catholicism, and many noble families con-verted. They were also expected to maintain standards of virtuous conduct within their own families and over their dependents.

The transformation of the Habsburg monarchy went far beyond the matter of insuring the future of the dynasty. It involved a shift in the whole cultural framework of the hereditary lands, away from "superstitious" beliefs, popular devotions, and communal social values towards a rigorous clerical control and an unquestioning loyalty to the ruler.[26] Of course, this shift never happened as smoothly as had been intended. It was a mostly external change that did not penetrate far into the spiritual consciousness of the self. Nonetheless, it set a pattern that was to be half-imitated, half-resisted in every other European monarchy.

It was accompanied by constitutional caution. Ferdinand's views on Imperial institutions were conservative by design, so that to call him a reforming absolutist, as many historians have, is misleading.[27] Among

German political writers of his time, the one whose work he most admired was Dietrich Reinking, professor at the Lutheran University of Gießen. Ferdinand granted high honours to Reinking and was said to have agreed completely with his writings.[28] Like Melchior Goldast, Reinking argued that the Holy Roman Empire was heir to Rome's empire. The emperor alone held sovereign power, and he was able to abrogate laws made by inferior bodies. Reinking added, however, that the emperor remained contractually bound to the Electors by his coronation oaths and Wahlkapitulationen and could even be sued in Imperial courts. This was not unified sovereignty in a Bodinian sense, and it cannot be regarded as strictly absolute.[29]

In keeping with Reinking's theories, Ferdinand always saw himself as supreme, but he was willing to observe the restraints imposed by the traditional constitutions of his realms. As archduke of Inner Austria in 1599, for example, he wanted to be considered *princeps absolutus*, or absolute prince. He interpreted this title as meaning there could be no appeal beyond him to the emperor. The Estates grudgingly recognized him as *rechten natürlichen Erbherrn*—true natural hereditary lord—while allowing him no sovereign rights over their consciences. The archduke accepted this compromise.[30] Twenty-two years later, Ferdinand acted more boldly as a constitutional innovator in Bohemia, where he could claim the rights of a conqueror after the defeat of the Protestant rebels. Bohemia's kingship was made hereditary rather than elective. This, however, was as far as the triumphant Habsburg ruler was willing to go. The Estates continued to meet, and no attempt was made to consolidate the administration of the diverse Czech provinces. Outside Bohemia, Ferdinand had no concrete plans for changing the political structures of his realms.[31]

Ferdinand presented himself as the protector of ancient rights within the Empire, not as their violator. Even his most incautious act, the 1629 Edict of Restitution, which restored church property in the Empire, was ostensibly designed "for the realization both of the religious and profane peace" and was justified under the terms of the Peace of Augsburg.[32] Ferdinand's publicity never emphasized radical political change. On the contrary, it endlessly reiterated his traditional legitimacy. The emperor's motto was *"Legitime certantibus corona"*—"to those who have just right goes the crown." His opponent Frederick of the Palatinate, on the other hand, was pilloried in Jesuit plays as the medieval tyrant Radißlaum, who tried to seize Bohemia from good Duke Wenceslaus. In Imperialist cartoons and satirical broadsheets of the Thirty Years' War, Frederick was crudely depicted as a homeless vagabond without roots or honour. The emperor, by contrast, was allegorized as the stolid Imperial eagle, symbol of the unity and continuity of the Reich.[33]

Was Ferdinand's carefully constructed image tainted by "reason of state"? He would have denied the accusation vehemently. He despised reason of state as impious and would have agreed with the definition of a good councillor proposed in *Princeps in compendio:* "a virtuous politician, an intelligent Christian, not Machiavellian."[34] Yet reason of state seemed to lie at the heart of the judicial murder of Albrecht von Wallenstein, duke of Friedland. To his many scholarly admirers, Wallenstein was a more "modern" and sympathetic figure than the emperor. Devoid of confessional zeal, he readily employed Protestant officers and was more interested in trade and finance than in doctrinal purity. His lavish and self-promoting artistic patronage rivalled that of Rudolf II; for example, the palace he built in Prague was the largest after the Hradschin. By 1634 Wallenstein was tired of war and sought to negotiate an end to it, which brought him to the brink of treason against the emperor. Aware of his plotting, the Privy Council ordered him to be arrested or, if necessary, killed as a convicted felon. A cabal of English, Scots, and Irish officers carried out the order, stabbing the ailing generalissimo in his room late at night during a portentous thunderstorm.[35]

Wallenstein's "modernity" has probably been exaggerated. He seems never to have formulated a clear vision of the Empire whose destiny he aspired to control. His impatience with legal niceties earned him many enemies within a Reich whose security rested on law and tradition. Ferdinand II was a more circumspect ruler; but, as Wallenstein's assassination showed, he was not above resorting on occasion to what Lipsius called "mixed prudence" and his enemies decried as "reason of state." The emperor preserved a veneer of legality in this case by not taking a direct part in the deliberations of his councillors, although everyone knew his wishes. If he used more than "a small deale" of deceit in dealing with his nemesis, Ferdinand was at least innocent in his own mind of having acted on Machiavellian principles. The emperor chose to interpret the generalissimo's death as a stroke of divine Providence, the answer to his prayers. His version of events was depicted in an extraordinary Jesuit play staged in 1635 before the Imperial heir, where Wallenstein appears as the blaspheming Julian the Apostate and his assassination is carried out by Christian soldiers acting on direct instructions from the Virgin Mary![36]

If Ferdinand did not espouse reason of state, it was because he had little conception of his Empire as a worldly entity with its own right to preservation. Did he even see it as a state? Elsewhere, the state would develop out of the idea of a corpus mysticum, so we may wonder where the emperor perceived the corpus mysticum of his realms to lie. The answer is not in his own Christ-like body, nor in the Imperial constitutions. In fact, the corpus mysticum of the renewed Habsburg monarchy seems to have rested in the body of Catholic believers, both within the Reich and in the Erblande. The emperor headed the temporal manifestation of this body and drew his power from the confessional conformity of his subjects. While this did not go far in building unified sovereignty, the collective idealization of authority in the Erblande was as rational and as thorough as in the other states of Europe. The lack of an overarching governing apparatus should not blind us to the centrifugal pull of ideological unity and personal discipline.

By the time he died in 1637, Ferdinand II's dream of constructing a confessionalized monarchy had not been achieved. Everywhere his plans were challenged by resistance and rebellion. Yet if the Imperial body was in pain, it was the pain of triumphant martyrdom. By the late 1630s much of Ferdinand II's ideological mission had in fact been accomplished. The religious doubts of the sixteenth century were forgotten, and the victory of Catholicism within the Erblande was assured. Rudolf II's magical museum was packed up in boxes and stored away—until the Swedes captured it, carrying *Vertumnus* to Stockholm. For the next three centuries, the Austrian Habsburgs remained resplendent examples of how the theatrical art of politics could transform piety into power.

## The Protestants Look for Joshua

In the third book of that fantastical and very nasty German fable *The Adventurous Simplicissimus*, the eponymous narrator, serving as a soldier during the Thirty Years' War, captures a well-dressed man who "told me plainly he was the great god Jupiter himself." Thinking him mad, Simplicissimus asks why the god has descended to earth. Jupiter informs him of his plan to punish a wicked world: " 'I will raise up a German hero that shall accomplish all with the edge of the sword; he shall destroy all evil men and preserve and exalt the righteous.' " The hero will restore the empire and bring " 'a perpetual peace between all nations.' " Diverse faiths will be reunited in " 'the true, holy Christian religion in accordance with Holy Writ.' " Jupiter ends his curious disquisition with a reflection on his own many fleas.[37]

Grimmelshausen's Jupiter must be either play-acting or mad. His zealous rhetoric serves to lampoon hopes of a German saviour who would rescue the Protestant cause, unite Calvinists with Lutherans, take command of the Empire, and impose divine order on a divided Europe—thus acting out what were widely expected to be the final scenes in the political theatre of this world. The dream of a righteous Protestant hero was in part a reaction to the Habsburg resurgence, in part a culmination of long-standing millenarian hopes.

The dream was sustained by a deeply entrenched Protestant confessional culture that bore similarities to Ferdinand II's programme but differed in its impetus and goals. Protestant culture derived political strength as much from the convictions of ministers and the lay elite as from the efforts of princes. Unlike Catholic reformism, it did not emphasize martyrdom or sacramental purification; rather, it placed its trust in military strength and envisioned righteous discipline as an aspect of social duty. The virtuous monarch was not a priestly or intercessionary figure who imitated Christ through personal sacrifice. On the contrary, the Protestant hero-king appeared on the political stage as a biblical judge or holy warrior who would carry out divine intentions with a terrible sword.

Protestants adopted a more dichotomous view of cultural representation than Catholics did. They found the sacred only in the language of Holy Writ, equating the profane with a seductive and false theatre of the world. In embracing one, the godly had to reject the other. This made them quicker than Catholics to condemn popular customs, quasi-pagan beliefs, and "superstitious" rituals. Thus, English Puritans battled constantly to enforce observance of the Sabbath, to suppress unruly popular festivals like May dancing, and to eliminate ungodly practices like church ales, fund-raising events where strong drink was served. Dutch Calvinists similarly railed against "those numerous and glaring abuses, by which the people are seduced from true holiness . . . such as *Carnivals, Comedies, Farces* of *strolling Comedians* and *Mountebanks, Hocus-pocus tricks, drunker Clubs, Dancing Schools,*" and so forth.[38] In Denmark, religious laws abolished drinking and dancing around the coffin at funerals, required women to wear long dresses and capes at church, and commanded that "no bishops or clergymen must break their beer cup on their neighbor's head."[39] Protestants were engaged in a constant public battle to assert the supremacy of the Word over other forms of cultural expression, whether collective or individual. For them, the mass culture of the baroque could only be acceptable if it rested on the bedrock of Scripture.

Although the ultimate aim of Protestant confessionalism was the conversion of the inner self, it asserted just as tight a control over the outward person as did Catholicism. All believers, whether they considered themselves regenerate or not, were obliged to adhere to common behavioral standards and turn away from vice. Within German Lutheran communities, as D. W. Sabean has shown, attendance at Communion was rigorously enforced by pastors, and "anyone not participating became labeled as stubborn, blasphemous, asocial."[40] The behaviour of the unregenerate was subjected to ministerial surveillance, community discipline, and public humiliation. This was seen as essential to what was called "police," which meant the proper administration of public order, in both society and the family.

By the early decades of the seventeenth century, police in the Protestant territories of Germany had become institutionalized through a steady stream of legislation. Many of these ordinances related to keeping the Sabbath, which entailed the suppression of games, pastimes, and drinking. Others dealt with parish schools, church attendance, or the enforcement of religious orthodoxy. Eventually, police laws were extended to include other social issues like bastardy, fornication, vagrancy, inheritance, public festivities, and forms of dress.[41] The historian Marc Raeff has observed that police became a more dynamic notion in the course of the century: "its aims no longer were to restore and correct abuses and defects but rather to create new conditions, to bring about changes and introduce innovations." Raeff sees this as the foundation of a "police state" that would eventually replace the German *Ständestaat,* or government by Estates. Before 1650, however, the Estates were enthusiastic proponents of police legislation. It was only after the Thirty Years' War—that great "caesura," as Volker Press put it, in the history of the Ständestaat—that social discipline increasingly became part of princely prerogative.[42]

Police, or godly social discipline, was a widespread collective endeavour, not simply defined from above. It had a voluntary as well as a coercive side, and its effects were far from uniform. As the revival of Habsburg power threatened Protestantism with destruction, however, police took on explicit military connotations. "Discipline," wrote one English divine in 1628, "is the chief commander of the camp-royal of God."[43] The faithful constituted an army of God that was enlisted in a life-or-death struggle with the forces of Satan. The destiny of the godly prince was to captain these legions. Many Lutheran and Calvinist rulers studied for the role by reading the moral writings of Justus Lipsius, who was so admired by the Habsburgs as well. What Protestants drew from Lipsius was his view that the highest form of virtue was found on the battleground. Protestant Neostoicism therefore encouraged a military version of police, based on new tactics, rigorous training, and conscript armies.[44]

The Protestants longed for a Joshua to command them. They remained suspicious of political artifice or theatricality, however, and wanted their champion to conform to a strict biblical typology. Before 1618, they were obliged to look not to monarchs but to princes who had swallowed the full demystifying draught of confessionalization. Many, including the radical political theorist Althusius, found their Joshua in the *stadholder* of the United Provinces, Prince Maurice of Nassau, quasi-hereditary commander of the Dutch forces. In him, Neostoic military prowess was combined with strict Calvinist values and disdain for the Habsburgs.[45] Still, he was not a real king, and he served a republic whose constitution was viewed with considerable alarm by conservative Protestants.

The confusion of Imperial politics after 1618 allowed three other Protestant rulers to imitate Maurice's example: Frederick of the Palatinate, who was briefly king of Bohemia, Christian IV of Denmark, and Gustavus II Adolphus of Sweden. All three appealed to confessional opinion by striding boldly into a public sphere of international image-making. All three sought to bind together Lutherans and Calvinists in a final contest for dominance in the Empire. What they found, however, was that confessional culture was not very effective in advancing the art of politics or forging a viable worldly alternative to the universal Catholic empire. Looking to the past, Frederick and Christian adopted dubious Renaissance mystifications. Looking to the future, Gustavus carefully practised reason of state, but saved his reputation for godliness through a premature death.

The most luckless of the three was Frederick V, Elector Palatine. He inherited a Lutheran territory whose confessional culture had already been forcibly altered by the prince. Frederick's father had become a Calvinist, curbing the authority of the Lutheran *Kirchenrat*, or Church Council.[46] From the first, therefore, Frederick V's own expansive projects were greeted with some suspicion by Lutherans. Yet in some minds, including his own, the young Elector was a prime candidate for the role of a Protestant messiah, which he claimed by accepting the kingship of Bohemia in 1618.

Bohemia's was a consecrated kingship, and Frederick seems to have enjoyed his new status as a sacral ruler. He also inspired a strange cult among a group of intellectuals who had imbibed all the mystical notions of Renaissance Neoplatonism. The mysterious Brotherhood of the Rosy Cross, or Rosicrucians, saw in the Elector Palatine the fulfilment of ancient prophesies. Their glorification of Frederick in emblematic prints and cryptic writings was in part an attempt to bridge differences among Protestants through a sort of natural philosophy that owed more to the Neoplatonist Giordano Bruno than to Luther.[47] This esoteric literature, an echo of the sacral pretensions of the court at Prague, was not the stuff to inspire affection in the minds of most Protestants. Even the mystic Jakob Boehme, an unorthodox Lutheran who resided in the Bohemian Crown lands, was not enthusiastic about his new ruler, and he remained doubtful that Frederick's reign heralded the advent of a "true German Emperor."[48] The Winter King of Bohemia lacked both confessional trustworthiness and traditional legitimacy, weaknesses that were endlessly exploited by his enemies. After the Habsburg recapture of Prague, he ended up a sad wanderer, looking desperately for allies among the German princes.

The other failed Protestant hero of the 1620s was Christian IV of Denmark, who as duke of Holstein was also a prince of the Empire. His Imperial dreams may have been fostered by his court surgeon, the political writer Henning Arnisaeus. As we have seen, Arnisaeus espoused a thoroughly desacralized Protestant monarchy. In keeping with such an image, Christian IV cultivated a reputation for being intensely devout. His motto was *"Regna firma pietas"* — "piety strengthens kingdoms." He patronized Lutheran clerics whose orthodox rigour verged on the austerity of Calvinism. He wanted to be known for his military virtue and was a keen reader of Lipsius. Immensely rich from the collection of tolls in the Sound (the entrance to the Baltic Sea) and the administration of extensive royal lands, Christian IV seemed to be marked out as a godly champion.[49]

Yet like his nephew Charles I of England, Christian was at heart a Renaissance monarch who longed to escape from the toils of confessionalism. In private life he was a heavy drinker, a womanizer, and a devotee of astrology. His court rivalled that of Elizabeth I in splendour and that of Rudolf II in its taste for the occult. He employed painters from all over Europe, including many Catholics, who decorated his palaces with scenes of classical heroism. He became an ardent patron of architecture and music—two arts cherished by Neoplatonists, because they were thought to express the mystical harmony of nature. Christian financed the efforts of the astronomer Tycho Brahe to map out the secrets of the natural universe, while his *Kapellmeister,* Heinrich Schütz, famous for his religious compositions, regaled the court with such profane delights as "Song of the Children of Venus."[50] Like other Renaissance monarchs, Christian had no conception of a state separate from his person, and he used his treasury like a private banking service. Even before the military disasters of the mid-1620s, his councillors had to intervene in order to draw a boundary between the finances of the king and those of the realm.[51]

Christian's visions also caused concern among the godly, because they seemed to violate the distinction between true and false representations. One night in December 1625 he saw the suffering Christ appear before him, wearing a crown of thorns. Like Ferdinand II's encounter with Jesus in 1619, the incident established a legitimizing connection between the king and the Son of God; so much so that, in a painting of his vision executed on royal command, Christ's face bears a striking resemblance to Christian IV's. This was too close to the sacral aura of Renaissance monarchy for some Lutherans. Theologians debated whether the king's vision had been sent by the devil—because he saw Jesus sitting down, while in Scripture the Saviour was described as standing. Before their deliberations were over,

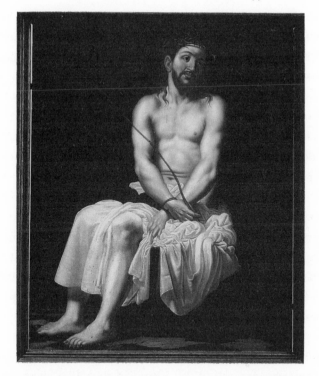

7. Anonymous, *Christ in Agony* (1625), painting.
Photo: The Danish Royal Collections, Rosenborg slot, Copenhagen.

Wallenstein's devastating invasion of Denmark in 1628 had ended the cosmic pretensions of the mercurial king Christian. Humiliated in the field, heavily indebted to his disgruntled nobles, he sank from international prominence.[52]

The German Protestants finally found a reliable warrior hero in 1630, when Gustavus II Adolphus of Sweden came galloping into the Empire. Gustavus was not only a sincerely pious Lutheran but also had genuine military skills. Unlike Christian IV, he did not see visions. Instead, he relied on the Word, and on his own messianic convictions. Firmly aligned with the orthodox Swedish clergy, he advocated severe religious discipline, encouraging the punishment of moral offenders through ice-cold drenchings, the stocks, and public whippings. His soldiers sang hymns on their way into battle and heard prayers twice a day, sermons once a week. Each company had a chaplain, as did each regiment.[53] The Swedish troops were made into good Protestants, inside and out.

For a short time it seemed as if Gustavus might realize his dimly conceived hope of gathering the Protestant territories of the Empire into a political confederation under his leadership—a Swedish Reich built on the ruins of the Holy Roman one. These were grand schemes that might portend the millennium, but—unlike Frederick V or Christian IV—Gustavus did not look to prophecy or alchemy to realize them. Rather, he depended on a Swedish national army raised through an organized conscription system, disciplined by martial law, and trained in the latest tactics.[54] Gustavus borrowed military concepts from Maurice of Nassau, and he once defined the perfect officer in finely chosen Neostoic terms: "I expect of him, under the article 'Virtue,' that he shall be of good life and conversation, diligent in ordering, laborious in performance, valorous in danger, various in his capacities, and swift in execution."[55] There was no hint given here that virtue was an art to be learned; rather, it was a quality intrinsic to the Christian self. How could God not give victory to such a king?

Gustavus II Adolphus was adored by German Protestants, both Lutherans and Calvinists, as their deliverer, the new Joshua or Gideon, David or Judas Maccabaeus, the Lion of the North. In him the godly saw a manifestation of the redeemed self. They identified with him completely. As the Swabian Calvinist preacher Johann Andreä recalled, "So much comfort did we derive from the happy progresses of the unconquerable hero, the King of Sweden."[56] The diarist Hans Heberle, a Lutheran shoemaker of Ulm, recorded a wonderful sign of Gustavus's coming: Protestants in Augsburg had seen a celestial army marching in the night sky, "and in front a mighty rider with a naked, shining sword. . . . This meant, that God wishes to rescue his people from misery."[57] A Protestant print of 1632 showed Gustavus, his features recognizable from hundreds of popular portrayals, riding the chariot of victory as angels hand him laurels and a crown. The deity himself "blesses his sword / As he uses it for God's honour." Other broadsheets and pamphlets depicted the Swede as Augustus or associated him with the Second Coming of Christ. A new star was seen in the skies to herald Gustavus's advance.[58] The millennial significance of his invasion was noted by a godly observer in England: "The papists now interpret the prophesies of the Revelation concerning Antechrist upon the king of Swede, and say he shall continew the 3 yeears etc., but I hope God hath raysed him to sitt thare in that stead, but not as that man-beast, I know, but

8. *The Swedish Progress* (1632), engraved broadsheet.
British Library callmark 1750 b 29 (47).
Photo: British Library, London.

the destroyer of that monster by God's blessing, or the preface to that greate worke."[59] To desperate Protestants, the Swedish king appeared not as a worldly conqueror but as a harbinger of the final days, when all human kingships would be dissolved and Christ would return to govern his people.

The messianic aura created around Gustavus, however, disguised the essentially worldly and political aims of his expedition. The Swedish king was not averse to the judicious exercise of reason of state in order to hasten the fulfilment of his mission. This was especially apparent in his dealings with Wallenstein and the French.[60] To sustain his claims on the international stage, moreover, Gustavus drew upon a source that was deeply offensive to the godly: the natural-law theories of Hugo Grotius, which we shall consider further in the next section. Whether his support of Grotius or his political scheming would have alienated some of his admirers in the end is of course a moot point. Gustavus II Adolphus was shot to death in battle with Wallenstein at Lützen in 1632. By then his conscript army was increasingly made up of mercenaries, and his treasury was filled with subsidies from Catholic France. Yet in Protestant memory, down to the nineteenth century and beyond, he remained the perfect confessional hero-king, who had mobilized every godly soul in his struggle to establish, not a worldly state, but a universal Christian polity. To his admirers he had come close to fulfiling the messianic dreams of Simplicissimus's Jupiter.

Only one Protestant monarch avoided becoming embroiled in the Imperial war and, for as long as he could, turned his back on the godly. James I of England was personally hostile to the values of messianic milita-rism, and he censored Neostoic writings, which he saw as veiled criticisms of his policies.[61] By rejecting the role of the holy warrior, however, he risked undoing the image of confessional kingship that his own writings had done so much to propagate.

Already mistrusted by the English political elite, James had turned for advice to a handsome young favourite, the duke of Buckingham, who was willing to flatter and cajole him. Self-interest and reason of state were Buckingham's guiding principles, and they made him many enemies, espe-cially among the godly.[62] The religious war in the Holy Roman Empire gave a new urgency to their criticisms. By all rights, James I should have led the forces of Protestantism against the Habsburg menace. He was father-in-law to Frederick of the Palatinate, brother-in-law to Christian of Denmark. He was the most powerful Protestant ruler in Europe. Yet in-stead of raising the banner of holy war, he tried to keep peace with Spain, allowing only a trickle of English money and troops to reach the be-leaguered German Protestants. He even sought to end the conflict by writing direct to the pope! The lack of a clear policy caused considerable confusion. As one Member of Parliament confided to Buckingham, "His Matyes ende is not knowen to any."[63] In 1623 Buckingham made a crazy attempt to secure peace by secretly travelling to Spain with Prince Charles, disguised as "Jack and Tom Smith." Their purpose was to woo the Spanish Infanta. A bemused Philip IV provided lavish entertainment for the pair, but no bride.[64]

One hundred crackling bonfires illuminated the return of Charles and Buckingham to London. The godly rejoiced at what they perceived to be a "blessed revolution"—the revival of an anti-Spanish policy. Vowing now that he was "a Protestant king," James gave in to the demands of the patriots who called for war.[65] Before real hostilities commenced, the old

king died in March 1625, and it was left to his son to deal with the financial
and political strains of warfare. Charles I, however, never expressed any
affinity for the role of a Calvinist warrior monarch. Why should he have?
Looking around Europe in the late 1620s, Charles's deeply conservative
mind might have found very little to admire in godly rulership, tainted as it
was by the writings of "demagogues" like Althusius. Charles wanted to
preserve Protestantism, but he did not wish to promote the agenda of
rebels. Is it any wonder that he began to see Calvinism itself as a threat to
monarchy? The failures of godly rulership in the Empire may have confirmed his preference for court culture over public theatre and his drift
towards the doctrine known as Arminianism, which was seen by many of
his subjects as no better than Popery.

## The Whole World Turned Arminian

The term *Arminianism* was derived from the name of the Dutch theologian, Jacobus Arminius. Rejecting the Calvinist doctrine that divine grace
provided salvation without human effort, Arminius was willing to allow
room for free will and good works. In other words, he made the inner conversion of the self more dependent on the outward behaviour of the person. Arminius also liberated Protestantism from its strict dependence on
the Word by sanctioning pious human acts as representations of the sacred.
In many ways the moderate views of his followers seemed to harken back
to humanism. The Christian self could have a part in deciding its own
destiny. No wonder the teachings of Arminius were abominated by strict
Calvinists, who saw them as just a step away from Catholicism. Maurice of
Nassau moved swiftly to repress them. An international synod held at
Dordrecht in 1618 denounced Arminian "innovations" and instructed min-
isters "to extirpate them as tares and weeds out of the Lord's Field."[66]

The Arminians were not so easily rooted out, and they soon began to
influence kings. One Arminian intellectual who escaped Prince Maurice's
vengeance—he was smuggled out of prison in a trunk full of books—was
the jurist Hugo Grotius. He took shelter in France, where he wrote his
famous *Rights of War and Peace*. Behind this work lies the Arminian conviction that human beings have broad opportunities for autonomous judgment and are not merely subjected to the will of God. In a stunning reversal

of the Calvinist conception of an all-powerful deity, Grotius maintained that natural law was "so unalterable, that it cannot be changed even by God himself."[67] The amazing unorthodoxy of this statement cannot have been lost on a mind as steeped in godliness as Gustavus II Adolphus. Yet Gustavus greatly admired Grotius, whom he made Swedish representative to France. Clearly, the Swedish Joshua was not content to depend solely on hopes of the millennium. He wanted an unshakeable natural foundation for his worldly ambitions, which he found in the work of a notorious anti-Calvinist.

Charles I went much further in his attraction to Arminianism. He promoted to bishoprics clerical moderates whose views made them equivalents of the Dutch Arminians.[68] These men had emerged out of an English school of humanist thought, and criticism of predestination was not always their main focus. They tended to lay more emphasis on the sacraments or on the dignity of priests and bishops. Like Dutch Arminians, however, they rejected strict Calvinism. William Laud, for example, attacked predestination for making God "the most fierce and unreasonable tyrant in the world." Compare this with the words of a moderate Dutch theologian in debate with a Calvinist: "You turn God into a tyrant and an executioner."[69] Such opinions caused fury among Calvinists on both sides of the North Sea.

King Charles embraced English Arminianism partly as an antidote to godly culture, a means of sanctioning his flamboyant artistic taste. James I's Calvinist reservations about the arts were discarded at his son's luminous court. Early in his reign the king posed as Apollo in a painting by Gerard Honthorst, which shows Buckingham as Mercury, presenting to him the seven Liberal Arts.[70] Charles sought to foster them all in the grand Renaissance manner of Queen Elizabeth. His fondness for acting in masques was shared by his French Catholic queen, Henrietta Maria, daughter of Henry IV. It was during Charles's reign that Inigo Jones perfected the theatrical production of masques, separating the stage from the audience through a proscenium arch and directing attention at the figure of the king through single-point perspective. Even Jones's erstwhile collaborator Ben Jonson denounced such innovations as "Idolatry." The radical puritan William Prynne used harsher words, going so far as to include Henrietta Maria in the category of "women actors, notorious whores."[71]

The intellectual underpinnings of court masques were more consistent with Arminianism than with Calvinism. Jones's stage resembled an altar, fenced off from the congregation by rails. The masque itself signified a partial return to the sacrificial theatre of the Mass, by which believers participated in the sufferings and triumphs of Christ's body. The triumphant power of love, which Kevin Sharpe has seen as essential to the Caroline masque, paralleled the Arminian insistence on divine love as the basis of salvation. Furthermore, the masque developed on a Neoplatonic assumption that "all the laws of nature have been understood and the attacks of mutability defeated by the rational power of the mind."[72] This was closer to the Arminian emphasis on human effort than to the Calvinist reliance on an inscrutable Providence.

Similarly, Charles's interest in the visual arts skirted the aesthetic boundaries of Protestantism. He was the greatest collector of paintings in seventeenth-century Europe. The most famous artists he patronized were two Flemish Catholics, Peter Paul Rubens and Anthony van Dyck. Rubens apotheosized the king's father on the gorgeous ceiling of the Banqueting House in Whitehall Palace, which could be seen as a crypto-Catholic sanctification of James I.[73] He also depicted Charles as St. George, probably in connection with the king's passionate interest in the Order of the Garter, whose badge is the saint's cross. The theme can only have been offensive to those who denigrated the worship of saints.[74] Van Dyck's paintings of Charles on horseback, striking the pose of a Roman emperor, were likewise meant to remind viewers of St. George, and perhaps of Christ, whose features in popular iconography resembled those of Charles.[75]

The king's lavish taste was meant to proclaim his own manliness and chivalric virtue before an admiring audience of courtiers.[76] It seems a sad compensation for his military inadequacies. Few would have noticed the irony at the time. Caroline court art, like all the productions of Renaissance monarchy, was intended for only a small group of well-heeled insiders who grasped its hidden meanings. It ignored mass culture and did not sustain a "public sphere" of discourse. In fact, great public celebrations were mostly abandoned during the course of Charles's reign. The king did not enjoy contact with his subjects; he even made the royal touch less accessible.[77] Outside the court, his private extravagances served as goads to those who had little wish to pay for them and may have found them redolent of Popery. Perhaps we should not contrast court culture too strongly with the

9. Anthony van Dyck, *Charles I on Horseback with M. De St. Antoine* (1633), painting. Buckingham Palace.

Photo: The Royal Collection, copyright 1998 Her Majesty Queen Elizabeth II.

culture of the godly. After all, courtiers with Puritan leanings danced in the king's masques and commissioned paintings from van Dyck. Nonetheless, it is hard to see how godliness could be reconciled with the artistic tastes of Charles I. In fact, no Protestant ruler anywhere in Europe rivalled the splendours of the Caroline court until the age of the prince regent.[78]

Charles made no secret of his desire to cast off the political mantle of Calvinist kingship. This goal became an obsession with him as a result of the conflict over the forced loan in 1626 and 1627. The loan was proclaimed in order to finance the war with Spain. Charles tried to justify the loan in terms that would appeal to the godly, drawing attention to "the late disaster (the chance of war) which hath fallen upon our dearest uncle the King of Denmark" and warning that "our common enemy will in an instant become master of all Germany." The response from Puritans, however, was recalcitrance. Pamphleteers stridently denounced the loan, warning that "subjects may disobey and refuse an unworthie Kinge his command or request if it be more then of duety wee ough unto him."[79] For the first time in Stuart England, the instruments of mass culture were directed against royal policy.

Charles did not forgive his godly critics. He amply rewarded Arminians for their loyalty to him during the forced-loan affair. One peer complained that "almost the whole world was turned Arminian."[80] In the raucous session of 1629 a subcommittee of the House of Commons drew up a set of resolutions that bluntly condemned "the subtle and pernicious spreading of the Arminian faction; whereby they have kindled such a fire of division in the very bowels of the State, as if not speedily extinguished, it is of itself sufficient to ruin our religion."[81] For Puritans, Arminianism meant subtlety, artifice, falseness, all the evils of an empty, idolatrous theatricality. Deeply offended, Charles ordered Parliament to adjourn, leading to the tumultuous scene in which Sir John Eliot and his supporters held down the Speaker while they read out three resolutions attacking Arminianism and unjust taxes.[82] This was a true godly theatre, representing divine will. It was also a scenario ominously reminiscent of Vienna in June 1619, although without a besieging army at the city gates.

In other kingdoms the political crisis might have led to insurrection, but in England public outrage was always mediated by the conservatism of parliamentarians whose deepest desire was to support the king.

Unfortunately, Charles kept pushing them too far, creating an ever-wider cultural gap. By the end of 1629 he was determined to rule without them, which is what he did for the next decade. The historian Kevin Sharpe has judged the period of "personal rule" a considerable success, at least down to 1637; but he underestimates the innovative aspects of the regime's religious policy, which proved shocking to many contemporaries.[83] As archbishop of Canterbury, William Laud suppressed Puritan preaching, censored writings about predestination, and promulgated ordinances concerning the "decent" placement of altars. This amounted to a concerted campaign against Calvinism.[84]

Another element in the anti-Calvinist programme was the reissuing of the Declaration of Sports, an old ordinance of King James that made certain festive activities lawful on the Sabbath. Puritans found it objectionable not only because it sanctioned maypoles, rush-bearings, and morris dances but also because it seemed to encourage the contempt of the common people for their godly superiors.[85] Indeed, the declaration provided the starting point for a popularly based "festive royalism" that was to have political importance over the next century; but this was far from its original intention. It condemned licentiousness, forbade "unlawful games" like bull-baiting, bear-baiting, and bowling, required church attendance, and stipulated that sports should train men for military service. Thus, the declaration was in keeping with police ordinances in the rest of Protestant Europe, although it gave the impression of a retreat from such controls.

Like so much in the English Arminian programme, the Declaration of Sports was a throwback to the humanist moderation of the Renaissance. In a confessional age, it seemed a confused and contradictory measure. The same lack of clear direction can be detected in Arminian political writings, which raised the mystical claims of sacral kingship to dizzying heights.[86] Robert Sybthorpe maintained that the king "doth whatsoever pleaseth him, where the *word of the King* is, there is *power.*" Matthew Wren hinted at the monarch's innate or natural divinity by stressing "the Image of God which is upon kings . . . the lively Image of his Divine Power." In a similar vein, Roger Maynwaring argued that royal power "is not meerely *humane*, but *Superhumane*, and indeed no lesse then a *Power Divine.*"[87] These writers went far beyond James I's mainstream Protestant views, envisaging a monarchy that was free of human weakness or confessional bonds.

Only one anti-Calvinist writer explored supreme power in terms that looked towards the rational state; but his chief work remained unpublished, perhaps because he knew how it would be received. Sir Robert Filmer was an obscure country gentleman who wrote *Patriarcha* around 1630. Like Bodin, Filmer traced the origins of government to patriarchal power. "I see not then," he wrote, "how the children of Adam, or of any man else, can be free from subjection to their parents. And this subjection of children is the only fountain of all regal authority, by the ordination of God himself."[88] The "natural duties" of a father were identical to those of a king: "We find them all one, without any difference at all but in the latitude or extent of them." The king could not be restrained by laws, for "as kingly power is by the law of God, so it hath no inferior law to limit it."[89]

Like Grotius, whose writings he knew but disapproved of, Filmer derived political power from immutable laws of nature, and he envisioned sovereignty as irresistible. "That power is called sovereign," wrote Grotius, "whose actions are not subject to the controul of any other power, so as to be annulled at the pleasure of any other human will."[90] For Grotius, natural liberty had been irretrievably lost through the acceptance of sovereignty; for Filmer, it had never existed. Grotius sought to extend the king's sphere of action beyond religious restraints. For his part, Filmer was convinced that not even the laws of God might interfere with the power of patriarchy: "Not only in human laws, but even in divine, a thing may be commanded contrary to law, and yet obedience to such a command is necessary."[91] The submission of the self to its ruler, therefore, was natural and inevitable rather than moral and voluntary. Such opinions placed Filmer alongside Grotius on the outer limits of Christian political thought, on the verge of rational authoritarianism.

*Patriarcha* was not typical of Arminian political writings. Nor can it be claimed that Bodinian sovereignty became the property of Charles I's apologists. The writer who made the most extensive use of Bodin was the anti-Arminian Sir John Eliot, in two treatises he penned while imprisoned for his conduct in the parliamentary session of 1629. The first was a paraphrase of the writings of Henning Arnisaeus; the second, a comparison of governance in society and the individual self, entitled *The Monarchie of Man*. Eliot affirmed that "Sovereignty cannot be yeilded to subjects: for then we should leave noe difference between them and their rulers, and that would bringe in Anarchie."[92] This was hardly the view of a revolutionary. Yet he also asserted of divine law that "noe Pope or prince can alter it, or take away. for it is iniury to god to presume to abrogate his lawe, yea it is treason against god."[93] The inviolability of religious truth and of the Christian self, or "Monarchie of Man," in which it was invested was what put Eliot at odds with his king.

In espousing sovereignty along with responsible subjection, Eliot was a harbinger of the rational state. The same cannot be said of Charles I and his Arminian allies, other than Filmer. Horrified by mass culture and the rough-and-tumble of political theatre, the Arminians turned back to humanist concepts of order, which their critics decried as flimsy justifications for reason of state. The Arminians did not provide convincing moral grounds for personal identification with the king's religious and cultural stance. The failure of their efforts would ultimately oblige a king who shunned publicity to defend himself publicly against the accusations of his own subjects.

## The Dilemma of Louis the Just

Charles I sought to escape from confessional culture. By contrast, Louis XIII was attracted to it, but with the memory of the Catholic League behind him, he knew that he could not embrace it without risk. Could the zealous aspirations of reformed religion be reconciled with royal authority? The *politiques*, or *bons français*, officers and dependents of the Bourbon state, answered negatively, just as the Arminians did in England. They deplored any surrender of sovereignty to the devout. The politique writer Guez de Balzac vilified the *dévots* as "those men strong in malice, who raise to the sky impure hands . . . all bloody from their parricides."[94] He had not forgotten Jacques Clément, or Ravaillac. Neither had his patron, Cardinal Richelieu, who guided the king's councils after 1630 in a humanist direction, deepening the cultural cleavage within the French elite.

Who were these dévots, whom Guez de Balzac feared so much? They were petty nobles and bourgeois, gentlemen and merchants, lawyers and office-bearers. Since the demise of the League, they had become more respectable; but their cultural values remained ascetic, inward-looking, and, by conventional standards, feminine. Among the devout were a remarkable number of prominent women: the famous Mère Angélique of Port-Royal convent; Jeanne de Chantal, founder of the Order of the Visitation; the mystic Barbe Acarie, who became Sister Marie de l'Incarnation; not to mention the Ursulines and a veritable holy regiment of Benedictine abbesses. Closely supervised by male protectors like St. Vincent de Paul and Cardinal Bérulle, these dévotes may have done little to change gender inequities, but their lives of submissive virtue were widely admired and imitated, by men as well as women. Scorning the public observances and saint's cults typical of popular worship, they cultivated self-discipline and a Christocentric piety based on private prayer. At the same time, they did not wholly withdraw from social life. Their spiritual guidebook was the *Introduction to the Holy Life* by St. François de Sales, which firmly admonished them to involve themselves in the world, even to the point of engaging in questionable amusements like dancing.[95]

The defeat of the League had turned the dévots away from the active purification of politics. They had even developed important ties to the court. The keeper of the seals, Michel de Marillac, was a famous example of a courtly dévot. He was uncle to Louise de Marillac, a laywoman who organized foundations for the sick and the poor. He was also a close friend of Marie de l'Incarnation, who once had a vision of the Virgin Mary in his presence. Still, the taint of "parricide," of undermining natural patriarchy and royal government, hung around him as it did all the devout. Marillac had supported the League as a headstrong youth. For her part, Marie de l'Incarnation had been married to a Parisian magistrate known as "the lackey of the League." Her female followers won the contempt of Pierre de l'Estoile as early as 1597, when they "ran about the town complaining of the Protestant preaching."[96] Although they had given up their wilder habits, the dévots continued to long for the rule of Catholic virtue, and they still hedged royal divinity within the boundaries of human fallibility. Cardinal Bérulle, who was Marie de l'Incarnation's cousin, wrote that monarchs should follow the divine will, not their own interests; and he addressed King Louis, with calculated reserve, as "a God not by essence, but by power, a God not by nature, but by grace."[97]

This self-reflective, spiritual, feminized Catholicism, so different in emphasis from Protestant confessional culture yet so similar in its methods, was a challenge to the masculine sway of French sovereignty. The challenge was expressed paradoxically—not in open resistance but through a language of personal salvation that exalted docility, meekness, simplicity, and other supposedly female qualities, quite the opposite of what was expected from the ruling elite of a warrior kingdom. The Bourbon monarchy could not simply stand firm in the face of such a movement, whose influence had seeped into all the muscles of governance. The public response of an agitated Crown, however, changed markedly over time—from appeasement to civil war, from confessionalization to humanist authoritarianism. It was a bewildering, disjointed performance, based more on the episodic scenarios of the *ballet de cour* than on the structural clarity of a classical drama.

Within four years of Louis XIII's accession the threat of rebellion had obliged the regent Marie de Médicis to forgo ritual declarations of sovereignty and turn to the Estates General. It was the only institution other than the Crown that could claim to represent the corpus mysticum of the whole nation, so its summoning was a partial surrender of sovereign authority. The last such assembly had supported the League. This one was supposed to forge political unity—in part by appeasing the dévots. Instead, it worsened everything. The clergy wanted ratification of the decrees of the Council of Trent; the lawyers of the Third Estate demanded that the clergy formally renounce the doctrine that the pope could depose the king. The regent refused to commit herself to any side. The debates of the Estates General led not to reform but to political paralysis.[98]

The monarch now had to reclaim by force his role as the natural centre of political order. The revival of sovereignty took the form of a struggle for control of the court between the king and his mother, whose female authority was denounced as "unnatural." Conflict was brought to a boil by a brutal act of reason of state: the assassination by the king's friends of Marie's advisor, the Maréchal d'Ancre. Guez de Balzac later exulted at how the court had been "purged of the shameful domination that established itself on the ruins of Royalty." Two subsequent rebellions in 1619 and 1620 by the queen mother's dévot supporters were soon defeated.[99] As in Henry IV's reign, sovereignty was established through violence. Yet it continued to lack a firm cultural basis, even in the king's inner circle. The court was still a morass of factional clientage, not a box garden of obedience and personal discipline. Seeking to tame its wildness, the king suddenly dropped the sword he had raised against the devout and instead instigated a public campaign of confessionalization, centred on the reduction of the Huguenots.

The shift towards confessional culture suited the royal temperament. The young Louis XIII was a pious Catholic, as happy at prayer as at the hunt. Although his sexual abstinence was arguably due to repressed homosexuality rather than asceticism, it was widely interpreted as an indication of his saintliness. "In one word, he has no concern for loving those pleasures which are common to men and beasts," wrote Guez de Balzac.[100] As befitted a king in an age of mass culture, he had no secret life; everything about him was transparently moral. Even today the glowing visage of Louis XIII can be seen in many paintings in French churches, where he is linked with veneration of the Eucharist or with Saint Louis, whose cult he restored in 1618. These works enhanced the confessional aspect of Louis's rulership by connecting his public face with the "explosion of images" characteristic of early seventeenth-century French Catholicism.[101]

King Louis's holy war against heresy was accompanied by a flood of publicity. The dramatist Pierre Corneille lauded the re-establishment of Catholicism in the Protestant principality of Béarn as a supreme example of confessional zeal. The king's valour "takes the honour of heaven as the aim of his victory, / And Religion fights Impiety, / It holds under its feet stamped-out Heresy, / Churches are its forts and its most beautiful trophy."[102] The king pressed on with military campaigns against the Huguenots, culminating in the siege and capture of the Protestant stronghold of La Rochelle. "The Huguenot republic had ceased to exist," wrote the historian A. D. Lublinskaya, who saw Louis's objectives in terms of sovereignty rather than confessionalism. For the king's publicists, however, fighting the Huguenots was an act of faith, amounting to a "second war of religion," to use Robert Sauzet's epithet. At Jesuit colleges, for example, Louis's victories were celebrated with allegorical ballets showing the triumphs of the true faith over heresy.[103]

Louis the Just, as he was popularly called, could now rival the emperor in the international theatre of confessional politics. "The Church has its revenge for its holy places that have been knocked down, and for its images that have been broken," Guez de Balzac noted with satisfaction.[104] Already the image of Louis's authority had shifted from brute strength to

Christian virtue. This emphasis on pious self-control might have signalled the spread of personal discipline at court and the beginning of a new phase in Elias's "civilizing process." But the path towards a "court society" remained blocked by the conflicting claims of confessionalism and sovereignty.

The marks of continuing cultural strife can be detected beneath the dazzling surfaces of the paintings that Peter Paul Rubens devoted in 1624 to the life of Marie de Médicis. In these twenty-four enormous allegorical canvases, Christian motifs are combined with a gorgeous Neostoic symbolism in order to glorify the piety and authority, not of the ruling monarch, but of his mother. Subtle parallels are repeatedly drawn between Marie and the Virgin Mary, between Henry IV and God. In the huge depiction of her coronation, the Queen Mother appears to receive her crown from Henry, who stands in a loge above her, framed like a holy icon. In other portrayals Marie seems to stand for ecclesia, the Church, itself—first oppressed, then militant, finally triumphant. Louis XIII is shown as a secondary figure, spatially dominated by his mother's presence. He even takes the part of her dutiful worshipper. As was quickly realized at the time, the artist had been instructed to chastise King Louis for his quarrels with his mother, who seems to exercise superior power here, in spite of Bodin or the Salic Law, which excluded female succession. The whole court was privy to the king's embarrassment, which some of its members evidently enjoyed. Rubens seems to suggest that Louis XIII can only achieve the destiny set for him by his divine father through submission to his mother, who incarnates the Church.[105]

In short, Louis's piety had not secured his authority, even at this own court. Yet he did not finally break with his mother and the dévots until he had reached the limits of moral reform. In 1629 he tried to purify French government through a massive ordinance presented to the Parlement of Paris. Scholarly attention has mostly focused on the potential administrative consequences of the ordinance, which would have limited the ability of the parlement to delay registration of royal edicts. A multitude of other changes, however, were included in the document, ranging from rules for clerical appointments and restrictions on patronage to the censorship of books and prohibitions against drunkenness and gambling. It was the most sweeping French police ordinance of the seventeenth century. The impetus

10. Peter-Paul Rubens, *Coronation of Marie de Médicis*, from *The Life of Marie de Médicis* (1624), painting. Louvre Museum.

Photo: Réunion des musées nationaux, Paris.

for this top-to-bottom government clean-up seems, not surprisingly, to have arisen from the zealous spirit of Michel de Marillac.[106]

Moral reform, however, had begun to threaten a delicate political balance. By trying to clean up patronage and corruption, the ordinance of 1629 was an affront to many great nobles and venal office-bearers.[107] The parlement did register Marillac's ordinance, under extreme pressure from the Crown; but its members declined to enforce what they derisorily referred to as the *Code Michau*, the "Mickey Code." Although the language of the devout was beginning to be heard in their ranks, the *parlementaires* were more interested in maintaining their own privileges than in the moral cleansing of the realm. Strongly imbued with humanist values, the judges were no puritans.[108]

Facing such opposition, confessionalization began to unravel. Marillac fell from office, and Richelieu became chief minister. The king now allowed himself to be carried into the scenario of a crusade against the Habsburg "Monster," as the cardinal moved towards French involvement in the Thirty Years' War. Richelieu explained to his master that "if the king resolves on war, he must leave aside all thought of repose, of saving money and of regulation within his kingdom."[109] Louis hoped to become "the most powerful monarch of the world and the most esteemed prince," the protector of Christendom, through the downfall of the Habsburgs. The purifying zeal of confessionalization gave way to the alluring Renaissance fantasy of restoring the empire of Charlemagne.[110]

The king remained personally devout, and he continued to sanction private efforts at Christian discipline. Confessionalization was promoted through the efforts of the Company of the Blessed Sacrament, which set up a secret system of religious surveillance throughout France. The company was a kind of clandestine alternative to the state, and it went much further towards disciplining the self than did state-sponsored police measures. It pursued not just external observance but also the inner purification of its elite membership. Within its cloistered confines the Catholic League's vision of the Christian polity had come true, and the ordering of the self was harmoniously united with obedience to the king.[111]

Outside the company, however, Richelieu held sway. The cardinal was no opponent of religious reform. He had vigorously pursued it as bishop of Luçon and in the Estates General. He opposed duelling, because "nothing is so contrary to Christianity as the unbridled rage of duels," and he favoured strict restraints on irregular marriages, one of the chief social goals of reformed Catholicism.[112] Furthermore, he was not committed to a policy of reason of state. As W. F. Church has shown, Richelieu was no disciple of the Machiavel, and if he practised "mixed prudence," it was because he saw it as compatible with Christian morality.[113] He was not much concerned about philosophical rationalism either, as he demonstrated in the famous case of demonic possession among the nuns of the Ursuline convent at Loudun. At a time when the Parlement of Paris was becoming increasingly sceptical about accusations of sorcery, Richelieu took the opposite approach. Although he privately doubted their validity, he encouraged the nuns in their diabolical allegations, which he used to destroy one of his political critics.[114]

Nonetheless, the cardinal had no sympathy with the spiritual fervour that was sweeping through the French church. In company with Laud, he was an enemy to passion in private life as well as in politics, and he saw proper religious belief as conducive to external order rather than internal purity. He advised the monarch that, "although devotion is necessary for kings, it ought to be devoid of all over-scrupulousness." He was particularly critical of the influence of women on government, "since their sex is more given to transports of devotion."[115] Richelieu was obsessed with restoring a classical grandeur whose basis was natural hierarchy. This was evident in the words of a memorial he drafted for the king in 1625: "Experience tells us that order maintains States in their splendour, just as, on the other hand, disorder causes their total ruin, and considering how the diverse troubles arising in the last several years in this kingdom have introduced and left confusion and disorder in all its parts; [we shall seek] to remedy this as much as we can, for the glory of God, the ease of our conscience, the welfare and tranquillity of our subjects, and the re-establishment of the grandeur of this State."[116] The cardinal saw order as dependent on nature, just as in a family. His goal was summed up by his admirer Guez de Balzac: "The State will be no more trouble to run than a well-regulated house."[117]

In many respects Richelieu was an old-fashioned humanist. He was fascinated by classical pedagogy and wanted to educate the sons of the nobility so as "to render them capable one day of serving the King and the State."[118] In religion, he sought to return to the peace that had preceded the League. As *proviseur* of the Sorbonne, he strenuously opposed any public debate over doctrinal issues—as did Laud over predestination. Richelieu promoted a cultural strategy that emphasized classical harmony over baroque tension. He made sure that the ballets de cour—the French equivalent of the masque—gave an impression of rhythmic composure within the state. Every gesture of the body on stage should reflect the triumph of order over passion.[119] Richelieu's creation of the Académie Française was intended to impose on French literature the classical rules of discipline and unity. As Marc Fumaroli has put it, the domain of the

Académie was "the language of the monarchy, which it sought to bring to a perfection worthy of the grandeur reconquered by the crown of France."[120]

Catholic dévots were driven towards opposition by Richelieu's humanist vision. They feared that his war policy would divide the universal Church, assist the Protestant heretics, and retard efforts at internal reform. Such apprehensions were not misplaced. Alain Lottin has argued that the hardships of war brought about a return to the uncontrolled popular devotions of pre-Tridentine days. "The political choice made by Richelieu and Louis XIII," Lottin concludes, "because of reason of state, effectively had . . . the disastrous consequences that the *dévots* feared for the future of Catholic reform in Europe." In fact, the most strident apologists for the conflict were episcopal careerists with little commitment to reform, like Bishop Cohon of Nîmes.[121] Yet there was no organized resistance to the cardinal's war. Indeed, by the mid-1630s the dévots were increasingly divided among themselves by Jansenism, which disdained any compromise with worldly values.

Cornelius Jansen, bishop of Ypres in the Spanish Netherlands, argued as Augustine had that salvation depended more on divine grace than on personal effort.[122] His followers retained the passionate, sensual language of Catholic mysticism but adopted an approach to personal conversion that was often associated with Protestantism. "This active grace by which God moves the heart of the just . . . is always joined to a delectation and to a secret pleasure which carries away the will," wrote the Abbé de St.-Cyran, spiritual advisor to the nuns of Port-Royal.[123] The Christian must examine the self for evidence of justification, not turn to worldly conventions. As Fumaroli has noted, St.-Cyran's inward-looking rhetoric joined dévot spirituality with the subjectivity of Montaigne; but it rejected the sovereign "I" of the humanist in favour of self-abandonment before the majesty of God.[124]

Nothing could have been further from the views of Richelieu, for whom good order was always linked to sovereignty over the self. His dislike of the new theology hardened in 1635, when Jansen wrote a pamphlet castigating French foreign policy for aiming "to reverse the true faith, to profane the mysteries and ceremonies, and to annihilate all that Jesus Christ established for the salvation of men." Furious, the cardinal imprisoned St.-Cyran, who remained in captivity until his death.[125] This was a chilling warning to Jansen's adherents. Yet Richelieu had to acknowledge the spreading reality of Jansenism, which he could not stamp out. It is a remarkable irony that the most insightful portraits of the cardinal were painted by a Flemish Jansenist, Philippe de Champaigne.

Richelieu did not break Champaigne's brush, but he did bend Corneille's pen. His treatment of the dramatist illustrates how the cardinal's humanist authoritarianism clashed not just with Jansenism but even with more conventional forms of Catholic mass culture. In spite of the war against Spain, the most popular drama of 1637 was *Le Cid* by Corneille, a play about a Spanish hero, based on a story retold by Juan de Mariana, the infamous upholder of tyrannicide. On the surface, *Le Cid* was hardly subversive. It showed the terrible consequences of duelling and elevated royal justice above aristocratic honour. Yet the plot tends to validate the sentiment voiced in it by an irate nobleman that "However great Kings may be, they are what we are, / They can make mistakes like other men." The king of Castile does not act very wisely in *Le Cid*. His interventions worsen the situation, and his opinions come close to Machiavellianism: "Time has often enough rendered legitimate / What seemed at first not able to be done without crime."[126]

*Le Cid* can be read as a Christian Neostoic critique of contemporary political morality. The offensive aspects of the play, however, became clear only after it had been performed at the Louvre and the Palais-Cardinal. It was attacked by the playwright Georges Scudéry for violating artistic unity and for plagiarism—in short, for being too Spanish. An ardent royalist, Scudéry added pointedly that Corneille "should treat the persons of Kings with more respect." Richelieu himself, now alerted to danger, pressured the Académie Française into judging the dispute. The result was a series of rebukes for Corneille on most of Scudéry's points, including the weak character of the king. Corneille learned his lesson and dedicated his next tragedy to the cardinal; but he did not forget the humiliation of *Le Cid*. After the death of his patron and former antagonist, the dramatist wrote a surprisingly honest epitaph: "He did me too much good to say ill of him, / He did me too much bad to say good of him."[127] In this terse statement Corneille summed up the ambiguity of Richelieu's cultural victories.

More amenable to the cardinal's humanist goals was Guez de Balzac, for whom order was reflected in a perfectly controlled literary style. He shocked Louis XIII and the theologians of the Sorbonne with his political treatise *Le prince,* in which he implied that the king was without vice and "capable, if I may say so, of rejuvenating the Universe."[128] Guez de Balzac shunned the vulgarity of mass culture, writing only for select audiences. He lavished fawning praise on the cardinal: "It will be through your prudence that there will be no more rebellions among us, nor tyranny among men. . . . That the people will leave Liberty, Religion and the Public good in the hands of its Superiors: & that from legitimate Government, & perfect obedience will be born that felicity which the *Politiques* search for, and which is the end of civil life."[129] Richelieu, in short, would realize the humanist promise of the sovereign self. For words like these, which should rightly have been bestowed on a king, Guez de Balzac was favoured with membership in the Académie Française.

His confident predictions, however, were not fulfilled; the people did not give Richelieu their trust. Marillac had once warned the cardinal that "the miseries and afflictions of the people of France, who were languishing under very great and incredible poverties, made peace desirable."[130] He was vindicated after 1635 by an explosion of peasant rebellions throughout France, protests against the exigencies of war. The *croquants* of Périgord went so far as to claim that high taxes were being levied "behind the king's back." Such expressions testified to a lack of support not just for the war but also for Richelieu's dominance. Provincial accents had not fully surrendered to a Parisian grammar of obedience.[131]

Like England, the French monarchy was lurching towards a showdown between the Crown and the godly, between classical order and mass culture, between humanism and the reformed Christian self. Before the storm broke, King Louis made a final attempt to appease the devout. In December 1637, following the suppression of the croquants, he signed an engagement placing his kingdom under the protection of the Virgin Mary. A desperate plea for peace at home, the so-called Vow of Louis XIII echoed Ferdinand II's invocations of Mary and was designed to convince the pious of the king's undiminished religious fervour. Two years later the birth of a royal heir was depicted in numerous paintings and prints that showed Queen Anne in the guise of the Virgin.[132] This symbolic surrender to female spiritual guidance was celebrated by popular processions throughout France. The masculine voice of sovereignty was temporarily muted,

11. Philippe de Champaigne, *Vow of Louis XIII* (1637), painting.
Photo: Musée des Beaux-Arts de Caen; Martine Seyve, photographer.

and the devout inched a little closer towards acceptance of a supreme human authority. The king's last shift, however, did not give security to France. Sovereignty could not stand on its own; but it had not been able to accommodate confessional culture either. The devout blamed this failure on Richelieu. In the end, even the pliable Guez de Balzac was disillusioned by his patron's manipulations, and he retired to his country estate, seeking an interior peace that his nation seemed to have lost.

## The King of Poland Fails to Smite His Enemy

The devout audience did not exist everywhere in Europe. In Poland the theatre of royal virtue was played out before empty seats. In Russia too a "public sphere" of discourse barely existed; but the Orthodox community set up its own fledgling version of royal theatre in the face of an outside religious threat. The results were a broadened sense of identification with the Crown, and the first stages of confessional reform. Developments in Eastern Europe confirmed the vital importance of a cultural exchange between monarchy and a godly public in the reformation of both the state and the self.

The Polish Commonwealth was more rent by religious division than any other monarchy in Europe. The protection of the gentry ensured the preservation of Calvinism, while Arianism flourished in the towns. The Arians doubted the divinity of Christ, and some of them preached in favour of communal property, personal equality, and non-allegiance to the state— messages antithetical to confessionalization, whether Catholic or Protestant. Their sectarian individualism presented a block not just to the state but to the religious disciplining of the common people as well.[133] Meanwhile, Counter-Reformation piety expanded very slowly on the local level. Jesuit theatrical productions had to contend not only against a thriving secular stage but also against a Protestant school theatre set up by the Bohemian exile Jan Comenius. Where it took hold, Catholic reform spread with the encouragement of the nobles themselves, especially through pilgrimages and devotions to the Virgin; but such practices did not supplant the pre-Tridentine popular religion of mystery plays, Christmas carolling, and semi-magical beliefs. Among the peasants, reformed Catholic culture made slow headway against the vestiges of paganism.[134]

King Sigismund III Vasa lacked the political power to reduce the disunity of his realms.[135] To be sure, the middle classes in urban areas often sided with the king against his noble opponents. But riots against Protestant chapels and the suppression of non-Catholic worship in royal towns failed to dislodge the heretics. When the royal chaplain, Piotr Skarga, warned the *Sejm* that God would inflict terrible punishments on Poland for its heresies, his words fell on deaf ears. In 1606 Sigismund faced the humiliation of a *rokosz*, or confederation, an armed insurrection by nobles who feared the imposition of Catholic confessionalization. The rokosz was directly aimed at the Jesuits, particularly Skarga, the "greatest disturber of the republic." "Our ancestors," the insurgents declared, "knew that they were born nobles rather than Catholics, that they were not descended from Levi, and

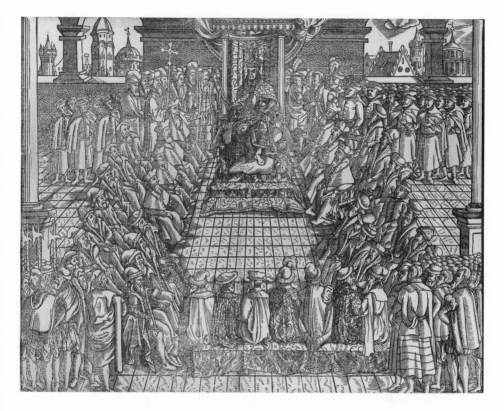

12. *The Polish Parliament,* from Alexander Guagninus, *Sarmati Europe Descriptio* (Cracow, 1578), engraving.

Photo: British Library, London.

that Poland is a political kingdom, not a clerical one."[136] The social and national identities of the elite superseded religious self-definition.

Sigismund's only big religious victory was won against Orthodoxy. Through the Union of Brest in 1595, Orthodox Ukrainians who rejected the new patriarchate of Moscow entered into communion with the Catholic Church.[137] Fifteen years later, soon after the suppression of the rokosz, the king's forces marched east towards Moscow. This sudden move seems to have been designed to bolster Sigismund's waning authority by by-passing the factious Sejm and focusing gentry attention on the common enemy, Orthodox Russia. The army's commander or hetman, Stanisłas Zółkiewski, recorded that "the expedition to Moscow was praised" in the *sejmiki,* or provincial assemblies, but he added knowingly that in the Sejm "it was neither proposed nor discussed."[138]

Żółkiewski did not see the expedition in confessional terms, and in his memoirs he never mentioned Catholicism as a motive for war. His own political goal was to stabilize Polish kingship by ensuring hereditary succession. Once he had reached Moscow, the hetman made an agreement with the boyar council that Sigismund's son, Crown Prince Władysłav, would become tsar. The boyars insisted on conversion to Orthodoxy, a point that Żółkiewski brushed aside in his account: "There was mention of the re-christening of the Crown Prince in the Muscovite faith and not a few other absurdities." He tried to convince Sigismund that making his son tsar would ensure his future election as king of Poland.[139] The staunchly Catholic king, however, baulked at the idea of his son turning Orthodox. His chancellor observed mockingly that "the heir has already been baptised; no other baptism has ever been recorded."[140]

As a well-educated man with humanist leanings, Hetman Żółkiewski may have been familiar with Bodin's *Six Books,* in which examples are cited of kings who united their "naturall" realms with those in which they had been elected, so as to "change an Aristocratique estate into a right Monarchie."[141] King Sigismund, however, had no desire to create sovereignty in Poland through a union with Muscovy. Like Ferdinand II, he dreamed of strengthening the monarchy by imposing Catholic standards of "virtuous conduct" on his subjects. He saw himself as a defender of the true faith, carrying the cross as well as the saber, which was how he was memorialized on a victory column in Warsaw.[142]

Sigismund proved to be no great warrior, however, and his eastern adventure ended in abject failure. He then began to turn his piety inwards, expressing it in his leisure hours through fussy allegorical paintings of religious subjects. His depiction as the harpist-king David in the royal chapel of the Carmelite Church at Cracow paid tribute to his artistic talents as well as his godly zeal. Yet Sigismund's court was never as brilliant as the courts of some of the great Polish-Lithuanian magnates, and he had little command over the methods of cultural dissemination. The Jagiellonian University at Cracow, for example, successfully resisted his attempts to hand it over to the Jesuits.[143]

Sigismund's last days in 1632 were marked by extraordinary personal devotions. When the king's will was read, it was noticed that "after the rebellion alias *Rokosz*" he had added to it a final statement "in which he protests openly before God that he was blamelessly innocent of giving cause for the spread of conspiracies in the Republic, either by a contract of change with the house of Austria, or by the lessening and abolition of all liberties, having God as witness of his innocence." It was a pathetic codicil. In the end, Sigismund wanted to be remembered as a politically correct Polish monarch, not as a would-be Bodinian sovereign or a creature of the Habsburgs. At least in death he found an audience. He was mourned even by the Arians, who mistook his caution for tolerance.[144]

His son Władysłav's reign was marked by numerous minor incidents of conflict between Catholics and members of other confessions. They culminated in a foolish attack by Arian students on a Catholic procession, which led to the closing of the famous Arian academy at Raków in 1638.[145] The king's official policy, however, tended towards a prudent, albeit un-easy, toleration, which is one reason why he is shown as the wise Solomon in the royal chapel at Cracow. His occasional dramatic gestures in the direction of Catholic confessionalization were quickly undone by the no-bility. In the late 1630s he founded the Order of the Immaculate Concep-tion, a seventy-two-member chivalric brotherhood limited to Catholic nobles who swore a special oath of allegiance to the monarch. Suspicious of the creation of a royalist party within the commonwealth, the Sejm de-manded the order's dissolution, and the king hastily complied.[146]

Władysław's troubles with the Sejm resembled Charles I's problems with Parliament; but in Poland the nobility never lost respect for the king, who was at least a brave commander in endless campaigns against the Russians and Turks. Thus, the commonwealth was held together by mili-tary enterprise rather than by confessional unity. Even Polish Arians, some of whom had shed their pacifism, exulted in Władysław's role as a warrior. A print of 1649 showed him riding on horseback like a Roman emperor through an elaborate triumphal arch.[147] If he was skilled at playing Caesar, however, he was less successful as Maecenas. His cultural endeavours, such as the introduction of Italian opera, did not have a wide impact. The popular theatre in Polish towns and the court theatres of the great nobles remained dominated by allegorical dramas and "minstrel comedies." The polite, sensuous charms of the opera, so similar in aesthetic purpose and political design to Jesuit morality plays, were confined to the royal theatre at Warsaw Castle.[148]

In contrast to the hero-king Władysław, the Russian tsars were saintly figures more than warrior leaders, and the preservation of religious conformity was always a main concern of their rulership. The confessional unity of Russia was essential to the development of a "public sphere" after 1605, when a series of tsars with questionable rights to the throne faced recurring crises of legitimacy. During this "Time of Troubles" the great boyar families competed for dominance at court, while the peasantry, resentful of the spread of serfdom, flocked to the standards of outrageous pretenders. Intervention by Catholic Poland finally rallied the Orthodox community behind a new dynasty, the Romanovs. In Moscow and the provinces a confessional public began to form—lacking almost all of the means of mass cultural production, to be sure, but bound together by a common ideological purpose. After 1619, moreover, the seeds of Orthodox confessionalization and of a reformed Christian selfhood were laid.

Boris Godunov, the "upstart" usurper, died in 1605 amid an uprising in favour of a pretender who claimed to be Dmitry, youngest son of Ivan the Terrible.[149] Assisted by a cabal of cynical Polish-Lithuanian nobles, who were buoyed by the image of a deliverer risen from the dead, and validated by rumours of miraculous signs like the mark of a white cross on his chest, the false Dmitry was able to take Moscow and proclaim himself tsar. Yet according to Isaac Massa, a Dutch merchant living in Moscow, Orthodox Muscovites were not much impressed by the impostor's new titles of "monarch" and "invincible."[150] To their disgust, Dmitry chose a Polish bride, who refused to be baptized into Orthodoxy. The tsarina was crowned in the cathedral, in the presence of Dmitry's Polish supporters. "Oh, how vexed the Muscovites were," exclaimed an amused Massa, "when they saw the Poles enter the church with plumes on their heads and weapons in their hands! . . . for they regard their churches as profaned by the presence of pagans." Foreign reports stress the religious basis of opposition to the false Dmitry. It was rumoured, for example, that he went unwashed to the cathedral, "followed by a pack of dogs." "Thus it dawned on them [the Russians] that they had been deceived," the diplomat Adam Olearius later noted.[151]

Soon the Orthodox would make Dmitry pay for his depravities. A group of boyars led by Vasily Shuisky raised up an angry crowd of Muscovites, to cries of "Death to the Poles! Let us take all they have!" Dmitry was caught trying to flee the palace and was hacked to death. His body was laid out on a table, "where the crowd came to rain insults for three days." After burial, the corpse was dug up by the infuriated citizens, who burned it and scattered the ashes. Many of Dmitry's Polish friends were brutally killed, and his wife's maids of honour were raped.[152] Through these rites of desecration committed against the bodies of the living and the dead, the community of the realm purified itself of the corrupting influence of the "Monster of Hell." As in the ceremonies of the Catholic League, behavioral conventions were violated so as to reassert, however paradoxically, the sacred foundations of moral order. René Girard's theories were never more brutally exemplified.

The Orthodox triumph, however, proved difficult to exploit. The new tsar, Vasily Shuisky, was merely the head of a boyar faction. He could not count on the loyalty of the peasants, many of whom sided with a new pretender, the second false Dmitry. He could not even count on his fellow boyars, some of whom invited King Sigismund to invade Russia. With Żółkiewski's army outside Moscow, the boyars deposed Shuisky and offered the throne to Crown Prince Władysław. For pious Russians this was the worst form of treachery—against religion itself. It was later remembered in a popular song that bewailed how "Many Russian boyars gave themselves to dishonor, / Gave themselves to dishonor, apostasized from Christ's faith."[153]

Those nobles who did not apostasize raised a provincial militia. Its organization may not have been much like the godly army of Gustavus II Adolphus, but it was similarly motivated by religious zeal. The militia recaptured Moscow in 1613 and set about to restore the monarchy. Following a procedure set under Boris Godunov, the choice of a new tsar was given to an electoral assembly, or *zemsky sobor*, consisting of representatives of the boyars, gentry, clergy, and towns, as well as the Crown and taxpaying peasants. Thus, the Orthodox *corpus mysticum* was assembled to give its sanction to a ruler steeped in the faith. After much factional wrangling, the Romanov clan emerged triumphant, and the sixteen-year-old Mikhail

Romanov was elected tsar. To legitimize this seemingly absurd choice, the tale was invented that the last Rurikid tsar had bequeathed the Russian throne to the Romanovs.[154]

Mikhail was not ruler of a Russian nation, a concept that had no broad significance in 1613. He was "most gentle tsar" of the Orthodox faithful, a religious community that had been bound together by years of struggle against the threat of Catholicism. His aim was to protect it, not to change it. As the historian R. O. Crummey has put it, "Mikhail's reign was a period of restoration. The government's central concern was to bring back the good old ways and to encourage the good old families."[155] In politics "the good old ways" meant that patronage, honours, and titles were lavished upon the chief boyars, while the local gentry continued to govern rural communities without much interference. In religion it meant the spread of popular miracle cults, which proliferated beyond the control of the church hierarchy.[156] Clearly, the Orthodox victory had not yet generated the disciplinary trends associated with confessional reform.

An Orthodox theatre of virtue, however, could be observed in the public ceremonial of the tsarist court. A pious routine of ritual observances was established by Tsar Mikhail's domineering father, the patriarch Filaret, who took the extraordinary title co-ruler. During a mission to Moscow in 1634, the German envoy Olearius recorded constant public religious occasions attended by the tsar, including processions, pilgrimages, and the veneration of icons or the cross. "The Russians exalt their Tsar very highly," Olearius observed, adding that they feared him "even more than God."[157] This was a crass exaggeration, but without doubt Mikhail's reign restored in the eyes of the community the tsar's tarnished reputation as protector of the faith.

The Catholic invasions had two other important confessional consequences. First, they connected the Russian monarchy with the religious politics of western Europe. Mikhail wrote to James I in 1617, seeking his support against the "unchristian" behaviour of Sigismund III, and in the 1630s he gave a small amount of economic support to Gustavus Adolphus.[158] Growing links with the rest of Christendom would later motivate Mikhail's successor to pursue a more intrusive approach to religion. Second, new contacts with Ukrainian Orthodoxy awakened in Russian clerics an ardent desire for reform, which began to make advances in the 1620s and 1630s through moralist religious writings and the first attempts to control popular religious practices. The tentative appearance of a mass culture can be discerned in the printing of religious books for public instruction, including a liturgy.[159] These were early signs of the confessional upheaval that was to come, through which a reformed Russian church would be fully subordinated to the power of the tsar.

## Politics of God, Government of Men

We have left until last the example of Spain, the heartland of what Maravall called "mass culture." To grasp why he saw Spain in this way, consider the Plaza Mayor. Three great public squares were laid out at the instigation of kings in the early seventeenth century: the Place Royale, now Place des Vosges, in Paris (1605–1611), the Plaza Mayor in Madrid (1617–1619), and Covent Garden in London (1630–1639). The public square was a stage-setting for monarchs to present themselves to their subjects. In France and England, however, the great squares rarely served this purpose. The Place Royale saw a spectacular equestrian carrousel in 1612; thereafter, it became little more than a fashionable address. Covent Garden never witnessed a royal event, and after 1656 it was the site of a fruit and vegetable market. Only the Plaza Mayor continued to host numerous state celebrations, including bullfights, the *autos de fé* of the Inquisition and the festivities that marked Prince Charles's visit to Madrid in 1623. After Philip II's death, the Spanish monarchy had come to depend on the mass culture of public occasions, which reaffirmed political unity, joining subject to ruler through shared experiences.[160]

It proved impossible, however, for a disjointed Spanish kingship to translate mass culture into an effective political authority. Significant discordances gradually emerged between the twin ideals of earthly power and spiritual purity. In addition, mass culture lent itself more to the outward projection than to the inner realization of confessional reform. The failure to surmount these difficulties contributed further to a widespread perception of Spanish "decline."[161]

Contemporary commentators interpreted "decline" as a predominantly moral issue. In addressing it, they followed two main paths. The *arbitristas*, or projectors, who flooded the king's councils with practical advice about how to cure Spain's maladies never gave up hope of reform through the imposition of effective policies by the Crown. Their humanist values often clashed with a Catholic idealism that called for a purified regime based on internalized piety. This was not a partisan conflict, as in France or England. It was a rift within minds as much as between them.

The arbitristas were lawyers, bureaucrats, and scholars, members of the broad class of *letrados,* the new educated elite of imperial Spain.[162] Their political thought owed much to the writings of the Italian ex-Jesuit Giovanni Botero, who had formulated an anti-Machiavellian conception of Christian reason of state. According to Botero, the preservation of the state depended upon "the exercise of the arts which win for a ruler the love and admiration of his people." While these arts might involve deceit as a means, the king should be guided in his ends by Christian morality—"God Himself has commanded that every ruler should have at his side a copy of His holy law and should observe it with the utmost care."[163] Thus, the royal actor was allowed to do some evil if it would lead to good. Such a position was hard to reconcile with the consistent moral transparency that the devout demanded of the reformed Christian self.

Like Botero, the arbitristas tended towards an outward, practical morality rather than spiritual interiority. Their proposals combined Boteran reason of state with a view of monarchy as the dynamic centre of an organic corpus mysticum. The king, according to the arbitrista Pedro Fernández de Navarette, was "the heart of the kingdom, which, giving to it spiritual vitality, conserves it in peace and justice." The monarchy, however, had been weakened by indulgence. "The sickness is extremely grave, but not incurable," Navarette cheerfully affirmed, adding that "as the major part of the infirmities of the realms has originated in the abundance of riches, badly spent and worse dissipated, it is unavoidable that . . . one prescribes for them temperance and frugality."[164] Navarrete targeted as examples of excess costly forms of dress, expensive jewels, grand buildings, luxurious meals, and too many coaches. The solution to these problems lay in a reform of public morality by the Crown. Although they were good Catholics, the arbitristas were not much interested in internal spiritual change; they tended to see moral decisions as rational and based on free will, a doctrine often associated with the Jesuit writer Luis de Molina.[165]

The values of the arbitristas percolated to wider audiences through the stage, where the theme of an ailing community looking to the monarch for practical action was a common motif during Philip III's reign. In Lope de Vega's celebrated play *Fuenteovejuna,* the tyranny of a vicious landlord leads to an uprising by justly outraged peasants, who cry "Long live King Ferdinand! Death to bad Christians and traitors!" Showing a stunning lack of Christian docility and self-control, the peasants murder their landlord. Although the killing takes place off-stage, such a scene probably could not have been enacted in France or England, where the vengeance of the villagers would have been seen as politically threatening and morally unjustifiable. Lope's peasants, however, represent a collective corpus mysticum that can act on its own in the absence of royal justice. When King Ferdinand finally appears, he cannot isolate the guilty among them and finally pardons them all in a splendid gesture of Christian reason of state.[166] Ferdinand the Catholic was the paragon of Christian rulership for the arbitristas, a model of "absolute excellence" for Botero, and "the major oracle of reason of state" for the Jesuit moralist Baltasar Gracián.[167] *Fuenteovejuna* leaves the disturbing impression that Philip III may not have equalled his ancestor's artful wisdom in dealing with the complaints of his subjects.

Other forms of profane literature reflected the same practical morality that was expressed by Lope and the arbitristas. Autobiographical works published by former soldiers (Cervantes himself penned one) concentrated on action and displayed little sense of introspection. Their prayers and devotions were focused on seeking divine assistance for worldly ends. While they saw themselves as reformed Christians, the soldier-writers had a meagre sense of internalized discipline. A similar absence of self-examination can be noted among the socially deviant heroes of picaresque novels.[168]

A more introspective and idealistic Catholic viewpoint was expressed by the brilliant and irascible Francisco de Quevedo Villegas. Attacking the arbitristas, he called for an end to "the calumnies of the innovators and the seditious" in his 1609 work *Spain Defended.* While he acknowledged a loss of virtue among his people, Quevedo ascribed this to personal sin, especially among women, the traditional targets of Catholic moralists. He identified the ultimate source of evil as "the forces of money . . . when poor, we conquered the riches of others: when rich, the same riches conquered us." Unlike Navarette, however, he saw the corruption of riches as caused by human avarice. Quevedo hurled at merchants and traders the studied contempt of an impecunious member of the lesser nobility. Spain would be ruined, he warned, "if the modesty and virtue and Christianity of don Felipe III, our lord, did not hold back these things with his example."[169]

Quevedo's moral idealism gave far more significance to the Christian self than did the arbitristas, as is evident in his remarkable *Politics of God, Government of Christ, Tyranny of Satan*. This treatise interprets quotations from the Gospels as examples of divine governance, and it urges the king to model himself totally on Christ: "The life, the death, the government, the severity, the clemency, the justice, the attentiveness of Christ our Lord present to Your Majesty such actions, that to imitate some and not others would show not free choice, but incapacity and criminality." He vilified the Boteran reason of state so admired by the arbitristas—"Lucifer, the rebellious angel, was its first inventor." Royal virtue was expressed not through successful policy but in good deeds, especially towards the poor; it should have no further aim than the service of God. Christian politics was not therefore a political "exercise of arts" but a personal movement of the spirit. It began when "God came and became flesh, and being made man he governed men. . . . He came to teach kings."[170] Like Bérulle, Quevedo wanted kingship to be a symbol of spiritual redemption.

Yet Quevedo was not a consistent dévot. His works were pervaded by an unresolved tension between Augustinian pessimism, convinced of human weakness, and a Neostoic striving for human perfectibility.[171] Quevedo was eccentric, but his bifurcated outlook may not have been uncommon among Castilian nobles and clerics, who wanted the monarchy both to symbolize Christian purity and to re-establish itself as an earthly empire. Indeed, these divided goals pervaded Spanish government under King Philip IV. The spiritual values of the so-called Government of Christ were enshrined at the royal court; but the actions of the chief minister, the count-duke of Olivares, were dominated by humanist concerns and resembled the shady dealings of a *pícaro*.

The king's minister was no Catholic idealist. Like Buckingham or Richelieu, Olivares was the "man of business" for a monarch who did not wish to sully himself with the political arts.[172] His dominance, however, was recognized as official in a way Buckingham's and Richelieu's was not. The *valimiento*, or chief ministership, had been formalized by Philip III, who allowed his long-serving *valido*, the duke of Lerma, to sign orders with the authority of the king.[173] Thus, the chief minister became the monarch's alter ego, the human image of a kingly power that was not supposed to be representable by anything except itself.

From the outset Olivares showed himself to be a reformer bent on rooting out the corruption and incompetence that had been spread by his predecessors. A great "council of councils," with the splendid title of *Junta Grande de Reformación*, was established in 1622; it drew up a spectacular programme of reform, ranging from the reduction of the royal household to the establishment of a banking system.[174] In the memorials he sent to his master the king, the count-duke sounded like an arbitrista. He praised Ferdinand II, idol of the projectors, and called for a programme of practical morality: "My Lord, the lack of obedience and lukewarmness of love and prevalence of selfish aims puts the service of Your Majesty in such a state today that if we do not heal ourselves with great care and attention, everything will fall down. This crown has enjoyed as kings great governors, the greatest of them the Catholic king; it is necessary to refresh that severity, as well as the desire, which we all hold, for doing it with calmness and without blood."[175] "Healing" meant severity, coercion, police. Among the recommendations of the Junta Grande was the closure of brothels and the suppression of licentious novels and plays.[176]

Olivares balanced such measures with programmes of moral education that would change the conduct of young nobles and make them "persons suitable for government, the state or war." The rest of the population would be forced to accept the virtue of labour, so that even vagabonds could be made useful: "The legless can work with their hands and the armless with their feet and so if they are not decrepit everyone has a job, justice has its place and the republic has great utility."[177] Like Richelieu, the count-duke did not permit charity to interfere with justice.

His vision was fixed on the ordered state, not on the Government of Christ. Olivares longed to make his master king of one Spain, not many. Hostile to national sentiments, no matter where they came from in the monarchy, he scorned the complaints of "patriots" like the Andalucian politician Mateo de Lisón y Viedma, who wanted the Cortes of Castile to mediate a reciprocal "conservation" of king and people.[178] Olivares's greatest scheme was the Union of Arms, which would have required a fixed military contribution from each of the Spanish kingdoms. The plan was rooted in the Neostoic conviction that military defence was the first duty of a ruler and the primary obligation of his subjects. The count-duke took Lipsius a stage further, arguing that divine, natural, and human law upheld the necessity of a common defence.[179] No customs, no traditions, no *fueros* were to stand in the way of the union. Olivares tried to promote his plan in the provinces of the monarchy, but to his dismay it was greeted with little warmth outside Castile and was shelved indefinitely.[180]

Like Richelieu and Laud, Olivares was a humanist rather than a puritan. He wanted good order, not godliness. Quevedo duly came to despise him. He viciously attacked the count-duke in his satirical piece *The Island of the Monopantos*. Olivares appears as the Jewish governor of the Monopantos, "men of quadruple malice, of perfect hypocrisy, of extreme dissimulation," who derive their principles from Machiavelli. The crude anti-Semitism that bubbles over in this work was stimulated by the count-duke's protection of Portuguese-Jewish bankers—a clear example, in Quevedo's mind, of his tepid commitment to confessional purity.[181] The accusation was not inaccurate. In spite of his deep personal piety, Olivares showed little desire to base his policies, whether internal or external, on Catholic confessionalism. He even gave secret military assistance to the French Huguenots and the Swiss Protestant Grisons.[182]

The count-duke did not set out to sacrifice religion on the altar of reason of state, and he was never a conscious Machiavellian. Nevertheless, he opposed at almost every turn the political influence of the church. He appointed a special junta in 1632 that declared a strict separation between temporal and spiritual power and justified royal resistance to undue papal interference. The decisions of this junta would later be used to justify the aggressive regalism of the Spanish Bourbons.[183] The perception that he was hostile to religion may have caused Olivares personal anxieties, fuelling his own morbid piety. Like so many other Spaniards, he was divided within himself between obedience to God and to the monarchy.

Philip IV was Olivares's partner in the formulation of policy, not his captive. He too was torn between humanist politics and Catholic devotion. The king was dedicated from birth to the task of reviving Spain's religious mission. He was christened with the name of St. Dominic, "scourge of heresy and founder of the Holy Inquisition"; his third name, Victor de la Cruz, proclaimed his crusading destiny.[184] As an adult he made war on the Dutch and English heretics and tried to reduce the frivolous opulence of his father's reign. In his private life, however, Philip was no paragon. A heavy drinker and habitual adulterer, he found the outward appearance of self-control easier to achieve than the inward discipline demanded by reformed religion.[185] This helps to explain his attraction to etiquette, the court ceremonial that the Habsburgs had partly invented, partly inherited from the medieval dukes of Burgundy. Philip chose to commit himself to the external rigours of etiquette, which allayed his moral qualms and gave a fleeting, theatrical reality to the "Politics of God."[186]

Norbert Elias argued that every aspect of mannerly conduct "bears witness to a particular structure of human relations, to a particular social structure, and to the corresponding forms of behavior."[187] The rules of etiquette, however, were meant to embody a divine rather than a worldly order. As Christina Hofmann has pointed out, Spanish court ceremony constituted a religious reality that "brought the king close to being a substitute for God."[188] Philip IV's obsessive regard for ceremony has to be interpreted in this light. The king was rarely seen, except at Mass; entry to his sleeping quarters was limited to gentlemen of the bedchamber. No other married men were allowed to sleep in his palaces. When he granted audiences to ambassadors, he stood motionless "like a statue." No one except grandees could wear a hat in his presence. He ate alone, in silence. Only the *mayordomo mayor*, or the leading grandee present, was allowed to give him water and a towel to wash his hands.[189] These rules were designed not only to preserve hierarchy and royal dominance but also to keep the king's person free from the pollution of worldly contact. They were forms of purification, intended to ward off those corroding social and political forces that the monarchy could not control.

The religious significance of etiquette was solemnly demonstrated every year on the Thursday before Easter, when the king of Spain washed and fed thirty poor men. The ceremony was held in memory of Christ's washing the feet of his apostles, as recounted in John 13:4–17. The thirty paupers were brought to the antechamber of the palace, inspected for disease, and bathed beforehand. The king then emerged from the royal chapel, in a procession headed by clerics carrying a cross. He removed his cape, hat, and sword and performed the washing. At the meal that followed, dishes were carried out by gentlemen of the bedchamber and their families, who handed them to the comptroller of the palace, who gave them to servants, who put them on a covered table and brought them to His Majesty. He then placed them before the paupers. After the meal, clothes and money were distributed.[190]

The Spanish foot-washing ritual was a theatrical performance, like a masque, or a ballet de cour, or one of the *autos sacramentales,* the religious plays favoured by King Philip. Following a carefully guided (if wordless) script, it presented a spectacle of royal piety. The king was carrying out the words of the Lord: "For I have given you an example, that ye should do as I have done to you" (John 13:15). His act of charity was real, and, unlike some of his royal counterparts elsewhere, he did actually wash the paupers' feet and serve them a meal. At least on the surface, the king's good deed was an example of perfect Christian conduct. Francisco Quevedo could have invented no more inspiring illustration of the Government of Christ.

Furthermore, by suggesting a special relationship between the king and Christ, the royal foot-washing indicated the exalted position of royalty. Yet we should remember that personal sacrality was always problematic in the Spanish monarchy. Philip could imitate Christ, but his nature was not divine. He was never allowed to forget that God would judge him not as a king but as an ordinary human being. Olivares once reminded him in a letter of how wrong it would be to believe "that it is much more to be king than man . . . follies which the most distracted mind would not say, because to be a man is above all the accidents of the world."[191] As a result, the king could only approach the image of God obliquely, through his deeds, his behaviour, his comportment.

Etiquette, therefore, did not bring about a transcendence of humanity in the king; rather, it constituted an acting-out of the divine role in human terms. This was what Diego Velázquez depicted in his naturalist portraits of Philip IV. Velázquez often showed the monarch dressed in black and wearing the restrained collar, or *golilla,* associated with his austere grandfather, Philip II; he also produced a seemingly informal painting of the king in hunting garb, which Jonathan Brown has described as "extraordinarily modest."[192] In all of these portraits, the viewer is supposed to

13. Diego Velázquez, *Philip IV in Hunting Garb* (c. 1635), painting.
Photo: Museo nacional del Prado, Madrid.

recognize the king's majesty in the rigid way he holds his body, in his direct gaze, or in his lack of vulgar emotions, not through any external symbols of power. Juan de Mariana wrote of the king: "Let the fullness of authority be present in his very nod; let dignity . . . shine forth from his very countenance and eyes." Quevedo agreed: "The eyes of the prince are his most powerful weapon."[193] Velázquez's paintings of King Philip are in keeping with this theme; they manifest sacred authority through an air of perfect human self-control. Like Christ, the king approaches us as a man.

That, at least, was how Philip IV liked to see himself. He was oblivious to the possibility that the motions of his body, or any aspect of his behaviour, might serve a self-interested reason of state. R. A. Stradling has accurately summed up his mentality: "The *truly* virtuous monarch, intent on doing only the work of God upon Earth, was . . . immune from the sin incurred by dabbling in the forbidden science of *Razón de Estado.*"[194] At the same time, there can be no doubt that royal etiquette was a politically contrived performance. It was artfully designed to suggest that a wholly externalized ritual act could take the place of heartfelt benevolence.

In the mid-1630s the king constructed a grand stage on which to enact the rituals of governance: the Buen Retiro palace on the outskirts of Madrid. For the first time in Christian Europe a whole royal residence was built to express a unified, carefully directed programme of publicity. Fittingly, it was created around a church, and to one observer it looked "more like a monastery than a royal dwelling." Was the palace the accomplishment of Quevedo's devout political hopes? Not quite. The Buen Retiro was a monument to empire, not a statement of piety, and its visual splendours were more worldly than spiritual. They depended on a heavy element of Neostoic militarism, notably in the enormous Hall of Realms, where paintings of victories were exhibited beneath the arms of the imperial territories. The Hall of Princely Virtue was the backdrop for a dozen paintings by Francisco Zurbarán showing the labours of Hercules, a favourite Lipsian symbol of classical virtue. Situated on the edge of a bustling capital rather than in the rocky wilderness of Philip II's Escorial, the Buen Retiro was obviously meant to impress public opinion, not to render homage to God. Its stunning effects, moreover, were politically illusory. The palace was a "monumental diversion," intended by Olivares to divert the king's attention away from menacing realities.[195] Clearly, it was not the visible fulfilment of a Christian ideal.

By the time the Buen Retiro was built, the Government of Christ was beginning to seem unattainable even in the most Catholic of monarchies. The perception of failure had begun to affect not only royal policy but also the reformation of the self. A century after the Council of Trent, Spain had achieved much in the confessional reshaping of popular beliefs and practices, but the reformed Christian self had not been yoked to central authority. The political limits of religious change were evident in the uneven impact of that most feared of Spanish institutions, the Holy Office of the Inquisition.

In the Inquisition the Spanish Crown had at its disposal a powerful instrument of confessionalization that was not available to any other monarchy. The Inquisition's campaigns against heretical writings, against Moriscos, and especially against *conversos*, or Jewish converts who had reverted to "judaizing" practices, are justly infamous. Less well known are its efforts to police the behaviour of so-called Old Christians. More than half of the cases that came before Inquisitorial courts in the sixteenth and seventeenth centuries dealt with blasphemy, bigamy, fornication, sodomy, bestiality, sorcery, witchcraft, magical practices, and the conduct of clerics. Wide-ranging studies of these offences have led historians like Bartolomé Bennassar and Jean-Pierre DeDieu to conclude that the Inquisition was highly successful in inculcating reformed Catholic values among the Spanish people. By the 1640s almost all of the Old Christians who appeared before the Holy Office in the Archbishopric of Toledo were familiar with the catechism, as shown by their recitation of basic prayers and of the Commandments. Most of them took confession and attended Mass.[196] The Inquisition also fought to control popular devotions, especially those centred on *beatas*, or holy women. As Mary Elizabeth Perry has shown, the mystical beatas of Seville were viewed by the Inquisitors as dangerous violators of religious and gender boundaries. By 1640 they had been effectively suppressed.[197]

The victory of the Inquisition in controlling the Christian self, however, was far from complete. Its influence often depended on the extent to which it reflected traditional values.[198] One area in which it did not meddle was marriage to close cousins. Although the prohibited degrees of consanguinity were strictly defined by the church, it was common in many areas of Spain (as at the Habsburg court) for cousins to marry.[199] Similarly, the Holy Office did not usually interfere with the proliferation of local saints' cults. After the opening of the Roman catacombs in the late sixteenth century, a great number of bones supposedly belonging to saints were exported to Spain as relics. The nobility and clergy of Galicia eagerly pursued this peculiar commerce, oblivious to the criticisms of theologians or the official post-Tridentine standards of authenticity for relics.[200]

On one occasion, the Inquisitors did try to stamp out a cult, with tumultuous results. Padre Francisco Simón was a popular priest in the town of Valencia who claimed supernatural powers of healing and prophecy. After his death in 1612 the town's governing elite supported a movement to have him canonized, and his memory was venerated in massive processions throughout the kingdom. The Inquisition, which had been suspicious of Padre Simón during his lifetime, obtained a royal edict ordering all images of him to be removed from churches. This prompted a riotous attack on the bishop of Valencia's palace. Although the cult gradually died out, the episode greatly discredited the Holy Office in Valencia, contributing to a decline in its authority.[201]

If the Inquisition was not capable of ensuring social control, neither was it an effective tool of political centralization. Henry Kamen has flatly maintained that "the tribunal rarely took any action which could even remotely be described as political, and it would consequently be quite false to regard it as an instrument of State."[202] While this may be an overstatement—the case of Padre Simón, for instance, can be regarded as political—it is clear that the Holy Office chose not to deal with anti-government dissent, even when the clergy was involved. Preaching on political themes was common in Spain, and at times it far exceeded the boundaries of what would have been acceptable in England or France. In 1624, as Olivares struggled to obtain support for the renewal of a hated tax, the worthy friars of Seville, the count-duke's native town, preached to the civic elite "not to consent upon any respect to such a destruction of their country."[203] In Catalonia the Inquisition had great difficulty in defending its own authority, let alone establishing that of the Crown. When the parish priest of a Pyrenean village was accused in 1632 of shooting at an informer for the

Holy Office, he simply refused to appear before the tribunal, asserting boldly that "he didn't recognize the Inquisition and didn't give a fig for it."[204] All in all, the Spanish Inquisition was more successful in encouraging confessionalism—the creation of a denominational identity—than in promoting confessionalization—the extension of secular authority and political identity through religious reform.

Maravall has characterized baroque culture, in Spain and throughout Europe, as an attempt to guide not only the outward behaviour but also the inner psychology of a broadly based, largely urban public.[205] At the centre of these efforts was the monarch—the *rey planeta,* or planet king, as Philip IV was called—around whom an ordered society was supposed to move like the stars, in perfect symmetry. This ideal formulation of baroque culture became an encompassing reality within the confines of the Buen Retiro, where the hieratic immobility of the royal body kept disaster at bay. In the rest of Philip IV's *monarquía,* however, the religious psychology of an unevenly reformed public was not so easily frozen into ritual obedience. As in other European kingdoms, mass culture entertained and edified the people, but it did not suddenly transform them into obedient subjects. Nor did it bring closer the humanist dream of a united, authoritarian monarchy. In Spain many educated minds had already begun to question their submission and re-examine their self-identity. Soon the cries of patriotism, which Olivares had so long feared, would be heard everywhere, and both the planet king and his monarchy would be plunged into agonies of inner conflict.

14. *Palm Sunday Festival, Moscow,* from Adam Olearius, *Voyages*
(Leyden, 1719), engraving.

Photo: British Library, London.

CHAPTER FOUR

# No King but King Jesus, 1637–1660

Kings, princes, monarchs, and magistrates seem to be most happy, but look into their estate,
you shall find them to be most encumbered with cares, in perpetual fear, agony, suspicion,
jealousy: that, as he said of a crown, if they knew but the discontents that accompany it, they
would not stoop to take it up.

—ROBERT BURTON, *The Anatomy of Melancholy* (1621)

ESUS RODE INTO Jerusalem like a king. As St. Matthew relates, he was mounted on an ass, and "a very great multitude spread their garments in the way; others cut down branches from the trees, and strawed them in the way." The crowd cried "Hosanna to the son of David: blessed is he that cometh in the name of the Lord" (Matthew 21:1–11). The image of the Messiah riding into the holy city to the acclaim of a godly people often recurred in the theatre of Christian monarchy, nowhere more so than in Russia.

Every year on Palm Sunday the tsar guided the patriarch of Moscow around the churches of the Kremlin. The tsar was on foot; the patriarch was mounted on a donkey, or perhaps, if the envoy Olearius is to be believed, on a horse "adorned with long ears, to make it resemble an ass." Clerics and boyars accompanied this procession, singing hosannas and waving palm branches, as large crowds of onlookers bowed their heads and crossed themselves.[1] Taking the role of Jesus, the patriarch affirmed that the church, the body of Christ, brought the community together in political harmony. The tsar's part was also indispensable; like the apostles, he led the way into the holy city.

On 1 June 1648, a few weeks after this elaborate ritual had been performed, the nineteen-year-old tsar Alexis was returning to Moscow from a pilgrimage when his entourage was met by a large crowd of towns-people. They held the bridle of the tsar's horse, offered him bread and salt—a sign of hospitality—and tried to read a petition denouncing the official in charge of civic administration. Olearius noted that this encounter was carefully planned in public meetings held in front of churches. The protesters certainly employed a striking religious symbolism. The tsar's procession into Moscow, like the Palm Sunday ride, paralleled the royal entry of Christ, but with the ruler in the starring role. This time the hands of the tsar's subjects, far from waving palms, had stopped his horse, forcing him to hear them. The corporate body of Orthodox believers had wel-comed the tsar to the holy city with a warning that he must cleanse the temple.

Alexis responded calmly, but some of his boyar retainers attacked the petitioners. The following day a huge crowd invaded the Kremlin, where a frightened tsar pledged to punish their oppressors. They went on to sack the houses of boyars and rich merchants. On 3 June they were back in the Kremlin, demanding the execution of Alexis's chief minister and former tutor, Boris Morozov. The tsar would not concede this, and the patriarch of Moscow was sent to plead with the crowd, which he did while holding up a revered icon of the Virgin. Then the tsar himself bravely appeared before the people, to beg for the life of his minister. In the end, Morozov was exiled, the salt tax was lowered, and Alexis agreed to call a national assem-bly, or *zemsky sobor*, a safer version of the corpus mysticum, to which he presented a new law code. It guaranteed equal justice for all his subjects—but at the same time, it gave legal recognition to serfdom.[2]

The Morozov riots had a variety of causes, but they took the form that they did for primarily religious reasons. As in the revolt against the false Dmitry, the moral purification of the realm was initiated by the Orthodox people, represented by male craftsmen and labourers. While they deferred to the authority of the ruler, they insisted that he lead their campaign for justice. Petitions from the Moscow gentry maintained that God had en-trusted to Alexis "the tsarist sword for the quelling of evildoers and the praise of the virtuous." Unlike the 1606 and 1612 revolts, however, the Morozov riots were directed against the minions of a tsar whose religious views were not in question. Alexis was not a false ruler, a tool of Poland and Rome. He was a legitimate and perfectly Orthodox monarch; yet his people were trying to influence his actions. In their petitions, they reminded him that he "was called to the tsardom by God himself, not by your own wish."[3] He should therefore cease to resist a collective will that was divinely inspired. What was the source of this growing moral confidence among the gentry and the *posadskie liudi*, or townsfolk, of Moscow?

It may have arisen from an ascetic revival in the Orthodox Church, which had produced groups of self-denying enthusiasts with names like the Zealots of God. Among the leading exponents of the new asceticism was the famous priest Avvakum, whose godly fervour led to frequent confrontations with oppressive local officials and with the quasi-pagan beliefs of the peasantry. The reformed Christian, according to Avvakum, "having through Truth understood Christ and by this gaining knowledge of God, denying himself, . . . succumbeth not to . . . seductions and worldly ways." The Christian became, like the tsar himself, an imitator of Christ, dedicated to rooting out evil wherever he saw it. In common with godly reformers elsewhere, Avvakum was particularly scandalized by ungodly sports: "There came to my village dancing bears with tambourines and domras, and I, sinner that I am, being zealous in Christ I drove them out."[4] It was no coincidence that within six months of the riots Alexis issued an instruction, to be read in every Russian church, outlawing "immoral" popular recreations like listening to itinerant minstrels or attending bear-baitings.[5] A timely sop to the godly, this counter Declaration of Sports may have been designed to placate those who had risen up in pious anger to punish the tsar's evil councillors.

Avvakum called on believers to bear witness to their inner spiritual experiences. "Speak," he advised, "seeking glory not for yourself but for Christ and the Mother of God."[6] With some modifications, this exhortation would not have been alien to a Quaker. It provides a link between the moral revolt in Russia and the godly revolution in England, between the Kremlin riots and the oddly moving little scene that took place eight years later in Bristol. On a rainy day in October 1656, the Quaker leader, James Nayler, re-enacted Christ's entry into Jerusalem by riding into town on an ass, preceded by female attendants who were waving branches, chanting hosannas, and spreading their garments before him. The unfortunate Nayler was arrested, taken to London, and tried for blasphemy by a Parliament that was determined to make his case an example of the dire consequences of religious toleration. He was sentenced to be whipped 310 times, branded on his forehead with a hot iron, and pierced through the tongue.[7]

The actions of Nayler and his followers would have been almost unthinkable a decade earlier. They were made possible by the defeat, trial, and execution of King Charles I, which for some marked a decisive rejection of royal mediation between God and the self. Various radical sects— Quakers, Fifth Monarchists, Ranters, and others—became prominent after the king was beheaded in January 1649. "The power and spirit of our Cause," wrote one Fifth Monarchist, "was great and high after the King's death, more than at any time before."[8] The execution of Charles I seemed to have provided the cataclysmic event that would initiate the thousand-year governance of the saints. Unlike the Fifth Monarchists, however, the Quakers did not aspire to godly rule. For the Friends, as they called themselves, the king's death had closed down the unholy theatre of politics for all time and shifted the burden of governance to the individual self. This did not mean that they renounced a public role or entirely rejected community in favour of individualism; but their struggle against Satan was an inner fight, not a political one, and only those who waged it could be considered part of the body of Friends.[9]

In his pamphlet *The Lamb's War*, written after his brutal punishment, Nayler explained this spiritual conflict in military terms: "At his appearance in his subjects he [Jesus, or the Lamb] puts spiritual weapons into their hearts and hands. . . . And thus the Lamb in them, and they in him, go out in judgment and righteousness to make war with his enemies, conquering and to conquer. Not as the prince of the world in his subjects, with whips and prisons, tortures and torments on the bodies of his creatures, . . . but he goes forth in the power of the Spirit with the Word of Truth."[10] Nayler implied that the holy war had not been won by Parliament. It could only be pursued by individual campaigns within each of the Lamb's "subjects." Avvakum might have approved of such an idea. Like the Russian ascetics, the Friends were excited by the possibility of immanent human sanctification, and they passed easily into states of ecstatic personal communication with God. They were certain of an inherent righteousness, which they generously recognized in all humanity. Nayler's ride at Bristol was meant to show the Christ-like perfection that was present within every soul—in the poor as well as the rich, in women as well as men.

Their aversion to communal politics, however, and the extent of their universality set Quakers apart from the Zealots of God. They were even willing to countenance a distinctly feminine spirituality, as Phyllis Mack has shown. In spite of their male leadership and acceptance of traditional family roles, the Quakers sanctioned public displays of religious zeal by women. Martha Simmonds, who accompanied Nayler at Bristol, had wandered through Colchester barefoot and in sackcloth, like an Old Testament prophet. She was not afraid to denounce male ministers, including Nayler himself, whom she once called "the head of the beast," throwing him into a deep depression.[11] The appearance of women who gave open testimony of their religious experiences, made critical judgments, and exercised prophetic powers would have horrified Avvakum. It was profoundly shocking to many in England, who took it as further evidence that the world was turning upside down, that the collapse of political order had brought a dangerous sectarian individualism to the fore.[12]

Both the Friends and the Morozov rioters drew upon the Christian self as a source of authority. The Morozov rioters, however, saw themselves as joined together in a mystical corporate body of believers, the Orthodox nation. The Friends, on the other hand, seemed to subvert corporate unity. They flourished amid the ruins of an English body politic whose authority was dispersed among the individual human elements of which it had been composed. Although neither group sought to overthrow existing forms of government, both were deeply threatening to worldly rulers, because they aimed to secure an earthly Jerusalem—externally and partially in one instance, internally and fully in the other.

The crowds in the Kremlin and the little band of Friends at Bristol took alternative paths towards the resolution of the same moral problem: how to bring life on Earth closer to the kingdom of God. This problem was at the heart of the several crises of the mid-seventeenth century: the crisis of nations, the crisis of states, the crisis of the self. Each was an aspect of a general disgust with human politics—the politics of Richelieu, Olivares, and Buckingham as well as of the local officials who persecuted Avvakum and the Quakers. In the end, however, the upheavals of the mid-seventeenth century did not throw open the gates of Jerusalem; rather, they aggravated political and sectarian conflicts, preparing the way for the approach of Leviathan, the rational state.

## The Lamb's Wars

Before about 1640, almost everyone agreed that kings should lead the way into the city of God. It was, after all, what the theatre of confessionalism had promised. It was what both the prophets and the Gospels had foretold: "Tell ye the daughter of Sion [Jerusalem], Behold, thy king cometh unto thee, meek, and sitting upon an ass" (Matthew 21:5). Every Christian monarch in Europe had re-enacted the glorious scene of Jesus entering the holy city. As Carmelo Lisón Tolosana has written of Philip II and Madrid, "the entrance of the king into the city between palms and olive branches on more than one occasion recalls that of Jesus Christ into Jerusalem."[13] Is this not also part of the message of van Dyck's huge painting of Charles I riding through a triumphal arch? Charles appears as the Christian king in glory, a Constantine entering the celestial city on a magnificent horse.[14]

According to the prophets, the entry into Jerusalem presaged a peaceable, universal kingdom extending "from sea even unto sea" (Zechariah 9:10). Many writers saw the Habsburg Empire as the fulfilment of the prophet Daniel's vision of a "fifth monarchy" (Daniel 7:13–14, 27). "Finally," explained the Spanish diplomat Don Diego de Saavedra Fajardo, "Daniel prophesies that there will be an eternal realm, which kings will serve and obey. This has been verified up to now . . . in the realms of Europe that have incorporated themselves in the crown of Spain." Similar millenarian hopes were also quite common among both Calvinists and Arminians, as William Lamont has shown. By the mid-seventeenth century, however, such predictions seemed to have been shattered or endlessly deferred by religious dissension, political machinations, and war. Instead of riding towards the millennium, kingly horsemen had stumbled into thickets or wandered onto dangerous paths. Some of them had postponed confessional reform; some could not attain it; some had pushed religious change in directions unacceptable to their subjects. No king had fulfiled biblical promises, and no kingdom could claim to be eternal. Saavedra Fajardo was forced to conclude that "what experience and the natural order of things show us is that empires are born, live and die."[15]

Throughout Europe the devout deplored the abundant failures of human governance and sought comfort in historical examples of individual fortitude. Quevedo immersed himself in the story of Job, the model of a patient king, which brought him back to Christian providentialism as well as to Neostoic resignation. "All this bloody confusion and show," he wrote, "which with death and arms astounds the whole world and bothers the open seas, doesn't move for you and me . . . they are the occult designs of eternal Providence."[16] Pierre Corneille found a less fatalistic source of political consolation in the letters of Saint Bernard of Clairvaux—"You who brought truth to our kings, / . . . [And made] Holiness reign over reasons of State / . . . For a second time, unite in this empire / The wisdom of the world with that of God."[17]

For many godly Protestants, however, the hope of just rulership had faded beyond repair. An age of tyranny had delayed the peaceable kingdom; Jerusalem was in ruins; its nemesis Babylon was flourishing. The German preacher Johann Andreä condemned "the depravity of the age of iron, in which we live," and lamented "so many and so thoughtless desertions of illustrious people to Babylon [the Catholic Church]!"[18] Meanwhile, in Scotland the godly trembled at the advances of Arminianism. "We are in great fears of a great and fearfull trial to come upon the kirk of God," wrote the Presbyterian minister Samuel Rutherford, "for these who would build their houses and nests upon the ashes of mourning Jerusalem, have drawn our King upon hard and dangerous conclusions upon those who are called Puritans, for the rooting them out."[19] An Austrian nobleman declared to the Polish Arians, "We shall never have Christian kings . . . a substitute for Christ would be only a usurper."[20] These were words of despair, which presaged a crisis.

By the mid-1630s, tremors of political anxiety had begun to penetrate even the sealed world of court entertainments. They had once depicted divine concord flowing from the presence of the king; now they showed rulers and heroes battling to enforce order in a troubled universe. In the *Ballet of the Prosperity of French Arms,* performed at Richelieu's Palais Cardinal in 1641, the Gallic Hercules met the denizens of an anarchic hell in mortal combat. Contrary to convention, the dancers did not descend from the stage to mingle with the spectators—perhaps because the audience was no longer trusted enough to participate in the scenes of royal triumph.[21] A year earlier the English court had been diverted by the masque *Salmacida spoliata,* which began with "a horrid scene . . . of storm and tempest. No glimpse of the sun was seen, as if darkness, confusion and deformity had

possessed the world and driven light to heaven." This sad condition was
blamed on the sins of the people—it was "the people's vice / To lay too
mean, too cheap a price / On every blessing they possess." King Charles
appeared amid military trophies and was joined by the queen, in "Amazo-
nian habits." Together they restored peace and obedience to the universe:
"All that are harsh, all that are rude, / Are by your harmony subdued."
Only then did the image of Jerusalem appear in the distance, as "the
suburbs of a great city."[22]

These court plays signalled deepening fears of disorder, which were
soon realized in a flood of popular rebellions. For the English earl of
Clarendon, the tumultuous events of the period constituted nothing less
than "a general combination, and universal apostasy in the whole nation
from their religion and allegiance."[23] Should this situation, reproduced in
other parts of Europe, be called a "general crisis"? The term carries with it
a lot of baggage. Historians were once captivated by the concept of a
general crisis spreading throughout the continent, perhaps even the world,
in the 1640s and 1650s. They traced it to growing populations, inadequate
production, extravagant courts, rising military expenditures, and mounting taxes. The allure of the general crisis has faded in the hothouse atmosphere created by the multiplication of specialist studies, but its charms
have not been entirely lost.[24] This chapter will try to revive them, by
arguing that the rebellions and upheavals of the mid-seventeenth century
in various parts of Europe had certain religious and intellectual features in
common. Such an assertion is of course controversial, and it has to be
carefully qualified.

The crisis of the mid-seventeenth century was "general" not because it
affected every aspect of life, or caused revolts everywhere in Europe, but
because it was generally observed and felt. "These days are days of shaking," a preacher told the English House of Commons in a sermon of 1643,
"and this shaking is universal."[25] With less enthusiasm, Albrycht Radziwiłł
glumly recorded in his memoirs for September 1649 that "now in all monarchies rebellions were excited," although he added that "certainly none
was more abused by its subjects than our Poland."[26] Referring to France,
but with all of Europe in mind, Queen Christina of Sweden worried about a
time when "neither king nor *parlement* have their proper power, but the
common man, the *canaille*, rules according to his fancy."[27] Such observa-

tions testify to an often fearful perception of sudden change that was more acute, more widespread and more globalized than in earlier periods.

Can we go a step further and ask whether there was a measure of consistency in the ideologies of revolt? Many historians would regard the question itself as tendentious. "I confess to feeling a certain scepticism," the late Denis Richet wrote, "with regard to the idea that there could have existed a unity of viewpoint between a Masaniello and a Jan de Witt, a Cromwell and a Cardinal de Retz."[28] His wariness was understandable. Nonetheless, all of the rebels Richet mentioned drew upon a common fund of political ideas. Witt, Cromwell, Retz, and Masaniello took advantage of conflicts between an erring monarchy and a godly nation. They imagined a state in which royal mediation was circumscribed or removed. All of them would have welcomed the title of patriot. Moreover, the rapid circulation of news within Europe meant that each group of insurrectionaries could build upon what it knew about its predecessors. In France during the uprising known as the Fronde, treatises were hastily written about the recent troubles of England, while eyewitness accounts of the revolution in Naples were quickly translated into English. The awareness of change brought about through mass culture was what chiefly distinguished this age of crisis from the 1560s or the 1590s.

The rebellions of the mid-seventeenth century were usually initiated by members of governing elites, often acting under popular pressure. Their aim was to reject reason of state and realize an ideal Christian polity. The corpus mysticum of the realm was forcibly dragged towards Jerusalem, with or without the compliance of its ruler. To be sure, the rebellious ideologies of the period were not by any means uniform, but they did have in common a tendency to appeal to an authority that was vested by God in the mystical body of the people rather than that of the monarch. Although kings had long claimed that the body politic was inseparable from their own persons, it was equated by rebel groups with a distinct national community, or *patria*.

By the late 1640s, however, the defence of the patria had degenerated into seemingly endless civil wars. Party politics and sectarian individualism threatened the unity, even the existence, of a collective corpus mysticum. In England, Naples, and the Dutch Republic, the body politic fragmented beyond repair. Elite minorities in those nations advocated the overthrow of monarchy—a revolution in the state—and the creation of what amounted to an oligarchical republic of virtue. Order in the republic would depend upon the male citizen, an independent, publicly engaged person, guided towards the common good by self-interest. For many in the privileged classes, however, this was too radical a break with the past. Their response to the breakdown of the corporate polity was a frantic search for a new source of unity—usually ending in a return to monarchy. In Barcelona and Naples, Paris and Westminster, kings came back; but they carried with them their own versions of the rejected republic of virtue, which would become the rational state.

It would of course be absurd to reduce the dynamics of rebellion to any single formulation. This chapter will draw out similarities in the ideas that motivated revolts of the period, but it will not seek to deny their peculiar characteristics. Strangely, a comparative approach of this kind has not often been attempted. Yet Roland Mousnier pointed to the appropriateness of such a perspective as long ago as 1949, when considering the causes of the Fronde. "The general opposition on financial issues," he wrote, "was first of all ideological and psychological. It was the idea of a defective government that rendered its financial policies unbearable more than the financial policies . . . which inspired the idea of a defective government."[29] For most Europeans of the mid-seventeenth century, opposition to misgovernance was not simply the result of economic pressures or social conflict; however vexing these issues were, they had to be filtered through the moral and religious beliefs that defined the Christian self. A defective government, in short, was demonstrably not on the road to Jerusalem.

## The Crisis of Nations

The rebels of the 1640s were patriots, not modern nationalists. They did not understand "the nation" in the same ways we do. Nevertheless, as J. H. Elliott has pointed out, they did have a conception of patria—the homeland or local community—that was important in motivating political resistance. "Given the existence of an idealized vision of the community," Elliott suggests, "movements of protest are likely to occur within the political nation when the discrepancy between the image and the reality comes to seem intolerably wide."[30]

Patriotism was not a natural social development. Whether it encompassed a whole province or was confined to a small geographical locality, the patria was a cultural construction, an "imagined community." It was created not merely by people living together, or by a shared awareness of familial, ethnic, and linguistic ties, but by the synthesis of diverse experiences and traditions into ideal forms. The cultural pull of the patria usually depended on three factors: the existence of distinct institutions; memories of a mythical past in which the whole community had supposedly been united; and a sense of collective destiny, often reinforced by providential or millenarian beliefs. Ethnicity, which was understood in mythic rather than "scientific" terms, could be subsumed within these factors. As for language, in an age when most people communicated in local dialects, a common tongue was more likely to be a result than a cause of national consciousness.[31]

Gustavus Adolphus of Sweden summed up the components of national identity in his farewell speech to the Riksdag in 1630. He told the assembled representatives of the nation that they were "the true heirs and descendants of the ancient Goths, who in their day conquered almost the whole earth."[32] Thus, he validated a myth of origins and of collective destiny in an address to the guardians of Sweden's unique constitution. This was an uncommon strategy for kings or their ministers, who were usually wary of national idealism, especially in composite monarchies where the king was normally absent from most of his provinces. In contrast to Gustavus Adolphus, the count-duke of Olivares treated patriotism derisorily: "I am not a national, which is a thing for children," he wrote in 1640. He viewed the empire as a supranational state, in contrast to his Andalusian critic Lisón y Vierma, who was praised as the "defender of the *patria.*"[33]

As Olivares realized, state policy and patriotism were often diametrically opposed. The humanist ideal of the state was temporal and authoritarian; its ultimate goals were uniformity and political order. The national ideal, on the other hand, pointed towards instability. It was based upon separateness, as typified in "ancient" laws, mythic histories, and the biblical rhetoric of a "chosen people." Although its educated proponents liked to draw upon classical examples of patriotic virtue, for most people the idea of the nation was drenched in religion. The patria comprised a corpus mysticum closely related to that of the church. "Love faithfully and tenderly the Church and the Nation which are both [your] inseparable mothers," Piotr Skarga exhorted his Polish countrymen in 1597; and he added that the nation was "your Jerusalem."[34] Patriotism exalted a sacred body politic, guided by Providence and free from the domination of outside powers, whether tyrannical lords, wicked ministers, or "foreign" kings.

The national ideal was not necessarily anti-monarchical. In the late 1640s, for example, self-styled patriots in the Swedish Riksdag upheld the constitutional authority of Queen Christina against the royal council, led by the meddlesome chancellor Axel Oxenstierna. Even in this case, however, patriotism entailed reform. The leaders of the Estates took the opportunity as representatives of the nation to make their own demands, including legal equality, the opening of government offices to all, and a *reduktion*, or restitution, of Crown lands that had been granted to nobles. Linking national unity with religious orthodoxy, some members of the clerical Estate called for a general consistory to define and enforce Lutheran doctrine.[35]

In many places the call for liberation of the patria simply bypassed royal mediation and spoke direct to the people. It often carried millenarian overtones, promising a release from worldly ties and taking on radical implications for self-identity and personal discipline. It could then become a frightening prospect to the educated elites who saw themselves as the guardians of national consciousness. Nobles and bourgeois who took up the cause of patriotic resistance could find crowds of artisans and rural labourers pushing them further towards reforming the mystical body than they were prepared to go. In most cases the outcome of these pressures was an elite reaction and the re-establishment of monarchy. In the end, the patria was seldom disentangled from the royal body. To understand why not, let us examine in greater detail the patriotic insurrections in the three Stuart kingdoms, Catalonia, Portugal, and the Ukraine.

## SCOTLAND, ENGLAND, AND IRELAND

By trying to impose a single religion on his English, Scottish, and Irish subjects, King Charles I succeeded only in raising against him three separate patriotic movements, based on the defence of confessional identity.

The English movement, however, was restrained by a cautious Parliament that saw itself as the protector of order. The rebellions in Scotland and Ireland were fomented by less regularly formed bodies (the Assembly of the Kirk, the Confederate Assembly) that claimed to represent the godly nation more directly. All three movements attempted to "rescue" Charles's multiple kingship from the snare of Arminianism.[36] Few envisaged the break-up of the three kingdoms or the possible empowerment of the Christian self.

The ideology of the Scottish revolt of 1637 was encapsulated in that extraordinary patriotic document the National Covenant. "This only is the true Christian faith and religion," it proclaimed, "received, believed and defended by many and sundry notable kirks and realms, but chiefly by the Kirk of Scotland . . . and therefore we abhor and detest all contrary religion and doctrine." True religion, in short, was found at its best in Scotland, a clear assertion of national uniqueness. The godly nation encompassed "majesty" and took precedence over obedience to the king's will. "Neither do we fear the foul aspersions of rebellion," the covenant continued, "seeing what we do is so well warranted, and ariseth from an unfeigned desire to maintain the true worship of God, the majesty of our King, and the peace of the kingdom." The Covenanters derived their theory of resistance from Althusius, using it to maintain the exceptional destiny of the Scots.[37]

The covenant was a response to the failure of Charles I's kingship. He had long been regarded in Scotland as an "uncounselled king," who depended for advice on the wrong people, particularly bishops. At his Scottish coronation in 1633, Charles's perceived attachment to "popish" ceremonies caused much negative comment.[38] Worse still was his attempt in 1637 to impose an Arminian prayer book, which "almost all our nobilitie and gentrie of both sexes, counts . . . little better then the Masse," according to the Ayrshire minister Robert Baillie.[39] The prayer book mobilized the Scots body politic, leading finally to the National Covenant, drawn up by godly clergymen and endorsed by nobles, lairds, and representatives of the towns or burghs.

"In seeking to assert the national sovereignty of the Scottish state," the historian Allan MacInnes has written, "the Covenanting Movement reacted consciously against the relegation of the kingdom to provincial status during the personal rule of Charles I."[40] Yet the Covenanters did not use terms like "sovereignty" or "the state." As MacInnes himself has shown, their national consciousness was based on Calvinist theology rather than Bodinian political theory.[41] For them the patria was a community of believers. This was why their revolt aspired to a universal Christian significance, and why they had no compunctions about intervening in English or Irish affairs. As Robert Baillie wrote to a general of the victorious Covenanting army, "God may be pleased to honour you with a farder successe, in helping the multitude of oppressed saints in England and Ireland: in dividing betwixt our gracious Sovereaigne and a handfull of wicked counsellors . . . they have beheld the church of France undone through their default; the churches of Germanie suchlyke; the house of Palatine in banishment these twenty years, and that of Denmark latelie."[42] This was not state-centred nationalism in the nineteenth-century sense; rather, it was a kind of patriotic messianism, which relegated the Crown to a permanent condition of dependency on the Protestant cause and the Christian self.

The political theology of the Covenanters swept like a whirlwind through what Baillie called "that flatt ayre of England."[43] Nehemiah Wallington, a godly turner of London who kept voluminous memoirs, gratefully recorded no fewer than thirteen ways in which God had granted the prayers of the righteous in 1640, all of which stemmed from the Scots rebellion. One blessing was the calling of a parliament that turned out to be full of allies of the Scots. Another was this: "Whereas before, our Bishops were liked, now they are much disliked, and are had in great detestation."[44] The Covenanters had designated a target for their English brethren: episcopacy, the seedbed of Arminianism. "All here, praised be God, goes according to our prayers, if we could be quyte [quit] of Bishops," Baillie wrote to his wife from London. In the streets of the city scores of prints and playlets were for sale in which the bishops, especially Laud, were lampooned as the instruments of popish tyranny.[45] The godly English nation would be brought to life through a wholesale purge of prelates, who obstructed contact between God and the self.

To end episcopacy, the "Root and Branch" petition was presented to Parliament in December 1640. Orchestrated by Puritan clergymen and with support from nineteen counties, it bore fifteen thousand signatures and warned that "the present wars and commotions" would continue "unless the prelates with their dependences be removed out of England." The petition, however, went much further than a call for presbytery. Like the covenant, it was a statement of national purpose. It delineated the outlines of a "government according to God's Word," a godly English polity incorporating public moral regeneration along with personal discipline and just commercial values. It called for reform of everything: vestments, altars, the Book of Sports; "idle, lewd and dissolute" ministers "which swarm like the locusts of Egypt over the whole kingdom"; "lascivious, idle and unprofitable books"; opinions favouring arbitrary monarchy; trade monopolies; "whoredoms and adulteries." In the new English Israel, the holy was to be completely separated from the unholy.[46] Root and Branch put the conservative gentlemen and peers of Parliament in a difficult position. Speaking on the petition in the Commons, the Puritan Sir Simonds D'Ewes supported many of its points but opined that "wee ought to proceed with great moderation. For doubtles the government of the church of God by godlie zealous and preaching Bishops had been most ancient, and I should reverence such a Bishop in the next degree to a King."[47] Could bishops be eliminated without undermining the whole consecrated hierarchy of church and state?

For the next year Parliament dithered over the issue. It passed piecemeal religious reforms, as if it aimed to build the godly nation in instalments. As for the king, he was increasingly treated by Parliament as if he were an incompetent or a minor, whose opinions did not have to be taken as commands. The legislature was now reclaiming the powers of kingship, which Charles had appeared to renounce by refusing to play his proper public role. But it could not yet decide how to rebuild Jerusalem.[48]

The stalemate in England was further aggravated in October 1641 by an unexpected event: an Irish Catholic uprising against Parliament and for the king. The rebellion in Ireland, like the rebellions in Scotland and England, was based on patriotic identity; but it was a fragile identity, created by political links recently forged across cultural boundaries. Half colony, half kingdom, Ireland was almost as religiously fragmented as Poland, and equally resistant to confessionalization from above. The Catholic population was divided between people of Gaelic descent and the so-called Old English, pre-Reformation settlers who had comprised the legal and bureaucratic class before the influx of Protestant plantation settlers.[49]

Old English support for a Catholic patriot rebellion was not inevitable. For a time they had joined in a different patriot coalition with Puritan settlers against the lord deputy Strafford, who had antagonized godly Protestants by introducing Arminian conformity. An unprecedented parliamentary alliance of Catholics and Protestants even made demands for legislative independence.[50]

This inter-confessional opposition, reminiscent of the coalition politics of the Polish Sejm, was wrecked by the rising of the Covenanters. Writing forty years later, the Old English earl of Castlehaven recalled that "the unexpected success of the *Scots* and the daily misunderstandings between the King and Parliament in *England,* gave at this time birth and life to the Irish Rebellion."[51] Catholic landowners, whether Old English or Old Irish, were convinced that victory for the Covenanters would lead to greater persecution and further Protestant plantations in Ireland. To justify their uprising, they resorted to a cunning invention: that Charles I had sent them a commission to form a Catholic army to fight his enemies. It was plausible enough to be widely accepted, by the king's Protestant critics as well as his Catholic friends.[52] The royalism of the Irish Confederates has often been dismissed as a sham, but in fact it provided a common political goal that was as important as religion in uniting them. To be sure, the king to whom they pledged allegiance was a benign myth. The real Charles I flatly denounced them as rebels. He agreed with the lords justices in Dublin, who were convinced that the insurgents "desire and labour to deprive him of his royal crown and dignity and to place over them some of themselves or some foreign prince."[53] Yet in their own minds, at least, the rebels remained true loyalists, fighting for the Crown as well as for religion.

The Catholic leaders set down their principles in the Confederation of Kilkenny, which was in some ways a reply to the National Covenant. The confederation, unlike the covenant, eschewed any semblance of rebellion against the king, to whom "all and every person and persons within this kingdom shall bear faith and true allegiance." On the other hand, it reasserted the privileges and restored the lands of the Catholic Church. Like the covenant, the confederation was a statement of national purpose, which defined an Irish kingdom as a legal and confessional, rather than an ethnic, community. In two of its articles ethnic distinctions were condemned, meaning "there shall be no distinction or comparison made betwixt Old Irish, and Old and New English." All were to be considered simply Irish—a statement of high idealism, then or now. The confederacy was recognized even by the lords justices as having set up "a national government." It might have provided the foundation for the emergence of an Irish state.[54]

The confederacy was far from a declaration of holy war against England or Protestantism. The Irish peasants who supported the rising, however, seem to have wanted a more thorough religious purification of the land. Although English tales of "massacres" by peasants in Ulster were grotesquely exaggerated, considerable violence did take place against the hated Protestant settlers. They were sometimes forced to run naked from their properties, which turned them into "savages," a term of abuse often used by settlers to describe the native Irish themselves.[55] Like French supporters of the Catholic League, the Ulster rebels tried to cleanse the body politic through the physical extirpation of heresy. This goal was not shared by the Old English elite, some of whom countenanced toleration for Protestants. Later, when the two sides of the Catholic cause split over making peace with the king, the Old English would be reviled in Gaelic verse as "the spurious children who wound the body of the church."[56] As was the case elsewhere, unprivileged social groups were more willing than members of the elite to enforce the confessional homogeneity of the nation through sacrificial violence.

Godly English observers like Nehemiah Wallington, whose brother-in-law was killed in Ireland, viewed the Catholic rebel as an unholy "Other," the antithesis of the Puritan self.[57] The threat of this Other caused the House of Commons, by a narrow majority, to pass a Grand Remonstrance, blaming "the subtile practice of the Jesuits" for "a malignant and pernicious design of subverting the fundamental laws and principles of government."[58] For many Puritans, however, the remonstrance was too vague to provide a charter for the English Israel. Unsatisfied, the City of London presented a monster petition against episcopacy in December 1641. Huge demonstrations in its favour culminated in riots. Several hapless prelates were abused by the angry crowds outside Parliament, while behind locked doors a frightened House of Commons voted to impeach the bishops for treason.[59]

The riots were later condemned by parliamentary leaders as the work of malicious sectarians, and the English national rebellion, the godly uprising against bishops, Arminians, and "Papists," never happened. Forestalled by an anxious and divided legislature, it was finally pre-empted by the king. Charles withdrew from London and began to raise a military force. In August 1642 he unfurled his banners at Nottingham and declared war on his own parliament. Thus, the threat of a patriotic rebellion was removed by the king's fomenting of the first English civil war.

The parliamentary response was typically conservative. The "two bodies" theory was revived, and Parliament claimed to be fighting against the king's natural body in order to preserve the mediating authority of his spiritual body.[60] This constituted a not very stirring call to national resistance. A few radicals took a less hesitant position. In his pamphlet *Lex, rex*, published in 1644, the Scottish Presbyterian Samuel Rutherford trumpeted the cosmic importance of the conflict: "I hope this war shall be Christ's triumph, Babylon's ruin." He argued that all sovereignty—a term he used explicitly—came from the people, not from divine selection, conquest, or patriarchal right. The corpus mysticum of the realm was also in the godly people, not in the king alone: "There is a dignity material in the people scattered, they being many representations of God and his image." *Lex, rex* gave substance to the worst nightmares of Sir Robert Filmer, by granting power to every Christian self. "Every man by nature is a free man born," Rutherford maintained, while "none are by nature kings."[61] He excoriated the assumption of an innate divinity in the royal body as an offence to God. Bluntly, unhesitatingly, Rutherford pointed the way towards a heavenly city that could be built out of the harmony of a multitude of particular consciences. The body politic would be held together simply by the strength of true religion over each mind.

Parliament ignored such radical advice. Instead, its members separated themselves further from the taint of popular sovereignty by adopting the Solemn League and Covenant, in which they swore "to preserve and defend the King's Majesty's person and authority," as well as to bring the Churches of England, Scotland, and Ireland "to the nearest conjunction and uniformity."[62] The Solemn League fell far short of the godly patriotism of Root and Branch, and in a nation already torn by religious factionalism it settled nothing. Many supporters of godly reform became deeply disturbed by what they saw as a charter of religious tyranny. Some of these troubled individuals would later become the instruments not just of a national revolt but of a revolution.

## CATALONIA

The leaders of the patriotic rebellions in Scotland and Ireland never seriously considered the possibility of creating a republic; neither, before 1647, did anyone of consequence in England. They could not imagine how the nation could be held together without monarchy. Their middling- and lower-class followers, however, may not have been so convinced. For them, the millenarian vision of "no king but king Jesus" may have been more palpable than it was for their social superiors. With God as its only monarch, the Christian self would truly be liberated. This was a recurring nightmare among the elite leaders of national rebellions. It hovered like a dark cloud over the nobles and urban oligarchs of Catalonia, whose political course in the great revolt of 1640 to 1652 was dictated almost as much by fear of the lower classes as by hatred of the policies of the king of Spain.[63]

The roots of national identity had existed for centuries in Catalonia. The province had its own political and judicial institutions. Although the *Corts*, or Estates, seldom met, fiscal affairs were dealt with by a six-man standing committee, the *Diputació*. A second binding factor in Catalonia's national identity was a myth of past greatness, a legendary history of constitutional autonomy and civic liberty that inspired patriotic writers like Francisco Gilabert.[64] As for a religiously based sense of destiny, at first glance the Catalans seem to have been no different in doctrine or practice from other Spanish Catholics. The upper classes of Barcelona eagerly read Castilian devotional literature.[65] Yet the religious outlook of the Catalans was still overwhelmingly determined by local forces. The Inquisition was weak and despised; the bishops, half of them Castilians, were not trusted. The parish clergy supplied the impetus behind confessional reform. Religion, moreover, was integral to the dissemination of a separate national identity. In 1636, for example, a provincial ecclesiastical council instructed the clergy to preach in the Catalan language.[66]

For rural labourers and urban artisans, the economic hardships that accompanied war with France after 1635, especially the billeting of troops, strengthened a conviction that the universal empire had failed and that the people of Catalonia were now justified by God in taking the future of their nation into their own hands. They translated these notions into violent action. In the spring of 1640, groups of rural labourers in towns and villages throughout the principality began to attack soldiers and tax officials. It was reported that the peasants had formed a "Christian army" to fight the Spanish troops, who were accused of desecrating churches. The Christian army had sent out a call to arms, assuring "all those of the Valleys and other Catalans" that the rebellion was directed from heaven: "We trust that you will not be lacking on this precise occasion especially where you know that it is to defend the Cause of Our Lord."[67]

On 22 May part of the Christian army entered the holy city to purify the temple. Rebellious peasants marched into Barcelona, bearing an image of Christ and shouting "Long live the King! Death to traitors! Down with bad government!" The first of these slogans may have been a reference to the divine king shown on their banner. A tense calm ensued in the city until the feast of Corpus Christi on 7 June, when hundreds of agricultural workers, or *segadors* (reapers), entered Barcelona for an annual hiring fair. Corpus Christi was a commemoration of the body of Christ, and hence of the Christian community. Its political connotations were widely exploited by Catholic rulers; but the crowd in Barcelona turned communal solidarity into a weapon against the king's representative. Their cries were "Long live holy mother Church, long live the king." Who was the real monarch on the feast of Christ's body? Whatever the answer, the segadors showed their anger at Philip IV by laying siege to the palace of his viceroy. The corpulent official fled to the beach, but he could not outrun the crowd and was beaten to death on the rocks.[68]

The respectable classes of Catalonia—the nobles, higher clerics, and "honoured citizens" of Barcelona—were both disturbed and excited by these events. They detested Olivares, his Union of Arms, and his billeting policy, but they refused to be forced into open rebellion by popular insurrections. The ecclesiastical *diputat* Pau Claris counselled a Neostoic fortitude to his fellow canons of the cathedral of Urgell: "This is a time when the entire province is without justice. . . . Therefore we must conduct our affairs in the light of reason of state [*raho de estat*] and prudence."[69] His advice summed up a practical politics that was not far removed from the humanism of Olivares himself. Claris, whose family were civic notables, exemplified the literate, cosmopolitan culture of the Barcelona oligarchy, the so-called honoured citizens who stood apart from the ignorant multitude.[70] His political outlook contrasted sharply with the "Politics of God" advocated by the segadors.

It would be wrong, however, to present the political culture of the Catalan elite in 1640 as detached from that of the common people. A religiously charged national identity was, to a large extent, shared by all Catalans, as Claris himself demonstrated before the Corts, which had been summoned in September 1640. In its first session he read out a history of the popular uprising that amounted to a justification. He condemned the behaviour of the Spanish troops stationed in Catalonia and particularly noted that "for the burnings of the holy sacrament which is the most detestable crime which the soldiers have committed, the most reverend bishop of Gerona has promulgated a sentence of excommunication against them." Although Claris deplored the "excesses" of the May and June riots, he did not question their motives.[71] What a difference from the English parliament's anaemic reaction to the riots of December 1641! The religious legitimation of the revolt continued with declarations of support from a special junta of theologians and the publication of a *Catholic Proclamation,* written by the Augustinian friar Gaspar Sala. It claimed that the Catalans had taken up arms to defend "home, life, honour, liberty, *patria,* laws, and above all holy temples, sacred images and the Most Holy Sacrament."[72] The rising was in defence of national identity, the body of Christ, and the Christian self.

This strong rhetoric did not mean that Sala was ready to throw off his king; in fact, his proclamation was addressed to "the pious Majesty of Philip the Great." Claris himself had concluded his speech to the Corts by offering faithful submission to the king. As late as December 1640, with a Spanish army advancing steadily into the principality, an offer of peace from Madrid might have been accepted, had not renewed rioting in Barcelona led to its rejection.[73] Once again the leaders of the revolt were pushed away from compromise by popular violence.

This time they sought refuge from the vengeance of Spain and the fury of the people in the arms of Louis XIII. In January 1641 the Corts was informed by the French king's diplomatic agent that "His Most Christian Majesty has given him power to admit [Catalonia] under his protection, provided that it reduces its government to the form of a republic." In other words, the principality had to form a legally separate entity in order to gain aid from France. Resolutions of the Corts and the Barcelona councillors created a republican state without ceremony or celebration. They certainly did not intend that power should revert to the common people. Six days later, facing the prospect of paying for war against Spain out of their own funds, the same bodies decided that a republic "appears to many not to be very effective or what the province needed." So they declared their obedience to Louis XIII of France, their newly chosen count of Barcelona.[74]

For the next eleven years Catalonia was a battleground for the forces of France and Spain. The *guerra dels segadors* turned into a civil war on two levels: between pro- and anti-Spanish Catalans, and between those who supported the king of France and those who did not. The village clergy encouraged resistance against the "heretical" troops of France, as they had formerly against those of Spain.[75] Amid this turmoil, patriotism continued to burn fiercely among lower-class Catalans. As late as the summer of 1651 the Barcelona tanner Miquel Parets bravely recorded in his diary that the retreat of a devastating plague was inspiring good patriots: "It gave great spirit to those who had not gone away to turn to the defence of the *pàtria* . . . everyone turned to Barcelona, that is, those who were good Catalans and who wanted to defend the *pàtria*."[76] He was over-optimistic; in October 1652 the city surrendered to its former master, Philip IV, and the revolt was over.

The councillors of Barcelona marked the end of a devastating war by deciding "to make a general procession as on the day of the Corpus and make a very great feast."[77] Thus, the honoured citizens tried to erase the political memory of a previous Corpus Christi by transferring its festivities to a celebration of their return to the monarchy of Spain. In the countryside, too, defeat channelled popular religious zeal into less insurrectionary paths. In an illuminating discussion of the religious implications of the guerra dels segadors, Joaquim Puigvert has drawn attention to the spread of devotions to the rosary and the Holy Sacrament during the rebellion.[78] These public observances had bound together the Catalan community in opposition to its enemies; but once peace had returned, they were used by local elites to reinforce social hierarchy and conformity. The same practices that had formerly highlighted the providential destiny of the patria now exemplified its subordination to the universal Church and, by implication, its obedience to the Church's chief servant, the king of Spain. Slowly but inexorably, the "Politics of God" guided the common people of Catalonia away from millenarian dreams and towards submission to the state.

## PORTUGAL

The rebellion in Portugal seemed quite different from that in Catalonia. An almost bloodless seizure of power at Lisbon, engineered by a noble cabal, ended Spanish rule in December 1640 and set on the throne the duke of Bragança as King João IV. The *Restauração,* or Restoration, was a lightning coup from above rather than a popular uprising. Nevertheless, it had ideological origins similar to those of other national rebellions.[79]

João Francisco Marques has discovered in sermons and religious writings of the Restoration period an enormous number of references to the Portuguese as a people specially designated by God for a worldwide spiritual mission. Such hopes were built upon a complex historical mythology. According to the "miracle of Ourique," the first king of Portugal had received a vision of Christ on the cross before a battle with the Moors. "Indeed," Jesus obligingly informed him, "I mean for you, and for your seed, to establish my rule [imperium] and to carry my name to foreign peoples."[80] In fulfilment of this prophecy, King Sebastian was killed while trying to invade North Africa in 1580. The decades of Spanish rule that followed were portrayed by later writers as a "Babylonian captivity" for the "new Israelites," the Portuguese people. The memory of the devout King Sebastian was inflated to messianic proportions; some believed he had not been killed at all, while others awaited his spiritual reappearance in a future ruler of his house.[81] The acclamation of the duke of Bragança in 1640 was seen as the culmination of "Sebastianism" and a reaffirmation of the miracle of Ourique. It was accompanied by further prodigies: angels carrying the Holy Sacrament were seen on the moon, and during a procession in honour of the new king, a figure of Christ freed his hand from the cross, as if to bless the liberation of his chosen people.[82] Enthusiastic religious writers, among them the famous Jesuit Antonio de Vieira, did not hesitate to identify Portugal with the "fifth monarchy" of the Book of Daniel, the universal kingdom that would precede the Second Coming.[83]

Resemblances between the religious mythology of the Portuguese monarchy and the dynastic ideology of the Habsburgs were not coincidental. The miracle of Ourique was a variant of the vision of Constantine. The prophecy of fifth monarchy was employed by Spanish imperial writers as well. By co-opting these myths, the kings of Portugal established their heaven-sent role as rivals to the Habsburgs. Yet there was an important difference between the propaganda of the two Crowns. The Portuguese royal legend was used to validate the global mission of the whole Catholic nation rather than the cosmic pre-eminence of the monarchy. The Restauração was viewed as a collective act of the divinely favoured Portuguese people, who had disposed of Spanish tyranny and restored a native kingship by universal consent. The Cortes of 1641 brought the religious definition of the nation into sharper focus by passing restrictive laws against converted Jews.[84] The new Israelites asserted their claim to heavenly sanction through threats of dispossession against an older chosen people.

In its effects on national identity, the Portuguese Restoration was one of the most unsettling of all the mid-century revolts, because it revived the Christian corpus mysticum on a populist and millenarian basis. Yet it was far from unsettling in its social implications. The nobility and clergy were accepted as the protectors of national traditions. As A. M. Hespanha has shown, the Cortes enshrined the privileges of the upper classes. The powers of the Crown were limited by the assumption of corporate rights, inherent in "the people" but exercised by landowners and ecclesiastics. Although the king described himself as absolute, his role was confined to the brokerage of patronage relations among the elite. The aristocracy behaved as if it had been to them that Christ promised an empire at Ourique.[85]

João IV did what he could to escape this situation, in part by considering a limited toleration for Protestants and Jews. As elsewhere, the politics of toleration pointed towards the undoing of the corpus mysticum and the possibility of sectarian individualism—in this case, with royal approval. The Portuguese aristocracy quickly suppressed the king's schemes. The debility of the Crown was put on show in 1668, when João's obnoxious son Afonso VI was forced to abdicate in favour of his brother, Pedro. To add insult to injury, the sexually confused Afonso lost not only his throne but also his wife, who after an embarrassing annulment married his more potent brother.[86] It is hard to imagine such a sordid affair taking place publicly in any other western European monarchy. In Portugal, the theatre of royal virtue had become a shambles.

Like other national uprisings of the mid-seventeenth century, the Portuguese Restoration was sustained by a religious conception of community. Unlike those other insurrections, however, it reinvigorated patriotism and empire under the auspices of the aristocracy. The thought of a nation without a king raised the spectre of anarchy and was abhorrent to the governing classes, but they installed a feeble monarchy and kept the means of mass culture—processions, public festivals, and so forth—under their own control. The confessional focus of the new regime, moreover, remained fixed on collective rather than personal devotions. The introspection and inner discipline that were elsewhere becoming typical of the reformed Catholic self emerged slowly in Portugal. In terms of ideological formation, therefore, the Restoration led to immobility. It retarded the creation of a rational state—until the ministry of Pombal built one by brute force a century later.

## The Ukraine

In contrast to the Portuguese Restoration, the uprising from 1648 to 1656 in the Ukraine fostered the development of a rational state, but not one founded on national identity. It was instead a tsarist state, based on shared Orthodoxy. In light of this, it might reasonably be claimed that the Ukrainian rising was not much of a national revolt at all.[87] It was led against the Polish Commonwealth by Cossacks under the command of their hetman, Bohdan Khmelnytsky. The Cossacks were runaway peasants who lived in military camps on the lower reaches of the Dnieper River, especially in the Zaporozhian Sich, or "fort beyond the rapids." In 1648 and 1649 they quickly overran the lands on the upper banks of the river, including the trading city of Kiev, and won support among settled peasants who resented the spread of serfdom. At first glance, Khmelnytsky's followers do not seem to have shared any of the defining features of national consciousness. The Ukraine, or "borderland," had never been a single state; few provincial institutions tied together this part of the Polish-Lithuanian Commonwealth; and the culture of the local nobility had been steadily Polonized.[88] The insurgents themselves had diverse origins, and strange allies. In his memoirs, the Polish magnate Albrycht Radziwiłł seldom failed to point out in horror that the *hostes Kozaci,* or Cossack enemies, were assisted by Muslim Tartars.[89]

In spite of this ungodly alliance, the unifying ideology of the Ukrainian rebellion was essentially religious. It rallied the orthodox, not only against Catholic Poland but also against the "heretical" Uniate Church and against Jews, who were subjected to terrible massacres. Rabbi Nathan Hanover, a survivor of these atrocities, saw them in strictly confessional terms. He referred to the settled Ukrainian peasants as "Greeks" and recorded with surprising compassion that "the nobles levied upon them heavy taxes, and some even resorted to cruelty and torture with the intent of persuading them to accept Catholicism."[90] The cause of preserving Orthodoxy also linked the Cossacks with the *bratstva,* or brotherhoods, of merchants and craftsmen that had initiated moral and educational reforms in many Ukrainian towns.[91] The religious nature of the revolt was bluntly expressed by Hetman Ivan Vyhovsky in a protest addressed to the Russian tsar in the late 1650s: "We, the entire Zaporozhian Army, declare and testify before God and the entire world with complete candour that the only cause and the only objective of the war that we undertook against the Poles was the defence of the holy Eastern Church and of our ancestral liberty."[92]

Vyhovsky's defence of Orthodoxy and Cossack "liberty" can be read as a statement of embryonic national consciousness, derived from religious conviction and inherited rights; but it also reveals a weak institutional basis. The rebels called their new polity "the Zaporozhian Army," and its foundation remained the Cossack regimental system, under an elected hetman.[93] As Khmelnytsky recognized, this was an inadequate substitute even for the feeble governing apparatus of the Polish monarchy. At Pereiaslav in January 1654 he told the assembled Cossack host that "we now see that we cannot live without a ruler" and asked them to agree to "let our Lord God join us to the Tsar's strong hand," which they promptly did without a single dissenting voice.

The Cossacks undoubtedly saw this as a contractual agreement, but when their officers asked the tsar's representative to take an oath that his prince would not violate Cossack freedoms, they met with a stiff rebuke. "To request an oath on behalf of the Sovereign is reprehensible," the

Cossacks were told; "it has never been practiced that an oath for the Sovereign be given to vassals but rather vassals give oaths to the Sovereign." The officers of the Zaparozhian Army accepted this tsarist haughtiness with some reluctance. It was the first sign of their subjection to an ever-expanding central authority. Khmelnytsky's successor, Hetman Vyhovsky, was soon driven to foment an unsuccessful insurrection against the tsar in hope of establishing a separate Ukrainian principality.[94]

Cossack resentment, which stemmed from their new ruler's obliviousness to their interests, was understandable; but so was the tsar's point of view. He was, after all, the leader by divine selection of the Orthodox community, within which the Ukrainians had no real claim to be considered a separate nation. If the Cossacks eventually acquiesced in this interpretation, it was because they did not possess a very clear sense themselves of how their faith might otherwise be preserved. Perhaps a rational Ukrainian state might have arisen out of a reunion between the Orthodox and Uniate churches, a trend encouraged by some magnates in the settled territories. Yet it was precisely this possibility that had caused the angry Cossacks to leap on their warhorses in the first place.[95] The Ukrainian problem was one common to all national rebellions: how was a religiously based political identity to be maintained without recourse to reason of state? Surely not by the Christian self alone, through some sort of confessional democracy. The only solution acceptable to social elites was to re-confer the authority of the community on a monarch. Under these circumstances, no king, not even João IV, was willing to recognize that the national collectivity could place permanent limits on him. The Cossacks, however, ultimately surrendered far more to the "high hand" of their hastily chosen ruler than the Portuguese, the Catalans, the Scots, or even the Irish were obliged to do.

## The Crisis of States

The national uprisings of the mid-seventeenth century did not aim to liberate the Christian self from royal mediation. Where this shocking possibility surfaced, as in Catalonia, it was quickly scuttled by ruling elites. In France, however, internal disorders in the late 1640s came closer to bringing about such a drastic change. In the United Provinces, Naples, and

England between 1647 and 1650, authority was actually transferred from a monarch to a republican state governed by a citizen oligarchy. Contemporaries were aware of the singular characteristics of these upheavals. Early accounts of the Neapolitan uprising of 1647 called it a *rivoluzione*, or revolution, without parallel in ancient or modern history; and it was soon connected with events in England and Holland. Dutch medals of the 1650s compared the fisherman Masaniello, who led the early stages of the revolt in Naples, to the English lord protector Oliver Cromwell, equating in a moral sense the guiding personalities who stood at the centre of two major revolutions.[96]

"Revolution" has a momentous resonance. Many scholars have complained that it is a vague or anachronistic term. Certainly it should not be inflated into some sort of metaconcept; but neither should it be rejected as a shibboleth.[97] Revolution can be defined as a fundamental change in the collective idealization of authority known as the state. Even in the seventeenth century the notions of revolution and the state were connected in political thought. They were both associated with Italian republicanism, particularly with Machiavelli. Although the reviled Florentine hardly used either word, he was deeply concerned with the process of change or corruption in the state. J. G. A. Pocock has dubbed the recurring incidence of this theme in political theory "the Machiavellian Moment."[98] Among Spanish and Italian writers of the seventeenth century, however, Giovanni Botero was a more congenial source, and we might rechristen the theme "the Boteran Moment." Botero defined the state as "a firm dominion over a people."[99] It was an ideal type of authority, presuming a just lordship over the community. The state was not, however, eternal. All states would eventually decay and fall, according to Botero, "because human affairs wax and wane as if by a law of nature, like the moon to which they are subject."[100]

The Boteran Moment surfaced again in Saavedra Fajardo's *Idea of a Politico-Christian Prince* of 1640, a series of political commentaries attached to emblematic illustrations. *Estado*, or state, was employed by Saavedra Fajardo to suggest the temporal and mutable qualities of human governance, in contrast to more fixed conventions like *república*, *reino*, and *monarquía*. The people cannot be made content, he argued, "when the State is in disharmony and a change of dominion is desirable." He frequently suggested parallels between state and "estate," by which he meant not only the territories of the Crown but also its physical condition or health. "Nothing is permanent in nature," he wrote, so that eventually every kingdom will arrive "at its ultimate estate."[101] A legacy of Renaissance humanism, the state implied an organic or natural mutability that might be at odds with the spiritual perfectionism of the Christian polity. The sources of the state's vitality and degeneration were among the secrets of nature, so it is not surprising that Saavedra Fajardo sought to explain them through emblems, the favourite devices of the Neoplatonists. One of his emblems showed a clock, representing "the government of a state," whose self-regulating mechanism operates in perfect unity and obedience. "The punishment of a state is up to the Holy Spirit," he noted, "and its blessing is that only one governs."[102]

Revolution was an aspect of the state's impermanence, a way of de-scribing its natural mutations. It had entered the common currency of Italian political discourse by the mid-seventeenth century, especially in republican Venice. Did this have anything to do with the controversy over Galileo, who had recently revived the heliocentric model of the universe first demonstrated in Copernicus's *Of the Revolutions of the Heavenly Spheres?* Ilan Rachum has argued that the emergence of revolutionary discourse had little to do with this debate; but it seems likely that Galileo's theory, which showed that the celestial mechanism was not perfect, had some indirect impact on contemporary political attitudes. Revolution had become a fashionable expression by the late 1640s, when it was included in book titles in order to increase sales. Popular tumults like the 1647 tax revolts in Palermo, for example, might be labelled *rivoluzioni* by writers eager to shock respectable readers. The Italophile Cardinal de Retz called various conspiracies to assassinate Richelieu "popular revolutions." Some writers represented revolutionary change as circular, leading back to an original point of constitutional origin—a comforting notion derived from Aristotle. Others were unclear about what course revolution might follow.[103]

Could states be constructed rationally, like Saavedra Fajardo's clock, so that if properly cared for they would never experience revolutions? The negotiators who put an end to the Thirty Years' War seem to have thought so. They defined the autonomy of new states, and confirmed the sov-ereignty of old ones, by recognizing the balance of military power. Their work was supposed to provide a permanent territorial settlement for the Empire.[104] For the first time, however, political order was not made dependent upon religious unity. On the contrary, the Treaties of Westphalia linked the preservation of states to the possibility of religious tolerance, justified in terms of "mixed prudence." "It is lawful by urgent necessity to enter into perpetual peace with heretics," conceded a Catholic publicist.[105]

The national revolts of the 1640s began in opposition to this sort of prudentialism. They were popular reactions against reason of state—indeed, against the whole concept of the state, which was becoming so widespread. A godly patriotism was presented as an antidote to the moral failures of humanist government and as the foundation of a Christian polity. In some cases, however, the leaders of rebellion had to consider another option, forced upon them by "urgent necessity": changing the form of government from monarchy into a republic of virtue, dominated by an oligarchy of responsible citizens.[106] For some, this was the only path towards political stability; for others, it was a terrible violation of the divine order reflected in both the body politic and the self. From either point of view it was a revolutionary step that established a new type of polity, a rational state in which every Christian was to some degree individually represented.

## THE FRONDE: A FAILED REVOLUTION?

The French civil wars from 1647 to 1653 are collectively called "the Fronde," a name derived from the slingshots used by rioters to break windows in Paris. The title may lend too great an appearance of unity to what was really a series of distinct revolts: the Fronde of the officers and *parlementaires,* the Fronde of the Paris bourgeoisie, the Fronde of the princes, the Fronde of Bordeaux. Were any of these revolutionary? Historians have had a hard time answering the question. Orest Ranum has stressed the revolutionary significance of lawbreaking by officers who were sworn to uphold the state.[107] All the same, it is hard to perceive how the Fronde was anything more than a potential revolution. Change in the state was debated, but not implemented. The revolutionary implications of the Fronde were undermined by fear among its own leaders of a revival of the turmoil of the religious wars, and by their self-interested adherence to the idea of a French state.

The Fronde took place in yet another period of great uncertainty about royal sovereignty. As in 1610 and again after 1715, the peculiar situation of a regency, when the king was not directly in charge, energized court factions and emboldened corporate bodies. Everyone could claim to be upholding the interests of a monarch who was too young to make decisions for himself. The regency also permitted a resurgence of the dévots in Paris. The city's popular preachers were now drawn towards the spiritual rigour of Jansen and St. Cyran.[108] The coadjutor bishop of Paris, Paul de Gondi, better known by his later title of Cardinal de Retz, delivered stirring sermons on human frailty and the need for moral regeneration. Earlier his preaching had earned him a rebuke as "a reckless fellow" from Richelieu. Gondi was indeed rash; although connected with the Jansenists of Port-Royal, he was a secret libertine, who confided that he had entered the clergy because he was disappointed in his other ambitions: "There was nothing to be done. That's what it takes to become a saint."[109] In any case, there were plenty of real saints among his bourgeois and noble listeners. By this time even some of the leading judges of the parlement had become noted for their piety. The elderly Pierre Broussel, acknowledged as the chief troublemaker among the parlementaires, had Jansenist leanings. He was praised in a popular print of 1648 for a virtue that "takes the title of Christian" rather than pagan—a swipe at the supposed irreverence and humanist values of the court.[110]

The immediate causes of the Fronde were not religious, but there was a confessional dimension, brooding and dangerous, to the confrontations of 1648 to 1653. Should it be called Jansenist? "The viewpoint which wants to see in it [Jansenism] a natural ally of the Fronde," René Taveneaux has cautiously noted, "is . . . neither inconsistent nor totally arbitrary." Christian Jouhaud has gone further: "Let us no longer fear to pronounce the word Jansenism."[111] Among most *Frondeurs*, to be sure, the word should not be applied too literally; it translated into an inward-looking and more rigorous Catholicism, not necessarily informed by Augustinian views on predestination. It was a piety that emphasized the grave responsibilities of the individual conscience and deplored the worldly religiosity of the

Jesuits. Cardinal Jules Mazarin, the king's chief minister, was horrified by it, and trembled at the thought of a *cabale des dévots*.[112]

The political onslaught of the parlementaires against Mazarin—and against the memory of Richelieu—can be seen as a moral struggle with Jansenist overtones. It began as a showdown between the judges and the financiers, or *partisans* (tax farmers), the supposedly low-born creatures who raised money for the cardinal's war. What did it matter that most of these speculators were actually from respectable office-bearing families, or that not a few of the judges had profited themselves from the "finance State"?[113] The *gens de finance* were seen as the moneylenders who had polluted the temple of state. Their diabolical corruption was denounced in highly charged religious language in a Frondeur pamphlet of 1649, the *Cathechism of the Partisans*. It heaped abuse on "the Partisans and all that sect of people" as if they were a bunch of heretics.[114] During the last desperate stages of the Fronde, as Jouhaud has shown, this paranoia about bloodsucking profiteers and fiscal "vampires" attached itself to a traditional religious target: the Jews, who were attacked in an outbreak of anti-Semitic pamphleteering in Paris.[115]

According to Frondeur propaganda, the financiers had perverted the morality of the whole state. Through their "Interest, Ambition and Avarice," royalty itself had been distorted, so that if God himself were to appear in glory on earth, "he would have difficulty finding a place, not in the king's household, but among the servants of a favorite."[116] The favourite was of course Mazarin—that "harpy made arrogant by the spoils and riches of this flourishing Kingdom," according to another print, which urged the Frondeurs to fight against him "like real Joshuas."[117] Thus, Mazarin became to the Fronde what Henry III had been to the Catholic League: an anti-Christ, the chief obstacle to the spiritual purification of the kingdom.

The moral crusade against the financiers reached its culmination in May 1648 when the leading parlementaires met with representatives of the other sovereign courts in the Chambre St. Louis of the Palais de Justice, for the purpose of reforming the kingdom. Some of them justified this extraordinary step by resorting to the convenient fiction of the king's two bodies. They argued that they were defending the mystical body of the king against the errors of his natural body, which was after all that of a minor.

# LE SALVT
# DE LA FRANCE,
## DANS LES ARMES DE LA VILLE DE PARIS.

A  *Le bon Genie de la France, conduisant sa Maiesté en sa flotte Royale.*

B  *Son Altesse le Prince de Conty, Generalissime de l'armée du Roy, tenant le timon du Vaisseau, accompagné des Ducs d'El-beuf, & de Beaufort, Generaux de l'armée, & du Prince de Marsillac, Lieutenant general de l'armée.*

C  *Les Ducs de Boüillon & de la Motte-Haudancour, Generaux, accompagnez du Marquis de Noirmontier, Lieutenant General de l'armée.*

D  *Le Corps du Parlement, accompagné de Messieurs de Ville.*

E  *Le Mazarin, accompagné de ses Monopoleurs, s'efforçant de renuerser la Barque Françoise, par des vents contraires à sa prosperité.*

F  *Le Marquis d'Ancre se voyant, en taschant de couler le Vaisseau à fond, faisant signe au Mazarin de luy prester la main dans sa premiere entreprise.*

15. *Le salut de la France dans les armes de la Ville de Paris* (1648),
engraved broadsheet.

Photo: Bibliothèque Mazarine, Paris; Jean-Loup Charmet, photographer.

The French judges may well have picked up the two-bodies theory from the debates raging across the Channel. It was clearly antithetical to the unitary conception of sovereignty and it might well have led to a republic of virtue, headed by the godly magistrates of the Chambre St. Louis, with the king reduced to a mere figurehead. Most parlementaires, however, were far from willing to jettison the Bourbon state, which had served them so well, in favour of an incoherent and foreign political theology. They merely sought to bring the existing regime under their own influence.[118] By accepting the rational permanence of the state, they renounced revolution.

Their plebeian supporters, on the other hand, had not yet given up the defence of the corpus mysticum, as they demonstrated when the queen decided to arrest Broussel. He was apprehended at the conclusion of a Te Deum mass in thanks for a recent military victory. It was a dramatic gesture, meant to suggest that the Frondeurs could not be trusted to carry on the war against Spain—and thus, perhaps, to associate them with bitter memories of the pro-Spanish Catholic League. Whatever its intention, the move was a disaster. The tradesmen and artisans of the city of Paris rose up in a new "day of the barricades" to defend Broussel, the "father of the people." Was this a spontaneous affirmation of a link between the Fronde and the League? Robert Descimon has doubted that the connection had much political significance.[119] Yet it is hard to determine exactly what the crowds had in mind. Retz recorded that the barricades were "bordered by flags and by all the arms that the League had left intact"—which gives a distinctly atavistic impression. He then went on to recount the famous story of the silver-gilt gorget that he saw around the neck of a militia officer. On it "was engraved the face of the Jacobin who killed Henry III, with this inscription: 'Saint Jacques Clément.'" Outraged, Retz seized the gorget and destroyed it with a hammer. "Everyone cried 'Long live the King!'," he recalled, "but the echo replied: 'No Mazarin!'"[120]

This is neither an implausible nor an insignificant story. The crowds at the barricades may well have been inspired by the same zeal for purifying the collective body politic that had motivated the League; and they may not have been reluctant to commemorate a movement that was abominated by the Bourbons. Was this why the city aldermen tried to give command of the militia to the duc d'Elbeuf, whose family had captained the armies of the League against Henry III and Henry IV? Elbeuf was heard to declare, in ominous tones, "that he would do much better than his cousin . . . had done for the League."[121] The League, however, had not confronted the issue of sovereignty. The Fronde of the people came closer to revolution, because the body politic that it sought to reform had absorbed so much of the rhetoric of Bodin.

What sort of government did the popular Fronde espouse? The five thousand Frondeur pamphlets called *Mazarinades* provide clues to this problem, but the messages expressed in them are not uniform. Hubert Carrier has tried patiently to examine their different audiences—from office-bearers and bourgeois to illiterate labourers. He has pointed out that "the *Mazarinades* are both a mirror where public opinion recognizes itself and a mould which shapes it." Christian Jouhaud, on the other hand, has seen them not as mirrors of opinion but as political acts that, like popular theatre, created an exaggerated appearance of reality in order to incite the audience to participation.[122] The effort to provide a "voice of the people," however, should not be minimized. Although they were never reluctant to shock, the authors of the Mazarinades sincerely believed that their views were in harmony with the common good and reflected public opinion.

Some of their writings bore fascinating resemblances to those of the League, combined with the newer language of sovereignty. These radical Mazarinades revived the idea of a mystical body of the people, an emanation of Christ's own body, and bestowed upon it a supreme authority derived from Bodin. One example of 1649 bore the portentous title *That the Voice of the People Is the Voice of God*. It advised the queen mother "to cherish all subjects, as members of the Sovereign," an extraordinary foreshadowing of the ideology of the rational state.[123] A 1653 pamphlet similarly evoked *The Voice of the People* in arguing "that these universal clamours were coming from a supernatural source, and that the very author of nature . . . was making heard his wishes by the voice of men."[124] In other words, the people spoke with the unquestionable authority of the divine sovereign. Like their predecessors of the 1590s, the more radical Frondeurs refused to recognize the physical sacrality of rulers. A king, suggested the author of a Mazarinade from 1650, "is a man elected by men." What if he turned against his people? The author grimly suggested that if the king, "instead of carrying out his office, troubles them [the people] by undue vexations, it is much more just that he perish like Saul, than that all the peoples that he dominates perish."[125] Thus, the language of Jacques Clément was joined to the idea that the people were supreme within the state.

Admittedly, the radical voice of the Fronde was only one strain among many. It was always subordinated to an equally pious but more moderate discourse that maintained the privileges of corporate bodies while refusing to resist the power of the king. Most of the Mazarinades were positively exuberant in their loyalty to the monarch. One pamphlet, *Christian and Political Discourse of the Power of Kings*, argued that religion and property were beyond the reach of the sovereign; but it also opined that "in the Political and Civil Body that is the Monarchical State, order must be inviolably observed."[126] The author ignored the possibility that order might have to be violated in order to protect what did not belong to the king.

The Fronde was ultimately defeated by such contradictions. In an ideological as well as a political sense, it was never able to detach itself from the Bourbon state. The system of Richelieu was hated, but its premises were accepted by the political elite as the only way of governing France. It is less certain whether this was also believed by the people, the urban shopkeepers and artisans who set up the barricades—let alone the peasants, whose views are unfathomable. The direction of the Fronde was never in their hands.[127]

Meanwhile, Louis XIV began to present his own conception of the state as a collective emanation of the majesty of his own person, not as a republic of virtue. Louis marked the attainment of his majority in September 1651 with a lit de justice attended by members of all the corporate bodies that had recently disturbed his government. The king was magnificently attired, and the Englishman John Evelyn, who watched the royal procession from Thomas Hobbes's window, said he looked "like a young Apollo."[128] His radiant appearance was supposed to convince Louis's assembled subjects of his divinely given power, which they could be part of only by accepting and reflecting it. This was a calculated reversal of the radical ideology of the Fronde. But the king's shining presence did not prevent the insurrection in Bordeaux, where the sovereignty of the people briefly became a reality.

In the spring of 1652 the Fronde of Bordeaux entered a radical phase called the *Ormée*, which came close to revolution.[129] It was brought about by a group of discontented lawyers and merchants who gathered under the *ormes*, or elm trees, of the town. When the *Ormistes* took over city government, they claimed divine sanction for their uprising through the miraculous apparition of a dove, which alighted in an elm during one of their meetings and then flew around the city churches. Their propaganda did not hesitate to assert that the dove gave "a very clear testimony of the providence of God, and of the assistance of the Holy Spirit for this Assembly."[130] A dove with the motto *Vox Populi, Vox Dei* became their official seal. Their manifesto announced "that the restoration of the French State cannot be made except by the People. The *grands* and the Magistrates are the accomplices and the supports of Tyranny." Therefore the Ormistes "have formed and given establishment to a Democratic Government."[131] The responsible Christian self would be freed from oppression by a divinely sanctioned democracy. The Holy Spirit was carrying the seed of a rational state—but one in which monarchy hardly figured.

The Ormée had the characteristics of both a national revolt and a state revolution. The Bordelais saw their region as a patria that enjoyed ancient and distinct privileges. Christian Jouhaud has pointed to the importance of this local patriotism in the works of the *Ormiste* priest and polemicist Geoffroy Gay.[132] In the miracle of the dove Gay discerned a providential sign of the collective mission of his people. Yet, like most supporters of the Ormée, he wanted to reform the whole kingdom of France, not to set Bordeaux apart from it. His rhetoric acknowledged the indivisibility of the state as well as the sovereignty of its people. Unfortunately, there was little agreement as to how these goals were to be reached. Some of the Ormistes were willing to listen to the English agent Edward Sexby, who recommended the declaration of a republic. Others considered an alliance with the Spanish—the option followed by the Catholic League in the 1590s. Most hoped that Louis XIV himself would agree to follow his people into the promised land of democratic revolution.[133]

The king had other ideas. He was a Bourbon to the core, and in the beseeching face of the Fronde he recognized only the horrible visage of the League. After retaking Paris for a third time in October 1652, he sent his armies to conquer the last important bastion of the Frondeurs. Revolutionary

Bordeaux fell in August 1653, and the leaders of the Ormée were executed or banished. Perhaps the dove still soared above the elm trees, but her quiet flight never again troubled the good order of the French state.

## REVOLUTION IN NAPLES

The Frondeurs had drawn near to the republic of virtue but had pulled back from it, fearing a revival of civil war. The leaders of other patriotic rebellions were sometimes more bold in asserting that the preservation of the body politic necessitated the overthrow of monarchy. Although this was presented as a conservative argument, it led to revolutionary assertions of state power and to rule by a chosen few. Instead of a reversion to a Christian theology of government, revolution produced oligarchy and debates about the locus of sovereignty. This was what happened at Naples in 1647 and 1648.[134]

Visiting Naples two years before the rising, John Evelyn witnessed one of the popular religious rituals by which Spanish authority was maintained: the viceroy's Lenten Carnival procession, "which was very splendid for the Reliques, Banners and Musique which accompanied the B: Sacrament."[135] The Blessed Sacrament, Christ's own body, corresponded to the corpus mysticum of the kingdom of Naples, now protected by the king of Spain. As in Catalonia, the royal office was understood as broadly contractual: for his authority to be recognized as legitimate, the king had to fulfil his moral obligations as a just ruler. The theory of contract, which had never carried much weight in most European monarchies, had been carefully preserved by political writers in southern Italy.[136] It was increasingly ignored, however, by the Neapolitan nobility, the dominant force in the government of the kingdom. A closed caste, largely exempt from taxes, the nobles had succeeded in tying the viceregal government to their own interests.[137]

Ironically, the future mastermind of the Neapolitan rebellion started out as a supporter of royal authority against the nobility. Giulio Genoino, a lawyer and cleric in minor orders, began his political career by urging the king to reform the corrupt and "luxurious" aristocracy.[138] The message of Genoino and his fellow reformers was patriotic, although not necessarily anti-Spanish. Like other movements based on national identity, patriotism

in Naples depended less upon opposition to the Crown than on the protection of local institutions, the generation of collective myths, and a belief in
providential destiny. This belief was usually the socially explosive element;
and so it proved in the summer of 1647 in the kingdom of Naples.

The Neapolitan revolt began in the provinces as a war of the peasantry
and the small-town middle classes against the nobility. The city of Naples
put itself at the head of this movement. The historian Rosario Villari has
downplayed the importance of religious factors in the uprising, with the
exception of hatred for the Jesuits.[139] Yet there is abundant evidence that
the strands of patriotism were bound together by religion. A contemporary
observer commented that the lower classes rose because they believed that
their leaders "are friends of God, led by the Holy Ghost, or guided by an
Angel." The manifestoes of revolt constantly called upon the protection of
Mary and the saints. At the height of the uprising, a crowd of armed
demonstrators entered a city church to beg protection from the saints
against "the tyrannies of bad government." Clerics took an active part in
directing the course of events. They were inspired by Cardinal Filomarino,
a pro-papal enemy of the aristocracy, who was acclaimed by the Neapolitan
crowd as "Liberator of the *Patria*."[140] When the republic was created, it
was said in Cosenza that the famous statue of the Madonna of the Carmine
had miraculously announced her protection of it. In nearby Torano local
priests sang a Te Deum to welcome republican troops. During the brutal
suppression of unrest four cathedral canons were executed in Nardò for
inciting the rebels; their heads were displayed on their choir stalls, *pour
encourager les autres*.[141]

As for the city of Naples, it had once been a powerhouse of reformed
Catholic piety but by the mid-1600s "was more a museum of the institutions of the Counter-Reformation than a centre of religious experience."[142]
The events of 1647 reinvigorated the city's spiritual zeal, along with its
patriotism. Peter Burke's study of the early stages of the revolt has stressed
the significance of popular religious beliefs in facilitating the rise of the
famous Masaniello. On 7 July, during commemorations of a feast of the
Virgin Mary at the Carmelite Church in the marketplace, a riot broke out
against taxation and high prices. The fisherman Tommaso Aniello, or
Masaniello, a member of a group that engaged in mock battles during the
festival, quickly emerged as leader of the rioters. Within a few days he had

been named "Captain-General of the People" by a frightened viceroy. The people acclaimed him as a "man sent from God," as a saint, even as a king. He was said to exercise an "absolute dominion" over the crowd, which obeyed him "like a sworn King, and its natural Lord." His supporters saw themselves as patriots struggling in a holy cause. After tearing one of Masaniello's enemies to pieces, they branded him a "rebel against the *Patria,* and traitor to the most faithful People." At the height of the fisherman's popularity, San Gennaro, patron of the city, reportedly appeared in the Carmelite Church holding a sword to defend his people. In the same church, on 16 July, Masaniello was assassinated by a group of grain merchants.[143]

The reign of Tommaso Aniello lasted only nine days, but his character was indelibly stamped on the whole revolt. To his supporters he was the common man who had become a king, a fisherman like the disciples of Christ, a sign of God's mercy to the poor. To his opponents he was a tool of natural destruction, the disturber of "a tempestuous sea."[144] Both aspects are presented in a remarkable painting by Micco Spadaro, who included *The Revolt of Masaniello* among a trio of large canvases depicting recent disasters that had struck Naples—the other two were an eruption of Mount Vesuvius in 1631 and the plague of 1656.[145] Masaniello is shown twice in the painting: as a would-be saint, preaching with a crucifix, and as a vainglorious warrior, parading in military costume. He is a two-faced messiah, undone by pride. The rage of his supporters is depicted as an elemental force of nature, registered in their violent and distorted gestures. Revolution is represented as a form of organic decay, a war within the body politic, produced by excessive passion in the unregulated bodies of the common people.

Spadaro's image of the uprising is deliberately misleading. From the beginning, Masaniello's rise was carefully managed and exploited by the aged Genoino and the reform party. Their purpose was not to tear down the state but to work with the viceroy in order to dislodge aristocratic control.[146] This strategy collapsed in August 1647, however, when a wave of riots broke out, led by disgruntled silk workers. Genoino opposed the new revolt and was sent into exile. Government fell under the control of radical lawyers, merchants, and minor nobles, many of them members of the so-called Academy of Idlers, a debating society in which classical

16. Domenico Gargiulo, called Micco Spadaro, *The Revolt of Masaniello* (c. 1656–60), painting. Museo nazionale di San Martino, Naples.

Photo: Soprintendenza per i beni artistici e storici di Napoli, Naples.

republican ideas had been discussed. Its most prominent alumnus was the rich lawyer and art collector Vincenzo D'Andrea, who headed the new regime. He found his own Masaniello in the illiterate blacksmith Gennaro Annese, who was named "Generalissimo of the Most Faithful People." After an unsuccessful Spanish attack in October, D'Andrea declared a republic. Appealing to the authority of "His Divine Majesty" (God, not Philip IV), as well as to the Virgin and the saints, he announced that "our Realm, and People [return] themselves to a state of liberty, free from all obligation, and servitude." This was a stunning proclamation of the emancipation of the Christian self.[147]

As a rational state, however, "the Most Serene Republic of this Kingdom of Naples" lacked a locus of sovereignty. Moderates wanted to imitate the Dutch and Venetian models, with a military commander holding supreme power. The position could not be held, of course, by a labourer like the vulgar Annese; he was succeeded by a high-born French adventurer, the duc de Guise, a descendant of both the chief of the Catholic League and the Angevin kings of Naples. Filomarino gave him clerical sanction by blessing his sword in the cathedral. D'Andrea, however, cherished a classical vision of the republic. He demanded the nomination of a senate of *virtuosi,* or leading citizens, that would share sovereignty with the duke. The Senate was eventually chosen in the spring of 1648, but by then it was evident that Guise wanted sole authority. This turned D'Andrea, Annese, and their friends against the "Royal Republic" and led them to welcome the return of Spanish rule.[148]

The republic had travelled far from the religious patriotism of Masaniello, into the domain of sovereignty and the state. A hostile writer recorded that the deluded people no longer spoke "of Religion, of Sermons, of Confession and other pious acts." No wonder that the Jesuits, guardians of good order in the mystical body of the church, hated the many-headed republican hydra from the first. The nobles who took up arms against it swore a crusading oath to the Jesuit martyr Saint Francis Xavier. The retaking of Naples was acclaimed as a mark of salvation by the supporters of Spain. The Society of Jesus asked the viceroy to reward its members for having rescued the city by their prayers.[149] Their spiritual counter-offensive was highly effective, and the republic never reappeared. It left behind, however, a legacy of state-centred reformism that would later be taken up by the Spanish themselves and culminate in the enlightened monarchy of the Neapolitan Bourbons. The republic also left behind the powerful image of Masaniello—the fisherman-king whose sufferings mirrored those of the Redeemer. His assumed sainthood had created a sacred underpinning for the creation of a rational republic. While they feared and despised the memory of Tommaso Aniello, the rulers of Europe would later struggle to repeat in their own realms the transforming effects of his myth.

## REVOLUTION IN ENGLAND

Only one event of the mid-seventeenth century could compete with the career of Masaniello in its impact on European consciousness: the execution of King Charles I of England on 30 January 1649. Albrycht

Radziwiłł included in his memoirs a long account of the horrible event, describing it as "truly a hidden sign from God" to fractious Poland. A Spanish minister wrote to Philip IV that the death of King Charles "should remind us that it is the people who raise up and give powers to kings for their own defense and preservation," a sound piece of advice that might have saved much trouble in Catalonia.[150] Dramatists used the fate of Charles I to argue that the people should rally to the Crown against the forces of Machiavellian self-interest. This was the message of Corneille's play *Pertharite*, which was inspired, as Georges Couton has shown, by events in England.[151] In his blood-soaked 1668 tragedy *Murdered Majesty*, the German playwright Andreas Gryphius showed a guiltless king opposed by fanatics whose real purpose is their own aggrandisement. At the end of the play, ghosts of Charles I roam the stage, crying out to the audience for revenge, which immediately ensues in the form of war, heresy, discord, suicide, and so on.[152]

The king's death inspired no plays in republican England, where Parliament had closed down the theatres.[153] In his own country, Charles's only stage was his scaffold, which he used to erase the memory of a failed kingship. It was a brilliant performance by a ruler who had never wanted to appear in the theatre of royal virtue. Like a Christian martyr, he forgave his enemies, proclaimed his innocence, called on his listeners to "give God his due by rightly regulating his Church." He declared his attachment to "liberty and freedom," but added that this "consists in having of government," in which the people have no share, for government "is nothing pertaining to them. . . . A subject and a sovereign are clean different things." His last public utterance was "Remember!"[154] Charles's scaffold speech was not meant to chastise the people; its intent was to convince them that, as Christians, they should restore royal sovereignty. It expressed an Anglican vision of godly monarchy, constructed on a framework of emotional identification with the ruler.

The king's final words, however, may be contrasted with an earlier and less pious reaction to the demands of his subjects. In the summer of 1642 Parliament had presented Charles with the Nineteen Propositions, which would have placed government under its authority. Charles did not reply with a reiteration of divine right but instead offered to endorse a mixed constitution in which "the laws are jointly made by a king, by a house of peers, and by a House of Commons chosen by the people." This balanced polity was based on "human prudence" rather than heavenly guidance — in fact, God was not even mentioned. If the Commons usurped royal prerogatives, it risked awakening "the common people," on whom its power depended. Should the people "discover this *arcanum imperii,* that all this was done by them, but not for them," they might "set up for themselves," even "destroy all rights and properties, all distinctions of families and merit," so that government would "end in a dark, equal chaos of confusion, and the long line of our many noble ancestors in a Jack Cade or a Wat Tyler."[155]

The king's *Answer to the Nineteen Propositions* was written under the direction of Lucius Cary, Viscount Falkland, an admirer of Grotius and Machiavelli who was called "the first Socinian in England." It presents a surprisingly rational depiction of the state, in which a purely natural sovereignty is shared by the Crown and the propertied classes on behalf of the people, but without their direct acquiescence.[156] Did Falkland's *Answer* represent the true Charles? Probably not; but until the last months of his life, the *Answer* was the public face of the prince and the chief theoretical document of his cause.

It was not, however, the reason men fought for him. Most of them took up arms primarily to prevent changes to religion and government, not to defend Charles's policies. A Cheshire royalist complained of the parliamentarians that "under pretext of reforming the Church, the true aime of such spirits is to shake off the yoke of all obedience."[157] Yet the king persisted in embracing the Machiavel, even after his war against Parliament was lost. As a prisoner, first of the Scots, then of Parliament, and finally of the army, he entered into an incredibly devious series of negotiations with every party in his three realms. Eventually, nobody trusted him, and Parliament prohibited any further addresses to him in January 1648.[158]

The English revolution of 1648 to 1649 was largely due to the political waywardness of King Charles, but he cannot bear the whole blame for it. By the mid-1640s a small group of influential parliamentarian writers had begun to propose a republican model of the rational state in response to the king's *Answer.* In his *Observations* of 1642, Henry Parker asserted that "Power is originally inherent in the people . . . our Kings receive all royalty from the people." He reviled "the Florentines [Machiavelli's] wretched Politiques," which he detected in the king's *Answer*. Towards the end of his treatise, however, Parker started to deploy a jarring language of interest, the state, and sovereignty: "That there is an Arbitrary power in every State somewhere tis true, tis necessary . . . every man has an absolute power over himself; but because no man can hate himself, this power is not dangerous, nor need to be restrayned; So every State has an Arbitrary power over it self, and there is no danger in it for the same reason. If the State intrusts this to one man, or few, there may be danger in it; but the Parliament is neither one, nor few, it is indeed the State it self."[159] Parliament, equivalent here to the state, is representative not of a unified Christian community but of the self-interest (or self-love) of each individual. On these grounds, it can claim an absolute sovereignty.

This shocking conclusion was not accepted by most parliamentarians, who wanted the legislature to share in power rather than monopolize it.[160] Nevertheless, the drift towards religious diversity began to incline radical opponents of the king towards a rhetoric of individual rather than corporate interest. They wanted Parliament to abandon religious unity and allow each person to decide doctrinal issues according to conscience. The legislature would then represent the sum total of individual reason instead of a mythical corpus mysticum and might truly become the sovereign authority in an English state. "It is not for you to assume a Power to controule and force Religion, or a way of *Church Government,* upon the People," one writer remonstrated to Parliament in 1645. If the Dutch example were followed, as he advised, then "all sorts of men might find comfort and contentment in your Government," which would "make this Nation a *State,* free from the Oppression of *Kings,* and the corruptions of the Court."[161]

The author was Richard Overton, who was pejoratively called a Leveller. Some scholars have seen the Levellers as secular radicals, but it might be more accurate to describe them as the harbingers of sectarian individualism. They had influence in the New Model Army, the military force created by Parliament to fight the king. The army saw itself as representing the people directly, in much the same way as the Covenanting or Confederate assemblies. Sectarianism proliferated within its ranks. By 1647 most of its regimental preachers were Independents, who rejected both Anglican and Presbyterian church discipline. The Putney debates, held by the army's General Council in October 1647, showed that at least some officers had also been won over to Leveller principles.[162]

The pro-Leveller officers at Putney argued that poor men (but not women, children, or perhaps servants) deserved the vote by "the Law of God," which "gave men reason." This proposal was not necessarily incompatible with monarchy, but during the debate Edward Sexby—who would later conspire to set up a republic in Bordeaux—complained, "I think we are going about to set up the power of kings, some part of it, which God would destroy." Even Lieutenant-General Cromwell admitted that "we all apprehend danger from the person of the King and from the Lords" and that it was not their intention "to preserve the one or the other, with a visible danger and destruction to the people and the public interest."[163]

The position of the Levellers was important not because Cromwell and the other generals embraced sectarian individualism but because they were willing to give it a hearing. This terrified moderate Presbyterians in Parliament and moderate Covenanters in Scotland, who were increasingly apprehensive about the growth of the sects. They entered into a secret engagement with the king, whose outcome was a second civil war. The New Model Army crushed both royalists and moderates, then purged its critics from Parliament.[164] It was a sign of continuing political uncertainty among the generals that as late as December 1648 they again met with the Levellers. Although the debate went nowhere, it seems to have been the only sustained constitutional discussion into which the army leaders entered before they set about to orchestrate the trial of the king.[165]

Charles I's judges deliberately chose not to rely upon the sectarian individualism of the Levellers or on any other precise legitimizing formula. The High Court of Justice indicted Charles for having "traitorously and maliciously levied war against the present Parliament, and the people therein represented." The indictment made no attempt to equate Parliament with the state or to define how it represented the people. Charles perceived at once that these omissions left the Court without any legal claim to judge him. He pointed out that "you never asked the question of the tenth man in the kingdom, and in this way you manifestly wrong even the poorest ploughman, if you demand not his free consent." These words might have come from the mouth of a Leveller. They imply that a sovereign parliament should represent individuals, not the collective corpus mysticum of the realm. At the same time, Charles never suggested that the kingdom's mystical body was vested in him, either. Instead, he portrayed himself as safeguarding "the true liberty of all my subjects." Even now, as the king faced death, he did not abandon the rhetoric of self-interest that had first appeared in his *Answer*.[166]

The High Court's refusal to answer Charles, and rationally define the new state, foreshadowed the ideological failure of the English republic; but it did not alter the king's fate. Ten days after his trial began, Charles stood on the snowy scaffold at Whitehall, acting out his final role as an imitator of Christ. The scene had been prefigured in an extraordinary work of royal hagiography, *Eikon Basilike*, subtitled "Portraiture of His Sacred Majesty in His Solitudes and Sufferings." Written by John Gauden, an Anglican minister, and corrected by Charles himself, *Eikon Basilike* was published six weeks after the execution. Its emblematic frontispiece shows Charles kneeling within a church, his eyes fixed on a heavenly crown, his hand clutching a crown of thorns. This is a sympathetic portrait as well as an emblem, and the viewer, who is placed within the open boundary of the church, is drawn to identify personally with the king's sorrows. The saintly monarch turns his back on worldly symbols and willingly accepts a martyrdom that is an inescapable part of his Christomimetic destiny.

The text of *Eikon Basilike* is divided, like the royal body, into "human" and "divine" parts. Each chapter contains a political argument, justifying the king's actions and condemning self-interest, followed by a deeply personal prayer acknowledging the king's sins and begging forgiveness for himself and his enemies. "I look upon my sins and the sins of my people, which are the tumults of our souls against Thee, O Lord, as the just cause of these popular inundations." In his prayers of atonement the king represents all his subjects, and the loyal reader is expected to subsume his or her Christian self in that of the monarch.[167] *Eikon Basilike*, therefore, makes a powerful appeal to the people to abandon sectarian individualism and reunite themselves as a political body through identification with the piety and suffering of their ruler. It was the same position taken by the king in his dying speech, although it differed markedly from the argument of his *Answer*.

17. Frontispiece from [John Gauden], *Eikon Basilike* (London, 1649), engraving.
Photo: British Library, London.

The parliamentary response to *Eikon Basilike* was restrained by a desire to avoid constitutional innovation. This weakness was evident in even the most brilliant of replies, John Milton's caustic *Eikonoklastes*. Milton unleashed a furious assault on the royal *corpus mysticum*. Political representation, he maintained, should be based on human and divine law, not on the idolatrous notions found in the king's false prayers. For Milton, "if the Parliament represents the whole Kingdom, as is sure anough they doe, then doth the King represent onely himself." He did not explain how Parliament represented the kingdom, or whom the Rump Parliament left by the purges of 1648 might represent. Nor did he attack the legality of monarchy. Seeking to show Parliament as the injured party, he condemned Charles for acting "as a Tyrant, not as as King of England, by the known Maxims of our Law." Yet if kingship was a false symbol, what maxims of law could have established it in the first place?[168]

Milton's attempt to rationalize parliamentary rule proved to be no match for the emotionally charged royal mediation of *Eikon Basilike*. The king's cause could also draw upon a hatred of Puritan reform that was already growing throughout the country. The abolition by Parliament of Christmas and maypoles, along with other objectionable signs of unruliness or "superstition," helped to link royalism with the survival of popular customs and recreations.[169] The monarch who had cast such opprobrium on the lower orders in his *Answer* became in death an object of popular veneration. His opponents were labelled as the worst sort of self-interested Machiavellians.

The regicides were obliged to uphold the hastily conceived state that the trial and execution of Charles I had created. With a mixture of horror and optimism, Andrew Marvell wrote of how "A bleeding head where they begun, / Did fright the architects to run; / And yet in that the State / Foresaw its happy fate."[170] This was putting the best face on it. In fact, the English republic had a distinctly unhappy future; it found only temporary security under the leadership of Lord Protector Cromwell, in whose divinely appointed person all the individual interests of a divided polity were supposedly represented. If a rational English state was born in 1649, it would not mature until the monarchy was restored.

## REVOLUTION IN THE DUTCH REPUBLIC

Unlike its English counterpart, the Dutch revolution of 1650 to 1651 aimed not to overthrow but to prevent the establishment of monarchy. The stadholder William II was accused of trying to set up royal government by imprisoning his critics and threatening a military coup against Amsterdam (his army got lost in a fog). From his own point of view the prince of

Orange was not changing the constitution; he was merely defending the prerogatives of the stadholder against Arminian "scoundrels" who had negotiated peace with Spain.[171] To his opponents his goal was to give himself the powers of a king. The resistance of the provincial Estates of Holland against the stadholder and their refusal, after his sudden death from smallpox, to recognize his infant heir, were defended through overtly anti-monarchist rhetoric. The Pensionary, or chief legal councillor, of Holland, Jan de Witt, vindicated the actions of the republicans by asking, "How can it be called freedom that anyone is born to the highest offices in a republic?"[172] Arguing that the "True Interest" of Holland lay in republicanism, the textile manufacturer Pieter de la Court vilified "*monarchy* and *monarchical rulers,*" meaning "such a state wherein one only person, tho' without right, yet hath the power to cause obedience to be given to all his orders."[173] Economic prosperity, he was convinced, depended upon preventing a monarchy.

Although both Orangists and republicans claimed to be constitutional conservatives, it was the latter who adopted revolutionary conceptions of sovereignty and of a federalist state. The Estates of Holland asserted that sovereign authority belonged to the provincial assemblies, not to any national government—not even to the Estates General of the United Provinces. The Grand Assembly of 1651, a meeting of provincial representatives held under the auspices of the Estates of Holland, virtually eliminated the office of stadholder. The outcome amounted to a new federal polity, based on biblical precedent: the Hebrew Republic, as it was called.[174] In the province of Holland, authority over domestic affairs passed entirely into the hands of the merchant patriciate—not, it should be noted, into those of "the sottish ill-natur'd rabble," as de la Court described them, "who always . . . are ready to impeach the aristocratical rulers of their republic."[175] This was hardly the democratic transformation that might have been expected from a "Hebrew Republic." It contrasts with the proclaimed liberation of the whole people in Naples, or even with the nominal inclusion of the Christian community in the Portuguese "New Israel." Yet it was, without doubt, a revolution.

It was made possible by a partial retreat from confessionalism. Although the Grand Assembly declared its loyalty to Calvinism, it sanctioned a broad toleration. The Reformed Church continued to operate as the public church of the United Provinces, but it was incapable of enforcing religious unity.[176] In Holland toleration already extended to Jews and, in practice at least, Catholics. For some time the confessional diversity of Amsterdam had been shocking visitors like John Evelyn, who wrote disapprovingly of "the Sectaries that swarm'd in this Citty, to which gaine made every new-fangle acceptable."[177] Pieter de la Court, by contrast, was confident that "the honest dissenting inhabitants, who fare well in this country, or possess any considerable estates . . . will be obliged by such liberty, easy and moderate government, to shew their gratitude to so good a magistracy."[178] The purpose of religious toleration was to protect rich immigrants and safeguard political stability, not to promote sectarian individualism. Nonetheless, it remained anathema to orthodox Calvinists, a powerful minority among the patriciate, who saw to it that confessional discipline was never completely abandoned. In 1654, for example, in angry response to Joost van den Vondel's play *Lucifer,* in which Satan is described as a stadholder, a Calvinist moral crackdown took place in Amsterdam. It netted such notorious violaters of good order as the painter Rembrandt.[179]

In the United Provinces, as in Naples and England, revolution did not lead to political harmony, even within the governing patriciate. The republicans strove hard to be godly, but they increasingly antagonized orthodox Calvinists. Their revolution, like others, became tied up in a language of sovereignty, state politics, and self-interest that seemed to their enemies to be impious and Machiavellian. Widely unpopular, the Dutch republic was characterised more by conflict than by consensus. In almost every respect the revolution in the United Provinces was the opposite of the national revolt in Portugal; but it established a resilient rational state, based on self-interest, that would survive the death of the "Hebrew Republic."

## The Crisis of the Self

The crises of the mid-seventeenth century did more than upset political systems. They had disturbing consequences for the Christian self as well, because they threatened royal mediation, shook up the hope of inner harmony within an orderly polity, and demanded a personal engagement with worldly affairs. The compromise between the self and the person, the Christian and the subject—the compromise framed by Augustine, developed over the Middle Ages, and tempered by the Reformations of the sixteenth century—seemed at last to be breaking down.

The most notorious assertion of its failure was found in the writings of the French philosopher René Descartes. He tried to reconstruct the broken order of the individual not from revelation or Scripture but from the necessity of God and the reason of his own mind. "I am not that structure of limbs that is called the human body," Descartes wrote. "But what then am I? A thing that thinks." The mind was sovereign; the rest of the universe, including the human body, consisted of physical extension that could be explained by mechanical principles. Out went Augustine's total reliance on divine agency; out went his acceptance of the body as the eternal repository of the soul. For some observers, out went Christianity as well. Although Descartes's method was designed to conquer doubt, many thought that it ended in religious scepticism.[180]

Few of Descartes's contemporaries responded to crisis in such drastic and unorthodox ways. Yet many of them found themselves in doubt about the relationship between the Christian self and a changing world. "I look around in every direction and all I see is darkness," wrote Blaise Pascal in his *Pensées*. "Nature has nothing to offer me that does not give rise to doubt and anxiety." This lack of external security led to an inward-looking attitude that Roger Smith has called "a heightened sense of self."[181] We can observe it in a variety of media, whether the introspective self-portraits of Rembrandt, the meditative poetry of Richard Crashaw, the devotions of Port-Royal, or the diaries and autobiographies produced in great numbers in the mid-seventeenth century.[182] In an age of upheaval in state and society, inwardness could nourish a radical subjectivity. The English republican James Harrington, for example, went so far as to assert that "the principles of authority . . . are internal and founded upon the goods of the mind."[183] Ultimately, however, the paths of self-examination mostly led back to worldly subjection.

Inwardness was not new. It could be traced back to Augustine, who recorded in his *Confessions* how "I wrangled with myself, in my own heart, about my own self . . . I probed the hidden depths of my soul and wrung its pitiful secrets from it." The saint's experience of divine grace followed an internal process of questioning.[184] Upholding Augustine's example, French Jansenists stressed the necessity of inner conscience; but this led them to criticize rather than to validate conventional religious practices. They derided external behavioral precepts like those of the Jesuits or the Neostoics, along with the public, communal devotions of popular Catholicism. In his *Provincial Letters* of 1657, Pascal offered an abrasive Jansenist critique of the moral laxity of Jesuit theology: "Since their morality is wholly pagan, natural powers suffice for its observance. . . . But to free the soul from worldly affections, to remove it from what it holds most dear, to make it die unto itself, to bring and unite it solely and immutably to God, this can only be the work of an almighty hand."[185] The compromises of a merely customary morality could not bring the light of grace into the soul.

The ultimate desire of the Jansenists was to deny the "hateful me," by which they meant the outward person. "*Sustained therefore by your grace,* I will speak of myself, as of a stranger, in whom I take no interest at all," declared the abdicated Queen Christina of Sweden, who was influenced by the *Provincial Letters*. The bliss of personal annihilation attracted many pious women and was expressed with single-minded precision by Pascal's sister Jacqueline. She wrote of how she must learn "not only to die in what touches my person, but also in all the interests of flesh and blood and human friendship, that is to say, to forget all that does not regard the salvation of souls, and no longer to involve myself in temporal affairs." She would then wait "in quietude" for "the sensible possession of grace, which is the beginning of glory."[186] Was it a coincidence that she set down these thoughts while the Fronde was raging around her?

In spite of their obsession with the death of the person, the Jansenists did not recommend that Christians renounce an active interest in social life, or even in politics. Blaise Pascal, for example, did not hesitate to give advice to kings. He told them that they should observe the same internalized moral imperatives as everyone else, "because while being God's ministers they are still men and not gods."[187] Antoine Arnauld, brother of Mère Angélique and spiritual heir of St.-Cyran, went further than his friend Pascal in denying that "the obedience which we owe to sovereigns could ever engage us to neglect what we owe to God, in approving what seems to us unjust."[188] This was a fearless affirmation of the primacy of inner judgment, informed by grace, over prudence or reason of state.

At the same time, the Jansenists did not justify rebellion. Although many of his acquaintances had supported it, Pascal complained of "the injustice of the Fronde, which sets up its alleged right against might." To be sure, the Christian self could not easily admire worldly monarchy, whose power was derived from force and folly; but neither should monarchy be resisted, because civil war was the worst of evils. Thus, the Jansenists moved from self-examination through criticism of existing authority towards a new pact with the ruler, a kind of temporal version of Pascal's famous wager on the existence of God. In the end it was more reasonable to bet on authority, because to reject it involved greater uncertainty. "Submission and use of reason; that is what makes true Christianity," wrote Pascal. The same formula, of course, made good subjects.[189]

Jansenism did not spread beyond the Pyrenees until the eighteenth century, but a similar, inward-looking reaction against moral laxity and human prudence emerged in Spain. On the stage, for example, inner judgment was praised as the basis of true justice. In Calderón de la Barca's play *The Mayor of Zalamea,* an internal moral code described as "honour" is allowed to set limits on worldly authority: "To the King property and life / We have to give; but honour / Is the patrimony of the soul, / And the soul is God's alone." If "honour" were replaced by "conscience," Arnauld himself would not have dissented from these sentiments. For Calderón true honour was an internal standard of behaviour, not a mere social convention. In Zalamea, unlike Lope's Fuenteovejuna, honour is upheld not by the community but by an upright official, the mayor, who tries and puts to death a soldier guilty of raping his daughter. Obliged to defend his actions before "the Prudent King" Philip II, the mayor argues that he has exercised an impartial justice which nobody can question. He willingly accepts the authority of the king, because there can be no distinction between his own "honour" and royal justice.[190]

Like Pascal, Calderón pointed towards the reasonableness of a pact between the inward-looking self and the monarch. This was an unspoken agreement, rooted in individual submission rather than membership in a corpus mysticum. It could be fulfilled only through a sense of personal identification with another, in whom one's inner values were reflected or represented. This went beyond the sacral mediation offered by medieval and Renaissance kings, and gestured towards the rational state.

The concept of identification, like that of inwardness, could be found in Augustine, who expressed it through the idea of public, or common, persons. He defined a public person as one who held universal moral significance—as he put it, a "Mediator in whom we can participate." For him, the term described only Adam and Christ, through whom all men died and were born again.[191] Radical Calvinists, however, believed that the deity had made a covenant with his saints that gave them the status of common persons. As Christopher Hill has shown, English sectarians became obsessed with this idea in the aftermath of the revolution of 1648 to 1649. The Fifth Monarchists, for example, announced that the saints should exert their public personhood by ruling over everyone else.[192] An even more egalitarian interpretation of common persons was espoused by the plebeian prophet Gerrard Winstanley, who believed that the covenant "makes a man to see Heaven within himself," through a spiritual connection with Christ. Winstanley was confident that "the same Spirit that filled every member of that one body, should in these last days be sent into whole mankind." Universal representation in Christ would make everyone equal, ending fleshly desire, covetousness, and private property.[193]

James Harrington also sought the basis of authority in "the image of God which is the soul of man," but he saw representative personhood as preserving order rather than liberating the self. The republican writer saw government as a reflection of economic interest, not common humanity, and he limited political participation to men who held property. Harrington's fictional commonwealth of Oceana is presided over by a Lord Archon, the state's founding legislator and military commander. The Lord Archon declares that "a commonwealth is a monarchy, where God is king, in as much as reason, his dictate, is her sovereign power."[194] He is the sole public person in Oceana, because he alone acts for God and represents everyone.

Harrington modelled the Lord Archon on Lord Protector Cromwell, who was widely perceived as a representative person, almost a substitute king. To reinforce his status, Cromwell even went through a strange "seating" ceremony in the English coronation chair.[195] He fascinated foreign observers, among them Queen Christina, who thought that if he was not sacred, he must be "hardly a mortal man."[196] Cromwell's authority rested not on popular approval but on his God-given ability to represent

198 · NO KING BUT KING JESUS

everyone. This was emphasized by the poet Marvell, who praised "Angelic Cromwell" for having single-handedly constructed the new Jerusalem— "And each one entered in the willing frame."[197] For Marvell as for Harrington, Cromwell was the republic's only common person, through whom each individual might share in a heaven-sent covenant.

Covenant theology was not accepted in Catholic Europe. Nevertheless, the identification of the self with representative others developed there as well, albeit in different ways. The Roman Catholic Church had long accorded such mediating status not only to Christ but also to the Virgin and the saints. In the seventeenth century, however, the concept of sainthood changed towards greater interiority and personalization. The Marian congregations, for example, propagated the saintly ideal of the Christian knight, whose exemplary combat was waged within himself as much as in the world.[198] Among the educated, devotions to the saints came to depend more on privately owned books and images than on public festivals. In churches, statues of the saints were no longer posed as if engaging in "holy conversation" with each other but were turned towards God or the faithful. The worshipper was drawn to identify, inwardly and personally, with the image of a particular holy figure, through whom he or she was represented to the divine power. The desired result was "conformity," meaning "a moment of contact . . . that the viewer felt with varied intensity."[199]

The tumults of the mid-seventeenth century accentuated the desire for such "conformity" among Catholics. In a passage that can be compared to the writings of Winstanley, Pascal wrote that the only true virtue was "to seek for a being really worthy of love in order to love him. But as we cannot love what is outside us, we must love a being who is within us but is not our own self." In other words, within each individual was a universal being in whom everyone was represented. Catholics who were more conventional than Pascal might transform the search for that being into a temporal adherence to a saintlike individual, whose image, both reflecting the self and internalized in it, could become the object of love.[200]

This provided a spiritual and emotional basis for loyalty to the representative figures who emerged from the revolts of the mid-seventeenth century in Catholic societies. Among them were Broussel, beloved "father of the people," and Pau Claris, who achieved virtual canonization in Catalonia after his sudden death in 1641. Giuseppe d'Alesi, a goldsmith who led the tax revolt in Palermo, rode around the town in a suit of armour, looking to his plebeian admirers like a perfect Christian knight.[201] Masaniello too was seen as a godly warrior. His quasi-sainthood was multilayered and could take various forms according to who was interpreting it. After death, for example, the fisherman was sometimes mystically feminized to resemble a "virgin of God," which implied that his nature was both sacrificial and universal.[202] In the wake of her conversion, Queen Christina turned out to be one of the most complicated Catholic representative persons of the period, an object both of love and revulsion. In popular literature and iconography she was variously reputed to be a saint, a freethinker, a dévote, a libertine, a goddess, a murderess, a universal monarch, and a lesbian. Historians have not yet sorted out the realities behind these conflicting roles.[203]

The rise in the 1640s of such subversive worldly saints was countered among the defenders of order by the adaptation of representative personhood to the strictures of obedience. For royalists, "conformity" with Christ and the saints became a prototype for inner acceptance of monarchical authority. Velázquez's *Las Meninas* is a magnificent realization of this theme. It addresses the issue of representative personhood from the point of view of a loyal courtier. The painter appears as a Christian knight, wearing the monk's habit of the crusading order of Santiago. He is the antithesis of Masaniello—not a self-styled saint but a warrior of the church. He stares intently at the true subjects of his work, the king and queen, who are seen as reflections in a mirror behind him. He remains subordinate to their fixed gaze, which only their offspring, the little princess, returns directly to them. His portrait of the royal couple, which is hidden from us, is clearly intended to serve his rulers, not to criticize or defy them. Although *Las Meninas* politely demands that we respect the moral authority of its creator, who looks at us with such confidence, it also calls for "conformity" with a kingship whose majesty we can only obliquely perceive.[204]

*Las Meninas* suggests that the king was a representative person, the "being who is within us but is not our own self," in Pascal's words. The monarch reflects not only God but also the divine element that is in the individual, so that every subject can recognize himself or herself in a royal

18. Diego Velázquez, *Las Meninas* (1656), painting.
Photo: Museo nacional del Prado, Madrid.

being who commands our love. Submission to the sovereign is an act of
surrender of the self to its own universalized human likeness. This pact,
however, is not made just with the king; it must also be made with the
collective entity that the king represents—that is, the state. Less formal
than a contract, more intimate than a treaty, the pact both facilitated the
restoration of monarchical order and laid the groundwork for the subjection of the Christian self to the rational state.

It also raised a frightening possibility: the extinction of Christian self-hood through its submersion in a state based on human reason. Educated minds of the mid-seventeenth century were not unaware of this prospect. They had been alerted to it through the pages of a notorious book by the English philosopher Thomas Hobbes. His *Leviathan* was an extreme statement of contractual monarchism, written in reaction to the English republic. For a century after its publication the argument of *Leviathan* would provide the devout with a sobering vision of what might happen if the Christian self fully committed itself to the preservation of a humanly constructed state.

*Leviathan,* which appeared in 1651, was the most terrifying political treatise of the century. In it Hobbes presents government as a monstrous creation of human artifice, "for by Art is created that great LEVIATHAN called a COMMON-WEALTH, or STATE, (in latine CIVITAS), which is but an Artificiall Man . . . in which, the *Soveraignty* is an Artificall *Soul.*" Nature itself is "Art," and human nature is just as artificial or mechanical as Leviathan, because it can be reduced to physical sensations, appetites, and self-love. Hobbes further suggests that persons are created by artifice, pointing out that *"Persona* in latine signifies the *disguise,* or *outward appearance* of a man." Covenants can be made with God only when the deity is humanly "personated," as by Moses or Christ. Yet such contracts tie the people to nothing, since "no man is obliged by a Covenant, whereof he is not Author." God made a covenant with Abraham, "not with any of his family, or seed," who were merely obliged to obey their patriarch. Thus, Hobbes debunks the notion of common personhood and rejects "rule by the saints."[205]

As for the commonwealth, "that *Mortall God,*" it is formed by a rational covenant whose foundations are fear of death and desire for security. The multitude "conferre all their power and strength upon one Man, or upon one Assembly of men, that may reduce all their Wills, by plurality of voices, unto one Will." This man or assembly becomes the sovereign, the only public person in the state. His rulership perfectly expresses natural laws. The liberty of his subjects consists "only in those things, which in regulating their actions, the Soveraign hath praetermitted," although one might justly resist a command to harm oneself physically. There can be no appeal from the sovereign to God, because divine

laws "are none but the Laws of Nature, whereof the principall is, that we should not violate our Faith, that is, a commandement to obey our Civil Sovareigns."[206]

Hobbes reversed standard royalist argument, building his assumptions about God and nature on the framework of the sovereign state rather than deriving the state from them. The result was a closed, machinelike universe, which left no room for the workings of divine grace. Hobbist morality has nothing to do with the individual perception of grace, which was so important to Calvinists and Jansenists. In fact, for Hobbes, individuals do not exist as public moral actors, except in the covenant by which they surrender themselves, or their "outward appearances," to an imaginary being, the commonwealth. Leviathan turns Augustine's City of God upside down. It is made up not of Christian subjects but of artificial persons; and it reflects an artificial nature, devised by a God who at times seems suspiciously artificial himself. Hobbes was no atheist, but he was not a conventional Christian either. His ultimate authority was himself. God was a necessary underpinning of his man-made state, and Christ merely a human representation of the deity, who blithely sacrifices him as a public scapegoat. Hobbes held an evident distaste for the notion of a personal Redeemer who might clog the machinery of Leviathan.[207]

The mechanical logic of *Leviathan* was generally hated by the devout, who saw in it a justification of power, no matter who held it. Hobbes did not defend divinely sanctioned monarchy but instead proposed a natural covenant of perfect order that bound the whole universe in a chain of inescapable representations. He stripped off the pious raiments of *Eikon Basilike*. Yet, maddeningly for the devout, he accurately discerned that the Christian self could find security only through a pact with the state. Hobbes was actually admired by many of his royalist contemporaries, including Charles II, to whom he was briefly tutor—"his Majestie had a good opinion of him, and sayd openly, That he thought Mr Hobbes never meant him any hurt."[208] That merry monarch regained his martyred father's throne with the collapse of the English republic in 1660. As he rode through the

---

19. Frontispiece from Thomas Hobbes, *Leviathan* (London, 1651), engraving.
Photo: British Library, London.

cheering throngs that welcomed him back, like Christ finally entering Jerusalem, did Charles entertain the dream of breaking the bonds of confessional politics and transforming his imperfect human self into the awesome shape of a Hobbist sovereign? Whether he held such illusions or not, the next thirty years would prove that the hour of Leviathan, or of something like him, was fast approaching.

# CHAPTER FIVE

# The Sign of the Artificial Man, 1660–1690

"Give us," said this people, "a king who moves."
The monarch of the gods sent them a crane,
Who munches them, who kills them,
Who gulps them down at his pleasure.
—LA FONTAINE, "The Frogs Who Ask for a King," *Fables,* 1668

HE REIGN OF Frederick III of Denmark began inauspiciously. His father, Christian IV, had sapped the wealth and authority of the Crown through disastrous military adventures. Frederick's accession was uncertain, due to the political dominance of the twenty-three nobles who sat on the Royal Council, or *Rigsråd.* Elected heir to the throne by the Rigsråd in July 1648, almost five months after the death of King Christian, he was obliged to agree to a charter that allowed the council to assume sovereignty in case the king broke his promises. To make matters worse, his treasury was empty, and he could not even be crowned until the royal headgear was returned from a bank in Hamburg, where it was being held as loan security. The bishop of Zeeland praised Frederick's God-given "unlimited power" at the coronation, but the king was essentially a captive of the high nobility.

For more than a decade thereafter the king reigned but the Rigsråd ruled in Denmark. Only a crisis, in the form of two devastating invasions by Sweden, toppled the power of the high nobles. The city of Copenhagen held out alone against the Swedes; and it was the burghers of the capital, together with the Lutheran clergy, who pushed through the Estates General of 1660 a proposal to declare the Crown hereditary. With the gates of Copenhagen locked and under double guard so that no nobleman could

20. Wolfgang Heimbach, *Proclamation of the Royal Law* (1665), painting.
Photo: The Danish Royal Collections, Rosenborg slot, Copenhagen.

escape, the Rigsråd was forced to annul the charter of 1648. Soon after, a system of collegial administration was created, and the king was formally acclaimed by the council and Estates as sovereign.[1]

The Danish national crisis had been resolved by a pact between patriotic subjects and a king who represented them.[2] The pact was codified in the *Kongelov*, or Royal Law, of November 1665. Grounded in religious terms, the law was influenced by Frederick's advisor Dietrich Reinking, former favourite of the emperor Ferdinand and a staunch defender of "empire and lordship conferred by God."[3] The preamble to the law marvelled at how "divine omnipotence" had caused the council and Estates "to give up their previous prerogatives and rights of election" and confer on the king hereditary right, "*Iura Maiestatis*, absolute power, sovereignty, and all royal privileges and regalia." Since "the best beginning is to begin with God," the first article of the law commanded the king's descendants to "honor, serve and worship God" through the Lutheran faith. They had to protect the church against "heretics, fanatics, and mockers of God." In exchange, the monarch was to be regarded "as the greatest and highest head on earth, above all human laws and knowing no other head or judge above him, either in spiritual or secular matters, except God." While he might "permit himself to be anointed publicly in the Church," he remained king by blood and would take no oaths to his subjects. He was to be sovereign of an undivided Norway and Denmark—a move towards the national unity favoured by Danish patriots. Described as "an eternal legacy," the Royal Law united the themes of sovereignty and confessional discipline.[4] As one of the earliest founding documents of the rational state, and perhaps the most succinct, it provides a fitting starting point for a chapter that will examine the impact of a new language of authority on the Christian self.

Did the Royal Law owe something to Hobbes? Some historians have thought so. Peder Schumacher, later Count Griffenfeld, the royal secretary who drafted the law, may have encountered Hobbes's writings while studying at Oxford; but as Knud Fabricius pointed out long ago, his English connections were mainly with anti-Hobbist royalists, and there is no evidence that he ever read *Leviathan*.[5] Nonetheless, the Royal Law does parallel Hobbes, not only in its brief invocation of contract theory but also in the surprising absence of any argument from tradition. Royal ancestors are not mentioned; neither are biblical kings or Roman emperors. This is more a declaration of change than a renewal of custom. Only the Royal Law itself, the original covenant between king and people, will remain unaltered. Everything else, even the Lutheran Church, will be "born again" in willing obedience. As in *Leviathan*, the covenant between God and the self has been appropriated to a political use, which deprives subjects of any possibility of resistance. The consent of the Estates simply ratifies the necessity of accepting the "eternal legacy"—meaning the permanence of the state. In the directives of the Royal Law, then, we may catch a furtive glimpse of Hobbes's "artificial man."

This did not mean that the law justified arbitrary royal control over the self, as was claimed by the Anglo-Irish writer Robert Molesworth in 1694. He observed Denmark through the eyes of a disgruntled sectarian individualist. Molesworth imagined the ideal polity neither as an organic whole nor as an artificial union but as a composition of freely connected parts. "Want of *Liberty* is a disease in any Society or Body Politick," he wrote, "like want of *Health* in a particular Person." He saw Denmark as afflicted by a "deplorable" condition of "Slavery," which "like a sickly Constitution, grows in time so habitual, that it seems no Burden nor Disease."

Molesworth put the blame on the clergy: "As long as the Priests are entirely dependent upon the Crown, and the People absolutely governed by the Priests in Matters of Conscience as they are here, the Prince may be as Arbitrary as he pleases without running any risque from his Subjects."[6] In reply, defenders of the Danish monarchy asserted that it was based on consensus rather than blind obedience. In the age of the rational state, Molesworth's individualistic conception of liberty was easily blasted as a "Romantick Notion."[7]

Molesworth certainly overstated the consequences of the Royal Law, which did not allow free rein to Danish kings. It created no specific powers that had not been claimed before. In fact, like other written constitutions, it subordinated supreme authority to the language of a particular document. We may see it as a move away from traditional authority, towards fixed rules of order. Eventually it would lead to further encroachments on time-honoured custom, of which Molesworth might have approved if he had learned more about them. Christian V's *Danske Lov* of 1683, which reduced provincial laws to a single national legal code, is an example of this.[8] The decline in prosecutions of witchcraft after 1660 is another. While the clergy continued to tremble at the name of the devil, who stared down malevolently from the wall paintings in a great many rural churches, a sceptical royal judiciary began to exclude ministers from the examination of accused witches and to stamp out witch trials. Reason of state also chipped away at religious intolerance, so that in 1685 French Calvinist *émigrés* were granted freedom of worship in Copenhagen and other parts of the kingdom.[9] The change from traditional governance promoted the emergence of a service aristocracy that separated itself from the past by adopting French fashions and using the Danish language rather than German as a form of polite address. The new elite would later find a brilliant spokesman in the historian, dramatist, and fervent admirer of the Royal Law, Ludvig Holberg.[10]

At the same time, not every aspect of the state was altered by reason. For example, the Danish monarch's private roads, or *kongeveje*, remained officially closed to regular traffic, although economic sense seemed to dictate that they should become public.[11] Similarly, rationalism had little to do with those parts of the Danske Lov dealing with plots against the king or the royal family. The conspirator's right arm was to be cut off and his body split on a wheel; if he fled from justice, the same punishment was to be administered to a likeness or effigy. Such provisions looked back to the belief that the polity was a corpus mysticum that should revenge itself by mutilating the bodies of its enemies. Treason was described as an abrogation of honour, not as an offence against the state. When Count Griffenfeld himself was brought to the scaffold in 1676, it was because he had violated *lèse majesté* by making disparaging personal remarks about the king in his private diary, not because he had betrayed the state.[12]

The persistence of such archaisms in the Danish state should make us wary of applying too broadly Weberian standards of rational authority. The pact between the king and his subjects did not make the state into a regulated, bureaucratic machine, a well-oiled clock. Similarly, it was not converted into an engine of war. Although Leon Jespersen has pointed out that Denmark after 1660 bore many resemblances to Otto Hintze's Machtstaat, or power-state, its military organization was always a means to ostensibly higher moral ends, such as social unity, the enforcement of personal discipline, and the promotion of national destiny.[13] The state rationalized these goals by giving them a political form and purpose; but it did not simply use religion as a justification for the pursuit of territorial interests.

In fact, as the Royal Law made clear, the Danish rational state was founded on religious identity, not on bureaucracy or military strength. What the burghers of Copenhagen, the clergy, and the lesser nobility had subscribed to in 1660 was a confessional agreement that linked the protection of their faith with the preservation of a sovereign monarchy with which every believer could identify. The Royal Law, in other words, rested on the internal consent of the Christian self. To be sure, not everyone was willing to invest their inner consciences in such an arrangement. Some sought the image of a godly, just, and customary polity elsewhere — especially in the recesses of their own memories. Such personal resistance to the state was exemplified in the most celebrated Danish prose work of the period, *Jammers Minde*, or *Sorrowful Memories*, by Princess Leonora Christina.

The princess was the half-sister of Frederick III. Her husband, Corfitz Ulfeldt, was a leader of the aristocratic opposition to the king. Imprisoned by Frederick on suspicion of treason in 1663, Leonora Christina spent the next twenty years in harsh and humiliating confinement, which she recorded in her prison memoirs. She was sustained in her afflictions by a recollection of God that she found inside herself: "I cannot recall to mind my sorrow and grief, my fears and distresses, without at the same time remembering the almighty power of God, who . . . has been my strength and help, my consolation and assistance." Supremely assured of divine grace, she was convinced that "it was God who Himself entered with me into the Tower-gate; it was He who extended to me His hand, and wrestled for me in that prison cell for malefactors, which is called 'the Dark Church.'"

Far from being demoralized by her fate, therefore, Leonora Christina was brimming with spiritual self-confidence. She became an admirer of "all the famous female personages, who were celebrated as true, chaste, sensible, valorous, virtuous, God-fearing, learned, and steadfast," which was how she saw herself. Her desire to laud exemplary women was nourished by a fierce national pride. Leonora Christina wrote to the well-known poet Thomas Kingo, as "a Danish Woman in the name of all Danish Women," to ask him to "exhibit in befitting honour the virtuous and praiseworthy Danish women." Her sense of female and national solidarity did not, however, extend to the irresponsible lower classes. She was continually shocked by the immorality of her plebeian attendants, especially by one who thought it was no sin to smother a sickly child so that she could marry again more easily. The princess was horrified by those who were guided by worldly expediency rather than by the directives of an internalized conscience.[14]

Leonora Christina made no pact with the rational state. Although she considered herself to be loyal to her brother the king and even wept when he died, she expressed no support for the Royal Law. Above all, she never acknowledged the authority of the state over her memory, or what we might call her imagination. Like St. Augustine, Leonora Christina sought God by looking into "the vast immeasurable sanctuary" of her memory. Her journal is presented as a book of remembrances. Amid the hardships of her imprisonment, she could still enjoy Christian freedom in her own mind. She found there a divine grace that kept her from surrendering herself fully to her captors.

For an innovative authority like that of the rational state, memory was bound to be an impediment. It was the repository of every political myth validated by "immemorial custom," from the corpus mysticum to the "nation of Israel." It had once been seen as the highest faculty of the mind, a mysterious terrain at the centre of the self in which sacred truths were hidden. Sages of the Renaissance explored the "art of memory" in order to penetrate the mysteries of the universe, including, among many wonders, the origins of language and the divine names of God.[15] Monarchy too had been amply provided with an array of mnemonic devices—sceptres, crowns, thrones—by which the mystery of the king's sacred body was remembered.

The advance of the printed word, a crucial element in the religious movements of the sixteenth century, shook the primacy of memory. It was forced to give way to the rationalizations of Scripture, to Tridentine decrees, and to written law. Symbols were replaced by more precise types of signs. This indicated a fundamental cultural change, which Michel de Certeau described as a shift from "the Spoken Word," based on memory and oral narrative, to a "Scriptural economy" of printed writing, associated with rationalism. Society, according to de Certeau, was increasingly thought of as a "blank page" on which history could continually be rewritten by thinkers obsessed with material "progress."[16] We do not have to accept the premise of a total break with the past, or a dichotomy between orality and writing, in order to appreciate that by 1650 educated culture no longer looked to the memory as a source of higher truths.

Around that time, imaginative memory came under withering fire from rationalists. Political events helped motivate their assault, because the crises of the period could be ascribed to the instability of the imagination. Descartes, the champion of "clear and precise ideas," wrote that "I could never approve of all of those trouble-making and quarrelsome types who . . . never cease in their imagination to effect some new reformation." The "art of memory," according to Descartes, led one "to speak without judgment concerning matters about which one is ignorant." Hobbes wrote off memory, along with the imagination, in a single chapter of *Leviathan,* reducing it to the fanciful combination of sense impressions.[17] For rational thinkers the path back to order, to a stable agreement between subject and ruler, did not lead through imaginative memory, which encompassed dangerous byways; it had to be found by reason or natural law and be marked out in precise language.

Concern with the precision of language became intense among rational philosophers of the late seventeenth century. Samuel Pufendorf wrote in 1673 that, as language was an "instrument of human society," everyone had a social duty "to denote each thing with one particular word and not another." He left no space at all for the imagination.[18] Language had to be expressed through rational signs, not by symbols referring to imaginary qualities. Antoine Furetière explained the semantic distinction between the two in his *Dictionnaire universel* of 1690: a sign was a "mark or visible character which denotes, which makes known something hidden, or secret," while a symbol was defined as a "type of emblem or representation of some moral thing, by the images or properties of natural things."[19] In short, signs revealed, while symbols hid. As the supreme instrument of human society, the king was a sign, the visible character of a majesty that denoted political order as well as the inner discipline of the self. In an indefinable way, the monarch remained a reflection of God, but he was more clearly understood as representing the state. Although his rulership might draw upon older notions of personal sacrality, it now also pointed towards a power based on universal human reason.

In Denmark, as we have seen, rational authority was written into the Royal Law. In most realms, however, kingship would not allow itself to be circumscribed by a single law. Rather, it was defined in the sphere of public discourse through a constant reiteration of the attributes of monarchical dominance, especially in written forms of panegyric and praise. We shall call this a royal language. In the late 1600s the royal language was highly specific and avoided the luxuriant, multivalent constructions that had been so vital to Renaissance monarchy. It tried to disengage the king from the ups and downs of politics and to place him in an immutable domain of permanent authority, the domain of the rational state.

Yet the impact of the royal language continued to depend on its public reception, which even in the age of "clear and precise ideas" was not wholly predictable. It could not succeed unless those on whom it relied were prepared to comply with its premises. Governing elites as well as the common people could not simply be coerced by force or brainwashed by the authority of the written word; they had to be swayed by the consistency of the king's representations and be convinced that he was the sign of a state in which every responsible subject was included. Mass culture still had a role in this, especially in evoking popular sympathy with the ruler or in elaborating the characteristics of some external "Other" who threatened to destroy the harmony of the realm. If the king violated the pact with his subjects, if he acted against their inner religious convictions, the royal language might still be challenged. The self could take back and exercise the imaginative memory that it had partially surrendered to the state.

To counter the dangers of such resistance, the royal language gradually established a rhetorical distance between itself and strict confessionalism. Some rulers carried the separation so far as to assert that the interests of the state took precedence over religious identity. This hitherto incredible claim is discussed in the third section of this chapter. It would be greeted by the devout with a disgust that verged on open opposition; but after 1660 there was little chance that they might turn the polity back towards the promise of Jerusalem. The final section of the chapter explains how the ideal of godly monarchy, the last vestige of Christian utopianism, collapsed into a state-centred rhetoric. By 1690 the earthly Jerusalem was no more. Out of its dust and ashes Leviathan had begun to emerge, as kings and subjects inscribed on the body politic the signs that would give him life.

## The Royal Language

### FRANCE

No single royal language dominated late seventeenth-century Europe, but that of King Louis XIV of France was the loudest of all. Its amplitude was built on the assumption of silence, especially concerning the recent past. Thus, it was generally understood that the Fronde would not be mentioned. Bishop Bossuet called the events of 1648 to 1653 "those things of which I would like to be able to be eternally silent."[20] Some of Louis XIV's advisors proposed that the parlement "remove from its registers all that happened during the troubles," but Jean-Baptiste Colbert, the controller general of finances, suggested that "it would be more glorious for the King" if the parlement "allowed itself, by the force of His Majesty's virtue, to bring them [the registers] itself to suppress them, without being asked."[21] In the end, the offensive records of the years of royal humiliation were not destroyed, and the lingering memory of the Fronde had to be drowned out by the king's own clamorous publicity.

Reason, that public voice proclaimed, was the foundation of the restored French state. The well-known *Memoirs for the Instruction of the Dauphin,* written by two secretaries with the assistance of the king, declared that "we see nothing in the world . . . which is not the plan and work of some rational mind."[22] The king viewed the state in rationalist terms as a collective entity separate from his body, rather than a mystical *dignitas* within him. He never said *"L'Etat, c'est moi"* and "never believed himself in any way to incarnate the State." Rather, he held the state like a piece of personal property—in fact, he could have said, *"L'Etat, c'est à moi."*[23]

This rationalism was not derived from Descartes, whose teachings were banned until late in the seventeenth century. Nor can it be directly ascribed to the writings of Hobbes. Although it had some influence in France, Louis XIV would have disdained Hobbes's *Leviathan* for its contractualism and impiety. Still, the devout bishop Bossuet (like Peder Schumacher in Denmark) came very close to the argument of Hobbes in explaining the origins of the state. He wrote of government as lying in "the unity of a people, when each renouncing his own will, transports and reunites it to that of the prince and the magistrate."[24] The pact between the self and the ruler was never more accurately described. To be sure, for Bossuet the moment of state formation was engineered by divine grace, not by natural law, contracts, or covenants. Yet the surrender of power by the individual to the state was just as inescapable and as morally rational for the bishop of Meaux as it was for the author of *Leviathan.*

The French version of the artificial man was entirely fixed and unalterable. It defied the theories of political mutation proposed by Spanish and Italian writers. Louis's *Memoirs* confidently asserted that "the most unscrupulous thinkers, the least affected by principles of equity, of goodness, and of honor seem to have predicted immortality for this state, insofar as it is humanly possible."[25] The "unscrupulous thinker" referred to here is of course Machiavelli, who is depicted (wrongly) as subscribing to a view of the French state as an "eternal legacy." Other royal publicists echoed the same conviction. "Princes must change, since men are mortal," wrote Bossuet, "but the government must not change; authority remains firm, counsels are connected and eternal."[26] Farewell, then, to the gloomy prognostications of Botero or Saavedra Fajardo: the monarchy of France would last for ever.

Admittedly, it lacked a Royal Law to define it for eternity. Instead, it had a fragmented customary constitution.[27] Louis XIV made even less reference to this dangerous collection of historical precedents than had his predecessors. His publicity ignored custom and history, concentrating instead on present manifestations of a supposedly continuous authority. For his own part, the king tried to behave as if the character of his rulership had always been the same. He gave no indication of having developed a sense of purpose over time or of having learned from past mistakes. The poet Nicolas Boileau went so far as to declare that the king had not had to mature at all: his "high wisdom / Is in no way the tardy fruit of a slow ageing."[28]

The denial of change implied that the king owed nothing to the past. In the *Memoirs*, the persona established for the king is depicted as without precedent. He hardly mentions any of his royal predecessors. Alexander the Great is given only one critical and one laudatory comment; the emperor Augustus is briefly praised. In recounting how he chose the sun as his emblem, Louis neglects to point out that it had been used extensively by Henry III and Louis XIII. His motto, "*Nec Pluribus Impar*" ("Not unequal to many"), was to be understood to apply to rulers of the past as well as the present.[29] Poets lauded Louis as a monarch who could be compared to no other. Dedicating his play *Alexander the Great* to the king, Jean Racine wrote of him that "we have never seen a king who at the age of Alexander has displayed the conduct of Augustus."[30] Could he even be the product of human reproduction? The royal historiographer Pierre Pellisson claimed in his "Panegyric to the King," delivered to the Académie Française in 1671, that "I have believed a thousand times that he was not born; but that he had been made our Master, as one without compare, more rational than any of his subjects."[31] Pellisson's comments studiously avoid historical comparisons, and they present the king's unalterable qualities as if they were rational truths.

Louis's unprecedented rulership soon began to manifest itself in great deeds, which were portrayed not as providential but as the direct products of the ruler's own exertions. Writing of the king's military triumphs of the 1670s in the Low Countries, Racine doubted "that fortune might have had some part in these successes, which were no more than the infallible consequence of an entirely marvellous conduct."[32] The king's "marvellous conduct" had to be revealed as if it were an uninterrupted sequence of brilliant domestic achievements and foreign exploits, wholly and effortlessly determined by the ruler himself. It was not an unfolding narrative or developing story; rather, it took the form of a series of episodes, each complete in itself, each representing a greater realization of the king's inherent glory. No wonder that the most elaborate expression of this royal history was not a written work—Racine's great projects remained in pieces—but a collection of medals celebrating the glorious events of the reign.[33]

The king liked to suggest that he was the ultimate author of his own publicity. He enjoyed the position of a distant executive producer, whose presence was generally unseen but always acutely felt by the artists who served him. This was the role he played in Molière's charming little comedy, *L'impromptu de Versailles*, where an exasperated playwright tries to cajole his company into rehearsing a new piece which the king has ordered at short notice. In the end, the comedians are excused from performing the play by a graceful reprieve from the monarch.[34] Unlike the actors fumbling over their lines, the king's commands, which begin and end everything, are certain.

Yet the royal voice is never heard in Molière's play, which was very fitting. Louis XIV did not want to be heard, because he had no desire to let mere words encapsulate his person. Even his *bons mots* seldom referred to himself. The royal language of praise and panegyric was for his subjects to employ in what were understood to be inadequate attempts to describe him. The king's own special means of communication was his own body. It appeared, for example, on a horse at the centre of the great equestrian carrousels of 1662 and 1664, to show that the whole world revolved around it. It rode again as Roger, the valorous knight of Ariosto's *Orlando Furioso*, in the magnificent tournament and spectacle of 1664 called the "Pleasures of the Enchanted Isle." Carefully trained and disciplined by the art of the dance, it shone like the sun in the lavish ballets de cour of the 1650s and 1660s. Jean-Pierre Néraudau has perceived in such public performances a "devaluation of the word," a deliberate avoidance of verbal expression, so that language would not be seen to encompass the person of the king.[35] The devaluation was deceptive, of course, since all these spectacles were acted out according to scripts, which told even the king what he was supposed to do.

Louis's public performances had mostly ceased by 1670. Was the king tired, or had he found that even a language of gestures was a denigration of his ineffable glory? We should not forget that the immediate audience for most royal theatre was restricted to the court; except during the carrousels and the infrequent royal entrées into Paris, few ordinary subjects had a chance to watch the king perform. They experienced his spectacles second-hand, through reading about them or seeing them represented in prints—in other words, through the public sphere rather than by direct experience. The move in the 1670s to the palace of Versailles, and to a permanent stage for the presentation of the royal body, did not therefore constitute a re-pudiation of the king's strategies of publicity; it simply made their locale and their incidence more regular, easing the strain on the royal physique. His subjects could still read about his every action and gaze upon graphic depictions of his majestic body.

The building of Versailles also allowed Louis to express himself through the "royal art" of architecture, a sort of writing with shapes in public space. Colbert was mostly responsible for conceiving Versailles. The minister had warned the king in 1665 that the palace, then no more than a hunting lodge, "reflects more the pleasure and diversion of Your Majesty than his glory." Over the next decade Colbert laboured mightily to transform it into a visual summation of the royal language: rational, disci-plined, eternal, unprecedented, free from the wild symbolic ornamentation of the baroque.[36] The palace and its surroundings were the harmonious domain of the king's body, a sign of his majesty and therefore of the state. Separate from him, but an extension of his sovereign self, the mini-state at Versailles was intended to mirror and enhance the daily rising and setting of the "Sun King." It envelopped Louis's body like a magnificent wrap-ping paper.[37]

At Versailles the royal language was officially designated by the *Petite Académie,* or Academy of Inscriptions, a committee of writers and artists that handled the official mottoes appearing on medals and statues of the king. Writing of the works of art displayed at the palace, Boileau noted that "it is in some way the King himself who speaks to those who come to see his Gallery." He recommended that inscriptions should not be laden "with a verbiage and a swelling of words, which being very bad in all cases, becomes completely unbearable in these places."[38] The royal language had to be simple, direct, and uncompromising. It also had to renounce vulgar or familiar terms, for as Boileau wrote, "there is nothing that makes a discourse more vile than low words."[39] Its effectiveness was measured by the specificity of its purpose and phrasing, not by its allusive or imaginative possibilities. It employed the aristocratic precision of signs, not the opaque, wordy, and vulgarizing rhetoric of symbols.

Versailles operated according to rules of etiquette, or *civilité*. Most of them were not new, but they reached a peak of formality and precision once the king was installed in the palace. The German-born Liselotte, duchesse d'Orléans (Madame Palatine), complained of Versailles that "for all their boasting about the famous French liberty, all diversions here are unbelievably stiff and constrained."[40] Norbert Elias interpreted the rigid ceremony of Louis's court as a kind of bonding between the king and the aristocracy, a means of rationalizing the constant struggle for prestige and status. In Elias's view, "the court society" established a code of aristocratic behaviour that upheld the hierarchical structure of the kingdom. In other words, it cemented a pact between nobles and the state. Pierre Bourdieu has further argued that such distinctions of manners do not simply reflect but actually "embody" a particular social order.[41] From this point of view, civilité produced the meaning of nobility, by stipulating what it meant to be a noble.

The etiquette of Versailles, however, was not just concerned with social distinction; like its model, the ceremony of the Habsburg court, it pointed back towards religious self-discipline. The qualities of a good courtier were defined in a manual of 1706 as "patience, politeness, no will at all; to listen to everything, never to report anything. Always to seem content."[42] This was a perversely twisted version of Christian submission. It gave the rituals that accompanied Louis XIV's daily routine—his rising, washing, eating, and so on—an aura of divine worship. In contrast to the moral earnestness of Jansenism, however, the civilité of Versailles was entirely external and had nothing to do with inner piety. The palace was the centre of an earthly cult, not a mirror of spiritual order. "The court is the most beautiful thing in the world at the rising of the King," wrote an admiring courtier, who did not confuse Versailles with heaven.[43] Nobody pretended that God rose, washed, and ate, as the king did. However reverential its ceremonies, French etiquette "embodied" a rational pact between the self and the state, not a mystical communion with the deity.

The royal language was not restricted to the court. It was disseminated beyond Versailles through elite cultural institutions like the Royal Academy of Music, whose intention, according to its organizers, was "to pacify and refine manners."[44] It also helped to generate an elite literary style that reflected a dissatisfaction with mutation, unfixedness, mere events, and tended towards epigrams, maxims, or reflections, aiming at irrefutable truths. Brevity, clarity, and precision became the hallmarks of good literary taste. Racine even made a list of Louis XIV's taciturn bons mots, as if they were perfect forms of expression.[45] Learned treatises depended less on sustained argument than on rapid exposition and dazzling assertion. In the "universal history" he wrote for the dauphin, Bossuet opined that "in order to understand everything," it was best to consult "a summary, where one sees, at a glance, all the order of the ages."[46]

In the reign of the Sun King everything was to be understood at a glance. La Bruyère prefaced his *Characters* with the remark that "as this work is only a simple instruction on the morals of men, and as it aims less to make them knowledgeable than to make them wise, we have excused ourselves from loading it with long and curious observations or with learned commentaries which render an exact account of antiquity."[47] Instead of lengthy tracts, the literary oracles of the reign preferred to present their opinions in short declamations, like the celebrated "Panegyrics of the King" pronounced before the Académie Française. The "curious observations" and sense of mutability and experiment that had been typical of Renaissance literature were now displaced. Bodin had written a mammoth tome on sovereignty, and Guez de Balzac had devoted a hefty treatise to it; La Bruyère gave it only a chapter, whose first recommendation was that one should submit to the government under which one is born, rather than question it.[48]

The shift away from extended investigation was most marked among the advocates of "modern" artistic genius, like Charles Perrault. His greatest production, other than his retold fairy tales, was a panegyrical oration entitled "The Century of Louis the Great." Asserting the superiority of French over Latin, of native perfection over Italian inventiveness, of *bon sens*—good judgment—over antique taste, Perrault claimed that the achievements of his own age surpassed those of the Greeks or Romans. "What can all Antiquity oppose to them / To equal their pomp and their variety?" he asked. Perrault's oration reflected a general aversion to historicity and foreshadowed the eighteenth-century belief in "progress." He was no relativist; the genius of the present excelled that of the classical past because all cultures shared the same values. Perrault even ignored any cultural differences between Christianity and paganism.[49]

The visual counterpart to this concise and authoritarian written language can be observed in the works of Charles Le Brun, First Painter to the king. The art historian Norman Bryson has argued that Le Brun's technique was "discursive, not figural," that it upheld "the centralising power of the text."[50] In other words, Le Brun's historical canvases have to be read as if they were written works. They strive to uphold the dominance of a single message, clearly formulated by the artist and instantly acknowledged by the viewer. Their iconographic references are deliberately precise and simple, to discourage a multiplicity of symbolic interpretations. Unlike Rubens, Le Brun did not implant a hidden moral programme in his paintings. His allegorical references are always transparent. Each face and body in his works can be scrutinized for obviously "legible" signs of inherent character.

One of the best known examples of Le Brun's method is *The Conquest of the Franche-Comté in 1674*. Designed for the *Grande Galerie* at Versailles, it records Louis XIV's invasion of this Spanish-ruled territory, which was eventually annexed to France. The painting is a jumble of allegorical figures representing everything from Victory and Glory to Fear, Winter, the fortress of Besançon and the river Doubs. A viewer who is aware of the title attached to each element of the composition can "read" the whole "text" very easily, without fear of ambiguity. Hercules, for example, stands for heroic valour; Mars, for the French Army (he has a fleur-de-lys on his shield). Amid the tumult, Louis XIV rises resplendent, dressed as Alexander the Great but representing his own unique glory. In this canvas he is a sign that refers only to itself.[51]

At this point we are in danger of mistaking the appearance of an unproblematic discourse of kingship for political reality. It is easy to forget that the effectiveness of the royal language always depended on the extent

21. Charles Le Brun, *The Conquest of the Franche-Comté in 1674* (1678–84), painting. Palace of Versailles.

Photo: Réunion des musées nationaux, Paris.

to which it was accepted by its audience, particularly the devout, who continued to insist that earthly rulers should be subordinated to God. The first entries in Furetière's dictionary under *king* and *sovereign* referred not to the French monarch but to God alone, who was *"King of Kings"* as well as "the only *Sovereign*, who has a Majesty, a goodness, a power *sovereign* and infinite." Yet at times, as we have seen, the publicity of Louis XIV made it appear as if the royal sign were self-created. The devout could not happily accept such overbearing suggestions; for, as La Bruyère pointedly remarked, in spite of all their "proud names," earthly kings could never send a single drop of water to the earth.[52]

Louis was observant and took his title of "Most Christian King" seriously. Nevertheless, he was neither as personally pious nor as morally upright as many of his subjects would have hoped. Significantly, Versailles was built around the king's apartments, not the chapel, which was finished last.[53] The actions of the *Grand Monarque* sometimes affronted the devout.

One of the first moves of his personal rule was to imprison Nicolas Foucquet, superintendant of finances, who was a member of the Company of the Holy Sacrament and had close relations with the dévots. Mme. de Sévigné, the great letter-writer, professed bewilderment at the king's vindictive treatment of her friend Foucquet: "Such rude and low vengeance could not issue from a heart like that of our master. They are using his name, and profaning it, as you see."[54] "They" meant Colbert and his allies, who were preparing the destruction of the company. Molière's *Tartuffe*, which ridiculed the dévots, signalled the attack. Furiously denounced by the company, the play was suppressed in 1664, but it reappeared in altered form three years later, with the protection of the Crown. By then the king and Colbert had compelled the company to dissolve.[55] Sovereignty seemed to have set itself at odds with the most assiduous promoters of religious surveillance over the self.

In the end, the dévots did not resist Colbert or the court. They stuck to the pact they had made after the Fronde. In keeping to it, however, they did not renounce their personal beliefs. Bossuet, once an energetic devotee of the Company of the Holy Sacrament, clung tenaciously to a strictly religious interpretation of monarchy, almost in spite of the profane images that emanated from his earthly master. The king, he wrote, must submit to law, both divine and human, or risk destroying the rule of justice. Bossuet did not employ the term *sovereignty* or imply that the state was a possession of the king.[56] Thus, without calling any attention whatsoever to his dissent, the God-fearing bishop set himself apart from Bodin and some of the assumptions on which the Bourbon state was based.

At least Bossuet was not a Jansenist. His religious motives were therefore not suspect and could be expressed with a certain freedom. Racine, on the other hand, had been raised at Port-Royal, and his heart never left its confines; while Boileau's religious sympathies are perfectly revealed in his "Third Epistle," a rumination on original sin dedicated to Antoine Arnauld.[57] Yet neither writer allowed personal convictions to interfere with service to a king whose distaste for Jansenism was palpable. They assiduously avoided treading on the disputed territory between religion and politics. Thus, although Racine did not shrink from writing about the Muslim prince Bajazet, none of his tragedies dealt with a Christian monarchy, and only his last two politically charged dramatic works are biblical.

Whatever advice his earlier plays gave to monarchs was deftly sewn into a non-Christian context.

Did the acquiescence of devout intellectuals extend to the common people as well? The answer might be derived from the evidence of popular literature, like the famed *Bibliothèque bleue* of Troyes. On the rough blue pages of these little chapbooks the godly prince of Bossuet's imagination was a prominent theme, and the figure of Charlemagne, the perfect Christian ruler, was encountered more often than that of Alexander the Great. The first Holy Roman Emperor was praised for spreading true religion, along with the glory of France, among pagans and infidels. How were such texts interpreted? Was King Louis seen as emulating the pious deeds of his ancestor, or as not measuring up to Charlemagne's example? Lending support to the former thesis, Roger Chartier contends that the *Bibliothèque bleue* was carefully edited for a respectable bourgeois public and reflected the "scriptural" values of learned culture, including political subordination. Yet it is hard to assess the impressions that stories of "Charles the Great" may have left in the minds of readers, especially as popular literature was drenched in a religiosity that might contrast with the rational strategies of royal representation.[58]

A smattering of evidence suggests that some of the ordinary subjects of Louis XIV wanted their ruler to conform more visibly to Christian virtue and piety. He should have been "the true father of his peoples," in the words of Alexandre Dubois, the parish priest of Rumegies near Tournai, who never called him an Alexander or an Apollo.[59] The king failed miserably as a biblical patriarch, according to the journal of Pierre Ignace Chavatte, a textile worker of Lille—admittedly, a town that became French only in 1667. Fervently Catholic and an avid reader of *canards*, or political leaflets, directed against the king of France, Chavatte was scandalized by what he judged to be Louis's lack of religious faith.[60] How far such opinions extended is unknown, but it is worth pointing out that there were still corners of the kingdom where the reforming zeal of the Catholic League had not faded from memory. In a remote vale near St. Malo, peasants honoured a statue of a "St. Dressmaker," representing a supporter of the League who became a hermit to escape the wrath of Henry IV. In another part of Britany flowed the miraculous waters of the "fountain of *Agonisants,*" where two monks had been killed by Bourbon troops in 1593.[61] It should not be assumed that the devotees of such shrines had fully accepted the rationalist premises of Louis XIV's sovereignty.

Yet they did not take up arms as often as they had before 1660. In part this was because the king left them alone and did not try to translate the royal language into an intrusive pattern of centralized authority. He was himself a tireless bureaucrat, but his realms were not united under one legal system, one form of administration, or one system of taxation. Although Colbert tried to encourage him towards "some greater design, as would be that of reducing all his kingdom under the same law," such a grand scheme was never undertaken.[62] The reform of administration was blocked by local authorities and endless conspiracies of the aristocracy. As for the parlements, although they were relatively quiet after 1660, they retained their own autonomy and were not shackled to the royal language. "Absolute" power, in short, was to a large degree a consoling myth. The king's practical authority was obtained only through accommodating a bewildering array of interest groups.[63]

The distinctions of court etiquette papered over this flimsy structure of governance. What they "embodied" was an ideal of the state, not the contradictions of the broader habitus or the actual distribution of power in the realm. At Versailles, no negotiation with the will of the monarch was possible; the king's favour, the only real prize, was distributed among his courtiers with apparent arbitrariness through the smallest of gestures. Within the confines of his palace and gardens Louis was able to act out his appointed role as an earthly god, freely bestowing an unearned grace upon his subjects. The ceremonies of his court emphasized the contingency of aristocratic privilege, not its immanence. Thus, the court memoirist Saint-Simon recorded that a certain nobleman, given a ducal title in fulfilment of a swiftly regretted royal promise, "could never please the king after he had been raised to it, and suffered throughout his life all the aversion that he [the king] could give him, which pulled the sting of having made him a duke in spite of himself." Saint-Simon conveys the sense of insecurity that afflicted the court nobility. It was not a feeling prevalent throughout elite society, however. As François Bluche reminds us, the tiny elite of anxious courtiers comprised no more than 5 percent of the French aristocracy.[64]

If the denizens of Versailles perceived any inconsistencies between the royal language and the governance of the kingdom, they did not mention them openly until after their master's death. Saint-Simon's loquacious *Memoirs* belong to the chatty and expansive eighteenth century, not to the golden age of the Grand Monarque, when brevity, clarity, and restraint were the guarantors of a fragile cultural order. Saint-Simon was too young to remember the terrible upheavals of the 1640s, which in most minds had confirmed the necessity of elite self-censorship and of tolerance for assertions of sovereignty. He seems never fully to have grasped to what extent the secure image of the Sun King, benignly casting down his radiance on a grateful people, depended on self-imposed silences: silences about the Fronde, silences about religion, and, finally, silences about the limitations on royal power.

## ENGLAND

In England, unlike in France, the features of the royal language were hotly contested. Charles II had to deal with Anglican royalists, who understood his powers in strictly confessional terms, and with sectarian individualists, who espoused a representative kingship reminiscent of Cromwell's Protectorate. Meanwhile, Charles himself espoused a natural definition of kingship. The result of these ideological divergences was renewed party struggle. In the long run, conflicts over the royal language could only be resolved by an agreement between the Crown and one of the two parties. Surprisingly, out of that pact arose a powerful English version of the rational state.[65]

Anglican royalists saw monarchy in the terms expressed by *Eikon Basilike,* as a confessional symbol in whose renewal every loyal subject had spiritually shared. John Evelyn wrote with emotion of the Restoration as "the Lords doing, *et mirabile in oculis nostris* [and wonderful in our eyes]." It was a providential event, "past all humane policy." He compared it to "the returne of the Babylonian Captivity," a collective national deliverance. Although royalists denied that the people had any direct role in bringing about the Restoration, they stressed personal identification with the Crown and imagined sovereignty as a divine gift that entailed the protection of a godly people. "It is therefore the sovereign power which supporteth the laws, and that is our Sovereign Lord the king," Sir Peter Leicester pointed out in 1677. "And this power is given him from God . . .

wherefore the king is called . . . God's officer or minister, not the people's officer." He added, however, that it was the royal duty to defend the "English Israel," a community founded on adherence to the church.[66]

In the wake of his Restoration, Charles II was careful to stick to the Anglican formulation of monarchy. By using the Royal Touch within a week of his return to London, he publicly affirmed the heavenly origins of his powers. His coronation in 1661 became a spectacular affirmation of his connection with the people, one that attracted huge crowds. "God has wrought a wonderful miracle in settling us as he hath done," the king told a satisfied Parliament soon after.[67] The Anglican language of kingship aimed to build up rational authority in a confessional state similar to that of Denmark; but it carried uncomfortable implications for Charles II. The suggestion that the king owed his throne to divine providence implied that he might in future be held accountable to it. Moreover, like his father, Charles had no desire to be king over Israel. He mistrusted godliness, no matter where it came from. "Men that were earnest Protestants were under the sharpness of his Displeasure, expressed by Rallery, as well as by other ways," wrote the marquess of Halifax, who knew him well.[68]

By the time of the Restoration, the king's chief advisor, Edward Hyde, earl of Clarendon, had begun to devise an alternative royal language, based on the claim that Charles's hereditary right was upheld by the laws of nature and reason. This approach was inspired by the intellectual legacy of Hyde's friend Lord Falkland, as well as by the theories of Grotius and Hobbes. The Arminian bishop Matthew Wren stated its premises in quasi-Hobbesian terms: "It was impossible to establish any *Government* without a *Sovereign* Power vested in some One Man or Assembly of Men. . . . And therefore every Particular Man was necessitated to part with his Native Power and intrust it with the *Sovereign,* whose Actions He did thereby Authorise and make his own."[69] Government, in other words, was a rational compact, not one made by a sympathetic identification of the subject with the monarch.

Natural kingship had dire implications for confessionalism, as was evident in the Declaration of Breda, the pact proposed by Charles to his subjects just before he left Holland for home in 1660. Careful readers cannot have failed to notice the wording of the king's claim to "that right which God and Nature hath made our due," followed by a grant of "a liberty to tender consciences," a gesture towards sectarian individualism. In a speech to Parliament a year later, Clarendon argued that for the English, monarchy "is as natural to them as their food or raiment." He condemned the "extravagancy" of adopting a republican government, "which they knew no more how to do, than the naked Indians know how to dress themselves in the French fashion."[70] The return of the hereditary king, in short, put to right all the natural distinctions of gender, hierarchy, and culture on which social order was based. Clarendon discreetly ignored confessional distinctions.

The language of natural kingship bore echoes of Bodin, who had placed sovereignty in the natural body of the king rather than in a spiritual persona. Some English writers, in fact, urged Charles to copy the Bourbon model of sovereign kingship.[71] Among them was John Dryden, whose 1660 poem *Astraea Redux* drew a parallel between Charles II's Restoration and the victory of "his famous grandsire" Henry IV over the Catholic League. The poet employed natural metaphors of conjugal sexuality to describe the relationship between Charles and his people, complaining that "our cross stars deni'd us Charles his bed / Whom our first flames and virgin love did wed." The king would return to consummate a marriage between himself and his people—the same image used by Henry IV at his coronation.[72]

Was natural kingship a pale imitation of Bourbon monarchy? Louis XIV certainly believed that his cousin Charles's "inclinations . . . drew him toward France." Bishop Gilbert Burnet later accused Charles of "selling his own country" to the French.[73] Recent historians, however, have cast doubt on such patriotic denunciations. Charles II did not aspire to establish a sovereign monarchy on the French model, which would have put him at odds with most of the governing classes.[74] Still, he imitated Bourbon publicity in trying to project a royal language based less on confessionalism than on natural obedience to his person. This strategy may have been particularly suitable in Scotland and Ireland, where the security of Charles's rulership depended on tenuous control over mutually hostile religious groups.[75]

In England natural kingship motivated publicists to devote considerable attention to the king's own nature—his manly character, good manners, and fine physique. "To the gracefulness of his deportment may be joined his easiness of access," wrote an admiring courtier, "his patience in attention, and the gentleness both in the tune and style of his speech; so that those whom either the veneration for his dignity or the majesty of his presence have put into an awful respect are reassured as soon as he enters into a conversation."[76] Charles carefully cultivated these attributes, so as to make them seem effortless. "There was at first as much of Art as Nature in his Affability," Halifax commented sagaciously, "but by Habit it became Natural."[77] Thus, the king became the prime example of an innate nobility, the cultural ethos of the resurgent English aristocracy.

Like Louis XIV, Charles II promoted such distinctions through his court, which became the hub of civilité and style. Its culture was based on French models; Charles even hired twenty-four violinists in imitation of Louis XIV's famous musical ensemble. The comte de Grammont described the English court as "an entire scene of gallantry and amusements, with all the politeness and magnificence, which the inclinations of a prince, naturally inclined to tenderness and pleasure, could suggest."[78] Charles played the part of "first gentleman of the realm" by trying to set standards of behaviour and appearance for his courtiers to imitate. For example, Samuel Pepys recorded how in 1666 the king dressed himself in a new vest, a prototype of the waistcoat—"it is a fashion the King says he will never change." Evelyn observed with satisfaction that it was designed "to leave the French mode," and he lauded it as "a comely, and manly habite." Within two days Pepys noticed "several persons of the House of Lords, and Commons too, great courtiers, who are in it" and by the end of four days observed that "the court is all full of Vests." This sudden change in dress was not merely frivolous; on the contrary, it was meant "to teach the nobility thrift" and also to demonstrate the king's manly constancy and leadership, although Evelyn rightly thought it "to[o] good to hold, it being impossible for us to leave the Monsieurs Vanitys in good earnest long."[79]

The natural kingship of Charles's court certainly had its acolytes. They included women who were willing to stomach relentless sexual degradation and embrace the dictates of nature—not just courtesans and actresses like Nell Gwyn but also a few spirited writers, such as the dramatist Aphra Behn, for whom a less puritanical moral climate opened up new career opportunities.[80] As with the salons of contemporary France, however, the involvement of women in worldly culture was deeply shocking to the devout. In response, Evelyn wrote a life of "that Blessed Saint," his pious, chaste, and docile friend Mrs. Godolphin, maid of honour to the duchess of York. It says much about Anglican political reticence that he chose not to publish it.[81]

As for men, natural kingship provided a template for self-definition among ambitious place seekers. The best known of them, of course, was Samuel Pepys, diarist, bureaucrat, musician, and chronic philanderer, whose position as clerk to the Navy Board placed him at the centre of state administration. The king became a sort of distant alter ego for the ambitious civil servant. An assumed correspondence in their personalities, for example, fuelled Pepys's strong sexual attraction to the king's mistress, Lady Castlemaine. He professed to pity her, "though I know well enough she is a whore"; he "glutted himself with looking on her"; finally, he dreamed that he lay with her "and was admitted to use all the dalliance I desired with her." He felt no moral compunctions about any of this. Pepys's diary is not a record of inner conscience but a candid and "scientific" exposition of his experiences, his desires, his foibles, his health, his fumbling debauches—the natural man in all his manifold aspects. Fittingly, its author became a member of the Royal Society, the scientific club which Charles II had founded so that gentlemen might explore "the whole of Nature" through experiment and conversation.[82]

Beyond court and government circles, the king's publicity also connected him with the values and beliefs of the common people—or at least with what they were imagined to be. His subjects were exposed to Charles's natural parts, especially his courage and resourcefulness, through romanticized accounts of his dramatic escape after the battle of Worcester in 1651.[83] The king also appeared in popular prints as a kind of "vegetation god" who ushered in the spring. Woodcuts of Charles hiding in the leaves of an oak tree integrated the royal body into a protective symbol of nature. His majesty remained visible through the luxuriant foliage, as if his presence had made it bloom. Similarly, the maypoles that reappeared in towns and villages throughout England at the Restoration celebrated the springtime revival of nature and monarchy. The pagan and amorous connotations of maypole dancing, so disgusting to Puritans, proclaimed the triumphant return of a festive royalism firmly planted (or so it seemed) in popular affection.[84]

Charles II's popularity, however, waned quickly. Unlike Louis XIV, he was not able to separate his public image from his private life. Natural kingship increasingly seemed to provide a licence for passions that were anything but edifying—gambling, drinking, swearing, and, above all, "whoring." By 1667 even the steady royalist John Evelyn was bemoaning to Pepys "the badness of the Government, where nothing but wickedness, and wicked men and women command the King." When riotous London apprentices pulled down local brothels in the following year, they meant to pass on a message to the court about its own vices.[85] By then, widespread rumours of sexual rapacity had begun seriously to besmirch the reputation of the monarch. "But whatever it cost I will have a fine whore," the king vows in a libellous ditty of 1670, "And when I am weary of her I'll have more." The courtier-poet Lord Rochester pilloried the libidinous obsessions of "the easiest King and best-bred man alive," who had apparently tossed the phallic authority of his kingship into the laps of "whores": "His scepter and his prick are of a length; / And she may sway the one who plays with t'other." Others were even more blunt. "C——t is the mansion house where thou dost swell," an indignant versifier wrote of the king's "lewd life" in 1677.[86] From such sources was born the infamous legend of "Old Rowley the King," who was dominated by base instincts and whose only thought was for his own pleasure.

The openness of Charles II's vices eventually disgusted even Pepys. By 1667 he could record with contempt "the silliness of the King, playing with his dog all the while, or his codpiece."[87] Pepys knew more about his ruler's weaknesses than most servants of Louis XIV would have known about their ruler's, because Charles II was unable to protect himself from the glare of publicity. Fed by factional conflict, publicity finally made a mockery of natural kingship. It catered to a public that in England was more literate and better informed than anywhere else in Europe, except Holland. A profusion of newspapers, pamphlets, broadsheets, printed songs, and chapbooks supplied entertainment and instruction to a multitude of readers of the middling classes, who might consult such literature in a growing number of coffee houses. Press censorship proved only sporadically effective, and the government was obliged to sponsor its own official newspapers.[88] As the king's chief propagandist, Sir Roger L'Estrange, put it in 1681, " 'Tis the Press that has made 'um *Mad*, and the *Press* must set 'um *Right* again."[89]

Mass publicity was seen as necessary to deal with the provocations of Papists and Presbyterians. They were the "Other" against whom Anglican identity was defined. In print the enemies of the nation were attacked as malevolent minorities, festering within the godly confines of the new Israel, whose only political recourse was to plot against harmony in church and state. Reports proliferated in the press of the most horrid conspiracies, hatched by republican sectaries or Jesuits. Few doubted, for example, that wicked "Papists" had started the great London fire of 1666. Publicity was a means of protection against such plots, a spotlight case on the clandestine machinations of the "Other." In urban taverns and coffee houses, newspapers were read aloud as a group activity bonding male citizens in a common outlook and common prejudices. Reading, therefore, was not just a private path to knowledge but also a way of arming the community against hidden threats.

The breakdown of Anglican consensus was brought about by the publication of the wildest conspiracy of all, the Popish Plot of 1678. In an avalanche of revelations, the ex-Catholic and petty criminal Titus Oates fantasized about a grandiose Jesuit scheme to assassinate the king and bring his Catholic brother James to the throne. Within months, the abhorrers of Popery had introduced a parliamentary bill to exclude the duke of York from the succession (hence their party name, "Exclusionists"). They also organized an unprecedented campaign of anti-Catholic publicity, including mass demonstrations in London on Queen Elizabeth's birthday, at which the pope and other villains were burned in effigy. Sure of success, the Exclusionists were profoundly shocked when the king decided to fight them.[90]

Charles allied himself with Anglican royalists who defended hereditary right and warned that the nightmare of a Commonwealth might come again. "The House of Commons is the rabble's god," declared an anti-Exclusionist song of 1680, "The courtier's scourge, the bishops' iron rod, / The Lords' vexation, and the King's, by God!"[91] By the early 1680s every town in England was politically split between the two sides, who gave each other the deliberately insulting names Whig (or Covenanting Scots cattle thief) and Tory (or Papist Irish thug). These malicious epithets were designed to vilify and marginalize the opposing faction as unpatriotic, non-Anglican, and essentially criminal—in other words, to give them the characteristics of the hated "Other."[92]

R. White Sculp.

The Exclusion Crisis was a contest over the language of kingship. For the Whigs the monarch was a common person in whom all Protestants might be represented. He was the sign of a rational state that was based on human law and sectarian individualism. He should accept the restrictions on hereditary succession laid down by Parliament, since "'tis by law alone / Your right's derived to our English throne." These were ideas left over from Cromwell's Protectorate. For Tories, by contrast, the king was a sign of Anglican confessional unity. They saw the state as founded on a collective religious identity and governed by a divinely appointed sovereignty.[93] In 1660 Charles might have preferred the Whigs, whose views on confessionalism were more compatible with his own. By the 1680s, however, he was older and more hated and would not permit anything to stand in the way of the legitimate Stuart heir. Faced with his implacable hostility, many Whigs turned to his illegitimate son, the duke of Monmouth, who claimed to represent the interests of all Protestants, and who possessed a natural charisma.[94]

The Exclusion Crisis ended in victory for the Tories, who dominated court and administration in the last years of the reign. They make the king into an instrument of their party dominance and equated political inclusion with adherence to the Anglican Church. These would remain the hallmarks of the rational state in eighteenth-century England. Yet the Tories also preserved aspects of sacral kingship. They encouraged Charles to reassert his spiritual connection with the Anglican community by touching scrofulitics, which he did no fewer than 8,577 times in 1682 and 1683.[95] By these means they tried to anchor the rational state to the popularity of quasi-magical traditions.

John Dryden celebrated the Tory victory in his poem *Absalom and Achitophel*, where Monmouth's "manly beauty" infuses the character of Absalom, an archetype of natural kingship. King David, flawed and weak, is saved from rebellion by the intervention of "a train of loyal peers." The poem concludes with the king's rediscovery of his divinely sanctioned authority: "Once more the godlike David was restor'd, / And willing

---

22. Robert White, *The Royal Gift of Healing*, from John Browne, *Adenochoiradelogin* (London, 1684), engraving.

Photo: British Library, London.

nations knew their lawful lord."[96] The words of the final line paraphrase Marvell's panegyric to the lord protector; they suggest not so much an emotional bond as a rational pact between king and people. As for the once-sprightly Charles II, he had become a grudging accomplice of the Tories or High Churchmen, whose direction over the state he had no choice but to accept. They could not, however, restrain "Old Rowley" from taking his last and best revenge on all his Protestant subjects when he became a Roman Catholic on his deathbed.

## THE EMPIRE AND *Erblande*

In England the royal language was unsettled, and the rational state emerged out of dissension. In the Holy Roman Empire the language of rulership was relatively stable, but did it lend itself to the creation of a rational state? By 1660 many educated Germans had come to the conclusion that the Empire was not a state, and could never be one. The jurist Hermann Conring debunked the notion that the *Reich* was the heir to the imperial authority of ancient Rome, and he argued that its laws should be determined separately within each of its territories. Similarly, Samuel Pufendorf deplored the Imperial constitutions as "monstrous" and irrational. He sought to expose "what diseases lie hidden in the bowels of Germany," preventing it from becoming a state. At best, Pufendorf opined, the empire might develop into a system of territorial sovereignties, which seemed to be the path laid out by the Treaties of Westphalia.[97]

These views were not shared by all Germans. Among its more humble subjects, the office of emperor continued to command loyalty and a degree of reverence. The pious Lutheran cobbler Hans Heberle, for example, quickly set aside the bitterness of the Thirty Years' War and began again to record in his diary events that related to the emperor and his family. Ever alert to divine portents, he marvelled in 1654 when the death of the Imperial heir was presaged by an earthquake and the appearance of a star. Three years later Heberle observed with great solemnity the passing of "our greatest leader, the ever-shining, highest and mightiest Roman Imperial Majesty," Ferdinand III. Apparently, he had entirely forgotten how Ferdinand had hammered the Protestant armies at Nördlingen.[98]

Heberle was not untypical. Historians have recently begun to suggest that the Treaties of Westphalia, which seemed to seal the downfall of the Reich, actually reinvigorated it in many minds. The emperor became the leader of a powerful network of spiritual princes, Imperial knights, and Catholic nobles; the Reichstag re-emerged as "an important institution of stabilisation, integration and security;" and abused peasants continued to use the Imperial law courts—the *Kammergericht* and *Hofrat*—to win economic concessions from local lords. According to Volker Press, there was "a consciousness of the *Reich*, embedded in the concrete interests of the common people."[99]

This consciousness was based partly on recollection of an idealized past, partly on hopes of future political justice. It imagined a memory-state, rooted in the desire of the Christian self for conformity and stability. The Imperial memory-state was never fully rationalized around the twin pillars of sovereignty and confessionalization. Its royal language depended more on occult symbols, like the prophetic events that edified Hans Heberle, than on precise signs. Yet it was powerful enough to attract so rational a mind as that of the philosopher G. W. Leibniz. He portrayed the emperor as the head of a "republic of Christendom" and "the defender, or rather the chief, or if one prefers the secular arm of the universal Church." These were traditional attributes of the Imperial office, but in Leibniz's formulation they became the basis for a tolerant polity in which every Christian might be represented. As for unified sovereignty, Leibniz wrote that it "lacks the aid of good writers," and he attacked "Hobbesian empires" as "neither possible nor desirable, unless those who must have supreme power are gifted with angelic virtues." He implied, as had Arnisaeus, that a rational state did not have to be dominated by a single sovereign authority.[100]

Was Leibniz's "republic of Christendom" a personal fantasy, or did the Habsburg emperors actively pursue it? Certainly they were not unaware of a persistent support among German Protestants, and in spite of their commitment to militant Catholicism within the *Erblande*, they never renounced the integrating, pan-Christian aura of the Imperial office. After 1648 they assiduously tried to revive it by proposing that the religious interests of all Christian subjects were represented in the emperor's person. The biblical prototype for this unifying princely role was King Solomon, who symbolized wisdom and virtue rather than zealous orthodoxy. The Habsburg heir Ferdinand IV was depicted as Solomon in an elaborate print of 1653, above the broadly appealing if ambiguous slogan "FOR GOD—FOR THE PEOPLE." His brother Leopold I was later shown in the same role in the decorations of the Jesuit Church in Vienna. A Jesuit play performed before the emperor Ferdinand III in 1656 praised Solomon for piety, justice, good counsel, and "busy industriousness"—not, it should be noted, for despising heresy. A year later, on the other side of the confessional divide, the Lutheran preacher J. B. Schupp, son-in-law of Dietrich Reinking, made Solomon the subject of a lengthy discourse on just Christian rulership.[101]

After 1663, Habsburg publicity was able to exploit a more emotional source of Christian unity: fear of the "Other," in the guise of the Turks, who had declared war on the emperor. Hans Heberle was moved to pray in 1667 that God "would protect and guard our Germany and the whole Roman Empire from the sworn enemy, the Turks and other foreign peoples."[102] A well-developed religious xenophobia enhanced the emperor's position as defender of the Christian Reich against its "sworn enemies." The siege of Vienna by Turkish forces in 1683 became the most dramatic event of the century for many Germans, Protestant as well as Catholic. The Jesuits of Cologne celebrated the stunning defeat of the Ottoman army with an historical play, *Vienna liberata*, which seems to have been aimed at a broadly Christian rather than strictly Catholic public.[103]

"God gives us his blessings there on all sides," the emperor Leopold I wrote in 1663 about the war in Hungary. "If God is with us, who can be against us?"[104] Throughout his long wars against the Turks, Leopold did everything he could to project the image of defender of a common Christian faith. In 1686 he issued a gold medal showing himself as Joshua, with the inscription "I give it to you, you will have the use of it; the godless people will be subjected to your power." The medal celebrated the fall of Budapest to the Imperial armies, and its motto was taken from a recent oratorio, *The Fall of the City of Jericho*, in which the biblical city represented the Hungarian capital. The figure of Joshua, of course, had been closely associated with Protestant godly rulership, especially with Gustavus Adolphus. Leopold's publicity further appropriated from the late Swedish king the unusual role of the Jewish liberator Judas Maccabaeus.[105] The emperor used such biblical parallels to engage all his Christian subjects in the titanic struggle against their common religious nemesis.

The Imperial language generated from Vienna was designed to pull both Catholic and Protestant subjects towards identification with a purposeful political entity, whose symbol was the emperor. This was the goal of royal languages everywhere. Still, we cannot call the Holy Roman Empire a rational state. The artificial man never took full shape there. His development was hampered by the weakness of Imperial institutions, confessional differences, and competition from territorial princes. Conring and Pufendorf, therefore, were correct in seeing the Empire as something less than a state; but it was able to survive in an age of competitive states because it was the object of the same personal attachment that sustained its rivals. Significantly, no territorial prince within the Reich was able to displace the emperor as a sign of Christian unity, and none of the princes enjoyed his international status.

Within the Habsburg Erblande, the royal language was uncontested, and personal identification with the ruler was more intense. As P. W. von Hornigk put it in his celebrated treatise on Austrian economic self-sufficiency, *Oesterreich über Alles,* "Salvation must come from the Princes of our people, for the people can do nothing without them."[106] For von Hornigk the emperor's leadership was perfectly compatible with rational self-interest. Leopold's own publicity, by contrast, continued to stress his confessional image as a model of piety and intercessor between God and a Catholic people. Nevertheless, by the late seventeenth century Habsburg confessionalism had begun to lean towards a more rational definition of authority.

This confessional rationalism was triumphally displayed in the *Pestsäule,* or plague column, erected in Vienna to commemorate the end of the decimating plague of 1679. A spiralling baroque fantasy, the column is topped by the Holy Trinity, who preside over angels carrying the symbols of rulership through cloudy billows. It does not look much like a monument to the rational state. Yet the viewer cannot take in the awesome spectacle of heaven; rather, we fix our gaze on the precisely rendered figure of the emperor Leopold, who kneels below the clouds, just above our heads. He alone touches the divine, and what floats above him is lodged in *his* imagination, not ours. Leopold's worldly authority is shown in the sword and armour he wears. He is clearly a sovereign as well as an intercessor. Around him the classically modelled base of the column is decorated with biblical motifs on friezes that resemble the pages of a book. The

Pestsäule, therefore, juxtaposes an unknowable divine order with the rational, "scriptural" (or written) order of the state. The column became the focal point for what may be called state devotions. Every day a religious procession marched out to it, accompanied by Imperial court musicians. What they were celebrating was not a spiritual event but a pact of obedience between Christian subjects and their ruler.[107]

Thus, beneath the baroque flourishes of Leopold's monarchy can be detected a royal language informed by reason and centred on the person of the emperor. As in France and England, the main source of this royal language was the court. R. J. W. Evans has noted that "central government was subsumed in a larger entity: the central court. Political operations were bound up with cultural ones."[108] H. C. Ehalt has argued that Leopold I's court rationalized aristocratic social structure by formalizing distinctions of rank and prestige as well as by distributing economic and titular favours. Unlike Versailles, however, the Viennese court did not disguise the confessional implications of etiquette, which came to resemble a kind of state liturgy. The emperor's person, for example, was treated more worshipfully than Louis XIV's. Leopold demanded the "Spanish reverence"—a deep bend of the knee—whenever his name was mentioned; he rejected the more perfunctory "French reverence." At Vienna, civilité was not made of manners alone; it was always consciously informed by supposedly higher values.[109]

The royal language can also be observed in the theatrical "mass culture" of Leopold's court. It took the forms of fantastic operas, lavish oratorios, and grandiose spectacles. Among them was the famous Roßballet of 1667, which imitated Louis XIV's equestrian carrousels—"for centuries nothing like it has been seen," chortled the emperor. He sponsored no fewer than four hundred feste teatrali for the edification of his subjects, who could experience them vicariously through prints and published accounts. The celebrations of his marriage to the Infanta of Spain went on for two full years! Most of these performances were accompanied by music, which was thought to be an art particularly edifying to moral sentiments. It

---

23. Matthias Rauchmiller, J. B. Fischer von Erlach and others, *The Pestsäule* (1682–92), Vienna.

Photo: Robert Haidinger, courtesy of Karin Hanta.

was under Leopold that Italian opera first thrived at the Viennese court and gained the characteristics of "maximum stability and persistent identity" that would last until the time of Mozart. The frequent use of classical motifs reminded audiences that their ruler was the successor to Rome, that his dominance was based on nature and reason as well as confessionalism. Thus, court entertainments articulated a royal language not far removed from that of Louis XIV.[110]

Beyond the confines of the court, the emperor encouraged a remarkable degree of rational intervention by local authorities in the lives of his subjects. These endeavours were often targeted at disciplining the poor. Vienna was provided with its first orphanage for boys, its first penitentiary workhouse, and its first street lamps, to combat crime. The Russian visitor Peter Tolstoi marvelled at the lights burning all night in the capital, and he greatly admired the hospital built outside the city, where "all are kept at the emperor's expense." Meanwhile, an Austrian law of 1679 paralleled English poor-law reforms in expelling beggars who could not prove residence in a parish.[111] These measures were forerunners of the social engineering that was widely adopted in the Habsburg lands during the eighteenth century.

On a broader level, Imperial publicists used the Turkish war as an opportunity to spread a message of necessary submission within the Erblande. The Turks were often depicted as more threatening in a moral than a military sense. "What is the Turk?" asked the fulminous court preacher Abraham a Sancta Clara. "You Christians, don't answer before you are informed! He is a replica of the antichrist; he is a vain piece of a tyrant; he is an insatiable tiger . . . he is an epicurean piece of excrement; he is a tyrannic monster."[112] All this vitriol did not mean that the Turks were inhuman; on the contrary, they were the worst examples of unbridled human excess and selfish appetite, due to their irrational religion. Abraham generously allowed them a few virtuous practices, like charity to the poor; but he vigorously maintained that they exemplified the antithesis of the inner moral values to which a Christian should aspire. The tenets of Mohammed, he asserted, resulted in tyranny, both within the self and in the state. Indeed, the Turks—and to some extent the Jews, who were expelled from Vienna in 1670—had largely replaced the Protestants as the demons of Habsburg propaganda.[113] They presented convenient stereotypes of

"Otherness," in opposition to which an authoritarian response was fashioned, centred on rational self-discipline.

Of course, theatrical publicity and bombastic preaching should not be mistaken for effective control. How great was the impact of Italian opera on the plains of Hungary? The emperor's cultural endeavours may have lent no more overall coherence to the Habsburg state than they did to the structure of the Hofburg, which remained a rambling and rather uninspired example of baroque architecture.[114] On an administrative level, Leopold created no new institutions to tie together his realms, and those that already existed, like the Imperial Privy Council, went into decline.[115] The provincial Estates of the Erblande retained considerable clout. In Bohemia they successfully hampered the implementation of Leopold's confessional programme by neglecting to restore church property or to reinstall priests in every parish.[116] In Hungary, the main battleground of the Turkish wars, Leopold suffered a more severe setback. His efforts to suppress Protestantism spurred the Hungarian nobles to support serious uprisings in 1664 and 1676. The outcome of these struggles was a constitutional compromise worked out in 1688 between the emperor and the noble-dominated Hungarian Estates. The crown of St. Stephen became hereditary in the house of Habsburg, and the Estates lost their right of armed resistance; but their other powers were preserved, and religious liberty was guaranteed in Transylvania. These were important concessions, which in some ways marked the limits of confessionalism and the rewriting of the state pact in one of the Habsburg lands.[117]

In spite of its partial failure in Hungary, the Habsburg state was much more than an imagined reality in the Erblande. It was based on the personal standards of "virtuous conduct" and confessional identity. Its patriarchal leadership emanated from the person of the emperor and travelled through the Catholic noble houses of Austria and Bohemia into peasant households. In an ideological sense, therefore, the Habsburg state was a broader manifestation of the Imperial house, the *domus nostra* that is so frequently mentioned in Leopold's personal correspondence. The emperor constantly exhorted his relatives "to promote the interest of our whole house," and he defended his own policy as "of service to the whole house."[118] The domus nostra provided a familial model of rulership that the state would follow for the next two centuries. Its pervasive ideological influence compensated for a chronic lack of centralized institutions in the Erblande. Stone by stone, the Austrian Habsburgs converted their Imperial house into a disjointed but still recognizable residence for the artificial man.

## SPAIN

Compared to that of their Austrian relations, the royal language of the Spanish Habsburgs seems barely discernible. This is partly because the late seventeenth century confronts us with what Henry Kamen has called "the Spain we do not know," a kingdom in apparent decline whose history is still largely unexplored. To some degree, King Charles II himself—known as *El Hechizado*, "the Bewitched"—is "the king we do not know." Even his uncle Leopold thought he should be exposed to the populace, so as to disprove French reports that he was "no little boy, but only a little girl." Charles has long been depicted as the sickly, mentally deficient result of two centuries of Habsburg inbreeding. His father was his mother's uncle, and in the previous six generations of his family, he had only forty-six forebears rather than the usual 126. Charles's intellectual failings were painfully apparent (for example, as an adult he wrote like a ten-year-old), but their importance may have been exaggerated. While he was without doubt a severely handicapped monarch, he was not a helpless one. He was capable of projecting a royal language when it was supplied to him by others.[119]

For most of his reign, however, Charles was constrained to reiterating the confessional rhetoric left to him by his father, Philip IV. It dwelled less on the state than on the exemplary piety of the monarch, and it offered no precise formulation of sovereignty. It was deeply influenced by the ascetic and submissive values of reformed Catholicism. After Olivares's downfall, Philip had become the devotee of a rigorist nun, Sister María de Agreda, who did not hesitate to chastise him for his frequent sins. To her the king wrote a stream of anxious letters, despairing that "if God does not help me, I am so frail, that I will never get rid of the obstructions of sin."[120] Sister María was celebrated for her ecstatic visions and mystical journeys that took her as far away as Mexico. Her political influence over the king contributed to an abandonment of humanist and state-centred goals.

As a result, the exequies for King Philip, who died in September 1665, emphasized not the glory of his earthly accomplishments but his attainment of a heavenly kingdom through devotion to the cross, the Eucharist, and the Virgin Mary. His body was placed beneath a gigantic catafalque surrounded by banners displaying hieroglyphic emblems. Most of them were macabre reminders of death and resurrection, replete with scythes, skulls, and open tombs; only a few referred obliquely to the succession, the token of continuity in the state. The royal crown and the sun are used in these designs as symbols of Philip's Christian self, not as representations of his monarchy. Moreover, the emblems are almost completely devoid of classical allusions. Catholic piety, not Neostoic prudence, upholds the king; and in turn, his redeemed soul will be a guide to Faith, shown as a blind woman holding the chalice and Host. By contrast, the catafalque prepared in Naples to commemorate the king's death concentrated on Philip's temporal glory, and the official elegy made incongruous classical references to him as a "true Atlas of religion"![121]

The heavy religious imagery of the Madrid exequies set a tone for the reign of Charles II. A further legacy from Philip IV to his son was an obsession with court etiquette. In 1647 the late king had appointed a *junta* to compile strict rules of precedence and decorum, which became a charter for Charles II's household. By determining the relative prestige of every office and title, however, the junta's work limited the king's ability to use favours and distinctions as a means of political control. Furthermore, because the ceremonial of the Spanish court concentrated on religious devotions rather than on the king's daily routine, contact with the royal person was far more difficult at Madrid than at Versailles or Vienna. All in all, the court of Charles II was a relic of the baroque past. It was less the "embodiment" of social relations than an approximation of divine order.[122]

Court art was similarly muted by a nostalgic piety, which can be observed in the paintings of Francisco de Herrera the younger or Claudio Coello.[123] In courtly entertainments, confessional themes predominated. The only exceptions were the light musical plays called *zarzuelas,* which were based on uplifting classical subjects. Like the operas performed at Versailles or Vienna, they were intended to refine the manners and morals of the nobility. Zarzuelas were confined to the private enjoyment of a select group of courtiers, however, and were not inflated into exemplary public spectacles.[124]

Outside the palace, the mass culture of Philip IV's reign continued to flourish, but it placed more value on spiritual purification than on political participation. Calderón edified the court and the general public with his *autos sacramentales,* one-act devotional plays that were performed in the royal presence on open stages in the streets of Madrid. These simple moral works did not contain any of the human tension or political rationalism of the *Mayor of Zalamea.* In them the character of "the Prince" exemplified religious duty, and on one occasion a monstrous figure of Leviathan was trotted out as a "symbol of sin!"[125] Perhaps the most typical "mass cultural" event of Charles II's reign was a grandiose Inquisitorial auto de fé of 1680, held before a delighted king in the Plaza Mayor. Deeply offended by any aspect of popular culture that seemed immoral or unorthodox, Charles even moved against the public stage, which had provided an important forum for humanist ideas. He closed down the theatres in Seville, although he did not dare to suppress those in Madrid.[126]

Charles's most notable public campaign was aimed at making the Immaculate Conception of the Virgin Mary into a dogma of the church. This doctrine removed Mary's birth from the taint of sexual intercourse and made her free of original sin. During Charles's reign, church paintings by Murillo and other Spanish artists spread amazing images of the Immaculate Conception to a wide audience. They would show a stunningly beautiful Virgin, posed as the Apocalyptic Woman of the Book of Revelation, riding on fluffy clouds and crowned by twelve stars symbolizing important events in her life. The Immaculate Conception was integrated into popular piety through devotions like the rosary processions, which started at Seville in 1690 and were at first exclusively male.[127] Making the Virgin into a kind of female deity rather than a compassionate human mother may have served as a way of distancing her from everyday life and of denying her some of the volatile representative status accorded to ordinary saints. She might then no longer inspire the dangerous visions claimed by mystic *beatas,* or give her blessings to Neapolitan rebels. At the same time, her ethereal purity consoled the imagination of a monarch who had begun to feel that nature and reason were the tools of the enemy.

The failure to develop a royal language may have been due as much to the king's mother, Queen Mariana, as to Charles himself. She was largely responsible for directing the government away from the reformism of the 1620s and 1630s. In turn, Mariana was manipulated by her brother, the emperor Leopold, who sent her constant political advice. His overriding purpose was not to rationalize the Spanish state but to hinder any attempts "to do damage to our house," which meant the interests of Vienna.[128] Accordingly, Mariana gave meticulous attention to the Habsburg religious mission and enshrined the memory of Philip IV. Prolonged mourning for her husband induced her to wear a nun's habit as her normal dress. Portraits of her in this garb epitomize the confessional trappings of power in what was essentially a branch office of domus nostra, another Habsburg memory-state.

As for the centralist visions of Olivares, they were left unrealized. The Spanish Empire became "a union of autonomous states," troubled by sporadic patriotic revolts—at Messina in 1675, in Catalonia from 1687 to 1691. Nevertheless, the dream of rational reform had not been abandoned by everyone. It nurtured the messianic ambitions of Don Juan, the king's illegitimate half-brother and Queen Mariana's rival. A manly swordsman like the earl of Essex, he forced his way into power by an aristocratic military coup in 1677 but died suddenly two years later. Reform gradually came back into fashion after 1680, as the Spanish economy sluggishly began to improve. Although the evidence is still unclear, the foundations of the Bourbon fiscal-military state in Spain may have been laid in this period.[129]

Meanwhile, growing dissatisfaction with the regime led to party divisions. In Spain as in England, the features of a rational state would eventually emerge out of prolonged factionalism. During the 1690s Charles's second wife, Mariana of Neuburg, led a *camarilla* of meddlesome German advisors against a clique of "patriotic" Spanish nobles. Each faction eagerly courted public opinion, and Madrid was bombarded with satires attacking one side or the other. "The most bloody pasquinades appear every day," the English ambassador Alexander Stanhope noted. "These most loyal subjects seem to have lost all manner of respect to Majesty." As in England during the 1670s, a sphere of public political discourse arose out of widespread fears that the weakness of the monarchy would lead to a breakdown of civil order.[130]

When food riots broke out in the capital on 28 April 1699, they quickly took on a political complexion. The rioters were openly encouraged by leading members of the court to demand the resignation of the chief minister. They marched on the royal palace of the Alcázar and demanded to see the monarch. Told by the queen that he was asleep, they answered,

"We do not believe it, for this is no time to sleep." As in an old trope of popular literature, they sought to awaken the somnolent king, so that he might repair the kingdom. Charles walked out onto the palace balcony, saluted them with his hat, bowed, and pardoned them. His gesture was splendidly theatrical, but it was that of a Christian gentleman rather than a sovereign.[131] He was still unable to articulate a royal language.

This was one of the last grand scenarios of Habsburg mass culture. Shortly after the riots the king became seriously ill. Facing the extinction of his lineage, he fell back on the spiritual supports that had been the chief props of his monarchy. He marched in the Corpus Christi procession, went to bullfights, visited the Marian shrine of Our Lady of Atocha. On 1 November 1700 the last Spanish Habsburg died.[132] In his testament, he left an undivided empire to the duc d'Anjou, grandson of Louis XIV. The text of the will gave precedence, however, to the king's religious concerns. It drew particular attention to the doctrine of the Immaculate Conception of Mary, "for which pious belief I have made with the Apostolic See all the efforts that I have been able . . . I have ordered it to be raised as a symbol on my royal standards." The king commanded his successors to take special care of El Escorial and begged them to "honour the Inquisition greatly." They were further charged to "govern things more by considerations of Religion than by respect to the political estate [*estado político*]," just as Charles himself had always "held it better and more convenient to be lacking in reasons of State [*razones de Estado*] than to dispense with and dissimulate about a point in matters that relate to Religion." Although he mentioned "my sovereignty and plenitude of power" and referred to his "absolute royal power . . . as King and sovereign lord," the context of such remarks made it clear that he was calling upon an authority that operated only in special circumstances.[133]

To the very end, Charles II's royal language was undermined by political debility and confessional preoccupations. His pious reticence inspired few memorials; happily, one of them is the splendid painting *La Sagrada Forma*, executed by Claudio Coello from 1685 to 1690 over the

---

24. Claudio Coello, *The Sacred Form* (1685–90), painting.
Monastery-Palace of El Escorial.

Photo: Patrimonio nacional, Madrid.

sacristy altar at El Escorial. This is a work of expiation, donated by the king in order to obtain a papal pardon for some supporters of Don Juan who had ransacked the monarchy while in pursuit of one of their political adversaries. King Charles is shown on his knees before the altar, venerating the Sacred Form of Gorinchem, a piece of the Eucharist that reportedly shed blood when trampled by Dutch Protestant rebels. The ungainly royal face seems to reflect the suffering Host, just as the painting itself seems perfectly to mirror what it depicts. Coello's altarpiece is a moving restatement of the Habsburg family myth, with Charles II playing Rudolf I. Yet its composition, placing the king below the prior of the monastery, displays the supremacy of the church over the Crown. Charles is glorified through the priest who holds up the Host. A further political message can be detected, containing perhaps a note of criticism. While the violence that gave birth to Coello's painting has been expunged from its untroubled surface, the canvas does contain a group portrait of the guilty noblemen, who crowd around the king. They pay him little attention and take no part in the royal communion with God, but their lurking presence is a reminder of where real authority lay in the memory-state of Charles II.[134]

## Beyond Confessionalism

The orthodox restraint of *The Sacred Form* contrasts with the confidence of Charles Le Brun's *Resurrection,* which once hung over the high altar of the now-vanished Paris church of the Saint Sépulcre. It shows Christ rising in triumph above the worshipful figures of Louis XIV and his ancestor Saint Louis. The king offers Christ his sceptre and helmet, symbols of a state that is his by divine appointment. He gazes at the great mystery of Christianity above the veil of the tabernacle, which divides heaven from earth, the sacred from the profane. A survival from medieval Imperial imagery, the veil alludes to the king's dual nature, both human and divine. The viewer approaches the sacred person of Louis XIV through the figure of his chief minister Colbert, who stands below him, staring out at us and pointing to the king.[135]

---

25. Charles Le Brun, *The Resurrection of Christ* (1676), painting.

Photo: Musée des Beaux-Arts, Lyons; copyright R. M. N. — OJEDA.

Unlike Coello, Le Brun gives no hint that the church mediates the relationship between king and God. Instead, Christ directly blesses the monarch's earthly sovereignty and its emanation, the state. The heavenly and worldly spheres on either side of the veil are not strictly separated. The triumphs of Louis XIV are confuted with the Resurrection, so that the soldiers writhing beneath the veil may either be those who guarded Christ's tomb or the conquered enemies of France. Christ's body seems to emerge out of the king's. Christ's rippling muscles and beaming countenance resemble a pagan statue of Apollo, a god whose iconography was particularly connected with Louis XIV. The deliberate mixing of sacred and profane themes is further apparent in the pile of treasure at the bottom of the canvas. It represents the money loaned to the king by the Mercers' Corporation for his military campaigns. In fact, it was the wealth of the mercers, not the prayers of the king, that had made Le Brun's Apollonian Christ rise up in glory over the altar of the Saint Sépulchre. How many works of sacred art announce the financial mechanisms by which they have been commissioned?

In this expression of religious zeal, therefore, we are faced with a visual rhetoric that is not purely confessional but quotes freely from the royal language and owes everything to the state—not to mention the deep pockets of the *gens de finance*. Of course, Louis XIV continued to regard God as the only source of his powers and to insist that his greatest duties were to religion. Unlike his father, however, Louis did not equate his servitude to God with service to the universal Church. If he advanced the cause of Catholicism, it was not as a means towards his own salvation, or even that of his subjects; rather, it was a state obligation. Such convictions led him to press in the 1680s towards the final phase of confessionalization in France, the defence of Gallican privileges and the extinction of Protestantism, "an evil that I had always regarded, and still regard, with sorrow."[136]

He was encouraged in these actions by the continuing success of religious reform. Indeed, the confessional disciplining of the French people reached an apogee in the late seventeenth century. The studies of Gabriel Le Bras on the diocese of Chalons and of Louis Pérouas on the diocese of La Rochelle have pointed to the period from 1650 to 1690 as a high point of reform, measured by episcopal ordinances, pastoral activity, the spread of catechism, and the level of communicants. It was only in these decades that Catholic preaching missions began to reach remote areas like rural Brittany.[137] Yves-Marie Bercé has suggested that the late seventeenth century saw an onslaught against popular religion in France, entailing clerical control over confraternities, the suppression of "immoral" festive rites (especially dancing), and a reduction in the number of feast days. Bishops with Jansenist leanings, like Caulet of Pamiers and Nicolas Pavillon of Alet, were especially keen participants in the crusade to stamp out offensive popular practices.[138]

The same trends can be observed elsewhere. Preaching missions in remote rural areas of Spain had begun much earlier, but it was not until the last half of the seventeenth century that the battle against "ignorance" seemed to be turning in the church's favour in places like Alpujarras and the Pyrenees.[139] In England efforts by local authorities to reform behaviour continued to accelerate after the Restoration. Anglican moralists picked up where Puritans had left off, especially in combating drunkenness and failure to observe the sabbath. The Church of England achieved considerable success; visitation records from various parts of England reveal very high numbers of parishioners taking Easter Communion in the 1670s.[140]

The politics of confessionalization, however, had become more complicated. In the aftermath of the Treaties of Westphalia, religious uniformity no longer appeared to be indispensable to the security of the state. Other solutions, perhaps even toleration, began to seem possible. Clerical emissaries of the emperor Leopold even entered into vague negotiations towards a reunion of the Catholic and Lutheran churches, in which prominent philosophers like Leibniz, Bossuet, and Arnauld played the part of intermediaries. To be sure, sectarian individualism was still generally deplored as conducive to anarchy. "Where ev'ry private man may save a stake, / Ruled by the Scripture and his own advice / Each has a blind bypath to Paradise," wrote John Dryden, a convert to Catholicism. Yet even he could accept a toleration sponsored by the monarch, which he described as "the Lion's peace."[141]

In short, the interests of the state had begun to assert themselves as paramount in the process of confessionalization. Louis XIV was not alone in claiming this ultimate supremacy. James II of England did the same, albeit by different means. He effectively tried to denationalize the Church of England by breaking its monopoly on religious worship. This would have reinvigorated confessional diversity under the auspices of an authoritarian monarchy acting as the protector of every "tender conscience." The pact between the state and the self would have been individualized to an extent unparalleled elsewhere. In spite of their different methods, Louis and James were similar in their state-centred approaches to confessionalism. Their efforts had been foreshadowed, however, by another ruler, of whom they knew almost nothing: Tsar Alexis of Russia. Like Louis XIV, Tsar Alexis wanted to establish royal dominance over a national church. Like James II, he espoused sweeping innovation and was strongly opposed by religious leaders who saw him as wrecking the whole basis of confessional unity.

It was quite a change from the late 1640s, when the reliance of the Romanov dynasty on the Orthodox community had been demonstrated by the tsar's surrender to the Morozov rioters. When in 1652 the tsar chose as patriarch the godly monk Nikon, religious reformers like Avvakum saw it as confirming the ruler's commitment to their programme. They later looked back with bitterness on Nikon's appointment. "Much could be said about his treachery!" Avvakum recorded. "When he was made patriarch, he wouldn't even let his friends into the Chamber of the Cross! And then he belched forth his venom!"[142] Nikon's great crime was to introduce a number of liturgical reforms, which he claimed to be Byzantine in origin. In fact, they were not ancient but in accordance with current Greek practice. This suggests that the long-term goal of the changes was to facilitate the unification of the main branches of Orthodoxy under the supreme authority of Moscow, which Nikon's supporters eagerly described as "the Third Rome." Avvakum and his supporters, however, could not accept the patriarch's "apostasy" on matters like the Greek use of three fingers rather than two in making the sign of the cross. This was not a merely "external" issue to believers, who recognized in every religious gesture an unalterable symbol of a higher reality.[143]

The tsar was a stronger supporter of the reforms themselves than he was of their author, whose extravagant claims to authority he resented. Nikon insisted on being addressed by the title *Velikii Gosudar'*, or Great Sovereign, which had previously been used only by Patriarch Filaret and seemed to put Nikon above the tsar. It was an annoying breach of a royal language that had begun to develop in Russia with the annexation of the

Ukraine and had found a clear, uncompromising voice in the negotiations at Pereiaslav. Designed to compete with those of western monarchies, the royal language could brook no diminution of the ruler's sovereignty. In a decisive show of power, Alexis forced Nikon to abdicate in 1658. The patriarch was furious. "You will have to give account to the Lord God for everything," he wrote threateningly to the tsar, who paid no attention. The patriarch was finally deposed by a religious court hand-picked by the angry monarch.[144]

Responsibility for upholding the liturgical reforms now passed to Alexis, but Avvakum and his followers remained unwilling to compromise, even with their ruler. Their views were labelled heretical in 1667 by a patriarchal council loaded with Greeks. Avvakum denounced the patriarchs to their faces as godless and "shamed the whore of Rome within them." His tongue was subsequently cut out, and he was sent into exile in the far north, where he was probably burned at the stake fifteen years later. By that time, the *Raskol*, or schism, of the Old Believers, who rejected Nikon's reforms, was blazing as wildly and brightly as the fires that brought martyrdom to its leader.[145]

The historian Michael Cherniavsky emphasised that the Raskol was both a religious and a political challenge to tsarism. Since the reforms were heretical, the ruler who upheld them had to be the Antichrist. For some Old Believers, like the monks of the famous Solovetskii monastery in the far north, this justified armed resistance against the tsar. It is possible that Old Belief was also a motivating factor in the massive peasant uprising led by Stenka Razin in the valleys of the Don and Volga in 1670 and 1671. Razin himself had twice visited the Solovetskii monastery, and he was joined by many of the "white clergy," or parish priests, who were more sympathetic to Old Belief than were most monks. Razin's supporters, however, seem to have desired a general moral turnaround in government—including the abolition of serfdom—rather than a specific end to liturgical reform. For the most convinced adherents of the Raskol, the logic of millennialism led not to rebellion but to self-immolation. By burning themselves in rituals of mass suicide, Old Believers purified their own bodies from any taint of association with the worldly body of the Antichrist.[146]

The Raskol amounted to a schism between the ideal of the ascetic body, the foundation of the Orthodox self, and the body of the sacred ruler, which to its critics had become nothing more than the sign of an unholy state. For his part, Alexis found himself caught in an unwanted cultural struggle. He had no great wish to move Russian government in the direction of the western rational state, but this was the effect of many of his initiatives after 1667. They included the encouragement of naturalistic icon-painting, the adoption of polyphonic music, and the building of the Kolomenskoe palace, whose walls were decorated with representations of Julius Caesar and Alexander the Great. The ideology of the court seemed increasingly hostile to traditional religion. Secular philosophy and the semi-westernized learning of the Ukrainian schools were openly defended by the court preacher Simeon Polotskii.[147] What influence the bizarre Croatian scholar Iurii Krizhanich may have had on Alexis remains undetermined, but his *Politika* of 1663 must have made Old Believers choke with rage. The wealth and military strength of the kingdom, not its spiritual purity, were Krizhanich's main concerns. He drew no distinction between political and religious authority, arguing that "in a state, the king represents the soul," rather than the head. He described Alexis as a Slavic Messiah, a new David.[148] Krizanich was indifferent to confessional rhetoric and hostile to the Orthodox promise of an otherworldly Jerusalem.

The gradual opening of Russian culture to western influences continued after the death of Alexis in 1676. His son Fedor was dominated by pro-Ukrainian advisors during his six-year reign. From 1682 to 1689 Alexis's daughter Sophia ruled as regent for her younger brothers, including the future Peter I. Although a keen reformer, Sophia was careful to preserve an aura of strict piety and to claim inspiration from the "Wisdom of God," for which she was named. The influx of foreign values, however, helped to liberate Sophia from the cloistered celibacy in which Russian princesses were expected to live. Her lover and chief minister, V. V. Golitsyn, broke so far with custom as to allow women to attend banquets at his palace, where they were surrounded by western furniture and scientific instruments. Sophia's physical freedom and self-control contrast starkly with the self-destructive devotion of legions of female Old Believers, whose only access to worldly authority was to make their bodies into symbols of resistance to the tsarist state.[149] Yet these pious women, most of them peasants, would no doubt not have exchanged their glorious martyrdom for all of Sophia's profane liberties.

Louis XIV was unaware of these events, but he was just as provocative as Alexis and Sophia in placing state interests above spiritual purity and the unity of the church. In the early 1670s he had deeply antagonized the Holy See by extending his right of *régale*, which allowed him to claim revenues and make nominations to benefices in vacant episcopal seats. This was an ambitious claim; even the king of England did not enjoy such control over money and offices in the church. According to Louis's publicists, moreover, the régale was an inherited privilege of sovereignty, not a grant from the pope. In 1680 an assembly of the clergy backed up this position, in spite of the protestations of the Jansenist bishops Caulet and Pavillon. "We are so closely attached to Your Majesty that *nothing is capable of separating us,*" the churchmen assured their king. A subsequent assembly in 1681 and 1682 endorsed the Gallican theses known as the Four Articles, which were edited by Bossuet. They declared that "kings are by the ordinance of God subject in matters temporal to no ecclesiastical power" and that authority in the Catholic Church lay not with the pope but with general councils and national assemblies. It was not an easy victory for the king; the Faculty of the Sorbonne, for example, refused to accept three of the Four Articles until pressured to recant. The response of the parish clergy to this crisis is hard to fathom, but Alexandre Dubois, *curé* of tiny Rumegies, supported the Four Articles in spite of his tendencies towards Jansenism.[150]

Gallicanism catered mainly to the officers, parlementaires, and aspiring bourgeois who regarded their interests as bound up with those of the state, and who resented papal intrusions into French affairs. By creating the impression of royal guidance over the church, however, Gallicanism enhanced a broad-based religious nationalism that would prove difficult to control in the future. Every compromise with the pope after 1682 could be viewed by Gallicans as a surrender of French sovereignty. This would pose a recurring constitutional problem for the Crown in the eighteenth century, one that would contribute to the political enfeeblement of the French monarchy.

Still, in the mid-1680s the king was full of confidence. Having been elevated to leadership of the church in France, Louis decided to manifest his powers by enacting confessional uniformity. He knew that French Protestants had lost their military strength and had been declining in numbers since his father's assault on them in the 1620s. By finishing them off with one legal blow, Louis would accomplish what the Habsburgs had failed to do in the Empire, and without making any concessions to the dévots. He would also wipe out the stain on royal sovereignty that was represented by the Edict of Nantes. It did not matter that his Protestant subjects were peaceful and loyal, that in some communities they were living in harmony with Catholics, or that the gradual method of securing conversion through offers of money was working relatively well.[151] In October 1685 the King's Council issued the infamous Edict of Fontaine-bleau, which revoked the Edict of Nantes, outlawed both public and private Protestant worship, and demanded that all Protestant children be raised in the Catholic faith. Pastors were obliged to convert but could continue to receive clerical privileges. The edict's last article, "almost nutty" in the judgment of Janine Garrisson, allowed adult Protestants who were not ready to convert to remain in France so long as they did not practice any religion at all—thus, "they had all identity taken away from them!"[152] Clearly, the intention of the edict was not so much to ensure the salvation of souls as to erase publicly any disruptive distinctions of faith among Louis XIV's subjects.

As everyone knows, the Edict of Fontainebleau was brutally enforced by troops in the notorious *dragonnades,* which prompted an illegal mass emigration of French Protestants out of "Babylon" and into foreign lands. Interestingly enough, the first use of dragoons to back up Louis XIV's religious policy had been in the diocese of Pamiers in 1680, where they were employed to suppress the Jansenist opponents of the régale.[153] Because religious unity was in the interest of the state, it could be maintained by the state's military power against any threat, whether Catholic or Protestant. To be sure, French Catholics initially applauded the Edict of Fontainebleau as genuinely inspired by faith rather than by reason of state. They agreed with Father Alexandre Dubois that Louis could have avoided sweeping action, "but his religion carried him beyond his interests."[154] Nevertheless, the perception slowly grew that the edict fostered external signs of religion rather than inner spirituality, that it led to false conversions and all manner of deceptions, that it might even have hurt the doctrinal purity of Catholicism. It certainly had a part in the steady rise of scepticism.[155]

There were definite parallels between King Louis's policy of religious coercion and James II's efforts at toleration. Both monarchs sought to bring about "Catholicism in one country," to set up a national confession beholden mainly to them rather than to Rome. Neither perceived any conflict between their political aims and the personal obligations of their faith. Both were authoritarian innovators who had little patience with religious qualms; both proceeded on what they perceived as rational principles of state interest. If James II disapproved of the Edict of Fontainebleau, it was because, like the pope and many other Catholics outside France, he thought it unwise and excessive. The English king assisted efforts to allow Huguenots to emigrate, and he privately told the Dutch envoy that "he detested Louis XIV's conduct as not being politic, much less Christian."[156]

James II's own behaviour, of course, was no more politic, and it was far more disastrous in its consequences. Although the king was not the wicked despot that his enemies made him out to be, he was certainly pig-headed and insensitive. Bishop Burnet rightly judged that his reign "was begun with great advantages, yet was so badly managed." At his accession, James II had the solid support of the Anglican Church hierarchy. Archbishop Sancroft even omitted Communion and altered the prayers at the coronation ceremony so as not to offend the king's Catholic faith. If the king wanted to rule through the High Churchmen, as his brother had, they were ready to serve him.[157] Their loyalty was fulsomely demonstrated in the summer of 1685 when they rallied against the duke of Monmouth, who had raised a rebellion in the west of England. Posing as both a natural king and a sacred one, Monmouth did not hesitate to use the Royal Touch; but those who were convinced were mostly Dissenters. "What your religion is I cannot tell, / But Protestants, I'm sure, can ne'er rebel," a Tory poet admonished them.[158]

If James had used his victory over Monmouth to marginalize the Dissenters further, he might have reigned much longer. Already, however, he was turning in the opposite direction. He wanted to escape from the Churchmen, even if it meant embracing former republicans. In April 1687 he stunned his Anglican supporters by issuing a Declaration of Indulgence, suspending the religious penal laws and informing "all our loving subjects, that . . . we do freely give them leave to meet and serve God after their own way and manner, be it in private houses or places purposely hired or built for that use." No restrictions were placed on such worship; nowhere was it even stipulated that it should be Christian. With a single command James had opened up the broadest religious toleration known anywhere in Europe. The king admitted that it was done for reasons of state, since persecution was contrary "to the interest of government, which it destroys by spoiling trade, depopulating countries and discouraging strangers." The best solution was to abandon all hope of confessional unity and lend state sanction to sectarianism.[159] This was precisely the same reasoning as that of the Dutch republicans.

With hindsight, it is clear that the Declaration of Indulgence was a stupendous blunder. The king, however, believed that he could gain powerful allies by extending toleration, and in fact his policy was welcomed by a number of leading Dissenters.[160] The High Church reaction, on the other hand, was unequivocally negative. It rested on the doctrine of passive obedience, which allowed subjects to refuse compliance with the unlawful commands of a ruler. After James ordered his declaration to be read aloud in parish churches, a phalanx of bishops subscribed to a letter refusing to carry out the king's will because it dispensed with existing laws.[161]

"This is a standard of rebellion," King James cried out furiously when he saw the bishops' petition. He insisted that the seven bishops who had drafted it be indicted for seditious libel. To his astonishment, they were acquitted. Evelyn remarked that as they came out of the court the bishops were met by a huge crowd of people "upon their knees . . . to beg their blessing: Bon fires made that night, and bells ringing, which was taken very ill at Court." A frenetic publicity campaign followed their release. Its purpose was to bring the king back to his senses, and into the still-loyal Tory embrace.[162] On the same day as the bishops' acquittal, however, a small group of unemployed politicians, mostly Whigs, sent an invitation to William of Orange to invade England and put the kingdom to rights.[163]

James II had failed to break the confessional foundations of English government, but his idea of state-sponsored religious toleration would later be taken up by Parliament. Thus, the subordination of religion to the state, which James had promoted with fatal results for his own rulership, was subsequently extended by his critics, without many positive consequences for the devout. Like confessional uniformity in France or doctrinal reform in Russia, toleration in the Stuart kingdoms would damage the prestige of the church and encourage the spread of disillusionment, scepticism, and doubt.[164]

In Russia, France, and England the artificial man was enlisted to overhaul the established patterns of religion. His labours threatened the whole Christian definition of the self, because he valued worldly interests over salvation, obedience over conscience, reason over memory. Like the Saviour in Le Brun's *Resurrection*, the body of the state was rising above the veil of religion; and with it was emerging an increasingly political, state-oriented understanding of identity. As yet, this identity mainly applied to those who played a direct part in government, but it would soon be spread to wider groups of subjects, often by military force.

The ascent of the state over the church could be violent, and it was always polarizing. Alexis was obliged to strike down Nikon and silence Avvakum; Louis XIV had to stifle critics of the régale, then clean out the buzzing hive of Huguenot preachers; James II was compelled to crush Monmouth and face down the bishops. In each case the state set itself apart from opponents on both sides of the confessional arena. It neatly squashed those who stood for further innovation or who represented sectarian minorities. On the other hand, its victory over the traditionalists—over Jansenism, Toryism, and Old Belief—was never complete. In the next century, as the state pushed further beyond confessional limits, conservatives would prove to be its greatest foes, and their resistance would propel it into ever more authoritarian gestures.

## The Last Godly Heroes

Alongside the rise of the rational state, the end of the seventeenth century witnessed what would prove to be the final attempts to establish monarchies that represented godly ideals. The last confessional hero-kings were Jan III Sobieski in Poland-Lithuania, Charles XI in Sweden, and William of Orange in the United Provinces, England, and Scotland. All were rulers of unstable regimes with powerful national legislatures. Each strove to secure loyalty by allying with public opinion against policies that were associated with reason of state. The dreams of the devout, however, failed to materialize. Jan III, who seemed to be the Joshua of his age, became ineffectual, while Charles XI and William III framed their own royal languages, reconciling themselves to the state power that they had formerly reviled. The Swedish and English regimes also allowed Samuel Pufendorf and John Locke to publish writings that sounded the death-knell of the mystical political body and heralded new conceptions of responsible subjection.

By the late 1600s Poland had little chance of becoming a rational state. The gentry, or *szlachta,* who dominated the national and local legislatures, and who had blocked every effort at confessionalization, would give no countenance to the idea of extending a sovereign authority over themselves, even after the "Deluge" of rebellion and invasion in mid-century. On the contrary, they seemed to grow more uncontrollable. The dreaded *liberum veto,* by which a single member of the *Sejm* could use his negative voice to block the passage of legislation, was first used in 1652. In the following century it would hamstring every plan to rationalize the Polish constitution.[165]

A devastating Swedish invasion, however, briefly revived the reformist aspirations of the Polish monarchy. In 1658 and again in 1661, magnates in the Sejm presented proposals for limiting the liberum veto, curtailing the influence of provincial *sejmiki* and providing for the election of a king in the lifetime of his predecessor. Whether these reforms might have created the framework for a rational monarchical state or for rule by the great lords is debatable. In the event, King Jan II Kazimierz did not back them wholeheartedly. He knew that he was not popular with the Polish gentry; even Jan Pasek, who loyally served him, accused the king of "listening to dishonest advisors . . . guided not by your welfare, but by their own interests . . . they have no conscience and no God in their hearts."[166] The king had no wish to spark an uprising, and in the end his hesitancy prevented reform. The only major change adopted by the Sejm in 1658 was religious: the Arians were ordered into exile, ending the era of broad toleration. This reflected the anti-Arian sentiments of most of the gentry and was no triumph for the state. Some even viewed the Arians as allies of the king.[167]

Instead of making a pact with the state, the szlachta increasingly fell back upon the ideals of so-called Sarmatism, derived from myths of aristocratic descent from an ancient Sarmatian warrior class. Sarmatism affected the dress, manners, and lifestyles of the Polish nobility, as well as their politics and their unreformed religious attitudes. It set the gentry apart from the despised peasantry; but it also bolstered distrust of the "cosmopolitan" magnates. The historian Janusz Tazbir describes Sarmatism as "a kind of defensive culture . . . an element of disintegration in national culture."[168] In Jan Pasek's *Memoirs* it appears as a strange imaginative mishmash, blending aristocratic haughtiness and pugnacious masculinity with old-fashioned Catholic piety, a smattering of classical knowledge, and a deep admiration for those who lived "in the manner of old Polish warriors." The Sarmatian noble hated the cultural and political influence of France, which was exercised through Jan Kazimierz's French queen, Louise Marie de Gonzague—that "*imperiosus* [sic] *mulier*" (domineering woman) in Pasek's judgment. "There were more Frenchmen in Warsaw than were kindling the fire of Cerberus," Pasek fumed. He recounted a revealing story of a public theatrical performance that took place in the capital when a Francophile Pole shot dead an actor playing the emperor Leopold. Some good old Polish knights then began shooting arrows at Frenchmen in the audience and wounded "Louis XIV."[169] Pasek saw nothing odd about this violent transgression of the boundary between representation and reality. Personal discipline was not one of the goals of Sarmatism. Rather, it licensed the imaginative memory of Polish noblemen to run riot.

In 1665 the Sarmatians rose against the Crown in a major rebellion led by Field Hetman Jerzy Lubomirski. Pasek did not join them, but his sympathies were with the rebels, and he gleefully quoted the defeated Lubomirski's words of surrender, which defiantly asserted that it was "His Royal Highness himself, along with his good advisors who have brought about this state of affairs in order to lay waste our fatherland." Exasperated, Jan Kazimierz abdicated to become abbot of St. Germain-des-Prés in Paris, which must have confirmed the suspicions of many Francophobe Polish nobles. The tide of Sarmatism ran high at the ensuing election diet, when French bribes and magnate pressure provoked anger from the assembled gentry. "We shall choose a king *ex gremio* [from our midst], such a one as God will make pleasing to our hearts," declared one bunch of representatives. To cries of "*Vivat Piast!*" (the Piasts were the original dynasty of Polish kings), the nobleman Michał Wiśniowecki was elected as monarch. The new king was a mere cipher, and he expired four years later, either from eating too many gherkins or from poison in his wild duck.[170]

At the next election diet, in Pasek's words, "once again God gave us a

26. Anonymous, *King Jan III Sobieski and his Family* (c. 1695), painting.
Photo: Wilanow Palace Museum, Warsaw.

Piast," in this case Field Hetman Jan Sobieski. He was in some respects
an unlikely hero for the Sarmatians. Married to a Frenchwoman, Marie-
Casimire de la Grange d'Arquien, known as "Marysieńka" and called
"Astrée" by her adoring husband, Sobieski was the candidate of the French
party among the magnates. Yet he had all the characteristics of a godly
Sarmatian warrior. Fearless in battle against the Turks and deeply pious in
the pre-Tridentine Polish fashion, Sobieski spoke with fervour of his nation as a land chosen by heaven: "Lord, you were formerly called God of
Israel: we call you with humble reverence God of Poland and of our *patria*,
God of arms and of phalanxes." No wonder Jan Pasek prayed that Sobieski
might found a whole dynasty of pious rulers: "May God make his lineage
strong, as He did once that of Abraham and may the crown not fall from
the heads of his descendants."[171]

As suited the gentry, Jan III's godly monarchy was not reformist, least
of all in pursuing sovereignty or confessionalization. When Protestant
mobs destroyed the Carmelite monastery in Gdansk or drove the Catholic

bishop out of Toruń, the king did nothing to punish them. At Mass in 1688 Sobieski heard a Carmelite preacher reprove him from the pulpit, alleging that "His Majesty cared little for God's honor, since he failed to intercede for the injustice done to Him and *contra ordinem equestrem*" — that is, he had failed to act against the gentry.[172] The king had indeed tried never to offend the gentry, but he could point to a signal occasion when he had defended God's honour: against the Turks at Vienna in 1683. The devout throughout western Europe were thrilled by the story of how the winged Polish knights, with their monarch at their head, had thundered down from the Kahlenberg, scattered the enemies of Christ, captured the grand vizier's tent, and seized the banner of the Prophet. The Polish triumph was celebrated with public festivities in Rome, Bologna, and Florence, while at Lille the diarist and textile worker Chavatte praised Sobieski as a Christian hero.[173]

By the 1690s, however, Sobieski was enormously fat and had run out of victories. The old warrior had been forced to accept as final the loss of the Ukraine to Russia. The liberum veto continued to undo any chance of constitutional reform. As Norman Davies points out, King Jan's magnificent palace at Wilanów (Villa Nova) was designed as a refuge from politics, not as a Polish Versailles, and Jan lived there "in the style of a wealthy nobleman, of a private citizen rather than a monarch." Although he named his youngest son after the emperor Constantine, Sobieski had little success in insuring a royal future for his progeny. Marysieńka opposed his dynastic efforts, and after his death in 1696 she refused to allow their eldest son, Jakub, to take the crown from her husband's body. The Russian traveller Peter Tolstoi saw Sobieski's body lying in state, with his portrait over the casket; he also noticed with typical Moscovite disdain that the nearby windows of the Sejm house were broken, "smashed at a discordant meeting, and there is discord in all affairs among the drunken Poles."[174] Like the kingship of Jan III, Sarmatism was a dead end for the ailing Polish Commonwealth, which had begun to resemble a nation without a state. A godly and militaristic kingship would now give way to political stagnation and rule by foreigners.

Why was the destiny of monarchy in Sweden so different? For a start, the Swedish Crown had been bolstered by Lutheran confessionalization. Under Queen Christina, moreover, a considerable royalist literature had begun to appear, lauding the monarch as the possessor of a supreme power, given by God. Christina's successor, Charles X, is even thought to have read Bodin. Yet sovereignty was not seen as contradicting the traditional legal constraints of Swedish "mixed monarchy." As Stellan Dahlgren has pointed out, Charles X "accepted the constitution to which he pledged himself at his coronation, although he did indeed give it an elastic inter-pretation." He initiated a limited *reduktion,* or resumption of Crown lands from the aristocracy, but was careful not to anger the great aristocrats who sat on his council.[175] At his death in 1660 the king bequeathed to his infant son a potentially powerful state authority. The reign of Charles XI began with clear advantages over that of Jan Sobieski.

Equally important to the development of the Swedish state were the cultural insecurities of the nation's ruling classes, which contrasted sharply with the Sarmatian self-confidence of the szlachta. The Swedes had a bad reputation around the Baltic as an impoverished, violent, and quasi-pagan people. Indeed, Jan Pasek saw them as a race of sorcerers.[176] The Swedish governing elite, often educated abroad, was painfully aware of such "bar-baric" characterizations and sought to counter them by adopting codes of Neostoic virtue and upper-class civilité. The "civilizing process" was ea-gerly promoted by Queen Christina, who introduced the French ballet at her court so that Swedish nobles would learn how to move their bodies in a proper manner.[177] Similar ideals were expressed in the poetry of Georg Stiernhielm, especially his long didactic work *Hercules.* Stiernhielm rose to noble rank through government office, and he saw aristocracy as resting on "Noble Virtues" rather than birth. Although his political views were closer to Althusius than to Bodin and his religion was highly unorthodox, Stiern-hielm's work was much admired by Charles X.[178]

Nils Runeby has suggested that in Sweden aristocratic manners went hand-in-hand with a strong central authority, because only the state seemed capable of imposing the values of good behaviour on a rude and backward society.[179] For most Swedes, however, the road out of "barba-rism" was still paved by religious belief. The Lutheran clergy looked to the monarchy, not to teach them how to dance but to lead the struggle for confessional purity. They wanted a godly king to burn out devils, not to laugh them away in sophisticated scorn. Mass executions of witches con-tinued in both Sweden and Finland into the mid-1680s, testifying to enduring fears of an underlying pagan "Other" that threatened to engulf the Lutheran nation.[180]

In habits and personality Charles XI certainly fitted the part of a godly Lutheran king. Pious and abstemious, he took one-course meals at his mother's house and indulged in few pleasures other than hunting bears. "It is fidelity and righteousness that I have pledged to my subjects, not intelligence or wisdom," he once remarked, thus distancing himself from the connivances of reason of state. He pressed hard for confessional reforms. The Canon Law of 1686 defined Lutheran orthodoxy, stigmatizing the liberal interpretations encouraged by Queen Christina and ruling out doctrinal compromise with Calvinism. Any public servant who lapsed from the faith was to be removed from office and exiled. The law made a basic knowledge of catechism necessary, not only for Communion but for marriage as well. The royal government further promised to punish breakers of the sabbath, impose religious censorship, and send to the stocks those who smoked in churchyards or talked too loudly during services. The consolidation of Lutheran religious identity was completed by the publication of a new catechism, a revised liturgy, and a standard hymnal.[181]

The centrepiece of Charles XI's policy, however, was a great work of state rationalization: the reduktion of 1680, by which the Riksdag transferred back to the Crown vast tracts of land that had been given to the nobility. Charles expressed his delight at the reduktion in a message to the Estates which maintained that "We, as a King of full age, to whom God has granted Our hereditary kingdom, to rule according to law and lawful statutes, are responsible for Our actions to God alone." Modestly hiding its own part in his triumphs, a 1689 resolution of the Riksdag confirmed that Charles and his heirs "have been set to rule over us as sovereign Kings, whose will is binding upon us all, and who are responsible for their actions to no man on earth, but have power and authority to govern and rule their realm as Christian Kings, at their own pleasure."[182] These devout formulae can be read as the charters of a Swedish royal language. They exalted a godly monarchy that would flourish within the structures of a rational state.

The reduktion did not wipe out the status of the nobility, but by securing royal finances it allowed the Crown to pay its servants and thus to infuse new blood into the elite. It also replaced military conscription with a contract system called *indelningsverket,* through which peasant villages were paid to supply and maintain soldiers. This enormously ambitious project directly linked every peasant family to a hitherto remote state. It added an element of military discipline to confessional control over the self.[183]

The rationalization of the Swedish state did not overturn existing forms of government. Charles XI continued to observe the fourteenth-century Land Law, which called for the monarch to consult his council and the Estates. Furthermore, as Michael Roberts has pointed out, the reform programme "was from beginning to end the creation of the *riksdag.*"[184] The Swedish Estates endorsed the expansion of royal authority because they saw it as raising the strength and civility of their nation. Yet while they continued to employ a religious language to justify their actions— even the reduktion was discussed in terms of divine law—the Estates sought to shift responsibility for enforcing standards of social morality from the church to the state. Clerical offences themselves were now to be tried in secular courts.

If the Swedish state can be linked to a particular political theory, it might be that of the German jurist Samuel Pufendorf. Invited by Charles XI to the University of Lund in 1667, Pufendorf became a privy councillor, secretary of state, royal historian, and tutor to the king's children. In 1673 he published *On the Duty of Man and Citizen According to Natural Law,* in which he served up some of the spicier tenets of *Leviathan* in a sauce that was more to Lutheran tastes. Like a good German Aristotelian, he began by arguing that human society preceded the state and was governed by natural laws of duty and obligation—to God, to oneself, and to others. Pufendorf acknowledged, however, that the savage Hobbist desires of human beings compelled the male heads of households to protect their families and property by forming a state, or *civitas,* which like Leviathan "is conceived as one person." Each member of this artificial man sacrifices natural liberty and becomes a citizen, who is wholly subjected to a sovereign authority (*imperium*) that stems from the state but is not identical with it. Pufendorf defined the "good citizen" (*civis*) as "one who promptly obeys the orders of those in power, one who strives with all his strength for the public good." Living in states is preferable to a natural existence, because citizens "are steeped from their earliest years in more suitable habits of behaviour and

THE SIGN OF THE ARTIFICIAL MAN · 267

discover the various skills by which human life has been improved and enriched." The sovereign who rules over these docile citizens is unaccountable and irresistible, yet bound to the duty of guarding public safety. As the sole representative of the artificial man, he "must forego pursuits that have no bearing on his office. Pleasures, amusements and idle pastimes must be cut back."[185]

Pufendorf might have been describing Charles XI, as man and monarch. Much in his treatise is reminiscent of the Swedish state, from its emphasis on the maintenance of orthodoxy to its endorsement of social "progress." Pufendorf's combination of contractualism with a strong manifestation of sovereignty reflected the constitutional rhetoric of the Riksdag. His concept of citizenship, moreover, foreshadowed indelningsverket. The duties of citizenship, like those of the Swedish recruiting system, were marks of participation in the state; both were based on an obligation to defend the public good, which was spread among all male members of the polity.

Like Charles XI, Prince William of Orange was a godly ruler who led a willing people—not into Jerusalem but towards the rational state. The darling of Dutch Calvinists, William's restoration as *stadholder* of Holland in 1672 was precipitated by popular panic over a French invasion. A crowd of his supporters tore the de Witt brothers to pieces, as if they hoped to reconstruct the body politic by dismembering the bodies of the architects of republican individualism. Yet the Prince of Orange never satisfied his supporters' desire for godly rule. Politically cautious, he kept former republicans in important civic offices and preserved a broad religious tolerance. To be sure, his concern with maintaining the rational state at home did not diminish his reputation abroad as the chief defender of Protestantism against Louis XIV. This international fame would catapult him towards usurping the English throne from his Catholic father-in-law, James II.[186]

In November 1688, when William waded ashore at the head of a Dutch army, he declared that he had come to England only "to preserve and maintain the established Laws, Liberties and Customs, and, above all, the Religion and Worship of God" from the threat of Catholicism.[187] He arrived as a godly hero, the nemesis of reason of state. He was lauded in popular verse not as a potential king but as a Protestant champion who would smash the Church of Rome: "Now welcome to our English shore, / And now we will engage-o, / To thump the Babylonish whore / And kick her trumpery out of door." Nobody was yet heard to proclaim "Orange for King."[188] Within a few weeks, however, James II had fled to France, and William had decided to claim his inheritance. The change of monarch was effected very quickly, from the top down and from the centre outwards. A "provisional government" of Whig peers meeting at the Guildhall asked William "to take upon you the administration of publick affairs." By the end of 1688, writes R. A. Beddard, "the dynastic revolution was essentially complete."[189] It remained to be legally packaged and sold to the broader political nation by the Convention, or proto-Parliament, that met in January 1689; and it might have been stopped if the Tories had put constitutional propriety before state security. Both Houses of the Convention finally voted in favour of an ambiguous resolution that King James, having subverted the constitution, broken the original contract with his people, violated the fundamental laws, and left the kingdom, "hath Abdicated the Government; and that the Throne is thereby Vacant." Tories were persuaded to accept this confusing statement by worries about the continuance of stable governance. They chose to safeguard the state by replacing the king.[190]

Meanwhile, the Whigs advanced a more rational interpretation of the revolution. A flood of pamphlets argued that James had been deprived of his throne by the people for breaking his original contract with them and that the Crown was held under certain legal conditions. Such views informed the Bill of Rights, which barred Catholics from the succession, abolished the royal power to suspend or dispense with laws, and declared William and his wife, Mary, to be joint rulers of England. The Bill of Rights helped give Parliament a permanent role in the state, but it also sanctioned a royal language, much used by William and by the Hanoverian kings, that could claim the prior consent of "the people" in advancing state interests.[191]

The new regime soon showed that it valued those interests above confessional unity. The Toleration Act of 1689 bestowed freedom of worship on Protestant Dissenters, while explicitly excluding enemies of the state, namely Roman Catholics and Arians. Compliance rested on taking an oath of loyalty to the Crown, not on an examination of doctrine.

Although it was the most restrictive grant of religious freedom in the seventeenth century, the act allowed the Church of England little control over who qualified for toleration. Thus, the state-centred rationalism of James II's Declaration of Indulgence was reshaped into a weaker but more politically workable form.[192]

The Glorious Revolution was not accepted by everyone in the three British kingdoms. The Jacobites, adherents of the exiled James II, emphatically rejected it, largely for confessional reasons. They fomented civil wars in Scotland and Ireland and concocted numerous conspiracies in England.[193] Many Tories felt the pull of Jacobitism, because they did not regard William and Mary as "rightful and lawful" rulers. A Kentish parson went so far as to tell his flock "that king William was only sett up by the mobile, and that he only prayed for him as he did for Turks, Jews and infidells."[194] An Irish Jacobite gentleman offered a similar analysis, tinged with national sentiments and the memory of 1641: "Why should the Catholicks of Ireland turn savages by destroying their lawful king without rhyme or reason? That is a behaviour more suitable to heretics . . . Ireland hath never acknowledged her king to be chosen by the people, but to succeed by birth; nor her king to be deposable by the people upon any cause of quarrel. She knows more righteous things, and scorns to make heretical England her pattern in the point of righteousness."[195] With the Jacobites constantly baying at his heels in all three kingdoms, it was impossible for William to hide the marks of innovation that had been left by the Glorious Revolution.

Whose interests did the English state represent? Soon after the Glorious Revolution, the Whig writer John Locke published a compelling if controversial answer.[196] In his *First Treatise of Government* he mocked Filmer's supposition that the patriarchal sovereignty of Adam could have been inherited by modern kings. The natural authority of fathers, derived by Filmer from Scripture as well as nature, was discarded in favour of a theory of state formation based entirely on subjective reasoning. In the *Second Treatise* Locke echoed English Levellers and Dutch republicans in proposing that political society consists of an amalgamation of individuals rather than an organic corpus mysticum. The central precept of this society was "property," by which Locke understood the person and the product of its exertions. He wrote that "every Man has a *Property* in his own *Person*.

This no Body has any Right to but himself. The *Labour* of his Body, and the *Work* of his Hands, we may say, are properly his." Worldly property, not inherent sacrality, defined the individual. Yet Locke also believed that the original state of nature was governed by a divinely bestowed reason rather than unbridled desire. This was a more conventionally Christian approach than that of Hobbes, and it made the owning of property an essential part of God's benevolent design.[197]

According to Locke, natural reason allowed men to preserve their property by forming political society, which comprised a single body, an artificial man: "For when any number of Men have, by the consent of every individual, made a *Community*, they have thereby made that *Community* one Body, with a Power to act as one Body." Locke departed from Grotius and Pufendorf, however, as well as from the opinions of most of the English ruling elite, in arguing that individuals did not have to sacrifice any of their natural rights to this collective body. "The Obligations of the Law of Nature, cease not in Society," so that government "can never have a power to take to themselves the whole or any part of the Subjects *Property*, without their own consent." If a government ever claimed such an "arbitrary" power, it could be dissolved by its own members.[198]

Locke was not very precise about whose consent was necessary to make up political society. Were women, children, and the poor, who had property only in their own persons, privy to the original contract? They could have been; Locke did not directly say. His writings bore traces of the Christian enthusiasm that had allowed Gerrard Winstanley to extend representative personhood to everyone, but it was also possible to read Locke as an advocate of rule by men who owned property. A similar ambiguity about who was represented by it—everyone, or just a privileged few?— would typify English government after 1688. The post-revolutionary state was an uncertain union of political, religious, and economic interests dominated by property owners. To this extent Locke's writings were prophetic.[199]

Like Peder Schumacher in Denmark or Bossuet in France, Pufendorf and Locke had successfully rehabilitated the artificial man. All had recognized what the sceptic Hobbes had refused to countenance: that a rationally constructed state was more likely to develop from a shared sense of moral duty than from naked self-interest. This meant that the artificial man could be reconciled with religious sentiment—but only by moulding the Christian self into the political personality of the responsible subject or citizen. The public life of the individual had to be concerned with civic duty, not spiritual purity. The godly nation would then metamorphose into a harmonious earthly polity, a rational state in which every property-owning *paterfamilias* was equally represented—while women and the poor might have to sacrifice whatever small share of political identity they had previously enjoyed.

The rational state continued to offend those who rejected compromise with an impure worldly authority or who clung to hopes of an idealized patriotism. But in most of Europe it had succeeded in gaining the acquiescence of the mainstream of the governing elite. They saw in the disciplining powers of the artificial man a guarantee that the popular rebellions of the mid-seventeenth century, with all their disruptive political, social, and personal consequences, would not be repeated. The elite were prepared to accept restraints on confessionalism and the imaginative memory. To be sure, Hobbes might no longer have recognized his creation, altered as it had been by political circumstances, by theoretical reconsiderations, and above all by the tenacity of Christian religious beliefs. Leviathan had metamorphosed into a state based on collective reason rather than self-centred fear. The artificial man was still distrusted by many of the devout, but he now beckoned to them with a sword in one hand, a cross in the other.

# CHAPTER SIX

# The State Remains, 1690–1715

I hold myself to be a blissful subject in the kingdom of the great author of all Nature. The world-edifice seems to me to be one country, which under the sceptre of this perfectly wise and good monarch has an abundance of all desirable goods.

—JOHANN CHRISTOPH GOTTSCHED,
*Der Biedermann*, no. 1, 1 May 1727

N THE MORNING OF 1 SEPTEMBER 1715, King Louis XIV died of gangrene at Versailles. Having been mortally ill for two weeks, and knowing well how a king should die, he had not lost the opportunity to bestow fitting farewells upon his family and courtiers. Some of his most celebrated dying words were delivered in a speech recorded by the marquis de Dangeau. They include this sentence: "*Je m'en vais, mais l'Etat demeurera toujours*" — "I am going away, but the State will always remain." So by the end of Louis's long reign, the state was no longer to be understood simply as a possession, or "a firm dominion over a people," or an emanation of sovereignty but as an eternal duty to the polity, a moral principle of "union and strength," as Louis put it later in the same speech. It encompassed the whole people as well as the royal body. Nobody spoke any more about transferring the dignitas of the corpus mysticum at the death of the king. For Louis as for his people, these magical entities had been rationalized into the undying state, a concept both corporeal and invisible, collective and particular, human and immortal.[1]

---

27. Giovanni Lorenzo Bernini, *Equestrian Statue of Louis XIV* (1671–77). Palace of Versailles.

Photo: Réunion des musées nationaux, Paris.

The state was now the animate force in French kingship. It passed from Louis to his successor at the moment of his death. The transition was marked by a brief ceremony, carried out as if by clockwork. An officer with a black plume appeared on the palace balcony and announced, "The king is dead!" He retired, changed to a white plume, went back onto the balcony and cried three times, "Long live King Louis XV!" These words, familiar since 1515 at the passing of French monarchs, were now pronounced at the hour of death, not at the royal funeral. The body of the dead king was immediately emptied of its former significance and became that of a mere person. It lay for a week at Versailles in a *lit de ciel* with a portrait of one of Louis's mistresses in the "sky" above him. Then it was moved through Paris to St. Denis. The lawyer Mathieu Marais was shocked at the public reaction: "The people regarded this as a festival, and, full of joy at having seen the King living, did not show all the pain that the death of so great a King should cause." A flood of libels excoriated the memory of the late monarch, attacking his person as well as his policies — "Here lies Louis the Little, / He whom the people raved about / . . . Don't pray God for his soul: / Such a monster never had one." By treating the dead king like any other hated public official, the citizens of Paris showed they had learned too well the message of the royal funeral: that it put to rest a mortal being whose powers of rulership were already gone. Accordingly, the corpse of Louis XIV lay under a catafalque at St. Denis, without an effigy, until the prayers were done and the casket could be installed in the Bourbon crypt.[2]

The king had gone away, and, with almost mechanical precision, he had been replaced. The state he had left behind, however, was not a machine. It was a moral force attached to a particular human body that was the living sign of its dominance over every individual. The personal configuration of state authority was ensured at a *lit de justice* on 12 September attended by the judges and all the officers of state, at which the chancellor, speaking for the five-year-old Louis XV, proclaimed the regency of Philippe, duc d'Orléans. The person of the king would continue to be treated with a quasi-religious reverence, in circumstances that verged on the ridiculous. For instance, even when he was not present at meals, courtiers had to bow towards the silver-gilt vessel in which the little ruler's napkins were kept. On the other hand, his body could be subjected to the close scrutiny of his subjects, as it was in February 1717 when Louis reached his seventh

birthday and his courtiers arrived at the Tuileries "to carry out the ceremony of stripping the King naked, so that they could all be witnesses of the
good state [état] of His Majesty, that he is male, in no way deformed and
well-fed."[3] In former centuries this ritual had served to assure the aristocracy that the Salic Law was observed, that the ruler would wield a strong
arm in defence of his kingdom, and that God had not cursed his body with
defects. By the early eighteenth century, however, it provided a public
assurance that the king conformed to the natural requirements for representing rational authority: maleness, independent motion, a pleasing
physique. As the point of contact between the state and the responsible
subject, the ruler could not be an invalid, a monster, or—in France at
least—a woman.

The state was not a machine; but for many observers, it was defined by
the same unbreakable laws of nature and reason that were applied to
science, mathematics, and mechanics. We have already observed the infil-
tration of such ideas into the royal language of Louis XIV. By the 1690s,
rationalism had been provided with a theological justification through the
writings of the priest Nicolas Malebranche. He was a member of the Oratory, the order founded by the devout Cardinal Bérulle; and his overriding
aim was to reunite Augustinian piety with the mechanical philosophy of
Descartes. For Malebranche, God was the cause of all movement and
extension in the universe: "It is only the creator who can be the mover,
only He who gives being to bodies, who can put them in the places they
occupy." The laws of nature and reason operated entirely through God.
Yet he could not violate them without creating an impossible contradiction
in himself. Thus, Malebranche vindicated the elevation of natural law
above the will of God, just as Grotius had, albeit without suggesting that
the deity could be subject to anything but himself. As for politics, Malebranche assured his readers that "God forms all societies, governs all
nations . . . by the general laws of the union of minds with His eternal
wisdom"—in short, by "sovereign Reason." The state is a product not of
human volition but of immutable rules of order, the same principles as
those that govern nature.[4]

According to Malebranche's philosophy, the pact between the state
and the self is not just natural but also inevitable. Human choice has no
role in it. Sympathetic identification between ruler and subject becomes

276 · THE STATE REMAINS

irrelevant, and no room is left for personal moral judgment of a government that is always moved, for good or ill, by the divine hand. This was a kind of benign Christian Hobbesianism. Antoine Arnauld immediately perceived that such ideas constituted a serious threat to the freedom of the Christian self: "Nothing," he wrote, "is more contradictory to St. Augustine." To the mind of Arnauld, Malebranche had debased the divine by seeing it in everything; he had restricted free grace by making it dependent on general laws; he had removed any difference between the perception of external objects and the internal communication of the self with God. Arnauld may have deduced that such ideas pointed towards deism, the belief that God, having created the universe, allowed it to operate like a clock, according to natural laws that did not require his direct intervention. Was it not significant that the Huguenot exile Pierre Bayle, whose famous *Dictionnaire* would become a sourcebook for deists, supported Malebranche against Arnauld's attacks?[5]

The fears of Arnauld may have been exaggerated. We now know, of course, that Bayle was not a deist but a rational Protestant; and Malebranche always considered himself to be a good Catholic.[6] Nonetheless, the cry of warning raised by the great Jansenist alerts us to a definite shift in European understanding towards a rationalism that was more natural than divine. By means of this shift, to quote Paul Hazard, "a new order of things began its course." Hazard placed Malebranche in the middle of a "crisis of European consciousness," which he dated between 1680 and 1715. Its result was to move intellectuals away from religious explanations towards scientific or natural ones. Admittedly, Hazard was extravagant in depicting the effects of this "crisis": "Never was there a greater contrast, never a more sudden transition than this! . . . One day, the French people, almost to a man, were thinking like Bossuet. The day after, they were thinking like Voltaire."[7] These are sweepingly imprecise generalizations (not least because we simply do not know what most French people were thinking); but they do evoke a certain reality, at least about the educated elite. Voltaire was a schoolboy at a Jesuit college in Paris when Bossuet died in the same city in 1704. Both men were raised as orthodox Catholics; neither was ever an atheist or a sceptic. Yet in their mature works they expressed fundamentally different conceptions of religion, reason, and nature. Between them lay the philosophical gulf traversed by Malebranche, Bayle, and others.

It was not a gulf that monarchy failed to cross. The Most Christian King Louis XIV had prepared the way for the rise of natural reason by striking down the advocates of spiritual autonomy. In particular, he had crushed Quietism, Jansenism, and millenarian Protestantism. Of them, Quietism was the most obnoxious to the rational state, because it allowed believers to retreat from the world. Introduced at Rome in the 1670s by the Aragonese priest Miguel de Molinos, it involved a renunciation of human moral action and the pursuit of a contemplative mysticism. Through submission to "the gentle yoke of the divine," according to Molinos, the self would attain a "divine knowledge," the "science of the saints," which seemed to impart a tremendous authority to the mystical initiate.[8]

Among those attracted to Molinos's theology was the remarkable French mystic Jeanne Guyon. She was one of the last defenders of the absolute primacy of the Christian self, which for her was essentially female. In her numerous books of spiritual advice, she urged a complete surrender to the will of God. She associated mystical transcendence with the conventional characteristics of women: passivity, subordination, meekness. Yet she was also vocal and proselytizing. At Grenoble, Guyon preached all day in the open air to large crowds of hearers and encouraged young working girls to labour in silence, "so as to talk with God." Her teachings were adopted within some Jansenist circles, profoundly affecting Archbishop Fénelon of Cambrai. Finally, however, she was thrown into the Bastille at the instigation of Bossuet, and her followers were suppressed as heretics.[9]

Quietism was perceived as incompatible with a monarchy that demanded the total compliance of its subjects. Soon the king began to detect its taint on every Jansenist. Throughout the 1690s, political pressure was building against what the priest Alexandre Dubois called "this phantom" of Jansenism. "One only had to be regular in his life and in his dress to be known as one," he complained. During the last years of his reign Louis wreaked awful vengeance on the ageing female inmates of Port-Royal, first by dissolving the Paris convent, then by destroying its buildings, finally by scattering the remains of deceased nuns in a common grave. Even this was not enough for the king. He pressured the pope to issue the bull *Unigenitus* in 1713, which condemned a series of Jansenist propositions. "May the all-powerful God turn this away!" prayed Father Dubois when the bull was publicised. A small group of bishops led by de Noailles, cardinal-archbishop of Paris, refused to accept *Unigenitus.* The Parlement of Paris registered it reluctantly. Jurists, always the protectors of sovereignty, bitterly complained that it contravened the Gallican Articles of 1682 and violated royal authority, in spite of the fact that the king had wanted it in the first place.[10]

After Louis's death, when the floodgates of political expression were opened, he was not spared the most scurrilous of epitaphs for his treatment of Jansenism. Voltaire himself was sent to the Bastille on a false accusation of having written the following lines: "I have seen the holy place degraded, / I have seen Port-Royal demolished, / I have seen the blackest actions, / That could ever happen."[11] Some worried observers were convinced that the days of the Catholic League were returning. The diarist Marais noted in September 1715 that members of religious orders were not allowed to enter the royal palace without a pass—"They are feared because of Jacques Clément, the Jacobin who assassinated Henry III."[12]

Unlike the virulent propaganda of the League, however, Jansenist libels contained a mixture of love and hate for the monarchy. They were marked by what Freud would have called emotional ambivalence towards the king. In her study of seditious words in eighteenth-century Paris, Arlette Farge has argued that expressions of contempt for the monarch were "the mirror image" of feelings of personal submission and attachment to him. As we have seen, internalized sentiments and "movements of the heart" were typical of Jansenists. They had wanted to love the king with their inner selves; now they reviled his person in furious verses.[13] As early as 1693, emotional ambivalence had suffused the anonymous letter addressed to Louis XIV by Archbishop Fénelon. In a terrible writ of condemnation, Fénelon told the king that he was no Christian: "You do not love God. You only fear him with the fear of a slave. It is Hell and not God whom you fear. . . . You relate everything to yourself as if you were God on earth." The only solution was for Louis "to humiliate yourself in order to convert, for you will never be a Christian except in humiliation." Yet Fénelon ended his harangue with a call for the king "to save the State," and he assured Louis that he "would give his life to see you such as God wants you."[14] Even the most disillusioned among the devout did not reject the hope that they could again submit to a ruler guided by Christian principles.

There was no Jansenist revolt, no new League. It was the Huguenots, not the Catholic devout, who tried to bring on the millennium in 1702 by raising an insurrection in the Cévennes. Protestant "prophets" or open-air preachers condemned the Crown's persecutions as a wicked attempt to end the freedom of the Christian self. "The King wants to make us renounce the word of God and renounce Eternal grace!" one of them declaimed, "but he is incapable of doing anything against the word of our Eternal One!" The rebel leader Jean Cavalier suggested that the king would be punished like the pharaoh who had persecuted the Jews. Yet the declarations of the so-called Camisards, like those of the Jansenists, mingled deep resentment for the king with a promise of heartfelt love. They continued to reiterate their loyalty to a crown that had betrayed them: "Like our fathers who were true subjects of the King, so also are we, just as our bodies and our goods and even our poor lives depend on him." Cavalier himself wrote that he would "submit myself to the service of my Prince if he has need, with all the submission possible, and with my person."[15] For Camisards as for Jansenists, the enemy was not the state but its erring human representative. As in the Fronde, this attitude contributed to defeat and a deeper silence. Once the Camisards had been suppressed, the French state's control over religious identity would not again be seriously shaken until the 1760s.

Throughout these confessional struggles, the supporters of natural reason stood behind Louis XIV. Bayle was a strong supporter of royal authority, as was Malebranche; and Voltaire himself was no enemy of the monarchical state. Like his early Jesuit mentors, he admired the Sun King and espoused a dynamic royalism.[16] Voltaire's successful public career, in fact, was made possible by the sanction given by the French state to rationalism in the last years of Louis XIV. If we had to determine a point at which this was manifested, it might be 1691, when the Cartesian sceptic Fontenelle was admitted to the Académie Française. Fontenelle championed a "mechanical" philosophy that "will have the universe to be in great what a watch is in little, and that everything in it should conduct itself by regular movements which depend on the arrangement of its parts."[17] A few years later he joined Malebranche in the Académie des Sciences and was eventually appointed to the highly selective Académie des Inscriptions. All of this happened before the death of Bossuet.

The promotion of Fontenelle signalled that there was room within the monarchy for outright rationalists, so long as they were loyal to the king and did not seek to divide his subjects. Louis XIV did not go so far as to re-establish toleration for Protestants, but Bayle was not totally misguided in hoping that his successors might do so. In 1715 Madame Palatine wrote of her son the regent that "if he could follow his own inclinations, no one in the world would be harassed for his religion."[18] When the state gave such honours to a writer like Fontenelle, who seemed to mock Christianity, was toleration unthinkable? Was the emergence of Voltaire unimaginable?

"God! What change in the Church and in the State after the death of Louis XIV!" wrote the abbé Louis Legendre in the mid-eighteenth century. "Would we have believed it if we hadn't seen it?"[19] In fact, the change began before 1715. The age of confessionalization was passing away, and with it were dying long-standing assumptions about the relationship between monarchy and religion. Like Malebranche's God, the king was becoming the source of all movement in a rational political universe. This chapter is a sketch of what happened at a crucial stage of that transition. In contrast to Hazard's treatment, it does not seek to explain the roots of a modernity that was not fully visible by 1715. It is a chapter of endings as much as of beginnings, because it pays attention to those who lost something in the "crisis of consciousness": those who, like Arnauld, continued vainly to champion the Christian self against the claims of the rational state. The devout were not opposed to reason, of course, but they were alarmed by what Fénelon called "corrupted" reason, which "restricts itself to present things that are so brief, and neglects the future that is eternal. . . . It abandons itself to malign and unjust maxims, it laughs at justice and simplicity."[20] Fénelon's terms of condemnation were exactly those by which the reign of Louis XIV was vilified in the libels that appeared after the king's death. Like the crowds that mocked the dead monarch, the devout resented a sovereignty that seemed to give them no choice but to accept everything that pertained to worldly interest.

Throughout Europe the devout were frightened by the neo-Cartesianism of Malebranche and Fontenelle, by the individualism of Bayle and the "natural religion" of Leibniz and Isaac Newton—not to mention the doctrines of freethinkers, sceptics, and atheists, whose influence they saw in every corner of the realm. As early as the 1670s the German

Lutheran minister Philip Jacob Spener had lamented the worldliness and "spiritual misery" of his era. Regarding earthly rulers, he complained of "how few there are who remember that God gave them their scepters and staffs in order that they use their power to advance the kingdom of God! ... How many of them there are who do not concern themselves at all with what is spiritual!" Like Fénelon, Spener wanted to direct the Christian self away from the world, towards "the inner man": "Our whole Christian religion consists of the inner man or the new man, whose soul is faith and whose expressions are the fruits of life."[21]

Other responses to the spiritual "defects" of the age were more aggressive. The English High Churchman Francis Atterbury bemoaned a time "when heresies of all kinds, when scepticism, Deism and atheism itself overrun us like a deluge." Atterbury detested these ways of thinking all the more because they had proven attractive to those who guided the state. His solution was the assertion of political control by the church over the state — culminating, perhaps, in the restoration of a Stuart Pretender.[22] In Spain the moral rearmament of the devout turned into a major insurrection against what was seen as the anti-religious ideology of the ruling Bourbon house. King Philip V was depicted as a puppet of France, the most impious and worldly nation in Europe: "France is neither Catholic, nor Protestant, nor Mohammedan, nor of any sect known up to now. It is a new universal hydra, composed of so many heads that it accommodates itself to everything that touches its interest." The French were even identified with the fearsome Muslim "Other": "France and the Turks, cunning, proud, insufferable, double-dealing, deceitful, persistent, vengeful, vainglorious." Bourbon government meant despotic rationalism in the polity and selfishness in the soul, consistent with the precepts of "Machiavellian books." This was a rhetoric that Atterbury or the Camisards could easily have understood.[23]

What united the jeremiads of the devout in France, Germany, England, and Spain was an insistence on the need for divine healing or grace. As we have seen, grace was an ambiguous concept. In earlier times it had released an explosive anti-authoritarianism in the minds of radical *Frondeurs* or Quakers or *Raskolniki*. On the other hand, it could also sustain the internal subjection of the Christian self to human governance. "Saint Paul wants us to honour kings, not only with an exterior and political submission, but with a real obedience and submission, interior and religious, forming a part of Christian piety," wrote the Jansenist Pasquier Quesnel.[24] Grace informed a pact of obedience that was compatible with God-given reason; but to rationalize subjection mechanically, to make it a necessary rule of nature, meant sacrificing the spiritual autonomy of the self, or, to use Fénelon's phase, "true liberty." The archbishop equated true liberty with an inner peace bestowed by grace. He quoted with approval the words of St. Paul, "Where the Spirit of the Lord is, there is liberty."[25] For the devout, therefore, the sovereignty of natural reason was not a deliverance; it was a kind of appropriation, by which they were deprived of some of the freedom to receive grace.

The decline of a theology of grace was crucial to the emerging ideology of the state. In a celebrated catchphrase, inspired by Weber, Fritz Hartung described the eighteenth century as bringing about "*eine Entzauberung der Monarchie von Gottes Gnaden,*" an end to the enchantment of monarchy by God's grace.[26] Hartung did not mean by this that kings ceased to claim divine approval for their actions or to follow rituals that linked their powers to those of the deity. The key to his perceptive statement is the word *Gnade,* or grace. It was a religious sentiment notably missing from Louis XIV's *Memoirs,* from his bons mots, or from his deathbed soliloquies—that is, until his very last utterance, which according to several witnesses was "O my God, come to my aid, hasten to help me."[27] As Arnauld maintained against Malebranche, grace had to be a personal, ineffable, and unpredictable quality. Unfettered by natural laws, it was felt in the heart, not reasoned out in the mind. It brought with it both a conviction of human unworthiness or "abjection" and a sudden awareness of the sacred—a "hierophany," to use Mircea Eliade's term. We might see it as an inner charisma, the last refuge of the imaginative memory. No wonder, then, that the Grand Monarque was so averse to it, until faced with his own extinction.

For the devout, participation in a state that did not depend on divine grace was a threat to their religious identity. This was what they apprehended from governments that grounded themselves in natural reason. For some groups of believers—the Raskolniki in Russia, the Huguenots in France—the dreaded possibility of losing part of their Christian identity had already been realized. It did not end there. As we shall see, the rationalization of religious identity occurred in virtually every European monarchy. What touched the Christian self so deeply, of course, was bound to affect ideas of the nation and the body. The nation was a collective political expression of the self. It held out millennial hopes that rested on acceptance of a specially designated grace. The body was the vehicle of the self and the repository of the soul. While tending to corruption, it could be raised to glory by the infusion of grace. The rational state could not easily abide these assumptions. It tried to absorb the nation within an overarching imperial sovereignty. At the same time, it deprived the body of its spiritual definition and made it a natural object of worldly discipline. In so doing, it may have encouraged kings to cast off some of their own sacred trappings and present themselves to their subjects as natural beings, a process that has been called desacralization.

All of these developments can be interpreted as signals of the impending Enlightenment that would sweep through the educated elites of Europe later in the eighteenth century. The Enlightenment will be foreshadowed throughout this chapter, as the culmination of the rational state and the beginning of a new configuration of power, in which nature and reason were aligned. For the devout this represented a final moral disaster. The "true liberty" of the Christian self seemed to have been overthrown by a natural reason that promised a different sort of liberty, as well as a different bondage. We of course have to acknowledge what the devout could not: that the Enlightenment drew heavily upon the established cultural values of reformed Christianity. It shared the preoccupation with the self, the obsession with internal discipline, and the loathing of "superstition" that were so marked among the godly. In fact, the language of the Enlightenment was sometimes plucked straight out of the literature of spiritual regeneration. It was the Jansenist Pierre Nicole—not Bayle or Leibniz or Malebranche—who first wrote that "there is nothing so similar to the effects of charity, as those of self-love . . . an enlightened self-love [*un amour-propre éclairé*], which knows its own interests, and which leads to the ends which reason proposes."[28] Nicole would have been shocked to discover how "enlightened self-love" was employed by future generations of intellectuals whom he would have regarded as no better than atheists. Like his friend Arnauld, he chose not to recognize how easily Christian identity could be applied to worldly purposes quite different from those for which grace had intended it.

## Rationalizing Religious Identity

The political rationalization of religious identity in the period after 1690 stemmed from the insistence that private as well as public morality should be attuned to the state's rational interests. What reformers aspired to was not by any means a secular identity but an identity in which the political influence of religion was confined to supporting the inner discipline of the responsible subject. This was the goal expressed by Peter I of Russia to a group of clerics, whom he exhorted "to preach morality to the people above all else, so that little by little superstition should be banished from his country and both God and himself better served by his subjects."[29] It was not a distant leap, however, from the tsar's position to the rational morality expressed by Madame Palatine: "To my mind those are holiest who do the least harm to their fellow man and who are just in their ways." She added scornfully that "this I do not find in the pious people here; on the contrary, no one in the world is more filled with bitter hatred."[30]

The rationalization of religious identity began before 1690, but it was widened and accelerated by conditions of war. In the quarter-century before Louis XIV's death, the monarchies of Europe became embroiled in a series of long-running military confrontations: the War of the League of Augsburg, the War of the Spanish Succession, the Great Northern War. These conflicts were waged on a larger scale and were far more expensive than previous wars. They demanded constant recruitment, formalized military training, and levels of fiscal and administrative organization never before seen.[31] Furthermore, although they had religious overtones, none was primarily a war of religion. Alliances were no longer made chiefly on denominational grounds. Religious priorities came second to military ones. Thus, it was state interests, not confessionalism, that guided Charles XII of Sweden through a reign of almost non-stop fighting. Unlike his predecessor Gustavus II Adolphus, Charles did not pretend that he made war in order to fulfill a religious mission or to unite all Protestants. He did not even hesitate to seek an alliance with the dreaded Turks.[32] The worldly morality of Otto

Hintze's Machtstaat was becoming manifest in the area of international conflict.

The conditions of war, or of impending war, allowed kings to embark on sweeping domestic measures that would have seemed rash or provocative in times of peace. Their edicts and proclamations multiplied, testifying to a conviction that written law could transform every aspect of custom and memory. The Christian assumption that human history was rapidly moving towards an impending millennium was discarded; instead, monarchs espoused the view that time was an endless march of progressive change. Nowhere was this more evident than in Peter I's decree of a new Russian calendar in 1699:

> To commemorate this happy beginning and the new century, in the capital city of Moscow, after a solemn prayer in churches and private dwellings, all major streets, homes of important people, and homes of distinguished religious and civil servants shall be decorated with trees, pines and fir branches. . . . Poor people should put up at least one tree, or a branch on their gates or on their apartment [doors] . . . friends should greet each other and the New Year and the new century as follows: when the Red Square will be lighted and shooting will begin . . . everyone who has a musket or any other fire arm should salute thrice or shoot several rockets or as many as he has.[33]

The calendar regulated the whole ritual year, whose temporal gradations were supposed to follow a divinely set pattern. To alter that pattern through law was to suggest that religious observances, even time itself, served human purposes and might be improved. The point was noted by an Austrian diplomat describing how the traditional New Year's ceremonies had been abandoned: "With the new-fangled ambition of our days, they were left unrevived as things worn-out and obsolete. It was considered that the worship of by-gone generations was needlessly superstitious in allowing majesty to be wrapped up with so many sacred rites."[34] By defining how everyone should act, moreover, the decree denied any distinction between private and public behaviour; both were under the scrutiny of a state whose reach seemed to be ubiquitous.

In their reforming proclamations, kings referred to the state as an entity with its own interests, to which everyone should contribute. An example can be found in the Spanish king Philip V's regalist decree of April 1709, which expelled the papal nuncio and prohibited any "commerce" with Rome. Philip ordered clerics to disregard any papal command which might lead to "inconvenience or harm to the common good and that of the State [*Estado*]."[35] The separation of state interests from those of religion marked a clear break with the ideology of Charles II's court. Philip's chief minister, Melchor de Macanaz, an indefatigable advocate of rational control, went further in his regalist proposal of 1713, the *Pedimento fiscal*. It claimed for the Crown full powers of appointment and jurisdiction over the church—in short, a complete appropriation of religious autonomy. The *Pedimento* justified royal dominance in terms of social utility, giving it the widest possible compass: "It is very appropriate to secular power, and to good political and economic governance, to agree to prevent all that which can disturb the peace among subjects." Churchmen "are obliged towards all that comprises or touches the public good of the State." Like Peter I, who drafted superfluous clerics into the army, Macanaz wanted to reduce everyone to equal subordination.[36]

Throughout Europe the rationalization of religious identity involved the cultural construction of the responsible subject. Although his attributes were not identical in every kingdom, he was imagined in similar ways. He bore the duty of allegiance as an individual rather than as a member of a collective body. He was expected to exercise self-discipline, both in his internal beliefs and in his external conduct. His religion was not to interfere in any way with his civil loyalty. He could even be allowed to hold views that did not accord with the religion of the state, so long as they were kept private. The English writer Joseph Addison explained in 1714 how such an upright character might be formed: "The most likely Method of rectifying any Man's conduct, is, by recommending to him the Principles of Truth and Honour, Religion and Virtue; and so long as he acts with an Eye to these Principles, whatever Party he is of, he cannot fail of being a good *Englishman*, and a Lover of his Country."[37] Women could not of course be responsible subjects. "Female Virtues are of a Domestick turn," Addison opined. "The Family is the proper Province for Private Women to Shine in."[38] Their participation in the state was indirect, through obedient support of their husbands and fathers.

For the responsible subject, political allegiance was as natural as family relationships. The Ukrainian cleric Feofan Prokopovich, Peter I's favourite preacher, elaborated on this assumption in a sermon of 1718. "And behold," he announced, "might there not be in the number of natural laws this one, that there are to be authorities holding power among nations? There is indeed!" Royal authority was derived from "the natural law written on man's heart by God."[39] Prokopovich wholly internalized subjection within the conscience of the responsible Christian. His God, like the God of Malebranche, was the prime mover of natural laws that directed the self unfailingly towards obedience. No rational resistance could be offered against them.

Although the virtues of the responsible subject were natural, they had to be drawn out by proper guidance. For this purpose, humanist pedagogy was again revived; but it was now applied to a wider constituency. Leibniz elaborated on its goals in a memoir addressed to "enlightened men of good intention": "To contribute truly to the happiness of men, one must enlighten their understanding; one must fortify their will in the exercise of virtues, that is, in the habit of acting according to reason; and one must, finally, try to remove the obstacles which keep them from finding truth and following true goods."[40] No ruler, of course, could dream at this point of embarking on the sort of educational project envisioned by Leibniz. It was as yet beyond the administrative capacity of any European state.[41] Nevertheless, kings could strengthen virtue through police ordinances; they could stamp out beliefs that led their subjects away from "true goods"; and they could root out impediments to reason—above all, "superstition" and custom.

The training of the responsible subject was always supposed to be informed by religion. No confessional movement was more effective in achieving this goal than Pietism. It developed out of the teachings of Spener, although he was more concerned with the impending kingdom of God than with forming good subjects for worldly regimes.[42] Before Spener's death, however, his follower August Hermann Francke had begun to direct the "inner man" towards the state. Francke was an indefatigable moral reformer whose orphanage, school, and manufacturing complex— or *Anstalt*—at Halle became the "World-centre of General-reformation." He was always what Hartmut Lehmann calls "a citizen of two worlds," the state and the spirit, and he had trouble choosing between them.[43] The Prussian state, however, was eager to appropriate his movement's inner policing and dedication to service. During a visit to the Anstalt in 1713,

King Frederick William I tried to sound Francke out as to where his primary allegiance lay and asked what he thought of wars:

> FRANCKE: Your Royal Majesty must protect the land, I, however, am called to preach: Blessed are the peacemakers. . . .
>
> KING: But the young people, are they not taught that they would catch the Devil if they became soldiers?
>
> FRANCKE: I know many Christian soldiers. I have more friends and protectors among soldiers than among the clergy.[44]

Francke's answers were somewhat evasive, but they pleased the king, who often heard what he wanted to hear. Frederick William now began to choose Pietists as army chaplains; soldiers and their wives were routinely catechized; and officer cadet training was remodelled on the Halle programme of self-discipline. As the historian Klaus Deppermann put it, "The Pietism of Halle trained subjects for the Prussian state who were obedient, competent and conscious of social responsibility."[45]

The moral guidance offered by Pietism was paralleled in England by a campaign for "reformation of manners," engineered by Dissenters and Low Church Whigs during the reign of William III. It aimed to stamp out vices like gambling and drinking as well as raise the religious tone of the nation. The English monarchy, like the Prussian, gave active encouragement to this "godly Revolution," which it saw as serving the interests of state discipline and police. It was no coincidence that the advocates of reformation of manners were often the strongest supporters of King William's war against Catholic France.[46] Meanwhile, in Peter I's Russia, the clerical academies of Kiev and Moscow played a role similar to that of Halle in disseminating an ideology of responsible subjection. The academicians stressed western ideals of rational self-control rather than Orthodox asceticism. They venerated Tsar Peter as their patron and protector. A print from the early eighteenth century shows admiring academicians standing before the tsar, who is dressed as "Pallas," a curious mixture of Apollo and Minerva. Arranged in soldierly ranks, with faces beaming, the students reveal that they are ready to accept the westernized wisdom bestowed on them by their godlike ruler.[47]

The religious formation of the responsible subject was designed to make him into an efficient servant of the state. His main duty, as Gerhard Oestreich noted, was to defend the polity, either by bearing arms or by

28. I. Shchyrsky, *Kievan Mohyla Academy* (c. 1698), engraving.
Photo: University of Toronto Press, Toronto.

otherwise contributing to military security.[48] The period from 1690 to 1715 saw a profusion of schemes for conscription, forced recruiting, and the raising of militia units. Many of these plans were modelled on the Swedish *indelningsverket*. The kings of Prussia, for example, built on the Swedish experience in developing a massive conscript army and a remarkably efficient system of military administration. Other realms, such as Piedmont-Savoy, followed their own paths towards a militarization of the relationship between ruler and subject. Even in England, where the standing army was highly controversial, the colossal war effort against France produced an extensive and highly intrusive fiscal-military state.[49]

In spite of its growing bureaucratic structures, however, the state remained intimately attached to the person of the ruler. The responsible subject did not bow down to an administrative apparatus, the mechanical limbs of the artificial man; rather, he owed allegiance to its living sign, a human ruler in whom he could still recognize an idealization of his own virtues. The kings of Europe were expected to exemplify good conduct in their actions, and to publicize it through their pronouncements. By 1715, however, the theatre of royal virtue had changed in three important ways. First, the authority expressed through monarchical publicity no longer relied so heavily on religious sources of legitimation. Coronation rituals illustrate the point. In 1697 Sweden's Charles XII was the first king in Europe to crown himself, rather than accepting his regalia from a bishop.[50] Four years later the Elector Frederick of Brandenburg appeared at the Castle Church in Potsdam with a crown already on his head and a sceptre in his hand. He then crowned his wife and proceeded to anoint himself with oil, "for His Majesty was not first attaining through the unction the royal dignity . . . but only proclaiming and confirming it."[51] Peter I distanced Russian state ideology from religion by shearing his own titles of theological epithets. In Spain Philip V systematically abandoned the confessional "mass culture" of the Habsburgs. He never attended an auto de fe, gave no support to the rosary processions, and insisted that autos sacramentales be staged in public theatres, without the king in attendance, rather than at royal palaces.[52]

The second change was a trend towards confessional moderation, derived from the vestiges of humanism and tending at times towards a politically motivated tolerance. Charles XII exemplified these qualities. It may be that in his mind, as an admiring biographer put it, "fear of God took first place," but the same writer tells us that his religion was simple, private, and "without bigotry." He later gained a reputation for freethinking, which was probably unjustified. Still, he was deeply interested in science and hostile to "superstition," prophecies, and intolerance of other faiths. Charles took refuge for several years among the Turks—an unthinkable step for a Christian ruler of earlier times—and he looked with considerable admiration on what he saw as the dedication of Muslims to the interests of the state.[53]

Frederick I of Prussia was a monarch of similar views. A Calvinist ruling over a Lutheran people, he shrugged off the implications of his own religion by accepting the role of good works in gaining salvation and called for his subjects to join with him in an evangelical union. By calling Huguenot immigrants to enter his realm, Frederick sanctioned a limited de facto toleration.[54] Although his successor, Frederick William I, allied himself with the Pietists, they could not count on the king's support on doctrinal issues, about which he was totally indifferent. Nor did Frederick William give the Pietists much backing in combating their rationalist foes at the University of Halle—foremost among them the Leibnizian philosopher Christian Thomasius. While the Prussian state made use of Pietism as a means of indoctrination, it never espoused the godly utopianism that lay behind the Anstalt.[55]

More surprising, perhaps, was the spread of toleration in the Habsburg lands and Russia. As Holy Roman Emperor after 1705, Joseph I moved towards alterations in the rigid confessional framework of Habsburg governance. He allowed Protestants to attend his court, accepted a Swedish plan for freedom of worship in Silesia, and ratified toleration in Hungary after suppressing the Rákóczi rebellion.[56] For his part, Peter I favoured limited tolerance of other Christian denominations and even Muslims, although his broad-mindedness did not extend to Jews. He allowed Old Believers to live unmolested in northern parts, so long as they paid double taxation on their lucrative commercial ventures. Thus, he extended to them a personal pact that was entirely based on economic self-interest. Peter's own religiosity was described with gushing enthusiasm by the Englishman John Perry, who depicted it as quasi-Protestant: "The *Czar* who has a more rational sense of God and Religion, seeing the stupid Folly, as well as Bigotry of his Subjects . . . has reduced the Number of his Saints in his own Houses of Residence wherever he is, to the Cross, or the Picture of our blessed Saviour only."[57]

A third element of change in the publicity of kingship was the use of classical imagery. The classicism of the period was designed less to convey hidden meanings to a court elite than to instruct a broad audience through a familiar, unchanging shorthand of reason and civility. The public assimilation of an imagined Greek or Roman past was particularly favoured in realms that were seen by their neighbours as "barbaric" or "uncivilized." In Prussia, for instance, Frederick I's desire to spread classical culture gained Berlin the nickname "Athens on the Spree." Frederick spent large sums of money on projects like an opera house and a painting academy. His grandson later condemned what he perceived as "the dissipation of a vain and prodigal prince; his court was one of the most superb of Europe." In fact, Frederick I had laid the cultural foundations of a monarchy that owed almost nothing to confessionalism.[58]

The same attachment to classicism as a mark of rational civility can be seen in Russia under Peter I. The architecture of ancient Rome, not that of traditional Orthodoxy, informed the public buildings of the new capital, St. Petersburg. By claiming the title of emperor, Peter tried to claim the heritage of Rome as well as of Byzantium. Roman gods and heroes appeared frequently, and sometimes incongruously, in the political propaganda of the academicians of Kiev and Moscow. For example, they celebrated the victory over the Swedes at Poltava in 1709 by designing huge commemorative arches on which the image of the triumphant tsar was festooned with classical references: Hercules, Mars, Perseus. While they longed to extirpate native paganism, the academicians associated responsible subjection with the pagan values of western antiquity—just as Swedish intellectuals had done in the days of Stiernhielm.[59]

Joseph I could claim a more direct link with the civilizing example of the Roman emperors. His image too was associated with an easily decipherable classicism. In the triumphal arches erected at Vienna in 1690 to celebrate his crowning as king of Rome, Joseph is depicted as a young sun god riding in a chariot above his admiring ancestors. The twin pillars of Habsburg rulership appear in these works as signs of a state power which rivals that of the ancients. The pillar designated as Prudence takes an equal place with that representing Religion.[60] The Viennese arches resembled an operatic set, which is not surprising, as Joseph was a lifelong patron of the opera. Epitomizing the classical culture of his reign, opera was prohibited by imperial licence from performance in popular theatres, because it was "more a matter for princes and kings than for shopkeepers and traders," in the judgment of the composer Johann Mattheson. Opera plots were usually derived from classical myth and history rather than from biblical stories, and attending operatic performances was supposed to have an immediate civilizing effect on the court nobility. The elaborate machinery of the operatic stage, moreover, was a sign of rational control; Fontenelle was not

alone in seeing its "wheels and counterweights" as metaphors for a mechanical universe. Did they not also reflect a state that increasingly worked
as if it were a machine, propelled by a classical rather than a confessional morality?[61]

Two rulers of the period do not seem to fit the model of royal publicity
that we have been considering. The emperor Charles VI, who succeeded
his morally wayward brother Joseph in 1711, restored the orthodox character of a court-based rulership. Frederick II of Prussia later described
Charles as "a good father, a good husband, but superstitious and big-
oted"—in short, a traditional Habsburg patriarch. In spite of this, Charles
did not discard toleration in the borderlands, and he favoured the benign
image of Solomon rather than that of a confessional champion. His publicity did not abandon a concern with state interests. His court became known
for grandiose musical performances that exalted his worldly rulership—
including annual commemorations of his military exploits in Spain.[62]
Charles's building projects, like his brother's, used the twin pillars of
Hercules to denote not just the Habsburg dynasty but the state. They
appear in Fischer von Erlach's plan for the Schönbrunn Palace and in front
of his famous *Karlskirche*, or Church of St. Charles Borromeo, in Vienna.
The two columns of Constance and Fortitude standing at the entrance to
the Karlskirche, apart from its main structure, announce that the imperial
state provides its subjects with access to religion. The neo-classical architecture of this new Temple of Solomon enshrined a rational harmony that
one art historian has called "quasi-Leibnizian."[63]

Queen Anne of England was an even more unlikely rationalist than
Charles VI. Her pronouncements exuded a fervent piety. In her accession
speech she declared, "I know my own heart to be entirely English"—
words that testified to a revival of the sympathetic pact between the Stuart
monarchy and the Anglican nation. A loyal daughter of the church, she
approved of the censuring of "Heretics" and the repression of "the impious
attempts lately made to subvert the foundation of the Christian Faith."[64]
Unlike her female predecessor Elizabeth I, she did not present herself as the
profane object of "courtly love"; instead, she adopted the image of a
"nursing mother," which conformed better to Protestant conceptions of
virtuous femininity.

Anne's publicity, however, was heavily influenced by ideas of natural

The Statue of Our Sovereign Lady QUEEN ANNE, being of y. finest
Marble, erected in Honour of Her Majesty at the West end of
S.t PAUL'S CATHEDRALL London.

29. *The Statue of Our Sovereign Lady Queen Anne* (c. 1712), engraving.
Pennant, vol. II, no. 101.

Photo: British Museum, London.

rulership. In his poem "Windsor Forest," the Catholic writer Alexander Pope praised her reign not as an Anglican millennium but as a restoration of nature and material plenty, using images that were derived from classicism and the literature of Charles II's court.[65] The queen might also represent an abstract concept of sovereign authority, as she did in numerous frozen-pose statues that still adorn public buildings in England today (more, perhaps, than of any other monarch before Victoria).[66] Anne's sense of policy was guided less by High Church idealism than by a realistic assessment of the restrictions placed on the royal language by party divisions. She understood that the Crown could no longer compete with factional publicity. She therefore kept her court frugal, hierarchical, and sober, like an Anglican household, but never made it the nerve centre of high culture.[67] Nor did she try to lead a High Church reaction, which would have deeply alienated the Whig aristocrats and merchants on whom the machinery of the state depended. In spite of her personal convictions, she allowed the only heresy case of her reign, against the Arian theologian William Whiston, to be dropped.

If the devout could not fully count on the political guidance of a monarch like Anne, where could they turn? Some withdrew into a private sphere of inner faith, outside the notice of the state. Among them were the surviving rural Protestants of Bohemia, who had given up on the hope of a Protestant saviour and, in the words of Marie-Elisabeth Ducreux, "manifested their particular identity by their reading and their attachment to the book."[68] Others raised the hopeless cry that Christian liberty had been betrayed by the king. Among them was the headstrong Swedish pastor who in 1698 was sentenced to life imprisonment (later cut to ten years by royal command) for publishing a sermon that criticized royal sovereignty.[69] A more widespread and organized resistance by the devout was found in Russia, England, and Spain, where it took the forms of counterpublicity, party struggles, and open rebellion.

In the minds of many Russians, Peter I's reforms amounted to a full-scale assault on Orthodoxy. His calendar decree was particularly resented. "They comply with this order out of mere Fear," noted Perry. Old Believers continued to mark the new year on the first of September.[70] In spite of his attempts to placate them, Peter was fiercely hated by many Raskolniki, who denounced him as the Antichrist. After the brutal suppression of a military revolt in 1698, however, armed uprising was not a viable option for opponents of the tsar. So his critics began to carve out a clandestine sphere of subversive discourse, producing colourful political caricatures that showed Peter as a hungry, smirking cat or an ungainly boy trying to shave off the beard of a dignified Raskolnik. Others who mistrusted the tsar's initiatives gathered around the heir to the throne, Peter's son Alexis, who was thought to be a traditionalist in religion.[71] The rationalization of Orthodox identity led to the entrenchment of divisions that would continue to disturb the state, not so much by insurrection as through periodic disruptions within the institutions of governance.

In England a High Church counter-offensive against the rational state began in the last years of William III's reign, under the slogan "The Church in Danger." The High Churchmen, or Tories, espoused a strictly confessional definition of participation in the polity. They called for revival of the clerical assembly known as Convocation, a sort of alternative Parliament, and for an end to "occasional conformity," by which Dissenters could qualify for office by taking the Anglican sacrament. The Tories enjoyed a broad basis of support among artisans and shopkeepers, both in London and provincial towns. The High Church party triumphed in 1710, when the Whigs bungled an attempt to impeach the impudent preacher Henry Sacheverell for his public attacks on toleration and the Glorious Revolution. An overwhelming victory for the Tories in the subsequent general elections seemed to signal the reversal of the settlement of 1689, perhaps including the restoration of a Stuart king.[72]

Ultimately, however, Queen Anne chose not to lead the Tories into the new dispensation. Instead, she and her ministers doggedly, and sometimes reluctantly, protected the fiscal, religious, and dynastic status quo from the furious attacks of Tory backbenchers. Unlike her uncle Charles II, the queen would not allow the Church party to dominate her. "You cannot wonder that I who have been ill used so many years should desire to keep myself from being again enslaved," she wrote to her chief minister in 1712.[73] Accordingly, at her death in August 1714, the British state was handed over intact to her Protestant successor: Georg Ludwig, Elector of Hanover, a German Lutheran, a friend of Leibniz, and a religious rationalist.

Within weeks of his accession, George I set in motion a full-scale takeover of Anglican identity, more radical than anything the kings of

Sweden or Prussia had ever attempted. The Tory party was flung from power and High Churchmen were replaced with Whigs at every administrative level, from the Treasury to commissions of the peace. Convocation was indefinitely suspended. Promotion to the episcopate was restricted to those willing to set doctrinal issues aside and express an unquestioning fidelity to the king, his ministers, and the ruling party. In despair, the Tory leaders called on the Stuart Pretender, James III, to rescue them; but his Jacobite adherents were crushed in the uprising known as the '15. Furious riots against the new regime at the coronation, and again in the summer of 1715, showed that George I was widely disliked by large numbers of the English people. It mattered little to him, because his rulership did not rest on bipartisan popularity. Its principal supports were the law, the Whig party, and a large standing army, maintained for domestic policing.[74] Meanwhile, the semblance of "moral revolution" was abandoned, and it was only with great reluctance that George was persuaded to continue paying for the "English tables" at the Halle Anstalt.[75]

Like the High Church reaction in England, the Spanish uprising against Philip V drew upon the fury of the lesser clergy, especially in Aragon. The archbishop of Zaragoza wrote that "the origin and cause of the sedition and rebellion in this kingdom have been friars and clergy, and particularly village priests who are the only directors of their flocks."[76] Minor clerics were responsible for the enthusiastic publicity of the Habsburg claimant, the archduke Charles. In one imaginative pamphlet, an enthusiastic friar claimed that planetary conjunctions clearly pointed to Charles as heaven's choice for king! Such otherworldly zeal was matched by a church organist who sang "*Salve,* Charles of the heavens" at evening services.[77] The state-centred policies of the Bourbon monarchy were utterly foreign to the mystical and highly personal religiosity expressed by adherents of the Habsburg cause.

In countering the rebels, Bourbon apologists tended to stress a rational obedience based on confessional identity. Bishop Belluga of Murcia praised Philip V as "a King chosen by the hand of God," an "Absolute Monarch and Supreme Legislator." Deluded priests who spread sedition, Belluga pointed out, were aiding the Protestant allies of the archduke and thereby introducing heresy into Spain.[78] This was a particularly effective accusation, which among secular writers might be represented as a deviation from nature. The marquess of San Felipe later recalled with prurient horror how the English troops had "profaned churches and sacred altars, making them theatres of lewdness." He accused the Protestants of desecrating the patriarchal foundations of society by dishonouring daughters and wives as well as by tempting weak-minded women and children to imbibe the "poison" of Luther and Calvin. For San Felipe the mixing of priestly and military roles among the insurgents was a further violation of natural order. He recorded how priests and religious in Catalonia, "taking off the sacred habits, dressed themselves in bandoliers and strapped on arms, and there was no atrocity, sacrilege and lewdness which they failed to commit."[79]

The rebels were defeated, but the principles they had espoused with such emotion did not quickly disappear. Unlike Hanoverian England, the Spanish state was not able fully to exploit its victory over the armies of the devout; on the contrary, it encountered a second line of entrenched resistance from religious loyalists like Belluga, angered by regalist policies that seemed to threaten confessionalism. Macanaz's *Pedimento,* intended only for consideration by the council, was leaked to the Inquisition by the minister's enemies and was swiftly condemned. King Philip abandoned his enlightened advisor, who was dismissed from office and banished. Two years later the king signed a concordat with the pope renouncing the more extreme forms of regalism. In spite of this retreat, partisan disputes between regalists and their opponents would continue to mark the slow advance of a Spanish state identity throughout the eighteenth century.[80]

In Spain as in England and Russia, the devout lost politically but could not be entirely defeated on a personal level. Paradoxically, therefore, the rationalization of religious identity, which sought to impose loyalty on the whole individual, widened a cleavage between the private self, still largely shaped by confessional values, and the public person, obliged to accept the rules of interest and expediency. To some extent this cleavage had been incipient since the Reformation. For two centuries it had proven increasingly difficult to "fear God and honour the king"—in other words, to reconcile inner devotion to religion with outer obedience to government. From the early 1700s onwards, the two obligations would pertain to more or less separate aspects of the individual. The development of the Christian self would be confined to private life, while everything that pertained to public duty would be governed by worldly principles of reason and nature. Out of this dualism was born the instability of the enlightened self, unable to reject religious belief but unwilling to place confessional principles ahead of the natural order of society. While such a divided identity did not produce the total submission that Louis XIV or Peter I had demanded, at least it provided an acquiescence that would not easily be disrupted. Meanwhile, the ideological dependence of the rational state on confessionalism would steadily diminish. Despite many attempts to halt that process over the past two hundred years, it has never been reversed.

## Appropriating National Identity

The state consumed religious identity in bits and pieces; it swallowed national identities whole. This was accomplished in several ways: first, through rituals that declared the essential unity of the state; second, through the state-sponsored standardization of national languages; third and most drastically, through the elimination of separate provincial or national institutions and the establishment of state unions that were more centralized. Thus, national sentiment was deprived of any formal means of political expression outside the purview of the state. The religiously based patriotism that had fomented so many upheavals was gradually submerged in an ideology of imperial destiny that would lead Europeans into an age of global expansion.

The rituals of unity were hardly new, but their significance as occasions for asserting a state identity was heightened in the last decades of the seventeenth century. For example, the Te Deum, or thanksgiving ceremony, was celebrated with increasing frequency in France after the majority of Louis XIV. Michèle Fogel has counted no fewer than ninety Te Deums between 1661 and 1715, of which fifty-seven took place after 1688. They combined a religious service with a strong message of political unity and were celebrated in exactly the same way throughout the kingdom, whether the ruler was present or not. In the Habsburg Erblande the Corpus Christi procession had a similar significance. It assembled the orders of society to commemorate a state-centred rite of unity, which was repeated in all parts of the realm. The Russian Peter Tolstoi, who in 1697 witnessed the feast of Corpus Christi at Vienna, described how the citizens "walked by ranks" to the cathedral of St. Stephen. The royal family followed, dressed in black and seated in magnificent coaches. The assembly then walked on foot to the Pestsäule, with the Host carried before them. Large contingents of troops, the guardians of the state, were always in view, and (strangely to our ears, perhaps) the march took place to the music of kettledrums and trumpets. As in the French Te Deum, the monarch was present at the Corpus Christi ritual in the capital, but his place was taken elsewhere by high-ranking local officials.[81]

If the state regularized the rituals by which unity was represented, it also sought to standardize the predominant means of cultural representation, the national language. Charles XII was deeply concerned for the "purity and status" of Swedish, and he wanted university lectures to be printed in the native tongue as well as in Latin. Peter I of Russia couched his decrees in a "simplified" state language that was deliberately non-religious and avoided the terminology of Old Church Slavonic. They were even printed in a new "civic alphabet" that was less ornate than ecclesiastical script.[82] The Spanish king Philip V was more systematic in his attempts at linguistic control. In 1713 he set up the Royal Academy of Language, which embarked on the daunting task of compiling an authoritative Castilian dictionary. Differing tongues and dialects had helped keep Spanish regional identities alive, so royal endorsement of the dictionary carried a strong message of centralism. In a similar vein, the Royal Council recommended that Castilian become the language of primary schooling and religious instruction in conquered Catalonia.[83] Once the elements of language had been fixed, they had to be taught. Although plans for a unified national education system belong mainly to the period after 1740, the groundwork for increasing state control over the instruction of children was already being laid in a few places, such as Denmark.

In two notable instances—Scotland and Catalonia—national institutions were actually abolished in this period, and in a third—the Ukraine—a process of abolition was set in motion. What replaced them in each case was what John Robertson has described as an imperial union, through which diverse territories were incorporated into a centralized yet expansive whole.[84] The Scottish union stemmed from a confessional polarization worsened by the Glorious Revolution. A convention led by Scots Presbyterian magnates declared in 1689 that James II had "forefaulted the Right to the Crown" by exercising "an arbitrary and despotick Power" in matters of religion. The refusal of some bishops to accept these words, and to swear the oath of allegiance to William and Mary, was used as a reason finally to abolish prelacy from the Scottish Kirk. About five hundred to six hundred Nonjuring ministers—half of the parish clergy—remained loyal to the episcopal establishment and King James. So did many Highland clan leaders, who joined Catholic clansmen in an abortive Jacobite rebellion.[85] Scottish Jacobitism thereafter became a patriotic cause, a form of opposition to the Presbyterian bosses who manipulated a corrupt Parliament.

For Scots Presbyterians, as for English Whigs, the solution to Jacobite unrest was the Act of Union of 1707, which abolished the Scottish Parliament. It was built on promises of political stability and commercial prosperity—in short, on reason of state and self-interest. Queen Anne herself instructed the Scottish Members of Parliament that the union would "secure your Religion, Liberty and property" as well as "increase your Strength, Riches and Trade."[86] Yet Scottish patriots, whatever their dynastic views, could not stomach it. Even so staunch a Whig as Andrew Fletcher of Saltoun refused to endorse the union, because it could ruin a fragile economy and make the Scots "a conquered people." The Jacobite patriot George Lockhart saw the union as purely a party measure: "The Whigs proposed to unite the Whigs in both kingdomes by this in a near and close allayance, and to wheedle us over to the succession."[87] Many English Tories also opposed the union because, in bringing together two kingdoms with different religions, it compromised the confessional basis of the state. How could Presbyterians be kept out of government in one part of Great Britain when they were dominant in the administration of the other part? This question may have been bothersome to some, but it ignored the rational state's tendency to override religious differences in order to safeguard order and obedience. In the end, the guarantor of state authority was military force, which was used to suppress a serious Highland uprising in 1715 and 1716.[88] The defeated Jacobites returned to plotting against the union. They would not surrender to it until after 1745.

Just as it inspired Scottish patriotism, religious enthusiasm was at the heart of Catalan nationalism. Like the Jacobites, adherents of the Habsburg claimant saw their struggle as one of Christian governance against atheistic tyranny. Carried away by a rhetoric of spiritual renewal, they even spoke of implementing social justice for the poor. In Valencia, for example, the archduke's supporters abolished feudal dues and encouraged a peasant uprising against oppressive landowners. Everywhere, the Habsburg cause became inseparable from the defence of provincial rights. The archduke Charles was praised as a Christ-like "Restorer of Catalan liberty," and his devotions at local shrines of the Virgin Mary were seen to symbolize his respect for the privileges of Aragon.[89] The aim of the insurgents, however, was not simply to preserve their own patria from the encroachments of Madrid but to impose a decentralized, federal model of government on the whole monarchy. As Pierre Vilar has pointed out, the commercial middle classes who led the revolt in Barcelona were "less separatist . . . with regard to Spain, than in a hurry to intervene in Spanish destiny." They sought to assert the political equality of Aragon with Castile and to purge Spain of "tyrannical" French influence. Inspired by a chiliastic sense of purpose, the Catalans resisted Philip to the bitter end, even after the archduke had returned to Vienna and his Protestant allies had given up the struggle. Barcelona fell to the Bourbon king only after a hard-fought siege in 1714.[90]

Philip V's response to the rising concentrated first and foremost on the destruction of national autonomy. He began in 1707 with a decree abolishing the *fueros*, or legal privileges, of Aragon and Valencia. This was legitimized in terms of a unitary kingship based on sovereign right as well as conquest. The decree proclaimed Philip's "absolute dominion" over Aragon and Valencia, denying their particularity by pointing out "the circumstance that they are included in the other realms that I so legitimately possess in this Monarchy, to which is now added the just right of conquest which my Arms have made of them lately because of their rebellion." The king further stipulated "that one of the principal attributes of Sovereignty is the imposition and derogation of laws." Sovereignty was presented as a legal principle inherent in Spanish kingship. Like divine power, it had attributes, not boundaries.[91]

The famous decree of January 1716 for the *Nueva Planta*, or new foundation, of Catalonia contained a briefer preamble, which simply placed the power to establish government in "my Sovereignty." In spite of such reticence, the consequences of the Nueva Planta were astonishingly far-reaching. The whole structure of Catalan law and administration—the *fueros, Corts,* and *Diputació*—were swept away, to be replaced by a royal *audiencia,* or supreme court, and local fiscal-judicial officers called *co-rregidores.* Cases in the audiencia were to be heard only in Castilian. This was a complete levelling of traditional constitutionalism, which went far beyond anything Olivares ever contemplated. Even the French Bourbons had never abolished a major provincial assembly, although they had detached particular territories from them. Unlike the elimination of the Scottish Parliament, moreover, the Nueva Planta was not just a legislative union but a full-scale annihilation of tradition.[92]

The Ukraine did not suffer quite so awful a fate, but its national identity was just as fully—if more gradually—appropriated by the Russian state after the rebellion of 1708. For Ukrainians the decision of the aged Cossack hetman Ivan Mazepa to support the Swedes against Peter I was the outcome of decades of chipping away at their privileges. As always, religion was a major source of grievance; the Ukrainians regarded the Russians as religiously ignorant and resented the fact that a number of their episcopal diocese had been placed under the control of the patriarch of Moscow. Mazepa, himself a graduate of the Kiev Academy, displayed his spiritual leadership over the Orthodox Ukrainian nation by sponsoring the building of numerous local churches in a style known as Cossack baroque. The immediate cause of his rebellion was the tsar's refusal to defend the Ukraine against a Polish Catholic invasion, which in the hetman's opinion violated the contract agreed to at Pereiaslav. The uprising quickly collapsed, however, and Mazepa fled to the Ottoman Empire. The tsar now began to reward his countrymen with offices, land, and trading privileges in the Ukraine. He formed a governing commission, dominated by his own creatures, that had powers over the new hetman.[93]

In all these cases, patriotism was caught up in an international political situation dominated by state interests rather than religion. This made it impossible for patriots to maintain the purity of their confessional motives. In fact, the Jacobites, the Catalans, and the Mazepists laid themselves open to charges of abetting the enemies of the true faith. The Jacobite candidate for the throne was a Roman Catholic upheld by France; the Catalans fought alongside the Protestant English and Dutch; and the hetman was denounced as a "Judas" who aided the Lutheran Swedes. Each group of patriots, therefore, had to justify its resistance in terms that made some allowance for reason of state—that is, for pursuing the moral evil of alliance with a religious "Other" in pursuit of a greater spiritual good. Without doubt, this weakened the patriot cause. On the other hand, the rationalization of religious identity by the state had smoothed the way for the undermining of separate national institutions and privileges. George I, Philip V, and Peter I were able to present themselves as the defenders of a moderate confessional settlement that was inseparable from the security of the state.

The Act of Union, the Nueva Planta, and the reduction of the Hetmanate set precedents that would be followed throughout the eighteenth century. They indicated the beginning of the end of composite monarchies and the rise of aggressive, imperial states. The impetus for this change came not so much from new theories of government as from cultural trends: in particular, the primacy of political over confessional allegiances, the appropriation of religious autonomy, and a decline of confidence in messianic promises of national religious destiny. Nevertheless, the immediate circumstances of each case of imperial unification were unusual, and they did not provide a pattern of reform that could be imitated elsewhere. The unified British state, for example, was not extended to Ireland. Instead, the anomalous, semi-colonial position of the Irish kingdom was prolonged, even after the defeat of the Jacobites in 1690. The Dublin Parliament, an entirely Protestant institution, was awkwardly managed by the Crown rather than abolished. Before long, the Protestant elite had itself became imbued with a strong patriotism that resented any interference from Westminster. Against the better judgment of William III, the Irish Protestants subjected their Roman Catholic compatriots to sweeping confiscations of property and further legal restrictions. No gestures of political inclusion were made towards a confessional majority that was regarded by the ruling elite as an uncivilized "Other." It may be wondered whether the state existed at all in Ireland; certainly it was no more than the accomplice of one side in a long-running conflict between two confessionally based versions of national consciousness.[94]

Similarly, imperial union did not embrace Hungary, where the defeat of the Rákóczi revolt might have led to a wholesale reduction of national privileges and the elimination of confessional diversity. As in Ireland, however, the Estates remained powerful in Hungary, and about half of the population continued to espouse Protestantism. An act of 1715 made the legal existence of Protestant churches dependent on the will of the sov-

THE STATE REMAINS · 305

ereign; but, like the Irish penal laws, it was passed by the Estates them-selves, not decreed by the ruler. The Hungarian nobles did not regard such concessions as sacrifices of their national identity or their constitutional "liberties." Imbued with patriotic warrior values that were redolent of Polish Sarmatism, they would resist the intrusions of the Habsburg state until the end of the century.[95]

We should be careful, therefore, not to overestimate the impact of the state on national identity. Nonetheless, in many parts of Europe, patriotism had by 1715 ceased to be a constant motivator of rebellion. Instead, it had begun to find a place within the conventional and non-violent discourse of institutional politics. This gradual taming of patriot sentiment could be observed in the various "Country" oppositions within the British Parlia-ment; in criticism of the French Regency by parlementaires and peers; in the publicity campaign launched by Spanish aristocrats against Queen Elisabeth Farnese; and in the party divisions that would emerge in Sweden after the death of Charles XII. In none of these instances did patriotism lead to armed revolt; rather, it operated within the bounds of acceptable political activity. Although the patriot mentality still stuck to a moral high road, after 1715 it was no longer so strongly imbued with religious princi-ples. The godly destiny of the "nation of Israel" was transformed into a more worldly imperialism whose purpose was to spread commerce and civility to the Americas, Asia, and Africa. By 1750, patriots were calling for more guidance from above, not less. They had begun to promulgate an ideal that would profoundly alter the image of European monarchy: the patriot king.

## Naturalizing the Body

The rational state had little direct interest in the soul. As yet, it had at its disposal few means of moulding the mind, although some of its propo-nents, like Leibniz or Peter I, grandly envisioned its future pedagogical mission. The main object of state discipline was the body. In dealing with it separately from the mind and the soul, Europe's rulers adhered to a sort of practical Cartesianism. Their methods, like those of Descartes, treated the body as a natural, social, and sometimes mechanical instrument. The body was never, of course, fully appropriated by the state, but it did come under increasing scrutiny and interference. The cultural ramifications of these efforts at control were labyrinthine, and the following pages will consider only a few of them. We shall then conclude with a discussion of the sacred status of the king's own body and the beginnings of a change that some historians have called desacralization.

The claims of the rational state over the body were made in ways that were not usually innovative, but their development reached an apogee in the late seventeenth and early eighteenth centuries. One of them was legal punishment. By 1715, communal, feudal, and private forms of justice had given way in most parts of Europe to the authority of royal law courts. Reforming monarchs had codified the laws of the realm in a series of major enactments, from Philip II's *Nueva Recopilación* of 1567 to Louis XIV's massive ordinance of 1670. Even in England, where customary law continued to operate in felony cases, legislative statutes like the Game Laws of the 1670s defined a growing multitude of criminal offences against property. As a result, when the bodies of criminals were hanged or pilloried or whipped around the market place, the king and his state were usually responsible for the form and severity of the punishment.

Once this control over justice had been secured, it was not long before governments began to apply the principles of reason to its procedures—not in order to alleviate the pains of the punished but to make sure that retribution fell on the heads and backs of the guilty. Torture, which had long been criticized as a poor method of reaching the truth, fell into disuse in Scotland after 1690 (when it was last used on a Jacobite conspirator). Charles XII discouraged it, and in 1722 it was abolished in Sweden. Frederick William of Prussia declared that it could not be used without the monarch's express consent. At the same time, the rules of civility were gradually being applied to the exercise of justice. Personal violence, which reflected badly on the noble character of a judge, was to be avoided. Educated people throughout Europe were shocked, therefore, at the report— probably false—that Peter I had decapitated some of the rebels of 1698 with his own hands.[96]

Another way in which the state claimed control over the body was through the incarceration of vagrants, the poor, and the sick in workhouses or hospitals. The "great confinement," as it has been called, began in the sixteenth century and was broadened as a result of the economic crisis of the early seventeenth century. Confinement usually involved only a temporary segregation from society and partial enclosure; but it could also include various forms of bodily correction and reform, such as whippings or forced labour. Initially, most "carceral" institutions were charities run by religious orders, as in Italy and Spain, or by local governments, as in England. By the late seventeenth century, however, the state was becoming more involved in them. The Habsburg emperors were particularly zealous in founding hospitals and *Zuchthäuse,* or workhouses; a statute establishing workhouses for beggars throughout Norway was enacted in 1683; Louis XIV had decreed in 1662 that hospitals for vagrants were to be set up in every French town. Such ambitious projects were never fully accomplished, but they indicate the increasing concern of the state with the disciplining of the poor.[97]

The military uniform represented a different method of state control over the body, one that offered rewards as well as penalties. Until the late seventeenth century, only palace guards had been issued with uniform dress by the monarch; other military units had been clothed at the discretion of their aristocratic commanders. By the 1690s, however, the entire French infantry was uniformed in white or grey coats, supplied by the king, while foreign regiments in the service of France wore red or blue. Buttons and facing colours were determined by state regulations. The Swedish army took the standardization of uniform to an extreme, clothing all infantry regiments in a plain blue *justaucorps* with yellow facings, breeches, and stockings. Almost every depiction of the adult Charles XII shows him wearing this simple military garb. Soon the Austrian, British, and Russian armies were uniformed. The soldiers of Spain continued to wear their colonel's colours, until the Bourbon monarchy imposed white coats on them. The noble Sarmatian cavalrymen of Poland, of course, wore into battle whatever dress they chose.[98]

Michel Foucault pointed to the costume of the soldier as evidence of the "docility" of the body in the "classical age."[99] Military uniform, however, was a means of personal identification as well as of control. It gave the common soldier some of the respectability and social status of priests or lawyers, the other groups that regularly wore a formal costume. Uniform enshrined the masculinity of the man-in-arms, gaining him the admiration of women and the jealousy of other men. It gave him a right to use

30. J. D. Swartz, *Charles XII* (1706), painting.
Photo: Statens Konstmuseer, Stockholm.

violence, which was not infrequent in civilian life. Finally, it displayed the soldier's personal commitment to the monarch. In these respects, the uniform signified not so much "docility" as participation (willing or not) in a state that compensated its servants with certain freedoms and the outward trappings of a higher worldly standing.

The disciplining of the body should not be exaggerated. The rational state did not aspire to some sort of totalitarian manipulation of the body; its efforts never remotely approached such a goal. It did not punish every criminal or lock up every beggar, and those who suffered at its hands were generally thought to benefit from such treatment. The "great confinement" was imagined as a labour of charity rather than a work of social engineering. Even the standardization of military dress was not wholly systematic, and it did not lead to complete physical uniformity; soldiers could still tilt their hats jauntily, grow moustaches, or keep buttons undone, giving themselves an air of individuality. Watteau's paintings of French infantrymen illustrate this point—the figures certainly do not all look alike. Still, it has to be recognized that no state before the late seventeenth century had been able to interfere so broadly, or at so many conjunctures, with the human body.

The attentions of the state were mostly applied to the bodies of deviants, the poor, and the lower classes. For those in the elite, the human physique was subjected to rules of civility or good manners, and also to the attentions of medical science. Civility was a means of distinction, not a coherent intellectual system. At certain times it treated the body as base and unpleasant, at others, as desirable and titillating. In any case, it saw the body as worldly and natural, not as the terrain of self-purification or of inner moral struggles. This tied in with contemporary trends in medicine. Cartesianism even led some thinkers, as Thomas Laqueur has shown, towards a mechanical or "biological" understanding of sexuality. What such changes amounted to was a decline of Christian conceptions of the body as the indispensable vehicle of the soul and the receptacle of a possible human sacrality. For most educated people, spirituality had become a thing of the mind, not of the body. The properties of the human frame could be examined scientifically, but they did not directly manifest the divine Being. Instead, they were the fruits of a benign and universal nature.[100]

By the early 1700s philosophers had begun to address the problem of replacing the body's religious significance with conventions of natural morality that would unite ethical principles and aesthetic judgments. In England the third earl of Shaftesbury argued for applying the same rules "in the mental or moral subjects as in the ordinary bodies or common subjects of sense." For him both beauty and rational virtue were the products of regularity. Conversely, Shaftesbury condemned religious enthusiasm as an irregularity in the body politic, "mental eruptions" that might "set all nature in an uproar." His polite philosophy had particular appeal to aristocratic Whigs, who were supporters of the rational state and critics of the physical sacrality of both kings and priests.[101] Shaftesbury did not, however, provide a satisfactory solution to the problem of natural ethics, which would continue to preoccupy educated minds throughout the century.

The naturalized body had wide-ranging consequences for European culture. Most of them belong to the period after 1715, but even in the early days of the French Regency we can note a growing fascination in court circles with natural shapes and sensuous images. Out of these would develop the rococo style, which spread rapidly throughout Europe. On a more mundane level, emphasis on the natural body encouraged the suppression of offensive odours and the pursuit of hygiene, which had not been matters of great concern to earlier generations. "At the court of Louis XV," Alain Corbin has noted, "etiquette prescribed the use of a different perfume every day." Courtiers became obsessed by rules of bodily decorum that pertained to physical relations among themselves and had little to do with veneration of the king's person. Meanwhile, sumptuary laws fell into abeyance as the display of variety and luxury in costume became an increasingly important "embodiment" of social distinction.[102]

Another cultural offshoot of the naturalized body was pornography, in both written and graphic forms. The unifying theme of pornography was that sexual urges were natural and could not be resisted. Treatises making this point proliferated in France during the last years of Louis XIV's reign, some of them with quite bizarre plots, like the often reprinted *Zombie of Great Peru*. The court aristocracy in the waning years of the Grand Monarque was thought to be saturated with licentiousness, and the period was a favourite setting for later pornographers, among them the marquis de Sade in his *120 Days of Sodom*. The reputation of the regency was worse; even the regent's mother complained of how the elite "find their only comfort in debauchery and distractions." Pornographic writers and artists did not seek to pillory such conduct. Rather, by associating it with elite behaviour, they were able to suggest that their philosophy was not entirely subversive; it could claim to uphold natural order, in the form of a hierarchy of sexual behaviour, with male aristocrats at its peak. Still, pornography did nothing to enhance the moral authority of kings. In an early and relatively restrained example—a life of Louis XIV's mistress, Louise de la Vallière, published at Cologne in 1685—the monarch's nature is depicted as simply human. "Men are always men," the author asserts, "and Kings are no more exempt than others from the tyranny of the passions."[103]

It was difficult to reconcile the naturalized body with the sacred body of the king. We may wonder, therefore, whether changes in conceptualizing the body in the early eighteenth century led towards what some historians have called desacralization.[104] It should be pointed out at once that no king anywhere in Europe wanted to cast off an iota of sacred authority before the eyes of his subjects; but this does not mean that sacrality was always essential to publicity. By 1715, royal funeral ceremonies—not just in France but in most European kingdoms—represented the king's body more as a human object than a divine one. This was reflected, for example, in the impressive but relatively simple catafalque designed by Fischer von Erlach for the funeral of Joseph I in 1711, installed in St. Stephen's Cathedral. The coffin was surmounted by an obelisk with the emperor's bust on it, surrounded by classical figures. In proclaiming the worldly reputation of the monarch rather than his piety or holiness, Joseph's catafalque contrasted with the funeral monuments of previous Habsburg rulers.[105]

As for the coronation, it remained a necessary ritual everywhere in Europe, but the sacred legitimation it bestowed was less essential to monarchies that invested natural authority in the king from the moment of his accession. Thus, while Charles II's crowning in 1661 was the most splendid of such occasions in England for a century and a half, it did not mark the beginning of his kingship. His brother's consecration rite was altered to suit a Catholic monarch, suggesting that the procedure was not inviolable. After the Glorious Revolution, political circumstances further limited the impact of the coronation. The hereditary legitimacy of English kings was now questionable, and their right to the throne rested on statutory law. The crowning ceremony therefore became more of a confirmation of constitutional propriety than a sacralization. Legitimists might even interpret it as a provocation; George I's coronation day was marred by anti-Hanoverian riots throughout England. The French coronation remained splendid, but it seems that the attention of its audience was no longer fixed on its spiritual elements. The diarist Barbier's account of the *sacre* of Louis XV in 1722, for example, dwells on it mainly as an expensive festival. He tells us that the diamond in the centre of the crown, as big as a pigeon's egg, was called "the *millionaire*" and that the camp built around Rheims to accommodate visitors did not fill up, because people thought it would be too crowded. Nowhere does he convey a sense of religious awe. Like many other anxious subjects, Barbier was more interested in the young king's natural body than in his sacredness—after all, if he died suddenly, the hated regent would claim the crown. Thus, we find Barbier describing the monarch as "very delicate" when he danced in a theatrical ballet and as "looking poorly and very pale" at a Te Deum just before the coronation.[106]

Sacredness had never counted for much among the territorial rulers of the Holy Roman Empire. Four of them became kings in this period: Victor Amadeus of Piedmont-Savoy, who was (briefly) king of Sicily; Augustus the Strong, Elector of Saxony and king of Poland-Lithuania; Frederick I, Elector of Brandenburg and king in Prussia; and George I, Elector of Hanover and king of Great Britain.[107] None of them projected much sense of personal divinity. Augustus was enamoured of big public festivals, but they were connected with secular themes like royal birthdays or the hunting season rather than with sacred rituals. Frederick was so indifferent to conventional marks of sacrality as to anoint himself with oil at his coronation, "since no one but he could confer on the Consecrator the power to anoint him."[108] George I disliked ceremony, according to his cousin Madame Palatine, who said of him that "he would have a better time at his *Göhrde* [hunting lodge] than in all his splendor in England." He refused to perform the Royal Touch, the ultimate expression of the king's sacred body, although it had been used—admittedly, without much fanfare—by his predecessor Queen Anne. The ceremony of the touch was kept in the church's liturgy for some time after 1715, indicating a reluctance to tamper with it, but the practice was never revived.[109]

Philip V of Spain and Peter I of Russia cultivated an air of informality rather than sacrality. The cloying religious ceremonialism of the Habsburg court was toned down and at times wholly discarded by Philip. When the duc de Saint-Simon visited Madrid on an embassy in 1721 and 1722, he was delighted by the openness of the royal couple, to whom he easily gained access. Queen Elisabeth Farnese, whose wit and intelligence he greatly admired, even told him, "with an air of kindness, that there should no longer be hours set for me, or etiquette." Soon after, he was received by Their Majesties very early in the morning, while they lay in bed—"the king, almost wholly lying down on pillows, with a little bed-jacket of white satin, the queen sitting up, a piece of tapestry-work in her hand." It is hard to imagine Philip IV—or, for that matter, Louis XIV—conceding such a privilege to anyone. Saint-Simon exaggerated in concluding "that there remained no vestige of the former etiquettes of this court," but his account makes it clear that the purifying rituals of Philip IV's time had been largely forgotten.[110]

Philip V's palace at La Granja de San Ildefonso displayed the new emphasis on domesticity and nature. In deliberate contrast to the nearby Escorial, the design of San Ildefonso did not follow a religious blueprint. Neither was it intended to provide a Versailles-like setting for the king's sacred body. Its model was Marly, the "cottage" where Louis XIV went to relax in semi-privacy. At San Ildefonso, the private life of the Spanish king and queen became their public image. They resided there as a couple. Their apartments were not separated, as was the case in most royal residences. They enjoyed strolling in the gardens full of magnificent fountains, with the surrounding *sierra* providing an overwhelming backdrop of "hideous beauty" (in Saint-Simon's words). San Ildefonso expressed a sense of natural harmony, reflected in the conjugal bliss of the royal pair as well as in the easy dominance of the king over his mountainous domain.[111]

For Peter I, informality could be achieved only through a disruptive break with the Orthodox past. As Michael Cherniavsky has shown, Peter rejected the image of "saint-prince" promulgated by his ancestors. Instead, he liked to be represented as naturally superior to others, and after Poltava he especially enjoyed the role of a great general. He tried to introduce western concepts of natural social relations at his court. He shocked many courtiers by allowing women to dine and dance in his presence. His second marriage in 1712, to the Lithuanian peasant Catherine Skavronka, took place in an irregular ceremony, without a priest. It was publicly celebrated with relatively informal rituals in which the theme of natural love was prominent. In raising the profile of his wife, Peter may have intended to deprecate the quasi-religious image of "Mother Russia," to whom the sovereign was symbolically wed in the popular imagination.[112]

Such behaviour seems to have aroused ambivalent sentiments in the tsar himself. Did they strengthen his power, or debase it? Was nature an acceptable foundation for an Orthodox monarchy? The internal tension created by such questions helps to explain the strange rituals of desecration acted out in private by the "Most Drunken Council," a society consisting of Peter and his intimate male friends. The Austrian secretary recorded with

31. Alexei Zubov, *The Wedding of Peter I and Catherine Alekseevna* (1712), etching.

Photo: State Pushkin Museum, Moscow, courtesy of Professor Richard Wortman.

disgust how "a sham Patriarch and a complete set of scenic clergy dedi-cated to Bacchus, with solemn festivities, the palace which was built at the tsar's expense." The figure of Bacchus wore a tin bishop's mitre but was otherwise naked; and the sign of the cross was "held up to mockery." The revellers even made fun of the Palm Sunday procession by leading a sham patriarch on a camel down to a wine cellar.[113] These antics may remind us of the freethinking insobriety of the regent Philippe d'Orléans's dinner parties. Both were anxious, furtive responses to a cultural milieu in which nature could not yet openly proclaim her dominion over the sacred. A more severe neurosis underlay the natural paradise of San Ildefonso, where the outward impression of conjugal bliss disguised King Philip's obsession with daily sexual intercourse, and his equally frequent visits to the confessional.

Nature could never fully absorb a royal body that had been shaped for sacrality. Even in the centuries after 1715 the shade of the king's sacred body continued to flit uneasily behind the images of natural rulership. In the age of democracy and mass publicity, a new kind of sanctity began to assert itself, based not so much on resemblance to the divine as on a close personal identification with the representative human characteristics of a royal figure. This sentiment enhanced Emperor Franz Josef's grand-fatherly image, as well as Queen Victoria's chosen role as "widow of Windsor." The sense of mass personal identification was not restricted to monarchs, however; in recent years, for example, it was bestowed upon Diana, Princess of Wales. Her royal status was derived from marriage, not from birth, and she was eventually deprived of it. To her legions of ad-mirers, however, she continued to represent a wholly natural royal per-sona, full of faults and weaknesses, in which they could readily see them-selves. Her body, both adored and pitied, was the sign of this ambiguous power. The outburst of grief that accompanied her funeral in Westmin-ster Abbey may be compared to the groans of the crowd that witnessed Charles I's execution at the Banqueting House a few hundred yards away. In both cases, a deeply emotional involvement arose out of sympathy with an ideal representative of the self. In the death of Charles I, however, his horrified subjects witnessed a desecration of the supreme earthly symbol of sacrality. Princess Diana's admirers, on the other hand, mourned her natu-ral qualities, which were widely interpreted as saintly but seemed to owe nothing to divine appointment. Sacredness was now a manifestation of popularity, not of God. Humanity had become its own object of veneration.

# CHAPTER SEVEN

# Conclusion

IMAGINE THREE KINGS ON HORSEBACK. The first is Philip IV of Spain, in the famous equestrian portrait by Velázquez that once decorated the Hall of Realms at the Palace of the Buen Retiro. Horse and rider are frozen in harmony, their bodies under absolute control, as they perform a perfect *levade*, an exercise right out of a riding manual. The king is shown in armour, but the idealized landscape gives no hint of real battles. Jonathan Brown has noted how Velázquez turns "fact into symbol" in this work by making a realistic portrait into an icon of rulership and Neostoic self-discipline. In its motionlessness, in its lack of referents beyond the figure itself, in its evocation of a light shining on the king's face that comes direct from God, Velázquez's homage to Philip IV is at once simple yet laden with mystery.[1]

Our second king is Louis XIV, nephew and son-in-law of Philip IV, in the marble relief by Antoine Coysevox that still decorates the Salon de la

---

32. Diego Velázquez, *Philip IV on Horseback* (1628–29), painting.
Photo: Museo nacional del Prado, Madrid.

33. Antoine Coysevox, *Equestrian Portrait of Louis XIV* (1681),
marble relief. Palace of Versailles.
Photo: Réunion des musées nationaux, Paris.

Guerre at the Palace of Versailles. Dressed as Alexander the Great, the Grand Monarque stares out of the relief with a look of complete composure, while his horse charges straight ahead in a stylized gallop, trampling over royal enemies. Louis seems to be directing his steed by will alone. In the sky above him, a female figure of Glory carries a crown down from the clouds. Coysevox's relief is not at all mysterious. It is presented not as a collection of symbolic clues but as an historical text adorned with signs as clear and unmistakable as the king's majestic expression. Louis represents himself, the greatest of monarchs; he incarnates the personal sovereignty of a Roman emperor, not a Christian ruler. His horse, however, seems worried and skittish. Its mane waves in the wind, its nostrils flare, and its head twists; we might think that it is apprehensive about charging into battle, that it fears the destiny into which the king is leading it.[2]

More than half a century later, almost exactly the same composition would reappear in an equestrian portrait of our third king: Philip V of Spain, grandson of Louis XIV and great-grandson of Philip IV. This time, the turning rider, agitated horse, and far-off battle were painted by Jean Ranc, a French-born court artist. For a royal portrait, it is a highly realistic scene; Ranc did not even flinch from including smoke and uniformed soldiers in his canvas. The only incongruously mythical note is the winged figure who flies above the royal head. The king himself wears contemporary military costume. He has a commanding presence, but he does not appear to symbolize anything beyond his own natural rulership, which claims to be neither typological nor definitive, neither Christian nor classical. His horse is clearly scared and perhaps a little out of control. Ranc's painting, rescued from a devastating fire at the Alcázar Palace in 1735, now hangs in the Prado Museum, not far from Velázquez's depiction of Philip IV, with whose spare and impassive poise it contrasts so markedly.[3]

Let us draw attention to a single point: the change in royal equestrian portraiture from a perfectly aligned levade, trot, or rear to a stance in which the body was turned and the horse agitated. This was not a stylistic triviality. It had a political significance for contemporary observers. "How well a king looks on horseback!" wrote a supporter of Philip V. "Whoever knows how to govern an animal, also will know how to govern a rational wit."[4] As Walter Liedtke has shown in a careful study of the theme, representations of the king on horseback were meant to demonstrate the ability

34. Jean Ranc, *Philip V on Horseback* (c. 1730), painting.
Photo: Museo nacional del Prado, Madrid.

to rule, with the horse standing for the kingdom or people. The poses were usually derived from Italian Renaissance models, which in turn were interpretations of classical originals. Thus, they implied an imperial Roman heritage, associated with Marcus Aurelius or Constantine. They may also have evoked the image of a Christian knight, claiming mastery over himself. The horse could be seen as the body, the rider as its soul. Together, the two comprised an integrated self. In all these connotations, the horse was supposed to be inseparable from its rider. It was fixed to the king by ties of possession, dominance, and identity. As in Velázquez's painting, the two faced in the same direction and moved as if they were one. There was, of course, never any question that the steed would throw its lord off its back.[5]

Before the eighteenth century the turned rider and agitated horse were not widely acceptable ways of representing rulership. Although ministers or noblemen might be shown exercising less than perfect form in directing their steeds, kings might not. The statues on horseback of Philip III, Philip IV, and Louis XIII by Pietro Tacca and of Charles I by Hubert Le Sueur illustrated the precise discipline of the riding schools, as did engravings of the equestrian carrousels held by Louis XIV in 1662, by Leopold I in 1667, and by Charles XI in 1672. Even prints of monarchs like Henry IV and Rudolf II riding furiously into battle always showed horse and rider in synchronized movement.[6] All of these images were meant to impress the public with the unbreakable unity and political fixity of king and people. While around them things might change and battles might rage, the monarch and his equine subject remained in a state of harmonious equilibrium and immobility.

Then came Bernini's statue of Louis XIV, executed between 1671 and 1677 but not delivered until 1685 (ill.27). It was commissioned by Colbert, who wanted it to resemble the sculptor's recent statue of Constantine's vision of the cross. In that startling work of baroque confessional art, the first Christian emperor looks up in rapture at the unseen cross, while his scared horse averts its eyes from the sight. It is a theatrical scene, depicting a crucial moment of religious and political transformation. Bernini's Constantine suggests that the Christian monarch must experience direct revelation from the Almighty, a spiritual state that will exalt him above his secular imperium, symbolized by the horse. Yet when asked to, the artist refused to show Louis XIV in this pose. He told Colbert that his

35. Giovanni-Lorenzo Bernini, *Equestrian Statue of Constantine* (1670). Vatican.
Photo: Fratelli Alinari, Florence.

statue of the king would be quite different, because it represented Louis "in an attitude of majesty, and of command." In other words, it was a depiction of sovereignty rather than Christian kingship. In the finished work, the classical figure of the rider is taken straight out of the familiar iconography of the Grand Monarque — he might have been painted by Le Brun. Only the horse remained the same as in the Constantine statue. In all of Bernini's sketches and models, as well as in the final version, Louis's horse seems to be out of control, turning its head in fright, just like the Christian emperor's. Was the artist trying to imply that King Louis was similarly leading his people towards some tremendous change that they were unable to understand?

The art historian Rudolf Wittkower suggested that Bernini's Louis was meant to be riding the mythological winged horse Pegasus up the "mountain of Virtue." It was a relatively obscure classical allusion, without a clear Christian relevance. The final version of the horse, moreover, has no wings. It seems as though the king has flown himself up the mountain, fulfilling through his dynamic will a destiny that the horse fears. Whatever meaning this perplexing work may have conveyed, the king did not like it. When he first saw the statue at Versailles, he found it "so badly done that he resolved not only to remove it from there, but even to have it broken up." Eventually he had it altered so as to depict the suicide of the Roman patriot Marcus Curtius—a distinctly non-Christian theme. Soon after, when he began to commission equestrian statues to decorate public squares throughout his kingdom, Louis chose works in which the horse was under his complete domination. After all, he wanted to proclaim his sovereignty as a stabilizing force, not as a kind of protean energy that would carry France towards an uncertain future.[7]

Louis's attitude was typical. No monarch in seventeenth-century Europe wanted to be thought of as an innovator, a risk taker, a daring adventurer. In spite of all their bold projects and reforms, they still aimed at preserving the harmony that was summed up in riding-school portraits of royal horsemen. They did not want to be seen astride Pegasus. Yet Bernini's statue was already exerting a strong influence over other artists long before it arrived at Versailles. Coysevox's relief owed something to it. Even Le Brun made a sketch for an equestrian monument similar to Bernini's, in which King Louis rides an agitated horse on top of a rock.[8] The project was never realized, but it shows that the imagination of the quintessential royal artist—and of Colbert, the quintessential royal minister—did not always march precisely in step with the more cautious mind of their master.

By the 1730s Jean Ranc did not have to hide what he owed to Bernini. His patron, Philip V, had used his sovereignty to shake Spain from top to bottom, abolishing the fueros, insulting the pope, unsettling the old Habsburg certainties, and creating the framework of a fiscal-military state. In different ways, similar things had been attempted by other monarchs on agitated horses: by William III of England, whom Godfrey Kneller painted in a turning pose on a nervous grey charger; by Charles XII of Sweden, whose depictions on dashing steeds appeared on everything from popular prints to tobacco-box lids; by Frederick I of Prussia, who commissioned the sculptor Andreas Schlüter to produce a jaunty equestrian monument to his father, the Great Elector; by the emperor Joseph I, often shown as driving a chariot pulled by furious horses; by Peter I of Russia, who would be commemorated at St. Petersburg by the sculptor Falconet in the most dramatic of all equestrian statues drawn out of Bernini's magnificent failure. None of these monarchs, to be sure, would have described his government in secular terms; none would have welcomed the idea that he was anything other than a Christian ruler. Yet all of them had abandoned the path of a strictly confessional, godly kingship. As Bernini seems to have realized in creating his different images of Constantine and of Louis XIV, monarchy in the late seventeenth century was flying away from grace and revelation, towards a rational ideal of virtue.

It had been pushed in that direction not by a sceptical reaction to religion among a jaded elite but by the pressure of changing religious beliefs, emanating from broadly-based confessional groups. The acquiescence of these groups was necessary for rulers to assert control over the Christian self, an outcome that was not achieved until Europe had passed through a series of unsettling ideological crises. Rational authority after 1660 was therefore constructed on a confessional basis; but it soon began to place state interests above religious unity and orthodoxy. At the same time, the cultural foundation of rulership was changed, from personal sacrality to the representation of collective will. Through these moves the devout were gradually elbowed towards the fringes of the state. Of course, they resented these developments, but their resistance to them became formal and domesticated. Eventually, devout opposition to the state would either be absorbed within an acceptable public sphere of political discourse or would take increasingly desperate forms on the margins of respectable society.

The Christian self was being transformed into the enlightened self. While the Augustinian and ascetic models of selfhood survived in western and eastern Europe as the basis of private discipline, their public manifestations were gradually submerged in the triumphant rhetoric of sovereignty and the state. The corpus mysticum was lost; millenarianism became a sign of dissidence or madness; representative personhood was tainted by rebellion; and the internal conscience was obliged to reconcile itself to the rational course of public affairs. Although every European polity retained an attachment to religion, the Christian self as constructed by Augustine or by Maximus Confessor would become increasingly irrelevant to the workings of governance.

This did not mean an absolute surrender of religious autonomy or the unbridled imposition of state discipline over the self. Rather, it resulted in a duality and unfixedness within the European concept of self that has lasted to the present. The origins of that duality can be observed in the ambivalence that runs through the journal of Alexandre Dubois, *curé* of Rumegies. Sympathetic to a vague Jansenism that he dared not even name, he was nonetheless hostile to anything that disturbed the peace of the church. In politics, although he was imbued with the spirit of local patriotism, he remained firmly loyal to the king of France. He was eager to lend clerical sanction to state policy whenever he could, as when he and other priests paraded with relics of St. Amand to celebrate the proclamation of the treaty of Ryswick. Yet he was enough of a local patriot to praise "the religion of the Walloons, which is the most regular and the most consistent with the spirit of Jesus Christ, chief of the true Church."[9]

As for the villagers to whom Dubois ministered, they had not been fully transformed from Christian subjects into citizens by 1715. Apart from tax collectors, they were little troubled by the agents of the state. They looked to their bishop as a local protector in the same way villagers elsewhere might look to a great lord or to provincial Estates. Yet the ideological groundwork for a metamorphosis in self-identity had taken shape, even in Rumegies. Composite loyalties and otherworldly attachments were being undermined; the sacred aura of kingship and of the human body had been palpably diminished; local authorities had been made into the instruments of unity within the state. The culmination of these changes lies outside the scope of this book, but the consciousness of every European was ultimately reoriented. The descendants of Father Dubois's parishioners would be expected to feel an internal commitment to a sovereign and unified French state, governing a distinct public sphere, while regulating beliefs and behaviours that were allowed to belong to private life. Through the eighteenth century and beyond, mind and body would be subjected, however unevenly and imperfectly, to ever more intrusive disciplines.

Without doubt, this was an alienating and disruptive process, marked by war, imperial expansion, and the suppression of popular beliefs, all carried out under the supposedly benign aegis of rational values. Without doubt it can be connected to later revolutionary terrors and the imposition of a rigid, state-defined nationalism. Still, we should not spend too much time mourning "the world we have lost," as if the manners of Christian Europe were somehow more gentle, its methods more humane. It should not be forgotten that the rise of the rational state also made it less likely that heretics would be tortured, witches burned, Jews massacred, the human body subjected to unspeakable pain for the sake of preserving the unity of the corpus mysticum. The return to such horrors in twentieth-century Europe—even at century's end, as in Bosnia—can be ascribed not to the effects of rationalism but to the revival of quasi-confessional concepts of nation or people, and their combination with the efficient mechanical and scientific apparatus of the state.

The transformation of the Christian self and the rise of the rational state were morally complex phenomena; they were not simply "good" or "bad" for everyone in equal measure. They were experienced variously within different social groups—as we see, for example, among educated women. In 1686 the teenaged English poet Sarah Fyge affirmed how " 'tis observed in all Religions, that Women are the truest Devotionists, and the most Pious, and more Heavenly than those who pretend to be the most perfect and rational Creatures." Did godly women have much to gain from military states that excluded them from all political participation and re-defined their subordination in natural terms? Nevertheless, some female writers, like Mme. de Scudéry, were already trying to turn reason in favour of their gender by espousing rational programmes of education for women. Others bitterly noted how the female Christian self was so often denounced as impure or demoted to a lower spiritual rank by the ministers of religion. In her maturity, even Sarah Egerton, formerly Fyge, wrote with scorn of how women had been reduced to "Slaves" by a "Tyrant Custom" sanctioned by "Priests of old."[10]

In terms of class relations as well, the balance sheet of the rational state was mixed. The poor and unskilled, both male and female, would be re-labelled by the state; once called "members in Christ," they were stamped as the products of social decay. They were removed from the inadequate shelter of religious charity and regimented into systems of institutional incarceration. Just above them in status, skilled artisans and shopkeepers were threatened by the encroachments of the state on custom and tradition. They became the staunchest defenders of national sentiments, the most fervent admirers of representative persons from Masaniello to the Stuart Pretender. Lesser landowners and peasants also opposed the centralizing tendencies of sovereign authority, and they felt excluded by a politics of interest. Yet the rational state would eventually bring distinct social and economic gains to all of these groups. Peasants in eighteenth-century France, for instance, began to look to the agencies of central government for support against landlords, as they had done for some time in the Habsburg Erblande.[11] The state could promise to everyone the best of all possible worlds, at least according to the rational calculus of human progress which its defenders promoted, and which they have bequeathed to us today. Of course, few in the early eighteenth century could have foreseen the future benefits of increased access to education, the growth of commercialism, and more salubrious prisons.

Was the rational state an indicator of a fundamental socio-economic shift? Perry Anderson has argued that "beneath its veneer this culture was more deeply penetrated than ever before by the ideas of the ascendant bourgeoisie."[12] It seems at first unlikely that such a level of underlying socio-economic similarity could be found in states as diverse as the Habsburg Erblande and England. In most cases, moreover, the state continued to rely on long-established aristocratic officials, not on newly recruited middle-class bureaucrats. Nevertheless, certain socially ambitious groups profited from the rational state throughout Europe: namely, military contractors and investors in public credit, who were drawn from the mercantile classes and from commercially minded elements in the landed elite. They were the main beneficiaries of higher expenditure on armaments and provisions, and it was they who backed government financial schemes like the *Wiener Stadtbank* and the Bank of England. They became the most convinced proponents of natural reason. For them, the state resembled a joint-stock company in which they held an individual interest. Thus, as Perry Anderson suggested, the expanding authority of European monarchy brought with it the rise of a capitalist mentality.

Even for those who most clearly profited from it, however, the rational state could be morally and religiously unsettling. Although he was a life-long courtier, the duc de Saint-Simon struggled at the outset of his memoirs with the vexing question of whether a Christian was permitted to write the profane history of states, which were so full of wicked examples. In the end, giving in to the rationalism by which he was able to justify all the compromises of his life, Saint-Simon rejected scruples that "so wound good sense and natural reason," and he began to chronicle the reign of Louis XIV.[13]

A different sort of moral dilemma was faced in 1694 by the English merchant and Dissenter Samuel Jeake the younger, who lived at Rye in Sussex. He suffered deep misgivings over whether he should subscribe to a government-run lottery, because like many of the godly he considered lotteries to be sinful. At last, after much deliberation, he was satisfied that it was "necessary for the support of the Government in the War against France" and "concluded this might be lawfull." It was a hard decision for a puritan conscience, no matter how steeped in profit-making it may have been.[14] For Jeake, as for Saint-Simon, surrender to a self-interested, natural reason was never easily purchased; it always demanded a spiritual price.

The moral account book of the self was not closed after 1715; even today debits and credits continue to stack up in the minds of responsible Europeans. By the mid-eighteenth century, however, the calculus of self-worth for many educated people was no longer primarily confessional. When Weipart Ludwig von Fabrice, counsellor to the Elector of Hanover and a devout Lutheran, recorded the birth of his son in 1683, he wrote in effusive German of how "the Almighty God in all mercy happily delivered my dear wife once more of her wifely burden." The child was baptized on the same day "and thereby was incorporated in the covenant of grace with his Redeemer Jesus Christ." Significantly, when the son, Friedrich Ernst von Fabrice, wrote his own memoirs fifty years later, he began them with a cursory "In N[omine] D[ei]!" before explaining bluntly that "I was born in Celle." He penned these words in French, the language of international reason. As the younger Fabrice recounted it, his life as a soldier and courtier contained no episodes of personal religious significance. If he is a representative example, then the centrality of Christian grace in defining the self had been almost entirely lost in only one generation.[15]

Finally, what has our discussion revealed about the theoretical configurations of power proposed by Weber, Marx, Elias, and Foucault? It has argued in favour of the dynamic role of religious and political ideals in constructing authority in early modern Europe. It has suggested that power was manifested through strategies of political action and publicity that involved wide segments of the population, not simply through the imposition of hegemonic concepts by an elite. No kind of cultural author-ity—whether over the body, the self, the state, the dictionary, or the uni-verse—can be understood as an unproblematic or unchallengeable totality. Within every type of dominance exist buried remnants of the past that refuse to be obliterated. They ensure that goals cannot be fulfilled, conflicts cannot be resolved, claims cannot be completely substantiated. The result is not a smoothly managed transition from one all-encompassing *episteme* to another but a series of traumatic lurches towards an idealized harmony that may never be achieved. Along the way, opportunities can arise for choosing a different direction, although to take them may compromise the overriding purpose of the journey.

Reformed Christians of the sixteenth and seventeenth centuries were sorely distressed by the bumpy and tortuous political road they were obliged to travel; but they rarely threw off their royal riders, because they could see no other way to maintain order within the church, the polity, and the self. Hoping, in St. Peter's words, to protect their fellowship, fear God, and honour the king, they flew up the mountain of Virtue, to deliver themselves not into the arms of the shining bridegroom Christ but into the mechanical embrace of the artificial man, the rational state. It was a journey in which Christian Europe died and enlightened Europe was born, already governed by its own dogmas, already full of an expansive energy and an overweening arrogance. Whether we admire or deprecate that headstrong Pegasus, the enlightened self, we should not fail to recognize that through its flight some part of you and me and everyone was carried away from the dream of heaven and into the harsh, uncertain light of the world.

# Notes

## Chapter One: Introduction

1. The painting is discussed in Harold E. Wethey, *El Greco and His School*, 2 vols. (Princeton, 1962), vol. 2, pp. 74–76.

2. Among them, Perry Anderson, *Lineages of the Absolutist State* (London and New York, 1974, 1989); J. H. Shennan, *The Origins of the Modern European State, 1450–1725* (London, 1974); J. H. Shennan, *Liberty and Order in Early Modern Europe: The Subject and the State, 1650–1800* (London, 1986); Charles Tilly, ed., *The Formation of National States in Western Europe* (Princeton, 1975); Kenneth H. F. Dyson, *The State Tradition in Western Europe: A Study of an Idea and Institution* (New York, 1980); Hendrik Spruyt, *The Sovereign State and Its Competitors: An Analysis of Systems Change* (Princeton, 1994). National studies include Philip Corrigan and Derek Sayer, *The Great Arch: English State Formation as Cultural Revolution* (Oxford, 1985); Stephen L. Collins, *From Divine Cosmos to Sovereign State: An Intellectual History of Consciousness and the Idea of Order in Renaissance England* (New York, 1989); Michèle Fogel, *L'état dans la France moderne de la fin du XVe au milieu du XVIIIe siècle* (Paris, 1992); James B. Collins, *The State in Early Modern France* (Cambridge, 1995); Marc Raeff, *Understanding Imperial Russia: State and Society in the Old Regime*, trans. A. Goldhammer (New York, 1984).

3. For example, Quentin Skinner, *The Foundations of Modern Political Thought*, 2 vols. (Cambridge, 1978); J. G. A. Pocock, *The Machiavellian Moment: Florentine Political Thought and the Atlantic Republican Tradition* (Princeton, 1975); Richard Tuck, *Philosophy and Government, 1572–1651* (Cambridge, 1993).

4. Norbert Elias, *The Germans: Power Struggles and the Development of Habitus in the Nineteenth and Twentieth Centuries*, ed. Michael Schröter, trans. Eric Dunning and Stephen Mennell (New York, 1996), pp. ix, 1–20; Pierre Bourdieu, *Distinction: A Social Critique of the Judgement of Taste*, trans. Richard Nice (Cambridge, Mass., 1984); Michel de Certeau, *The Practice of Everyday Life*, trans. Steven Rendall (Berkeley, 1984), p. 59.

5. For example, see Ralph E. Giesey, "Models of Rulership in French Royal Ceremonial," in Sean Wilentz, ed., *Rites of Power: Symbolism, Ritual, and Politics since the Middle Ages* (Philadelphia, 1985), pp. 41–64, and David Cannadine, "Introduction: Divine Rights of Kings," in David Cannadine and Simon Price, eds., *Rituals of Royalty: Power and Ceremonial in Traditional Societies* (Cambridge, 1987), pp. 1–19.

6. A. M. Hocart, *Kingship* (London, 1927, 1969), and his *Kings and Councillors*, ed.

Rodney Needham (Chicago, 1936, 1970); Clifford Geertz, *Negara: The Theater-State in Nineteenth-Century Bali* (Princeton, 1980), esp. pp. 4–19, 98–120, and his "Centers, Kings, and Charisma: Reflections on the Symbolics of Power," in Wilentz, ed., *Rites of Power*, pp. 13–38.

7. For different approaches, see Roger Chartier, *Cultural History: Between Practices and Representations*, trans. Lydia Cochrane (Ithaca, N.Y., 1988), pp. 1–16; Clifford Geertz, "Thick Description: Toward an Interpretive Theory of Culture," in *The Interpretation of Cultures* (New York, 1973), pp. 3–30.

8. J. G. A. Frazer, *Lectures on the Early History of Kingship* (London, 1905); Hocart, *Kingship*, p. 7. For similar interpretations, all indebted to Frazer, see Margaret Murray's unconvincing *The Divine Right of Kings* (London, 1960); Harold Nicolson, *Monarchy* (London, 1962); and *The Sacral Kingship: Contributions to the Central Theme of the VIIIth International Congress for the History of Religions (Rome, April 1955)* (Leiden, 1959).

9. Sigmund Freud, *Totem and Taboo and Other Works*, in James Strachey and Anna Freud, eds., *The Standard Edition of the Complete Psychological Works of Sigmund Freud*, 24 vols. (New York, 1953–63), vol. 13, pp. 1–162.

10. Contrasting approaches to the issue are presented in Walter Hubatsch, *Das Zeitalter des Absolutismus, 1600–1789* (Brunswick, 1962), and John Miller, ed., *Absolutism in Seventeenth-Century Europe* (New York, 1990), pp. 1–20. See also two thoughtful essays in Ragnhild Hatton, ed., *Louis XIV and Absolutism* (London, 1976): E. H. Kossmann, "The Singularity of Absolutism," pp. 3–17, and G. Durand, "What Is Absolutism?" pp. 18–36.

11. J. G. A. Frazer, *The Golden Bough*, 3d ed., 13 vols. in 8 parts (reprint New York, 1990), pt. 1, vol. 2, p. 377; Keith Thomas, *Religion and the Decline of Magic* (New York, 1971), pp. 46–50, 153–54, 636–40. See also Bronislaw Malinowski, *"Magic, Science, and Religion" and Other Essays* (Glencoe, Ill., 1948), pp. 17–148, as well as the critique of Thomas and Malinowski in Stanley Jeyaraja Tambiah, *Magic, Science, Religion, and the Scope of Rationality* (Cambridge, 1990), pp. 20–24, 65–83.

12. G. W. F. Hegel, *Hegel's Philosophy of Right*, ed. and trans. T. M. Knox (Oxford, 1952, 1967), pp. 183, 185.

13. Max Weber, *Economy and Society: An Outline of Interpretive Sociology*, ed. Guenther Roth and Claus Wittich, 2 vols. (Berkeley, 1968, 1978), vol. 1, pp. 215–41; quotations on pp. 227, 231.

14. Ibid., p. 241.

15. Ibid., pp. 243–54. For further considerations on charisma, see Max Weber, *The Sociology of Religion*, trans. Ephraim Fischoff (New York, 1963), pp. 2–3.

16. For example, Otto Brunner, "Von Gottesgnadentum zum Monarchischen Prinzip: Der Weg der europäischen Monarchie seit dem hohen Mittelalter," in his *Neue Wege der Verfassung- und Sozialgeschichte*, 2d. ed. (Göttingen, 1956, 1968), pp. 160–86; Reinhard Bendix, *Kings or People: Power and the Mandate to Rule* (Berkeley, 1978); Michael Mann, *The Sources of Political Power*, 2 vols. (Cambridge, 1986, 1993).

17. Several important essays by Hintze are translated in Felix Gilbert, ed., *The Historical Essays of Otto Hintze* (New York, 1975), especially "Calvinism and Raison d'Etat in Early Seventeenth-Century Brandenburg," pp. 88–154, "The Formation of States and Constitutional Development: A Study in History and Politics," pp. 157–77, and "Military

Organization and the Organization of the State," pp. 178–215 (quotations from pp. 201, 215); see also Otto Hintze, "Wesen und Wandlung eines modernen Staates," in *Gesammelte Abhandlungen zur Staats-, Rechts- und Sozialgeschichte Preussens*, vol. 1: *Staat und Verfassung*, ed. Gerhard Oestreich (Göttingen, 1962), pp. 470–96. A further discussion of the Machtstaat is in Otto Heinrich von der Gablentz, "Macht, Gestaltung und Recht: Die drei Wurzeln des politischen Denkens," in Hanns Hubert Hofmann, ed., *Die Entstehung des modernen souveränen Staates* (Cologne, 1967), pp. 52–72.

18. See Weber, *Sociology of Religion*, esp. ch. 10; also Max Weber, *The Protestant Ethic and the Spirit of Capitalism*, trans. Talcott Parsons (New York, 1958), pp. 13–31.

19. The quotations are from *The Civil War in France*, *The German Ideology*, and *Manifesto of the Communist Party*, as printed in Robert C. Tucker, ed., *The Marx-Engels Reader*, 2d. ed. (New York, 1978), pp. 629, 160–61, 475.

20. Anderson, *Lineages of the Absolutist State*, p. 40.

21. Friedrich Engels, *The Origin of the Family, Private Property, and the State*, ed. Michele Barrett (Harmondsworth, Middlesex, 1972, 1985), pp. 138–41, 161–62, 179–81, 188–90.

22. Norbert Elias, *The Civilizing Process*, trans. Edmund Jephcott, 2 vols. (New York, 1978, 1982), and *The Court Society*, trans. Edmund Jephcott (New York, 1983). Discussions of his work can be found in Chartier, *Cultural History*, pp. 71–94, and Giuliano Crifò, "Tra sociologia e storia: Le scelte culturali di Norbert Elias," in Sergio Bertelli and Giuliano Crifò, eds. *Rituale, ceremoniale, etichetta* (Milan, 1985), pp. 261–78.

23. Michel Foucault, *Madness and Civilization: A History of Insanity in the Age of Reason*, trans. Richard Howard (New York, 1965); *The Order of Things: An Archaeology of the Human Sciences* (New York, 1973); *Discipline and Punish: The Birth of the Prison*, trans. Alan Sheridan (New York, 1979); and *The History of Sexuality*, trans. Alan Sheridan, 3 vols. (New York, 1980–85). Michael Kelly, ed., *Critique and Power: Recasting the Foucault/Habermas Debate* (Cambridge, Mass., 1994), contains several valuable essays.

24. Emil Durkheim, *The Elementary Forms of the Religious Life*, trans. J. W. Swain (Glencoe, Ill., 1954), pp. 36–42, 409–24.

25. Mircea Eliade, *The Sacred and the Profane: The Nature of Religion*, trans. W. R. Trask (New York, 1959), pp. 11–12, 70; see also Bryan S. Rennie, *Reconstructing Eliade: Making Sense of Religion* (New York, 1996), pp. 7–33.

26. René Girard, *Violence and the Sacred*, trans. Patrick Gregory (Baltimore, 1972).

27. Emmanuel Levinas, "Difficult Freedom," in Seán Hand, ed., *The Levinas Reader* (Oxford, 1989, 1996), p. 260.

28. Jacques Derrida, *The Gift of Death*, trans. David Wills (Chicago, 1995), p. 2.

29. Julia Kristeva, *Pouvoir de l'horreur: Essai sur l'abjection* (Paris, 1980), p. 72; for a discussion, see Diane E. Prosser MacDonald, *Transgressive Corporeality: The Body, Poststructuralism, and the Theological Imagination* (Albany, N.Y., 1995), ch. 4.

30. See Elizabeth Alvilda Petroff, *Body and Soul: Essays on Medieval Women and Mysticism* (New York, 1994), and Caroline Walker Bynum, *Fragmentation and Redemption: Essays on Gender and the Human Body in Medieval Religion* (New York, 1991).

31. Worthy of note, however, are Alan Macfarlane, *The Origins of English Individualism* (Oxford, 1978); Charles Taylor, *Sources of the Self: The Making of Modern Identity* (Cambridge, 1989); Philippe Ariès and Georges Duby, gen. eds., *A History of Private Life*,

trans. Arthur Goldhammer, 5 vols. (Cambridge, Mass., 1987–90); Roy Porter, ed., *Rewriting the Self: Histories from the Renaissance to the Present* (London, 1997).

32. Marcel Mauss, "A Category of the Human Mind: The Notion of Person; The Notion of Self," trans. W. D. Halls, in Michael Carrithers, Steven Collins, and Steven Lukes, eds., *The Category of the Person: Anthropology, Philosophy, History* (Cambridge, 1985), pp. 1–25.

33. Erving Goffman, *The Presentation of Self in Everyday Life* (New York, 1959), esp. pp. 238–55. A similar approach, emphasizing verbal transactions, is found in Vincent Crapanzano, "On Self Characterization," in James W. Stigler, Richard A. Schweder, and Gilbert Herdt, eds., *Cultural Psychology: Essays on Comparative Human Development* (Cambridge, 1990), pp. 401–23.

34. Richard A. Schweder and Edmund J. Bourne, "Does the Concept of the Person Vary Cross-culturally?" in A. J. Marsella et al., eds., *Cultural Conceptions of Mental Health* (New York, 1982), pp. 158–99; Melford E. Spiro, "Is the Western Conception of the Self 'Peculiar' within the Context of the World Cultures?" *Ethos* 21, no. 2 (1993): 107–53. Clifford Geertz rejects the term *holism*, without providing a very convincing alternative, in "Person, Time, and Conduct in Bali," in his *Interpretation of Cultures*, pp. 360–411.

35. See Sigmund Freud, *Civilization and Its Discontents*, in Strachey and Freud, eds., *Complete Works of Freud*, vol. 21, pp. 57–145; Jacques Lacan, *Ecrits* (Paris, 1966), pp. 93–100.

36. Natalie Zemon Davis, *The Return of Martin Guerre* (Cambridge, Mass., 1983).

37. William of St. Thierry, "The Nature of the Body and Soul," trans. Benjamin Clark, in Bernard McGinn, ed., *Three Treatises on Man: A Cistercian Anthropology* (Kalamazoo, Mich., 1977), p. 141.

38. St. Augustine, *Concerning the City of God against the Pagans*, trans. Henry Bettenson (Harmondsworth, Middlesex, 1972), book 13, ch. 22, p. 535. See also Pierre Chaunu, *La mort à Paris: XVIe, XVIIe et XVIIIe siècles* (Paris, 1978), pp. 83–112; Peter Brown, *The Body and Society: Men, Women, and Sexual Renunciation in Early Christianity* (New York, 1988); Caroline Walker Bynum, *The Resurrection of the Body in Western Christianity, 200–1336* (New York, 1995), pp. 94–104.

39. Thomas Aquinas, *The Soul*, trans. John Patrick Rowan (St. Louis, 1951), pp. 26–27; Bynum, *Resurrection of the Body*, pp. 259–71.

40. Jaroslav Pelikan, *The Christian Tradition*, vol. 1: *The Spirit of Eastern Christendom (600–1700)* (Chicago, 1974), pp. 10–16, 249–50.

41. St. Augustine, *Confessions*, trans. R. S. Pine-Coffin (Harmondsworth, Middlesex, 1961), book 1, ch. 20, p. 40.

42. Jacques Le Goff, *The Birth of Purgatory*, trans. Arthur Goldhammer (Chicago, 1984); Bynum, *Resurrection of the Body*, pp. 280–83.

43. Emmanuel Le Roy Ladurie, *Montaillou: The Promised Land of Error*, trans. Barbara Bray (New York, 1979), pp. 306–26; Bynum, *Resurrection of the Body*, pp. 215–20.

44. For an overview, see Marty Newman Williams and Anne Echols, *Between Pit and Pedestal: Women in the Middle Ages* (Princeton, 1992), chs. 7–10.

45. Margery Kempe, *The Book of Margery Kempe*, ed. and trans. B. A. Windeatt (Harmondsworth, Middlesex, 1985, 1994), p. 38; Bynum, *Resurrection of the Body*, pp. 334–41.

46. Jacob Burckhardt, *The Civilization of the Renaissance in Italy*, trans. S. G. C. Middlemore (New York, 1960), part 2, pp. 120–44; Giovanni Pico della Mirandola, "Oration on the Dignity of Man," trans. Elizabeth Livermore Forbes, in Ernst Cassirer, Paul Oskar Kristeller, and John Herman Randall Jr., eds., *The Renaissance Philosophy of Man* (Chicago, 1948), p. 225.

47. Michel de Montaigne, "Of Presumption," in *The Complete Essays of Montaigne*, trans. Donald Frame (Stanford, 1965), p. 499.

48. Stephen Greenblatt, *Renaissance Self-Fashioning: From More to Shakespeare* (Chicago, 1980), p. 9.

49. See John Hale, *The Civilization of Europe in the Renaissance* (New York, 1993), chs. 8–9; Margaret L. King, *Women of the Renaissance* (Chicago, 1991), ch. 3.

50. Montaigne, "Apology for Raymond Sebond," in *Complete Essays*, p. 457. For a recent re-evaluation of the Renaissance self, see Peter Burke, "Representations of the Self from Petrarch to Descartes," in Porter, ed., *Rewriting the Self*, pp. 17–28.

51. Benvenuto Cellini, *The Autobiography of Benvenuto Cellini*, trans. George Bull (Harmondsworth, Middlesex, 1956), p. 224.

52. Thomas à Kempis, *The Imitation of Christ* (London, 1960), book 2, ch. 5, p. 56.

53. John Donne, "Holy Sonnets," no. 2, ll. 5–8, in Louis L. Martz, ed., *English Seventeenth-Century Verse*, vol. 1 (New York, 1963, 1969), p. 79.

54. The chief sources for this section are E. E. Rich and C. H. Wilson, eds., *The Cambridge Economic History of Europe*, vol. 4: *The Economy of Expanding Europe in the Sixteenth and Seventeenth Centuries* (Cambridge, 1967), and *The Cambridge Economic History of Europe*, vol. 5: *The Economic Organization of Early Modern Europe* (Cambridge, 1977); Fernand Braudel, *Civilization and Capitalism, Fifteenth to Eighteenth Century*, vol. 1: *The Structures of Everyday Life*, trans. Sian Reynolds (London, 1981); Richard Bonney, *The European Dynastic States, 1494–1660* (Oxford, 1991); William Doyle, *The Old European Order, 1660–1800* (Oxford, 1978); Shennan, *Origins of the Modern European State*.

55. J. H. Elliott, "A Europe of Composite Monarchies," *Past and Present* 137 (1992): 48–71; Conrad Russell, *The Causes of the English Civil War* (Oxford, 1990), ch. 2; also H. G. Koenigsberger, *"Dominium regale or Dominium politicum et regale,"* in his *Politicians and Virtuosi: Essays in Early Modern History* (London, 1986), pp. 1–25, and the essays in Mark Greengrass, ed., *Conquest and Coalescence: The Shaping of the State in Early Modern Europe* (London, 1991).

56. Peter Sahlins, *Boundaries: The Making of France and Spain in the Pyrenees* (Berkeley, 1989).

57. Robert Muchembled, *Popular Culture and Elite Culture in France, 1400–1750*, trans. Lydia Cochrane (Baton Rouge, 1978, 1985); Peter Burke, *Popular Culture in Early Modern Europe* (New York, 1978), chs. 8–9.

58. Among the many studies of the European churches in this period are R. N. Swanson, *Religion and Devotion in Europe, c. 1215–c. 1515* (Cambridge, 1995); John Bossy, *Christianity in the West, 1400–1700* (Oxford, 1985); Jean Delumeau, *Catholicism between Luther and Voltaire*, trans. Jeremy Moiser (London, 1977); R. Po-chia Hsia, *Social Discipline in the Reformation: Central Europe, 1550–1750* (London, 1989).

## Chapter Two: The Sickness of the Royal Body, 1589–1610

1. Pierre de L'Estoile, *The Paris of Henry of Navarre*, ed. and trans. Nancy Lyman Roelker (Cambridge, Mass., 1958), pp. 180–82; Martha W. Freer, *Henry III, King of France and Poland: His Court and Times*, 3 vols. (London, 1858), vol. 3, pp. 369–70, 372, 380–81; Pierre Chevallier, *Henri III: Roi Shakespearien* (Paris, 1985), pp. 696–706; Denis Crouzet, *Les guerriers de Dieu: La violence au temps des troubles de religion (vers 1525–vers 1610)*, 2 vols. (Seyssel, 1990), vol. 2, pp. 485–92; Orest Ranum, "The French Ritual of Tyrannicide in the Late Sixteenth Century," *Sixteenth Century Journal* 11 no. 1 (1980): 69–70; Roland Mousnier, *The Assassination of Henry IV*, trans. Joan Spencer (New York, 1973), pp. 213–15.

2. Etienne Pasquier, *Lettres historiques pour les années 1556–1594*, ed. D. Thickett (Geneva, 1966), p. 431. Pasquier is discussed in Donald R. Kelley, *Foundations of Modern Historical Scholarship: Language, Law, and History in the French Renaissance* (New York, 1970), ch. 10.

3. Pasquier, *Lettres historiques*, pp. 311–12.

4. Ibid., p. 447.

5. Ralph Giesey, *The Royal Funeral Ceremony in Renaissance France* (Geneva, 1960).

6. For the economic crisis, see Peter Clark, ed., *The European Crisis of the 1590s: Essays in Comparative History* (London, 1985).

7. Michel De Certeau, *The Practice of Everyday Life*, trans. Steven Rendall (Berkeley, 1984); p. 139; Lyndal Roper, *Oedipus and the Devil: Witchcraft, Sexuality, and Religion in Early Modern Europe* (London, 1994), p. 21.

8. For discussions of the body that emphasize medical thought rather than religion, see Michel Foucault, *The History of Sexuality*, trans. Alan Sheridan, 3 vols. (New York, 1980–85), vol. 3; Thomas Lacqueur, *Making Sex: Body and Gender from the Greeks to Freud* (Cambridge, Mass., 1990); Anthony Fletcher, *Gender, Sex, and Subordination in England, 1500–1800* (New Haven, 1995), chs. 2–5.

9. Peter Brown, *The Body and Society: Men, Women and Sexual Renunciation in Early Christianity* (New York, 1988); Caroline Bynum, *Holy Feast and Holy Fast: The Religious Significance of Food to Medieval Women* (Berkeley, 1987), chs. 1–2.

10. St. Augustine, *Concerning the City of God against the Pagans*, trans. Henry Bettenson (Harmondsworth, Middlesex, 1972), book 22, ch. 24, pp. 1071, 1073; Brown, *Body and Society*, ch. 19.

11. William of St. Thierry, "Nature of the Body and Soul," trans. Benjamin Clark, in Bernard McGinn, ed., *Two Treatises on Man: A Cistercian Anthropology* (Kalamazoo, Mich., 1977), p. 131.

12. St. Augustine, *On Christian Doctrine*, trans. D. W. Robertson Jr. (New York, 1958), book 3, ch. 31, p. 120; Walter Ullmann, *Medieval Political Thought* (Harmondsworth, Middlesex, 1975), pp. 101–2; I. S. Robinson, "Church and Papacy," in J. H. Burns, ed., *The Cambridge History of Medieval Political Thought, c. 350–c. 1450* (Cambridge, 1988), pp. 252–55.

13. Bynum, *Holy Feast and Holy Fast*, pp. 264–65.

14. Ernst Kantorowicz, *The King's Two Bodies: A Study in Medieval Political Theology* (Princeton, 1957, 1981), pp. 194–206.

15. Ullmann, *Medieval Political Thought*, pp. 53—58, and his *Growth of Papal Government in the Middle Ages* (London, 1955, 1962), pp. 28—31; but see also Francis Oakley, "Celestial Hierarchies Revisited: Walter Ullmann's Vision of Medieval Politics," *Past and Present* 60 (1973): 3—48; R. K. Leyser, *Rule and Conflict in an Early Medieval Society* (Oxford, 1989), pp. 77—107; P. D. King, "The Barbarian Kingdoms," in Burns, ed., *Cambridge History of Medieval Political Thought*, pp. 127—29.

16. Kantorowicz, *King's Two Bodies*, ch. 3; Ullmann, *Growth of Papal Government*, ch. 5; Karol Gorski, "Le roi-saint: Un problème d'idéologie féodale," *Annales: Economies, sociétés, civilisations* 24, no. 2 (1969): 370—76; Janet Nelson, "Kingship and Empire," in Burns, ed., *Cambridge History of Medieval Political Thought*, pp. 241—42.

17. J. N. Figgis, *The Divine Right of Kings* (Cambridge, 1896, 1914), ch. 2; Ullmann, *Growth of Papal Government*, ch. 9; Colin Morris, *The Papal Monarchy: The Western Church from 1050 to 1250* (Oxford, 1989), chs. 5—7.

18. Kantorowicz, *King's Two Bodies*, pp. 207—32; Jeanine Quillet, "Community, Counsel, and Representation," in Burns, ed., *Cambridge History of Medieval Political Thought*, pp. 539—41.

19. John of Salisbury, *Policraticus*, ed. and trans. Cary J. Nederman (Cambridge, 1990), book 5, ch. 2, pp. 66—67; Kantorowicz, *King's Two Bodies*, pp. 199—200; H. Liebeschütz, "John of Salisbury and Pseudo-Plutarch," in *Journal of the Warburg and Courtauld Institutes* 6 (1943): 33—39, and a further note by Arnaldo Momigliano in ibid. 12 (1949): 189—90; Georges Duby, *The Three Orders: Feudal Society Imagined*, trans. Arthur Goldhammer (Chicago, 1980), pp. 264—66.

20. Marc Bloch, *The Royal Touch*, trans. J. E. Anderson (New York, 1989), chs. 1, 2; Louis Rougier, "Le caractère sacré de la royauté en France," in *The Sacral Kingship* (Leiden, 1959), pp. 609—19.

21. Bloch, *Royal Touch*, ch. 7; Giesey, *Royal Funeral Ceremony*, ch. 10.

22. See Georges Duby, ed., *A History of Private Life*, vol. 2: *Revelations of the Medieval World*, trans. Arthur Goldhammer (Cambridge, Mass., 1988), pp. 14—17; Duby, *The Three Orders*, p. 353.

23. J. H. Burns, *Lordship, Kingship, and Empire: The Idea of Monarchy, 1400—1525* (Oxford, 1992), chs. 2—3, and his "Fortescue and the Political Theory of *Dominium*," *Historical Journal* 28, no. 4 (1985): 777—97, esp. p. 782.

24. Hermann Meinert, *Von Wahl und Krönung der deutschen Kaiser zu Frankfurt am Main* (Frankfurt am Main, 1956), pp. 5—34; Gerd Kleinheyer, *Die Kaiserlichen Wahlkapitulationen: Geschichte, Wesen, und Funktion* (Karlsruhe, 1968), ch. 1.

25. Norman Davies, *God's Playground: A History of Poland*, 2 vols. (Oxford, 1981), vol. 1, pp. 331—36 (quotation on p. 335); Antoni Mączak, "The Culture of Power in the Commonwealth of the Sixteenth and Seventeenth Centuries," in J. K. Fedorowicz and Henryk Samsonowiez, eds., *A Republic of Nobles: Studies in Polish History to 1864* (Cambridge, 1982), pp. 109—34, esp. p. 128; Andrzej Wycański, "The System of Power in Poland, 1370—1648," in Antoni Mączak, Henryk Samsonowicz, and Peter Burke, eds., *East-Central Europe in Transition: From the Fourteenth to the Seventeenth Century* (Cambridge, 1985), pp. 140—52.

26. Teofilo F. Ruiz, "Unsacred Monarchy: The Kings of Castile in the Late Middle Ages," in Sean Wilentz, ed., *Rites of Power: Symbolism, Ritual and Politics since the Middle*

*Ages* (Philadelphia, 1985), pp. 109–44; Ralph Giesey, *If Not, Not: The Oath of the Aragonese and the Legendary Laws of Sobrarbe* (Princeton, 1968), chs. 1, 6.

27. Burns, *Lordship, Kingship, and Empire*, p. 77.

28. J. H. Elliott, "Power and Propaganda in the Spain of Philip IV," in Wilentz, ed., *Rites of Power*, p. 148, and his *Imperial Spain, 1469–1716* (Harmondsworth, Middlesex, 1963, 1985), pp. 249–51.

29. C. Lisón Tolosana, *La imagen del rey: Monarquía, realeza y poder ritual en la casa de los Austrias* (Madrid, 1992), pp. 59–111.

30. Jaroslav Pelikan, *The Christian Tradition*, vol. 1: *Spirit of Eastern Christendom (600–1700)* (Chicago, 1974), pp. 254–70; Georgios I. Mantzardis, *The Deification of Man: St. Gregory Palamas and the Orthodox Tradition*, trans. Liadain Sherrard (New York, 1984); George P. Fedotov, *The Russian Religious Mind*, vol. 2: *The Middle Ages*, ed. John Meyendorff (Belmont, Mass., 1975), pp. 265–84, 302–15.

31. D. M. Nicol, "Byzantine Political Thought," in Burns, ed., *Cambridge History of Medieval Political Thought*, pp. 51–79; J. B. Aufhauser, "Die sakrale Kaiseridee in Byzanz," in *The Sacral Kingship* (Leiden, 1959), pp. 531–42.

32. Michael Cherniavsky, *Tsar and People: Studies in Russian Myths* (New Haven, 1961), ch. 1, esp. pp. 6, 28–29; Richard S. Wortman, *Scenarios of Power: Myth and Ceremony in Russian Monarchy*, 2 vols. (Princeton, 1995 and forthcoming), vol. 1, pp. 24–30.

33. Richard Pipes, *Russia under the Old Regime* (London, 1974), pp. 64–70. There is a critique of Pipes's view of Russian "patrimonialism" in Alexander Yanov, *The Origins of Autocracy: Ivan the Terrible in Russian History*, trans. Stephen Dunn (Berkeley, 1981), pp. 111–19. H. H. Rowen has argued that France was also a "patrimonial" kingdom in *The King's State: Proprietary Dynasticism in Early Modern France* (New Brunswick, N.J., 1980).

34. Marc Szeftel, "The Title of the Muscovite Monarch up to the End of the Seventeenth Century," *Canadian-American Slavic Studies* 13, nos. 1–2 (1979): 59–81, and his "L'autocratie moscovite et l'absolutisme français au XVIIe siècle: Parallèles et divergences (réflections comparatives)," *Canadian-American Slavic Studies* 16, no. 1 (1982): pp. 45–62; also Isabel de Madariaga, "Autocracy and Sovereignty," *Canadian-American Slavic Studies* 16, nos. 3–4 (1982): 369–87, and her "Tsar into Emperor: The Title of Peter the Great," in Robert Oresko, G. C. Gibbs, and H. M. Scott, eds., *Royal and Republican Sovereignty in Early Modern Europe: Essays in Memory of Ragnhild Hatton* (Cambridge, 1997), pp. 351–81.

35. Paul Bushkovitch, *Religion and Society in Russia: The Sixteenth and Seventeenth Centuries* (Oxford, 1992), p. 42.

36. Robert O. Crummey, *The Formation of Muscovy, 1304–1613* (London, 1987), pp. 139, 168, 211; Ruslan G. Skrynnikov, *Boris Godunov*, ed. and trans. Hugh F. Graham (Gulf Breeze, Fla., 1982), ch. 4; Bushkovitch, *Religion and Society*, ch. 1.

37. The subject is vast. The Italian courts are discussed and beautifully illustrated in Sergio Bertelli, Franco Cardini, and Elvira Garbero Zorzi, eds., *The Courts of the Italian Renaissance*, trans. Mary Fitton and Geoffrey Culverwell (New York, 1985). For pan-European views, see Sydney Anglo, "The Courtier: The Renaissance and Changing Ideals," in A. G. Dickens, ed., *The Courts of Europe: Politics, Patronage, and Royalty, 1400–1800* (London, 1977), pp. 33–53, as well as the essays in Bertelli and Crifò, eds., *Rituale, ceremoniale, etichetta*, and Hugh Trevor-Roper, "The Culture of the Baroque Courts," in

A. Buck et al., eds., *Europäische Hofkultur im 16. und 17. Jahrhundert*, 3 vols. (Hamburg, 1981), vol. 1, pp. 11–23. An interesting study with broad implications is Tibor Klaniczay, "Gli antagonismi tra Corte e società in Europa centrale: la Corte transilvanica alla fine del XVI secolo," in Marco Cattini and Marzio A. Romani, eds., *La Corte in Europa* (Brescia, 1983), pp. 31–58.

38. Tommaso Campanella, *The City of the Sun: A Poetical Dialogue*, ed. and trans. Daniel J. Donno (Berkeley, 1981), p. 123; Rodolfo de Mattei, *Il pensiero politico Italiano nell'età della Controriforma*, 2 vols. (Milan, 1982), vol. 1, ch. 13; Anthony Pagden, "Tommaso Campanella and the Universal Monarchy of Spain," in his *Spanish Imperialism and the Political Imagination: Studies in European and Spanish-American Social and Political Theory, 1513–1830* (New Haven, 1990), pp. 37–63.

39. The most extensive comparative study of this phenomenon remains Frances Yates, *Astraea: The Imperial Theme in the Sixteenth Century* (London, 1975); but see also Roy Strong, *Art and Power: Renaissance Festivals, 1450–1650* (Berkeley, 1984), and Marie Tanner, *The Last Descendant of Aeneas: The Habsburgs and the Mythic Image of the Emperor* (New Haven, 1993), chs. 4–6. For Neoplatonic political ideas, see de Mattei, *Il pensiero politico italiano*, vol. 1, ch. 8.

40. Thomas à Kempis, *The Imitation of Christ* (London, 1960), book 3, ch. 43, p. 148.

41. Martin Luther, "A Sermon on the Estate of Marriage," in Jaroslav Pelikan and Helmut Lehmann, gen. eds., *Luther's Works*, 55 vols. (Philadelphia, 1962–), vol. 44, ed. James Atkinson, pp. 9–10. See also Steven Ozment, *When Fathers Ruled: Family Life in Reformation Europe* (Cambridge, Mass., 1983), ch. 1; Heiko A. Oberman, *Luther: Man between God and the Devil* (New Haven, 1989), pp. 272–83; John Bossy, *Christianity in the West, 1400–1700* (Oxford, 1985), pp. 116–25.

42. Martin Luther, "Temporal Authority: To What Extent It Should Be Obeyed," in *Luther's Works*, vol. 45, ed. Walther Brandt, p. 91. On Lutheran political thought, see Skinner, *Foundations*, vol. 2, ch. 1; Francis Oakley, "Christian Obedience and Authority, 1520–1550," in J. H. Burns and Mark Goldie, eds., *The Cambridge History of Political Thought, 1450–1700* (Cambridge, 1991), pp. 163–75; Thomas A. Brady Jr., "Luther and the State: The Reformer's Teaching in Its Social Setting," in James D. Tracy, ed., *Luther and the Modern State in Germany* (Kirksville, Mo., 1986), pp. 31–44; and Eric W. Gritsch, "Luther and the State: Post-Reformation Ramification," in ibid., pp. 45–59.

43. Henning Arnisaeus, *Doctrina politica* (Amsterdam, 1643), pp. 27, 187–90, 197–261, 265–69; Horst Dreitzel, *Protestantischer Aristotelismus und absoluter Staat: Die "Politica" des Henning Arnisaeus (ca. 1575–1636)* (Wiesbaden, 1970), pp. 143–56, 170–259, 328–35; Otto von Gierke, *The Development of Political Theory*, trans. Bernard Freyd (New York, 1966), pp. 161–62, 203 nn. 94–95.

44. Thomas Munck, *Seventeenth-Century Europe, 1598–1700* (London, 1990), p. 62; Benito Scocozza, *Christian IV* (Copenhagen, 1987), pp. 51–65, 121; John A. Gade, *Christian IV, King of Denmark and Norway* (London, 1928), pp. 61–62; Paul Douglas Lockhart, *Denmark in the 30 Years' War: King Christian IV and the Decline of the Oldenburg State* (Selsingrove, 1996), ch. 2.

45. Michael Roberts, *The Early Vasas: A History of Sweden, 1523–1611* (Cambridge, 1968), pp. 404–11, 412–26; Nils Runeby, *Monarchia mixta: Maktfördelningsdebatt i Sverige under den tidigare stormaktstiden* (Stockholm, 1962), pp. 45–78; Ingun Montgomery, "The

338 · NOTES TO PAGES 49–51

Institutionalization of Lutheranism in Sweden and Finland," in Ole Peter Grell, ed., *The Scandinavian Reformation: From Evangelical Movement to Institutionalization of Reform* (Cambridge, 1995), pp. 162–67.

46. Jean Calvin, *Institutes of the Christian Religion*, ed. J. T. McNeill, trans. F. L. Battles, 2 vols. (Philadelphia, 1960), vol. 1, p. 289, vol. 2, pp. 1252, 1481–82. Yet he later praised human bodies as "in their essence, good creations of God." William J. Bouwsma, *John Calvin: A Sixteenth-Century Portrait* (New York, 1988), p. 134.

47. Jules Bonnet, ed., *Letters of John Calvin*, trans. M. R. Gilchrist, 4 vols. (New York, 1858, 1972), vol. 4, p. 349.

48. Calvin, *Institutes*, vol. 2, p. 1489.

49. Ibid., vol. 2, p. 1515. While consistent with Quentin Skinner's views in *Foundations*, vol. 2, pp. 191–94, this interpretation differs from the discussion in Bouwsma, *Calvin*, ch. 13.

50. The Lutheran origins of "resistance theory" are pointed out in Skinner, *Foundations*, vol. 2, pp. 194–238.

51. *Vindiciae contra tyrannos*, in Julian H. Franklin, ed., *Constitutionalism and Resistance in the Sixteenth Century* (New York, 1969), p. 160. An older translation of the whole treatise is in Harold Laski, ed., *A Defense of Liberty Against Tyrants* (Gloucester, Mass., 1924, 1963). For Calvinist political thought, see Robert M. Kingdon, "Calvinism and Resistance Theory, 1550–1580," in Burns and Goldie, eds., *Cambridge History of Political Thought, 1450–1700*, pp. 193–218; D. R. Kelley, *The Beginning of Ideology: Consciousness and Society in the French Reformation* (Cambridge, 1981), pp. 307–28; Skinner, *Foundations*, vol. 2, pp. 322–38.

52. *Vindiciae contra tyrannos*, p. 143.

53. For Buchanan, see Skinner, *Foundations*, vol. 2, pp. 339–48; J. H. Burns, "George Buchanan and the Anti-Monarchomachs," in Nicholas Phillipson and Quentin Skinner, eds., *Political Discourse in Early Modern Britain* (Cambridge, 1993), pp. 3–22; and for Dutch republicanism, Martin van Gelderen, *The Political Thought of the Dutch Revolt, 1555–1590* (Cambridge, 1992), as well as the tracts he has edited in *The Dutch Revolt* (Cambridge, 1992). Dutch influence in Britain is considered in Hugh Dunthorne, "Resisting Monarchy: The Netherlands as Britain's School of Revolution in the Late Sixteenth and Seventeenth Centuries," in Oresko, Gibbs, and Scott, eds., *Royal and Republican Sovereignty*, pp. 125–48.

54. Frederick S. Carney, ed. and trans., *The Politics of Johannes Althusius* (Boston, 1964), pp. 106–7; also von Gierke, *Development of Political Theory*, pp. 33–52; Hanns Gross, *Empire and Sovereignty: A History of the Public Law Literature in the Holy Roman Empire, 1599–1804* (Chicago, 1973), pp. 103–19. For the impact of Althusius in Sweden, see Runeby, *Monarchia mixta*, pp. 39–41, 126–28, 132–33, 150–51, 168–70.

55. Carney, ed., *Politics of Althusius*, pp. 127, 155, 188. Barclay and Du Plessis Mornay, by contrast, had denied that God made a separate covenant with the prince.

56. See Maurice Lee Jr., *Great Britain's Solomon: James VI and I in His Three Kingdoms* (Urbana, Ill., 1990), pp. 31–35.

57. Lee, *Great Britain's Solomon*, pp. 53, 79; Jenny Wormald, "Ecclesiastical Vitriol: The Kirk, the Puritans, and the Future King of England," in John Guy, ed., *The Reign of Elizabeth I: Court and Culture in the Last Decade* (Cambridge, 1995), pp. 126–49. James

later avenged himself on the Presbyterians by bolstering episcopacy: Maurice Lee Jr., *Government by Pen: Scotland under James VI and I* (Urbana, Ill., 1980), ch. 5.

58. Jean Delumeau, *Catholicism between Luther and Voltaire*, trans. Jeremy Moiser (London, 1977), esp. pp. 43–59; and his *Sin and Fear: The Emergence of a Western Guilt Culture, 13th–18th Centuries*, trans. Eric Nicholson (New York, 1990), esp. ch. 16; also, John Bossy, "The Counter-Reformation and the People of Catholic Europe," *Past and Present* 47 (1970): 64–70, and A. D. Wright, *The Counter-Reformation: Catholic Europe and the Non-Christian World* (New York, 1982), chs. 2, 6.

59. Louis Chatellier, *The Europe of the Devout: The Catholic Reformation and the Formation of a New Society*, trans. John Birrell (Paris, 1989), p. 108.

60. Pedro de Rivadeneira, *Tratado de la religión y virtudes que debe tener el príncipe Cristiano para gobernar y conservar sus Estados*, in Vicente de la Fuente, ed., *Obras escogidas del Padre Pedro de Rivadeneira*, Biblioteca de Autores Españoles, 60 (Madrid, 1919), pp. 466, 507, 518.

61. Rivadeneira, *Tratado del príncipe Cristiano*, pp. 475, 485, 504. The image of the ruler as minister of God is further discussed in Raymond Darricau, "La spiritualité du prince," *XVIIe Siècle* 62–63 (1964): 78–111.

62. Juan de Mariana, *The King and the Education of the King*, trans. G. A. Moore (Washington, 1948), p. 150.

63. Francisco Suárez, *Tractatus de legibus, ac Deo legislatore*, in James Brown Scott, ed., *Selections from Three Works of Francisco Suárez*, trans. G. L. Williams, A. Brown, and J. Waldron, Carnegie Classics of International Law, 2 vols. (Oxford, 1944), vol. 2, book 3, ch. 2, pp. 374–75.

64. Suárez, *De legibus*, book 3, ch. 4, pp. 384–87; also his *Defensio fidei Catholicae*, book 6, ch. 4, p. 705, and *De bello*, disp. 13, sec. 8, pp. 854–55, all in Brown Scott, ed., *Selections from Suárez*, vol. 2. See also Bernice Hamilton, *Political Thought in Sixteenth-Century Spain* (Oxford, 1963), chs. 2–3; J. P. Sommerville, "From Suárez to Filmer: A Reappraisal," *The Historical Journal* 25, no. 3 (1982): 525–35.

65. Auguste Berga, *Un prédicateur de la cour de Pologne sous Sigismond III: Pierre Skarga (1536–1612)* (Paris, 1916), pp. 332–60; Czeslaw Milosz, *The History of Polish Literature*, 2d ed. (Berkeley, 1983), pp. 90–95.

66. Janusz Tazbir, "La Polonisation du Catholicisme," in his *La république nobiliaire et le monde: Etudes sur l'histoire de la culture Polonaise à l'époque du baroque*, trans. Lucjan Grobelak (Wrocław, 1986), p. 138.

67. William Allen, *A True, Sincere, and Modest Defense of English Catholics That Suffer for Their Faith Both at Home and Abroad*, in *The Execution of Justice in England by William Cecil* and *A True Sincere and Modest Defense of English Catholics*, ed. Robert M. Kingdon (Ithaca, N.Y., 1965), p. 204.

68. His *An Apologie for the Oath of Allegiance, A Premonition to all Christian Monarches, Free Princes and States*, and *A Defence of the Right of Kings, against Cardinall Perron* are all reprinted in C. H. McIlwain, ed., *The Political Works of James I* (Cambridge, Mass., 1918), pp. 71–268.

69. Ernst W. Zeeden, *Die Entstehung der Konfessionen: Grundlagen und Formen der Konfessionsbildung im Zeitalter der Glaubenskämpfe* (Munich, 1965); Heinz Schilling, "Die Konfessionalisierung im Reich: Religiöser und Gesellschaftlicher Wandel in Deutschland

zwischen 1555 und 1620," *Historische Zeitschrift* 246 (1988): 1–45. In English, see Heinz Schilling, "The Reformation and the Rise of the Early Modern State," pp. 21–30, and Karlheinz Blaschke, "The Reformation and the Rise of the Territorial State," pp. 61–75, both in Tracy, ed., *Luther and the Modern State;* also R. Po-chia Hsia, *Social Discipline in the Reformation: Central Europe, 1550–1750* (London, 1989), esp. ch. 4; Bossy, *Christianity in the West*, pp. 153–61.

70. Hsia, *Social Discipline*, pp. 183–84; Keith Thomas, *Religion and the Decline of Magic* (New York, 1971), ch. 3; Wolfgang Reinhard, "Gegenreformation als Modernisierung? Prolegomena zu einer Theorie des konfessionellen Zeitalters," *Archiv für Reformationsgeschichte* 68 (1977): 226–52.

71. Anna Coreth, *Pietas Austriaca: Ursprung und Entwicklung barocker Frömmigkeit in Österreich* (Munich, 1959), p. 19.

72. For Charles's ambitions, see Yates, *Astraea*, ch. 1; Strong, *Art and Power*, pp. 75–97; and for an excellent account of the end of the reign, M. J. Rodríguez-Salgado, *The Changing Face of Empire: Charles V, Philip II, and Habsburg Authority, 1551–9* (Cambridge, 1988).

73. R. J. W. Evans, *The Making of the Habsburg Monarchy, 1550–1700* (Oxford, 1979), ch. 1.

74. Thomas DaCosta Kaufmann, "Arcimboldo's Imperial Allegories: G. B. Fonteo and the Interpretation of Arcimboldo's Painting," *Zeitschrift für Kunstgeschichte* 29 (1976): 275–96; his "Arcimboldo and Propertius: A Classical Source for Rudolf II as Vertumnus" *Zeitschrift für Kunstgeschichte* 38 (1985): 117–23; his "Allegories and Their Meaning," in *The Arcimboldo Effect: Transformations of the Face from the Sixteenth to the Twentieth Century* (New York, 1987), pp. 89–109; and his *School of Prague: Painting at the Court of Rudolf II* (Chicago, 1988), pp. 164–72.

75. Piero Falchetta, ed., "Anthology of Sixteenth-Century Texts," in *The Arcimboldo Effect*, p. 186.

76. Kaufmann, *School of Prague*, pp. 10–17; Thomas DaCosta Kaufmann, *Court, Cloister, and City: The Art and Culture of Central Europe, 1450–1800* (Chicago, 1995), pp. 185–203; Sven Alfons, "The Museum as Image of the World," in *The Arcimboldo Effect*, pp. 67–85.

77. The best treatment of this subject is in R. J. W. Evans, *Rudolf II and His World* (Oxford, 1972), chs. 6–7. Rudolf's musical patronage, however, seems to have been relatively orthodox: see Carmelo Peter Comberiati, *Late Renaissance Music at the Habsburg Court* (New York, 1987).

78. Flachetta, ed., "Anthology," *The Arcimboldo Effect*, p. 189. For hieroglyphics at Rudolf's court, see Evans, *Rudolf II*, pp. 269–70. The *Corpus hermeticum*, a mystical work popular among Rudolfine scholars, hinted obscurely that "the very quality of the speech and the [sound] of Egyptian words have in themselves the energy of the objects they speak of." Brian P. Copenhaver, ed. and trans., *Hermetica: The Greek "Corpus hermeticum" and the Latin "Asclepius"* (Cambridge, 1992), p. 58.

79. Evans, *Rudolf II*, ch. 2; Andrew Weeks, *Boehme: An Intellectual Biography of the Seventeenth-Century Philosopher and Mystic* (Albany, N.Y., 1991), pp. 48–51.

80. Volker Press, "The Imperial Court of the Habsburgs from Maximilian I to Ferdinand III, 1493–1657," in Ronald G. Asch and Adolf M. Birke, eds., *Princes, Patronage, and*

*the Nobility: The Court at the Beginning of the Early Modern Age* (Oxford, 1991), pp. 289–312; and his "Habsburg Court as Center of the Imperial Government," *Journal of Modern History* 58, Supplement (Dec. 1986): pp. 23–45, esp. pp. 31–36.

81. Melchior Goldast, *Monarchia S. Romani Imperii, sive tractatus de iurisdictione imperiali seu regia, & pontificia seu sacerdotali,* 3 vols. (Graz, 1611–14, reprint 1960), vol. 1, preface; Kleinheyer, *Die Kaiserliche Wahlkapitulationen,* pp. 1, 70; Evans, *Making of the Habsburg Monarchy,* p. 66. For the Protestant view of Imperial institutions, see Heinz Duchhardt, "Der Kampf um die Parität im Kammerrichteramt zwischen Augsburger Religionsfrieden und 30-jahrigem Krieg," *Archiv für Reformationsgeschichte* 69 (1978): 201–18, and Winfried Schulze, "Majority Decision in the Imperial Diets of the Sixteenth and Seventeenth Centuries," *Journal of Modern History* 58, Supplement (Dec. 1986): 46–63.

82. Victor von Klarwill, ed., *The Fugger Newsletters, 1568–1605,* trans. Pauline de Chary (London, 1924), pp. 173–74, 207–8.

83. Hans Sturmberger, *Georg Erasmus Tschernembl: Religion, Libertät und Widerstand* (Graz, 1953), pp. 100–1, 141–226; Zeeden, *Entstehung der Konfessionen,* pp. 161–63.

84. Ricardo García-Villoslada, "Felipe II y la Contrarreforma Catolica," in Ricardo García-Villoslada, ed., *Historia de la iglesia en España,* part 3: *La iglesia en la España de los siglos XV y XVI,* 2 vols. (Madrid, 1980), vol. 2, pp. 3–106.

85. Henry Kamen, *The Phoenix and the Flame: Catalonia and the Counter-Reformation* (New Haven, 1993), ch. 2. A contrasting assessment is found in Sara T. Nalle, *God in La Mancha: Religious Reform and the People of Cuenca, 1500–1650* (Baltimore, 1992), pp. 32–56. The local context of the Spanish Counter Reformation is further discussed in William Christian, *Local Religion in Sixteenth-Century Spain* (Princeton, 1981), and Jodi Bilinkoff, *The Avila of St. Teresa: Religious Reform in a Sixteenth-Century City* (Ithaca, N.Y., 1989).

86. José de Sigüenza, *Historia de la Orden de San Jerónimo,* 2 vols. (Madrid, 1907), vol. 2, pp. 405, 660–71; René Taylor, "Architecture and Magic: Considerations on the Idea of the Escorial," in Howard Hibbard, ed., *Essays in the History of Architecture Presented to Rudolf Wittkower* (New York, 1967), pp. 81–109; René Taylor, "Hermeticism and Mystical Architecture in the Society of Jesus," in Rudolf Wittkower and B. B. Jaffe, eds., *Baroque Art: The Jesuit Contribution* (New York, 1972), pp. 63–97; Catherine Wilkinson-Zerner, *Juan de Herrera, Architect to Philip II of Spain* (New Haven, 1993), pp. 50–51, 104.

87. Carlos M. N. Eire, *From Madrid to Purgatory: The Art and Craft of Dying in Sixteenth-Century Spain* (Cambridge, 1995), pp. 255–365; Rosemarie Mulcahy, *The Decoration of the Royal Basilica of El Escorial* (Cambridge, 1994), pp. 208–10; Tanner, *Last Descendant of Aeneas,* chs. 7–12. Tanner overemphasizes the sacral element in Spanish kingship.

88. Wilkinson-Zerner, *Juan de Herrera,* pp. 42–45; Sigüenza, *Historia de la Orden de San Gerónimo,* vol. 2, p. 577; but see George Kubler, *Building the Escorial* (Princeton, 1982), pp. 128–30.

89. Geoffrey Parker, *Philip II* (London, 1979), pp. 50–51; but Henry Kamen, *Philip II* (New Haven, 1997), pp. 223–24, suggests that he wore black because he was frequently in mourning.

90. Claude Chauchadis, *Honneur, morale et société dans l'Espagne de Philippe II* (Paris, 1984), chs. 2, 5; quotation on p. 60. Court life is evoked in Parker, *Philip II,* ch. 3; M. J. Rodríguez-Salgado, "The Court of Philip II of Spain," in Asch and Birke, eds., *Princes,*

*Patronage, and the Nobility*, pp. 205–44; and J. H. Elliott, "The Court of the Spanish Habsburgs: A Peculiar Institution?" in his *Spain and Its World, 1500–1700* (New Haven, 1989), pp. 142–61.

91. Even J. H. Elliott, who has generally opposed the use of the term *crisis*, employed it for the 1590s in his *Imperial Spain*, pp. 285–300. For the economic crisis, see James Casey, "Spain: A Failed Transition," in Clark, ed., *European Crisis of the 1590s*, pp. 209–28.

92. Quoted in Kamen, *The Phoenix and the Flame*, p. 80.

93. Richard L. Kagan, *Lucrecia's Dreams: Politics and Prophecy in Sixteenth-Century Spain* (Berkeley, 1990), pp. 79–83, 123–28, 154–55; Kamen, *Philip II*, pp. 281–83.

94. For these events, see Elliott, *Imperial Spain*, pp. 277–84; Parker, *Philip II*, pp. 183–90; Kamen, *Philip II*, pp. 284–95; Giesey, *If Not, Not*, pp. 232–37; Stephen Haliczer, *Inquisition and Society in the Kingdom of Valencia, 1478–1834* (Berkeley, 1990), pp. 46–48; Henry Kamen, *Inquisition and Society in Spain in the Sixteenth and Seventeenth Centuries* (Bloomington, Ind., 1985), pp. 242–48; Xavier Gil, "Crown and Cortes in Early Modern Aragon: Reassessing Revisionisms," *Parliaments, Estates, and Representations* 13, no. 2 (Dec. 1993): 109–22; and the colourful account in Gregorio Marañón, *Antonio Pérez, "Spanish Traitor,"* trans. C. D. Ley (London, 1954), pp. 248–94.

95. The passage is from G. B., *A Fig for the Spaniard, or Spanish Spirits* (London, 1591), reprinted in Gustav Ungerer, ed., *A Spaniard in Elizabethan England: The Correspondence of Antonio Pérez's Exile*, 2 vols. (London, 1975), vol. 1, p. 40. See also ibid., vol. 1, p. 13; Elliott, *Imperial Spain*, p. 278; Kagan, *Lucrecia's Dreams*, pp. 88–90, 95–101.

96. Johann van Oldenbarnevelt, in Herbert H. Rowen, ed., *The Low Countries in Early Modern Times* (London, 1972), p. 109. For the toleration of Protestant merchants, see Antonio Domínguez Ortiz, "El primer esbozo de tolerancia religiosa en la España de los Austrias," in his *Instituciones y sociedad en la España de los Austrias* (Barcelona, 1985), pp. 184–91.

97. "Act in Restraint of Appeals," in Geoffrey Elton, ed., *The Tudor Constitution: Documents and Commentary* (Cambridge, 1960), p. 344. For the evolution of such ideas, see John W. McKenna, "How God Became an Englishman," in Delloyd J. Guth and John W. McKenna, eds., *Tudor Rule and Revolution: Essays for G. R. Elton from His American Friends* (Cambridge, 1982), pp. 25–42.

98. J. S. Neale, *Elizabeth I and Her Parliaments*, 2 vols. (London, 1953, 1957), vol. 1, pp. 65–66.

99. David Loades, *The Tudor Court* (Totowa, N.J., 1987), pp. 182–83.

100. Sydney Anglo, *Spectacle, Pageantry, and Early Tudor Policy* (Oxford, 1969), pp. 351–52; Susan Frye, *Elizabeth I: The Competition for Representation* (Oxford, 1993), ch. 1; John N. King, "The Royal Image, 1535–1603," in Dale Hoak, ed., *Tudor Political Culture* (Cambridge, 1995), pp. 127–32. A sceptical view of the social impact of the Tudor royal cult is found in Sydney Anglo, *Images of Tudor Kingship* (London, 1992).

101. Quoted in Kantorowicz, *King's Two Bodies*, p. 7. Marie Axton, *The Queen's Two Bodies: Drama and the Elizabethan Succession* (London, 1977), chs. 1–4, suggests that the doctrine may have been devised to insure the succession of Mary, Queen of Scots. The succession problem is further discussed in Howard Nenner, *The Right to Be King: The Succession to the Crown of England, 1603–1714* (Chapel Hill, N.C., 1995), chs. 1–2.

102. F. W. Maitland, "The Crown as Corporation," in his *Selected Essays*, ed. H. D. Hazeltine, G. Lapsley, and P. H. Winfield (Cambridge, 1936), pp. 109–11.

103. Patrick Collinson, *The Elizabethan Puritan Movement* (London, 1967), pp. 195–96, and his *Religion of Protestants: The Church in English Society 1559–1625* (Oxford, 1982), pp. 29–31.

104. Yates, *Astraea*, part 2, esp. pp. 112–26; Frye, *Elizabeth I*, ch. 2; Roy Strong, *The Cult of Elizabeth* (London, 1977), pp. 114–63.

105. For the avoidance of factional conflicts, see Simon Adams, "Eliza Enthroned? The Court and Its Politics," in Christopher Haigh, ed., *The Reign of Elizabeth I* (London, 1983), pp. 55–77, and his "Favourites and Factions at the Elizabethan Court," in Asch and Birke, eds., *Princes, Patronage, and the Nobility*, pp. 265–87. Elizabeth was careful to keep her Privy Chamber female and relatively free from faction: Pam Wright, "A Change in Direction: The Ramifications of a Female Household, 1558–1603," in David Starkey, ed., *The English Court: From the Wars of the Roses to the Civil War* (London, 1987), pp. 147–72.

106. Edmund Spenser, *The Faerie Queene*, ed. Thomas P. Roche Jr. and C. Patrick O'Donnell Jr. (New Haven, 1978), book 3, preface, p. 383.

107. For Elizabeth's appearances in the poem, see Robin Headlam Wells, *Spenser's Faerie Queene and the Cult of Elizabeth* (London, 1983); Louis Adrian Montrose, "The Elizabethan Subject and the Spenserian Text," in Patricia Parker and David Quint, eds., *Literary Theory/Renaissance Texts* (Baltimore, 1986), pp. 303–40; David Lee Miller, *The Poem's Two Bodies: The Poetics of the 1590 "Faerie Queene"* (Princeton, 1988).

108. See Frye, *Elizabeth I*, ch. 3; Carole Levin, *"The Heart and Stomach of a King": Elizabeth I and the Politics of Sex and Power* (Philadelphia, 1994); Diana E. Henderson, "Elizabeth's Watchful Eye and George Peele's Gaze: Examining Female Power Beyond the Individual," in Louise Olga Fradenburg, ed., *Women and Sovereignty* (Edinburgh, 1992), pp. 150–69.

109. See Collinson, *The Religion of Protestants*, ch. 5; Keith Wrightson, *English Society, 1580–1680* (London, 1981), ch. 3.

110. David Cressy, *Bonfires and Bells: National Memory and the Protestant Calendar in Elizabethan and Stuart England* (Berkeley, 1989), ch. 7. The quotation from the pamphlet *The Spanish Masquerado* is on p. 123.

111. Simon Adams, "The Patronage of the Crown in Elizabethan Politics: The 1590s in Perspective," in Guy, ed., *The Reign of Elizabeth I*, pp. 20–45; R. B. Outhwaite, "Dearth, the English Crown, and the 'Crisis of the 1590s,'" in Clark, ed., *European Crisis of the 1590s*, pp. 23–43; Peter Lake, *Moderate Puritans and the Elizabethan Church* (Cambridge, 1982), pp. 201–42.

112. Richard Hooker, *Of the Laws of Ecclesiastical Polity*, ed. A. S. McGrade and Brian Vickers (London, 1975), pp. 140–41, 348, 360. Peter Lake argues that Hooker was the first "Anglican" in *Anglicans and Puritans? Presbyterianism and English Conformist Thought from Whitgift to Hooker* (London, 1988), pp. 145–238. See also J. P. Sommerville, "Richard Hooker, Hadrian Saravia, and the Advent of the Divine Right of Kings," *History of Political Thought* 4 (1983): 229–45.

113. The best treatment of the revolt is in M. E. James, "At a Crossroads of the Political Culture: The Essex Revolt, 1601," in his *Society, Politics, and Culture: Essays in*

*Early Modern History* (Cambridge, 1986), pp. 416–65; see also Paul E. J. Hammer, "Patronage at Court, Faction, and the Earl of Essex," in Guy, ed., *The Reign of Elizabeth I*, pp. 65–86, and Fritz Levy, "The Theatre and the Court in the 1590s," in ibid., pp. 274–300. Pérez's relations with Essex can be followed in Ungerer, ed., *A Spaniard in Elizabethan England*. The earl did not attend the performance of Shakespeare's play.

114. Neale, *Elizabeth I and Her Parliaments*, vol. 2, p. 389; R. P. Sorlien, ed., *The Diary of John Manningham of the Middle Temple, 1602–1603* (Hanover, N.H., 1976), p. 221. For further evidence of disillusionment, see Robert Ashton, ed., *James I by His Contemporaries* (London, 1969), pp. 76–77.

115. Jenny Wormald, "James VI and I, *Basilikon doron*, and the *Trew Law of Free Monarchies:* The Scottish Context and the English Translation," in Linda Levy Peck, ed., *The Mental World of the Jacobean Court* (Cambridge, 1991), pp. 36–54. A different approach to James's works can be found in J. P. Sommerville, "James I and the Divine Right of Kings: English Politics and Continental Theory," in ibid., pp. 55–70.

116. James VI and I, *The Trew Law of Free Monarchies: Or the Reciprock and Mutuall Duetie betwixt a Free King, and His Naturall Subjects,* in McIlwain, ed., *Political Works of James I*, pp. 54–55, 64.

117. James VI and I, *Basilikon doron,* in McIlwain, ed., *Political Works of James I*, pp. 12–18; Wormald, "James VI and I," p. 51, citing the researches of P. W. M. Blayney.

118. Raymond Crawford, *The King's Evil* (Oxford, 1911), pp. 82–85; Bloch, *The Royal Touch*, pp. 191–92; and for Protestant attitudes to royal healing, Thomas, *Religion and the Decline of Magic*, pp. 192–99.

119. Kantorowicz, *King's Two Bodies*, pp. 14–16; Axton, *Queen's Two Bodies*, p. 145. For the Scottish union project, see R. C. Munden, "James I and 'the growth of mutual distrust': King, Commons, and Reform, 1603–4," in Kevin Sharpe, ed., *Faction and Parliament: Essays on Early Stuart History* (London, 1978), pp. 43–72; Brian P. Levack, *The Formation of the British State: England, Scotland, and the Union, 1603–1707* (Oxford, 1987), esp. ch. 2.

120. Samuel Daniel, "A Panegyrick Congratulatory," in John Nichols, ed., *The Processes, Processions, and Magnificent Festivities of King James the First*, 4 vols. (London, 1828), vol. 1, p. 131.

121. Linda Levy Peck, *Court Patronage and Corruption in Early Stuart England* (London, 1990), chs. 2–4. The sale of honours was laid bare in Lawrence Stone, *The Crisis of the Aristocracy, 1558–1641* (Oxford, 1965), ch. 3. For the role of favourites in the royal household, see Neil Cuddy, "The Revival of the Entourage: The Bedchamber of James I, 1603–1625," in Starkey, ed., *The English Court*, pp. 173–225.

122. Stephen Orgel, *The Jonsonian Masque* (Cambridge, Mass., 1965), ch. 2; also his *Illusion of Power: Political Theater in the English Renaissance* (Berkeley, 1975), pp. 59–77. The texts of all the Stuart court masques are printed in Stephen Orgel and Roy Strong, *Inigo Jones: The Theatre of the Stuart Court*, 2 vols. (Berkeley, 1973). See also Leeds Barroll, "The Court of the First Stuart Queen," in Levy Peck, ed., *Jacobean Court*, pp. 191–208, and Jerzy Limon, "The Masque of Stuart Culture," in ibid., pp. 209–29.

123. D. H. Willson, *King James VI and I* (Oxford, 1956, 1967), p. 274; Cressy, *Bonfires and Bells*, ch. 9.

124. Natalie Zemon Davis, "The Rites of Violence," in *Society and Culture in Early*

*Modern France* (Stanford, 1975), pp. 152–87; also Janine Estèbe and Natalie Zemon Davis, "The Rites of Violence: Religious Riot in Sixteenth-Century France," *Past and Present* 67 (1975): 127–35, and Crouzet, *Les guerriers de Dieu,* vol. 1, chs. 4–5.

125. Jacqueline Boucher, *Société et mentalités autour de Henri III,* 4 vols. (Lille, 1981), pp. 955–1115, 1223–1329, and her "La commistione fra Corte e Stato in Francia sotto gli ultimi Valois," in Cattini and Romani, eds., *La Corte in Europa,* pp. 93–130; Yates, *Astraea,* pp. 121–72, 222–24, and her *Valois Tapestries* (London, 1959, 1975), pp. 51–108; Strong, *Art and Power,* pp. 98–125; Margaret McGowan, *L'art du ballet de cour en France, 1581–1643* (Paris, 1963, 1978), ch. 3; Jean-François Solnon, *La cour de France* (Paris, 1987), pp. 75–159.

126. Crouzet, *Les guerriers de Dieu,* vol. 1, ch. 6, vol. 2, pp. 30–62.

127. Montaigne, "Of Moderation," in *The Complete Essays of Montaigne,* trans. Donald Frame (Stanford, 1965), p. 146. Also Boucher, *Société et mentalités,* pp. 1354–64; Yates, *Astraea,* pp. 173–207, and her *French Academies of the Sixteenth Century* (London, 1947), ch. 8.

128. De L'Estoile, *The Paris of Henry of Navarre,* pp. 135–36; for royal debauchery, see pp. 139–40.

129. Ibid., pp. 146–52; Chevallier, *Henri III,* pp. 628–38; Salmon, *Society in Crisis,* ch. 10. See also the debate in Robert Descimon and Elia Barnavi, "La Ligue à Paris: Une révision," *Annales* 37, no. 1 (1982): 72–127.

130. Denis Crouzet, "La représentation du temps à l'époque de la Ligue," *Revue historique* 270, no. 548 (1983): pp. 297–388, and his *Les guerriers de Dieu,* vol. 2, chs. 16–18; Yates, *Astraea,* p. 196 and plate 40, and her *French Academies,* p. 221; Robert R. Harding, "The Mobilization of Confraternities Against the Reformation in France," *Sixteenth-Century Journal* 11, no. 2 (1980): 93–94.

131. De L'Estoile, *The Paris of Henry of Navarre,* pp. 173–74.

132. Boucher, *Société et mentalités,* pp. 1332–34; also Crouzet, *Les guerriers de Dieu,* vol. 2, pp. 543–52.

133. De L'Estoile, *The Paris of Henry of Navarre,* p. 177.

134. François Cromé, *Dialogue d'entre le Maheustre et le Manant,* ed. Peter M. Ascoli (Geneva, 1977), p. 54. The attempted suppression of this book by the Guise faction is recounted in De L'Estoile, *The Paris of Henry of Navarre,* pp. 245–47. A discussion of the pamphlet's main ideas can be found in F. J. Baumgartner, *Radical Reactionaries: The Political Thought of the French Catholic League* (Geneva, 1975), pp. 210–20.

135. Salmon, "Catholic Resistance Theory," in Burns and Goldie, eds., *Cambridge History of Political Thought, 1450–1700,* pp. 229–30; David A. Bell, "Unmasking a King: The Political Uses of Popular Literature Under the French Catholic League, 1588–9," *Sixteenth-Century Journal* 20, no. 3 (1989): 371–86.

136. Different interpretations of Henry's conversion are provided in Yves Cazaux, *Henri IV ou la grande victoire* (Paris, 1977), and Michael Wolfe, *The Conversion of Henri IV: Politics, Power, and Religious Belief in Early Modern France* (Cambridge, Mass., 1993).

137. Montaigne, "Of the Art of Discussion," in *Complete Essays,* p. 720.

138. Paul Lawrence Rose, "Bodin and the Bourbon Succession to the French Throne, 1583–1594," *Sixteenth-Century Journal* 9, no. 2 (1978): 75–98.

139. Jean Bodin, *On Sovereignty: Four Chapters from the Six Books of the Common-*

*wealth,* ed. and trans. Julian H. Franklin (Cambridge, 1992), p. 1. This is the best English translation, but for the complete work readers must still consult *Six Bookes of the Commonweale,* trans. Richard Knolles, ed. K. D. McRae (Cambridge, Mass., 1962, reprint of 1606 ed.), where this quotation is on p. 85. For analysis of Bodin's thought, see Julian H. Franklin, *Jean Bodin and the Rise of Absolutist Theory* (Cambridge, 1973); Skinner, *Foundations,* vol. 2, pp. 284–301.

140. Bodin, *Six Bookes* (1606 ed.), p. 8. For the legal consequences of Bodin's patriarchalism, see Sarah Hanley, "Engendering the State: Family Formation and State Building in Early Modern France," *French Historical Studies* 16, no. 1 (1989): 4–27.

141. Bodin, *Six Bookes* (1606 ed.), p. 20.

142. Ibid., p. 112; Bodin, *On Sovereignty,* p. 44. Bodin may have invented this succinct formulation of a traditional principle: Giesey, *Royal Funeral Ceremony,* p. 182.

143. Fundamental law is explained in Roland Mousnier, *The Institutions of France under the Absolute Monarchy,* 2 vols. (Chicago, 1979), vol. 2, pp. 649–53. On the role of parlements in the sixteenth century, see J. H. Shennan, *The Parlement of Paris* (London, 1968), ch. 7, and Sarah Hanley, *The Lit de Justice of the Kings of France: Constitutional Ideology in Legend, Ritual, and Discourse* (Princeton, 1983). The treatment of the parlement under the Catholic League is detailed in De L'Estoile, *The Paris of Henry of Navarre,* pp. 198–215, and Nancy Lyman Roelker, *One King, One Faith: The Parlement of Paris and the Religious Reformations of the Sixteenth Century* (Berkeley, 1996), chs. 11–14.

144. The speech is reprinted in Cazaux, *Henri IV,* pp. 373–79.

145. Giesey, *Royal Funeral Ceremony,* p. 182; Hanley, *Lit de Justice,* p. 180.

146. Nannerl O. Keohane, *Philosophy and the State in France: The Renaissance to the Enlightenment* (Princeton, 1980), pp. 125–26; Howell A. Lloyd, *The State, France, and the Sixteenth Century* (London, 1983), pp. 162–68; Charles Loyseau, *A Treatise of Orders and Plain Dignities,* ed. and trans. Howell A. Lloyd (Cambridge, 1994), pp. xx–xxii; Mousnier, *Institutions,* vol. 1, pp. 645–46, 661–62—the quotation from Loyseau, *Traité des seigneuries,* is on p. 646.

147. Bodin, *On Sovereignty,* p. 18; the quote also appears in *Six Bookes* (1606 ed.), p. 95. Similarly, conciliarists of the fifteenth century had been able to reconcile "absolute" kingship with constitutionalism; see Burns, *Lordship, Kingship, and Empire,* ch. 6.

148. Giesey, *Royal Funeral Ceremony,* ch. 10, suggests that this change dates from 1610, but he does not mention the events of 1589.

149. Richard A. Jackson, *Vive le roi! A History of the French Coronation from Charles V to Charles X* (Chapel Hill, N.C., 1984), pp. 45–46, 85–90, 125–27.

150. Bloch, *Royal Touch,* pp. 193–95.

151. Solnon, *La cour de France,* ch. 8.

152. Corrado Vivanti, "Henri IV, the Gallic Hercules," *Journal of the Warburg and Courtauld Institutes* 30 (1967): 176–97; Edmund H. Dickerman and Anita M. Walker, "The Choice of Hercules: Henry IV as Hero," *Historical Journal* 39, no. 2 (1996): 315–37; Jacques Hennequin, *Henri IV dans les oraisons funèbres ou la naissance d'une légende* (Paris, 1977), pp. 145–60, 185–98; Jean-Pierre Babelon, "L'image du roi," in *Henri IV et la reconstruction du royaume* (Paris, 1989), pp. 193–212; Yates, *Astraea,* p. 210; Mousnier, *Assassination of Henry IV,* pp. 245–49; Crouzet, *Les guerriers de Dieu,* vol. 2, pp. 569–85.

153. David Buisseret, *Henry IV* (London, 1984), pp. 70–74, 121–23; Janine [Estèbe]

Garrisson, *L'Edit de Nantes et sa révocation: Histoire d'une intolérance* (Paris, 1985), pp. 15–27; Vivanti, "Henry IV, the Gallic Hercules," pp. 192–97.

154. Hanley, *Lit de Justice*, ch. 10; Giesey, *Royal Funeral Ceremony*, pp. 180–92.

155. Maximilien de Béthune, duc de Sully, *Mémoires*, 9 vols. (London, 1768), vol. 8, p. 33.

156. Hanley, *Lit de Justice*, pp. 263–66; Jackson, *Vive le roi!*, pp. 148–65. For the sun and other images of French royalty, see Anne-Marie Lecoq, "La symbolique de l'état: Les images de la monarchie des premiers Valois à Louis XIV," in Pierre Nora, ed., *Les lieux de mémoire*, part 2: *La nation*, 2 vols. (Paris, 1986), vol. 2, pp. 145–92.

157. Jackson, *Vive le roi!*, pp. 131–48; Hanley, *Lit de Justice*, pp. 261–63, 266.

158. Roland Mousnier, *La vénalité des offices sous Henri IV et Louis XIII*, 2d. ed. (Paris, 1971), pp. 594–605; J. Russell Major, *Representative Government in Early Modern France* (New Haven, 1980), chs. 9–10.

159. Ribadeneira, *Tratado del príncipe cristiano*, p. 456; Geoffrey Parker, *The Dutch Revolt* (Harmondsworth, Middlesex, 1979), pp. 242–43; Rowen, ed., *Low Countries in Early Modern Times*, pp. 105–8.

160. Dreitzel, *Protestantischer Aristotelismus*, pp. 143–44, 186–88, 219–20, 242–43; Arnisaeus, *Doctrina politica*, pp. 14–15, 271–72; Gross, *Empire and Sovereignty*, pp. 170–79; von Gierke, *Development of Political Theory*, pp. 164–67.

161. Sorlien, ed., *Diary of John Manningham*, p. 216.

162. Nichols, ed., *Progresses of James I*, vol. 1, pp. 11, 15; Wormald, "James VI and I," p. 43, and Linda Levy Peck, "The Mentality of a Jacobean Grandee," in Levy Peck, ed., *Jacobean Court*, pp. 150–51; Ward Allen, ed., *Translating for King James* (Kingsport, Ill., 1969), pp. 90–91.

163. Jackson, *Vive le roi!*, p. 90. For a comparison of sovereignty in seventeenth-century Spain, France, and England, see Stephan Skalweit, "Das Herrscherbild des 17. Jahrhunderts," *Historische Zeitschrift* 184 (1957): 65–80.

## Chapter Three: The Theatre of Royal Virtue, 1610–1637

1. The events of the rebellion in Bohemia are recounted in Geoffrey Parker, ed., *The Thirty Years' War* (London, 1984), pp. 23–49; J. V. Polisensky, *The Thirty Years' War* (London, 1971), pp. 66–100; and Hans Sturmberger, *Aufstand in Böhmen: Der Beginn der Dreißigjährigen Krieges* (Munich, 1959), pp. 7–14, 35–64. See also Jaroslav Pánek, "The Religious Question and the Political System of Bohemia before and after the Battle of the White Mountain," in R. J. W. Evans and T. V. Thomas, eds., *Crown, Church, and Estates: Central European Politics in the Sixteenth and Seventeenth Centuries* (New York, 1991), pp. 129–48, and Winfried Schulze, "Estates and the Problem of Resistance in Theory and Practice in the Sixteenth and Seventeenth Centuries," in ibid., pp. 158–75.

2. Johann Franzl, *Ferdinand II.: Kaiser im Zwiespalt der Zeit* (Graz, 1978), p. 200; Anna Coreth, *Pietas Austriaca: Ursprung und Entwicklung barocker Frömmigkeit in Österreich* (Munich, 1957), pp. 38–39; Robert Bireley, *Religion and Politics in the Age of Counterreformation: Emperor Ferdinand II, William Lamormaini, S.J., and the Formation of Imperial Policy* (Chapel Hill, N.C., 1981), pp. 14–15, 102; Hans Sturmberger, *Georg Erasmus Tschernembl: Religion, Libertät und Widerstand* (Graz, 1953), pp. 276–315.

3. Marie Tanner, *The Last Descendant of Aeneas: The Habsburgs and the Mythic Image of the Emperor* (New Haven, 1993), ch. 10; Elida Maria Szarota, ed., *Der Jesuitendrama im deutschen Sprachgebiet: Eine Periochen-Edition*, 7 vols. in 4 parts (Munich, 1979–87), part 1, vol. 1, pp. 62–63; Jean-Marie Valentin, *Le théâtre des Jésuites dans les pays de langue allemande: Salut des âmes et ordre des cités*, 3 vols. (Frankfurt am Main, 1978), vol. 2, p. 654.

4. Tanner, *Last Descendant of Aeneas*, pp. 202, 300 n. 52; *Obsigende Gottseeligkeit: Das ist Flavius Constantinus der Grosse* (Vienna, 1659), reprinted in Szarota, *Das Jesuitendrama*, part 3, vol. 5, pp. 1049–61 (quotation on p. 1050). The occasion for both performances was the elevation of each prince to the title of King of the Romans, or heir to the Empire. For a 1653 print of Ferdinand IV, King of the Romans, as Constantine, see Friedrich B. Polleross, *Das sakrale Identifikationsporträt: Ein höfischer Bildtypus vom 13. bis zum 20. Jahrhundert*, 2 vols. (Worms, 1988), vol. 1, p. 248, vol. 2, plate 99.

5. Henry Bertram Hill, ed. and trans., *The Political Testament of Cardinal Richelieu* (Madison, Wis., 1961), p. 68.

6. Michèle Fogel, *Les cérémonies de l'information dans la France du XVIe au milieu du XVIIIe siècle* (Paris, 1989), pp. 11–19.

7. Miguel de Cervantes Saavedra, *The Adventures of Don Quixote*, trans. J. M. Cohen (Harmondsworth, Middlesex, 1950, 1986), p. 429.

8. Jürgen Habermas, *The Structural Transformation of the Public Sphere: An Inquiry into a Category of Bourgeois Society*, trans. Thomas Burger (Oxford, 1989), esp. chs. 2–3; also Fogel, *Cérémonies de l'information*, pp. 411–29.

9. Heinz Kindermann, *Theatergeschichte Europas*, vol. 3: *Das Theater der Barockzeit* (Salzburg, 1959), pp. 13–21; Konrad Repgen, "Uber die Geschichtsschreibung des dreißigjährigen Krieges: Begriff und Konzeption," in Konrad Repgen and Elisabeth Müller-Luckner, eds., *Krieg und Politik, 1618–1648: Europäische Probleme und Perpektiven* (Munich, 1988), pp. 11–16.

10. José Antonio Maravall, *Culture of the Baroque: Analysis of a Historical Structure*, trans. Terry Cochran (Minneapolis, 1986), pp. 233–41. Robert Muchembled, *Popular Culture and Elite Culture in France, 1400–1750*, trans. Lydia Cochrane (Baton Rouge, 1978, 1985), ch. 6, further contrasts "mass culture" with popular culture; but the two were not always clearly distinct.

11. For criticisms of Machiavelli, see Robert Bireley, *The Counter-Reformation Prince: Anti-Machiavellianism or Catholic Statecraft in Early Modern Europe* (Chapel Hill, N.C., 1990).

12. Valentin, *Le théâtre des Jésuites*, vol. 1, pp. 178–204, 247–57; Kindermann, *Theatergeschichte*, vol. 3, pp. 440–84; R. Po-chia Hsia, *Social Discipline in the Reformation: Central Europe, 1550–1750* (London, 1989), pp. 94–8; John Bossy, "The Mass as a Social Institution," *Past and Present* 100 (Aug. 1983): 29–61.

13. Justus Lipsius, *Sixe Bookes of Politickes or Civil Doctrine*, trans. William Jones (London, 1594; reprint Amsterdam, 1970), book 1, chs. 2–3, book 4, chs. 2–4.

14. Ibid., book 2, chs. 4, 16, book 6, ch. 5; the quotations are on p. 114.

15. Ibid., p. 64. For a different interpretation of his views, see Richard Tuck, *Philosophy and Government, 1572–1651* (Cambridge, 1993), pp. 45–64.

16. Gerhard Oestreich, *Neostoicism and the Early Modern State* (Cambridge, 1982), chs. 1–7; Bireley, *Counter-Reformation Prince*, ch. 4.

17. Bireley, *Counter-Reformation Prince*, pp. 79–80; Oestreich, *Neostoicism*, pp. 96–101; Coreth, *Pietas Austriaca*, p. 12; Hans Sturmberger, *Kaiser Ferdinand II. und das Problem der Absolutismus* (Vienna, 1957), p. 6; Franz Bosbach, ed., *Princeps in compendio*, in Konrad Repgen, ed., *Das Herrscherbild im 17. Jahrhundert* (Münster, 1991), pp. 79–114.

18. *Pater-familias evangelicus: Der evangelische Hausvater* (Augsburg, 1625), reproduced in Szarota, *Das Jesuitendrama*, part 1, vol. 1, pp. 533–56. For his patronage of the Jesuit theatre, see Kindermann, *Theatergeschichte*, vol. 3, pp. 486–89.

19. Bireley, *Religion and Politics*, pp. 12–13, 14, 101, 104; Coreth, *Pietas Austriaca*, 23–24, 28–29, 48–51; Kraus, "Das katholische Herrscherbild," p. 15; Valentin, *Le théâtre des Jésuites*, vol. 2, pp. 655–58; Polleross, *Das sakrale Identifikationsporträt*, vol. 1, pp. 158, 235, vol. 2, plates 35, 156; Robert Bireley, "Confessional Absolutism in the Habsburg Lands in the Seventeenth Century," in Charles W. Ingrao, ed., *State and Society in Early Modern Austria* (West Lafayette, Ind., 1994), p. 37. For the significance of Corpus Christi, see John Bossy, *Christianity in the West, 1400–1700* (Oxford, 1985), pp. 71–72.

20. *Princeps in compendio*, p. 110; Polleross, *Das sakrale Identifikationsporträt*, vol. 1, pp. 134–35, vol. 2, plate 25.

21. Szarota, *Das Jesuitendrama*, part 1, vol. 1, pp. 64–66; *Hermenigildus Martyr* (Ingolstadt, 1623, Augsburg, 1626), reproduced in ibid., part 3, vol. 1, pp. 467–77, 479–93; Polleross, *Das sakrale Identifikationsporträt*, vol. 1, p. 289.

22. R. J. W. Evans, *The Making of the Habsburg Monarchy, 1550–1700* (Oxford, 1979), ch. 10; Bireley, "Confessional Absolutism," p. 45; Inge Gampl, *Staat- Kirche- Individuum in der Rechtsgeschichte Österreichs zwischen Reformation und Revolution* (Vienna, 1984), pp. 4, 18, 29–30; Brian P. Levack, *The Witch-Hunt in Early Modern Europe* (London, 1987), pp. 95, 127, 175, 178–79, 198–99.

23. Muchembled, *Popular Culture*, ch. 5; Jean Wirth, "Against the Acculturation Thesis," in Kaspar von Greyerz, ed., *Religion and Society in Early Modern Europe, 1500–1800* (London, 1984), pp. 66–78. The element of persuasion in Catholic reformation is emphasized in Marc Foster, *The Counter-Reformation in the Villages: Religion and Reform in the Bishopric of Speyer, 1560–1720* (Ithaca, N.Y., 1992).

24. Hermann Rebel, *Peasant Classes: The Bureaucratization of Property and Family Relations under Early Habsburg Absolutism, 1511–1636* (Princeton, 1983), esp. pp. 121–98, 230–84.

25. Evans, *Making of the Habsburg Monarchy*, pp. 92–96, 169–80, 204–10, 240–46; Georg Heilingsetzer, "The Austrian Nobility, 1600–1650: Between Court and Estates," in Evans and Thomas, eds., *Church and Estates*, pp. 245–60; Charles W. Ingrao, *The Habsburg Monarchy, 1618–1848* (Cambridge, 1994), pp. 41–44; Henry Frederick Schwarz, *The Imperial Privy Council in the Seventeenth Century* (Cambridge, Mass., 1943), ch. 5.

26. The best overall description of this process is in Evans, *Making of the Habsburg Monarchy*, chs. 2–3; see also Karl Vocelka, "Public Opinion and the Phenomenon of Sozialdisziplinierung in the Habsburg Monarchy," in Ingrao, ed., *State and Society*, pp. 119–38.

27. Gunther Franz, "Glaube und Recht im politischen Denken Kaiser Ferdinands II.," *Archiv für Reformationsgeschichte* 49 (1958): 258–69, argues for an absolutist interpretation, while Sturmberger, *Kaiser Ferdinand II.*, pp. 45–46, identifies Ferdinand with a form of "confessional absolutism." Religious motives are stressed in Robert Bireley, "Ferdinand II: Founder of the Habsburg Monarchy," in Evans and Thomas, eds., *Crown, Church,*

*and Estates,* pp. 220–44, and in Andreas Kraus, "Das katholische Herrscherbild im Reich, dargestellt am Beispiel Kaiser Ferdinands II. und Kurfürst Maximilians I. von Bayern," in Repgen, ed., *Das Herrscherbild,* pp. 1–25; but Bireley moderates his stance in "Confessional Absolutism," pp. 36–53.

28. Hauke Jessen, *"Biblische Policey": Zum Naturrechtsdenken Dietrich Reinkings* (Freiburg, 1962), pp. 28–30; Roland Mousnier, "The Exponents and Critics of Absolutism," in J. P. Cooper, ed., *The New Cambridge Modern History,* vol. 4: *The Decline of Spain and the Thirty Years' War, 1609–48/59* (Cambridge, 1970), p. 109.

29. Jessen, *"Biblische Policey,"* pp. 17–24; Otto von Gierke, *The Development of Political Theory,* trans. Bernard Freyd (New York, 1966), pp. 159, 203 n. 92, n. 93; Evans, *Making of the Habsburg Monarchy,* p. 282.

30. Bireley, "Confessional Absolutism," pp. 38–39. The Emperor's relations with the Estates are considered in Hans-Bernhard Neumann, "The Impact of the Counter-Reformation on the Styrian Estates, 1578–1628," *Austrian History Yearbook* 15–16 (1979–80): 47–59; Winfried Schulze, "Das Ständewesen in den Erblanden der Habsburger Monarchie bis 1740: Von dualistischen Ständestaat zum organisch-föderativen Absolutismus," in Peter Baumgart and Jürgen Schmädeke, eds., *Ständetum und Staatsbildung in Brandenburg-Preussen* (Berlin, 1983), pp. 263–79.

31. Evans, *Making of the Habsburg Monarchy,* pp. 67–79, 198–200; Sturmberger, *Kaiser Ferdinand II.,* pp. 24–31, 39–44; but see Franz, "Glaube und Recht," pp. 262–65; Schwarz, *Imperial Privy Council,* ch. 3; Gunter Barudio, *Der teutsche Krieg, 1618–1648* (Frankfurt am Main, 1985), pp. 291–97.

32. Bireley, *Religion and Politics,* chs. 3–5; Gerhard Benecke, ed., *Germany in the Thirty Years' War* (New York, 1979), p. 14.

33. Bireley, *Religion and Politics,* pp. 12–13; Szarota, *Das Jesuitendrama,* part 1, vol. 1, p. 68; *Ritterlicher Kampff: In welchem der heylige Wenceslaus Herzog inn Böhem wider den Tyrannen Radißlaum von den Englen beschützt und verfochten worden* (Augsburg, 1636), reproduced in Szarota, *Das Jesuitendrama,* part 3, vol. 2, pp. 999–1006; W. A. Coupe, "Political and Religious Cartoons of the Thirty Years' War," *Journal of the Warburg and Courtauld Institutes* 25 (1962): 71, 74.

34. *Princeps in compendio,* p. 92. For Ferdinand's views on reason of state, see Franz, "Glaube und Recht," p. 262; Sturmberger, *Kaiser Ferdinand II.,* pp. 32–38; Bireley, *Religion and Politics,* pp. 200–204.

35. Golo Mann, *Wallenstein: His Life Narrated,* trans. Charles Kessler (New York, 1976), pp. 790–844. The original German version, *Wallenstein: Sein Leben erzählt* (Frankfurt am Main, 1971), contains a thorough bibliography of the vast literature on the "Wallenstein problem." See also Barudio, *Der teutsche Krieg,* pp. 298–302, and Parker, ed., *Thirty Years' War,* pp. 256–57, n. 7, and 294–95. For Wallenstein's architectural projects, see Thomas DaCosta Kaufmann, *Court, Cloister, and City: The Art and Culture of Central Europe, 1450–1800* (Chicago, 1995), pp. 249–55.

36. *Maria Virgo Blasphemarium Victrix, sive Julianus Apostata ob blasphemias divinus interemptus* (Vienna, 1635), in Szarota, ed., *Das Jesuitendrama,* part 2, vol. 1, pp. 831–45, part 2, vol. 2, p. 2289.

37. H. J. C. von Grimmelshausen, *The Adventurous Simplicissimus,* trans. A. T. S. Goodrick (Lincoln, Neb., 1962), pp. 170–80.

38. Christopher Hill, *Society and Puritanism in Pre-Revolutionary England* (London, 1964, 1969); David Underdown, *Revel, Riot, and Rebellion: Popular Politics and Culture in England, 1603–1660* (Oxford, 1985); David Underdown, *Fire from Heaven* (London, 1993); Herbert H. Rowen, ed., *Low Countries in Early Modern Times* (London, 1972), p. 138.

39. Gade, *Christian IV*, pp. 131–32, 166–67; Jens Glebe-Møller, "Fromhed styrker rigerne: Skole- og kirkepolitik under Christian IV," in Svend Ellehøj, ed., *Christian IVs verden* (Copenhagen, 1988), pp. 249–76; Thorkild Lyby and Ole Peter Grell, "The Consolidation of Lutheranism in Denmark and Norway," in Ole Peter Grell, ed., *The Scandinavian Reformation: From Evangelical Movement to Institutionalization of Reform* (Cambridge, 1995), pp. 126–41.

40. David Warren Sabean, *Power in the Blood: Popular Culture and Village Discourse in Early Modern Germany* (Cambridge, 1984), p. 58. Lyndal Roper warns against overestimating such disciplinary tactics in "Drinking, Whoring, and Gorging: Brutish Indiscipline and the Formation of Protestant Identity," in her *Oedipus and the Devil: Witchcraft, Sexuality, and Religion in Early Modern Europe* (London, 1994), pp. 145–67.

41. Marc Raeff, *The Well-Ordered Police State: Social and Institutional Change through Law in the Germanies and Russia, 1600–1800* (New Haven, 1983), pp. 56–92; and for sexual police, Isabel V. Hull, *Sexuality, State, and Civil Society in Germany, 1700–1815* (Ithaca, N.Y., 1996), ch. 2.

42. Raeff, *Well-Ordered Police State*, pp. 50, 146–66; Oestreich, *Neostoicism*, ch. 9; Volker Press, "Formen des Ständewesens in den deutschen Territorialstaaten des 16. und 17. Jahrhunderts," in Baumgart and Schmädeke, eds., *Ständetum und Staatsbildung*, pp. 280–318, as well as his "Vom Ständestaat zum Absolutismus: 50 Thesen zur Entwicklung des Ständewesens in Deutschland," in ibid., pp. 319–26.

43. Quoted in Hill, *Society and Puritanism*, p. 214.

44. Oestreich, *Neostoicism*, chs. 7, 9; also Geoffrey Parker, *The Military Revolution: Military Innovation and the Rise of the West, 1500–1800* (Cambridge, 1988), pp. 20–22.

45. Oestreich, *Neostoicism*, ch. 5; Herbert Rowen, *The Princes of Orange: The Stadholders in the Dutch Republic* (Cambridge, 1988), ch. 2. For Protestant ideals of rulership, see Heinz Duchhardt, "Das protestantische Herrscherbild des 17. Jahrhunderts im Reich," in Repgen, ed., *Das Herrscherbild*, pp. 26–42.

46. Volker Press, *Calvinismus und Territorialstaat: Regierung und Zentralbehördern der Kurpfalz, 1559–1619* (Stuttgart, 1970), pp. 114–29, 369–478.

47. Frances Yates, *The Rosicrucian Enlightenment* (London, 1972), esp. chs. 1–7; Barudio, *Der teutsche Krieg*, pp. 228–30.

48. Weeks, *Boehme*, pp. 127–42. For attempts to justify Frederick's resistance to the Emperor, see Sturmberger, *Tschernembl*, pp. 336–62.

49. Oestreich, *Neostoicism*, pp. 112–13; Horst Dreitzel, *Protestantischer Aristotelismus und absoluter Staat: Die "Politica" des Henning Arnisaeus (ca. 1575–1636)* (Wiesbaden, 1970), p. 26; Scocozza, *Christian IV*, pp. 122, 124–25; Douglas Lockhart, *Denmark in the 30 Years' War: King Christian IV and the Decline of the Oldenburg State* (Selsingrove, 1996), ch. 3; David Kirby, *Northern Europe in the Early Modern Period: The Baltic World, 1492–1772* (London, 1990), pp. 198–200; T. K. Derry, *A History of Scandinavia* (Minneapolis, 1979), pp. 114–19.

50. Charlotte Christensen, "Christian IVs Renæssance: Billedkunsten i Danmark, 1588–1648," in Ellehøj, ed., *Christian IVs verden*, pp. 302–35; Kjeld de Fine Licht, "Arkitektur: Manierismens fortsættelse," in ibid., pp. 336–77; Ole Kongsted, "Den verdslige »Rex Splendens«: Musikken som repræsentativ kunst ved Christian IVs hof," in ibid., pp. 433–64; Kindermann, *Theatergeschichte*, vol. 3, pp. 563–68.

51. E. Ladewig Petersen, *Christian IV's pengeudlån til Danske adelige: Kongelige foretagervirksomhed og adelige goeldsstiftselse, 1596–1625* (Copenhagen, 1974), and his "War, Finance, and the Growth of Absolutism: Some Aspects of the European Integration of Seventeenth-Century Denmark," in Göran Rystad, ed., *Europe and Scandinavia: Aspects of the Process of Integration in the Seventeenth Century* (Lund, 1983), pp. 33–45.

52. Scocozza, *Christian IV*, pp. 136–37; Heiberg, *Christian IV*, p. 430; Lockhart, *Denmark in the 30 Years' War*, pp. 137, 172; Alex Wittendorf, "»Fire stolper holder et skidehus«: Tidens forestillingsverden," in Ellehøj, ed., *Christian IVs verden*, pp. 233, 238.

53. Michael Roberts, *Gustavus Adolphus: A History of Sweden, 1611–1632*, 2 vols. (London, 1953, 1958), vol. 1, pp. 399–405, vol. 2, pp. 241–42; Nils Ahnlund, *Gustav Adolf the Great*, trans. Michael Roberts (Princeton, 1940), pp. 136–38, 259–67; Montgomery, "The Institutionalization of Lutheranism," pp. 167–72.

54. See Roberts, *Gustavus Adolphus*, vol. 2, ch. 3, as well as three of his pieces collected in *Essays in Swedish History* (London, 1967): "Gustav Adolf and the Art of War," pp. 56–81; "The Political Objectives of Gustav Adolf in Germany, 1630–2," pp. 82–110; and "The Military Revolution, 1560–1660," pp. 195–225. See also Günter Barudio, *Gustav Adolf der Große: Eine politische Biographie* (Frankfurt am Main, 1982, 1985), pp. 385–404, and Sven Lundkvist, "Die schwedischen Kriegs- und Friedenziele, 1632–1648," in Repgen and Müller-Luckner, eds., *Krieg und Politik*, pp. 219–40. The socio-economic consequences of the military state are examined in Sven A. Nilsson, *De stora krigens tid: Om Sverige som militärstat och bondesamhälle* (Uppsala, 1990), pp. 150–77, 226–44; in Jan Lindegren, "The Swedish 'Military State,' 1560–1720," *Scandinavian Journal of History* 10 (1985): 305–36; and in Parker, *The Military Revolution*, pp. 52–55.

55. Quoted in Roberts, *Gustavus Adolphus*, vol. 2, p. 238. For Lipsian influence in Sweden, see Oestreich, *Neostoicism*, pp. 109–12; Nils Runeby, *Monarchia mixta: Maktfördelningsdebatt in Sverige under den tidigare stormaktstiden* (Stockholm, 1962), pp. 49–50, 102, 104–5, 123–24, 160–62, 164–65.

56. Paul Antony, ed., *Johann Valentin Andreä—ein schwäbischer Pfarrer im dreißigjährigen Krieg* (Heidenheim an der Brenz, 1970), p. 63; also Polleross, *Das sakrale Identifikationsporträt*, vol. 1, pp. 93–95.

57. Gerd Zillhardt, ed., *Der dreißigjährige Krieg in zeitgenössischer Darstellung: Hans Heberles "Zeytregister" (1618–1672)* (Ulm, 1975), pp. 126–27. The significance of such portents in inculcating public discipline is explained in John Theibault, "Jeremiah in the Village: Prophecy, Preaching, Pamphlets, and Penance in the Thirty Years' War," *Central European History* 27, no. 4 (1994): 441–60.

58. William A. Coupe, *The German Illustrated Broadsheet in the Seventeenth Century*, 2 vols. (Baden-Baden, 1967), vol. 1, pp. 78–82, vol. 2, plate 38; [Alexander Gil], *The New Star of the North Shining upon the Victorious King of Sweden* (London, 1632, reprint Norwood, N.J., 1976).

59. Arthur Searle, ed., *Barrington Family Letters, 1628–1632*, Camden Society, 4th series, vol. 28 (London, 1983), p. 238.

60. For opposing interpretations of Gustavus's attitude towards reason of state, see Ahnlund, *Gustav Adolf*, pp. 267–75, and Barudio, *Gustav Adolf*, pp. 257–67.

61. J. H. M. Salmon, "Seneca and Tacitus in Jacobean England," in Linda Levy Peck, ed., *The Mental World of the Jacobean Court* (Cambridge, 1991), pp. 169–88; Malcolm Smuts, "Court-Centred Politics and the Uses of Roman Historians, c. 1590–1630," in Kevin Sharpe and Peter Lake, eds., *Culture and Politics in Early Stuart England* (Stanford, 1993), pp. 21–43.

62. The best biography is Roger Lockyer, *Buckingham* (London, 1981). For different views of the opposition, see Conrad Russell, "Parliamentary History in Perspective, 1604–1629," in his *Unrevolutionary England, 1603–1642* (London, 1990), pp. 31–57; Derek Hirst, "Court, Country, and Politics before 1629," in Kevin Sharpe, ed., *Faction and Parliament: Essays on Early Stuart History* (London, 1978), pp. 105–37.

63. G. P. V. Akrigg, ed., *Letters of James VI and I* (Berkeley, 1984), pp. 383–85; Conrad Russell, "The Foreign Policy Debate in the House of Commons in 1621," in his *Unrevolutionary England*, p. 79; Simon Adams, "Foreign Policy and the Parliaments of 1621 and 1624," in Sharpe, ed., *Faction and Parliament*, pp. 139–64.

64. Thomas Cogswell, *The Blessed Revolution: English Politics and the Coming of War, 1621–1624* (Cambridge, 1989), pp. 6–53; the court festivities are described in Antonio Rodríquez Villa, *Etiquetas de la casa de Austria* (Madrid, 1913), pp. 119–30.

65. Cogswell, *Blessed Revolution*, chs. 4–7; Conrad Russell, *Parliaments and English Politics, 1621–1629* (Oxford, 1979), ch. 3.

66. Rowen, ed., *Low Countries*, pp. 129, 141; Peter Geyl, *The Netherlands in the Seventeenth Century*, 2 vols. (New York: 1961), vol. 1, pp. 38–83; Jonathan Israel, *The Dutch Republic: Its Rise, Greatness, and Fall, 1477–1806* (Oxford, 1995), pp. 393–95; Nicholas Tyacke, *Anti-Calvinists: The Rise of English Arminianism, c. 1590–1640* (Oxford, 1987), ch. 4.

67. Hugo Grotius, *The Rights of War and Peace*, trans. A. C. Campbell (New York, 1901), book 1, ch. 1, para. 10, p. 22, book 1, ch. 2, para. 5, p. 36; Tuck, *Philosophy and Government*, pp. 190–201.

68. The fullest accounts is in Tyacke, *Anti-Calvinists*, chs. 2–7. See also his "Puritanism, Arminianism, and Counter-Revolution," in Conrad Russell, ed., *The Origins of the English Civil War* (London, 1973), pp. 119–43, as well as Hugh Trevor-Roper, "Laudianism and Political Power," in his *Catholics, Anglicans, and Puritans* (London, 1987), pp. 40–119; Andrew Foster, "Church Policies of the 1630s," in Richard Cust and Anne Hughes, eds., *Conflict in Early Stuart England: Studies in Religion and Politics, 1603–1642* (London, 1989), pp. 193–223. Tyacke's views are sharply criticized in Kevin Sharpe, *The Personal Rule of Charles I* (New Haven, 1992), pp. 275–308, and Julian Davies, *The Caroline Captivity of the Church: Charles I and the Remoulding of Anglicanism, 1625–1641* (Oxford, 1992), ch. 3.

69. Tyacke, *Anti-Calvinists*, pp. 266–70; Geyl, *The Netherlands*, vol. 1, p. 43; but see Davies, *Caroline Captivity of the Church*, ch. 2.

70. For overviews of court culture, see Peter W. Thomas, "Charles I of England: The

354 · NOTES TO PAGES 104–108

Tragedy of Absolutism," in A. G. Dickens, ed., *The Courts of Europe: Politics, Patronage, and Royalty, 1400–1800* (London, 1977), pp. 190–211; Sharpe, *Personal Rule*, pp. 209–35. Davies, *Caroline Captivity of the Church*, ch. 1, connects court culture with the king's religious ideas.

71. Stephen Orgel and Roy Strong, *Inigo Jones: The Theatre of the Stuart Court*, 2 vols. (Berkeley, 1973), vol. 2, pp. 1–75; R. M. Smuts, *Court Culture and the Origins of a Royalist Tradition in Early Stuart England* (Philadelphia, 1987), pp. 162–68 and ch. 9; Sharpe, *Personal Rule*, pp. 227–33, 647–48; Martin Butler, *Theatre and Crisis, 1632–1642* (Cambridge, 1984), ch. 5; and for Jonson's reservations about court entertainments, Martin Butler, "Ben Jonson and the Limits of Courtly Panegyric," in Sharpe and Lake, eds., *Culture and Politics*, pp. 91–115.

72. Kevin Sharpe, *Criticism and Compliment: The Politics of Literature in the England of Charles I* (Cambridge, 1987), ch. 5; Orgel and Strong, *Inigo Jones*, vol. 1, p. 13.

73. Mark Morford, *Stoics and Neostoics: Rubens and the Circle of Lipsius* (Princeton, 1991), pp. 204–10. Roy Strong, however, has argued that Inigo Jones came up with the ceiling's design: see his *Britannia triumphans: Inigo Jones, Rubens, and Whitehall Palace* (London, 1980).

74. Smuts, *Court Culture*, pp. 247–49; Sharpe, *Personal Rule*, pp. 219–22.

75. Roy Strong, *Van Dyck: Charles I on Horseback* (New York, 1972), ch. 4; Sharpe, *Personal Rule*, pp. 224–27.

76. Kevin Sharpe, "The Image of Virtue: The Court and Household of Charles I, 1625–1642," in his *Politics and Ideas in Early Stuart England* (London, 1989), pp. 147–73; J. S. Adamson, "Chivalry and Political Culture in Caroline England," in Sharpe and Lake, eds., *Culture and Politics*, pp. 161–97.

77. Judith Richards, " 'His Nowe Majestie' and the English Monarchy: The Kingship of Charles I before 1640," *Past and Present* 113 (1986): 70–96.

78. For different viewpoints on this issue, see Smuts, *Court Culture*, chs. 7–9; P. W. Thomas, "Two Cultures? Court and Country under Charles I," in Russell, ed., *Origins*, pp. 168–93; and Sharpe, *Criticism and Compliment*, ch. 1, as well as his "Culture, Politics, and the English Civil War," in Sharpe, ed., *Politics and Ideas*, pp. 279–316.

79. Samuel Rawson Gardiner, ed., *The Constitutional Documents of the Puritan Revolution, 1625–1660*, 3d ed. (Oxford, 1906), pp. 51–52; Richard Cust, *The Forced Loan and English Politics, 1626–1628* (Oxford, 1987), p. 179.

80. Quoted in Russell, *Parliaments and English Politics*, p. 392.

81. Gardiner, ed., *Constitutional Documents*, p. 79.

82. This session is discussed in Christopher Thompson, "The Divided Leadership of the House of Commons in 1629," in Sharpe, ed., *Faction and Parliament*, pp. 245–84; Russell, *Parliaments and English Politics*, pp. 396–416; and L. J. Reeve, *Charles I and the Road to Personal Rule* (Cambridge, 1989), ch. 3.

83. Sharpe, *Personal Rule*, pp. 952–54. A contrasting interpretation of the origins of personal rule is presented in Reeve, *Charles I and the Road to Personal Rule*, chs. 7–9.

84. Tyacke, *Anti-Calvinists*, ch. 8; Foster, "Church Policies," pp. 210–14; Sharpe, *Personal Rule*, pp. 333–45; Davies, *Caroline Captivity of the Church*, chs. 4, 6.

85. Gardiner, *Constitutional Documents*, pp. 99–103; Hill, *Society and Puritanism*,

pp. 193–95; Underdown, *Revel, Riot, and Rebellion,* pp. 65–68; Sharpe, *Personal Rule,* pp. 351–60; Davies, *Caroline Captivity of the Church,* ch. 5.

86. See J. G. A. Pocock, *The Ancient Constitution and the Feudal Law* (Cambridge, 1957, 1967), chs. 2–3; Cust, *Forced Loan,* pp. 62–67; J. P. Sommerville, *Politics and Ideology in England, 1603–1640* (London, 1986), pp. 127–31.

87. Robert Sybthorpe, *Apostolike Obedience* (London, 1627), pp. 10–11; [Matthew Wren], *A Sermon Preached before the Kings Majestie On Sunday the seventeenth of February last, at White-Hall* (Cambridge, 1627), pp. 27–28; Roger Maynwaring, *Religion and Allegiance* (London, 1627), part 1, pp. 10, 13.

88. Sir Robert Filmer, *Patriarcha and Other Writings,* ed. Johann Sommerville (Cambridge, 1991), p. 7. For the date of composition, see ibid., pp. xxxii–iv, and Richard Tuck, "A New Date for Filmer's *Patriarcha,*" *Historical Journal* 29 (1986): 183–86. Filmer's work is discussed in Sommerville, *Politics and Ideology,* pp. 31–32; Gordon Schochet, *Patriarchalism and Political Thought: The Authoritarian Family and Political Speculation and Attitudes, Especially in Seventeenth-Century England* (Oxford, 1975), chs. 7–8; W. J. Daly, *Sir Robert Filmer and English Political Thought* (Toronto, 1979).

89. Filmer, *Patriarcha,* pp. 12, 35.

90. Grotius, *Laws of War and Peace,* book 1, ch. 3, para. 7, p. 62.

91. Filmer, *Patriarcha,* p. 43. Grotius, however, made an exception for obedience to commands directly repugnant to divine law in *Rights of War and Peace,* book 1, ch. 3, para. 9, p. 69.

92. Sir John Eliot, *De jure majestatis: or Political Treatise of Government,* ed. A. B. Grosart (London, 1882), p. 99. See also Harold Hulme, *The Life of Sir John Eliot* (New York, 1957), ch. 16; J. N. Ball, "Sir John Eliot and Parliament, 1624–1629," in Sharpe, ed., *Faction and Parliament,* pp. 173–207; Sommerville, *Politics and Ideology,* pp. 157–58.

93. Sir John Eliot, *The Monarchie of Man,* ed. A. B. Grosart, 2 vols. (London, 1879), vol. 2, p. 42; Eliot, *De jure majestatis,* p. 110.

94. Jean-Louis Guez de Balzac, *Le prince,* in L. Moreau, ed., *Oeuvres de J.-L. de Guez, sieur de Balzac,* 2 vols. (Paris, 1854), vol. 1, pp. 44–48.

95. Henry Phillips, *Church and Culture in Seventeenth-Century France* (Cambridge, 1997), ch. 1; Chatellier, *Europe of the Devout,* ch. 8; René Taveneaux, *Le Catholicisme dans la France classique, 1610–1715,* 2 vols. (Paris, 1980), vol. 2, ch. 12; Elisabeth Labrousse and Robert Sauzet, "La lente mise en place de la réforme Tridentine (1598–1661)," in Jacques le Goff and René Rémond, gen. eds., *Histoire de la France réligieuse,* vol. 2: *Du Christianisme flamboyant à l'aube des Lumières* (Paris, 1988), pp. 322–443.

96. Labrousse and Sauzet, "La lente mise en place," p. 344; De L'Estoile, *The Paris of Henry of Navarre,* p. 285.

97. W. F. Church, *Richelieu and Reason of State* (Princeton, 1972), p. 94; Raymond Darricau, "La spiritualité du prince," *XVIIe Siècle,* 62–63 (1964): 80.

98. J. Michael Hayden, *France and the Estates General of 1614* (Cambridge, 1974), pp. 216–17; Pierre Blet, *Le clergé de France et la monarchie: Etude sur les Assemblées Générales du clergé de 1615 à 1666* (Rome, 1959), pp. 40–82; Roland Mousnier, *La vénalité des offices sous Henri IV et Louis XIII,* 2d ed. (Paris, 1970), pp. 608–27; Roger Chartier and

Denis Richet, eds., *Représentation et vouloir politique: Autour des Etats-Généraux de 1614* (Paris, 1982); Joseph Bergin, *The Rise of Richelieu* (New Haven, 1991), pp. 127–45.

99. Guez de Balzac, *Le prince*, pp. 95–96; Victor-Louis Tapié, *France in the Age of Louis XIII and Richelieu*, trans. D. M. Lockie (New York, 1975), ch. 3; A. Lloyd Moote, *Louis XIII, the Just* (Berkeley, 1989), chs. 4–5. On the queen's supporters, see J. Russell Major, "The Revolt of 1620: A Study of Ties of Fidelity," *French Historical Studies* 14, no. 3 (1986): 391–408.

100. Pierre Chevallier, *Louis XIII, roi cornélien* (Paris, 1979), pp. 411–55; Guez de Balzac, *Le prince*, p. 59.

101. Polleross, *Das sakrale Identifikationsporträt*, vol. 2, pp. 257–58; Phillips, *Church and Culture*, pp. 47–58; René Pillorget, "L'image du prince dans la France du XVIIe siècle," in Repgen, ed., *Das Herrscherbild*, pp. 52–53.

102. "Les triomphes de Louis le Juste XIIIe du nom, roi de France et de Navarre," in Pierre Corneille, *Oeuvres complètes*, ed. Georges Couton, 2 vols. (Paris, 1984), vol. 2, p. 435; Christiane Desplat, "Louis XIII and the Union of Béarn to France," in Mark Greengrass, ed., *Conquest and Coalescence: The Shaping of the State in Early Modern Europe* (London, 1991), pp. 68–83; J. Russell Major, *Representative Government in Early Modern France* (New Haven, 1980), pp. 446–59.

103. A. D. Lublinskaya, *French Absolutism: The Crucial Phase, 1620–29* (Cambridge, 1968), p. 219 and ch. 4; Robert Sauzet, *Contre-Réforme et Réforme Catholique en Bas-Languedoc: Le diocèse de Nîmes au XVII siècle* (Brussels, 1979), pp. 165–210; Janine Garrisson, *L'édit de Nantes et sa révocation: Histoire d'une intolérance* (Paris, 1985), ch. 3; Margaret McGowan, *L'art du ballet de cour en France, 1581–1643* (Paris, 1963, 1978), pp. 216–20.

104. Guez de Balzac, *Le prince*, p. 21.

105. Ronald Forsyth Millen and Robert Erich Wolf, *Heroic Deeds and Mystic Figures: A New Reading of Rubens' Life of Maria de' Medici* (Princeton, 1989), esp. chs. 6, 11.

106. For the ordinance, see Major, *Representative Institutions*, pp. 512–18; Roland Mousnier, *The Institutions of France under the Absolute Monarchy*, 2 vols. (Chicago, 1979), vol. 2, pp. 602–3; Mousnier, *La vénalité des offices*, pp. 649–51; Richard Bonney, *Political Change in France under Richelieu and Mazarin, 1624–1661* (Oxford, 1978), pp. 34–35; Robin Briggs, "Richelieu and Reform: Rhetoric and Political Reality," in Joseph Bergin and Laurence Brockliss, eds., *Richelieu and His Age* (Oxford, 1992), pp. 92–93.

107. The best treatment of patronage is in Sharon Kettering, *Patrons, Brokers, and Clients in Seventeenth-Century France* (Oxford, 1986); see also Arthur L. Herman Jr., "The Language of Fidelity in Early Modern France," *Journal of Modern History* 67, no. 1 (1995): 1–24.

108. Marc Fumaroli, *L'age de l'éloquence: Rhétorique et «res literaria» de la Renaissance au seuil de l'époque classique* (Geneva, 1980), pp. 427–74.

109. Quoted in Chevallier, *Louis XIII*, p. 366. The term *Monster* was applied to the Habsburgs by Guez de Balzac, *Le prince*, p. 108.

110. Pierre Grillon, ed., *Les papiers de Richelieu: Section politique intérieure, correspondance et papiers d'état*, 6 vols. (Paris, 1975), vol. 4, p. 24; see also Hermann Weber, " 'Une bonne paix': Richelieu's Foreign Policy and the Peace of Christendom," trans. Robert Vilain, in Bergin and Brockliss, eds., *Richelieu and His Age*, pp. 45–69.

111. Raoul Allier, *La cabale des dévots (1627–1666)* (Geneva, 1902, 1970), pp. 45–47; Alain Tallon, *La Compagnie du Saint-Sacrement (1629–1667): Spiritualité et société* (Paris, 1990), pp. 51–61, 129–30.

112. Bergin, *Rise of Richelieu*, ch. 3; Joseph Bergin, "Richelieu and His Bishops? Ministerial Power and Episcopal Patronage under Louis XIII," in Bergin and Brockliss, eds., *Richelieu and His Age*, pp. 175–202; Grillon, ed., *Papiers de Richelieu*, vol. 1, pp. 257–58; Hill, ed., *Political Testament*, pp. 22–26; V. G. Kiernan, *The Duel in European History: Honour and the Reign of Aristocracy* (Oxford, 1988), pp. 74–77.

113. Church, *Richelieu and Reason of State*, esp. pp. 416–30, 505–13.

114. Robert Mandrou, *Magistrats et sorciers en France au XVIIe siècle: Une analyse de psychologie historique* (Paris, 1980), pp. 210–19, 226–45, 264–84, 313–63; Robin Briggs, "Witchcraft and the Community in France and French-Speaking Europe," in his *Communities of Belief: Cultural and Social Tension in Early Modern France* (Oxford, 1989), pp. 7–65.

115. Hill, ed., *Political Testament*, pp. 34–35, 70–75.

116. Grillon, ed., *Papiers de Richelieu*, vol. 1, pp. 248–49.

117. Guez de Balzac, *Le prince*, p. 22.

118. Grillon, ed., *Papiers de Richelieu*, vol. 1, pp. 267–68; Laurence Brockliss, "Richelieu, Education, and the State," in Bergin and Brockliss, eds., *Richelieu and His Age*, pp. 237–72; Ellery Schalk, *From Valor to Pedigree: Ideas of Nobility in France in the Sixteenth and Seventeenth Centuries* (Princeton, 1986), pp. 181–99.

119. McGowen, *L'art du ballet de cour*, pp. 176–90; Jean-François Solnon, *La cour de France* (Paris, 1987), pp. 224–29.

120. Fumaroli, *L'age de l'éloquence*, p. 647; Brockliss, "Richelieu, Education, and the State," pp. 252–61; and Fogel, *Cérémonies de l'information*, pp. 293–326, for the evolution of a "state language."

121. Alain Lottin, *Lille: Citadelle de la Contre-Réforme? (1598–1668)* (Dunkirk, 1984), p. 315; Sauzet, *Contre-Réforme et Réforme catholique*, pp. 216–44.

122. Jean Orcibal, ed., *Les origines du Jansénisme*, vol. 1: *Correspondance de Jansénius* (Louvain, 1947); Antoine Adam, *Du mysticisme à la révolte: Les Jansénistes du XVIIe siècle* (Paris, 1968), pp. 71–146; Phillips, *Church and Culture*, pp. 196–201.

123. Quoted in Jean Orcibal, *St. Cyran et le Jansénisme* (Paris, 1961), p. 123. See also Jean Orcibal, *Les origines du Jansénisme*, vol. 2: *Jean Duvergier de Hauranne, Abbé de Saint-Cyran et son temps* (Paris, 1948).

124. Fumaroli, *L'age de l'éloquence*, pp. 632–46.

125. René Taveneaux, ed., *Jansénisme et politique* (Paris, 1965), p. 54, 56–59; Orcibal, *Saint-Cyran et le Jansénisme*, pp. 27–38.

126. Corneille, *Le cid*, in his *Oeuvres complètes*, vol. 1, pp. 689–777. The quotations are from 1:4, ll. 151–52; 5:7, ll. 1839–40. This interpretation relies on David Clarke, *Pierre Corneille: Poetics and Political Drama under Louis XIII* (Cambridge, 1991), pp. 17–37, 136–66; but see also Michel Prigent, *Le héros et l'état dans la tragédie de Pierre Corneille* (Paris, 1986).

127. For the *Querelle du cid*, see Corneille, *Oeuvres complètes*, pp. 779–820, 1456–66; Clarke, *Corneille*, pp. 41–52; and for Scudéry's royalism, Pillorget, "L'image du prince," p. 45.

128. Guez de Balzac, *Le prince*, pp. 81, 188; Pierre Walter, "Jean-Louis Guez de Balzac's *Le prince*—A Revaluation," *Journal of the Warburg and Courtauld Institutes* 20 (1957): 215–48; Church, *Richelieu and Reason of State*, pp. 238–61; F. E. Sutcliffe, *Guez de Balzac et son temps* (Paris, 1959); Margaret McGowan, "Guez de Balzac: The Enduring Influence of Rome," in Keith Cameron and Elizabeth Woodrough, eds., *Ethics and Politics in Seventeenth-Century France* (Exeter, 1996), pp. 41–54.

129. H. Bibas and K.-T. Butler, eds., *Les premières lettres de Guez de Balzac, 1618–1627*, 2 vols. (Paris, 1934), vol. 2, p. 21.

130. Quoted in Mousnier, *La vénalité des offices*, p. 654.

131. Boris Porchnev, *Les soulèvements populaires en France au XVIIe siècle* (Paris, 1972), pp. 55–96; Roland Mousnier, *Peasant Uprisings in Seventeenth-Century France, Russia, and China*, trans. Brian Pearce (New York, 1970), pp. 32–113; Yves-Marie Bercé, *History of Peasant Revolts: The Social Origins of Rebellion in Early Modern France*, trans. Amanda Whitmore (Ithaca, N.Y., 1991), pp. 248–51; Robin Briggs, "Popular Revolt in Its Social Context," in *Communities of Belief*, pp. 115–53.

132. Chevallier, *Louis XIII*, pp. 539–48; Tapié, *France in the Age of Louis XIII and Richelieu*, pp. 374–75; Polleross, *Das sakrale Identifikationsporträt*, vol. 2, pp. 127–29, 145–46.

133. Stanislas Kot, *Socinianism in Poland: The Social and Political Ideas of the Polish Antitrinitarians in the Sixteenth and Seventeenth Centuries*, trans. E. M. Wilbur (Boston, 1957), chs. 5–9; Janusz Tazbir, *A State without Stakes: Polish Religious Toleration in the Sixteenth and Seventeenth Centuries* (New York, 1973), chs. 7–8; Janusz Tazbir, "The Polish Reformation as an Intellectual Movement," in Samuel Fiszman, ed., *The Polish Renaissance in Its European Context* (Bloomington, Ind., 1988), pp. 111–26.

134. Norman Davies, *God's Playground: A History of Poland*, 2 vols. (Oxford, 1981), vol. 2, ch. 6; J. Umiński, "The Counter-Reformation in Poland," and F. Nowak, "Sigismund III, 1587–1632," in W. F. Reddaway et al., eds., *The Cambridge History of Poland*, vol. 1: *From the Origins to Sobieski (to 1696)* (Cambridge, 1950), chs. 19, 21; Janusz Tazbir, "La Polonisation du Catholicisme," in his *La république nobiliaire et le monde*, trans. Lucjan Grobelak (Wrocław, 1986), pp. 124–56; Czeslaw Milocsz, *The History of Polish Literature*, 2d ed. (Berkeley, 1983), pp. 96–108, 125–26; Kindermann, *Theatergeschichte*, vol. 3, pp. 594–99, 601–5.

135. For an assessment of Poland as a thriving proto-democracy, see Józef Siemeński, "Polish Political Culture in the Sixteenth Century," in Władysław Czapliński, ed., *The Polish Parliament at the Summit of Its Development (Sixteenth–Seventeenth Centuries)* (Wrocław, 1985), pp. 53–84 (an essay first published in 1932). A more balanced picture is found in Antoni Mączak, "Polish Society and Power System in the Renaissance," in Fiszman, ed., *The Polish Renaissance*, pp. 17–33.

136. Quoted in Davies, *God's Playground*, vol. 1, p. 342; see also Auguste Berga, *Un prédicateur de la cour de Pologne sous Sigismond III: Peter Skarga (1536–1612)* (Paris, 1916), pp. 252–57; Tazbir, *State Without Stakes*, pp. 111–12.

137. Orest Subtelny, *Ukraine: A History*, 2d ed. (Toronto, 1994), pp. 99–102.

138. Stanislas Zólkiewski, *Expedition to Moscow*, trans. and ed. Jedrzej Giertych (London, 1959), p. 51.

139. Ibid., pp. 91, 113.

140. Quoted in Ruslan G. Skrynnikov, *The Time of Troubles: Russia in Crisis, 1604–1618*, ed. and trans. Hugh Graham (Gulf Breeze, Fla., 1988), p. 104.

141. Bodin, *Six Bookes of the Commonweale*, trans. Richard Knolles (Cambridge, Mass., 1962, reprint of 1606 ed.), pp. 723–29. The quotation is on p. 726.

142. Kaufmann, *Court, Cloister, and City*, pp. 245–46.

143. Hugh Trevor-Roper, ed., *The Age of Expansion: Europe and the World, 1559–1660* (London, 1968), p. 247, plate 13; Polleross, *Das sakrale Identifikationsporträt*, vol. 1, p. 104; Julian Krzyzanowski, *A History of Polish Literature*, trans. Doris Ronowicz (Warsaw, 1978), p. 142.

144. Albrycht Stanisław Radziwiłł, *Memoriale rerum gestarum in Polonia, 1632–1656*, ed. Adam Przyboś and Roman Zelewski, 5 vols. (Wrocław, 1968–74), vol. 1, pp. 17–18; Kot, *Socinianism in Poland*, pp. 135–36.

145. Radziwiłł, *Memoriale*, vol. 2, pp. 260–61, 266, vol. 3, pp. 2–4; Milosz, *History of Polish Literature*, p. 115; Kot, *Socinianism in Poland*, p. 167; Tazbir, *State without Stakes*, pp. 189–93.

146. W. Czapliński, "The Reign of Wladyslaw IV, 1632–48," in Reddaway et al., eds., *Cambridge History of Poland*, vol. 1, pp. 494, 497; Davies, *God's Playground*, vol. 1, p. 240; Radziwiłł, *Memoriale*, vol. 2, pp. 240, 252; Polleross, *Das sakrale Identifikationsporträt*, vol. 1, p. 115.

147. Kot, *Socinianism in Poland*, pp. 138–45; Krzyzanowski, *History of Polish Literature*, pp. 145–50 and plate 9.

148. Milosz, *History of Polish Literature*, pp. 148–51; Kaufmann, *Court, Cloister, and City*, pp. 246–49; Kindermann, *Theatergeschichte*, vol. 3, pp. 599–601; Władysław Czapliński, "Das Theater am Hofe des polnischen Wasas," in A. Buck et al., eds., *Europäischer Hofkultur im 16. und 17. Jahrhundert*, 3 vols. (Hamburg, 1981), vol. 2, pp. 295–300; Milos Velimirović, "Warsaw, Moscow, and St. Petersburg," in George J. Buelow, ed., *The Late Baroque Era: From the 1680s to 1740* (Englewood Cliffs, N.J., 1994), pp. 436–37.

149. Skrynnikov, *Boris Godunov*, ch. 12.

150. Isaac Massa, *A Short History of the Beginnings and Origins of These Present Wars in Moscow under the Reign of Various Sovereigns down to the Year 1610*, ed. and trans. G. Edward Orchard (Toronto, 1982), p. 131; Maureen Perrie, *Pretenders and Popular Monarchism in Early Modern Russia* (Cambridge, 1995), pp. 63–69; Zólkiewski, *Expedition to Moscow*, pp. 39–40; Skrynnikov, *Time of Troubles*, pp. 13–14, 31–32.

151. The most reliable account is in Skrynnikov, *Time of Troubles*, pp. 32–35. The quotations here are from Massa, *Short History*, pp. 132–33, and Samuel H. Baron, ed., *The Travels of Olearius in Seventeenth-Century Russia* (Stanford, 1967), p. 186.

152. Massa, *Short History*, pp. 136–42, 144–45; Baron, ed., *Travels of Olearius*, pp. 186–87; Perrie, *Pretenders and Popular Monarchism*, ch. 3; Skrynnikov, *Time of Troubles*, pp. 37–41.

153. Quoted in Skrynnikov, *Time of Troubles*, p. 167; see also Perrie, *Pretenders and Popular Monarchism*, chs. 6–7.

154. Skrynnikov, *Time of Troubles*, pp. 265–80.

155. Robert O. Crummey, *Aristocrats and Servitors: The Boyar Elite in Russia, 1613–1689* (Princeton, 1983), p. 27.

156. Valerie A. Kivelson, *Autocracy in the Provinces: The Muscovite Gentry and Political*

*Culture in the Seventeenth Century* (Stanford, 1996), pp. 3–9, ch. 6; Paul Bushkovitch, *Religion and Society in Russia: The Sixteenth and Seventeenth Centuries* (Oxford, 1992), ch. 5.

157. Baron, ed., *Travels of Olearius*, pp. 72–75, 174.

158. S. Konovalov, "Seven Russian Royal Letters (1613–23)," *Oxford Slavonic Papers* 7 (1957): 119; Parker, *Thirty Years' War*, pp. 123, 262 n. 5.

159. Bushkovitch, *Religion and Society*, pp. 52–56 and ch. 6; Pierre Pascal, *Avvakum et les débuts du Raskol* (Paris and La Haye, 1938, 1969), ch. 1.

160. McGowan, *L'art du ballet de cour*, pp. 70–71, 129; John Summerson, *Georgian London* (London, 1945), pp. 13–17; R. Malcolm Smuts, "The Court and Its Neighbourhood: Royal Policy and Urban Growth in the Early Stuart West End," *Journal of British Studies* 30 (April 1991): 117–49, esp. pp. 135–47; Hugh Thomas, ed., *Madrid: A Traveller's Companion* (New York, 1990), pp. 161–70; Rodríguez Villa, *Etiquetas de la casa de Austria*, pp. 119–30; José Dileito y Piñuela, *El rey se divierte* (Madrid, 1964), pp. 181–94; Maravall, *Culture of the Baroque*, ch. 3.

161. For the socio-economic foundations of "decline," see José María Jover Zamora, gen. ed., *Historia de España*, vol. 23: *La crisis del siglo XVII: La población, la economía, la sociedad* (Madrid, 1989). Henry Kamen offers a sceptical view in "The Decline of Spain: A Historical Myth?" *Past and Present* 81 (1978): 24–50.

162. J. H. Elliott, "Self-Perception and Decline in Early Seventeenth-Century Spain," *Past and Present* 74 (1977): 41–61; R. A. Stradling, *Philip IV and the Government of Spain, 1621–1665* (Cambridge, 1988), pp. 13–14; R. L. Kagan, *Students and Society in Early Modern Spain* (Baltimore, 1974), chs. 4–6.

163. Giovanni Botero, *The Reason of State*, trans. P. J. and D. P. Waley (London, 1956), pp. 12, 63–64. His views and influence are discussed in Bireley, *Counter-Reformation Prince*, ch. 3, and in Tuck, *Philosophy and Government*, pp. 78–81. See also J. A. Fernández-Santamaría, *Reason of State and Statecraft in Spanish Political Thought, 1595–1640* (Lanham, Md., 1983).

164. Pedro Fernández Navarrete, *Conservación de monarquías*, in *Obras de Don Diego de Saavedra Fajardo y del Licenciado Pedro Fernández Navarrete*, Biblioteca de Autores Españoles, 25 (Madrid, 1920), pp. 495, 544.

165. For Molinism, see Melquiades Andrés Martín, "Pensamiento teologico y vivencia religiosa en la Reforma Española (1400–1600)," in Ricardo García-Villoslada, ed., *Historia de la iglesia en España*, part 3: *La iglesia en la España de los siglos XV y XVI*, 2 vols. (Madrid, 1980), vol. 2, pp. 323–26; Julio Caro Baroja, *Las formas complejas de la vida religiosa (religión, sociedad y carácter en la España de los siglos XVI y XVII)* (Madrid, 1978), ch. 21; Jean Delumeau, *Catholicism between Luther and Voltaire*, trans. Jeremy Moiser (London, 1977), p. 101.

166. Lope de Vega, *Fuenteovejuna*, trans. William E. Colford (New York, 1969). See also Richard A. Young, *La figura del rey y la institución real en la comedia Lopesca* (Madrid, 1979); Noel Salomon, *Recherches sur le thème paysan dans la «comedia» au temps de Lope de Vega* (Bordeaux, 1965), pp. 862–92.

167. Elliott, "Self-Perception and Decline," p. 50; Botero, *Reason of State*, p. 15; Baltasar Gracián, *El Politico Don Fernando el Católico* (1640), in his *Obras completas*, ed. Arturo del Hoyo (Madrid, 1960), p. 37. See also Angel Ferrari, *Fernando El Católico en Baltasar Gracián* (Madrid, 1945), ch. 5.

168. Margarita Levisi, "Golden Age Autobiography: The Soldiers," in Nicholas Spadaccini and Jennaro Talens, eds., *Autobiography in Early Modern Spain* (Minneapolis, 1988), pp. 97–117; Anthony N. Zahareas, "The Historical Function of Picaresque Autobiographies: Toward a History of Social Offenders," in ibid., pp. 129–62; Miguel de Cervantes Saavedra, "Curriculum Vitae," in ibid., pp. 247–80.

169. Francisco Quevedo, *España defendida, y los tiempos de ahora, de las calumnias de los noveleros y sediciosos,* in Luis Astrana Marín, ed., *Obras completas de Don Francisco de Quevedo Villegas: Obras en prosa* (Madrid, 1932), pp. 273–301, esp. 299–300.

170. Quevedo, *Política de Díos, Gobierno de Cristo Nuestro Señor,* in Astrana Marín, ed., *Obras de Quevedo: Prosa,* pp. 307, 312, 368. Strangely, Fernández-Santamaría, *Reason of State and Statecraft,* pp. 48–51, links this work with the "realist" school of Spanish political writers.

171. Quevedo's Neostoicism is discussed in Henry Ettinghausen, *Francisco de Quevedo and the Neostoic Movement* (Oxford, 1972), and in Karl Alfred Blüher, *Seneca in Spanien: Untersuchungen zur Geschichte der Seneca-Rezeption in Spanien vom 13. bis 17. Jahrhundert* (Munich, 1969), pp. 326–63. Neither devotes much attention to the *Política de Díos.* For Quevedo's letters to Lipsius, see Luis Astrana Marín, ed., *Epístolario completo de D. Francisco de Quevedo-Villegas* (Madrid, 1946), pp. 1–9. The impact of Lipsius in Spain can be judged from Alejandro Ramírez, ed., *Epístolario de Justo Lipsio y los Espanoles (1577–1606),* 2d ed. (St. Louis, 1966).

172. For a comparison, see J. H. Elliott, *Richelieu and Olivares* (Cambridge, 1984).

173. A thorough account of the *valimiento* is found in Francisco Tomás y Valiente, "El gobierno de la monarquía y la administración de los reinos en la España del siglo XVII," in José María Jover Zamora, gen. ed., *Historia de España,* vol. 25: *La España de Felipe IV: El gobierno de la monarquía, la crisis de 1640 y el fracaso de la hegemonía europea* (Madrid, 1982), pp. 107–17.

174. Gregorio Marañón, *El Conde-Duque de Olivares: La pasión de mandar* (Madrid, 1936), chs. 21–22; J. H. Elliott, *The Count-Duke of Olivares: The Statesman in an Age of Decline* (New Haven, 1986), pp. 115–24.

175. J. H. Elliott and José de la Peña, eds., *Memoriales y cartas del conde-duque de Olivares,* 2 vols. (Madrid, 1978–80), vol. 2, p. 75. Marañón, *El conde-duque,* pp. 107–8, mentions his credulity when presented with "projects."

176. Elliott, *Count-Duke of Olivares,* pp. 104–6, 187; Elliott and de la Peña, eds., *Memoriales y cartas,* vol. 2, p. 156; Marañón, *El conde-duque,* pp. 310–11.

177. Elliott, *Count-Duke of Olivares,* p. 537; J. H. Elliott, "The Court of the Spanish Habsburgs: A Peculiar Institution?" in his *Spain and Its World, 1500–1700* (New Haven, 1989), pp. 157–58; Elliott and de la Peña, eds., *Memoriales y cartas,* vol. 2, pp. 70, 81–82, 160–65 — the quotations are on pp. 87, 176–77.

178. Jean Vilar, "Formes et tendances de l'opposition sous Olivares: Lisón y Viedma, defensor de la patria," *Mélanges de la casa de Velázquez* 7 (1971): 263–94.

179. Ramírez, ed., *Epístolario de Justo Lipsio,* pp. 121–30, 166–67; Elliott and de la Peña, eds., *Memoriales y cartas,* vol. 1, pp. 184–85; Stradling, *Philip IV,* pp. 60–63, for Olivares and Lipsius.

180. Elliott and de la Peña, *Memoriales y cartas,* vol. 2, pp. 173–97; Elliott, *Count-Duke of Olivares,* ch. 7. The limitations of the Spanish military system before the Union of

Arms are detailed in I. A. A. Thompson, *War and Government in Habsburg Spain, 1560–1620* (London, 1976).

181. Francisco Quevedo, *La hora de todos y la fortuna con seso*, in his *Obras completas: Prosa*, pp. 259–63; Elliott, *Count-Duke of Olivares*, pp. 556–57.

182. For the Huguenots and Grisons, see Elliott, *Olivares and Richelieu*, pp. 126–27, and for Olivares's personal religious views, Marañón, *El conde-duque*, pp. 170–84.

183. The text of this revealing document is printed in Quintín Aldea, *Iglesia y estado en la España del siglo XVII* (Comillas, 1961), pp. 247–399. Church-state relations are further analyzed in Aldea's "Iglesia y estado en la epoca barroca," in Jover Zamora, gen. ed., *Historia de España*, vol. 25, pp. 529–633, and by Antonio Domínguez Ortiz, "Regalismo y relaciones iglesia-estado en el siglo XVII," in Antonio Mestre Sanchis, ed., *Historia de la iglesia en España*, part 4: *La iglesia en la España de los siglos XVII y XVIII* (Madrid, 1979), pp. 77–84.

184. Martin Hume, *The Court of Philip IV*, 2d ed. (London, n.d.), pp. 8–12; Stradling, *Philip IV*, p. 5.

185. Deleito y Piñuela, *El rey se divierte*, pp. 17–29. For court expenditures, see Antonio Domínguez Ortiz, "Los gastos del corte en la España del siglo XVII," in his *Crisis y decadencia de la España de los Austrias* (Barcelona, 1969, 1973), pp. 75–96.

186. For the Burgundian court, see C. A. J. Armstrong, "The Golden Age of Burgundy," in Dickens, ed., *Courts of Europe*, pp. 55–75; and Werner Paravicini, "The Court of the Dukes of Burgundy: A Model for Europe?" in Ronald G. Asch and Adolf M. Birke, eds., *Princes, Patronage, and the Nobility: The Court at the Beginning of the Early Modern Age* (Oxford, 1991), pp. 69–102. Spanish court etiquette is discussed in Lisón Tolosana, *La imagen del rey*, pp. 115–70; Rodríguez Villa, *Etiquetas de la casa de Austria;* Christina Hofmann, *Das spanische Hofzeremonielle von 1500–1700* (Frankfurt am Main, 1985); J. H. Elliott, "Philip IV of Spain: Prisoner of Ceremony," in Dickens, ed., *Courts of Europe*, pp. 169–89; Elliott, "Court of the Spanish Habsburgs," pp. 142–61; J. E. Varey, "The Audience and the Play at Court Spectacles: The Role of the King," *Bulletin of Hispanic Studies* 61 (1984): 399–406.

187. Norbert Elias, *The Civilizing Process*, trans. Edmund Jephcott, 2 vols. (New York, 1978, 1982), vol. 1, pp. 53–84 (quotation on p. 59), vol. 2, pp. 229–333.

188. Hofmann, *Spanische Hofzeremonielle*, p. 23.

189. Rodríguez Villa, *Etiquetas de la casa de Austria*, pp. 15–16; Elliott, "Court of the Spanish Habsburgs," pp. 147–50; Deleito y Piñuela, *El rey se divierte*, p. 108.

190. Rodríguez Villa, *Etiquetas de la casa de Austria*, pp. 97–98. Similar forms of the Holy Thursday ritual were found in England and France. Elizabeth I left the foot-washing to her yeomen of the laundry, but her Stuart heirs restored the royal role. French kings always performed the washing ceremony themselves, as Henry IV did after his entry into Paris in 1594. John Cannon and Ralph Griffiths, *The Oxford Illustrated History of the British Monarchy* (Oxford, 1989), p. 622; Pierre De L'Estoile, *The Paris of Henry of Navarre*, ed. and trans. Nancy Lyman Roelker (Cambridge, Mass., 1958), p. 262.

191. Elliott and de la Peña, eds., *Memoriales y cartas*, vol. 2, pp. 245–46. The moral distinction between "king" and "man" was first suggested by Fadrique Furió Ceriol in 1556: Fernández-Santamaría, *Reason of State and Statecraft*, pp. 116, 133–34 n. 98.

192. Jonathan Brown, *Velázquez: Painter and Courtier* (New Haven, 1986), pp. 44–47, 132; Antonio Domínguez Ortiz, Alfonso E. Pérez Sánchez, and Julián Gállego, *Velázquez* (New York, 1989), pp. 88–103, 172–77. Even Velázquez's painting of Bacchus with his acolytes, which has been interpreted as an allegory of Spanish kingship, is entirely natural in its presentation; see Steven N. Orso, *Velázquez, "Los Borrachos," and Painting at the Court of Philip IV* (Cambridge, 1993), ch. 4.

193. Juan de Mariana, *The King and the Education of the King*, trans. G. A. Moore (Washington, 1948), p. 193; Quevedo, *Política de Dios*, p. 317.

194. Stradling, *Philip IV*, p. 303.

195. Jonathan Brown and J. H. Elliott, *A Palace for a King: The Buen Retiro and the Court of Philip IV* (New Haven, 1980), pp. 8–9, 71, 86, ch. 6; Luis Díez del Corral, *Velázquez, la monarquía e Italia* (Madrid, 1979), pp. 47–55, 63–76; Morford, *Stoics and Neostoics*, pp. 208–10.

196. Bartolomé Bennassar et al., *L'Inquisition Espagnole, XVe–XIXe siècles* (Paris, 1978); Jean-Pierre DeDieu, "The Inquisition and Popular Culture in New Castile," in Stephen Haliczer, ed., *Inquisition and Society in Early Modern Europe* (Totowa, N.J., 1987), pp. 129–46, and his "Christianization in New Castile: Catechism, Communion, Mass, and Confirmation in the Toledo Archbishopric, 1540–1650," trans. Susan Isabel Stein, in Anne J. Cruz and Mary Elizabeth Perry, eds., *Culture and Control in Counter-Reformation Spain* (Minneapolis, 1992), pp. 1–24; Steven Haliczer, *Inquisition and Society in the Kingdom of Valencia, 1478–1834* (Berkeley, 1990), ch. 8.

197. Mary Elizabeth Perry, *Gender and Disorder in Early Modern Seville* (Princeton, 1990), ch. 5, and her articles "Beatas and the Inquisition in Early Modern Seville," in Haliczer, ed., *Inquisition and Society*, pp. 147–68, and "Magdalens and Jezebels in Counter-Reformation Spain," in Cruz and Perry, eds., *Culture and Control*, pp. 124–44. See also María Helena Sánchez Ortega, "Women as Source of 'Evil' in Counter-Reformation Spain," in Cruz and Perry, eds., *Culture and Control*, pp. 196–215; Claire Guilhem, "L'Inquisition et la dévaluation des discours féminins," in Bennassar et al., *L'Inquisition Espagnole*, pp. 197–240.

198. See Nalle, *God in La Mancha*, pp. 56–69, 118–33; Henry Kamen, *Inquisition and Society in Spain in the Sixteenth and Seventeenth Centuries* (Bloomington, Ind., 1985), ch. 11, and his *Phoenix and the Flame: Catalonia and the Counter-Reformation* (New Haven, 1993), ch. 5.

199. James Casey, *The Kingdom of Valencia in the Seventeenth Century* (Cambridge, 1979), p. 211; Kamen, *Phoenix and the Flame*, pp. 304–6; Aldea, *Iglesia y estado*, pp. 123–54, which documents the lucrative system of dispensations. The Inquisition's treatment of marriage cases is discussed in Jean-Pierre DeDieu, "Le modèle sexuel: La défense du mariage chrétien," in Bennassar et al., *L'Inquisition Espagnole*, pp. 313–38.

200. José Luis Bouza Alvarez, *Religiosidad Contrarreformista y cultura simbólica del barroco* (Madrid, 1990), pp. 23–169. For the cultural significance of such cults, see William Christian, *Local Religion in Sixteenth-Century Spain* (Princeton, 1981), chs. 2–3; Caro Baroja, *Las formas complejas*, pp. 77–106; Sara T. Nalle, "A Saint for All Seasons: The Cult of San Julián," in Cruz and Perry, eds., *Culture and Control*, pp. 25–50.

201. Haliczer, *Inquisition and Society in Valencia*, pp. 51–56.

202. Kamen, *Inquisition and Society,* p. 244; but see Bartolomé Bennassar, "Pour l'état, contre l'état," in Bennassar et al., *L'Inquisition Espagnole,* pp. 371–88, and Domínguez Ortiz, "Regalismo," pp. 113–21.

203. Elliott, *Count-Duke of Olivares,* p. 153. For a different view of preaching as a means of social control, see Gwendolyn Barnes-Karol, "Religious Oratory in a Culture of Control," in Cruz and Perry, eds., *Culture and Control,* pp. 51–77.

204. Quoted in Kamen, *Phoenix and the Flame,* p. 260.

205. Maravall, *Culture of the Baroque,* pp. 126–45, 226–47.

## Chapter Four: No King but King Jesus, 1637–1660

1. Samuel H. Baron, ed., *The Travels of Olearius in Seventeenth-Century Russia* (Stanford, 1967), pp. 99–100; Paul Bushkovitch, *Religion and Society in Russia: The Sixteenth and Seventeenth Centuries* (Oxford, 1992), pp. 41–42.

2. This account is based on Baron, ed., *Travels of Olearius,* pp. 203–14; Leo Loewenson, "The Moscow Rising of 1648," *Slavonic and East European Review* 27 (1948): 146–56; Robert O. Crummey, *Aristocrats and Servitors: The Boyar Elite in Russia, 1613–1689* (Princeton, 1983), pp. 83–88; Valerie Kivelson, *Autocracy in the Provinces: The Musovite Gentry and Political Culture in the Seventeenth Century* (Stanford, 1996), pp. 216–40; Philip Longworth, *Alexis, Tsar of All the Russias* (New York, 1984), pp. 38–53. For urban society in the early seventeenth century, see J. Michael Hittle, *The Service City: State and Townsmen in Russia, 1600–1800* (Cambridge, Mass., 1979), pp. 46–69.

3. Kivelson, *Autocracy in the Provinces,* pp. 242–48.

4. Avvakum, *The Life Written by Himself,* ed. and trans. Kenneth N. Brostrom (Ann Arbor, Mich., 1979), pp. 38, 46; Pierre Pascal, *Avvakum et les Débuts du Raskol* (Paris and La Haye, 1938, 1969), pp. 99–147.

5. Longworth, *Alexis,* pp. 54–55.

6. Avvakum, *Life,* p. 112.

7. Hugh Barbour, *The Quakers in Puritan England* (New Haven, 1964), pp. 63–64.

8. Christopher Feake, quoted in Christopher Hill, *The Experience of Defeat: Milton and Some Contemporaries* (New York, 1984), p. 54. The best overview of radical religious movements is provided by Christopher Hill, *The World Turned Upside Down: Radical Ideas during the English Revolution* (Harmondsworth, Middlesex, 1975).

9. William Lamont, *Godly Rule: Politics and Religion, 1603–60* (London, 1969), p. 167; Barbour, *Quakers in Puritan England,* ch. 7.

10. James Nayler, *The Lamb's War Against the Man of Sin* (1658), in Hugh Barbour and Arthur O. Roberts, eds., *Early Quaker Writings, 1650–1700* (Grand Rapids, Mich., 1973), pp. 106–7.

11. Phyllis Mack, *Visionary Women: Ecstatic Prophecy in Seventeenth-Century England* (Berkeley, 1992), pp. 197–208.

12. See Keith Thomas, "Women and the Civil War Sects," *Past and Present* 13 (1958): 42–62; Sharon L. Arnoult, "The Sovereignties of Body and Soul: Women's Political and Religious Actions in the Civil War," in Louise Olga Fradenburg, ed., *Women and Sovereignty* (Edinburgh, 1992), pp. 228–49. The relationship of gender order to social order is

discussed in Susan Dwyer Amussen, *An Ordered Society: Family and Village in England, 1560–1725* (Oxford, 1988), chs. 4–5.

13. C. Lisón Tolosana, *La imagen del rey: Monarquía, realeza y poder ritual en la Casa de los Austrias* (Madrid, 1992), p. 170.

14. Oliver Millar, *Van Dyck in England* (London, 1982), pp. 50–52.

15. Diego de Saavedra Fajardo, *Corona gótica, castellana y austriaca, políticamente ilustrada* (1645), in *Obras de Don Diego de Saavedra Fajardo y del Licensiado Pedro Fernández Navarrete*, Biblioteca de Autores Españoles, 25 (Madrid, 1920), p. 387; Franz Bosbach, "Die Habsburger und die Entstehung des dreißigjährigen Krieges: Die 'Monarchia universalis,'" in Konrad Repgen and Elisabeth Müller-Luckner, eds., *Krieg und Politik, 1618–1648: Europäische Probleme und Perspektiven* (Munich, 1988), pp. 151–68; Lamont, *Godly Rule*, chs. 1–2.

16. Francisco de Quevedo, *La constancia y paciencia del Santo Job en sus perdidas, enfermedades y persecuciones* (1641), in Luis Astrana Marin, ed., *Obras Completas de Don Francisco de Quevedo Villegas: Obras en Prosa* (Madrid, 1932), pp. 978–1026; and "Epistolario," in ibid., p. 1578.

17. Pierre Corneille, "A Saint Bernard" (1648), in *Oeuvres complètes*, ed. Georges Couton, 2 vols. (Paris, 1984), vol. 2, p. 623.

18. Paul Antony, ed., *Johann Valentin Andreä—ein schwäbischer Pfarrer im dreißigjährigen Krieg* (Heidenheim an der Brenz, 1970), p. 140.

19. Quoted in Margaret Steele, "The 'Politick Christian': The Theological Background to the National Covenant," in John Morrill, ed., *The Scottish National Covenant in Its British Context* (Edinburgh, 1990), p. 34.

20. Quoted in Stanislas Kot, *Socinianism in Poland*, trans. E. M. Waller (Boston, 1957), p. 173.

21. Margaret McGowen, *L'art du ballet de cour en France, 1581–1643* (Paris, 1963, 1978), pp. 186–90.

22. Sir William Davenant and Inigo Jones, *Salmacida spoliata*, in Steven Orgel and Roy Strong, *Inigo Jones: The Theatre of the Stuart Court*, 2 vols. (Berkeley, 1973), vol. 2, pp. 729–34.

23. Edward Hyde, earl of Clarendon, *Selections from the History of the Rebellion and the Life by Himself*, ed. G. Huehns (Oxford, 1956), p. 1.

24. The classic statements of the "general crisis" thesis are found in E. J. Hobsbawm, "The Crisis of the Seventeenth Century," in Trevor Aston, ed., *Crisis in Europe, 1560–1660* (London, 1965), pp. 5–58; H. R. Trevor-Roper, "The General Crisis of the Seventeenth Century," in ibid., pp. 59–95; Henry Kamen, *The Iron Century: Social Change in Europe, 1550–1660* (London, 1971), chs. 9–12; Theodore K. Rabb, *The Struggle for Stability in Early Modern Europe* (New York, 1975); the introduction to Geoffrey Parker and Lesley M. Smith, eds., *The General Crisis of the Seventeenth Century* (London, 1978), pp. 1–25; and Neils Steensgard, "The Seventeenth-Century Crisis," in Aston, ed., *Crisis in Europe*, pp. 26–56. For an area too often neglected, see Sheilagh C. Ogilvie, "Germany and the Seventeenth-Century Crisis," *Historical Journal* 35, no. 2 (1992): 417–41. Conrad Russell examined the comparative effects of wartime finance in "Monarchies, Wars, and Estates in England, France, and Spain, c. 1580–c. 1640," in his *Unrevolutionary England*,

*1603–1642* (London, 1990), pp. 121–36. H. G. Koenigsberger declared the debate over, and the "general crisis" theory proven untenable, in "The Crisis of the Seventeenth Century: A Farewell?" in his *Politicians and Virtuosi: Essays in Early Modern History* (London, 1986), pp. 149–68.

25. Quoted in Kamen, *Iron Century*, p. 307.

26. Albrycht Stanisław Radziwiłł, *Memoriale rerum gestarum in Polonia, 1632–1656*, ed. Adam Przyboś and Roman Zelewski, 5 vols. (Wrocław, 1968–74), vol. 4, p. 141.

27. Quoted in Michael Roberts, "Queen Christina and the General Crisis of the Seventeenth Century," in Aston, ed., *Crisis in Europe*, p. 196.

28. Denis Richet, "Où situer la Fronde parmi les troubles européens des années 1640 à 1650?" in Roger Duchêne and Pierre Ronzeaud, eds., *La Fronde en questions* (Aix-en-Provence, 1989), p. 127.

29. Roland Mousnier, "Quelques raisons de la Fronde: Les causes des journées révolutionnaires parisiennes de 1648," in his *La plume, la faucille et le marteau: Institutions et société en France du Moyen Age à la Révolution* (Paris, 1970), p. 300.

30. J. H. Elliott, "Revolution and Continuity in Early Modern Europe," in Parker and Smith, eds., *Crisis of the Seventeenth Century*, pp. 126. See also Rosario Villari, "The Rebel," in Rosario Villari, ed., *Baroque Personae*, trans. Lydia Cochrane (Chicago, 1995), pp. 112–19; Xavier Gil, "Noves visions sobre velles realitats de las relacions entre la capital i el territoris a les monarquies europees dels segles XVI i XVII," in Albert Rossich and August Rafanell, eds., *El barroc català* (Barcelona, 1989), pp. 23–45.

31. There is an enormous literature on nationalism, including Hans Kohn, *The Idea of Nationalism: A Study in Its Origin and Background* (New York, 1944); Benedict Anderson, *Imagined Communities: Reflections on the Origin and Spread of Nationalism*, 2d ed. (New York, 1991); John Breuilly, *Nationalism and the State*, 2d ed. (Chicago, 1993). Both Ernest Gellner, *Nations and Nationalism* (Ithaca, N.Y., 1983), and Eric Hobsbawm, *Nations and Nationalism since 1789: Programme, Myth, Reality* (Cambridge, 1990), restrict the term to the period after 1789; but see Mary G. Dietz, "Patriotism," in Terence Ball, James Farr, and Russell L. Hanson, eds., *Political Innovation and Conceptual Change* (Cambridge, 1982), pp. 177–93, and Adrian Hastings, *The Constitution of Nationhood: Ethnicity, Religion, and Nationalism* (Cambridge, 1997).

32. Michael Roberts, ed., *Sweden as a Great Power, 1611–1697: Government: Society: Foreign Policy* (London, 1968), p. 15. See also Kurt Johannesen, *The Renaissance of the Goth in Sixteenth-Century Sweden: Johannes and Olaus Magnus as Politicians and Historians*, trans. James Larson (Berkeley, 1991), p. 221; Bengt Ankarloo, "Europe and the Glory of Sweden: The Emergence of a Swedish Self-Image in the Early Seventeenth Century," in Göran Rystad, ed., *Europe and Scandinavia: Aspects of the Process of Integration in the Seventeenth Century* (Lund, 1983), pp. 237–44; Erik Ringmar, *Identity, Interest, and Action: A Cultural Explanation of Sweden's Intervention in the Thirty Years' War* (Cambridge, 1996), ch. 6; Nils Ahnlund, *Gustav Adolf the Great*, trans. Michael Roberts (Princeton, 1940), pp. 131–34; Günter Barudio, *Gustav Adolf der Große: Eine politische Biographie* (Frankfurt am Main, 1982, 1985), pp. 302–9.

33. J. H. Elliott and José de la Peña, eds., *Memoriales y cartas del conde duque de Olivares*, 2 vols. (Madrid, 1978–80), vol. 1, p. 43; Gregorio Marañón, *El conde-duque de Olivares: La pasión de mandar* (Madrid, 1936), pp. 295–98; J. H. Elliott, *The Count-Duke of*

*Olivares: The Statesman in an Age of Decline* (New Haven, 1986), pp. 191–200; Jean Vilar, "Formes et tendances de l'opposition sous Olivares: Lisón y Viedma, defensor de la patria," *Mélanges de la casa de Velázquez* 7 (1971): 294.

34. Auguste Berga, *Un prédicateur de la cour de Pologne sous Sigismond III: Pierre Skarga (1536–1612)* (Paris, 1916), pp. 333, 340.

35. Roberts, "Queen Christina and the General Crisis," pp. 195–221; Roberts, ed., *Sweden as a Great Power,* pp. 40–43, 98–110; Nils Runeby, *Monarchia mixta: Maktför-delningsdebatt i Sverige under den tidigare stormaktstiden* (Stockholm, 1962), pp. 310–38; Curt Weibull, *Christina of Sweden* (Stockholm, 1931, 1966), pp. 25–50; Sven Stolpe, *Christina of Sweden,* trans. Alec Randall and Ruth Mary Bethell (New York, 1966), pp. 111–14.

36. Conrad Russell, *Causes of the English Civil War* (Oxford, 1990), ch. 2, and his *Fall of the British Monarchies, 1637–1642* (Oxford, 1991), ch. 2.

37. S. R. Gardiner, ed., *The Constitutional Documents of the Puritan Revolution, 1625–1660,* 3d ed. (Oxford, 1906), pp. 124–34; Edward J. Cowan, "The Making of the National Covenant," in Morrill, ed., *Scottish National Covenant,* pp. 68–89; Steele, "The 'Politick Christian,'" in ibid., pp. 31–67; Allan I. MacInnes, *Charles I and the Making of the Covenanting Movement, 1625–1641* (Edinburgh, 1991), ch. 7. The best history of the rebellion is David Stevenson, *The Scottish Revolution, 1637–1644: The Triumph of the Covenanters* (London, 1973).

38. Maurice Lee Jr., *The Road to Revolution: Scotland under Charles I, 1625–37* (Urbana, Ill., 1985), ch. 4; MacInnes, *Charles I and the Covenanting Movement,* chs. 3–5; Peter Donald, *An Uncounselled King: Charles I and the Scottish Troubles, 1637–41* (Cambridge, 1990), ch. 1.

39. David Laing, ed., *The Letters and Journals of Robert Baillie, A.M., Principal of the University of Glasgow, 1637–1662,* 3 vols. (Edinburgh, 1862), vol. 1, p. 4.

40. MacInnes, *Charles I and the Covenanting Movement,* p. 204.

41. Ibid., pp. 16–22; also I. M. Smart, "The Political Ideas of the Scottish Covenanters, 1638–88," *History of Political Thought* 1, no. 2 (1980): 167–93.

42. Laing, ed., *Letters of Baillie,* vol. 1, p. 264.

43. Ibid., vol. 1, p. 118.

44. Nehemiah Wallington, *Historical Notices of Events Occurring Chiefly in the Reign of Charles I,* ed. R. Webb, 2 vols. (London, 1869), vol. 1, pp. 134–35. For Wallington's political views, see Paul S. Seaver, *Wallington's World: A Puritan Artisan in Seventeenth-Century London* (Stanford, 1985), ch. 6.

45. Laing, ed., *Letters of Baillie,* vol. 1, p. 298; Butler, *Theatre and Crisis,* pp. 236–46.

46. Gardiner, ed., *Constitutional Documents,* pp. 137–44; Russell, *Fall of the British Monarchies,* pp. 180–95; Russell, *Causes of the English Civil War,* pp. 118–26; Anthony Fletcher, *The Outbreak of the English Civil War* (New York, 1981), ch. 3.

47. Wallace Notestein, ed., *The Journal of Sir Simonds D'Ewes, from the Beginning of the Long Parliament to the Opening of the Trial of the Earl of Strafford* (New Haven, 1923), p. 139.

48. Russell, *Fall of the British Monarchies,* chs. 7, 9, 11; Fletcher, *Outbreak of the English Civil War,* ch. 4; Caroline M. Hibbard, *Charles I and the Popish Plot* (Chapel Hill, N.C., 1983), chs. 8–9.

49. Nicholas Canny, *Kingdom and Colony: Ireland in the Atlantic World, 1560–1800*

(Baltimore, 1988), ch. 1; Ciarán Brady, "The Decline of the Irish Kingdom," in Mark Greengrass, ed., *Conquest and Coalescence: The Shaping of the State in Early Modern Europe* (London, 1991), pp. 94–115; Aidan Clarke, *The Old English in Ireland, 1625–42* (Ithaca, N.Y., 1966), chs. 2–3, and his "Selling Royal Favours, 1628–32," in T. W. Moody, F. X. Martin, and F. J. Byrne, eds., *A New History of Ireland*, vol. 3: *Early Modern Ireland, 1534–1691* (Oxford, 1976), pp. 233–42.

50. Hugh Kearney, *Strafford in Ireland, 1633–41* (Manchester, 1959); Aidan Clarke, "The Government of Wentworth, 1632–40," and "The Breakdown of Authority, 1640–41," in Moody, Martin, and Byrne, eds., *New History of Ireland*, vol. 3, pp. 243–88; M. Perceval Maxwell, *The Outbreak of the Irish Rebellion of 1641* (Montreal, 1994), ch. 3.

51. James Tuchet, earl of Castlehaven, *Review: or his Memoirs of his Engagements and Carriage in the Irish Wars* (London, 1684, reprint Delmar, N.Y., 1974), p. 22. Political connections across the Irish Sea are discussed in David Stevenson, *Scottish Covenanters and Irish Confederates: Scottish-Irish Relations in the Mid-Seventeenth Century* (Belfast, 1981), and in M. Perceval-Maxwell, "Ireland and Scotland, 1638 to 1648," in Morrill, ed., *Scottish National Covenant*, pp. 193–211.

52. Clarke, *Old English*, pp. 156–65; Conrad Russell, "The British Background to the Irish Rebellion of 1641," in his *Unrevolutionary England*, pp. 263–79; Maxwell, *Outbreak of the Irish Rebellion*, ch. 6.

53. Historical Manuscripts Commission, *Calendar of the Manuscripts of the Marquess of Ormonde, K.P., Preserved at Kilkenny Castle*, new series, 2 vols. (London, 1903), vol. 2, p. 74.

54. Edmund Curtis and R. B. McDowell, eds., *Irish Historical Documents, 1172–1922* (New York and London, 1943, 1968), pp. 148–52; Patrick J. Corish, "The Rising of 1641 and the Catholic Confederacy," in Moody, Martin, and Byrne, eds., *New History of Ireland*, vol. 3, pp. 297–303; Historical Manuscripts Commission, *Ormonde*, vol. 2, p. 246. For the view that this was a "pre-nationalist" conflict, see Jerrold I. Casway, *Owen Roe O'Neill and the Struggle for Catholic Ireland* (Philadelphia, 1984).

55. See Hilary Simms, "Violence in County Armagh, 1641," in Brian MacCuarta, ed., *Ulster 1641: Aspects of the Rising* (Belfast, 1993), pp. 123–38; Canny, *Kingdom and Colony*, pp. 60–65; Maxwell, *Origins of the Irish Rebellion*, pp. 216–33.

56. Patrick J. Corish, "Ormond, Rinuccini, and the Confederates, 1645–9," in Moody, Martin, and Byrne, eds., *New History of Ireland*, vol. 3, pp. 327–31.

57. Wallington, *Historical Notices*, vol. 2, pp. 295–308.

58. Gardiner, ed., *Constitutional Documents*, pp. 202–32; Russell, *Fall of the British Monarchies*, ch. 10; Fletcher, *Outbreak of the English Civil War*, ch. 6; Hibbard, *Charles I and the Popish Plot*, pp. 213–16.

59. Coates, ed., *Journal of Sir Simonds D'Ewes*, pp. 270–73, 353, 356, 364–67; Brian Manning, *The English People and the English Revolution* (Harmondsworth, Middlesex, 1978), ch. 4.

60. See Janelle Greenberg, "Our Grand Maxim of State, 'The King Can Do No Wrong,'" *History of Political Thought* 12, no. 2 (1991): 209–28.

61. [Samuel Rutherford], *Lex, rex* (1644), in A. S. P. Woodhouse, ed., *Puritanism and Liberty: Being the Army Debates (1647–9) from the Clarke Manuscripts with Supplementary Documents* (London, 1938), pp. 199–212.

62. Gardiner, ed., *Constitutional Documents*, pp. 267–71.

63. The best account of the outbreak of the rebellion remains J. H. Elliott's magisterial *Revolt of the Catalans: A Study in the Decline of Spain (1598–1640)* (Cambridge, 1963); but for events beyond 1640, see José Sanabre, *La acción de Francia en Cataluña en la pugna por la hegemonía de Europa (1640–1659)* (Barcelona, 1956). Eulogio Zudaire Huarte gave a pro-Spanish interpretation in *El conde-duque y Cataluña* (Madrid, 1964). More recent views are offered in A. Simón Tarrés, "La revuelta catalana de 1640: Una interpretación," in A. Simón Tarrés et al., *1640: La monarquía hispánica en crisis* (Barcelona, 1992), pp. 17–24, and Eva Serra, "1640: Un revolució política: La implicació de les institucions," in Eva Serra et al., *La revolució catalana de 1640* (Barcelona, 1991), pp. 3–65.

64. Elliott, *Revolt of the Catalans*, chs. 2–3; Víctor Ferro, *El dret públic català: Les institucions a Catalunya fins al Decret de Nova Planta* (Vic, 1987), chs. 1, 2, 5–6; Pierre Vilar, *La Catalogne dans l'Espagne moderne: Recherches sur les fondements économiques des structures nationales*, 3 vols. (Paris, 1962), vol. 1, pp. 625–33; James Amelang, *Honored Citizens of Barcelona: Patrician Culture and Class Relations, 1490–1714* (Princeton, 1986), ch. 1; Joan-Pau Rubiés, "Reason of State and Constitutional Thought in the Crown of Aragon, 1580–1640," *Historical Journal* 38, no. 1 (1995): 1–28.

65. For Catalan culture, see Amelang, *Honored Citizens of Barcelona*, ch. 5; Henry Kamen, *The Phoenix and the Flame: Catalonia and the Counter-Reformation* (New Haven, 1993), ch. 7; Kenneth Browne, "El barroc literari català i castella: Contextos, textos i intertextos," in Rossich and Rafanell, eds., *Barroc català*, pp. 513–30; Albert Rossich, "Subordinació i originalitat en el barroc literari català: Alguns parallelismes," in ibid., pp. 531–66; August Rafanell, "Notes sobre la interferència lingüística en la literatura catalana del barroc," in ibid., pp. 611–30.

66. Kamen, *Phoenix and the Flame*, ch. 4 and pp. 362–73; Ferro, *Dret públic català*, pp. 24–25, 127–36; Joaquim M. Puigvert i Sola, "Guerra i Contrareforma a la Catalunya rural del segle XVII," in Serra et al., *La revolució catalana*, pp. 112–16; Joan Busquets, "Bisbes espanyols y francesos a Catalunya durant la guerra dels segadors," in Rossich and Rafanell, eds., *Barroc català*, pp. 61–87; Sanabre, *Acción de Francia*, pp. 15–19; Simón Tarrés, "La revuelta catalana," p. 35, citing the work of Rosa María González Peiró on Catalan preachers; Ricard Garcia Càrcel, *Pau Claris: La revolta catalana* (Barcelona, 1985), pp. 37–47.

67. "Copia de la carta que los villanos del motín embían por los lugares," in Zudaire, *El conde-duque y Cataluña*, p. 457. For the rural riots, see ibid., ch. 11; Elliott, *Revolt of the Catalans*, pp. 418–29; Xavier Torres i Sans, "Segadors i miquelets a la revolució catalana (1640–1659)," in Serra et al., *La revolució catalana*, pp. 66–81.

68. Elliott, *Revolt of the Catalans*, pp. 429–30, 445–51; Sanabre, *Acción de Francia*, pp. 63–71; Zudaire, *El conde-duque y Cataluña*, ch. 13; P. Basili de Rubí, ed., *Les Corts Generals de Pau Claris: Dietari o procés de Corts de la Junta General de Braços* (Barcelona, 1976), pp. 110–12.

69. Quoted in Elliott, *Revolt of the Catalans*, pp. 471–72. Claris's leadership of the revolt is discussed in Garcia Càrcel, *Pau Claris*, pp. 69–125.

70. Amelang, *Honored Citizens of Barcelona*, ch. 8.

71. Rubí, ed., *Les Corts Generals*, pp. 108–21. The work of this Corts is discussed in Serra, "1640: Un revolució política," pp. 44–62.

72. Quoted in Puigvert i Sola, "Guerra i Contrareforma," p. 100; see also Elliott, *Revolt of the Catalans*, p. 507, and Garcia Càrcel, *Pau Claris*, pp. 90–92.

73. Rubí, *Les Corts Generals*, pp. 120–21, 291–93; Sanabre, *Acción de Francia*, pp. 87–104, 123–24; Elliott, *Revolt of the Catalans*, pp. 519–21.

74. Rubí, *Les Corts Generals*, pp. 412–13, 426–31; Sanabre, *Acción de Francia*, pp. 131–34.

75. Sanabre, *Acción de Francia*, pp. 273–94, 319–37, 458–99; Vilar, *Catalogne dans l'Espagne moderne*, pp. 633–36; Torres i Sans, "Segadors i miquelets," pp. 81–96; Jordi Vidal, "La guerra dels segadors a la Vall d'Aran (1640–1643): Revolta popular i conflicte polític," in Serra et al., *La Revolució catalana*, pp. 192–210.

76. Miquel Parets, *Dietari d'un any de pesta: Barcelona 1651*, ed. James M. Amelang and Xavier Torres i Sans (Barcelona, 1989), p. 67.

77. Ibid., pp. 72–73; Josep M. Torras i Ribé, "El projecte de repressió dels Catalans de 1652," in Serra et al., *La revolució catalana*, pp. 241–90; Vilar, *Catalogne dans l'Espagne moderne*, vol. 1, pp. 636–38.

78. Puigvert i Solà, "Guerra i Contrareforma," pp. 116–32.

79. Accounts in English of these events include Vitorino Magalhaes Godinho, "Portugal and Her Empire," *The New Cambridge Modern History*, vol. 5: *The Ascendancy of France* (Cambridge, 1961), pp. 384–97; A. H. de Oliveira Marques, *History of Portugal*, 2 vols. (New York, 1972), vol. 1, pp. 322–33; H. P. Livermore, *A New History of Portugal*, 2d ed. (1976), pp. 170–85; J. H. Elliott, "The Spanish Monarchy and the Kingdom of Portugal, 1580–1640," in Greengrass, ed., *Conquest and Coalescence*, pp. 48–67.

80. João Francisco Marques, *A parenética portuguesa e a Restauracão, 1640–1668: A revolta e a mentalidade*, 2 vols. (Oporto, 1989), vol. 2, pp. 109–45; also Raymond Cantel, *Prophétisme et messianisme dans l'oeuvre d'Antonio Vieira* (Paris, 1960), ch. 2 and pp. 249–51.

81. Marques, *Parenética portuguesa*, vol. 2, pp. 147–65; also Luís Reis Torgal, *Ideologia política e teoria do estado na Restauracão*, 2 vols. (Coimbra, 1981), vol. 2, pp. 303–28.

82. Marques, *Parenética portuguesa*, vol. 1, pp. 105–7, vol. 2, pp. 227–35.

83. Ibid., vol. 2, pp. 167–91; Torgal, *Ideologia política*, vol. 1, pp. 303–28, vol. 2, pp. 269–77; Cantel, *Prophétisme et messianisme*, ch. 3 and pp. 142–50.

84. António M. Hespanha, "La «restauracão» portuguesa en los capítulos de las Cortes de Lisboa de 1641," in Simón Tarrés et al., *1640*, pp. 141–42.

85. Ibid., pp. 123–68; A. M. Hespanha, *Vísperas de Leviatan: Instituciones y poder político (Portugal siglo XVII)*, trans. Fernando Jesús Bouza Alvarez (Madrid, 1989), pp. 233–42, 392–414; Torgal, *Ideologia política*, vol. 2, pp. 24–43.

86. Livermore, *History of Portugal*, pp. 185–96; *Mémoires de Monsieur d'Ablancourt, envoyé de Sa Majesté Très-Chrétienne Louis XIV en Portugal* (Amsterdam, 1701), pp. 335–52.

87. On Ukrainian national identity, see Andrzej Kamiński, "Polish-Lithuanian Commonwealth and Its Citizens (Was the Commonwealth a Stepmother for Cossacks and Ruthenians?)" in Peter J. Potichnyj, ed., *Poland and Ukraine: Past and Present* (Edmonton, 1980), pp. 32–57; Harvey Goldblatt, "Orthodox Slavic Heritage and National Consciousness: Aspects of the East Slavic and South Slavic National Revivals," in Ivo Banac and Frank E. Sisyn, eds., "Concepts of Nationhood in Early Modern Eastern Europe," *Har-*

*vard Ukrainian Studies* 10, nos. 3–4 (1986): 336–47; Teresa Chynczewska-Hennel, "The National Consciousness of Ukrainian Nobles and Cossacks from the End of the Sixteenth to the Mid-Seventeenth Century," in ibid., pp. 377–92; Zenon E. Kohut, "The Development of a Little Russian Identity and Ukrainian Nationality," in ibid., pp. 559–76.

88. Orest Subtelny, *Ukraine: A History*, 2d ed. (Toronto, 1994), pp. 105–38; Norman Davies, *God's Playground: A History of Poland*, 2 vols. (Oxford, 1981), vol. 1, pp. 463–68; M. Korduba, "The Reign of John Casimir, 1648–54," in W. F. Reddaway et al., *The Cambridge History of Poland*, vol. 1: *From the Origins to Sobieski (to 1696)* (Cambridge, 1950), pp. 503–17; Leo Okinshevich, *Ukrainian Society and Government, 1648–1781* (Munich, 1978), pp. 9–16; C. Bickford O'Brien, *Muscovy and the Ukraine: From the Pereislavl Agreement to the Treaty of Andrusovo, 1654–1667* (Berkeley, 1963), pp. 12–20.

89. Radziwiłł, *Memoriale*, vol. 4, pp. 14–17.

90. Nathan Hanover, *Abyss of Despair (Yeven Metzulah): The Famous Seventeenth-Century Chronicle Depicting Jewish Life in Russia and Poland During the Chmielnicki Massacres of 1648–1649*, trans. Abraham J. Mesch (New Brunswick, N.J., 1983), p. 28; Bernard Weinryb, *The Jews of Poland: A Social and Economic History of the Jewish Community in Poland from 1100 to 1800* (Philadelphia, 1972), ch. 9.

91. William K. Medlin and Christos G. Patrinelis, *Renaissance Influences and Religious Reforms in Russia: Western and Post-Byzantine Impacts on Culture and Education (Sixteenth to Seventeenth Centuries)* (Geneva, 1971), pp. 99–149; Paul Robert Magosci, *A History of Ukraine* (Seattle, 1996), ch. 11; Subtelny, *Ukraine*, pp. 96–99.

92. "Ivan Vyhovsky's Manifesto to Foreign Rulers on the Reason for His Break with Moscow," in John Besarab, *Pereiaslav 1654: A Historiographical Study* (Edmonton, Alberta, 1982), p. 259. The religious basis of the rebellion is also stressed in Frank E. Sysyn, "Ukrainian-Polish Relations in the Seventeenth Century: The Role of National Consciousness and Conflict in the Khmelnytsky Movement," in Potichnyj, ed., *Poland and Ukraine*, pp. 58–82.

93. Okinshevich, *Ukrainian Society*, pp. 16–21, 66–81; Magosci, *History of Ukraine*, ch. 18.

94. "The Diplomatic Report of Vasilii Buturlin," in Besarab, *Pereiaslav*, pp. 250–57; also, O'Brien, *Muscovy and the Ukraine*, pp. 20–64; Subtelny, *Ukraine*, pp. 134–36; Okinshevich, *Ukrainian Society*, pp. 23–28; Longworth, *Alexis*, pp. 88–89.

95. See F. Sysyn, *Between Poland and the Ukraine: The Dilemma of Adam Kysil, 1600–1653* (Cambridge, Mass., 1985).

96. Alessandro Giraffi, *An Exact Historie of the Late Revolutions in Naples and of their Monstrous Successes not to be Parallel'd by any Ancient or Modern History*, trans. James Howell (London, 1650); Nessipio Liponari, *Relatione della rivolutioni popolari sucesse nel Distretto, e Regno di Napoli* (Padua, 1648); Rosario Villari, "Masaniello: Contemporary and Recent Interpretations," *Past and Present* 108 (1985): 125–32.

97. The best discussion of the history of the term *state* is in Quentin Skinner, "The State," in Ball, Farr, and Hanson, eds., *Political Innovation*, pp. 90–131; see also Charles Tilly, "Reflections on the History of European State-Making," in Tilly, ed., *Formation of National States*, pp. 12–46. For *revolution* in a seventeenth-century context, see Lawrence Stone, *The Causes of the English Revolution, 1529–1642* (New York, 1972), pp. 3–25; and for a broader treatment, John Dunn, "Revolution," in Ball, Farr, and Hanson, eds.,

*Political Innovation,* pp. 333–56. The debate among Spanish historians about *state* is outlined in Simón Tarrés, "La revuelta catalana," p. 26, n. 40.

98. Niccolò Machiavelli, *The Prince,* in *Machiavelli: The Chief Works and Others,* trans. Allan Gilbert, 3 vols. (Durham, N.C., 1958, 1989), vol. 1, pp. 89–92, and his *Discourses on the First Decade of Titus Livius,* in ibid., vol. 1, pp. 197–99, 210–11, 238–43; Pocock, *Machiavellian Moment,* chs. 6–7.

99. Giovanni Botero, *The Reason of State,* trans. P. J. and D. P. Waley (London, 1956), p. 3; Robert Bireley, *The Counter-Reformation Prince: Anti-Machiavellianism or Catholic Statecraft in Early Modern Europe* (Chapel Hill, N.C., 1990), p. 51.

100. Botero, *Reason of State,* pp. 5–6, 11.

101. Diego de Saavedra Fajardo, *Idea de un principe politico-Cristiano* (1642), in *Obras de Saavedra Fajardo y Fernández Navarrete,* pp. 15, 105, 159.

102. Ibid., pp. 151–52. A century earlier, the clock image had been used to represent a well-ordered kingdom in Antonio de Guevara, *Relox de principes,* ed. Emilio Blanco (Madrid, 1994), pp. 38–39.

103. Ilan Rachum, "Italian Historians and the Emergence of the Term 'Revolution,' 1644–1659," *History* 80, no. 259 (1995): 191–206; Cardinal de Retz, *Mémoires,* in his *Oeuvres,* ed. Marie-Thérèse Hipp and Michel Pernot (Paris, 1984), p. 153.

104. Fritz Dickmann, *Der Westfälische Frieden,* 3d ed. (Münster, 1959, 1972), pp. 6–9, 206–12; see also Bernd Mathias Kremer, *Der Westfälische Friede in der Deutung der Aufklärung* (Tübingen, 1989), pp. 46–50; Heinz Duchhardt, "Imperium und regna im Zeitalter Ludwigs XIV," *Historische Zeitschrift* 232, no. 3 (1981): 561–62, 577–78.

105. *Pro pace perpetua Protestantibus danda consultatio catholica* (Freiburg, 1648), p. 11; Kremer, *Der Westfälische Friede,* pp. 39–42.

106. For the history of this republican option, see H. G. Koenigsberger, "Republicanism, Monarchism, and Liberty," in Robert Oresko, G. C. Gibbs, and H. M. Scott, eds., *Royal and Republican Sovereignty in Early Modern Europe: Essays in Memory of Ragnhild Hatton* (Cambridge, 1997), pp. 43–74.

107. Orest Ranum, *The Fronde: A French Revolution, 1648–1652* (New York, 1993), pp. 5–9. That the Fronde was not a revolution is the opinion of E. H. Kossmann, *La Fronde* (Leiden, 1954), and of A. Lloyd Moote, *The Revolt of the Judges: The Parlement of Paris and the Fronde, 1643–1652* (Princeton, 1971); but see Hubert Méthivier, *La Fronde* (Paris, 1984), p. 8.

108. Richard M. Golden, *The Godly Rebellion: Parisian Curés and the Religious Fronde, 1652–1662* (Chapel Hill, N.C., 1981), ch. 4.

109. Retz, *Mémoires,* pp. 137, 158; J. H. M. Salmon, *Cardinal de Retz: The Anatomy of a Conspirator* (London, 1969), ch. 4.

110. "Le vray portraict du Père du peuple et le grand support de la France," reproduced in Hubert Carrier, *La presse de la Fronde (1648–1653): Les Mazarinades: La conquête de l'opinion* (Geneva, 1989), p. 222; also Lucien Goldmann, *The Hidden God: A Study of the Tragic Vision in the Pensées of Pascal and the Tragedies of Racine,* trans. Philip Thody (London, 1964), ch. 6.

111. René Taveneaux, ed., *Jansénisme et politique* (Paris, 1956), p. 15; Christian Jouhaud, *Mazarinades: La Fronde des mots* (Paris, 1985), p. 183; also Alexander Sedgwick,

*Jansenism in Seventeenth-Century France: Voices from the Wilderness* (Charlottesville, Va., 1977), ch. 3.

112. Raoul Allier, *La cabale des dévots (1627–1666)* (Geneva, 1902, 1970), pp. 324–46.

113. Robert Descimon and Christian Jouhaud, "La Fronde en mouvement: Le développement de la crise politique entre 1648 et 1652," *XVIIe Siècle* 145 (1984): 306–12; Daniel Dessert, *Argent, pouvoir et société au grand siècle* (Paris, 1984), pp. 82–109.

114. *Catéchisme des Partisans, ou résolutions théologiques, touchant l'imposition, levée et employ des finances* (Paris, 1649), in Hubert Carrier, ed., *La Fronde: Contestation démocratique et misère paysanne: 52 Mazarinades*, 2 vols. (Paris, 1982), vol. 2, no. 1, p. 26.

115. Jouhaud, *Mazarinades*, ch. 3.

116. *Catéchisme des Partisans*, p. 3.

117. "Le salut de la France, dans les armes de la Ville de Paris," in Carrier, *La presse de la Fronde*, p. 416.

118. Moote, *Revolt of the Judges*, ch. 5; Ranum, *The Fronde*, pp. 95–97, 121–46; Christine Vicherd, "Des raisons idéologiques de l'échec du Parlement de Paris," in Duchêne and Ronzeaud, eds., *La Fronde en questions*, pp. 319–27; Retz, *Mémoires*, p. 205.

119. Robert Descimon, "Les barricades frondeuses (26–28 août 1648)," in Duchêne and Ronzeaud, eds., *La Fronde en questions*, pp. 245–61; Ranum, *The Fronde*, pp. 156–69. Descimon also notes that barricades were set up in 1636 to resist a possible Spanish attack on Paris.

120. Retz, *Mémoires*, p. 230; Simone Bertière, "L'image de la Ligue dans les *Mémoires* du Cardinal de Retz," in Keith Cameron and Elizabeth Woodrough, eds., *Ethics and Politics in Seventeenth-Century France* (Exeter, 1996), pp. 55–64.

121. Ranum, *The Fronde*, pp. 188–93; Retz, *Mémoires*, pp. 274–85; the quotation is on p. 274.

122. Carrier, *La presse de la Fronde*, pp. 33, 82–86, 389–439; Jouhaud, *Mazarinades*, ch. 4.

123. *Que la voix du peuple est la voix de Dieu* (Paris, 1649), in Carrier, ed., *La Fronde: 52 Mazarinades*, vol. 1, no. 4.

124. *La voix du peuple, à Monseigneur le Prince Conty* (Paris, 1653), reprinted in Eckart Birnstiel, *Die Fronde in Bordeaux, 1648–1653* (Frankfurt am Main, 1985), p. 323.

125. *De la puissance qu'ont les roys sur les peuples, et du pouvoir des peuples sur les roys* (Paris, 1650), in Carrier, ed., *La Fronde: 52 Mazarinades*, vol. 1, no. 15, pp. 16–17, 18.

126. *Discours chrétien et politique de la puissance des rois* (Paris, n.d.), in Carrier, ed., *La Fronde: 52 Mazarinades*, vol. 1, no. 5, pp. 3, 7, 19–26.

127. The later phases of the revolt can be followed in Ranum, *The Fronde*, pp. 169–24, 271–302; Moote, *Revolt of the Judges*, chs. 6–10.

128. John Bowle, ed., *The Diary of John Evelyn* (Oxford, 1985), pp. 142–43.

129. Its history can be followed in Ranum, *The Fronde*, chs. 7–8; Birnstiel, *Die Fronde in Bordeaux*, ch. 1; Sal Westrich, *The Ormée of Bordeaux* (Baltimore, 1972), chs. 1–2, 5–7.

130. [Geoffroy Gay], *Histoire véritable d'une colombe qui a paru miraculeusement en un lieu appellé l'Ormaye de Bordeaux, proche la ville* (Paris, 1652), reprinted in Birnstiel, *Die Fronde in Bordeaux*, pp. 242–47. The propaganda of the Ormée is discussed in ibid., pp. 171–93, Westrich, *The Ormée*, pp. 48–59, and Jouhaud, *Mazarinades*, ch. 7.

131. *Le manifeste des Bourdelois* (Paris, 1652), reprinted in Birnstiel, *Die Fronde in Bordeaux*, pp. 248–52.

132. Jouhaud, *Mazarinades*, p. 200.

133. Birnstiel, *Die Fronde in Bordeaux*, pp. 191–92, 341–47; Westrich, *The Ormée*, pp. 56–57.

134. Neapolitan patriotism is discussed in Rosario Villari, "Revoluciones periféricas y declive de la monarquía española," trans. Mireia Carol, in Simón Tarrés et al., *1640*, pp. 169–82; for revolutionary ideology, see Pier Luigi Rovito, "La rivoluzione constituzionale di Napoli (1647–48)," *Rivista storica italiana* 98 (1986): 367–462.

135. Bowles, ed., *Diary of Evelyn*, pp. 90, 94–95.

136. Rodolfo de Mattei, *Il pensiero politico italiano nell'età della Controriforma*, 2 vols. (Milan, 1982), vol. 2, pp. 211–19; Rovito, "Rivoluzione constituzionale," pp. 383–86; *Il cittadino fedele* (1647), reprinted in Rosario Villari, ed., *Per il re o per la patria: La fedeltà nel seicento* (Rome, 1994), pp. 41–57.

137. Rosario Villari, *The Revolt of Naples*, trans. James Newell and John A. Marino (Cambridge, Mass., 1967, 1993), pp. 56–60; H. G. Koenigsberger, "The Italian Parliaments from Their Origins to the Early Eighteenth Century," in his *Politicians and Virtuosi: Essays in Early Modern History* (London, 1986), pp. 44–46; Tommaso Astarita, *The Continuity of Feudal Power: The Caracciola di Brienza in Spanish Naples* (Cambridge, 1992), ch. 6.

138. Michelangelo Schipa, *Masaniello* (Bari, 1925), pp. 27–64; Villari, *Revolt of Naples*, p. 101; Villari, "Interpretations of Masaniello," p. 123; Vittor Ivo Comparato, "Toward the Revolt of 1647," in Antonio Calabria and John A. Marino, eds., *Good Government in Spanish Naples* (New York, 1990), pp. 275–316.

139. Villari, *Revolt of Naples*, pp. 174–75; Villari, "Interpretations of Masaniello," pp. 121–22; also Pier Luigi Rovito, *La rivolta dei notabili: Ordinamenti municipali e dialettica dei ceti in Calabria citra, 1647–1650* (Napoli, 1988), ch. 1. Aurelio Musi, *La rivolta di Masaniello nella scena politica barocca* (Naples, 1989), pp. 41, 181–211, argues that the revolt was essentially urban and failed in the provinces.

140. Comparato, "Toward the Revolt of 1647," p. 316; *Manifesto del regno*, in Villari, ed., *Per il re*, pp. 83–84; Innocenzo Fuidoro, *Successi historici raccolti dalla sollevatione di Napoli dell'anno 1647*, eds. Anna Maria Giraldi and Maria Raffaeli (Milan, 1994), pp. 52–53; Rovito, "Rivoluzione constituzionale," pp. 395–97; Romeo De Maio, *Pittura e Controriforma a Napoli* (Bari, 1983), pp. 80, 151–52; Liponari, *Relatione delle revolutioni*, pp. 276, 278.

141. Rovito, *La rivolta dei notabili*, pp. 115, 198–204, 237; Benedetto Croce, *History of the Kingdom of Naples*, trans. Frances Frenaye, ed. H. Stuart Hughes (Chicago and London, 1925, 1970), p. 126.

142. Romeo De Maio, "The Counter-Reformation and Painting in Naples," in Clovis Whitfield and Jane Martineau, eds., *Painting in Naples, 1606–1705: From Caravaggio to Giordano* (New York, 1982), p. 32; also De Maio, *Pittura e Controriforma*, p. 28.

143. Peter Burke, "The Virgin of the Carmine and the Revolt of Masaniello," *Past and Present* 99 (1983): 3–21; Alessandro Giraffi, "The Neapolitan Revolution," in Brendan Dooley, ed. and trans., *Italy in the Baroque: Selected Readings* (New York, 1995), pp. 239–75; Liponari, *Relatione delle rivolutioni*, pp. 143, 152, 254; Schipa, *Masaniello*, pp. 65–119; Musi, *Rivolta di Masaniello*, pp. 111–44.

144. Musi, *Rivolta di Masaniello,* pp. 144–54; *Dialogo politico per la morte di Masaniello nella sollevatione della città di Napoli,* in Villari, ed., *Per il re,* pp. 103–4.

145. De Maio, *Pittura e Controriforma,* pp. 157–58; Whitfield and Martineau, eds., *Painting in Naples,* pp. 249, 252–54; Francis Haskell, *Patrons and Painters: A Study in the Relations between Art and Society in the Age of the Baroque,* 2d. ed. (New Haven, 1963, 1980), p. 139.

146. These points are stressed by Rosario Villari in his critique of Burke's cultural analysis: see Villari, *Revolt of Naples,* pp. 153–70; Villari, "Interpretations of Masaniello," pp. 116–22.

147. Vittorio Conti, ed., *Le leggi di una rivoluzione: I bandi della Republica Napoletana dell'ottobre 1647 all'aprile 1648* (Naples, 1983), pp. 32–33.

148. Schipa, *Masaniello,* pp. 120–59; Rovito, "Rivoluzione constituzionale," pp. 388–89, 407–49; Musi, *Rivolta di Masaniello,* pp. 163–80, 213–52; Fuidoro, *Successi historici,* pp. 272–74; Conti, ed., *Leggi di una rivoluzione,* pp. 198, 283–91.

149. Rovito, *La rivolta dei notabili,* p. 116; Louis Chatellier, *The Europe of the Devout: The Catholic Reformation and the Formation of a New Society,* trans. John Birrell (Paris, 1989), pp. 122–23; Fuidoro, *Successi historici,* p. 472; De Maio, "Counter-Reformation and Painting," p. 35.

150. Radziwiłł, *Memoriale,* vol. 4, pp. 116–18; R. A. Stradling, *Philip IV and the Government of Spain, 1621–1665* (Cambridge, 1988), p. 301.

151. *Pertharite, Roi des Lombards,* in Couton, ed., *Oeuvres de Corneille,* pp. 713–84, 1496–1507; Georges Couton, *Corneille et la Fronde: Théâtre et politique il y a trois siècles* (Clermont-Ferrand, 1951), pp. 79–103.

152. Andreas Gryphius, *Ermorderte Majestät, oder Carolus Stuardus, König von Groß Britannien,* in Andreas Gryphius, *Gesamtausgabe der deutschsprachigen Werke,* part 4: *Trauerspiele,* vol. 1, ed. Hugh Powell (Tübingen, 1964), pp. 63–139—the quote is from p. 73, ll. 485–86.

153. Butler, *Theatre and Crisis,* pp. 95–99.

154. "King Charles his Speech, made upon the Scaffold at Whitehall," in J. P. Kenyon, ed., *The Stuart Constitution, 1603–1688: Documents and Commentary,* 2d ed. (Cambridge, 1986), pp. 293–95.

155. Kenyon, ed., *Stuart Constitution,* pp. 18–20.

156. Hugh Trevor-Roper, "The Great Tew Circle," in his *Catholics, Anglicans, and Puritans* (London, 1987), pp. 166–230; Huehns, ed., *Selections from Clarendon,* pp. 49–67; John Aubrey, *Aubrey's Brief Lives,* ed. Oliver Lawson Dick (Harmondsworth, Middlesex, 1949, 1982), pp. 152–55; J. G. A. Pocock, *The Machiavellian Moment: Florentine Political Thought and the Atlantic Republican Tradition* (Princeton, 1975), pp. 361–66; Corinne Comstock Weston and Janelle Renfrow Greenberg, *Subjects and Sovereigns: The Grand Controversy over Legal Sovereignty in Stuart England* (Cambridge, 1981), pp. 35–43.

157. See Tuck, *Philosophy and Government,* pp. 260–78; John Morrill, *The Revolt of the Provinces: Conservatives and Radicals in the English Civil War, 1630–1650* (London, 1976), pp. 48–50—quotation on p. 49; Ronald Hutton, "The Royalist War Effort," in John Morrill, ed., *Reactions to the English Civil War, 1642–1649* (London, 1983), pp. 51–66.

158. See Robert Ashton, *Counter-Revolution: The Second Civil War and Its Origins, 1646–1648* (New Haven, 1994), ch. 1.

159. [Henry Parker], *Observations upon some of his Majesties late Answers and Expresses* (London, 1642), in William A. Haller, ed., *Tracts on Liberty in the Puritan Revolution, 1638–1647*, 3 vols. (New York, 1933), vol. 2, pp. 1, 5, 19, 34; Michael Mendle, *Henry Parker and the English Civil War: The Political Thought of the Public's "Privado"* (Cambridge, 1995), ch. 4; Richard Tuck, *Philosophy and Government, 1572–1651* (Cambridge, 1993), pp. 226–40; Pocock, *Machiavellian Moment*, pp. 368–71.

160. Weston and Greenberg, *Subjects and Sovereigns*, pp. 44–86.

161. [Richard Overton], *A Remonstrance of Many Thousand Citizens, and other Freeborn People of England, To their owne House of Commons* (London, 1646), in Haller, ed., *Tracts on Liberty*, vol. 3, pp. 12, 16.

162. Austin Woolrych, *Soldiers and Statesmen: The General Council of the Army and Its Debates, 1647–1648* (Oxford, 1987), pp. 18–23; but see Mark Kishlansky, *The Rise of the New Model Army* (Cambridge, 1979), pp. 284–91, and his "Ideology and Politics in the Parliamentary Armies, 1645–9," in Morrill, ed., *Reactions to the English Civil War*, pp. 163–83.

163. "The Putney Debates," in Woodhouse, ed., *Puritanism and Liberty*, pp. 53, 55–56, 62, 103, 104–5; Woolrych, *Soldiers and Statesmen*, chs. 9–10.

164. Gardiner, ed., *Constitutional Documents*, pp. 347–53; Ashton, *Counter-Revolution*, chs. 8–9.

165. "The Whitehall Debates," in Woodhouse, ed., *Puritanism and Liberty*, pp. 125–78; Woolrych, *Soldiers and Statesmen*, pp. 338–39; Underdown, *Pride's Purge*, pp. 198–200.

166. Gardiner, ed., *Constitutional Documents*, pp. 371–76; Underdown, *Pride's Purge*, pp. 182–93.

167. Philip Knachel, ed., *Eikon Basilike: The Portraiture of His Sacred Majesty in His Solitudes and Sufferings* (Ithaca, N.Y., 1966), p. 36. The impact of the work on royalist propaganda is discussed in Lois Potter, *Secret Rites and Secret Writings: Royalist Literature, 1641–1660* (Cambridge, 1989), ch. 5.

168. John Milton, *Eikonoklastes* (1649), ed. Merritt K. Hughes, in *Complete Prose Works of John Milton*, 8 vols. (New Haven, 1953–82), vol. 3, pp. 362–68, 410, 458; also, Christopher Hill, *Milton and the English Revolution* (London, 1977), pp. 171–81.

169. See John Morrill, "The Church in England, 1642–9," in Morrill, ed., *Reactions to the English Civil War*, pp. 89–114; Ashton, *Counter-Revolution*, ch. 7; Claire Cross, "The Church in England, 1646–1660," in G. E. Aylmer, ed., *The Interregnum: The Quest for Settlement, 1646–1660* (London, 1972), pp. 99–120; David Underdown, *Revel, Riot, and Rebellion: Popular Politics and Culture in England, 1603–1660* (Oxford, 1985), chs. 8–9.

170. Andrew Marvell, "An Horatian Ode upon Cromwell's Return from Ireland," in Elizabeth Story Donno, ed., *Andrew Marvell: The Complete Poems* (Harmondsworth, Middlesex, 1981), p. 56, ll. 69–72.

171. The events of 1650 to 1654 are examined in Peter Geyl, *The Netherlands in the Seventeenth Century*, 2 vols. (New York, 1961), vol. 2, pp. 13–37, and his *Orange and Stuart, 1641–1672*, trans. Arnold Pomerans (New York, 1939, 1969), pp. 55–125; Herbert H. Rowen, *The Princes of Orange: The Stadholders in the Dutch Republic* (Cambridge, 1988), chs. 4–5; Jonathan Israel, *The Dutch Republic: Its Rise, Greatness, and Fall, 1477–*

*1806* (Oxford, 1994), chs. 25, 29; J. L. Price, *Holland and the Dutch Republic in the Seventeenth Century: The Politics of Particularism* (Oxford, 1994), pp. 154-71.

172. Herbert H. Rowen, ed., *The Low Countries in Early Modern Times* (London, 1972), p. 196.

173. [Pieter de la Court and Jan de Witt], *The True Interest and Political Maxims of the Republic of Holland*, trans. John Campbell (London, 1746, reprint New York, 1972), p. 313. De la Court and his brother Johan are discussed in J. L. Price, *Culture and Society in the Dutch Republic during the Seventeenth Century* (New York, 1974), pp. 198-203, and in Eco Haitsma Muller, "The Language of Seventeenth-Century Republicanism in the United Provinces: Dutch or European?" in Anthony Pagden, ed., *The Languages of Political Theory in Early-Modern Europe* (Cambridge, 1987), pp. 179-97.

174. Geyl, *The Netherlands*, vol. 2, pp. 19-25; Price, *Holland and the Dutch Republic*, pp. 211-20; G. Groenhuis, *De predikanten: De sociale positie van de gereformeerde predikanten in de Republiek der Verenigde Nederlanden voor 1700* (Groningen, 1977), pp. 81-92.

175. De la Court, *True Interest*, p. 334. For Dutch aversion to democracy, see A. T. van Deursen, *Plain Lives in a Golden Age: Popular Culture, Religion, and Society in Seventeenth-Century Holland*, trans. Maarten Ultee (Cambridge, 1991), ch. 12.

176. Groenhuis, *De predikanten*, pp. 13-14; Price, *Culture and Society*, pp. 29-34; Israel, *The Dutch Republic*, ch. 27; van Deursen, *Plain Lives*, ch. 15.

177. Bowle, ed., *Diary of John Evelyn*, p. 21. The complicated position of Catholics is explained in van Deursen, *Plain Lives*, ch. 16.

178. De la Court, *True Interest*, pp. 320-21.

179. Joost van den Vondel, *Lucifer*, trans. Leonard Charles van Nappen (Greensboro, N.C., 1917); Simon Schama, *The Embarrassment of Riches: An Interpretation of Dutch Culture in the Golden Age* (Berkeley, 1988), pp. 113-21; Price, *Holland and the Dutch Republic*, pp. 70-80; Groenhuis, *De predikanten*, pp. 18-21.

180. René Descartes, *Meditations on First Philosophy*, trans. John Cottingham (Cambridge, 1986), pp. 18-19; Peter Dear, *Mersenne and the Learning of the Schools* (Ithaca, N.Y., 1985), ch. 5; Richard Popkin, *The History of Scepticism from Erasmus to Spinoza* (Berkeley, 1960, 1979), chs. 9-10; Stephen Gaukroger, *Descartes: An Intellectual Biography* (Oxford, 1995), pp. 11-12, 184-86, 207-8, 309-21.

181. Blaise Pascal, *Pensées*, ed. and trans. A. J. Krailsheimer (Harmondsworth, Middlesex, 1966), p. 162; Roger Smith, "Self-Reflection and the Self," in Roy Porter, ed., *Rewriting the Self: Histories from the Renaissance to the Present* (London, 1977), pp. 49-57.

182. For autobiographies of the period, see Paul Delany, *British Autobiography in the Seventeenth Century* (London, 1969); Philippe Lejeune, *L'autobiographie en France* (Paris, 1971), pp. 108-11.

183. James Harrington, *The Commonwealth of Oceana*, in J. G. A. Pocock, ed., *The Political Works of James Harrington* (Cambridge, 1977), p. 169.

184. St. Augustine, *Confessions*, trans. R. S. Pine-Coffin (Harmondsworth, Middlesex, 1961), book 8, chs. 11-12, p. 177.

185. Blaise Pascal, *The Provincial Letters*, trans. A. J. Krailsheimer (Harmondsworth, Middlesex, 1967), letter 5, pp. 77-78; also Antoine Adam, *Du mysticisme à la révolte: Les Jansénistes du XVIIe siècle* (Paris, 1968), pp. 193-227.

186. Pascal, *Pensées*, p. 229; Christina, queen of Sweden, *Apologies*, ed. Jean-François de Raymond (Paris, 1994), p. 75; Jacqueline Pascal, *Pensées edifiantes sur le mystère de la mort de Notre-Seigneur Jésus-Christ*, reprinted in Victor Cousin, *Jacqueline Pascal* (Paris, 1884), pp. 143, 160.

187. Pascal, *Provincial Letters*, letter 14, p. 209; Goldmann, *The Hidden God*, pp. 148–60.

188. Antoine Arnauld, *Apologie pour les Catholiques*, in Taveneaux, ed., *Jansénisme et politique*, p. 87.

189. Pascal, *Pensées*, pp. 52, 83.

190. Calderón de la Barca, *El alcalde de Zalamea* (Madrid, 1994), act 1, ll. 873–76, act 3, ll. 917–18. For his theological views, see Rafael María de Hornedo, "Teatro e iglesia en los siglos XVII y XVIII," in Antonio Mestre Sanchis, ed., *Historia de la iglesia en España*, part 4: *La iglesia en los siglos XVII y XVIII* (Madrid, 1979), pp. 317–18; and for negative portrayals of male honour in his plays, Melveena McKendrick, "Calderón and the Politics of Honour," *Bulletin of Hispanic Studies* 70, no. 1 (1993): 135–46.

191. St. Augustine, *Concerning the City of God against the Pagans*, trans. Henry Bettenson (Harmondsworth, Middlesex, 1972), book 9, ch. 16, p. 361.

192. Christopher Hill, "Covenant Theology and the Concept of 'A Public Person,'" in his *Collected Essays of Christopher Hill*, 3 vols. (Amherst, Mass., 1985–86), vol. 3, pp. 300–21; P. G. Rogers, *The Fifth Monarchy Men* (London, 1966), ch. 2; B. S. Capp, *The Fifth Monarchy Men: A Study in Seventeenth-Century English Radicalism* (London, 1971), ch. 6.

193. Gerrard Winstanley, *The New Law of Righteousness Budding Forth, To Restore the Whole Creation from Bondage of the Curse* (1649), in George H. Sabine, ed., *The Works of Gerrard Winstanley* (Ithaca, N.Y., 1941), pp. 161, 204, 226. Winstanley's theology is discussed in Christopher Hill, "The Religion of Gerrard Winstanley," in his *Collected Essays*, vol. 2, pp. 185–252.

194. Harrington, *Oceana*, pp. 169–70, 338; Pocock, *Machiavellian Moment*, pp. 383–400; Christopher Hill, "James Harrington and the People," in his *Puritanism and Revolution* (Harmondsworth, Middlesex, 1958, 1986), pp. 289–302; Rabb, *English Face of Machiavelli*, ch. 6; Mark Goldie, "The Civil Religion of James Harrington," in Pagden, ed., *Languages of Political Theory*, pp. 197–222.

195. Austin Woolrych, *From Commonwealth to Protectorate* (Oxford, 1982), pp. 364–68; Percy Ernest Schramm, *A History of the English Coronation* (Oxford, 1937), trans. L. G. Wickham Legg, p. 101.

196. Bulstrode Whitlocke, *A Journal of the Swedish Embassy in the Years 1653 and 1654*, ed. Charles Morton, 2 vols. (London, 1855), vol. 1, p. 318.

197. Andrew Marvell, "The First Anniversary of the Government under His Highness the Lord Protector, 1655," in Donno, ed., *Complete Poems*, pp. 126–37, ll. 33–35, 76, 126, 161–64. See also Blair Worden, "The Politics of Marvell's Horatian Ode," *Historical Journal* 27, no. 3 (1984): 525–47; William Lamont, "The Religion of Andrew Marvell: Locating the 'Bloody Horse,'" in Conal Condren and A. D. Cousins, eds., *The Political Identity of Andrew Marvell* (Aldershot, Hants., 1990), pp. 135–56.

198. Jean Delumeau, *Catholicism between Luther and Voltaire*, trans. Jeremy Moiser (London, 1977), pp. 43–47; Chatellier, *Europe of the Devout*, p. 8.

199. Sara T. Nalle, *God in La Mancha: Religious Reform and the People of Cuenca, 1500–1650* (Baltimore, 1992), pp. 141–54; Michèle Ménard, *Une histoire des mentalités religieuses aux XVIIe et XVIIIe siècles: Mille retables de l'ancien diocèse du Mans* (Paris, 1980), pp. 393–96; Giovanni Careri, "The Artist," in Villari, ed., *Baroque Personae*, p. 294; René Taveneaux, *Le Catholicisme dans la France classique, 1610–1715*, 2 vols. (Paris, 1980), vol. 2, pp. 368–79.

200. Pascal, *Pensées*, p. 222; also Jean Mesnard, "Pascal et le 'moi haïssable,'" in George Craig and Margaret McGowan, eds., *Moy qui me voy: The Writer and the Self from Montaigne to Leiris* (Oxford, 1989), pp. 19–29.

201. For the Sicilian revolt, see H. G. Koenigsberger, "The Revolt of Palermo in 1647," in his *Estates and Revolutions: Essays in Early Modern European History* (Ithaca, N.Y., 1971), pp. 253–77; Denis Mack Smith, *A History of Sicily: Medieval Sicily, 800–1713* (London, 1968), pp. 211–19; Luis A. Ribot, "Las revueltas sicilianas de 1647–1648," in Simón Tarrés et al., *1640*, pp. 183–99.

202. De Maio, *Pittura e Controriforma*, pp. 153–59; Fritz Saxl, "The Battle Scene Without a Hero: Agniello Falcone and His Patrons," *Journal of the Warburg and Courtauld Institutes* 3 (1939–40): 84–85 and plate 15a.

203. Conflicting interpretations of Christina are presented in Weibull, *Christina of Sweden*, pp. 51–91; Stolpe, *Christina of Sweden*, pp. 80–105, 115–173; Sven Stolpe, *Från Stoicism till mystik: Studier i Drottning Kristinas Maximer* (Stockholm, 1959), chs. 4–5; Susanna Akerman, *Queen Christina of Sweden and Her Circle: The Transformations of a Seventeenth-Century Philosophical Libertine* (Leiden, 1991), esp. chs. 2, 9, 11, and her "On the Impossibility of Abdicating: Queen Christina of Sweden and the Spiritual Crown," in Louise Olga Fradenburg, ed., *Women and Sovereignty* (Edinburgh, 1992), pp. 212–27.

204. Jonathan Brown, *Velázquez: Painter and Courtier* (New Haven, 1986), pp. 253–64; Michel Foucault, *The Order of Things: An Anthropology of the Human Sciences* (New York, 1973), ch. 1; Luis Díez del Corral, *Velázquez, la monarquía e Italia* (Madrid, 1979), pp. 97–104.

205. Thomas Hobbes, *Leviathan*, ed. Richard Tuck (Cambridge, 1996), pp. 9, 112–15, 323.

206. Ibid., pp. 120, 148, 151, 404.

207. See Tuck, *Philosophy and Government*, ch. 7; also A. P. Martinich, *The Two Gods of Leviathan: Thomas Hobbes on Religion and Politics* (Cambridge, 1992), which argues that Hobbes was more or less a conventional Calvinist.

208. Aubrey, *Brief Lives*, p. 231; also Quentin Skinner, "The Ideological Context of Hobbes's Political Thought," *Historical Journal* 9, no. 3 (1966), pp. 286–317; Perez Zagorin, "Clarendon and Hobbes," *Journal of Modern History* 57, no. 4 (1985): 593–616; Mark Goldie, "The Reception of Hobbes," in J. H. Burns and Mark Goldie, eds., *The Cambridge History of Political Thought, 1450–1700* (Cambridge, 1991), pp. 589–615.

## Chapter Five: The Sign of the Artificial Man, 1660–1690

1. Thomas Munck, *The Peasantry and the Early Absolute Monarchy in Denmark, 1660–1708* (Copenhagen, 1979), pp. 39–49; Knud Fabricius, *Kongeloven: Dens tilblivelse og plads i samtidens natur- og arveretlige udvikling* (Copenhagen, 1920, reprint, 1971),

pp. 95–98; E. Ladewig Petersen, "War, Finance, and the Growth of Absolutism: Some Aspects of the European Integration of Seventeenth-Century Denmark," in Göran Rystad, ed., *Europe and Scandinavia: Aspects of the Process of Integration in the Seventeenth Century* (Lund, 1983), pp. 46–49; Peter Brandt, "Von der Adelsmonarchie zur königlichen «Eingewalt»: Der Umbau der Ständegesellschaft in der Vorbereitungs- und Frühphase des Dänischen Absolutismus," *Historische Zeitschrift* 250, no. 1 (1990): 33–55; Gunnar Olsen and Finn Askgaard, *Danmarks Historie*, vol. 8: *Den Unge Enevælde, 1660–1721* (Copenhagen, 1970), pp. 11–46; David Kirby, *Northern Europe in the Early Modern Period: The Baltic World, 1492–1772* (London, 1990), pp. 207–14; T. K. Derry, *A History of Scandinavia* (Minneapolis, 1979), pp. 131–38.

2. The patriot theme is explored in Harald Ilsoe, "Danskeme og deres fædreland: Holdninger og opfattelsen, c. 1550–1700," in Ole Feldbæk, ed., *Danske identitetshistorie*, vol. 1: *Fædreland og modersmål, 1536–1789* (Copenhagen, 1991), pp. 53–6.

3. [Dietrich Reinking], *Jus feciale armatae Daniae* (Copenhagen, 1657), p. ii; Hauke Jessen, *"Biblische Policey": Zum Naturrechtsdenken Dietrich Reinkings* (Freiburg, 1962), pp. 37–57.

4. Key sections of the Law are translated in Ernst Ekman, "The Danish Royal Law of 1665," *Journal of Modern History* 29, no. 2 (1957): 102–7. See also Fabricius, *Kongeloven*, pp. 137–41, 207–23, 314–16; Munck, *Peasantry and Early Absolute Monarchy*, pp. 49–58; Brandt, "Von der Adelsmonarchie," pp. 55–60; Horst Dreitzel, *Protestantischer Aristotelismus und Absoluter Staat: Die "Politica" des Henning Arnisaeus (ca. 1575–1636)* (Wiesbaden, 1970), pp. 407–11. A nationalistic Norwegian interpretation of the Law, equating it with *danskdom*, is found in Halvdan Koht, *Inn i Einveldet, 1657–1661* (Oslo, 1960).

5. Fabricius, *Kongeloven*, pp. 16–20.

6. Robert Molesworth, *An Account of Denmark in the Year 1692* (London, 1694), preface and pp. 75, 251. See also Caroline Robbins, *The Eighteenth-Century Commonwealthman* (New York, 1959, 1968), pp. 98–109; Gerald Aylmer, "English Perceptions of Scandinavia in the Seventeenth Century," in Rystad, ed., *Europe and Scandinavia*, pp. 190–91.

7. [William King], *Animadversions on a Pretended Account of Denmark* (London, 1694), pp. 78–82; [Jodocus Crull], *Denmark Vindicated* (London, 1694), pp. 3, 215.

8. Olsen and Askgaard, *Danmarks historie*, vol. 8, pp. 273–76; Derry, *History of Scandinavia*, p. 139.

9. Jens Christian V. Johansen, "Denmark: The Sociology of Accusations," in Bengt Ankarloo and Gustav Henningsen, eds., *Early Modern European Witchcraft: Centres and Peripheries* (Oxford, 1990), pp. 338–65; and Hans Eyvind Naess, "Norway: The Criminological Context," in ibid., pp. 367–82; Thorkild Lyby and Ole Peter Grell, "The Consolidation of Lutheranism in Denmark and Norway," in Ole Peter Grell, ed., *The Scandinavian Reformation: From Evangelical Movement to Institutionalization of Reform* (Cambridge, 1995), p. 143.

10. Munck, *Peasantry and Early Absolute Monarchy*, pp. 50, 53–57, 59, 239–43; Knud J. V. Jespersen, "Social Change and Military Revolution in Early Modern Europe: Some Danish Evidence," *Historical Journal* 26, no. 1 (1983): 1–13; Brandt, "Von der Adelsmonarchie," pp. 60–71; Kirby, *Northern Europe in the Early Modern Period*, pp. 270–79; Peter Burke, *Popular Culture in Early Modern Europe* (New York, 1978), p. 278; Ole

Feldbæk, "Fædreland og indfodsret: 1700–tallets Dansk identitat," in Feldbæk, *Danske identitetshistorie,* vol. 1, pp. 112–18; Fabricius, *Kongeloven,* pp. 358–59.

11. Alex Wittendorf, "Public Roads and Royal Privilege: The Development of the Road System in Denmark and the King's Private Roads," *Scandinavian Journal of History* 1 (1976): 243–64.

12. Eckman, "Danish Royal Law," p. 107; Derry, *History of Scandinavia,* pp. 138–40, 146; Olsen and Askgaard, *Danmarks historie,* vol. 8, pp. 168–74.

13. Leon Jespersen, "The *Machtstaat* in Seventeenth-Century Denmark," *Scandinavian Journal of History* 10 (1985): 271–304; and for Norway, Oystein Rian, "State and Society in Seventeenth-Century Norway," in ibid., pp. 337–63. These essays were originally published in E. Ladewig Petersen, ed., *Magtstaten i Norden i 1600–tallet og dens sociale konsekvenser* (Odense, 1984).

14. Leonora Christina, *Memoirs of Leonora Christina, Daughter of Christian IV of Denmark, Written during her Imprisonment in the Blue Tower at Copenhagen, 1663–1685,* ed. and trans. F. E. Bunnètt, 3d ed. (London, 1872), pp. 87, 169, 247–48, 273–74. For the original, see *Jammers Minde,* ed. Vagn Lundgaard Simonsen (Copenhagen, 1964).

15. Frances Yeats, *The Art of Memory* (Chicago, 1966); see also Jacques Le Goff, "Memory," in his *History and Memory,* trans. Steven Rendall and Elizabeth Claman (New York, 1992), pp. 51–99.

16. Michel de Certeau, *Practice of Everyday Life,* trans. Steven Rendall (Berkeley, 1984), chs. 6 and 10; see also Roger Chartier, "The Practical Impact of Writing," in Roger Chartier, ed., *A History of Private Life,* vol. 3: *Passions of the Renaissance,* trans. Arthur Goldhammer (Cambridge, Mass., 1989), pp. 111–59.

17. René Descartes, *Discourse on Method,* trans. Donald A. Cress (Indianapolis, 1980), pp. 8–9; Thomas Hobbes, *Leviathan,* ed. Richard Tuck (Cambridge, 1996), pp. 16–19; Yeats, *Art of Memory,* pp. 373–75.

18. Samuel Pufendorf, *On the Duty of Man and Citizen According to Natural Law,* ed. James Tully, trans. Michael Silverthorne (Cambridge, 1991), pp. 78–79.

19. Antoine Furetière, *Le dictionnaire universel,* ed. Alain Rey, 3 vols. (The Hague, 1690, reprint Paris, 1978), under "signe" and "symbole." For the importance of signs in Jansenist thought about the world, see the dense discussion in Louis Marin, *La critique du discours: Sur la «Logique de Port-Royal» et les «Pensées» de Pascal* (Paris, 1975).

20. Jacques-Bénigne Bossuet, *Oraison funèbre du très haut et très puissant Prince Louis de Bourbon, Prince de Condé, premier prince du sang,* in his *Oeuvres,* ed. Abbé Velat and Yvonne Champailler (Paris, 1961), p. 198. For an oblique sculptural reference to the Fronde, see Nathan T. Whitman, "Myth and Politics: Versailles and the Fountain of Latona," in John C. Rule, ed., *Louis XIV and the Craft of Kingship* (Columbus, Ohio, 1969), pp. 286–301.

21. Pierre Clément, ed., *Lettres, instructions et mémoires de Colbert,* 8 vols. (Paris, 1861–82), vol. 6, p. 17.

22. Louis XIV, *Mémoires for the Instruction of the Dauphin,* ed. and trans. Paul Sonnino (New York, 1970), p. 59.

23. François Bluche, *Louis XIV* (Paris, 1986), pp. 122–23; Herbert H. Rowen, *The King's State: Proprietary Dynasticism in Early Modern France* (New Brunswick, N.J., 1980), ch. 4.

24. Jacques-Bénigne Bossuet, *Politique tirée des propres paroles de l'Ecriture Sainte,* ed. Jacques Le Brun (Paris, 1967), p. 18.

25. Louis XIV, *Mémoires,* p. 101.

26. Bossuet, *Politique tirée de l'Ecriture Sainte,* p. 22.

27. Roland Mousnier, "Comment les Français du XVIIe siècle voyaient la constitution," in his *La Plume, la faucille et le marteau: Institutions et société en France du Moyen Age à la Révolution* (Paris, 1970), pp. 43−56; also François Dumont, "French Kingship and Absolute Monarchy in the Seventeenth Century," in Ragnhild Hatton, ed., *Louis XIV and Absolutism* (London, 1976), pp. 55−84.

28. Nicolas Boileau, *Satires,* in his *Oeuvres complètes,* ed. Françoise Escal (Paris, 1966), p. 9.

29. Louis XIV, *Mémoires,* pp. 3−10, 80, 103−4, 220; Jean-Pierre Néraudau, *L'Olympe du Roi Soleil: Mythologie et idéologie royale au grand siècle* (Paris, 1986), pp. 35−45.

30. Jean Racine, *Alexandre le Grand,* in his *Oeuvres complètes,* vol. 1: *Théâtre-poésies,* ed. Raymond Picard (Paris, 1950), p. 176.

31. Paul Pellisson, "Panégyrique au Roi Louis XIV prononcé le 3. fevrier 1671," in Pierre Zoberman, ed., *Les panégyriques du roi prononcés dans l'Académie Française* (Paris, 1991), p. 102. For the panegyrics, see Nicole Ferrier-Caverivière, *L'image de Louis XIV dans la littérature française de 1660 à 1715* (Paris, 1981), pp. 101−6.

32. Jean Racine, "Eloge historique du roi sur ses conquêtes depuis l'année 1672 jusqu'en 1678," in his *Oeuvres complètes,* vol. 2: *Prose,* ed. Raymond Picard (Paris, 1966), p. 235.

33. Ferrier-Caverivière, *L'image de Louis XIV,* pp. 218−26; Louis Marin, *Portrait of the King,* trans. Martha M. Houle (London, 1988), pp. 39−88, 121−37; Peter Burke, *The Fabrication of Louis XIV* (New Haven, 1992), pp. 62−63, 97−98, 118−19, 206−8.

34. Jean-Baptiste Molière, *Oeuvres complètes,* ed. Georges Couton, 2 vols. (Paris, 1971), vol. 1, pp. 669−98. See also Jean Rohou, "L'influence de Louis XIV sur la vie littéraire: Pour un bilan critique," in Keith Cameron and Elizabeth Woodrough, eds., *Ethics and Politics in Seventeenth-Century France* (Exeter, 1996), pp. 245−55.

35. Néraudau, *L'Olympe du Roi Soleil,* pp. 80−84, 119−34; Jean-Marie Apostolidès, *Le roi machine: Spectacle et politique au temps de Louis XIV* (Paris, 1981), pp. 11−19, 40−46, 93−113; Régine Astier, "Louis XIV, 'Premier Danseur,'" in David Lee Rubin, ed., *Sun King: The Ascendancy of French Culture during the Reign of Louis XIV* (Washington, 1992), pp. 73−102; Molière, *Les plaisirs de L'île enchantée,* in his *Oeuvres complètes,* vol. 1, pp. 749−67, 820−29; Louis XIV, *Mémoires,* pp. 101−3.

36. Clément, ed., *Lettres de Colbert,* vol. 5, p. 269; Guy Walton, *Louis XIV's Versailles* (Chicago, 1986), chs. 6−10.

37. Apostolidès, *Le roi machine,* pp. 86−92, 135−37; Néraudau, *L'Olympe du Roi Soleil,* ch. 6; Edouard Pommier, "Versailles, l'image du souverain," and Hélène Himmelfarb, "Versailles, fonctions et légendes," in Pierre Nora, ed., *Lieux de Mémoire,* part 2: *La Nation,* 2 vols. (Paris, 1986), vol. 2, pp. 193−234, 235−92.

38. Boileau, "Discours sur le stile des inscriptions," in his *Oeuvres complètes,* p. 612; also, Bluche, *Louis XIV,* pp. 246−47; Burke, *Fabrication of Louis XIV,* pp. 58−59.

39. Boileau, *Réflexions critiques* (1692−4), réflexion 9, in his *Oeuvres,* p. 532.

40. Elborg Forster, ed. and trans., *A Woman's Life in the Court of the Sun King: Letters of Liselotte von der Pfalz, 1652–1722* (Baltimore, 1984), p. 34.

41. Norbert Elias, *The Court Society,* trans. Edmund Jephcott (New York, 1983), chs. 5–7; Pierre Bourdieu, *Distinction: A Social Critique of the Judgement of Taste,* trans. Richard Nice (Cambridge, Mass., 1984), pp. 467–70; Jean-François Solnon, *La Cour de France* (Paris, 1987), chs. 12–16; Jacques Levron, "Louis XIV's Courtiers," in Hatton, ed., *Louis XIV and Absolutism,* pp. 130–53.

42. Quoted in Franklin L. Ford, *Robe and Sword: The Regrouping of the French Aristocracy after Louis XIV* (New York, 1953, 1965), p. 10.

43. Quoted in Solnon, *La cour de France,* p. 321.

44. Robert M. Isherwood, *Music in the Service of the King: France in the Seventeenth Century* (Ithaca, N.Y., 1973), pp. 170–203.

45. Racine, "Notes et fragments," in his *Oeuvres Complètes,* vol. 2, p. 281.

46. Jacques-Bénigne Bossuet, *Discours sur l'histoire universelle,* in his *Oeuvres,* p. 666.

47. Jean de La Bruyère, *Les Caractères de Théophraste traduits du Grec avec les caractères ou les moeurs de ce siècle* (Paris, 1993), p. 24.

48. Ibid., p. 221.

49. See Hubert Gillot, *La querelle des anciens et des modernes en France* (Geneva, 1914, 1968), pp. 309–22, 454–70; Ferrier-Caverivière, *L'image de Louis XIV,* pp. 351–79; Apostolidès, *Le roi machine,* pp. 116–22; Néraudau, *L'Olympe du Roi Soleil,* pp. 73–80; Burke, *Fabrication of Louis XIV,* pp. 126–27.

50. Norman Bryson, *Word and Image: French Painting of the Ancien Régime* (Cambridge, 1980), p. 33.

51. Jacques Thuillier and Jennifer Montagu, *Charles Le Brun, 1619–1690: Peintre et dessinateur* (Paris, 1963), pp. 118–19; Michel Gareau and Lydia Beauvais, *Charles Le Brun, First Painter to Louis XIV,* trans. Katrin Sermat (New York, 1992), pp. 70–71.

52. La Bruyère, *Les Caractères,* p. 386; Ferrier-Caverivière, *L'image de Louis XIV,* pp. 246–49.

53. Furetière, *Dictionnaire universel,* under "Roy" and "Souverain"; Louis XIV, *Mémoires,* pp. 57–61; Walton, *Louis XIV's Versailles,* pp. 148–50, 195–209; Friedrich B. Polleross, *Das sakrale Identifikationsporträt: Ein höfischer Bildtypus vom 13. bis zum 20. Jahrhundert,* 2 vols. (Worms, 1988), vol. 1, pp. 257–58. A different interpretation of the king's religiosity is given in Ferrier-Caverivière, *L'image du Roi,* pp. 80–86, and Bluche, *Louis XIV,* pp. 564–91.

54. Daniel Dessert, *Foucquet* (Paris, 1987), pp. 189–95; Mme. de Sévigné, *Correspondance,* ed. Roger Duchêne, 3 vols. (Paris, 1972), vol. 1, p. 80.

55. Georges Couton's preface to *Tartuffe* in Molière, *Oeuvres complètes,* pp. 833–81, is of great value; also Raoul Allier, *La cabale des dévots (1627–1666)* (Geneva, 1902, 1970), chs. 19–20; René Chatellier, *The Europe of the Devout: The Catholic Reformation and the Formation of a New Society,* trans. John Birrell (Paris, 1989), ch. 9; Alain Tallon, *La Compagnie du Saint-Sacrement (1629–1667): Spiritualité et société* (Paris, 1990), pp. 129–39.

56. Bossuet, *Politique tirée de l'Ecriture Sainte,* pp. 63–67, 71, 92, 96–97.

57. Henri Busson, *La religion des classiques* (Paris, 1948), pp. 5–66; Raymond Picard, *La carrière de Jean Racine* (Paris, 1956), pp. 25–31, 447–68; Boileau, "Epistre 3," in his

*Oeuvres complètes*, pp. 110–12. For Jansenism in this period, see Antoine Adam, *Du mysticisme à la révolte: Les Jansénistes du XVIIe siècle* (Paris, 1968), pp. 261–91; Alexander Sedgwick, *Jansenism in Seventeenth-Century France: Voices from the Wilderness* (Charlottesville, Va., 1977), ch. 5.

58. Robert Mandrou, *De la culture populaire aux XVIIe et XVIIIe siècles: La bibliothèque bleue de Troyes* (Paris, 1964, 1975), pp. 146–72; Geneviève Bollème, ed., *La bibliothèque bleue: La littérature populaire du XVIIe au XIXe siècle* (Paris, 1970), pp. 192–95; Geneviève Bollème, ed., *La Bible bleue: Anthologie d'une littérature «populaire»* (Paris, 1975), pp. 164–67; Roger Chartier, "The *Bibliothèque bleue* and Popular Reading," in his *Cultural Uses of Print in Early Modern France*, trans. Lydia G. Cochrane (Princeton, 1987), pp. 240–64.

59. Henri Platelle, ed., *Journal d'un curé de campagne au XVIIe siècle* (Paris, 1965), p. 90.

60. Alain Lottin, *Chavatte, ouvrier Lillois: Un contemporain de Louis XIV* (Paris, 1979), pp. 178–98.

61. Michel Lagrée, "1532–1840," in Jean Delumeau, ed., *Le diocèse de Rennes* (Paris, 1979), p. 152.

62. Clément, ed., *Lettres de Colbert*, vol. 6, pp. 14–15; Dessert, *Argent, pouvoir et société*, pp. 325–38; Dessert, *Fouquet*, ch. 8; Roger Mettam, *Power and Faction in Louis XIV's France* (Oxford, 1988), pp. 268–308; John C. Rule, "Louis XIV, roi bureaucrate," in Rule, ed., *Louis XIV and the Craft of Kingship*, pp. 3–101.

63. Mettam, *Power and Faction*, pp. 12–44, 96–101, 266–67; William Beik, *Absolutism and Society in Seventeenth-Century France: State Power and Provincial Aristocracy in Languedoc* (Cambridge, 1985), chs. 8–9, 13; Klaus Malettke, *Opposition und Konspiration unter Ludwig XIV* (Göttingen, 1976), pp. 224–76, 325–33; Jean Meuvret, "Fiscalism and Public Opinion under Louis XIV," in Hatton, ed., *Louis XIV and Absolutism*, pp. 199–225; Albert M. Hamscher, *The Parlement of Paris after the Fronde, 1653–1673* (Pittsburgh, 1976), chs. 5–6.

64. Duc de Saint-Simon, *Mémoires*, 8 vols. (Paris, 1983), vol. 1, p. 271; Bluche, *Louis XIV*, pp. 520–22.

65. Recent assessments of the Restoration settlement include Ronald Hutton, *The Restoration: A Political and Religious History of England and Wales, 1658–1667* (Oxford, 1985), pp. 181–84; Ronald Hutton, *Charles I, King of England, Scotland, and Ireland* (Oxford, 1989), ch. 8; Paul Seaward, *The Cavalier Parliament and the Reconstruction of the Old Regime, 1661–1667* (Cambridge, 1989), ch. 3 and pp. 162–95; Tim Harris, *Politics under the Later Stuarts: Party Conflict in a Divided Society, 1660–1715* (London, 1993), pp. 6–7; John Spurr, *The Restoration Church of England, 1646–1689* (New Haven, 1991), pp. 34–51.

66. John Bowle, ed., *The Diary of John Evelyn* (Oxford, 1985), pp. 182, 184; John Spurr, " 'Virtue, Religion, and Government': The Anglican Uses of Providence," in Tim Harris, Paul Seaward, and Mark Goldie, eds., *The Politics of Religion in Restoration England* (Oxford, 1990), pp. 29–47; John Kenyon, ed., *The Stuart Constitution 1603–1688: Documents and Commentary*, 2d ed. (Cambridge, 1986), p. 459.

67. Harold Weber, *Paper Bullets: Print and Kingship under Charles II* (Lexington, Ky., 1996), pp. 50–67; Gerald Reedy, "Mystical Politics: The Imagery of Charles II's Corona-

tion," in Paul J. Korshin, ed., *Studies in Change and Revolution: Aspects of English Intellectual History, 1640–1800* (Menston, Yorks., 1972), pp. 19–42; Sir Arthur Bryant, ed., *The Letters, Speeches, and Declarations of King Charles II* (London, 1935, 1968), p. 114.

68. George Savile, marquess of Halifax, "A Character of King Charles II," in Walter Raleigh, ed., *The Complete Works of George Savile, First Marquess of Halifax* (Oxford, 1912), pp. 188–90; Hutton, *Charles II*, pp. 455–57.

69. Matthew Wren, *Monarchy Asserted or The State of Monarchical & Popular Government in Vindication of Considerations Upon Mr Harrington's Oceana* (Oxford, 1659), p. 77.

70. Kenyon, ed., *Stuart Constitution*, pp. 331, 348.

71. For the development of such ideas, see Corinne Comstock Weston and Janelle Renfrow Greenberg, *Subjects and Sovereigns: The Grand Controversy over Legal Sovereignty in Stuart England* (Cambridge, 1981), chs. 4, 6; also Schochet, *Patriarchalism*, ch. 7.

72. John Dryden, "Astraea Redux," in Earl Miner, ed., *Selected Poetry and Prose of John Dryden* (New York, 1969), pp. 12, 14, ll. 19–20, 99–100. On D'Urfé's *L'Astrée*, see Elias, *Court Society*, pp. 246–51, 255–66; and on Dryden's politics, Steven N. Zwicker, *Politics and Language in Dryden's Poetry: The Arts of Disguise* (Princeton, 1984), ch. 3, as well as Michael McKeon, *Politics and Poetry in Restoration England: The Case of Dryden's "Annus Mirabilis"* (Cambridge, Mass., 1975).

73. Louis XIV, *Mémoires*, p. 27; Gilbert Burnet, *History of His Own Times*, ed. Thomas Stackhouse (London, 1906), p. 220; David Ogg, *England in the Reign of Charles II*, 2 vols. (London, 1934, 1963), vol. 1, ch. 9.

74. See John Miller, "The Potential for Absolutism in Later Stuart England," *History* 69, no. 2 (1984): 187–207; J. R. Jones, *Charles II: Royal Politician* (London, 1987), pp. 187–90.

75. See Julia Buckroyd, *Church and State in Scotland, 1660–81* (Edinburgh, 1980), ch. 3; S. J. Connolly, *Religion, Law, and Power: The Making of Protestant Ireland, 1660–1760* (Oxford, 1992), pp. 5–32; J. G. Simms, "The Restoration, 1660–85," in T. W. Moody, F. X. Martin, and F. J. Byrne, eds., *A New History of Ireland*, vol. 3: *Early Modern Ireland* (Oxford, 1976), ch. 17.

76. Sir Samuel Tuke, quoted in Ogg, *England in the Reign of Charles II*, vol. 1, p. 148.

77. Halifax, "Character of King Charles II," p. 200.

78. Peter Holman, *Four and Twenty Fiddlers: The Violin at the English Court, 1540–1690* (Oxford, 1993), ch. 12; Sir Walter Scott, ed., *Memoirs of the Court of Charles the Second, by Count Grammont* (London, 1853), p. 173.

79. Bowle, ed., *Diary of John Evelyn*, pp. 216–17; Robert Latham and William Matthews, eds., *The Diary of Samuel Pepys*, 11 vols. (Berkeley, 1970–82), vol. 7, pp. 320, 324, 328; E. S. de Beer, "King Charles II's Own Fashion: An Episode in Anglo-French Relations, 1666–1670," *Journal of the Warburg and Courtauld Institutes* 2 (1938–39): 105–15; Diana de Marly, "King Charles II's Own Fashion: The Theatrical Origins of the English Vest," *Journal of the Warburg and Courtauld Institutes* 37 (1974): 378–82.

80. Steven N. Zwicker, "Virgins and Whores: The Politics of Sexual Misconduct in the 1660s," in Conal Condren and A. D. Cousins, eds., *The Political Identity of Andrew Marvell* (Aldershot, Hants., 1990), pp. 85–110; Hilda L. Smith, *Reason's Disciples: Seventeenth-Century English Feminists* (Urbana, Ill., 1982), ch. 3; Angeline Goreau, *Reconstructing Aphra: A Social Biography of Aphra Behn* (New York, 1980).

81. Bowles, ed., *Diary of John Evelyn*, p. 216; John Evelyn, *The Life of Mrs. Goldolphin*, ed. Harriet Sampson (London, 1939), p. 7. For a French parallel, see Carolyn C. Lougee, *Le paradis des femmes: Women, Salons, and Social Stratification in Seventeenth-Century France* (Princeton, 1976).

82. Latham and Matthews, eds., *Diary of Samuel Pepys*, vol. 1, p. 144; vol. 3, pp. 139, 175; vol. 6, p. 191. For the Royal Society, see Michael Hunter, *Science and Society in Restoration England* (Cambridge, 1981), ch. 2.

83. See Richard Ollard, *The Escape of Charles II after the Battle of Worcester* (London, 1966); "An Account of His Majesty's Escape from Worcester, Dictated to Mr. Pepys by the King Himself" and "The Boscobel Tracts," in Scott, ed., *Memoirs of Count Grammont*, pp. 455–536.

84. David Underdown, *Revel, Riot, and Rebellion: Popular Politics and Culture in England, 1603–1660* (Oxford, 1985), ch. 10; David Cressy, *Bonfires and Bells: National Memory and the Protestant Calendar in Elizabethan and Stuart England* (Berkeley, 1989), pp. 64–65, 171–72; Tim Harris, *London Crowds in the Reign of Charles II: Propaganda and Politics from the Restoration until the Exclusion Crisis* (Cambridge, 1987), pp. 38–39.

85. Latham and Matthews, eds., *Diary of Samuel Pepys*, vol. 8, p. 181; Tim Harris, "The Bawdy House Riots of 1668," in *Historical Journal* 29, no. 4 (1984): 537–56; Hutton, *The Restoration*, pp. 185–90.

86. "The King's Vows," in George deF. Lord, ed., *Poems on Affairs of State: Augustan Satirical Verse, 1660–1714*, vol. 1: *1660–78* (New Haven, 1963), p. 161, ll. 37, 39; Lord Rochester, "A Satyr on Charles II," in David M. Vieth, ed., *The Complete Poems of John Wilmot, Earl of Rochester* (New Haven, 1968), p. 60, ll. 11–12, 14–15; [John Lacy], "Satire," in Lord, ed., *Poems on Affairs of State*, vol. 1, p. 426, l. 13; also, Weber, *Paper Bullets*, pp. 88–127; Rachel Weil, "Sometimes a Scepter is Only a Scepter: Pornography and Politics in Restoration England," in Lynn Hunt, ed., *The Invention of Pornography: Obscenity and the Origins of Modernity, 1500–1800* (New York, 1993), pp. 125–53.

87. Latham and Mathews, eds., *Diary of Samuel Pepys*, vol. 8, p. 421.

88. See David Cressy, *Literacy and the Social Order: Reading and Writing in Tudor and Stuart England* (Cambridge, 1980), chs. 4, 6; James Sutherland, *The Restoration Newspaper and Its Development* (Cambridge, 1986), ch. 1; Lois G. Schwoerer, "Liberty of the Press and Public Opinion, 1660–1695," in J. R. Jones, ed., *Liberty Secured? Britain Before and After 1688* (Stanford, 1992), pp. 199–220; Steven Pincus, " 'Coffee Politicians Does Create': Coffeehouses and Restoration Political Culture," *Journal of Modern History* 67 (1995): 807–34.

89. [Sir Roger L'Estrange], *The Observator*, no. 1, Wednesday, 13 April 1681, reprinted in Violet Jordain, ed., *Selections from the Observator*, Augustan Reprint Society, vol. 141 (Los Angeles, 1970), p. 9.

90. J. P. Kenyon, *The Popish Plot* (London, 1972); Harris, *Politics under the Later Stuarts*, pp. 83–94; Harris, *London Crowds*, ch. 5; Hutton, *Charles II*, ch. 13; John Miller, *Popery and Politics in England, 1660–1688* (Cambridge, 1973), pp. 169–88; J. R. Jones, *The First Whigs: The Politics of the Exclusion Crisis, 1678–83* (Oxford, 1961), ch. 3.

91. "The Character," in Elias F. Mengel, ed., *Poems on Affairs of State*, vol. 2: *1678–82* (New Haven, 1965), p. 139, ll. 100–2. For Tory publicity, see Harris, *London Crowds*, ch. 6;

NOTES TO PAGES 231-235 · 387

for hereditary right, Howard Nenner, *The Right to be King: The Succession to the Crown of England, 1603–1714* (Chapel Hill, N.C., 1995), chs. 5–6.

92. J. R. Jones, "Parties and Parliaments," in Jones, ed., *Restored Monarchy*, pp. 48–70; Jones, *First Whigs*, chs. 4–5; Robert Willman, "The Origins of 'Whig' and 'Tory' in English Political Language," *Historical Journal* 17, no. 2 (1974): 247–64.

93. The quotation is from "Popish Politics Unmasked," in Mengel, ed., *Poems on Affairs of State*, vol. 2, p. 389, ll. 222–23. Tory rhetoric is further discussed in Tim Harris, " 'Lives, Liberties, and Estates': Rhetorics of Liberty in the Reign of Charles II," in Harris, Seaward, and Goldie, eds., *Politics of Religion*, pp. 217–41; Harris, *Politics under the Later Stuarts*, pp. 86–102.

94. Bowle, ed., *Diary of John Evelyn*, p. 277; Jones, *First Whigs*, pp. 124–26, 136–37; Harris, *London Crowds*, pp. 115–17, 158–61; Weber, *Paper Bullets*, pp. 77–81.

95. Hutton, *Charles II*, ch. 15; Miller, *Popery and English Politics*, ch. 9; Crawfurd, *King's Evil*, p. 112. Jones, *Charles II*, ch. 8, however, sees the king as gaining independence after 1682.

96. John Dryden, "Absalom and Achitophel," in Mengel, ed., *Poems on Affairs of State*, vol. 2, pp. 458, l. 22, 462, l. 150, 493, ll. 1030–31.

97. Hermann Conring, *Der Ursprung des deutschen Rechts*, trans. Ilse Hoffmann-Meckenstock, ed. Michael Solleis (Frankfurt am Main, 1994), pp. 237–49; "Severinus de Monzambano" [Samuel Pufendorf], *De statu Imperii Germanici*, ed. Fritz Salomon (Weimar, 1910), p. 146; Hanns Gross, *Empire and Sovereignty: A History of the Public Law Literature in the Holy Roman Empire, 1599–1804* (Chicago, 1973), ch. 8; Leonard Krieger, *The Politics of Discretion: Pufendorf and the Acceptance of Natural Law* (Chicago, 1965), pp. 178–87.

98. Gerd Zillhardt, ed., *Der dreißigjährige Krieg in zeitgenössischer Darstellung: Hans Heberles "Zeytregister" (1618–1672)* (Ulm, 1975), pp. 251–52, 253.

99. Karl Otmar von Aretin, *Das Reich: Friedensgarantie und europäisches Gleichgewicht, 1648–1806* (Stuttgart, 1986), pp. 55–75, and his "Die Großmächte und das Klientelsystem im Reich am Ende des 18. Jahrhunderts," in Antoni Mączak, ed., *Klientelsysteme im Europa der Früher Neuzeit* (Munich, 1988), pp. 66–67; Anton Schindling, "Der westfälische Frieden und der Reichstag," in Hermann Weber, ed., *Politische Ordnungen und soziale Kräfte im alten Reich* (Wiesbaden, 1980), pp. 113–53, and his "Development of the Eternal Diet in Regensburg," *Journal of Modern History* 58, Supplement (1986): 564–75; Heinz Duchhardt, "International Relations, the Law of Nations, and the Germanies: Structures and Changes in the Second Half of the Seventeenth Century," in Charles W. Ingrao, ed., *State and Society in Early Modern Austria* (West Lafayette, Ind., 1994), pp. 286–97; Volker Press, "Von der Bauernrevolten des 16. zur konstitutionellen Verfassung des 19. Jahrhunderts: Die Untertanenkonflikte in Hohenzollern-Hechingen und Ihre Lösung," in Weber, ed., *Politische Ordnungen*, pp. 85–112; also Bernd Mathias Kremer, *Der westfälische Friede in der Deutung der Aufklärung* (Tübingen, 1989), pp. 51–70; R. J. W. Evans, *The Making of the Habsburg Monarchy, 1550–1700* (Oxford, 1979), ch. 8.

100. G. W. Leibniz, "Caesarinus Fürstenerius (De suprematu principum Germaniae)," in *Political Writings*, ed. and trans. Patrick Riley (Cambridge, 1972, 1988), pp. 111, 114, 120.

388 · NOTES TO PAGES 236–240

101. Polleross, *Das sakrale Identifikationsporträt*, vol. 1, p. 117, vol. 2, plate 21; *Regiae virtutes seu initia regni Salomonis* (Vienna, 1656), reprinted in Elida Maria Szarota, ed., *Das Jesuitendrama im deutschen Sprachgebiet: Eine Periochen Edition*, 7 vols. in 4 parts (Munich, 1979–87), part 2, vol. 1, pp. 51–62; Joachim Whalley, "Obedient Servants? Lutheran Attitudes to Authority and Society in the First Half of the Seventeenth Century: The Case of Johann Balthasar Schupp," *Historical Journal* 35, no. 1 (1992): 27–42.

102. Zillhardt, ed., *Der dreißigjährige Krieg*, pp. 251–52, 253, 267.

103. *Vienna anno 1683 liberata* (Köln, 1684), in Szarota, ed., *Das Jesuitendrama*, part 3, vol. 3, pp. 763–65. The siege is described in John P. Spielman, *The City and the Crown: Vienna and the Imperial Court* (W. Lafayette, Ind., 1993), pp. 145–55.

104. Alfred Francis Pribram and Moriz Landwehr von Pragenau, eds., *Privatbriefe Kaiser Leopold I an den Graf Pötting, 1662–1673*, in *Fontes rerum Austriacarum*, 56–57, 2 vols. (Vienna, 1903), vol. 1, pp. 53–54.

105. Polleross, *Das sakrale Identifikationsporträt*, vol. 1, pp. 92–5, vol. 2, plate 12. For the Hungarian wars, see John P. Spielman, *Leopold I of Austria* (London, 1977), chs. 8–12; Charles W. Ingrao, *The Habsburg Monarchy, 1618–1848* (Cambridge, 1994), pp. 64–87.

106. P. W. von Hornigk, *Oesterreich über Alles, wenn es nur will* (1684), in C. A. Macartney, ed., *The Habsburg and Hohenzollern Dynasties in the Seventeenth and Eighteenth Centuries* (New York, 1970), p. 78.

107. Anna Coreth, *Pietas Austriaca: Ursprung und Entwicklung barocker Frömmigkeit in Österreich* (Munich, 1959), p. 15; Spielman, *City and the Crown*, pp. 137–45; Thomas DaCosta Kaufmann, *Court, Cloister, and City: The Art and Culture of Central Europe, 1450–1800* (Chicago, 1995), pp. 298–99; Peter Tolstoi, *The Travel Diary of Peter Tolstoi, A Muscovite in Early Modern Europe*, ed. and trans. Max J. Okenfuss (DeKalb, Ill., 1987), p. 56.

108. Evans, *Making of the Habsburg Monarchy*, p. 152.

109. Hubert Ch. Ewalt, *Ausdrucksformen absolutischer Herrschaft: Der Wiener Hof im 17. und 18. Jahrhundert* (Vienna, 1980), pp. 22–25, 63–108, 114–32, 147–57; also, Jürgen von Kruedener, *Die Rolle des Hofes im Absolutismus* (Stuttgart, 1973), pp. 30–72; R. J. W. Evans, "The Austrian Habsburgs: The Dynasty as a Political Institution," in A. G. Dickens, ed., *The Courts of Europe: Politics, Patronage, and Royalty, 1400–1800* (London, 1977), pp. 142–45; John P. Spielman, "Status as Commodity: The Habsburg Economy of Privilege," in Ingrao, ed., *State and Society*, pp. 110–18.

110. Pribram and von Pragenau, eds., *Privatbriefe Leopold I*, vol. 1, pp. 282, 283 n. 3; Heinz Kindermann, *Theatergeschichte Europas*, vol. 3: *Das Theater der Barockzeit* (Salzburg, 1959), pp. 490–510; H. G. Koenigsberger, "Music and Religion in Early Modern European History," in his *Politicians and Virtuosi: Essays in Early Modern History* (London, 1986), pp. 179–210; Lorenzo Bianconi, *Music in the Seventeenth Century*, trans. David Bryant (Cambridge, 1987), pp. 228–31.

111. Karl Vocelka, "Public Opinion and the Phenomenon of *Sozialdisziplinierung* in the Habsburg Monarchy," in Ingrao, ed., *State and Society*, pp. 133–34; Paul Bernard, "Poverty and Poor Relief in the Eighteenth Century," in ibid., p. 241; Tolstoi, *Travel Diary*, pp. 55, 58–60.

112. Quoted in Robert A. Kann, *A Study in Austrian Intellectual History: From Late Baroque to Romanticism* (New York, 1960, 1973), p. 74.

113. Ibid., pp. 75–80; Spielman, *City and the Crown*, pp. 129–33, and his *Leopold I*, pp. 75–76.

114. The view that Leopold's Hofburg made little architectural impact, expressed by Hellmut Lorenz in "The Imperial Hofburg: The Theory and Practice of Architectural Representation in Baroque Vienna," in Ingrao, ed., *State and Society*, pp. 93–109, can be balanced against Thomas DaCosta Kaufmann's more positive opinion in *Court, Cloister, and City*, pp. 271–73.

115. Henry Frederick Schwarz, *The Imperial Privy Council in the Seventeenth Century* (Cambridge, Mass., 1943), pp. 143–90; Evans, *Making of the Habsburg Monarchy*, pp. 148, 163, 297–98; Kann, *Study in Austrian Intellectual History*, pp. 28–31.

116. Evans, *Making of the Habsburg Monarchy*, ch. 6; Jean Bérenger, "The Austrian Lands: Habsburg Absolutism under Leopold I," in John Miller, ed., *Absolutism in Seventeenth-Century Europe* (New York, 1990), pp. 161–65.

117. Spielman, *Leopold I*, chs. 6, 8, 13 (quotation is on p. 63); Pribram and von Pragenau, eds., *Privatbriefe Leopold I*, vol. 2, p. 267; Evans, *Making of the Habsburg Monarchy*, ch. 7; Bérenger, "Austrian Lands," pp. 166–73; Kálmán Benda, "Habsburg Absolutism and the Resistance of the Hungarian Estates in the Sixteenth and Seventeenth Centuries," in R. J. W. Evans and T. V. Thomas, eds., *Crown, Church, and Estates: Central European Politics in the Sixteenth and Seventeenth Centuries* (New York, 1991), pp. 123–28; Macartney, ed., *Habsburg and Hohenzollern Dynasties*, pp. 85–87.

118. Pribram and von Pragenau, eds., *Privatbriefe Leopold I*, vol. 2, pp. 232, 297, and references in Index to "Habsburg, Haus."

119. Henry Kamen, *Spain in the Later Seventeenth Century* (London, 1980), ch. 1 and pp. 20–22; Luis Antonio Ribot Garcia, "La España de Carlos II," in Pere Molas Ribalta, ed., *Historia de España Menéndez Pidal*, vol. 28: *La transición del siglo XVII al XVIII: Entre la decadencia y la reconstrucción* (Madrid, 1993), pp. 63–69; Pribram and von Pragenau, eds., *Privatbriefe Leopold I*, vol. 1, p. 68.

120. On Jansenism in Spain, see Isaac Vázquez, "Las controversias docrinales postridentinas hasta finales del siglo XVII," in Antonio Mestre Sanchis, ed., *Historia de la iglesia en España*, vol. 4: *La iglesia en los siglos XVII y XVIII* (Madrid, 1979), pp. 443–55; for Sister María, see Joaquín Pérez Villanueva, "Sor María de Agreda y Felipe IV: Un epistolario en su tiempo," in ibid., pp. 359–417 (quotation on p. 370); Mario Rosa, "The Nun," in Rosario Villari, ed., *Baroque Personae*, trans. Lydia Cochrane (Chicago, 1995), pp. 215–19; José Deleito y Piñuela, *El rey se divierte* (Madrid, 1964), pp. 29–34; Martin Hume, *The Court of Philip IV*, 2d ed. (London, n.d.), pp. 379–84; R. A. Stradling, *Philip IV and the Government of Spain, 1621–1665* (Cambridge, 1988), pp. 269–76, 303–4, 347–48.

121. Steven Orso, *Art and Death at the Spanish Court: The Royal Exequies for Philip IV* (Columbia, Mo., 1989), passim; for the hieroglyph of blind Faith, see p. 103 and fig. 45. An account of the funeral ceremonies, by the wife of the English ambassador, can be found in "The Memoirs of Ann, Lady Fanshawe," in John Loftis, ed., *Memoirs of Lady Halkett and Lady Fanshawe* (Oxford, 1979), pp. 176–78. The Neapolitan exequies are described in Romeo De Maio, *Pittura e Controriforma a Napoli* (Bari, 1983), pp. 257–60.

122. See Orso, *Art and Death*, pp. 13–26; Yves Bottineau, "Aspects de la cour d'Espagne au XVIIe siècle: L'etiquette de la chambre du roi," *Bulletin hispanique* 74, nos. 1–2 (1972): 138–57; John E. Varey, "Processional Ceremonial of the Spanish Court in the

Seventeenth Century," in Karl-Hermann Körner and Klaus Rühl, eds., *Studia Iberica: Festschrift für Hans Flasche* (Bern, 1973), pp. 643–56.

123. Edward J. Sullivan, *Baroque Painting in Madrid: The Contribution of Claudio Coello with a Catalogue Raisonné of His Works* (Columbia, Mo., 1986), ch. 1; Jonathan Brown, *The Golden Age of Painting in Spain* (New Haven, 1991), ch. 13.

124. Juan Velez de Guevara, *Los celos hacen estrellas*, ed. J. E. Varey and N. D. Shergold (London, 1970), Introduction, pp. cv–cviii. For performances of Calderón's plays at the Viennese court, see Pribram and von Pragenau, eds., *Privatbriefe Leopold I*, vol. 1, pp. 276, 278 n. 10, 344; vol. 2, pp. 207, 208 n. 8.

125. Pedro Calderón de la Barca, *Lo que va del hombre a Dios* (1681?), in Eduardo González Pedroso, ed., *Autos sacramentales desde su origen hasta fines del siglo XVII*, Biblioteca de Autores Españoles, vol. 58 (Madrid, 1916), pp. 509–11; Kindermann, *Theatergeschichte*, vol. 3, p. 234.

126. Kamen, *Spain in the Later Seventeenth Century*, ch. 11; Rafael María de Hornedo, "Teatro e iglesia en los siglos XVII y XVIII," in Mestre Sanchis, ed., *Historia de la iglesia*, part 4, pp. 329–31.

127. Coreth, *Pietas Austriaca*, pp. 54–59; Marina Warner, *Alone of All Her Sex: The Myth and the Cult of the Virgin Mary* (New York, 1976), chs. 16–17; Suzanne L. Stratton, *The Immaculate Conception in Spanish Art* (Cambridge, 1994), pp. 47–52, 88–137; Antonio Mestre Sanchis, "Religión y cultura en el siglo XVIII español," in Mestre Sanchis, ed., *Historia de la iglesia*, part 4, p. 595.

128. Pribram and von Pragenau, eds., *Privatbriefe Leopold I*, vol. 1, p. 176.

129. Kamen, *Spain in the Later Seventeenth Century*, chs. 2, 13–14 (quotation on p. 22); Ribot García, "España de Carlos II," pp. 71–144, 163–203; Dennis Mack Smith, *A History of Sicily: Medieval Sicily, 800–1713* (London, 1968), ch. 22; Joaquim Albareda i Salvadó, "Catalunya a finals del sigle XVII: La continuitat de la revolta," in Eva Serra et al., eds., *La revolució catalana de 1640* (Barcelona, 1991), pp. 296–302.

130. [Lord Mahon], ed., *Spain under Charles the Second, or, Extracts from the Correspondence of the Hon. Alexander Stanhope, British Minister at Madrid, 1690–1699* (London, 1840), p. 143.

131. For the riots, see [Mahon], ed., *Spain under Charles the Second*, pp. 129–34; Vicente Bacallar y Sanna, Marqués de San Felipe, *Comentarios de la guerra de España e historia de su Rey Felipe V, el Animoso*, ed. Carlos Seco Serrano, Biblioteca de Autores Españoles, vol. 99 (Madrid, 1957), pp. 7–8; Ribot García, "La España de Carlos II," pp. 130–34; Kamen, *Spain in the Later Seventeenth Century*, p. 390.

132. [Mahon], ed., *Spain under Charles the Second*, pp. 141, 150–51; San Felipe, *Commentarios*, p. 7; José Luis de la Peña, ed., *Testamento de Carlos II* (Madrid, 1982), Introduction by Antonio Domínguez Ortiz, pp. xlvi–xlvii.

133. De la Peña, ed., *Testamento de Carlos II*, pp. 9, 15, 25, 31–35, 73, 83, 89, 185.

134. Sullivan, *Baroque Painting in Madrid*, ch. 4; Brown, *Spanish Painting*, pp. 300–2.

135. The painting is reproduced and described in Thuillier, *Charles Le Brun*, pp. 96–99. For the veil of the tabernacle, see Ernst Kantorowicz, *The King's Two Bodies: A Study in Medieval Political Theology* (Princeton, 1957), pp. 61–78.

136. Louis XIV, *Mémoires*, pp. 55, 57–58.

137. Gabriel Le Bras, *Études de sociologie religieuse*, 2 vols. (Paris, 1955–56), vol. 1, pp. 54–68; Louis Pérouas, *Le diocèse de La Rochelle de 1648 à 1724: Sociologie et pastorale* (Paris, 1964), chs. 3–4; Lagrée, "1532–1840," pp. 131–43.

138. Yves Marie Bercé, *Fête et révolte: Des mentalités populaires du XVIe au XVIIe siècle* (Paris, 1976), pp. 142–59; Elisabeth Labrousse and Robert Sauzet, "La lente mise en place de la réforme tridentine (1598–1661)," in Jacques Le Goff and René Rémond, gen. eds., *Histoire de la France réligieuse*, vol. 2: *Du Christianisme flamboyant à l'aube des Lumières* (Paris, 1988), pp. 434–43; Robin Briggs, "*Idées* and *mentalités:* The Case of the Catholic Reform Movement in France," in his *Communities of Belief: Culture and Social Tension in Early Modern France* (Oxford, 1989), pp. 364–80.

139. Henry Kamen, *The Phoenix and the Flame: Catalonia and the Counter-Reformation* (New Haven, 1993), pp. 435–36; Manuel Morán and José Andrés-Gallego, "The Preacher," in Villari, ed., *Baroque Personae*, pp. 152–56.

140. Fletcher, *Reform in the Provinces*, p. 277; Jonathan Barry, "Popular Culture in Seventeenth-Century Bristol," in Barry Reay, ed., *Popular Culture in Seventeenth-Century England* (London, 1988), pp. 70–76; Peter Laslett, *The World We Have Lost* (London, 1965), p. 71; G. V. Bennett, *The Tory Crisis in Church and State, 1688–1730: The Career of Francis Atterbury, Bishop of Rochester* (Oxford, 1975), p. 8.

141. Jean Orcibal, *Louis XIV et les Protestants* (Paris, 1951), pp. 58–61, 181–82; Leibniz, *Political Writings*, pp. 188–91; John Dryden, "The Hind and the Panther," in Miner, ed., *Selected Poetry and Prose*, p. 361, part 2, ll. 123–25, p. 379, part 3, l. 27.

142. Avvakum, *The Life Written by Himself*, ed. and trans. Kenneth N. Brostrom (Ann Arbor, Mich., 1979), p. 52. For Nikon, see Nickolaus Lupinin, *Religious Revolt in the Seventeenth Century: The Schism of the Russian Church* (Princeton, 1984), ch. 5; Paul Meyendorff, *Russia, Ritual, and Reform: The Liturgical Reforms of Nikon in the Seventeenth Century* (Crestwood, N.J., 1991), pp. 81–93.

143. Pierre Pascal, *Avvakum et les débuts du Raskol* (Paris and La Haye, 1938, 1969), pp. 190–227; Meyendorff, *Russia Ritual, and Reform*, pp. 225–27; Frederick C. Conybeare, *Russian Dissenters* (New York, 1921, 1962), pp. 41–59; Arthur Voyce, *The Art and Architecture of Medieval Russia* (Norman, Okla., 1967), pp. 233–40.

144. Philip Longworth, *Alexis Tsar of All the Russias* (New York, 1984), pp. 122–31, 137–42, 167–72, 177–81; Meyendorff, *Russia, Ritual, and Reform*, pp. 98–101; Harry T. Hionides, *Paisius Ligarides* (New York, 1972), p. 69.

145. Longworth, *Alexis*, pp. 166–67, 174–75, 183–85; Lupinin, *Religious Revolt*, ch. 9; Avvakum, *Life*, pp. 92–93; Pascal, *Avvakum*, pp. 360–402, 544–46.

146. Michael Cherniavsky, "The Old Believers and the New Religion," *Slavic Review* 25, no. 1 (1966): 1–39; Paul Avrich, *Russian Rebels, 1600–1800* (New York, 1972), pp. 95–97, 120; Longworth, *Alexis*, pp. 195–96, 200–2; Robert O. Crummey, *The Old Believers and the World of Antichrist: The Vyg Community and the Russian State, 1694–1855* (Madison, Wis., 1970), pp. 16–25, 39–57.

147. James H. Billington, *The Icon and the Axe: An Interpretive History of Russian Culture* (New York, 1970), pp. 144–49; Paul Bushkovitch, *Religion and Society in Russia: The Sixteenth and Seventeenth Centuries* (Oxford, 1992), pp. 163–72; Longworth, *Alexis*, pp. 203–28; Voyce, *Art and Architecture of Medieval Russia*, pp. 174–75, 240–41, 339.

392 · NOTES TO PAGES 254–258

392 · NOTES TO PAGES 254–258

148. John M. Leitche and Basil Dmytryshyn, eds., *Russian Statecraft: The "Politika" of Iurii Krizhanich* (Oxford, 1985), pp. 9–84, 183; Ivan Golub, "The Slavic Idea of Juraj Krizanić," *Harvard Ukrainian Studies* 10, nos. 3–4 (1986): 438–91.

149. Lindsey Hughes, *Sophia, Regent of Russia, 1657–1704* (New Haven, 1990), pp. 16–22 and chs. 5–7; Elizabeth Kristofovich Zelensky, " 'Sophia the Wisdom of God': The Function of Religious Imagery during the Regency of Sofia Alekseevna of Muscovy," in Louise Olga Fradenburg, ed., *Women and Sovereignty* (Edinburgh, 1992), pp. 192–211.

150. Pierre Blet, *Les assemblées du clergé et Louis XIV, de 1670 à 1673* (Rome, 1972), pp. 117–420; Robin Briggs, "Church and State from Henry IV to Louis XIV," in *Communities of Belief*, pp. 208, 216–18; Elisabeth Labrousse and Robert Sauzet, "Au temps du Roi-Soleil," in Le Goff and Rémond, eds., *Histoire de la France religieuse*, vol. 2, pp. 526–28; "Declaration of the Clergy of France on the Ecclesiastical Power, 19 March 1682," in H. G. Judge, ed., *Louis XIV* (London, 1965), pp. 69–70; Platelle, ed., *Journal d'un curé de campagne*, pp. 65–67.

151. Orcibal, *Louis XIV et les Protestants*, ch. 2; Elisabeth Labrousse, *«Une foi, une loi, un roi?»: Essai sur la révocation de l'Edit de Nantes* (Paris, 1985), ch. 8; Janine Garrisson, *L'Edit de Nantes et sa révocation: Histoire d'une intolérance* (Paris, 1985), ch. 5; Labrousse and Sauzet, "Au Temps du Roi-Soleil," pp. 477–83; Gregory Hanlon, *Confession and Community in Seventeenth-Century France: Catholic and Protestant Coexistence in Aquitaine* (Philadelphia, 1993).

152. Garrisson, *L'Edit de Nantes*, pp. 9–13; Labrousse and Sauzet, "Au Temps du Roi-Soleil," pp. 483–92; and for an unusual defence of the king, see Bluche, *Louis XIV*, pp. 598–613.

153. Orcibal, *Louis XIV et les Protestants*, pp. 69–74, 81–90; Labrousse, *Une foi*, ch. 9; Labrousse and Sauzet, "Au Temps du Roi-Soleil," pp. 492–503; Garrisson, *L'Edit de Nantes*, pp. 203–62; Bluche, *Louis XIV*, pp. 614–20.

154. Platelle, ed., *Journal d'un curé de Campagne*, p. 70; Orcibal, *Louis XIV et les Protestants*, ch. 5.

155. Orcibal, *Louis XIV et les Protestants*, pp. 159–67; Bluche, *Louis XIV*, p. 620.

156. Maurice Ashley, *James II* (London, 1977), pp. 186–87; John Miller, *James II: A Study in Kingship* (London, 1978, 1989), pp. 144–45; Miller, *Popery and Politics*, ch. 12, for James's relations with the papacy; and for a different opinion of his attitude towards the Huguenots, R. D. Gwynn, "James II in the Light of His Treatment of Huguenot Refugees in England," *English Historical Review* 92 (1977): 820–33.

157. Burnet, *History of His Own Times*, p. 222; Percy Ernest Schramm, *A History of the English Coronation* (Oxford, 1937), pp. 102, 106–7; Miller, *James II*, ch. 10; Harris, *Politics under the Later Stuarts*, pp. 119–23.

158. Robin Clifton, *The Last Popular Rebellion: The Western Rising of 1685* (London, 1984); "The Country's Advice to the Late Duke of Monmouth and Those in Rebellion with Him," in Galbraith M. Crump, ed., *Poems on Affairs of State*, vol. 4: *1685–8* (New Haven, 1968), p. 39, ll. 31–32.

159. John Miller, "James II and Toleration," in Eveline Cruickshanks, ed., *By Force or by Default? The Revolution of 1688–9* (Edinburgh, 1989), pp. 8–26; Miller, *Popery and Politics*, chs. 10–11; Miller, *James II*, pp. 148–57; Ashley, *James II*, ch. 14; Kenyon, ed., *Stuart Constitution*, pp. 389–91.

160. See J. R. Jones, "James II's Whig Collaborators," *Historical Journal* 7, no. 1 (1960): 65–73; J. R. Jones, *The Revolution of 1688 in England* (London, 1972), pp. 98–118; Miller, *James II*, pp. 167–75.

161. Mark Goldie, "The Political Thought of the Anglican Revolution," in Robert Beddard, ed., *The Revolutions of 1688* (Oxford, 1991), pp. 102–36; and his "Theory of Religious Intolerance in Restoration England," in Ole Peter Grell, Jonathan I. Israel, and Nicholas Tyacke, eds., *From Persecution to Toleration: The Glorious Revolution and Religion in England* (Oxford, 1991), pp. 331–68; George Hilton Jones, *Convergent Forces: Immediate Causes of the Revolution of 1688 in England* (Ames, Iowa, 1990), ch. 1; J. R. Western, *Monarchy and Revolution: The English State in the 1680s* (London, 1972), pp. 229–33.

162. Miller, "James II and Toleration," p. 21; Jones, *Convergent Forces*, ch. 2; Harris, *Politics under the Later Stuarts*, pp. 128–31; Bowle, ed., *Diary of John Evelyn*, p. 359; "A New Catch in Praise of the Reverend Bishops," in Crump, ed., *Poems on Affairs of State*, vol. 4, p. 230, ll. 5–6.

163. Miller, *James II*, pp. 189–99; Ashley, *James II*, pp. 233–48; Western, *Monarchy and Revolution*, ch. 8.

164. See John Redwood, *Reason, Ridicule, and Religion: The Age of Enlightenment in England, 1660–1750* (London, 1976), pp. 36–48.

165. Norman Davies, *God's Playground: A History of Poland*, 2 vols. (Oxford, 1981), vol. 1, pp. 345–47; Władysław Czapliński, "The Principle of Unanimity in the Polish Parliament," in Władysław Czapliński, ed., *The Polish Parliament at the Summit of Its Development (Sixteenth-Eighteenth Centuries)* (Wrocław, 1985), pp. 111–19.

166. Maria A.J. Swiecicka, ed. and trans., *The Memoirs of Jan Chrysostom z Gosławic Pasek* (Warsaw, 1978), p. 402; Stefania Ochmann, "Plans for Parliamentary Reform in the Commonwealth in the Middle of the Seventeenth Century," in Czapliński, ed., *Polish Parliament*, pp. 163–87; Robert I. Frost, *After the Deluge: Poland-Lithuania and the Second Northern War, 1655–1660* (Cambridge, 1993), ch. 5; W. Tomkiewicz, "The Reign of John Casimir, 1654–68," in W. F. Reddaway et al., eds., *The Cambridge History of Poland*, vol. 1: *From the Origins to Sobieski (to 1696)* (Cambridge, 1950), pp. 518–31; Andrzej Kamiński, "Polish-Lithuanian Commonwealth and Its Citizens (Was the Commonwealth a Stepmother for Cossacks and Ruthenians?)," in Peter J. Potichnyj, ed., *Poland and Ukraine: Past and Present* (Edmonton, 1980), p. 41.

167. Janusz Tazbir, *A State Without Stakes: Polish Religious Toleration in the Sixteenth and Seventeenth Centuries* (New York, 1973), pp. 196–97; Kamiński, "Polish-Lithuanian Commonwealth," pp. 35–36.

168. Janusz Tazbir, "Le sarmatisme et le baroque européen," in his *La république nobiliaire et le monde: Etudes sur l'histoire de la culture polonaise à l'époque du baroque*, trans. Lucjan Grobelak (Wrocław, 1986), pp. 7–27 (quotations on p. 22); Janusz Tazbir, "Culture of the Baroque in Poland," in Antoni Mączak, Henryk Samsonowicz and Peter Burke, eds., *East-Central Europe in Transition: From the Fourteenth to the Seventeenth Century* (Cambridge, 1985), pp. 167–80; Adam Zamoyski, *The Polish Way: A Thousand-Year History of the Poles and Their Culture* (New York, 1987, 1994), pp. 197–205.

169. Swiecicka, ed., *Memoirs of Jan Pasek*, pp. 344–47; for his tribute to "old Polish warriors," see pp. 160–67.

170. Davies, *God's Playground*, vol. 1, pp. 343–45, 468–72; Swiecicka, ed., *Memoirs of Jan Pasek*, pp. 367, 406–15.

171. Janusz Tazbir, "Le Rempart: Place de la Pologne en Europe," in his *La république nobiliaire*, pp. 87, 92 (Sobieski quotation); Swiecicka, ed., *Memoirs of Jan Pasek*, p. 443. For biographical details, see Davies, *God's Playground*, vol. 1, pp. 473–80; O. Forst de Battaglia, "Jan Sobieski, 1674–96," in Reddaway et al., eds., *Cambridge History of Poland*, vol. 1, ch. 24; Zamoyski, *The Polish Way*, pp. 185–88; Otton Laskowski, *Sobieski, King of Poland*, trans. F. C. Anstruther (Glasgow, 1944).

172. Tazbir, *State Without Stakes*, p. 202; Swiecicka, ed., *Memoirs of Jan Pasek*, p. 527. The Latin part of this passage may be more correctly translated in Catherine S. Leach, ed. and trans., *Memoirs of the Polish Baroque: The Writings of Jan Chryzostom Pasek, A Squire of the Commonwealth of Poland and Lithuania* (Berkeley, 1976), p. 295, where the preacher is said "to rail against the Chamber of Deputies."

173. Pasek was not at Vienna, but an account based on his nephew's eyewitness testimony is in Swiecicka, ed., *Memoirs of Jan Pasek*, pp. 473–83; see also Tazbir, "Aux yeux des étrangers," in his *La république nobiliare*, p. 205; Lottin, *Chavatte, ouvrier Lillois*, pp. 290–93; Davies, *God's Playground*, vol. 1, pp. 480–86.

174. Andrzej Sulima Kamiński, *Republic vs. Autocracy: Poland-Lithuania and Russia, 1686–1697* (Cambridge, Mass., 1993), pp. 189–200; Davies, *God's Playground*, vol. 1, pp. 488–89; Kaufmann, *Court, Cloister, and City*, pp. 285–88; Laskowski, *Sobieski*, p. 232; Tolstoi, *Travel Diary*, pp. 32–33.

175. Nils Runeby, *Monarchia mixta: Maktfördelningsdebatt in Sverige under den Tidigare Stormaktstiden* (Stockholm, 1962), pp. 339–77, 448–69; Stellan Dahlgren, "Charles X and the Constitution," in Michael Roberts, ed., *Sweden's Age of Greatness, 1632–1718* (London, 1973), pp. 174–202; Stellan Dahlgren, *Karl X och Reduktion* (Norstedts, 1964), pp. 156–79, 409–14; Michael Roberts, "Charles X and His Council: 'Dualism' or Co-operation?" in his *From Oxenstierna to Charles XII: Four Studies* (Cambridge, 1991), pp. 55–99.

176. Swiecicka, ed., *Memoirs of Jan Pasek*, p. 141; Maria Bogucka, "Sweden and Poland: Economic, Socio-political, and Cultural Relations in the First Half of the Seventeenth Century," in Rystad, ed., *Europe and Scandinavia*, pp. 164–67.

177. Kindermann, *Theatergeschichte*, vol. 3, pp. 573–76.

178. Allan Ellenius, "Konst och miljö," in Stellan Dahlgren et al., *Kultur och samhälle i stormaktstidens Sverige* (Stockholm, 1967), pp. 60–64, 69–84; Lars Gustafsson, "Litteratur och miljö," in ibid., pp. 100–8; Runeby, *Monarchia mixta*, pp. 122–33, 458–59; Alrik Gustafson, *A History of Swedish Literature* (Minneapolis, 1961), pp. 84–90; Georg Stiernhielm, "Hercules," in Bernt Olsson, ed., *Svensk litteratur*, vol. 1: *Från runorna till 1730* (Stockholm, 1993), pp. 277–97.

179. Nils Runeby, "Barbarei oder Zivilität? Zur Entwicklung einer organisierten Gesellschaft in Schweden im 17. Jahrhundert," in Rystad, ed., *Europe and Scandinavia*, pp. 203–18; but see also Eva Osterberg, "Violence among Peasants: Comparative Perspectives on Sixteenth- and Seventeenth-Century Sweden," in ibid., pp. 257–75.

180. Bengt Ankarloo, "Sweden: The Mass Burnings (1668–1676)," in Ankarloo and Hennigsen, eds., *Early Modern European Witchcraft*, pp. 285–317; Antero Heikkinen and Timo Kervinen, "Finland: The Male Domination," in ibid., pp. 319–38.

181. Michael Roberts, ed., *Sweden as a Great Power, 1611–1697: Government: Society:*

*Foreign Policy* (London, 1968), pp. 120–30; Michael Roberts, "The Swedish Church," in Roberts, ed., *Sweden's Age of Greatness*, pp. 168–70; Claude Nordmann, *Grandeur et liberté de la Suède (1660–1792)* (Paris, 1971), pp. 117–19; Robert Murray, *A Brief History of the Church of Sweden: Origins and Modern Structure* (Stockholm, 1961), trans. Nils G. Sahlin, pp. 46–47; Kirby, *Northern Europe in the Early Modern Period*, p. 275.

182. Michael Roberts, "Charles XI," in his *Essays in Swedish History* (London, 1967), pp. 247, 258–59; Roberts, ed., *Sweden as a Great Power*, pp. 80, 89; Nordmann, *Grandeur et liberté*, pp. 73–80; Günter Barudio, *Absolutismus: Zerstörung der «Libertären Verfassung»: Studien zur «Karolinischen Eingewalt» in Schweden zwischen 1680 und 1693* (Wiesbaden, 1976); A. F. Upton, "The Riksdag of 1680 and the Establishment of Royal Absolutism in Sweden," *English Historical Review* 403 (1987): 281–308; A. F. Upton, "Sweden," in Miller, ed., *Absolutism in Seventeenth-Century Europe*, pp. 111–17; Kirby, *Northern Europe in the Early Modern Period*, pp. 218–21.

183. Kurt Agren, "Rise and Decline of an Aristocracy: The Swedish Social and Political Elite in the Seventeenth Century," *Scandinavian Journal of History* 1 (1976): 55–80; Kurt Agren, "The *Reduktion*," in Roberts, ed., *Sweden's Age of Greatness*, pp. 237–64; Alf Aberg, "The Swedish Army, from Lützen to Narva," in ibid., pp. 268–70; Sven A. Nilsson, *De stora krigens tid: Om Sverige som Militärstat och Bondesamhälle* (Uppsala, 1990), pp. 245–70; Roberts, "Charles XI," pp. 248–57; Nordmann, *Grandeur et liberté*, pp. 87–91.

184. Michael Roberts, "On Aristocratic Constitutionalism in Swedish History, 1520–1720," in his *Essays in Swedish History*, pp. 15–16, 36–37; Roberts, "Charles XI," p. 246; Upton, "The Riksdag of 1680," p. 307.

185. Pufendorf, *On the Duties of Man and the Citizen*, pp. 132–34, 137, 146–47, 151; Krieger, *Politics of Discretion*, chs. 4, 7; Horst Denzer, *Moralphilosophie und Naturrecht bei Samuel Pufendorf* (Munich, 1972), pp. 176–81, 185–88, 216–71, 296–324.

186. For accounts of William's rise to power, see Peter Geyl, *Orange and Stuart, 1641–1672*, trans. Arnold Pomerans (New York, 1939, 1969), pp. 377–400; Herbert H. Rowen, *The Princes of Orange: The Stadholders in the Dutch Republic* (Cambridge, 1988), pp. 121–30; Stephen B. Baxter, *William III* (London, 1966), ch. 7.

187. E. N. Williams, ed., *The Eighteenth-Century Constitution, 1688–1815: Documents and Commentary* (Cambridge, 1960), pp. 10–16; W. A. Speck, *Reluctant Revolutionaries: Englishmen and the Revolution of 1688* (Oxford, 1988), ch. 4; Jones, *Revolution of 1688*, ch. 10.

188. "The Prince of Orange's Triumph," in Crump, ed., *Poems on Affairs of State*, vol. 4, p. 295; Lois Schwoerer, "Propaganda in the Revolution of 1688–9," *American Historical Review* 82, no. 4 (1977): 843–74.

189. Robert Beddard, ed., *A Kingdom without a King: The Journal of the Provisional Government in the Revolution of 1688* (Oxford, 1988), pp. 65, 166; also Robert Beddard, "The Unexpected Whig Revolution of 1688," in Beddard, ed., *The Revolutions of 1688*, pp. 18–42.

190. Speck, *Reluctant Revolutionaries*, ch. 5; Beddard, "Unexpected Whig Revolution," pp. 60–101; Lois Schwoerer, "A Jornall of the Convention at Westminster begun the 22 of January 1688/9," *Bulletin of the Institute for Historical Research* 49, no. 120 (1976): 242–63; *The Debate at large, between the House of Lords and House of Commons* (London, 1695, reprint Dublin, 1972), pp. 111, 143.

191. Lois G. Schwoerer, *The Declaration of Rights, 1689* (Baltimore, 1981), chs. 1–4, 14–16; Mark Goldie, "The Revolution of 1689 and the Structure of Political Argument: An Essay and an Annotated Bibliography of Pamphlets on the Allegiance Controversy," *Bulletin of Research in the Humanities* 83 (1980): 473–564; Williams, ed., *Eighteenth-Century Constitution,* pp. 26–33.

192. Burnet, *History of His Times,* p. 306; Williams, ed., *Eighteenth-Century Constitution,* pp. 42–46; Jonathan I. Israel, "William III and Toleration," in Grell, Israel, and Tyacke, eds., *From Persecution to Toleration,* pp. 129–70; Speck, *Reluctant Revolutionaries,* pp. 184–87; Harris, *Politics under the Later Stuarts,* pp. 179–80.

193. See Daniel Szechi, *The Jacobites: Britain and Europe, 1688–1788* (Manchester, 1994); Paul K. Monod, *Jacobitism and the English People, 1688–1788* (Cambridge, 1989); Bruce Lenman, *The Jacobite Risings in Britain, 1689–1746* (London, 1980); and for the Jacobite court in exile, Edward Gregg, "Monarchs without a Crown," in Robert Oresko, G. C. Gibbs, and H. M. Scott, eds., *Royal and Republican Sovereignty in Early Modern Europe: Essays in Memory of Ragnhild Hatton* (Cambridge, 1997), pp. 382–422.

194. Narcissus Luttrell, *A Brief Relation of State Affairs from September 1678 to April 1714,* 6 vols. (Oxford, 1857), vol. 1, p. 88. For similar views among the Scots Episcopalians, see Bruce Lenman, "The Scottish Episcopal Clergy and the Ideology of Jacobitism," in Eveline Cruickshanks, ed., *Ideology and Conspiracy: Aspects of Jacobitism, 1688–1759* (Edinburgh, 1982), pp. 36–48.

195. John T. Gilbert, ed., *A Jacobite Narrative of the War in Ireland, 1688–1691* (Dublin, 1892, reprint Shannon, 1971), p. 183. See also J. G. Simms, *Jacobite Ireland, 1685–91* (London, 1969); Patrick Kelly, "Ireland and the Glorious Revolution: From Kingdom to Colony," in Beddard, ed., *Revolutions of 1688,* pp. 163–82.

196. The best treatment of Locke's radical politics is in Richard Ashcraft, *Revolutionary Politics and Locke's Two Treatises of Government* (Princeton, 1986). Locke's religious views are discussed in John Marshall, *John Locke: Resistance, Religion, and Responsibility* (Cambridge, 1994); but compare this with Ian Harris, *The Mind of John Locke: A Study of Political Theory in Its Intellectual Setting* (Cambridge, 1994). See also Macpherson, *Political Theory of Possessive Individualism,* ch. 5; John Dunn, *The Political Thought of John Locke: An Historical Account of the Argument of the 'Two Treatises of Government'* (Cambridge, 1969), chs. 7–14.

197. John Locke, *Two Treatises of Government,* ed. Peter Laslett (Cambridge, 1960, 1988), "Second Treatise," pp. 287–88; Pufendorf, *On the Duty of Man,* p. 86. The religious connotations of the "Second Treatise" are discussed in Marshall, *John Locke,* ch. 6, and Harris, *Mind of John Locke,* ch. 7.

198. Locke, *Two Treatises,* "Second Treatise," pp. 289–90, 331, 357–58, 361.

199. For a different interpretation, see J. C. D. Clark, *English Society, 1688–1788: Ideology, Social Structure, and Political Practice during the Ancien Régime* (Cambridge, 1985), esp. ch. 2.

## Chapter Six: The State Remains, 1690–1715

1. François Bluche, *Louis XIV* (Paris, 1986), chs. 29–30, quotation on p. 891; John B. Wolf, *Louis XIV* (New York, 1968), pp. 617–19.

NOTES TO PAGES 274–278 · 397

2. Jean Buvat, *Journal de la Régence (1715–1723)*, ed. Emile Campardon, 2 vols. (Paris, 1865), vol. 1, p. 47; Mathieu Marais, *Journal et Mémoires ... sur la Régence et le règne de Louis XV (1715–1737)*, ed. M. de Lescure, 4 vols. (Paris, 1863–68, reprint Geneva, 1967), vol. 1, pp. 192–93; Bluche, *Louis XIV*, pp. 981–82; Ralph Giesey, *The Royal Funeral Ceremony in Renaissance France* (Geneva, 1960), p. 164; N. R. Johnson, *Louis XIV and the Age of Enlightenment: The Myth of the Sun King from 1715 to 1789*, in Haydn Mason, ed., *Studies in Voltaire and the Eighteenth Century*, vol. 172 (Oxford, 1978), ch. 3.

3. Michel Antoine, *Louis XV* (Paris, 1989), pp. 40–41, 56–57; Buvat, *Journal de la Régence*, vol. 1, pp. 247–48.

4. Nicolas Malebranche, *Dialogues on Metaphysics and Religion*, ed. Nicholas Jolley, trans. David Scott (Cambridge, 1997), pp. 116–17, 227.

5. Steven M. Nadler, *Arnauld and the Cartesian Philosophy of Ideas* (Princeton, 1989), pp. 18–34, 179–84; Antoine Arnauld, "Quatrième lettre d'Arnauld à Malebranche," in Nicolas Malebranche, *Receuil de toutes les réponses à Monsieur Arnauld*, in André Robinet, gen. ed., *Oeuvres complètes de Malebranche*, 20 vols. (Paris, 1962–67), vols. 8–9, pp. 1188–1201.

6. See Elisabeth Labrousse, *Bayle* (Oxford, 1983), and her "Reading Pierre Bayle in Paris," in Alan Charles Kors and Paul J. Korshin, eds., *Anticipations of the Enlightenment in England, France, and Germany* (Philadelphia, 1987), pp. 7–16.

7. Paul Hazard, *The European Mind: The Critical Years (1680–1715)*, trans. J. Lewis May (New Haven, 1953), pp. xv, 447.

8. Miguel de Molinos, *Guía espirituál* (1675), reprinted in José Angel Valente, *Ensayo sobre Miguel de Molinos* (Barcelona, 1974), pp. 78, 234–37; Sven Stolpe, *Från Stoicism till Mystik: Studier i Drottning Kristinas Maximer* (Stockholm, 1959), pp. 232–67; Romeo De Maio, *Pittura e Controriforma a Napoli* (Bari, 1983), pp. 112–17; Clovis Whitfield and Jane Martineau, eds., *Painting in Naples, 1606–1705: From Caravaggio to Giordano* (New York, 1982), p. 248.

9. Françoise Mallet-Joris, *Jeanne Guyon* (Paris, 1978); François de la Mothe-Fénelon, *Réponse de Monseigneur l'Archévêque de Cambrai à l'écrit de Monseigneur l'Evêque de Meaux intitulé Relation sur le quiétisme*, in his *Oeuvres*, ed. Jacques Le Brun, 2 vols. (Paris, 1983), vol. 1, pp. 1099–1199.

10. Henri Platelle, ed., *Journal d'un curé de campagne au XVIIe siècle* (Paris, 1965), pp. 77–78, 80, 174; Antoine Adam, *Du mysticisme à la révolte: Les Jansénistes du XVIIe siècle* (Paris, 1968), pp. 295–330. The term *phantom* was frequently used to denigrate the campaign against Jansenism; see Johnson, *Louis XIV and the Age of Enlightenment*, p. 85.

11. Marais, *Journal*, vol. 1, p. 189; Buvat, *Journal de la Régence*, vol. 1, pp. 99–100, 277–78, 511–17.

12. Marais, *Journal*, vol. 1, p. 204.

13. Arlette Farge, *Subversive Words: Public Opinion in Eighteenth-Century France*, trans. Rosemary Morris (University Park, Pa., 1994), pp. 125–50.

14. [Fénelon], *Lettre à Louis XIV*, in his *Oeuvres*, vol. 1, pp. 543–51; see also Roland Mousnier, "Les idées politiques de Fénelon," in *La plume, la faucille et le marteau: Institutions et société en France du Moyen Age à la Révolution* (Paris, 1970), pp. 77–92; Nicole Ferrier-Caverivière, *L'image de Louis XIV dans la littérature française de 1660 à 1715* (Paris, 1981), pp. 288–305.

15. Philippe Joutard, ed., *Les Camisards* (Paris, 1976), pp. 90, 156; Jean Cavalier, *Mémoires sur la guerre des Camisards*, ed. and trans. Frank Puaux (Paris, 1987), pp. 136, 250; also Charles Garrett, "Spirit Possession, Oral Tradition, and the Camisard Revolt," in Marc Bertrand, ed., *Popular Traditions and Learned Culture in France* (Saratoga, Calif., 1985), pp. 43–61.

16. Johnson, *Louis XIV and the Age of Enlightenment*, pp. 59, 85–86; François Marie Arouet de Voltaire, *Le siècle de Louis XIV*, ed. Antoine Adam, 2 vols. (Paris, 1969).

17. Bluche, *Louis XIV*, p. 729; Bernard le Bovier de Fontenelle, *Entretiens sur la pluralité des mondes*, in his *Oeuvres complètes*, ed. G.-B. Depping, 3 vols. (Paris, 1818, reprint Geneva, 1968), vol. 2, p. 11.

18. Elborg Forster, ed. and trans., *A Woman's Life in the Court of the Sun King: Letters of Liselotte von der Pfalz, 1652–1722* (Baltimore, 1984), p. 202.

19. Quoted in Johnson, *Louis XIV and the Age of Enlightenment*, p. 111.

20. [Fénelon], "Sur la raison," in his *Oeuvres*, vol. 1, p. 764.

21. Philip Jacob Spener, *Pia desideria*, trans. Theodore G. Tappert (Philadelphia, 1964), pp. 31–32, 43, 116.

22. G. S. Holmes and W. A. Speck, eds., *The Divided Society: Parties and Politics in England 1694–1716* (London, 1967), p. 116; also G. V. Bennett, *The Tory Crisis in Church and State, 1688–1730: The Career of Francis Atterbury, Bishop of Rochester* (Oxford, 1975), ch. 3.

23. *Clarín de la Europa, hipocresía descifrada, España advertida, verdad declarada* (Barcelona, 1706), reprinted in María Teresa Pérez Picazo, *La publicística española en la guerra de sucesión*, 2 vols. (Madrid, 1966), vol. 2, pp. 61, 82.

24. [Pasquier Quesnel], *La discipline de l'église* (1689), in René Taveneaux, ed., *Jansénisme et politique* (Paris, 1956), p. 132.

25. Fénelon, "De la vraie liberté," in his *Oeuvres*, vol. 1, pp. 688–89.

26. Fritz Hartung, "Die aufgeklärte Absolutismus," in Hanns Hubert Hoffman, ed., *Die Entstehung des modernen souveränen Staates* (Cologne, 1967), p. 170. Hartung actually quoted the phrase from Franz Schnabel.

27. Duc de Saint-Simon, *Mémoires*, 8 vols. (Paris, 1983), vol. 5, pp. 468, 1352 nn. 5–6. The words are similar to those of the Vulgate version of Psalm 69 (*"Domine, ad adjuvandum me festina"*), which were sung at vespers.

28. Pierre Nicole, *Essais de morale*, in Maurice Catel, ed., *Les écrivains de Port-Royal* (Paris, 1962), p. 334; also, Dale van Kley, "Pierre Nicole, Jansenism, and the Morality of Enlightened Self-Interest," in Kors and Korshin, eds., *Anticipations of the Enlightenment*, pp. 69–85.

29. Quoted in James Cracraft, *The Church Reform of Peter the Great* (Stanford, 1971), p. 26.

30. Forster, ed., *A Woman's Life*, p. 76.

31. Military reform in this period is further examined in André Corvisier, *Armies and Societies in Europe, 1494–1789* (Bloomington, Ind., 1979); M. S. Anderson, *War and Society in Europe of the Old Regime, 1618–1789* (London, 1988); Jeremy Black, *European Warfare, 1660–1815* (New Haven, 1993), ch. 8.

32. Claude Nordmann, *Grandeur et liberté de la Suède, 1660–1792* (Paris, 1971),

pp. 145–226; Otto Haintz, *König Karl XII. von Schweden*, 2 vols. (Berlin, 1936, 1951), vol. 2, chs. 2–5.

33. "Decree on a New Calendar," in Basil Dmytryshyn, ed., *Modernization of Russia under Peter I and Catherine II* (New York, 1974), p. 10; see also Marc Raeff, *The Well-Ordered Police State: Social and Institutional Change through Law in the Germanies and Russia* (New Haven, 1983), pp. 181–250.

34. Johann-Georg Korb, *Diary of an Austrian Secretary of Legation at the Court of Peter the Great* (London, 1863, reprint London, 1968), trans. Count MacDonnell, pp. 159–60; see also Reinhard Wittram, *Peter I: Czar und Kaiser*, 2 vols. (Göttingen, 1963), vol. 2, ch. 12.

35. The decree is printed in Antonio Mestre Sanchis, ed., *Historia de la iglesia en España*, part 4: *La iglesia en la España de los siglos XVII y XVIII* (Madrid, 1979), pp. 795–96. It is discussed in Teófanes Egido, "El regalismo y las relaciones iglesia-estado en el siglo XVIII," in ibid., pp. 162–69; Alfredo Martínez Albiach, *Religiosidad hispana y sociedad borbonica* (Burgos, 1969), pp. 445–50; and Antonio Mestre Sanchis, "La iglesia y el estado," in José María Jover Zamora, gen. ed., *Historia de España*, vol. 29: *La epoca de los primeros Borbones* (Madrid, 1985), pp. 284–89.

36. Melchor de Macanaz, *Testamento politico: Pedimento fiscal*, ed. F. Maldonado de Guevara (Madrid, 1972), pp. 100, 104, 112, 119–20; Carmen Martín Gaite, *El proceso de Macanaz: Historia de un empapelmiento* (Barcelona, 1969, 1988), ch. 10; Henry Kamen, "Melchor de Macanaz and the Foundations of Bourbon Power in Spain," *English Historical Review* 80, no. 317 (1965): 699–716; for comparison, Cracraft, *Church Reform of Peter the Great*, pp. 97–107.

37. [Joseph Addison], *The Spectator*, no. 556, 18 June [1714], in Joseph Addison and Richard Steele, *Selected Essays from "The Tatler," "The Spectator," and "The Guardian,"* ed. Daniel McDonald (Indianapolis, 1973), pp. 555–56.

38. [Addison], *The Spectator*, no. 81, 2 June 1711, in ibid., p. 252.

39. Feofan Prokopovich, "Sermon on Royal Authority and Honour," in Marc Raeff, ed., *Russian Intellectual History: An Anthology* (New York, 1966), pp. 19–20.

40. G. W. Leibniz, "Memoir for Enlightened Persons of Good Intention," in his *Political Writings*, ed. and trans. Patrick Riley (Cambridge, 1972, 1988), p. 105.

41. For popular schooling in central Europe, see James Van Horn Melton, *Absolutism and the Eighteenth-Century Origins of Compulsory Schooling in Prussia and Austria* (Cambridge, 1988), ch. 1.

42. See Klaus Deppermann, *Der hallesche Pietismus und der preußische Staat unter Friedrich III. (I.)* (Göttingen, 1961), pp. 34–61; Hartmut Lehmann, "Der Pietismus im alten Reich," *Historische Zeitschrift* 214 (1972): 78–82; Johannes Wallmann, *Philipp Jakob Spener und die Anfänge des Pietismus*, 2d ed. (Tübingen, 1986), pp. 324–54; Richard Gawthrop, *Pietism and the Making of Eighteenth-Century Prussia* (Cambridge, 1993), ch. 5.

43. Carl Hinrichs, *Preußentum und Pietismus: Der Pietismus in Brandenburg-Preußen als religiös-soziale Reformbewegung* (Göttingen, 1971), pp. 29–61 (quotation on p. 47), 69–117, 301–51; Gawthrop, *Pietism*, p. 87; Hartmut Lehmann, "Pietismus und soziale Reform in Brandenburg-Preußen," in Oswald Hanser, ed., *Preußen, Europa und das Reich* (Cologne, 1987), pp. 103–21, esp. p. 118.

44. "Der Besuch König Friedrich Wilhelms I. in den franckeschen Stiftungen in Halle," in Jochen Klepper, ed., *Der König und die Stillen im Lande* (Witten, 1957), p. 30.

45. Gawthrop, *Pietism*, chs. 6–7, 9–10; Lehmann, "Der Pietismus," pp. 85–89; Melton, *Absolutism and Compulsory Schooling*, ch. 2; Deppermann, *Der hallesche Pietismus*, p. 173.

46. D. W. R. Bahlman, *The Moral Revolution of 1688* (New Haven, 1957); John Spurr, "The Church, the Societies, and the Moral Revolution of 1688," in John Walsh, Colin Haydon, and Stephen Taylor, eds., *The Church of England, c. 1689–c. 1833: From Toleration to Tractarianism* (Cambridge, 1993), pp. 127–42; Tony Claydon, *William III and the Godly Revolution* (Cambridge, 1996), pp. 28–63 and ch. 3.

47. Max J. Okenfuss, "The Jesuit Origins of Petrine Education," in J. G. Garrard, ed., *The Eighteenth Century in Russia* (Oxford, 1973), pp. 113–20.

48. Gerhard Oestreich, *Neostoicism and the Early Modern State* (Cambridge, 1982), chs. 14–15.

49. F. C. Carsten, *The Origins of Prussia* (Oxford, 1954), ch. 16; Hans Rosenberg, *Bureaucracy, Aristocracy, and Autocracy: The Prussian Experience, 1660–1815* (Boston, 1958), chs. 1–3; Walter Barberis, "Die Bildung der 'milizia paesana' in Piemont: Zentrale Gewalt und lokale Verhältnisse zwischen dem 16. und 17. Jahrhundert," in Antoni Mączak, ed., *Klientelsysteme in Europa der Früher Neuzeit* (Munich, 1988), pp. 261–97; Geoffrey Symcox, *Victor Amadeus II: Absolutism in the Savoyard State, 1675–1730* (London, 1983), and his "From Commune to Capital: The Transformation of Turin, Sixteenth to Eighteenth Centuries," in Robert Oresko, G. C. Gibbs, and H. M. Scott, eds., *Royal and Republican Sovereignty in Early Modern Europe: Essays in Memory of Ragnhild Hatton* (Cambridge, 1997), pp. 242–69; Western, *Monarchy and Revolution*, ch. 10; John Brewer, *The Sinews of Power: War, Money, and the English State, 1688–1783* (New York, 1988), chs. 3–5.

50. Ragnhild Hatton, *Charles XII of Sweden* (London, 1968), p. 80.

51. C. A. Macartney, ed., *The Habsburg and Hohenzollern Dynasties in the Seventeenth and Eighteenth Centuries* (New York, 1970), pp. 275–92; Peter Baumgart, "Die preußische Königskrönung von 1701, das Reich und die europäische Politik," in Hanser, ed., *Preußen, Europa und das Reich*, pp. 65–86; Albert Waddington, *L'acquisition de la couronne royale de Prusse par les Hohenzollern* (Paris, 1888), pp. 273–83; Linda and Marsha Frey, *Frederick I: The Man and His Times* (New York, 1984), pp. 60–63.

52. Marc Raeff, *Understanding Imperial Russia: State and Society in the Old Regime* (New York, 1984), trans. Arthur Goldhammer, p. 6; Louise K. Stein, "The Iberian Peninsula," in George J. Buelow, ed., *The Late Baroque Era: From the 1680s to 1740* (Englewood Cliffs, N.J., 1994), p. 416.

53. Hans Villius, ed., *Ogonvittnen: Karl XII* (Stockholm, 1960), p. 124; François-Marie Arouet de Voltaire, *The History of Charles XII, King of Sweden* (New York, 1976), trans. Antonia White, pp. 238–39; R. M. Hatton, *Charles XII of Sweden* (London, 1968), pp. 81, 84, 217–18, 430–32, 566 n. 22.

54. Frey and Frey, *Frederick I*, pp. 119–38.

55. Hinrichs, *Preußentum und Pietismus*, pp. 301–51; Günter Birtsch, "Friedrich Wilhelm I. und die Anfänge der Aufklärung im Brandenburg-Preußen," in Hanser, ed., *Preußen, Europa und das Reich*, pp. 87–102.

NOTES TO PAGES 291–295 · 401

56. Charles W. Ingrao, *In Quest and Crisis: Emperor Joseph I and the Habsburg Monarchy* (West Lafayette, Ind., 1979), pp. 15–16, 29–30, 156–57.

57. Cracraft, *Church Reform of Peter the Great*, pp. 64–79; Robert O. Crummey, *The Old Believers and the World of Antichrist: The Vyg Community and the Russian State, 1694–1855* (Madison, Wis., 1970), chs. 5–6; M. S. Anderson, *Peter the Great* (London, 1978), pp. 106–9; John Perry, *The State of Russia, under the Present Czar* (London, 1716, reprint London, 1967), p. 223.

58. Frey and Frey, *Frederick I*, pp. 92–108, 119–38; Frederick II, "Mémoires pour servir à l'histoire de la Maison de Brandenbourg," in *Oeuvres de Frédéric le Grand*, 30 vols. (Berlin, 1846–56), vol. 1, p. 123.

59. James Cracraft, *The Petrine Revolution in Russian Architecture* (Chicago, 1988), ch. 6; Isabel de Madariaga, "Tsar into Emperor: The Title of Peter the Great," in Oresko, Gibbs, and Scott, eds., *Royal and Republican Sovereignty*, pp. 375–81; Richard S. Wortman, *Scenarios of Power: Myth and Ceremony in Russian Monarchy*, 2 vols. (Princeton, 1995 and forthcoming), vol. 1, pp. 42–51. For the growth of western influence on Russian visual arts under Peter I, see James Cracraft, *The Petrine Revolution in Russian Imagery* (Chicago, 1997), ch. 4.

60. Hans Aurenhammer, *J. B. Fischer von Erlach* (Cambridge, Mass., 1973), pp. 46–50; Hubert Ch. Ewalt, *Ausdrucksformen absolutischer Herrschaft: Der Wiener Hof im 17. und 18. Jahrhundert* (Vienna, 1980), p. 113; Friedrich B. Polleross, *Das sakrale Identifikationsporträt: Ein höfischer Bildtypus vom 13. bis zum 20. Jahrhundert*, 2 vols. (Worms, 1988), vol. 1, p. 119.

61. Susan Wollenberg, "Vienna under Joseph I and Charles VI," in Buelow, ed., *The Late Baroque Era*, pp. 333–42; Lorenzo Bianconi, *Music in the Seventeenth Century*, trans. David Bryant (Cambridge, 1987), p. 227; Fontenelle, *Entretiens sur la pluralité des mondes*, p. 10.

62. J. W. Stoye, "Emperor Charles VI: The Early Years of the Reign," in *Transactions of the Royal Historical Society*, 5th series, 12 (1962): 63–84; Frederick II, "Histoire de mon temps," in Adolf Köcher, ed., *Memoiren der Herzogin Sophie nachmals Kurfürstin von Hannover* (Leipzig, 1879), p. 162; Polleross, *Das sakrale Identifikationsporträt*, pp. 119–20; Wollenberg, "Vienna under Joseph I and Charles VI," p. 329.

63. Aurenhammer, *Fischer von Erlach*, pp. 50–57, 131–43; Ehalt, *Ausdrucksformen absolutischer Herrschaft*, pp. 102, 197 n. 113; Thomas DaCosta Kaufmann, *Court, Cloister, and City: The Art and Culture of Central Europe, 1450–1800* (Chicago, 1995), pp. 291–94, 300–2.

64. Beatrice Curtis Brown, ed., *The Letters and Diplomatic Instructions of Queen Anne* (London, 1935, 1968), pp. 330–31.

65. Alexander Pope, *Windsor Forest*, in Aubrey Williams, ed., *Selected Poetry and Prose of Alexander Pope* (Boston, 1969), p. 66, ll. 37–42, p. 74, ll. 326–28. The politics of this poem are discussed in Howard Erskine-Hill, *Poetry of Opposition and Revolution: Dryden to Wordsworth* (Oxford, 1996), pp. 63–71.

66. They include examples in London, Westminster, Windsor, Kingston-upon-Thames, Oxford, Winchester, Southampton, Minehead, Barnstaple, Worcester, Leeds, and Manchester.

67. Edward Gregg, *Queen Anne* (New York, 1980, 1984), chs. 5–6; R. O. Bucholz, *The Augustan Court: Queen Anne and the Decline of Court Culture* (Stanford, 1993).

68. Marie-Elisabeth Ducreux, "Reading unto Death: Books and Readers in Eighteenth-Century Bohemia," in Roger Chartier, ed., *The Culture of Print: Power and the Uses of Print in Early Modern Europe*, trans. Lydia Cochrane (Princeton, 1989), pp. 191–229.

69. Hatton, *Charles XII*, p. 84.

70. Perry, *The State of Russia*, p. 236.

71. Cherniavsky, "Old Believers and the New Religion," pp. 23–33; James Cracraft, "Opposition to Peter the Great," in E. Mendelsohn and M. Shatz, eds., *Imperial Russia, 1700–1917: Essays in Honor of Marc Raeff* (DeKalb, Ill., 1988), pp. 22–36.

72. Bennett, *Tory Crisis*, chs. 3–4; Tim Harris, *Politics under the Later Stuarts: Party Conflict in a Divided Society, 1660–1715* (London, 1993), ch. 7; Geoffrey Holmes, *British Politics in the Age of Anne*, rev. ed. (London, 1987), ch. 2; Ruth Perry, *The Celebrated Mary Astell: An Early English Feminist* (Chicago, 1986), ch. 7; Geoffrey Holmes, *The Trial of Doctor Sacheverell* (London, 1973).

73. Brown, ed., *Letters of Queen Anne*, p. 393; Gregg, *Queen Anne*, chs. 13–14; Daniel Szechi, *Jacobitism and Tory Politics, 1710–14* (Edinburgh, 1984).

74. Ragnhild Hatton, *George I, Elector and King* (London, 1978), ch. 7; Paul Monod, *Jacobitism and the English People, 1688–1788* (Cambridge, 1989), ch. 7; Harris, *Politics under the Later Stuarts*, ch. 8; Linda Colley, *In Defiance of Oligarchy: The Tory Party, 1714–60* (Cambridge, 1982), ch. 7.

75. Hinrichs, *Preußentum und Pietismus*, pp. 117–19; W. R. Ward, "The Eighteenth-Century Church: A European View," in Walsh, Haydon, and Taylor, eds., *The Church of England*, p. 296.

76. Henry Kamen, *The War of Succession in Spain, 1700–15* (Bloomington, Ind., 1969), pp. 264–65, 276–77, 307–8; Martínez Albiach, *Religiosidad hispana*, pp. 66–76; Pérez Picazo, *La publicística española*, vol. 1, pp. 58–63.

77. Brother José Arias, *Manifiesto astrologico del verdadero rey de España* (Barcelona, 1706), reprinted in Pérez Picazo, *La publicística española*, vol. 2, pp. 147–51; Teófanes Egido Lopez, *Opinión pública y oposición al poder en la España del siglo XVIII (1713–1759)* (Valladolid, 1971), p. 313 n. 181.

78. Bishop Luís Belluga, *Carta que el illustrisimo Señor D. Luís Belluga, obispo de Cartagena, del Consejo de Su Majestad, escribe a los fieles de su obispado* (Murcia, 1706), reprinted in Pérez Picazo, *La publicística española*, vol. 2, pp. 5, 15, 16–18; see also Egido López, *Opinión pública*, pp. 310–13.

79. San Felipe, *Comentarios*, pp. 97, 104, 122.

80. Gaite, *El Proceso de Macanaz*, chs. 17–20 (quotation on pp. 113–14); Egido, "Regalismo," pp. 145–49; Vicente Bacallar y Sanna, Marqués de San Felipe, *Comentarios de la guerra de España e historia de su Rey Felipe V, el Animoso*, ed. Carlos Seco Serrano, Biblioteca de Autores Españoles, vol. 99 (Madrid, 1957), pp. 258–59.

81. Michèle Fogel, *Les Cérémonies de l'information dans la France du XVIe au milien du XVIIIe siècle* (Paris, 1989), pp. 133–245, 443–50; Peter Tolstoi, *The Travel Diary of Peter Tolstoi, A Muscovite in Early Modern Europe*, ed. and trans. Max J. Okenfuss (DeKalb, Ill., 1987), pp. 60–64.

82. Hatton, *Charles XII*, p. 432; Anderson, *Peter I*, pp. 114–15.

83. Yves Bottineau, *L'art de cour dans l'Espagne de Philippe V, 1700–1746* (Bordeaux,

1961), pp. 300–1; W. N. Hargreaves Mawdsley, ed., *Spain under the Bourbons, 1700–1833* (Columbia, S.C., 1973), pp. 59–60; Joaquim de Camps i Arboix, *El Decret de Nova Planta* (Barcelona, 1963), p. 21.

84. John Robertson, "Empire and Union: Two Concepts of the Early Modern European Political Order," in John Robertson, ed., *A Union for Empire: Political Thought and the British Union of 1707* (Cambridge, 1995), pp. 3–37.

85. Gordon Donaldson, ed., *Scottish Historical Documents* (New York, 1970), pp. 252–61; P. W. J. Riley, *King William and the Scottish Politicians* (Edinburgh, 1979), esp. chs. 1–2; Bruce Lenman, *The Jacobite Risings in Britain, 1689–1746* (London, 1980), ch. 1; Colin Kidd, "Religious Realignment between the Restoration and Union," in Robertson, ed., *A Union for Empire*, pp. 145–68; Paul Hopkins, *Glencoe and the End of the Highland War* (Edinburgh, 1986), chs. 10–13.

86. Brown, ed., *Letters of Queen Anne*, p. 191.

87. Andrew Fletcher, "An Account of a Conversation Concerning a Right Regulation of Governments for the Common Good of Mankind," in his *Political Works*, ed. John Robertson (Cambridge, 1997), p. 195; Paul H. Scott, *Andrew Fletcher and the Treaty of Union* (Edinburgh, 1992), chs. 13–16; Daniel Szechi, ed., *Letters of George Lockhart of Carnwath, 1698–1712*, Scottish Historical Society, 5th series, vol. 2 (Edinburgh: 1989), pp. 34, 61; William Ferguson, *Scotland's Relations with England: A Survey to 1707* (Edinburgh, 1977), ch. 9.

88. For the politics of union, see P. W. J. Riley, *The Union of England and Scotland: A Study in Anglo-Scottish Politics of the Eighteenth Century* (Manchester, 1978), pp. 215–45; Ferguson, *Scotland's Relations with England*, chs. 13–14. Its theoretical justifications can be followed in John Robertson, "An Elusive Sovereignty: The Course of the Union Debate in Scotland, 1698–1707," in Robertson, ed., *A Union for Empire*, pp. 198–227.

89. Kamen, *War of Succession*, pp. 275–300; Martínez Albiach, *Religiosidad hispana*, p. 73 n. 140; Antonio Mestre Sanchis, "Religión y cultura en el siglo XVIII español," in Mestre Sanchis, ed., *Historia de la iglesia*, part 4, p. 591; John Lynch, *Bourbon Spain, 1700–1808* (Oxford, 1989), pp. 40–41.

90. Pierre Vilar, *La Catalogne dans l'Espagne moderne: Recherches sur les fondements économiques des structures nationales*, 3 vols. (Paris, 1962), vol. 1, p. 678; James Amelang, *Honored Citizens of Barcelona: Patrician Culture and Class Relations, 1490–1714* (Princeton, 1986), pp. 221–22; Joaquim Albareda i Salvadó, "Catalunya a finals del segle XVII: La continuitat de la revolta," in Eva Serra et al., eds., *La revolució Catalana de 1640* (Barcelona, 1991), pp. 312–17.

91. For the text of the decree, see José Luis Gómez Urdáñez et al., eds., *Historia de España*, vol. 12: *Textos y documentos de historia moderna y contemporánea* (Barcelona, 1985), pp. 13–14. The effects of the Nueva Planta in Aragon and Valencia are considered in Francisco Cánovas Sánchez, "Los decretos de Nueva Planta y la nueva organización política y administrativa de los países de la corona de Aragón," in José María Jover Zamora, gen. ed., *Historia de España*, vol. 29, pp. 7–40.

92. The full text of the decree is printed in Joaquim de Camps i Arboix, *El decret de Nova Planta* (Barcelona, 1963), pp. 47–58; a shortened version is in Gómez Urdáñez et al., eds., *Textos y documentos de historia moderna*, pp. 20–24. Its significance is discussed in Cánovas Sánchez, "Los decretos de Nueva Planta," pp. 41–64; Victor Ferro, *El dret públic*

*català: Les institucions a Catalunya fins al decret de Nova Planta* (Vic, 1987), pp. 450–60; and Joan Mercader i Riba, *Felip V i Catalunya* (Barcelona, 1968), pp. 25–33.

93. Orest Subtelny, "Mazepa, Peter I, and the Question of Treason," *Harvard Ukrainian Studies* 2 (1978): 158–83; Orest Subtelny, *Ukraine: A History,* 2d ed. (Toronto, 1994), pp. 156–67; Paul Robert Magosci, *A History of Ukraine* (Seattle, 1996), ch. 19; Cracraft, *Petrine Revolution in Architecture,* pp. 93–97.

94. S. J. Connolly, *Religion, Land, and Power: The Making of Protestant Ireland, 1660–1760* (Oxford, 1992), pp. 74–84; James I. McGuire, "The Irish Parliament of 1692," in Thomas W. Bartlett and D. W. Hayton, eds., *Penal Era and Golden Age: Essays in Irish History, 1690–1800* (Belfast, 1979), pp. 1–31; J. G. Simms, *The Williamite Confiscations in Ireland, 1690–1703* (London, n.d.), pp. 158–62.

95. Linda Frey and Marsha Frey, *Societies in Upheaval: Insurrections in France, Hungary, and Spain in the Early Eighteenth Century* (Westport, Conn., 1987), ch. 3; Henry Marczoli, *Hungary in the Eighteenth Century* (Cambridge, 1910), pp. 310–11; Béla K. Király, *Hungary in the Late Eighteenth Century* (New York, 1969), pp. 118–19.

96. Bruce Lenman and Geoffrey Parker, "The State, the Community, and the Criminal Law in Early Modern Europe," in V. A. C. Gatrell, Bruce Lenman, and Geoffrey Parker, eds., *Crime and the Law: The Social History of Crime in Western Europe since 1500* (London, 1980), pp. 11–48; Edward Peters, *Torture,* 2d ed. (Philadelphia, 1996), ch. 3; Hatton, *Charles XII,* pp. 121–22; Korb, *Diary of an Austrian Secretary,* p. 252; Anderson, *Peter the Great,* pp. 45–46.

97. Robert Jütte, *Poverty and Deviance in Early Modern Europe* (Cambridge, 1994), pp. 169–77; Robert M. Schwartz, *Policing the Poor in Eighteenth-Century France* (Chapel Hill, N.C., 1988), ch. 2; Pierre Ronzeaud, *Peuple et représentations sous le règne de Louis XIV* (Aix-en-Provence, 1988), pp. 77–97.

98. Richard Knötel, Herbert Knötel d. J., and Herbert Sieg, *Handbuch der Uniformkunde: Die militärische Tracht in ihrer Entwicklung bis zur Gegenwart* (Hamburg, 1937, 1971), pp. 1–4; John Mollo, *Military Fashion: A Comparative History of the Uniforms of the Great Armies from the Seventeenth Century to the First World War* (London, 1972), chs. 1–2; Hatton, *Charles XII,* p. 218.

99. Michel Foucault, *Discipline and Punish: The Birth of the Prison,* trans. Alan Sheridan (New York, 1979), pp. 135–36.

100. Thomas Laqueur, *Making Sex: Body and Gender from the Greeks to Freud* (Cambridge, Mass., 1990), pp. 154–63; Roy Porter, "Barely Touching: A Social Perspective on Mind and Body," in G. S. Rousseau, ed., *The Languages of Psyche: Mind and Body in Enlightenment Thought* (Berkeley, 1990), pp. 45–80.

101. Anthony Ashley Cooper, earl of Shaftesbury, *Characteristics of Men, Manners, Opinions, Times, etc.,* ed. John Robinson (London, 1900), pp. 12, 251; Lawrence E. Klein, *Shaftesbury and the Culture of Politeness: Moral Discourse and Cultural Politics in Early Eighteenth-Century England* (Cambridge, 1994).

102. J. H. Shennan, "Louis XV: Public and Private Worlds," in A. G. Dickens, ed., *The Courts of Europe: Politics, Patronage, and Royalty, 1400–1800* (London, 1977), pp. 305–7; Alain Corbin, *The Foul and the Fragrant: Odour and the French Social Imagination* (Cambridge, Mass., 1986), p. 74; Daniel Roche, *The Culture of Clothing: Dress and Fashion in the Ancien Régime,* trans. Jean Birrell (Cambridge, 1996), esp. ch. 3.

103. Margaret C. Jacob, "The Materialist World of Pornography," in Lynn Hunt, ed., *The Invention of Pornography: Obscenity and the Origins of Modernity, 1500–1800* (New York, 1993), pp. 157–202; *Dictionnaire des oeuvres érotiques: Domaine français* (Paris, 1971), pp. 443–48; Marquis de Sade, *The 120 Days of Sodom and Other Writings,* ed. and trans. Austyn Wainhouse and Richard Seaver (New York, 1966), p. 191; Forster, *A Woman's Life,* p. 263; Geneviève Bollème, ed., *La bibliothèque bleue: La littérature populaire du XVIIe au XIXe siècle* (Paris, 1970), pp. 198–203.

104. See Jeffrey Merrick, *The Desacralization of the French Monarchy in the Eighteenth Century* (Baton Rouge, 1990); Roger Chartier, "A Desacralized King," in his *Cultural Origins of the French Revolution,* trans. Lydia Cochrane (Durham, 1991), pp. 111–35.

105. Aurenhammer, *Fischer von Erlach,* pp. 120–22.

106. Percy Ernest Schramm, *A History of the English Coronation* (Oxford, 1937), pp. 102–11; Monod, *Jacobitism,* pp. 173–79; E. J. F. Barbier, *Journal historique et anecdotique du règne de Louis XV,* ed. A. de la Villegille, 4 vols. (Paris, 1847–56, reprint New York, 1966), vol. 1, pp. 70, 136, 156–57.

107. For the long-standing royal pretensions of the Savoyard house, see Robert Oresko, "The House of Savoy in Search for a Royal Crown in the Seventeenth Century," in Oresko, Gibbs, and Scott, eds., *Royal and Republican Sovereignty,* pp. 272–350.

108. George J. Buelow, "Dresden in the Age of Absolutism," in Buelow, ed., *Late Baroque Era,* pp. 216–29; Velimirović, "Warsaw, Moscow, and St. Petersburg," in ibid., pp. 439–40; Macartney, ed., *Habsburg and Hohenzollern Dynasties,* p. 287.

109. Forster, ed., *A Woman's Life,* p. 196; Bloch, *Royal Touch,* pp. 390–92; Raymond Crawfurd, *The King's Evil* (Oxford, 1911), pp. 144–53.

110. Yves Bottineau, *L'art de cour dans l'Espagne de Philippe V* (Bordeaux, 1960), pp. 164–96; Saint-Simon, *Mémoires,* vol. 8, pp. 56, 62, 275.

111. Bottineau, *L'art de cour,* pp. 374–82, 415–36; Saint-Simon, *Mémoires,* vol. 8, pp. 428–32.

112. Michael Cherniavsky, *Tsar and People: Studies in Russian Myths* (New Haven, 1961), pp. 72–74; Wortman, *Scenarios of Power,* vol. 1, pp. 56–59; Joanna Hubbs, *Mother Russia: The Feminine Myth in Russian Culture* (Bloomington, Ind., 1988), pp. 200–6.

113. Korb, *Diary of a Secretary of Legation,* pp. 255–56; Perry, *State of Russia,* pp. 238–40; Cracraft, *Church Reforms of Peter the Great,* pp. 10–14.

## Chapter Seven: Conclusion

1. Jonathan Brown, *Velázquez: Painter and Courtier* (New Haven, 1986), pp. 107–16; Walter Liedtke, *The Royal Horse and Rider: Painting, Sculpture, and Horsemanship, 1500–1800* (New York, 1989), pp. 18–35.

2. Liedtke, *The Royal Horse and Rider,* pp. 284–5; Guy Walton, *Louis XIV's Versailles* (Chicago, 1986), pp. 104, 115; Peter Burke, *The Fabrication of Louis XIV* (New Haven, 1992), pp. 78, 80.

3. Yves Bottineau, *L'art de cour dans l'Espagne de Philippe V, 1700–1746* (Bordeaux, 1961), pp. 443–49.

4. *Lucifer en visita y el diablo en residencia* (Madrid, n.d.), in María Teresa Pérez

Picazo, *La publicística española en la guerra de sucesión*, 2 vols. (Madrid, 1966), vol. 2, pp. 126–7.

5. Liedtke, *The Royal Horse and Rider*, pp. 37–47; Kevin Sharpe, *The Personal Rule of Charles I* (New Haven, 1992), p. 227.

6. Liedtke, *The Royal Horse and Rider*, pp. 204–5, 208, 210–11, 224, 226, 276, 288–89; John P. Spielman, *Leopold I of Austria* (London, 1977), plate 8; Allan Ellenius, "Konst och miljö," in Stellan Dahlgren et al., *Kultur och samhälle i stormaktstidens Sverige* (Stockholm, 1967), p. 66.

7. Liedtke, *The Royal Horse and Rider*, pp. 180–87; Rudolf Wittkower, *Gian Lorenzo Bernini: The Sculptor of the Roman Baroque*, 3d ed. (Ithaca, N.Y., 1955, 1981), pp. 23–24, 251–56, plates 110–15, and his "Vicissitudes of a Dynastic Monument: Bernini's Equestrian Statue of Louis XIV," in Millard Meiss, ed., *Essays in Honor of Erwin Panofsky*, 2 vols. (New York, 1961), vol. 1, pp. 497–531; Hans Kauffmann, *Giovanni Lorenzo Bernini: Die figürlichen Kompositionen* (Berlin, 1970), pp. 278–89; Burke, *Fabrication of Louis XIV*, pp. 92–97.

8. Liedtke, *Royal Horse and Rider*, p. 284.

9. Henri Platelle, ed., *Journal d'un curé de campagne au XVIIe siècle* (Paris, 1965), pp. 73–74, 118–19.

10. Sarah Fyge Field Egerton, "The Female Advocate" and "The Emulation," in Moira Ferguson, ed., *First Feminists: British Women Writers, 1578–1799* (Bloomington, Ind., 1985), pp. 155, 169; Georges Mongrédien, *Mme. de Scudéry et son salon* (Paris, 1946).

11. Hilton L. Root, *Peasants and King in Burgundy: Agrarian Foundations of French Absolutism* (Berkeley, 1987).

12. Perry Anderson, *Lineages of the Absolutist State* (London and New York, 1974, 1989), p. 57.

13. Duc de Saint-Simon, *Mémoires*, 8 vols. (Paris, 1983), vol. 1, pp. 7–11.

14. Michael Hunter and Annabel Gregory, eds., *An Astrological Diary of the Seventeenth Century: Samuel Jeake of Rye, 1652–1699* (Oxford, 1988), p. 232.

15. Rudolf Grieser, ed., *Die Memoiren des Kammerherrn Friedrich Ernst von Fabrice (1683–1750)* (Hildesheim, 1956), pp. x, 12 n. 1, 68–69.

# Index

Estates (*continued*)
  207; General of France, 25, 30, 72, 112; General of the Netherlands, 78–79, 192; government by, 96; Hungarian, 241, 304, 305; of Holland, 192. *See also* Cortes; Corts; Parliament; Reichstag; Riksdag; Sejm; *sejmiki; ¿emsky sobor*
etiquette: 12, 45, 135–36, 138, 218–19, 224, 239, 244, 274–75, 310, 312, 313
Evans, R. J. W.: 57, 239
Evelyn, John: 178, 180, 193, 225, 228–9, 230, 258
Exclusion crisis: 231, 233

Fabrice: Friedrich Ernst von, 327; Weipart Ludwig von, 327
Falconet, Etienne Maurice: 323
Falkland, Lucius Cary, viscount: 186, 226
Farge, Arlette: 278
Fedor, tsar of Russia: 254
Fénelon, François de la Mothe-, archbishop of Cambrai: 277, 278, 280, 282
Ferdinand II, Holy Roman Emperor: 81–82, 86–93, 120, 206; and reason of state, 92–93; publicity of, 88–89
Ferdinand II, king of Aragon: 131, 133
Ferdinand III, Holy Roman Emperor: 89, 234, 235
Ferdinand IV, king of the Romans: as Solomon, 235–36
Fernández de Navarette, Pedro: 130, 132
fifth monarchy: predictions of, 148, 165; believers in, 146, 197
Filaret, patriarch of All Russia: 128, 252
Filmer, Sir Robert: 109, 110, 160, 269
Filomarino, Cardinal Ascanio: 181, 184
Finland: 25, 264
Fischer von Erlach, J. B.: 293, 311
Fletcher, Andrew, of Saltoun: 301
Fogel, Michèle: 83, 299
Fontenelle, Bernard Le Bovier de: 279–80, 292–93
Fortescue, Sir John: 42
Foucault, Michel: 13, 307, 328
Foucquet, Nicolas: 222
France: denounced, 281; government of, 6, 24, 28, 29, 30, 78–79, 215, 224, 255–56, 273; Fronde in, 169, 172–80, 213; financiers of, 174, 250; Gallican church in, 255; monarchy in, 39–40, 41, 69–79, 110–120, 213–25, 255–56, 273–80, 299; religious wars in, 34–36, 70–73, 110–11
Francke, August Hermann: 287–88
Frazier, Sir J. G. A.: 7, 8

Frederick I, king in Prussia: 290–91, 292, 323; coronation of, 290, 312; patronage of, 291–92, 323
Frederick II, king of Prussia: quoted, 292, 293
Frederick III, king of Denmark: 205–6, 209, 210
Frederick V, Elector Palatine: 91–92, 96, 97, 100, 102
Frederick William I, king of Prussia: 288, 291
Freud, Sigmund: 8, 12, 17–18, 61, 278
Fronde: 151, 152, 172–80, 195, 213, 225, 279, 281; and Catholic League, 174, 176–7, 179; in Paris, 172–74, 176–7, 179. *See also* Ormée
Fumaroli, Marc: 117, 118
funeral ceremony: in France, 35–36, 75, 77–78, 274, 311; in Holy Roman Empire, 311; in Spain, 242–43; in Poland, 263
Furetière, Antoine: 212, 221

Galilei, Galileo: 171
Garrisson, Janine (Estèbe): 256
Gauden, John: 189
Gay, Geoffroy: 179
Geertz, Clifford: 4
general crisis: 150–51
Genoino, Giulio: 180, 182
George I, king of England: 296–97, 304, 311, 312
Girard, René: 14–15, 71, 88, 127
Godolphin, Margaret: 228–29
Goffman, Erving: 17
Goldast, Melchior: 58, 91
Golitsyn, V. V.: 254
grace: 23, 195, 203, 276, 282, 284, 327
Gracián, Baltasar: 131
Greco, El, (Domenikos Theotokopoulos): 1, 3–4
Greenblatt, Stephen: 22
Griffenfeld, Peder Schumacher, count: 207, 209, 214, 270
Grimmelshausen, H. J. C. von: 94
Grotius, Hugo: 101, 103–4, 109, 186, 226, 270, 276
Gryphius, Andreas: 84, 185
Guez de Balzac, Jean-Louis: 110, 112, 113, 117, 119–20, 121, 219
Guise: family, 70; Henri de Lorraine, duke of, 72; Henri de Lorraine, duke of, and duke of Naples, 184
Gustavus II Adolphus, king of Sweden: 96, 97, 99–102, 103, 127, 128, 153, 284; images of, 100–101, 236
Guyon, Jeanne: 277
Gwyn, Nell: 228